ATLAS OF FINANCE

ATLAS OF FINANCE

Mapping the Global Story of Money

BY

Dariusz Wójcik

AND

Panagiotis Iliopoulos **Stefanos Ioannou** **Liam Keenan** **Julien Migozzi**

Timothy Monteath **Vladimír Pažitka** **Morag Torrance** **Michael Urban**

WITH MAPS & GRAPHICS BY

James Cheshire **Oliver Uberti**

YALE UNIVERSITY PRESS
NEW HAVEN AND LONDON

Yale University Press books may be purchased in quantity for educational, business, or promotional use. For information, please e-mail sales.press@yale.edu (U.S. office) or sales@yaleup.co.uk (U.K. office).

Designed by Oliver Uberti.
Set in Dagny, Ingeborg, Venus, Cheltenham, and Peristyle type.
Printed in Slovenia.

Library of Congress Control Number: 2023941211
ISBN 978-0-300-25305-4 (hardcover : alk. paper)

A catalogue record for this book is available from the British Library.

This paper meets the requirements of ANSI/NISO Z39.48-1992 (Permanence of Paper).

10 9 8 7 6 5 4 3 2 1

TO ANIA, MARIA,
AND ZBIGNIEW

Contents

1 HISTORY & GEOGRAPHY 7

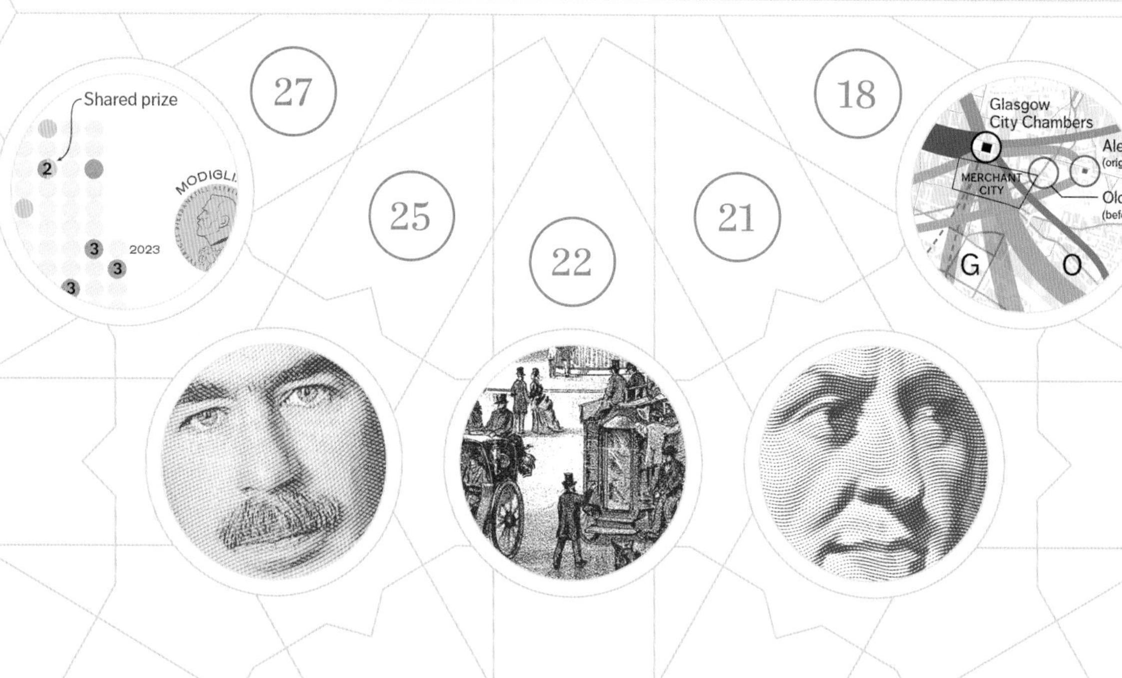

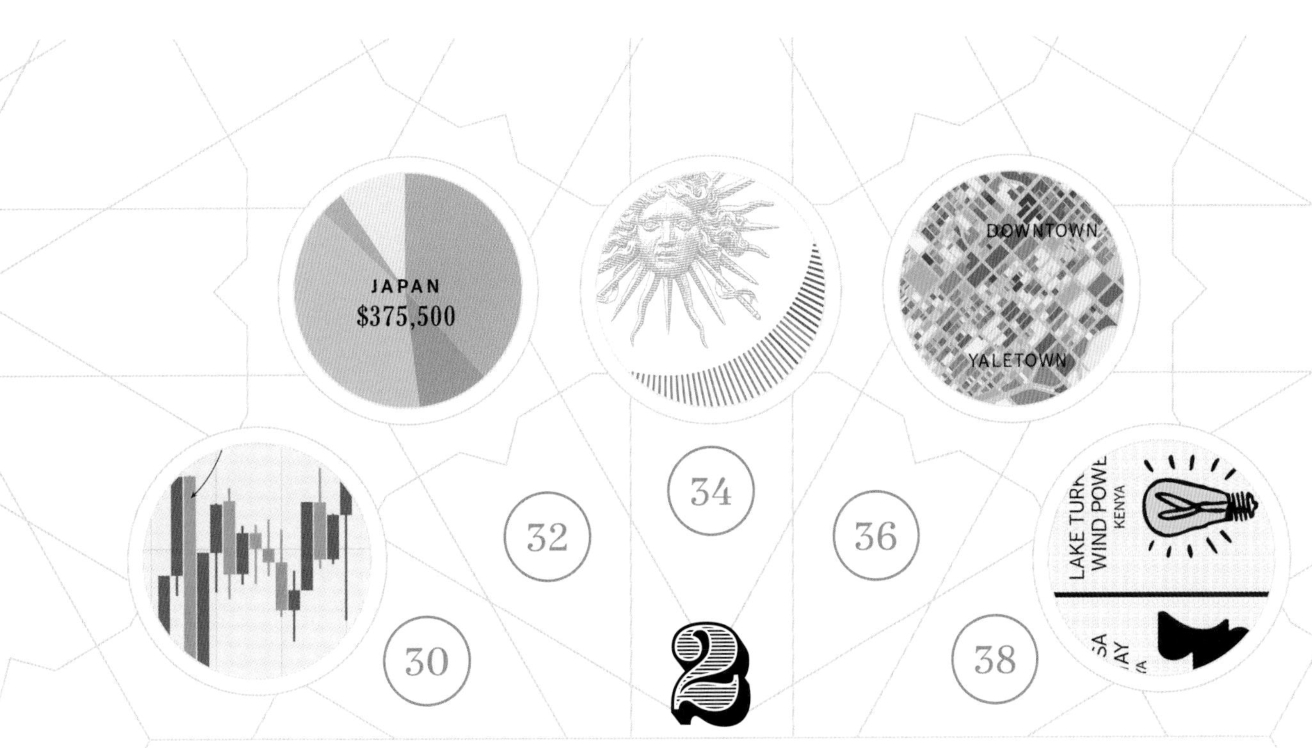

2

ASSETS & MARKETS 29

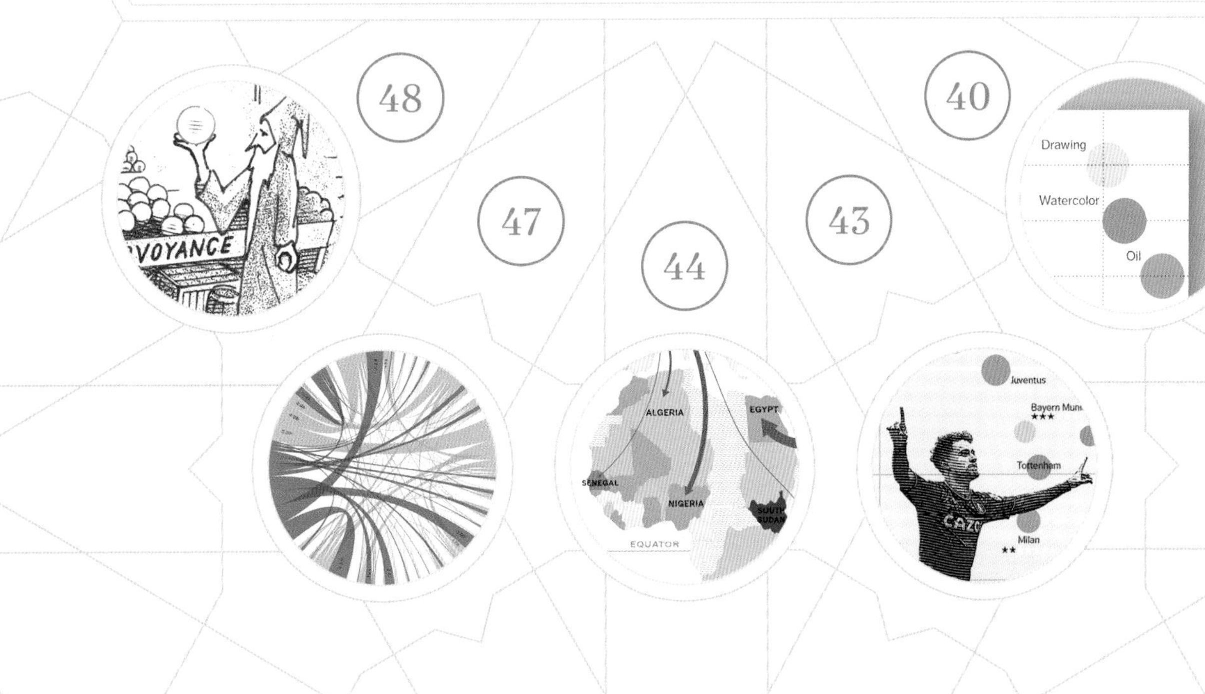

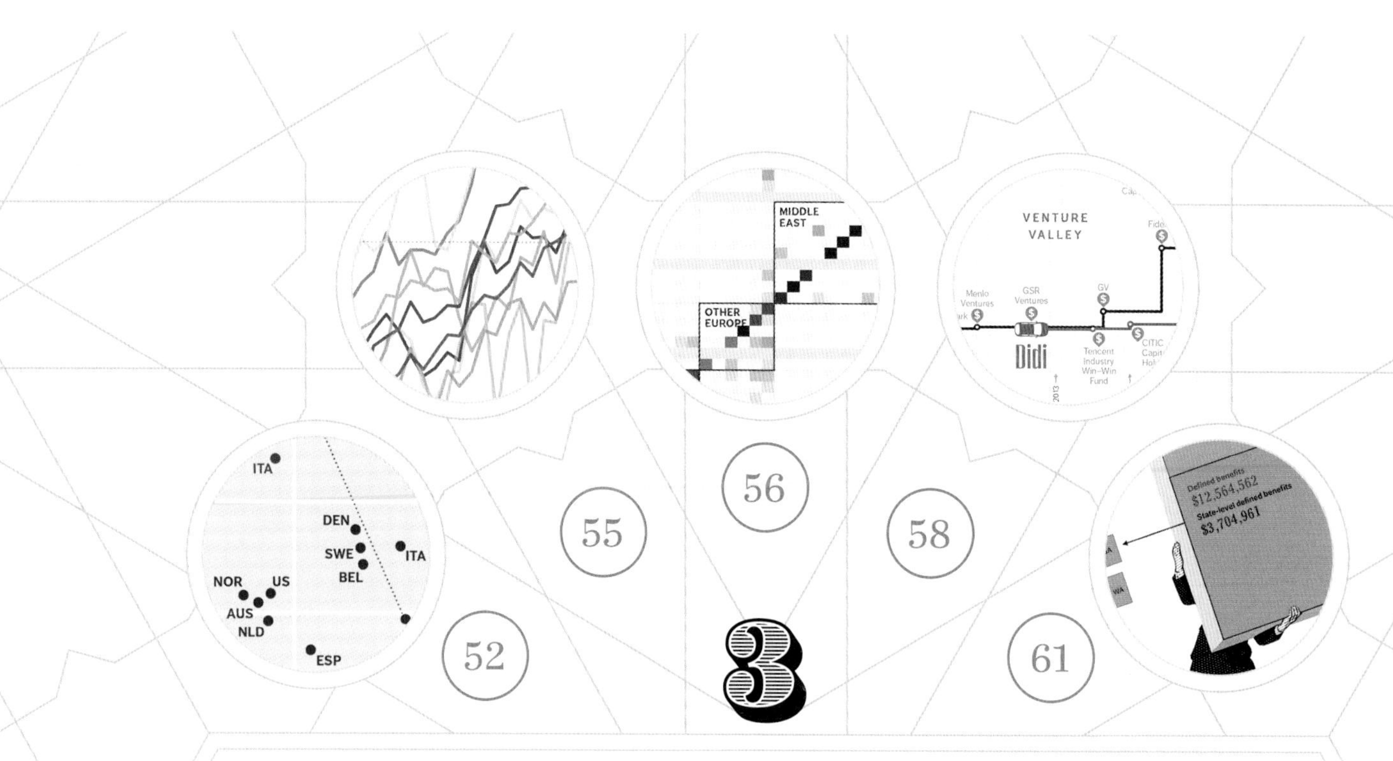

INVESTORS & INVESTMENTS 51

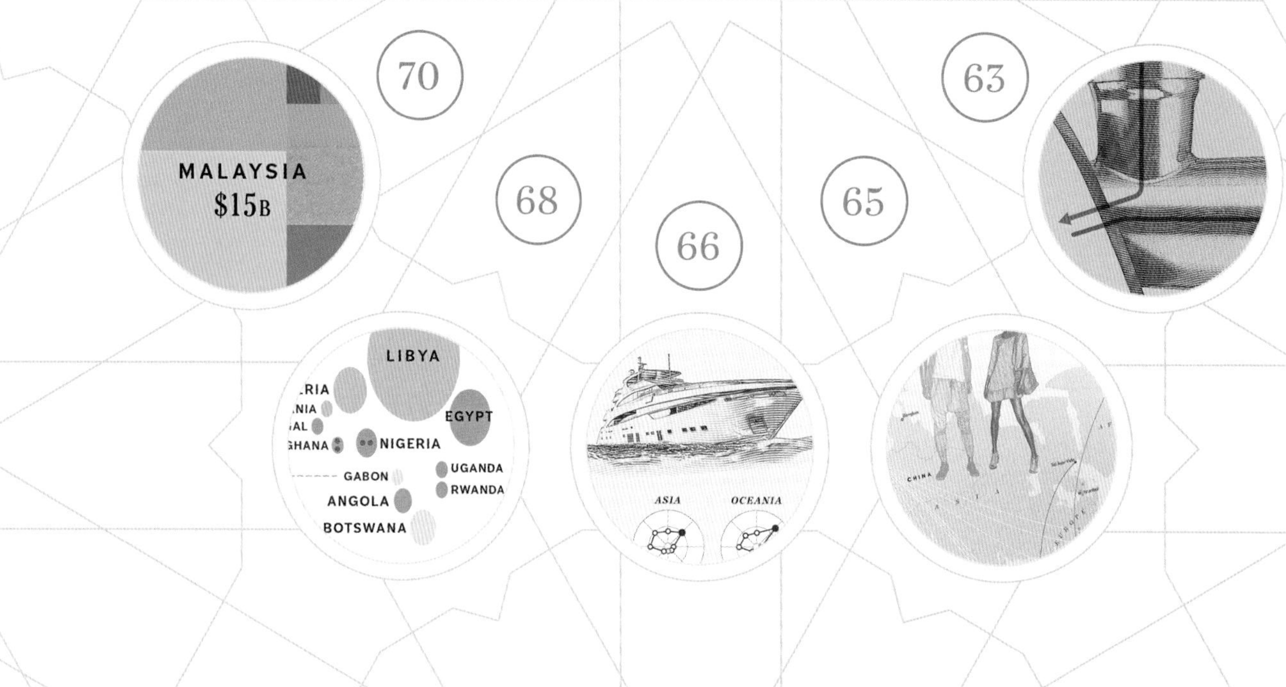

4 INTERMEDIATION & TECHNOLOGY 73

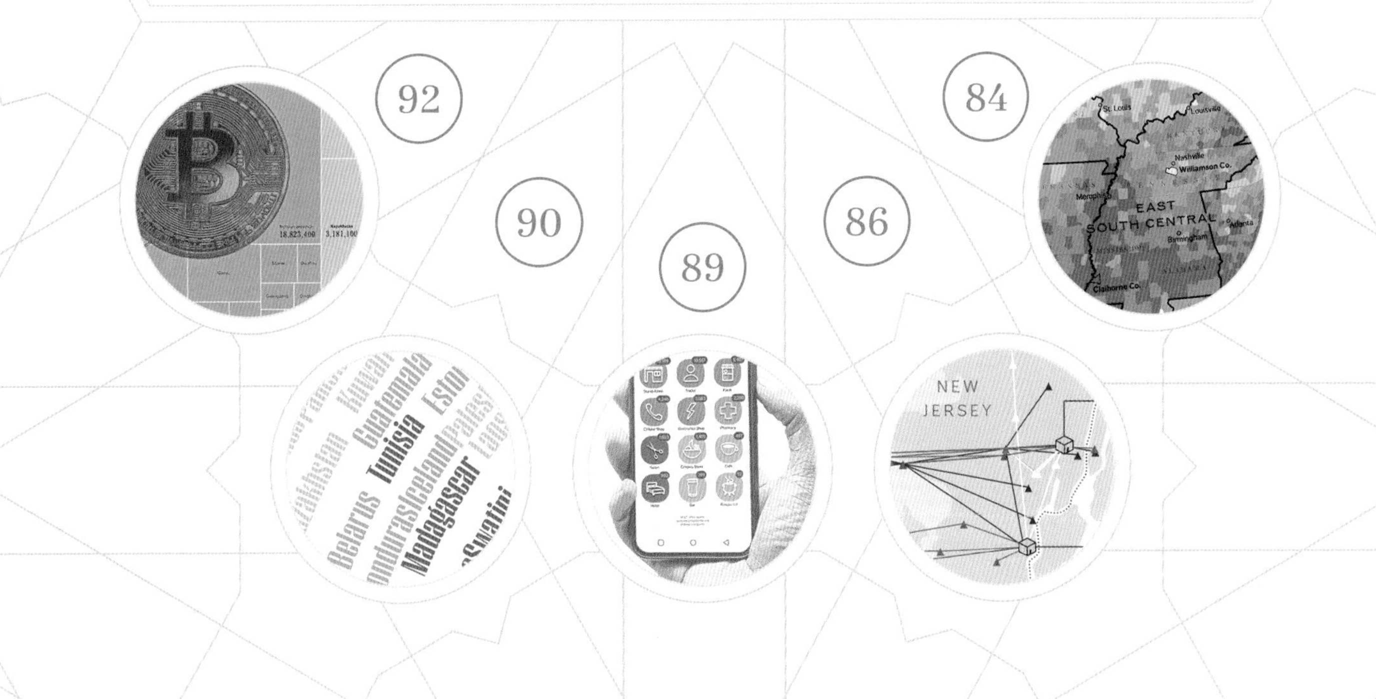

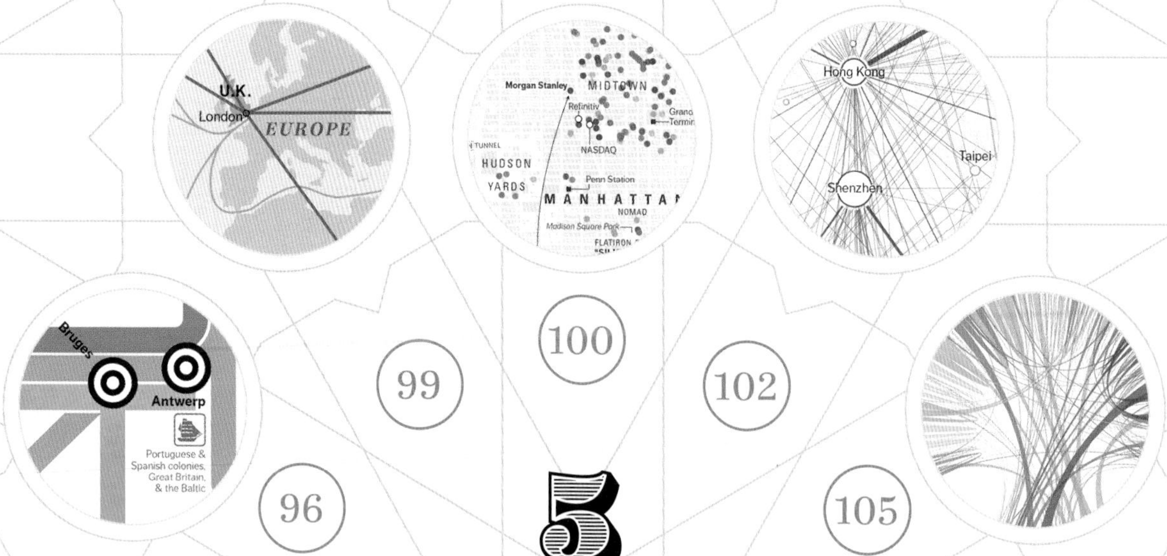

5
CITIES & CENTERS 95

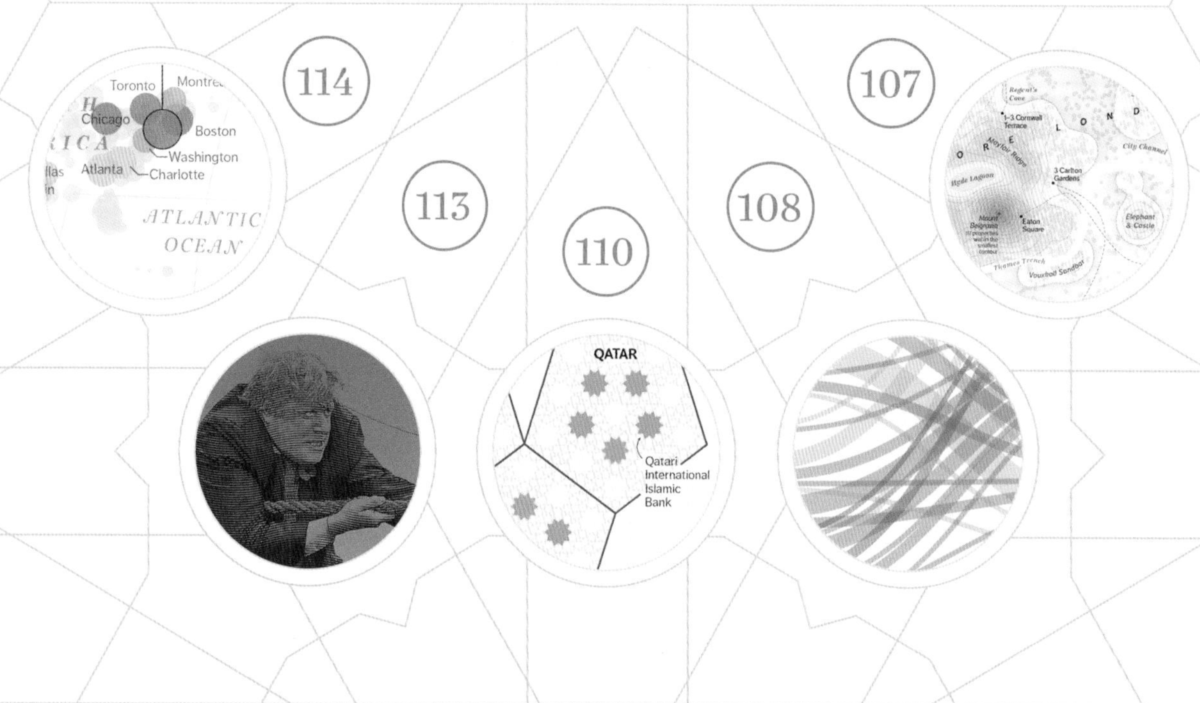

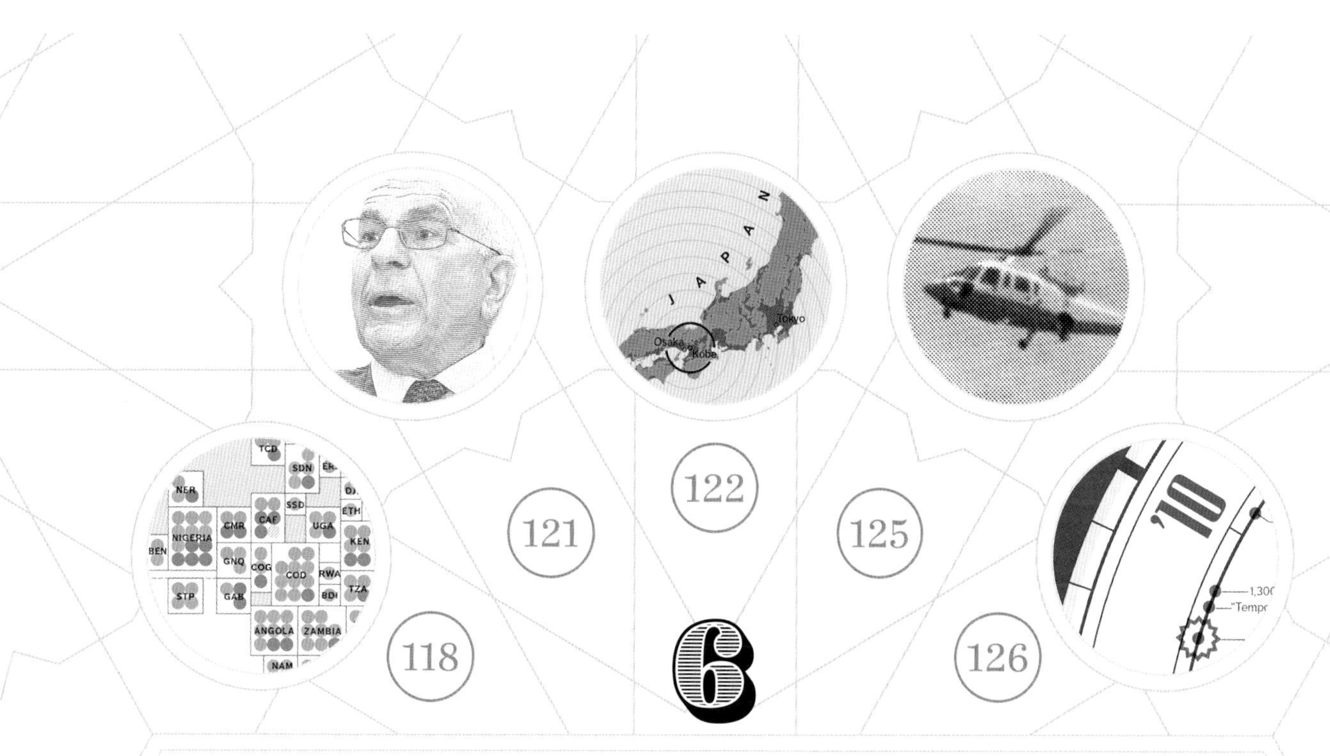

6 BUBBLES & CRISES 117

7

REGULATION & GOVERNANCE 141

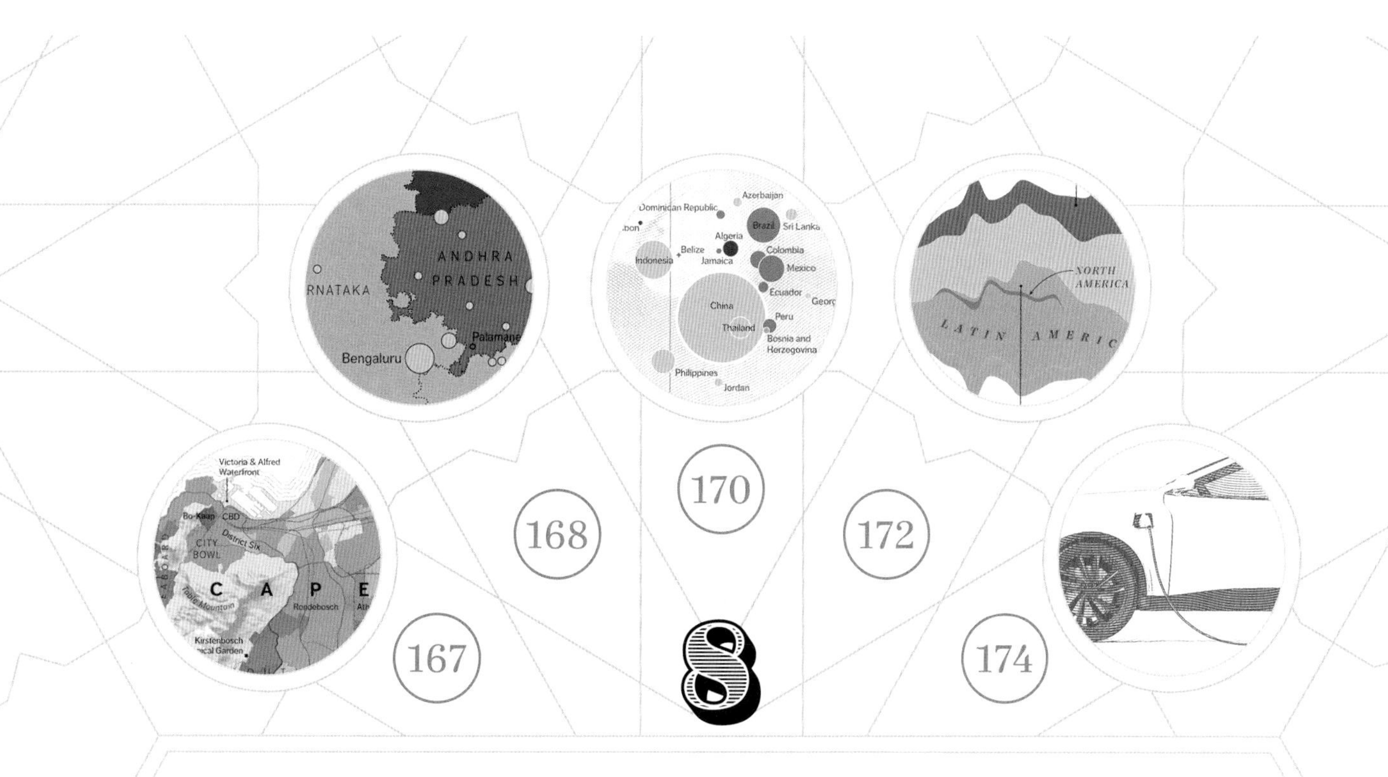

8 SOCIETY & ENVIRONMENT 165

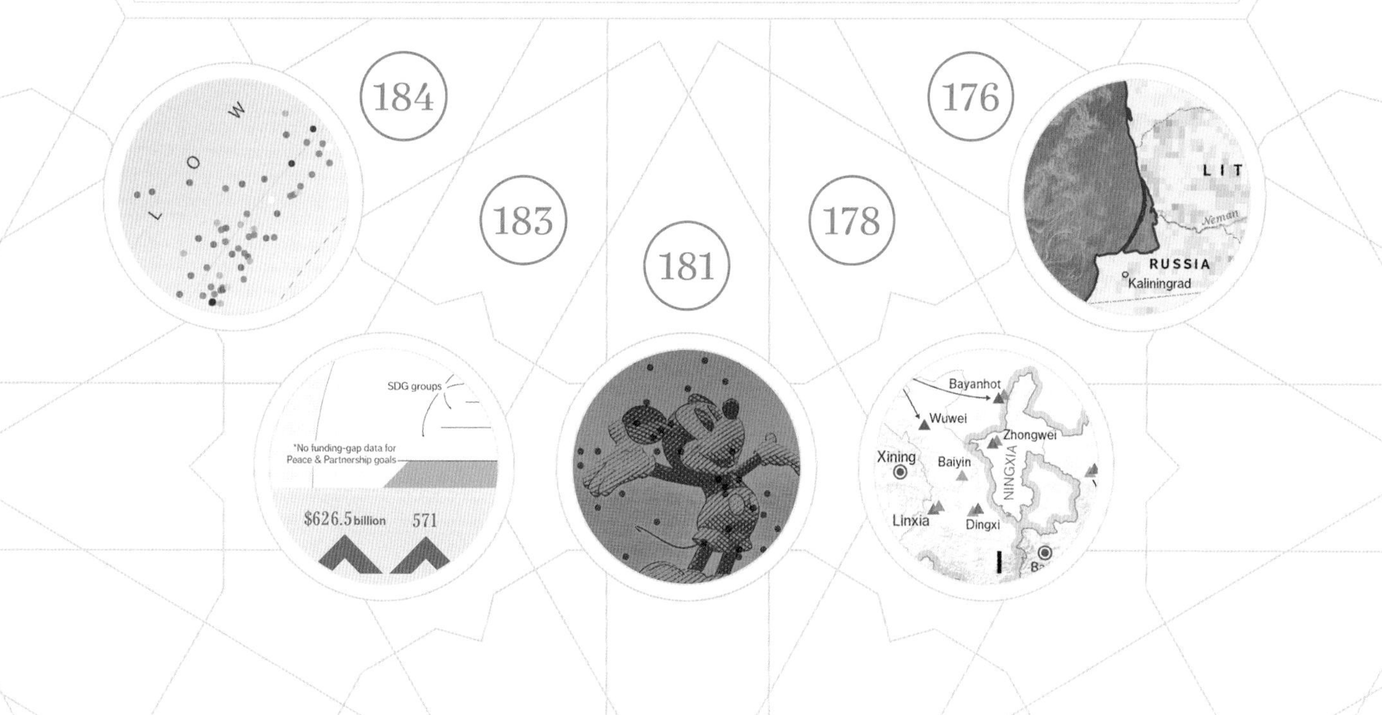

INTRODUCTION

Demystifying Finance

A PARADOX LIES in the very nature of finance. Money is abstract, fungible, and increasingly digital; it can change hands in an instant and without much friction. At the same time, money leaves bulky, tangible, and lasting footprints. Every building, street, and pipe in every town, city, and country is created and maintained with money, and every business and non-business organization follows financial calculations. Due to its paradoxical nature, most people consider money and finance arcane, something to leave to experts and technocrats, economists and bankers. Such an attitude is not only unhelpful but also dangerous. In 1920, the German economic sociologist Max Weber described money as a weapon in the struggle for economic existence. If we want to understand our economic existence and fight for a better future, we must understand money and finance.

So first, let us define our terms. We can define finance broadly as a system of human-environment relationships in which people interact with and experience each other and their environment through the medium of money. Over millennia, money has taken different forms, from shells and grains to coins, paper bills, and now, digital currency. Ultimately, money is anything that can simultaneously act as a medium of exchange, unit of account, and store of value. How well something works as money depends on how reliably it can perform all three functions. A fine painting may store value well, but few people count in Picassos, and it would not be easy to buy flour with one. Put differently, a painting lacks liquidity—the ease and speed with which it can be exchanged for other things. A cryptocurrency in contrast may be easy and quick to use, but if it is highly volatile, it is not a good store of value. To perform its functions, money must be trusted.

As a system of relationships, finance has immense transformative power. We can use it to pool private and public resources to invent a new vaccine and fight a pandemic. Likewise, it can enable one person to take control of a technological platform, affecting relationships among billions of people. Day to day, finance transforms work into labor, measured with wages, salaries, and bonuses (for the privileged few, often in the form of stocks and other financial instruments). A home becomes real estate, beset with taxes and upkeep. The whole environment becomes a set of assets, with its preservation or extinction driven by financial value and cost-benefit analyses. Life becomes a ledger of assets and liabilities. Time itself assumes financial value through the calculation of interest earned and owed. The future becomes a financial risk-return calculation that can be moderated with insurance and other financial risk-management techniques. Finance binds space and time together; it links places just as it links the past, present, and future.

The transformative power of finance has been crucial in our evolution from groups of hunter-gatherers to agricultural settlements, which in turn begat cities, countries and colonies, and our current global and digital networks. This does not mean that finance is indispensable to humanity. Indigenous Australians used a bartering network that spanned a whole continent, prospering without money and finance for 50,000 years or so until the plunderous West showed up on their shores. Unmediated by finance, their human-environment relationships represent, in the words of the novelist Mudrooroo, "the unity of the people with nature and all living creatures and life forms." As such, money and finance can be seen as the scissors that cut the umbilical cord connecting us to Mother Nature. Like the gods who gave Midas the power to turn everything he touched into gold, finance has given us the power to make everything about money. And like Midas, whose power eventually starved him, humanity is destroying the natural resources necessary for our sustenance.

So how do we avoid the Midas curse and re-harness the power of finance for the common good? In our view, the path to this goal traverses the fields of geography, cartography, and data visualization. Call it "finviz." Financial economics and the financial industry have long been obsessed with charts of fluctuating prices, but they have

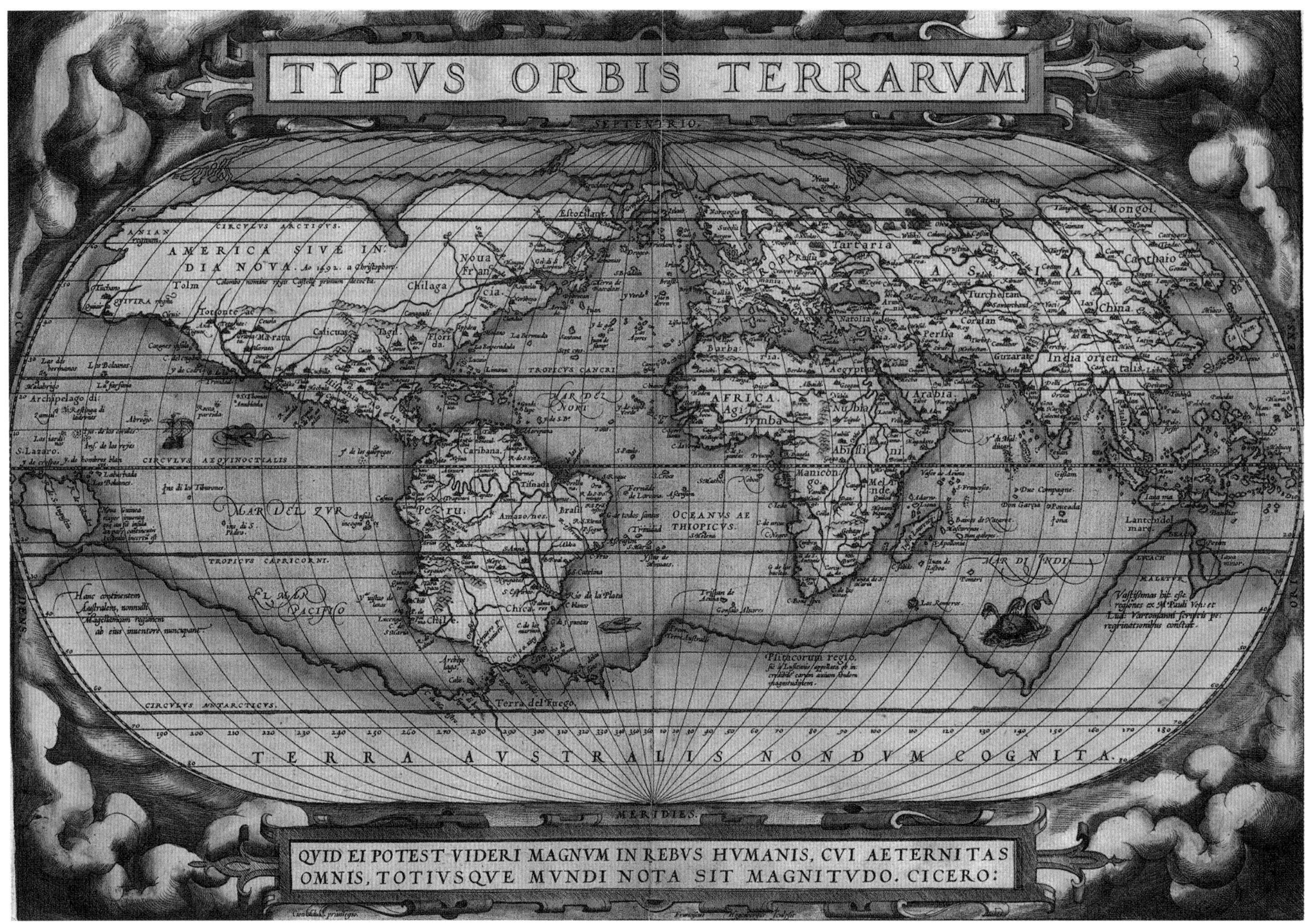

largely eschewed the broader patterns and impacts of finance. We need to map and visualize them in creative and critical ways if only because it's nearly impossible to solve problems you cannot see.

A Brief History of Finviz

The histories of maps and money have long been intertwined, from maritime maps facilitating trade with a New World to Google Maps dictating directions to a new restaurant. Along the way, maps have appeared on banknotes and stock certificates, sometimes to reassert national, regional, or local identity or to evoke images of the projects to be funded through the issuance of such certificates. Maps on coins are rarer due to their smaller size. Ancient Greek coins featured local produce, such as apples from Melos or roses from Rhodes, while ancient Roman coins often depicted temples, monuments, or urban landmarks such as the Colosseum or Circus Maximus. Spheres that may be interpreted as globes have been found on coins from both civilizations, with the oldest known example (c. 300 BCE) unearthed in Uranopolis in northern Greece. Today, you can find maps on coins circulating in Algeria, Nepal, and Turkmenistan and on the US Mint's fifty state quarters, fifteen of which include the distinctive shape of a state in their designs.

It's no coincidence that the greatest European mapmakers of the fifteenth, sixteenth, and seventeenth centuries all lived and worked in Europe's leading international financial centers. Fra Mauro created his *mappa mundi*—a fastidiously illustrated map containing much of the geographical knowledge of his time—around 1450 in Venice (see page xvi); Abraham Ortelius created the first modern atlas, *Theatrum Orbis Terrarum*, in 1570 in Antwerp (above); and Joan Blaeu created his larger and more comprehensive *Atlas Maior* in 1662 in Amsterdam (above right). These were not the most powerful cities of their era, nor were they necessarily the

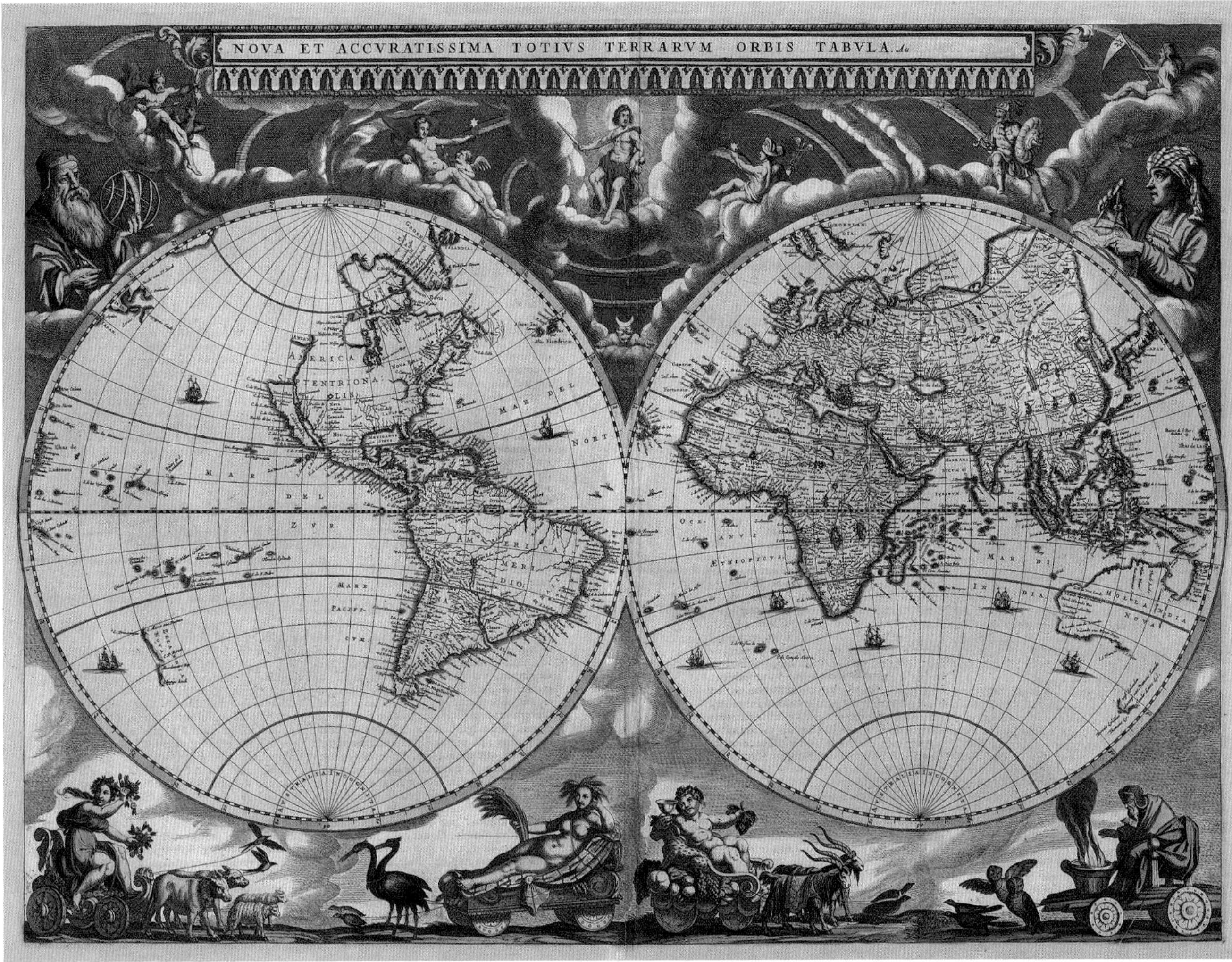

largest; each had just over 100,000 inhabitants. However, all three were arguably the most connected cities in Europe via trade and financial transactions. Along with their goods, traders brought information about distant parts of the world (e.g., Japan on Fra Mauro's map, the emerging contours of Australia in Ortelius's atlas, or Tierra del Fuego at the tip of South America on Blaeu's). The supply of information in Venice, Antwerp, and Amsterdam met the demand, with large and diverse communities of merchants and financiers, financial exchanges, and banks all hungry for an edge over their competition. Hotbeds of money, information, and talent, these cities hosted thriving publishing industries, scientists, and artists with relatively little censorship—fertile ground for a budding cartographer to bear fruit. For example, as both a major port and financial center, Antwerp made it easy for Abraham Ortelius to travel abroad, raise funds, collect maps, study the cartographic-mathematical inventions of Gerardus Mercator, and draw inspiration from artists like Albrecht Dürer and Pieter Breugel the Elder.

One of the more imaginative examples of financial cartography appeared in *The Great Mirror of Folly*, a book published in the Netherlands in 1720. The engraving features a map of an imaginary island, drawn as the "crazy head" of a jester (see page 4). The River Seine delineates the edge of the jester's cap, and in the middle, near where one might expect to find the fool's tiny brain, is a splotch labeled "Quinqempoix." That was the name of a narrow Parisian street on which speculators traded shares of the Mississippi Company, a monopolistic trader in the French colonies in North America and the West Indies, pumping up the share price to stratospheric heights in 1719 before a total collapse the following year. The "crazy head" island also features places like "Deception City," while little islands around it are called "Despair," "Poverty," and "Sadness." The map satirically condemns one of the biggest booms and busts in financial history.

The modern financial industry also shapes global finance and its maps. For instance, the concept of BRICS (Brazil, Russia, India, China, and South Africa) as the locomotives of global economic growth and terms like *emerging economies* and *developed markets* categorically divide the world into haves, have-nots, and almost-haves. But I have a more personal example of the close relationship between finance and cartography.

Financing an Atlas

I came to St Peter's College at the University of Oxford as a visiting student from Poland in 1998. The college is on New Inn Hall Street, site of the old Oxford Mint. In 1644, King Charles I was waging a civil war against Parliament, so he moved his court from London to Oxford. In need of resources, he established the mint to turn silver plates and cutlery from Oxford and Cambridge colleges into coins. One of the first ones minted that year was the Oxford Crown (see right), on which you can see a cityscape dotted with churches, colleges, and the Bodleian Library, a trove that today holds nearly two million maps and twenty thousand atlases. There are atlases of everything and anything—an atlas of bells; an atlas of dinosaur adventures; an atlas of countries that do not exist; a phantom atlas; atlases of beer, coffee, chocolate, and wine; an atlas of curiosities; an atlas of monsters—and yet no atlas of finance. Searching online, the closest I could find was a coin atlas, tracking the evolution of coinage in over a hundred countries. Still, coins represent just a small part of financial phenomena.

Charles I and his need for cash came to mind recently while I was walking from the School of Geography and the Environment at Oxford University, where in 2010 my mentor, Gordon L. Clark, and I first began envisioning an atlas of finance. Thoroughly researched, full-color atlases are enormously expensive to produce. As in the days of Mauro, Ortelius, and Blaeu, we quickly realized that to make one you need access to capital. Asking for college silver was not an option, so the project remained a fantasy for years.

Then in 2016, I received a grant from the European Research Council for a project called Cities in Global Financial Networks: Financial and Business Services and Development in the 21st Century, which you will see cited throughout the atlas as CityNet. The EU funding suddenly made our dream possible and gave me the means to hire the postdoctoral researchers who would become my co-authors, along with award-winning cartographers James Cheshire and Oliver Uberti. As part of the CityNet project, we analyzed millions of data points and hundreds of interviews with finance practitioners around the world. We published research articles and books. We also built on our interdisciplinary background in geography (Liam Keenan, Julien Migozzi), economics (Stefanos Ioannou, Vladimír Pažitka), political economy (Panagiotis Iliopoulos), and sociology (Timothy Monteath), as well as experience from the financial sector (Michael Urban, Morag Torrance). Armed with such resources, we were finally ready to fill the gap in the market—and on bookshelves—for a volume that unites money and maps, finance and geography.

Thus it is with great joy that I welcome you to the *Atlas of Finance*—the first book-length collection of maps and graphics dedicated to demystifying the world of finance. We begin with the origins and history of finance and how this history is a story of human civilization itself, with its economies, politics, ideas, and cultures. Chapters 2 to 5 chart the evolution, structures, and mechanisms of finance from four complementary perspectives: assets and markets, investors and investments, intermediation and technology, and the geographical footprint of finance. Chapter 6 examines the destructive power of finance as manifested in financial instability, bubbles, and crises. Chapter 7 then addresses various ways in which regulation and governance can harness this power. Lastly, we conclude with a long-term look at the impacts finance continues to have on society and the environment. As a whole, *Atlas of Finance* is a statement of financial geography, combined with data science, digital humanities, economics, social sciences, and design. While we reveal how finance can improve lives and unleash human potential, we do not shy away from finance's complex and often problematic relationship with civilization, noting its contributions to inequality, instability, and environmental degradation.

The atlas is the product of its place and time. We were certainly influenced by our European and North American perspectives, just as we were impacted by the hot financial topics of the early 2020s, including fintech and Bitcoin. However, we made much effort to transcend such biases, with attention to the history and geographical variation of each phenomenon depicted within. We aimed for a diversity of financial topics, historical periods, and geographical coverage as well as a range of map projections, colors, and types of visualization. We wanted the richness of the book itself to communicate how finance penetrates every nook and cranny of the world.

The book you are holding is the product of over twelve thousand hours of work. It has been one of the most labor-intensive and most creative projects of our lives. In addition to the efforts of my co-authors, nearly two hundred Oxford student interns assisted us with data collection, coding, analysis, and literature surveys. All contributed to the atlas and gained insight into this novel way of studying finance. As such, the atlas has already contributed to education. In fact, much of the painstaking scholarship that underpins every page is leading to future research publications on inequality and diversity in finance, global financial governance and technology, and sustainable finance.

Just as modern anatomy managed to map the human body, accelerating the development of modern medicine, we hope the patterns mapped in this atlas will inspire new thinking about finance. We hope the atlas serves as an inspiration for students and scholars across disciplines and as a resource for finance professionals in the private and public sector, including regulators and policymakers. Ultimately, we hope *Atlas of Finance*, unique in scale and scope, will contribute to a lasting change in the way you view both your money and your world.

Dariusz Wójcik
Sydney and Broadbeach, December 2022

If all the economists were laid end to end, they'd never reach a conclusion.

GEORGE BERNARD SHAW

History & Geography

The history of money and finance dates to the first cities in Mesopotamia. It has since evolved through trade, imperial conquest, globalization, and colonialism. Its evolution has always been the product of its environment. The greatest economic thinkers of the eighteenth, nineteenth, and twentieth centuries were influenced by financial developments around them. Despite financial globalization, the production of financial science remains geographically concentrated—and biased.

Sumerian Sums **Welcome to Uruk, about 3200–3000 BCE! Use our guide to decipher one of the world's oldest surviving financial artifacts.**

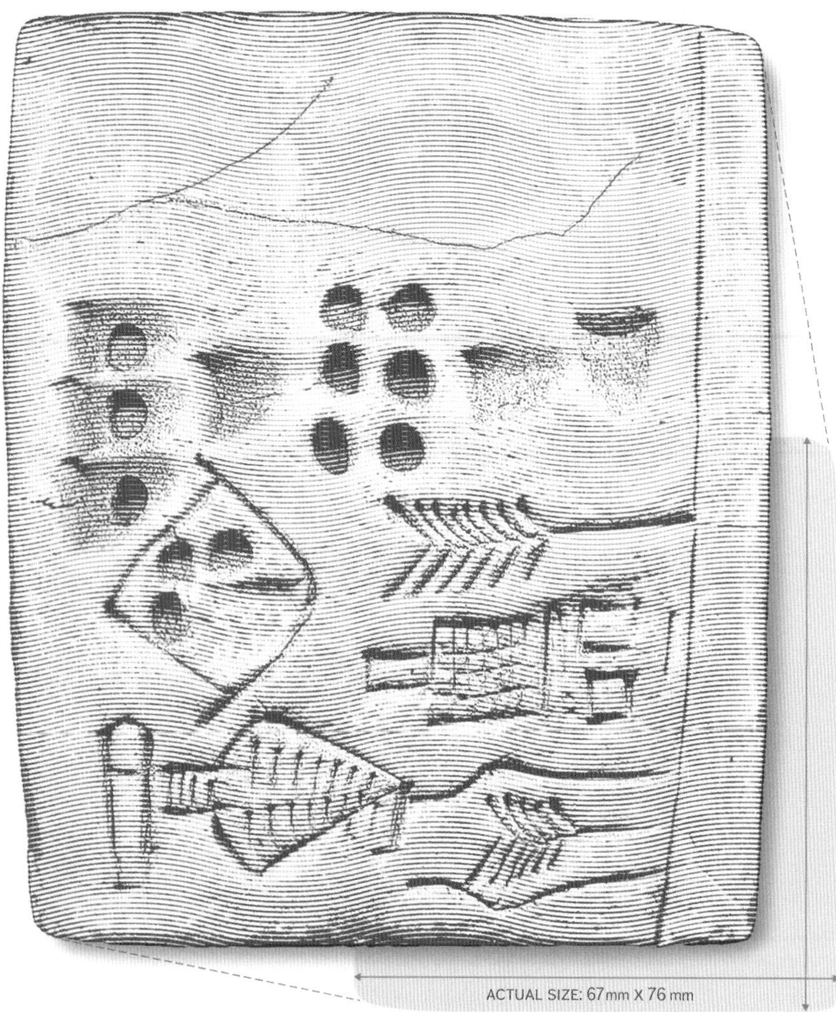

QUANTITY

In the Sumerian numeral system, the markings highlighted in red above indicate 28,086 units, or approximately 134,813 liters, of barley. Such a vast quantity reflects the needs of Uruk as a large city as well as a redistribution and production system to satisfy those needs. The precise number reflects the strictures and efficiency of Sumerian administration.

9000

900

300

30

5

1

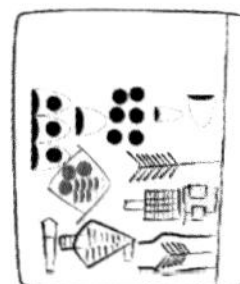

ACCOUNTING PERIOD

For administrative purposes, Sumerians used a calendar with twelve months of thirty days each, which facilitated financial calculations because 360 is divisible by many numbers. To adjust this system to a longer solar year, they would add an additional month, typically every three years. This explains the thirty-seven-month accounting period on the tablet.

10 months

1 month

10 days

1 day

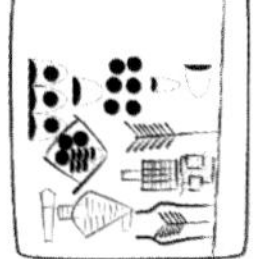

SIGNATURE

The oldest known signature in the world belongs to Kushim, a priest-manager at the Temple of Inanna (pictured above right). Inanna was a goddess and patron deity of Uruk; Kushim oversaw deliveries of barley and malt for beer production. As a Sumerian proverb states: "Enlil's temple is a summation of accounts. The temple manager is its overseer."

Location of the Sumer civilization in ancient Mesopotamia

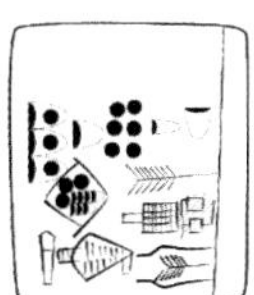

PRODUCT

Barley was the main crop of ancient Mesopotamia and the main subject of proto-cuneiform tablets. Sumerians also used it as a medium of exchange alongside imported silver; they settled accounts by measuring capacity or weight. Coins were invented elsewhere around 600 BCE, by which time Uruk had long been in decline and was about to be buried in the sand.

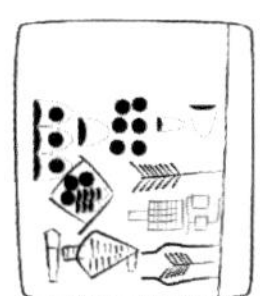

FUNCTION

Inscribed over a partially erased sign, this area of the tablet is hard to decipher. Popular accounts claim that if we rotate this symbol 90 degrees clockwise, we see a brick building with a chimney, representing a brewery; others claim it signifies a final account of the transaction. The lines could be a representation of the Sumerian accounting system, a bit like an ancient Excel spreadsheet.

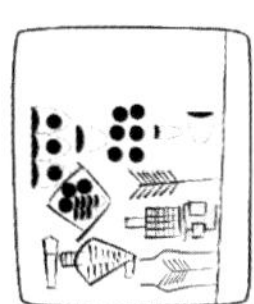

USE OF BARLEY

Proto-cuneiform did not use verbs, so this sign is as difficult to interpret as the function of the document. Some claim that if we rotate the symbol 90 degrees clockwise, we see barley in a bottle, representing beer. Sumerians invented beer and drank it often because fermentation made it safer to consume than water. Reading all six symbols together, we can interpret this tablet as Kushim confirming the delivery of 28,086 units of barley over thirty-seven months to produce beer.

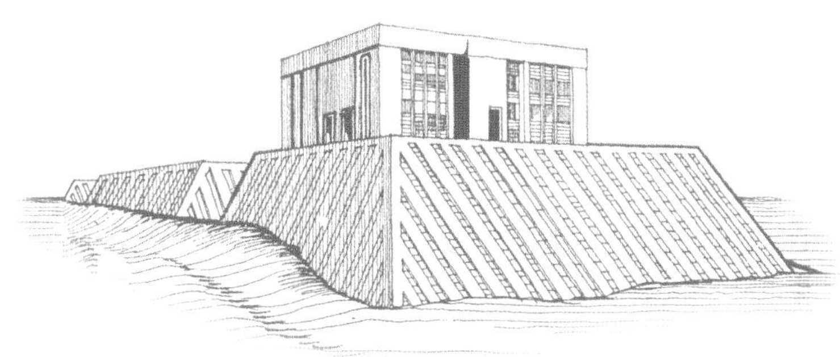

Clay Foundations

Innovations in measuring, writing, and accounting in ancient Mesopotamia laid the foundations for the development of finance and civilization.

THE ORIGIN OF FINANCE dates back to Sumerian culture in the fourth millennium BCE, when a favorable physical climate filled the "land between rivers" with resources: marshes full of fish, fowl, and construction materials; fertile alluvial plains for garden crops; irrigable plains for cereal cultivation; and vast peripheral areas for grazing. Rivers and plains, in conjunction with another Sumerian invention—the wheel—facilitated movement of goods and people. Thanks to all these factors, Sumerian farmers could produce much more than they needed for subsistence. The resulting surplus led to the creation of cities with large populations, social hierarchy, trade, and division of labor. Around 3100 BCE Uruk had approximately forty thousand inhabitants, making it likely the largest city in the world at the time.

Maintaining such a complex social organization required human ingenuity. Sumerians created ways to count, measure time, and represent things with symbols, thus inventing the earliest script in human history. Using a reed stylus, they impressed signs into the soft surface of clay tablets that they later sun-hardened or baked. These markings eventually developed into a writing system known as cuneiform in the third millennium BCE. Signs used earlier, like those translated at left, are known as proto-cuneiform. Sumerian elites used proto-cuneiform almost exclusively for accounting purposes to aid in the administration of their city-states; for example, to record and plan the delivery of grain for beer production.

Naming, counting, recording, and planning, Sumerians paved the path for the calculation of values, determination of property rights, taxation, investment, lending, insurance, and more. The simple tablet shown here—acquired at auction for US$229,000 in 2020—thus represents proto-finance, which evolved into the multi-trillion-dollar system we discuss throughout this atlas.

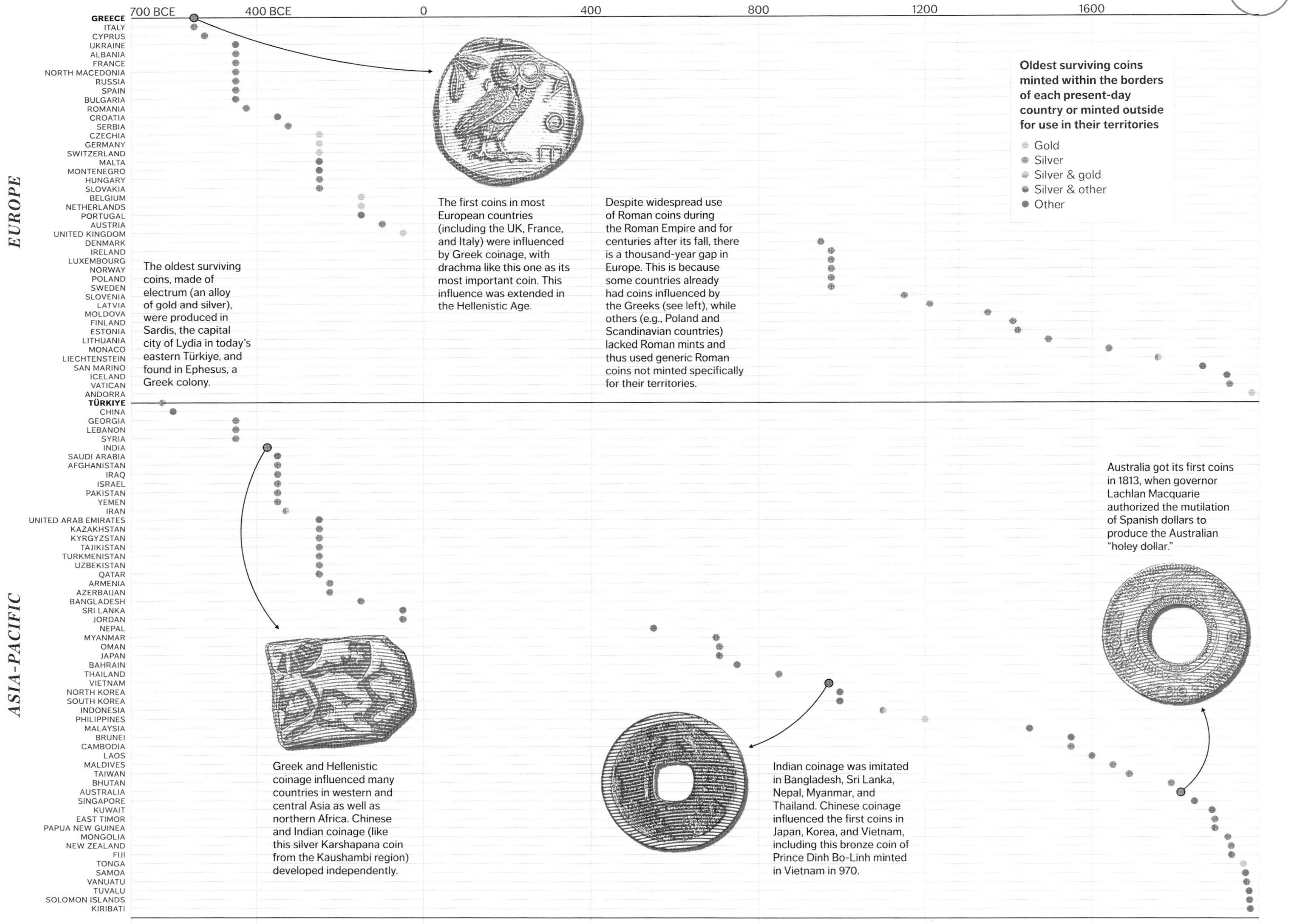

Oldest surviving coins minted within the borders of each present-day country or minted outside for use in their territories

- Gold
- Silver
- Silver & gold
- Silver & other
- Other

700 BCE | 400 BCE | 0 | 400 | 800 | 1200 | 1600

EUROPE

GREECE
ITALY
CYPRUS
UKRAINE
ALBANIA
FRANCE
NORTH MACEDONIA
RUSSIA
SPAIN
BULGARIA
ROMANIA
CROATIA
SERBIA
CZECHIA
GERMANY
SWITZERLAND
MALTA
MONTENEGRO
HUNGARY
SLOVAKIA
BELGIUM
NETHERLANDS
PORTUGAL
AUSTRIA
UNITED KINGDOM
DENMARK
IRELAND
LUXEMBOURG
NORWAY
POLAND
SWEDEN
SLOVENIA
LATVIA
MOLDOVA
FINLAND
ESTONIA
LITHUANIA
MONACO
LIECHTENSTEIN
SAN MARINO
ICELAND
VATICAN
ANDORRA

ASIA-PACIFIC

TÜRKIYE
CHINA
GEORGIA
LEBANON
SYRIA
INDIA
SAUDI ARABIA
AFGHANISTAN
IRAQ
ISRAEL
PAKISTAN
YEMEN
IRAN
UNITED ARAB EMIRATES
KAZAKHSTAN
KYRGYZSTAN
TAJIKISTAN
TURKMENISTAN
UZBEKISTAN
QATAR
ARMENIA
AZERBAIJAN
BANGLADESH
SRI LANKA
JORDAN
NEPAL
MYANMAR
OMAN
JAPAN
BAHRAIN
THAILAND
VIETNAM
NORTH KOREA
SOUTH KOREA
INDONESIA
PHILIPPINES
MALAYSIA
BRUNEI
CAMBODIA
LAOS
MALDIVES
TAIWAN
BHUTAN
AUSTRALIA
SINGAPORE
KUWAIT
EAST TIMOR
PAPUA NEW GUINEA
MONGOLIA
NEW ZEALAND
FIJI
TONGA
SAMOA
VANUATU
TUVALU
SOLOMON ISLANDS
KIRIBATI

The oldest surviving coins, made of electrum (an alloy of gold and silver), were produced in Sardis, the capital city of Lydia in today's eastern Türkiye, and found in Ephesus, a Greek colony.

The first coins in most European countries (including the UK, France, and Italy) were influenced by Greek coinage, with drachma like this one as its most important coin. This influence was extended in the Hellenistic Age.

Despite widespread use of Roman coins during the Roman Empire and for centuries after its fall, there is a thousand-year gap in Europe. This is because some countries already had coins influenced by the Greeks (see left), while others (e.g., Poland and Scandinavian countries) lacked Roman mints and thus used generic Roman coins not minted specifically for their territories.

Greek and Hellenistic coinage influenced many countries in western and central Asia as well as northern Africa. Chinese and Indian coinage (like this silver Karshapana coin from the Kaushambi region) developed independently.

Indian coinage was imitated in Bangladesh, Sri Lanka, Nepal, Myanmar, and Thailand. Chinese coinage influenced the first coins in Japan, Korea, and Vietnam, including this bronze coin of Prince Dinh Bo-Linh minted in Vietnam in 970.

Australia got its first coins in 1813, when governor Lachlan Macquarie authorized the mutilation of Spanish dollars to produce the Australian "holey dollar."

Metallic Money

The global spread of coinage tells a history of civilization.

SHELLS, GRAINS, METALS, and other materials have been used as money since the invention of finance. Of all these materials, metals—particularly the precious variety—gained most popularity due to their malleability, durability, and intrinsic value (e.g., as jewelry). Standardizing the use of metals as money by weighing them, marking them, and checking their purity led to the invention of coinage. Minted in a variety of ways including striking, punching, and casting metals, they were mainly used in wholesale transactions but with time penetrated retail trade and everyday lives, transforming economy and society.

Although evidence for the oldest use of precious metals as money comes from ancient Mesopotamia and Egypt, the oldest surviving coins come from Asia Minor, in today's eastern Türkiye. From there metal coins, struck mainly in silver, spread through the ancient Greek and Roman worlds around the Mediterranean basin, across Europe, western Asia, and northern Africa. Independently from European developments, coins cast in bronze emerged in China, and coins punched in silver emerged in India. Coinage then spread through eastern and southern Asia. European colonizers, mainly the Spanish, introduced coinage to the Americas in the sixteenth century, using silver and gold mined in the region. Other colonizers, mainly British and French, introduced coins in sub-Saharan Africa, Australia, and Oceania. While silver had been the main material of the first coinage in most countries, in the mid-nineteenth century it gave way to aluminum, copper, nickel, tin, and their combinations. Since then, banknotes printed for larger denominations have replaced the need for using expensive silver or gold.

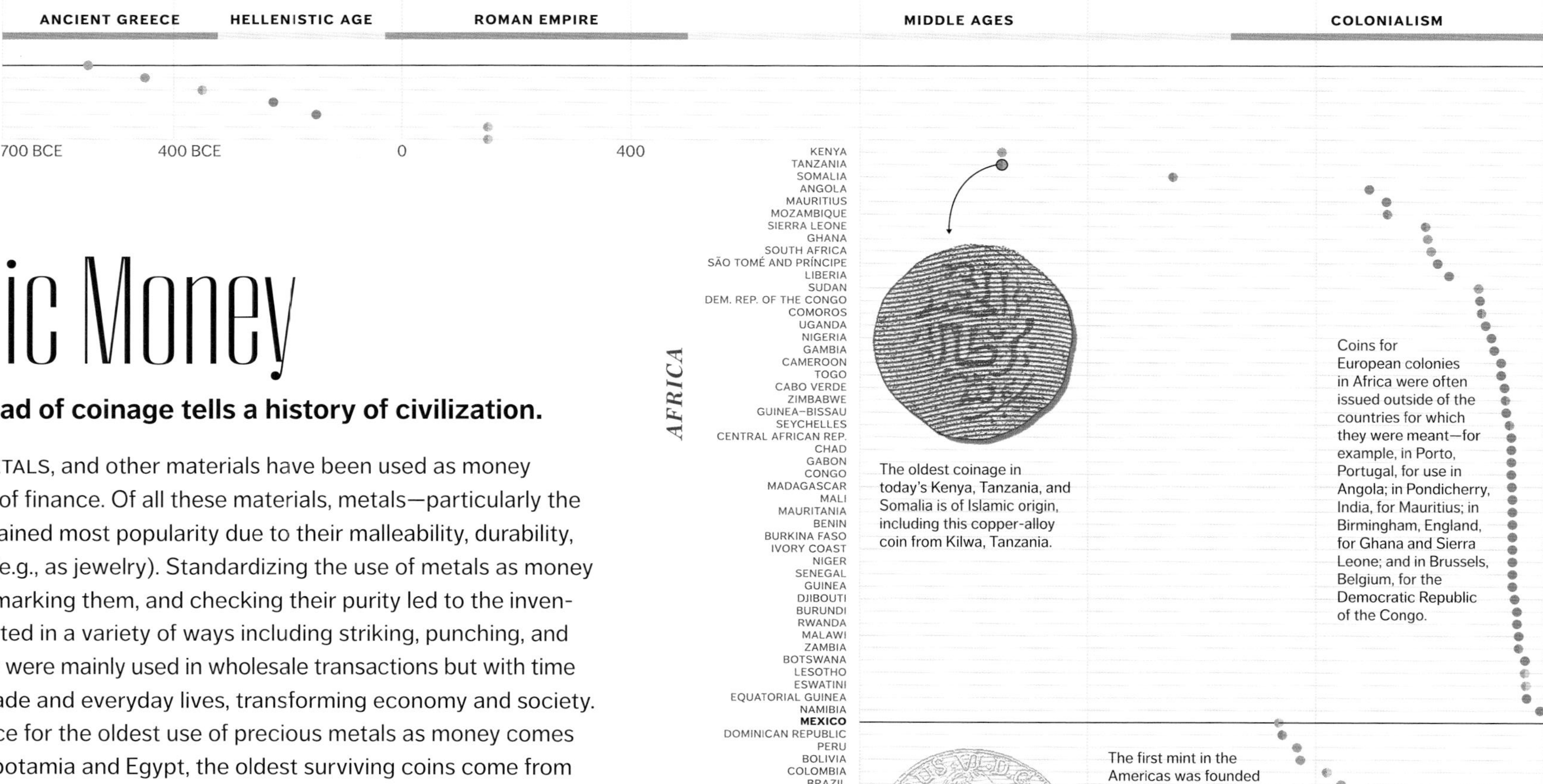

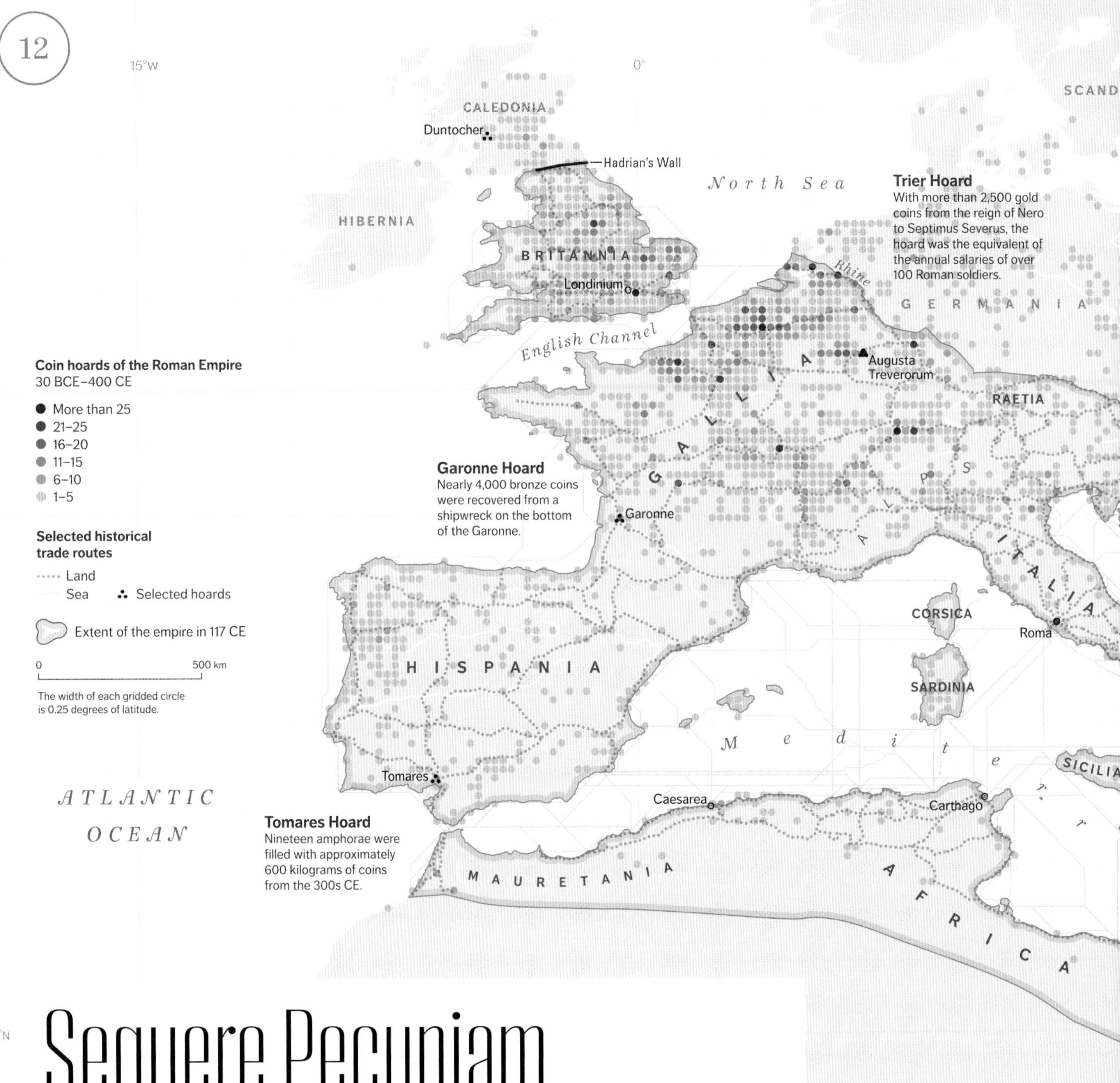

Sequere Pecuniam

The influence of Roman coins extended far beyond their empire.

THE LATIN SAYING *sequere pecuniam* (follow the money) means that if you want to get to the bottom of a matter, you must understand monetary flows related to it. In this spirit, to understand finance in the Roman Empire, we can follow coin hoards from that period.

The Roman Republic adopted Greek-style coinage as the Romans expanded into southern Italy and its Greek colonies. When Rome defeated Carthago in the Second Punic War, the production of coinage intensified, with the silver *denarius* as the main currency. Roman imperial coinage evolved into a system of gold, silver, and bronze coins. The face value of the most valuable coin (the gold *aureus*) was 1,600 times greater than the smallest (the copper *quadrans*), allowing flexibility in use. Coinage was dominated by the state, and the emperor was by far the richest person. The gradual displacement of local coins with Roman coins took over five hundred years. It was only in the 290s CE that the Roman world finally achieved a monopoly of standardized imperial coinage.

The map shows a high density of coin hoards along historical trade routes and around major cities. There are plentiful hoards along frontiers, such as the Rhine and the

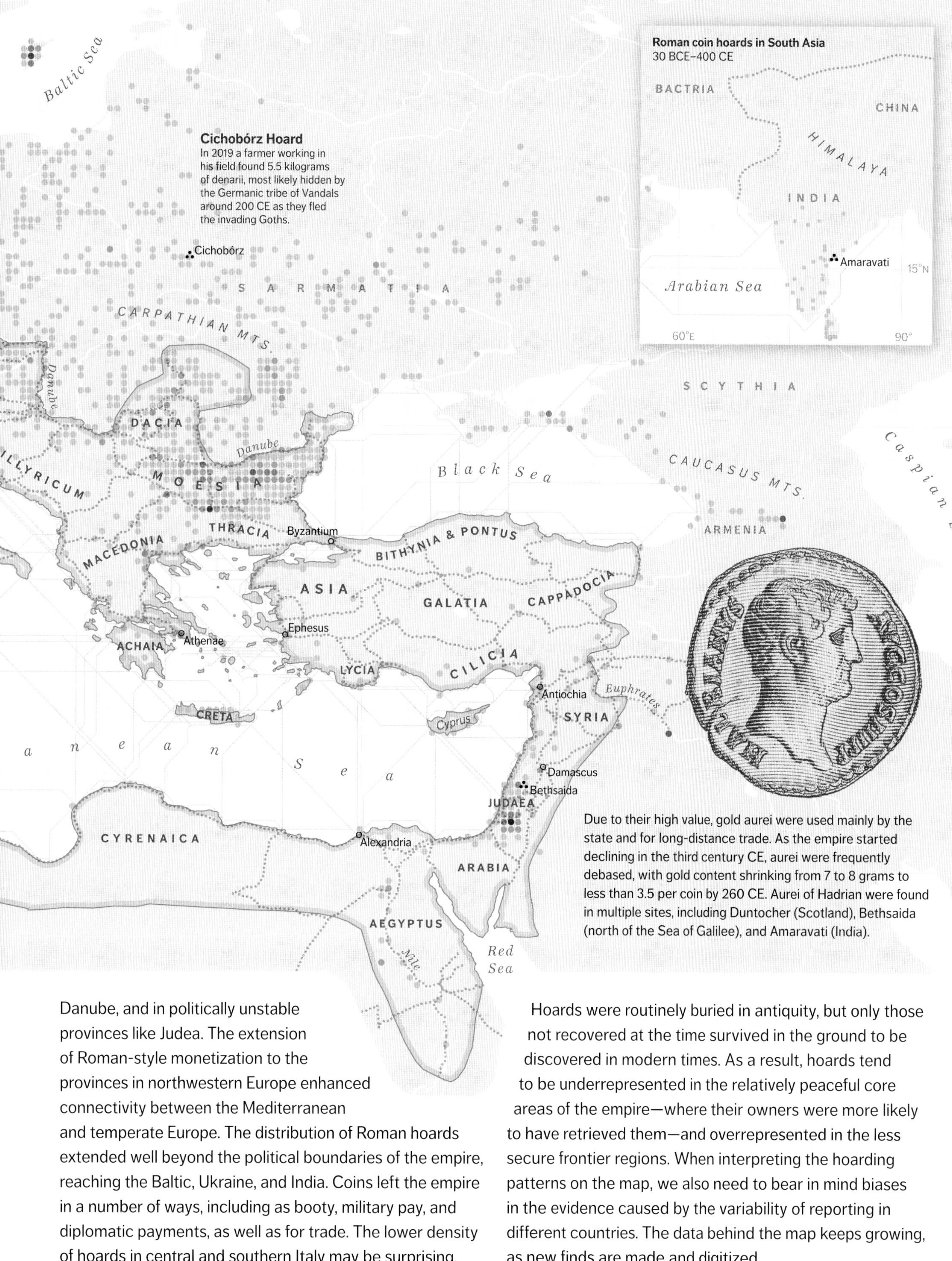

Due to their high value, gold aurei were used mainly by the state and for long-distance trade. As the empire started declining in the third century CE, aurei were frequently debased, with gold content shrinking from 7 to 8 grams to less than 3.5 per coin by 260 CE. Aurei of Hadrian were found in multiple sites, including Duntocher (Scotland), Bethsaida (north of the Sea of Galilee), and Amaravati (India).

Danube, and in politically unstable provinces like Judea. The extension of Roman-style monetization to the provinces in northwestern Europe enhanced connectivity between the Mediterranean and temperate Europe. The distribution of Roman hoards extended well beyond the political boundaries of the empire, reaching the Baltic, Ukraine, and India. Coins left the empire in a number of ways, including as booty, military pay, and diplomatic payments, as well as for trade. The lower density of hoards in central and southern Italy may be surprising.

Hoards were routinely buried in antiquity, but only those not recovered at the time survived in the ground to be discovered in modern times. As a result, hoards tend to be underrepresented in the relatively peaceful core areas of the empire—where their owners were more likely to have retrieved them—and overrepresented in the less secure frontier regions. When interpreting the hoarding patterns on the map, we also need to bear in mind biases in the evidence caused by the variability of reporting in different countries. The data behind the map keeps growing, as new finds are made and digitized.

Like many financial words, the Chinese character for "buy" was derived from the shape of a cowrie snail with a striped shell and two antennae.

Yuan and Its Ancestors

For more than a thousand years, Chinese money has influenced the world, first as coins, then paper.

DESPITE TODAY'S HEATED DEBATE on the internationalization of the Chinese currency and its future global influence, little attention is paid to the history of Chinese money. From seashores to the Silk Road, this map highlights eleven key points in its evolution and influence.

The Chinese initially used commodity money, such as silk and cowrie shells. These continued to circulate after the invention of coins in the middle of the first millennium BCE. The invention of the world's oldest paper money followed centuries later, around 1000 CE. Sophisticated ideas on the role of money in economy and society accompanied this millennia-long story of financial innovation. As a collection of essays from the Zhou dynasty found in the ancient city of Linzi stated, "If you grasp three coins, there is nothing to warm you. If you eat them, there is nothing there to nourish you. [Yet] the former kings used them to store up goods, to manage men, and to pacify the world."

Chinese paper money spread with the Mongol Empire. Marco Polo's account helped the idea of paper money spread further west and into Europe. In fact, chapter 24 of *The Travels of Marco Polo* is entitled "How the Great Kaan Causeth the Bark of Trees, Made into Something like Paper, to Pass for Money Over All His Country."

Chinese coins dominated much of East Asia and trade in South Asia. The Japanese government even stopped casting its own coins between 958 and 1635. However unlikely it is that Vietnam or Korea, not to mention Japan, would replace its domestic currencies with yuan in the twenty-first century, we should know that if they did, it would not be the first time.

Cowrie shell

SHELLS

DYNASTIES

商周

The oldest artifacts of Chinese financial history come from the tomb of Fu Hao, a female general of the Shang dynasty. They are cowrie shells discovered in Anyang (**1**). *The cowries were light and durable, and came from the Indian Ocean, which means their supply was limited, thus enhancing their value. Cowrie shells were used widely in ancient China before and after the Shang. In fact, they were used in Yunnan until the 1300s CE. The first record confirming the use of cowrie shells comes from the inscription inside the He Zun wine vessel from the Zhou dynasty found in Luoyang* (**2**).

SILK

DYNASTIES

唐

During the Tang dynasty, the capital Chang'an (**4**) *was a bustling financial center on the Silk Road, with financiers exchanging currencies, taking deposits, and making loans. Silk functioned as both a traded good and as money alongside coins and other commodities. A contract from 661 CE discovered in Turfan* (**5**) *records a loan of thirty bolts of bleached silk at a monthly interest of four bolts.*

COINS

DYNASTIES

周唐宋元大明大清

The oldest coins made in China were found in Linzi (**3**)*, the capital of Qi state. They were called* ***daobi****, made of bronze, and shaped like knives with the inscription "Construct the Nation," emphasizing the nation-building role of money. Chinese coins spread to the east and south. Prior to 1100 CE, all coins in Korea* (**6**) *were Chinese; the first coins minted in Japan, circa 708 CE* (**7**)*, were based on Chinese-style coins; and in Southeast Asia* (**8**)*, Chinese coins played a big part in trade. In Vietnam they circulated alongside local currency, while further south they were found in ports such as Kota Cina and Temasik and on shipwrecks like that of the Intan, which sank in the early 10th c. CE. The most common Chinese coin found in East and Southeast Asia is the Tang dynasty copper* ***Kaiyuan Tongbao****.*

PAPER

DYNASTIES

宋元大明大清

During the Song dynasty in today's Sichuan province, inflation caused by excessive minting of coins was so high that a pound of salt cost a pound and a half of iron coins. This incited a rebellion in 993 CE, with rebels capturing Chengdu (**9**) *and closing mints. When the Song recaptured the city, there was a shortage of coinage, and trade was based on privately issued bills of exchange called* ***jiaozi****. Gradually their issuance was centralized by the government. Khublai Khan, the founder of the Yuan dynasty, reunified China as part of the Mongol Empire, with the seat in Dadu (Beijing)* (**10**)*, and introduced* ***yuan****. Mongols spread paper money to western Asia. In 1294 CE paper notes imitating yuan were printed in Tabriz* (**11**)*.*

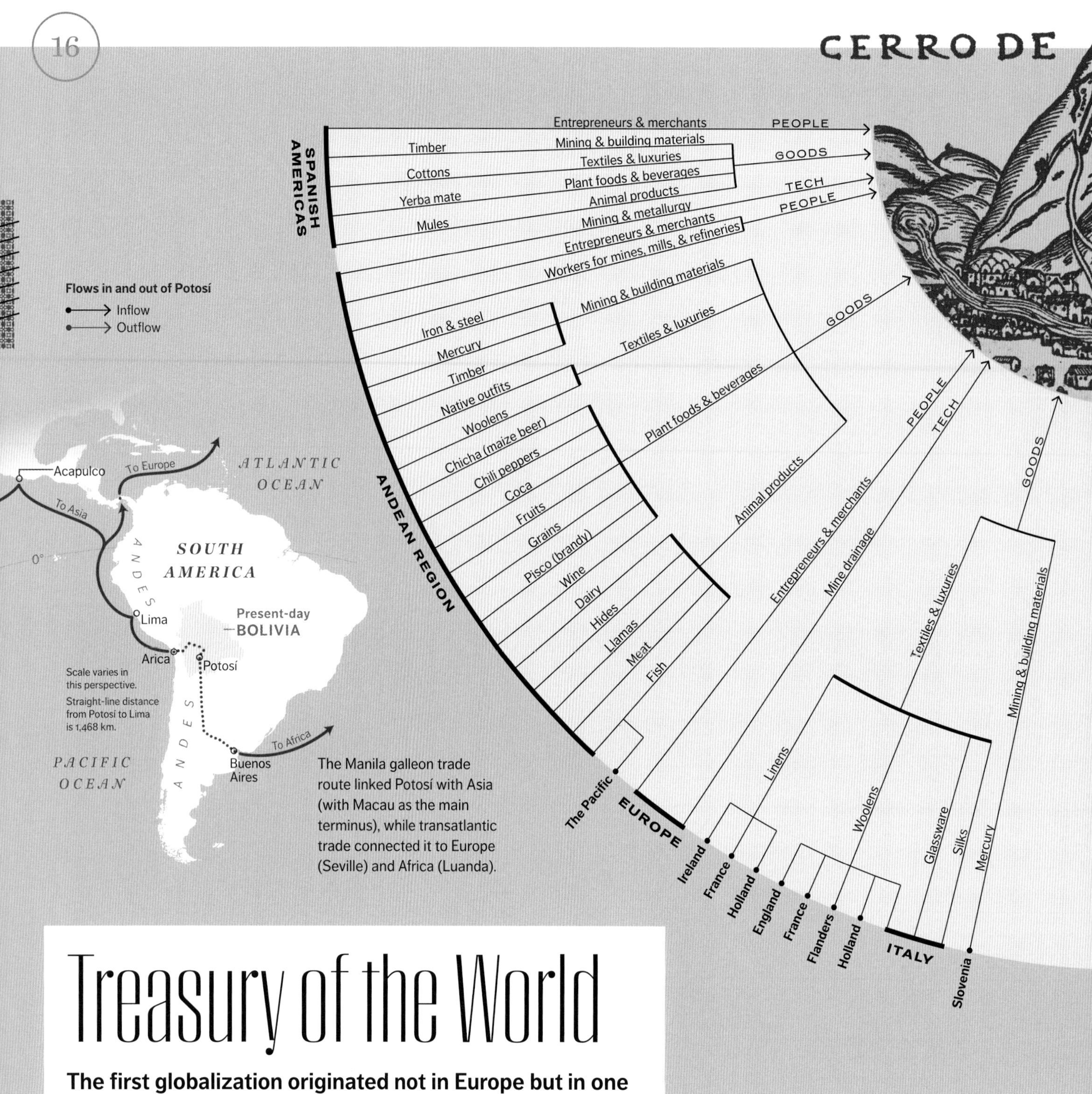

The Manila galleon trade route linked Potosí with Asia (with Macau as the main terminus), while transatlantic trade connected it to Europe (Seville) and Africa (Luanda).

Treasury of the World

The first globalization originated not in Europe but in one of the highest and most isolated cities in the world.

IN 1545, A NATIVE ANDEAN MINER named Diego Gualpa stumbled upon the world's richest silver deposit on a hill near Potosí, over 4,000 meters above sea level in an isolated part of today's Bolivia. Soon thousands of miners were working in the crevices of Cerro Rico, or "rich peak," then under control of the Spanish Empire, which had conquered this territory from the Incas. In 1561 Philip II of Spain decreed Potosí an imperial town. Over the next century Cerro Rico produced about half the world's silver, and Potosí became the largest city of the Americas, with a population close to 150,000. Charles V, Holy Roman emperor and king of Spain, christened Potosí the "treasury of the world."

As a seemingly inexhaustible source of silver, Potosí became the hub in a network of flows with unprecedented scale and scope. Potosí attracted people and goods from several continents, and its silver made the Spanish real the world's first global currency. More than just serving the Spanish Empire, Potosí stimulated economic activity globally. Its legend traveled the world, fueling the creation of colonial enterprises such as the British South Sea

POTOSI

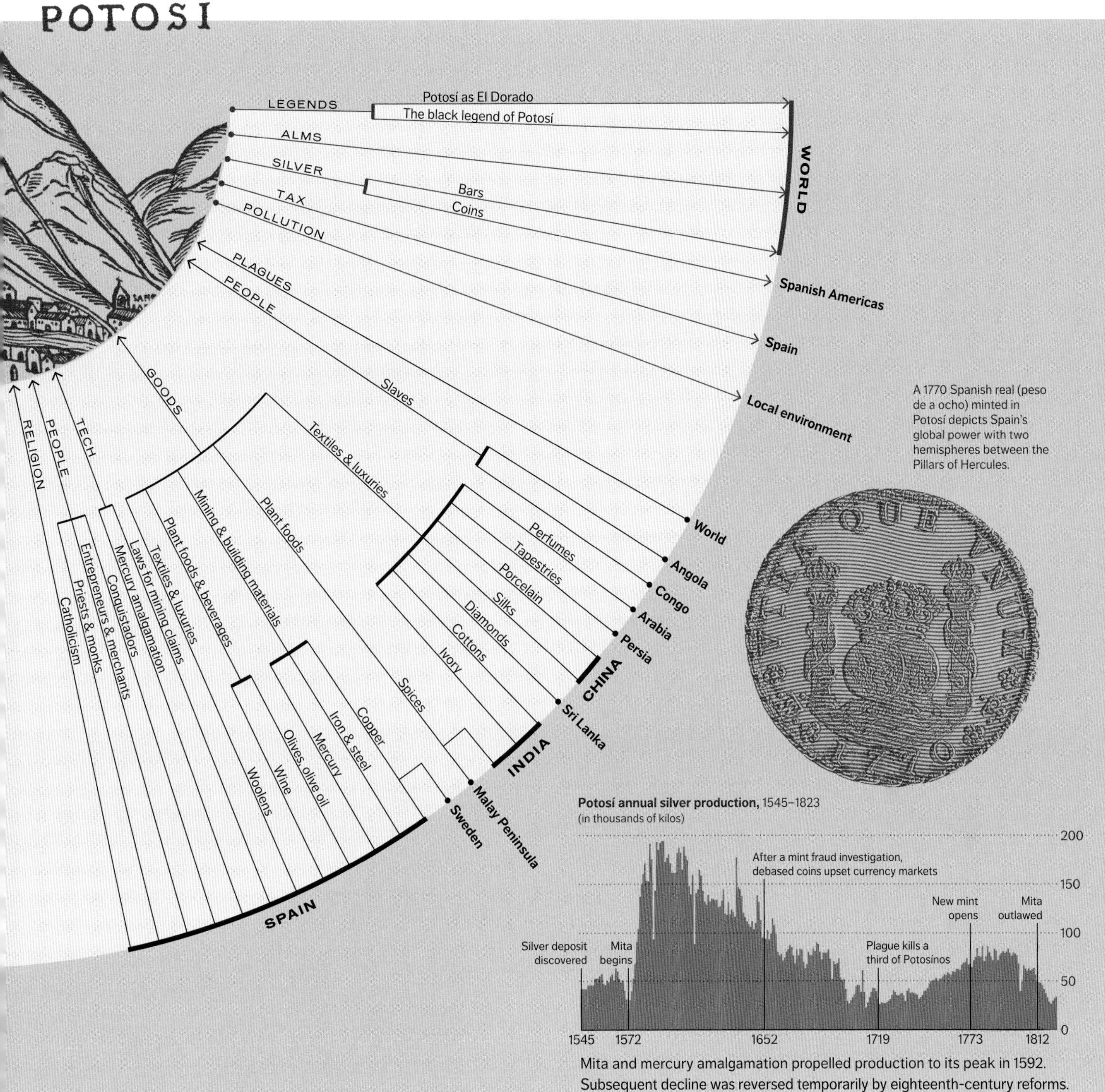

A 1770 Spanish real (peso de a ocho) minted in Potosí depicts Spain's global power with two hemispheres between the Pillars of Hercules.

Mita and mercury amalgamation propelled production to its peak in 1592. Subsequent decline was reversed temporarily by eighteenth-century reforms.

Company, which searched in vain for El Dorado before going bust in 1720.

All this happened at an unimaginable human and environmental cost. In 1572 Viceroy Francisco de Toledo imposed *mita*—a mandatory rotational labor system—on Andean villages, drafting up to fifteen thousand men a year. Some had to march, often with their families, hundreds of kilometers to Potosí. Many thousands died young in Potosí's silver mines, mills, and refineries. Toledo also introduced mercury amalgamation to refine silver, which revolutionized productivity but led to the deadly pollution of water, air, and soil. This contributed to the black legend of Potosí, with Cerro Rico described as the "blood mountain" and "mouth of hell" that "ate men." While Potosí thrived, its Andean hinterland suffered. The depletion of the silver deposit and the fall of the Spanish Empire led to the decline of Potosí. In 1825 Simón Bolívar proclaimed Bolivian independence from Cerro Rico. "If Potosí was an environmental disaster and a moral tarpit," says historian Kris Lane, "it was also a monument to human ingenuity and survival."

Who Paid for This?

Pathbreaking audits document financial flows connecting Glasgow City Council and University of Glasgow to slavery.

THE BRITISH TRAFFICKED over three million African people to the Americas between 1556 and 1810. Enslaved Africans were first treated by law as mobile (chattel) and later as immobile assets (real estate), so they could be permanently tied to plantations. The state-sanctioned slavery underpinned a transatlantic system of commerce, which contributed to the development of metropolitan economies across Great Britain, particularly at ports along the western seaboard such as Glasgow.

Between 1700 and 1815, around 90,000 Scots emigrated to North America, particularly to Virginia, Maryland, and North Carolina, centers of tobacco production enabled by slavery. Prominent Glasgow merchants known as "tobacco lords" imported American tobacco and re-exported it globally. After the American Revolution, the merchants switched to sugar from the West Indies (mainly Jamaica, but also Antigua, Barbados, Grenada, St. Vincent, Trinidad and Tobago) as well as from British Guiana and Brazil in South America. Many Glaswegians were plantation owners and enslavers, and some trafficked enslaved Africans. Much of the slavery-derived wealth of Glasgow came from the sugar trade, dominated by the city's "sugar aristocracy." Glasgow merchants also imported cotton produced by enslaved Africans and exported cotton and linen textiles worldwide, facilitating Scotland's Industrial Revolution.

Pathbreaking historical audits published since 2018 have revealed the slavery money connections of two leading institutions in Glasgow: the municipal government and the university. The government invested in the Company of Scotland, which trafficked enslaved Africans in the Indian Ocean, and received reimbursement when the company was dissolved. It borrowed money from the enslaver and governor of Virginia, Laurence Dinwiddie, who lived in Germiston House. It also received donations derived from slavery in the West Indies, North America, and South America, including in the form of schools, houses, and a library. Though home to leading abolitionists, the University of Glasgow likewise collected significant donations from people who profited from slavery. In the late 1860s such donations helped the university move and expand from the Old College site to the new campus. Asking "who paid for this?" is an essential step toward acknowledging and repairing history.

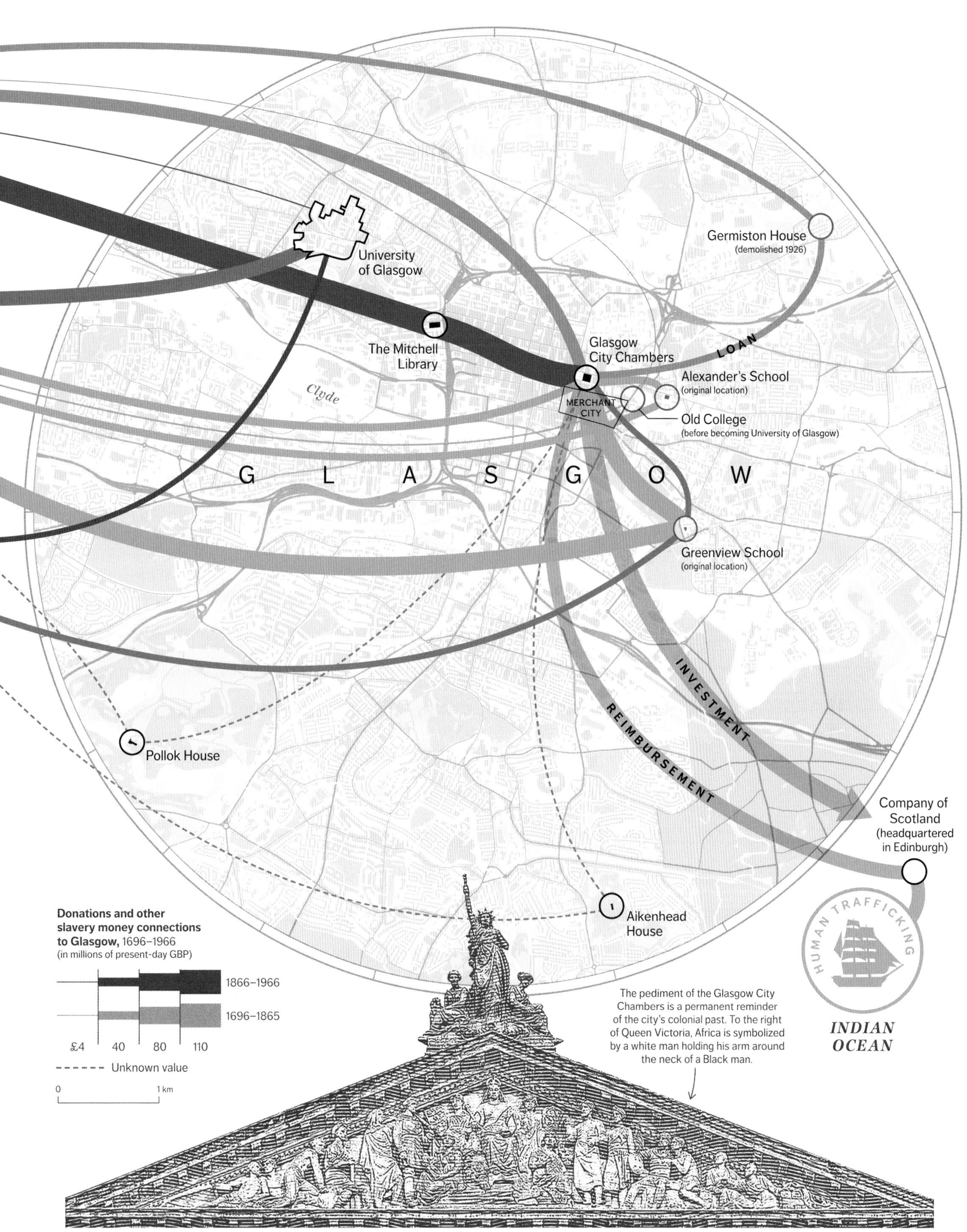

The pediment of the Glasgow City Chambers is a permanent reminder of the city's colonial past. To the right of Queen Victoria, Africa is symbolized by a white man holding his arm around the neck of a Black man.

At Amsterdam, however,
no point of faith is better
established than that for
every guilder, circulated
as bank money, there is a
correspondent guilder in
gold or silver to be found in
the treasure of the bank.
Adam Smith
1723–1790

OLD TOWN HALL, AMSTERDAM

Adam Smith, Financial Geographer

Known as the founder of modern economics, Smith also offers pioneering insights on money, finance, and financial centers.

NO HISTORY OF FINANCE would be complete without discussing three of its most influential thinkers: Adam Smith, Karl Marx, and John Maynard Keynes. On the following pages, we explore their ideas and how they changed the financial world. Adam Smith (1723–1790) is known most for his analysis of the division of labor and his advocacy of the invisible hand of the market. Few would associate him with finance, fewer still with geography. Nonetheless, a close reading of his main work, *The Wealth of Nations*, reveals insights on both.

Smith believed in the benefits of competition in financial markets and praised the ability of commercial banks to issue their own money without guarantees from the state. However, for Smith, the benefits of free financial markets were anything but automatic. Writing about the confidence in the "fortune, probity, and prudence of a particular banker" that is required for turning paper into money, he emphasized the role of trust in finance. He also advised against excessive creation of paper money, talking about the "Daedalian wings" of bank money, which can never be as secure as the solid ground of gold and silver. He was skeptical about companies with publicly traded stocks because stock markets separate owners from managers and leave investors open to abuse by the latter. In his view, some bank and market regulation is necessary for financial stability. Nobody before had described both the benefits and shortcomings of free financial markets with such attention to both economic and social factors.

In Smith's time, Amsterdam was still ahead of London as a financial center. To understand how international finance worked, Smith corresponded with Henry Hope, founder of Amsterdam-based Hope & Co., the leading bank of the eighteenth century. In an analysis befitting a financial geographer, Smith discussed factors that helped explain Amsterdam's financial prowess, including its location, information, expertise, foreign trade, quality of institutions, and trust. For example, merchants exporting grains from Baltic countries or wine from Portugal found Amsterdam an ideal place for transshipping their goods and financing their trade. He described the pioneering role of the Bank of Amsterdam in providing money guaranteed by the state, thus functioning like a modern central bank. The quotes at left stress how the reliability of this bank generated trust that served Amsterdam as a financial powerhouse. Its power may have since declined, but Smith's ideas endure.

Money in a World of Contradictions

Marx put money at the center of his analysis of capitalism and his ideology to abolish it.

IN HIS MAGNUM OPUS, *CAPITAL*, Karl Marx (1818–1883) analyzed capitalism as a never-ending expansion of markets enabled by the use of money. At the heartless center of it all, he saw a cycle wherein money buys means of production, such as land, labor, and raw materials; these produce goods and services, which are sold for profits; and profits are then reinvested in the cycle to make more money.

Marx wrote *Capital* in London. Quotes on the right illustrate his observations on the concentration of financial power in the city. While cities further north like Birmingham, Glasgow, and Manchester were centers of manufacturing in his time, London was the undisputed capital of capitalism because it was the center of government, empire, and money. He saw capitalists, who own the means of production, as the ruling class, collaborating with governments, which support the accumulation of profits, for example, by protecting private property. With government backing, capitalists can thus exploit labor and the natural environment. Marx's key insight was that capitalism ultimately contradicts itself. While promoting innovation and economic growth, it generates its own crises, as an addiction to profit leads to overproduction, the goods of which exploited workers cannot afford to buy, all while capitalists hoard excessive wealth. And money feeding the cycle in the form of credit only exacerbates capitalism's tendency toward crisis. Therefore, reading Marx offers a profound critique of the system we live in now and the centrality of finance in this system. If he were alive today, Marx would not be surprised by debates on how London casts a shadow on the development of other regions of the UK. Problems of excessive financial centralization still affect many countries.

Marx wanted his diagnosis of capitalism to change the world. His *Manifesto of the Communist Party,* co-authored with Friedrich Engels and published before *Capital,* identified money as a problem society needs to overcome. It complained that even family had been reduced to a "mere money relation" and called for "centralization of money and credit in the hands of the state through a national bank with state capital, and the suppression of all private banks and bankers." A communist revolution, he predicted, would make money superfluous. Countries that tried to nationalize their whole financial systems hardly succeeded. However, Marx's warnings about money alienating people from each other and their environment are timeless.

The rural depositor imagines he is simply depositing with his banker, and also imagines that when the banker makes loans it is to private individuals whom he knows. He does not have the remotest suspicion that the banker puts his deposit at the disposal of a London bill broker, over whose operations neither of them have the slightest control.

THE ROYAL EXCHANGE, LONDON

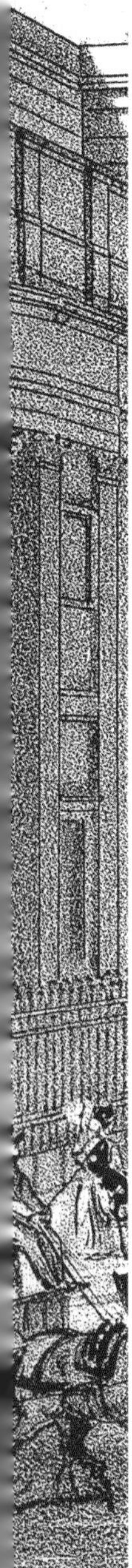

In this paper world, the real price and its real elements are nowhere to be seen, but simply bullion, metal coin, notes, bills and securities. This distortion is particularly evident in centers such as London, where the monetary business of an entire country is concentrated.

Karl Marx
1818–1883

In a system of production where the entire interconnection of the reproduction process rests on credit, a crisis must evidently break out if credit is suddenly withdrawn and only cash payment is accepted . . . the ultimate basis of the entire crisis being the expansion of [bills of exchange] far beyond the social need.

The outstanding fact is the extreme precariousness of the basis of knowledge on which our estimates of prospective yield have to be made. . . . If we speak frankly, we have to admit that our basis of knowledge for estimating the yield ten years hence of a railway, a copper mine, a textile factory, the goodwill of a patent medicine, an Atlantic liner, a building in the City of London amounts to little and sometimes to nothing.
The social object of skilled investment should be to defeat the dark forces of time and ignorance which envelop our future. The actual, private object of the most skilled investment today is "to beat the gun," as the Americans so well express it, to outwit the crowd, and to pass the bad, or depreciating, half-crown to the other fellow.
John M. Keynes
1883–1946
When he purchases an investment, the American is attaching his hopes, not so much to its prospective yield, as to a favorable change in the conventional basis of valuation, i.e. he is, in the above sense, a speculator. Speculators may do no harm as bubbles on a steady stream of enterprise. But the position is serious when enterprise becomes the bubble on a whirlpool of speculation.

Finance as a Beauty Contest

Written shortly after the financial crash of 1929, Keynes's *General Theory* offers a sharp critique of finance-led capitalism and Wall Street.

IF SMITH CAPTURED the spirit of capitalism and Marx probed its dark side, John Maynard Keynes (1883–1946) watched its descent into chaos and proposed ways to save it, while being actively involved in major events of his era.

He first rose to international fame following World War I at the Paris Peace Conference of 1919, when he resigned from the British delegation in protest of the terms of the treaty, which imposed a heavy debt on Germany. According to Keynes, this would damage German economic prospects, breed resentment, and lead to another war. He wasn't wrong.

Having witnessed the Wall Street crash of 1929, Keynes likened the stock market to a casino, dominated by short-term speculation. In other words, while the average market participant suffered from a lack of knowledge, professional financial investors spent too much energy trying to beat the market instead of examining the long-term yield of an investment. To Keynes this was like trying to guess the winner in a beauty contest, with judges trying to guess who other judges think has the most beautiful face instead of just choosing the most beautiful face. As a result, he felt values established in financial markets strayed too far from fundamentals. Consider people investing (and losing) fortunes in cryptocurrencies and crypto-assets just because they think other people will buy them too.

Published after the Great Depression of the 1930s, his book *General Theory of Employment, Interest and Money* explained why government intervention in the economy is necessary. Keynes thought that excessive optimism, which he called "animal spirits," drove investment and the economy forward. But when the public's spirits become overwhelmed by uncertainty, he felt governments needed to step in and spend money on investments to maintain demand for goods and services and prevent mass unemployment. If necessary, government intervention should include printing money.

Keynes lived through the shift of power from Great Britain to the United States. As World War II was ending, he proposed the creation of a world central bank, an international payments agency, and a new global currency. The World Bank and International Monetary Fund were influenced by his ideas, but the international currency system based on the US dollar fell short of his radical proposals. While the US's financial might prevailed over Keynes's policy suggestions, the power of his ideas may yet outlive it.

The FINANCIAL SCIENCE PRODUCTION LADDER

All nineteen people awarded the Nobel Memorial Prize in Economic Sciences for contributions to research on finance are or were white males who obtained their PhD in the US and worked there at the time of award.

Nobel Prizes awarded for contributions to financial economics, by affiliation at time of award

University of Chicago

Stanford University

Yale University

MODIGLIANI 1985 **MIT** · MARKOWITZ 1990 **CUNY** · MERTON 1997 **Harvard** · SCHOLES 1997 **LTCM** · AKERLOF 2001 **UC-Berkeley** · BERNANKE 2022 **Brookings** · DYBVIG 2022 **WashU**

Winners of the Nobel Memorial Prize in Economic Sciences, 1969–2023

For financial economics
- Born in the US
- Born outside the US

For other contributions

Shared prize

1969

2

3

3

3

3

2023

Out of twenty editors-in-chief of the top ten journals in finance (as of March 2021), only five were women and only three were based outside the US (at London Business School, Trinity College Dublin, and Utrecht University).

Editors-in-chief of the ten most cited journals in finance, by gender and country of affiliation

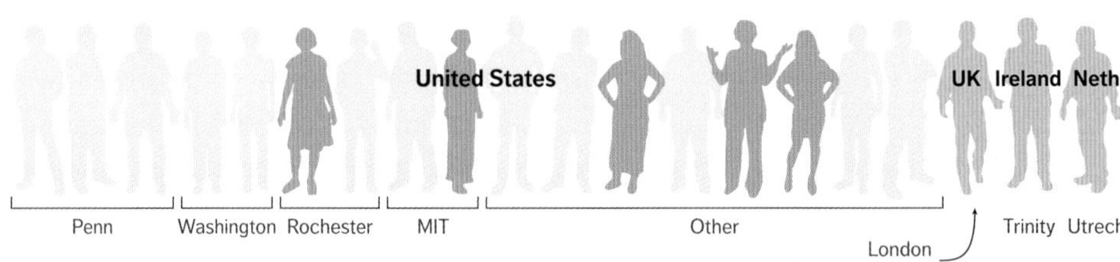

Out of 195 authors of the 100 most cited publications on finance (as of March 2021), only eleven were women, and 172 worked in the US. More authors were from the University of Chicago than from the whole world outside the US.

Authors of the 100 most cited papers on finance, by country of affiliation at the time of publication

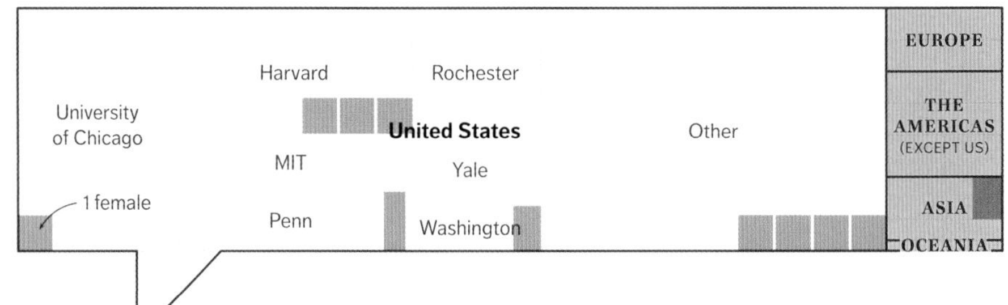

Based on the affiliation of authors, the US has the largest output of published papers on finance. Publishing by authors outside the US is growing fast, with China's output tripling between 2012 and 2019, but North America and Western Europe combined still accounted for more than 50 percent of papers in 2019.

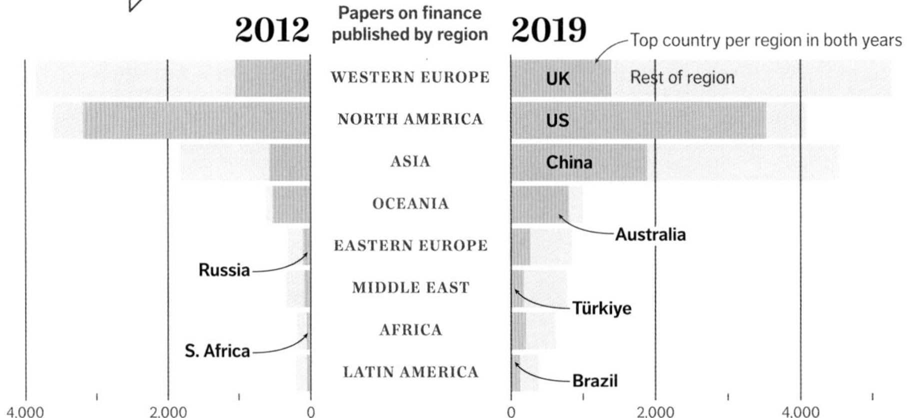

Made in the USA

Despite a rapid growth in publications from the rest of the world, the US still dominates the production of financial economics.

ADVANCEMENT IN THE SCIENCES can be thought of as a tall ladder. Publications are the first rung—"publish or perish," as the saying goes in academia. To gain influence, however, publications need citations. Other researchers need to read them and consider them significant enough to cite in their own work. Journal editors play a crucial part in the publication process by overseeing the review of submitted papers and managing the peer-review process. Ultimately it is up to them whether a paper is accepted or rejected. Some journals are so competitive and prestigious that a single publication in them can get you a job or tenure. At the very top of the ladder are prizes for papers, books, and lifetime achievements, the most coveted of which is the Nobel. Most researchers never become journal editors; very few win prizes.

The graphics on the left show that the production of science in finance is highly US- and male-dominated, particularly on higher rungs of the ladder. While the share of lead authors working in the US at the time of publication fell from 29 percent of all papers published on finance in 2012 to 20 percent in 2019, the share of US-affiliated authors among the authors of the 100 most cited papers of all time was 88 percent in 2021. The share of US-affiliated researchers among the editors-in-chief of the top ten journals was 85 percent. Women constituted only 6 percent of the authors of the most cited papers and 25 percent of the editors-in-chief.

At the top of the ladder, the Nobel Memorial Prize in Economic Sciences was awarded fifty-five times (between 1969 and 2023) to ninety-three laureates, with nineteen recognized for contributions to financial science. All nineteen were or are white males working in the US. Only three were born outside the US (Myron Scholes and Robert Mundell in Canada; Franco Modigliani in Italy). Some of them also worked for the financial sector. Scholes, for example, founded a hedge fund, which collapsed after the Asian financial crisis.

As such, financial research is possibly the most US- and male-dominated of all academic disciplines. It is hard to think of another area of the financial industry with such gender and geographical biases. This embedded lack of diversity produces research biased against developing countries and disadvantaged parts of society, which can affect education, public policy, and business strategy. Meanwhile, the nonexistence of Nobel Prizes for social sciences (other than economics) and humanities (other than literature) pushes much more diverse research on finance off the ladder.

2
CAZO
AVFC
AVFC

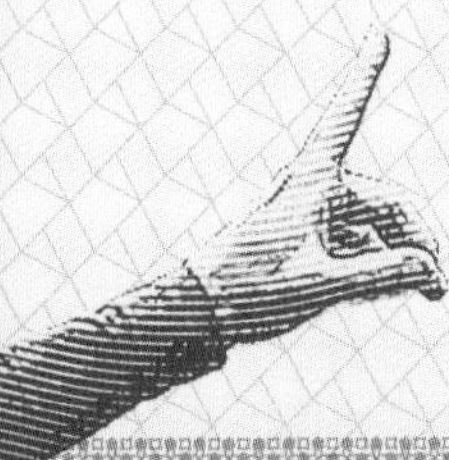

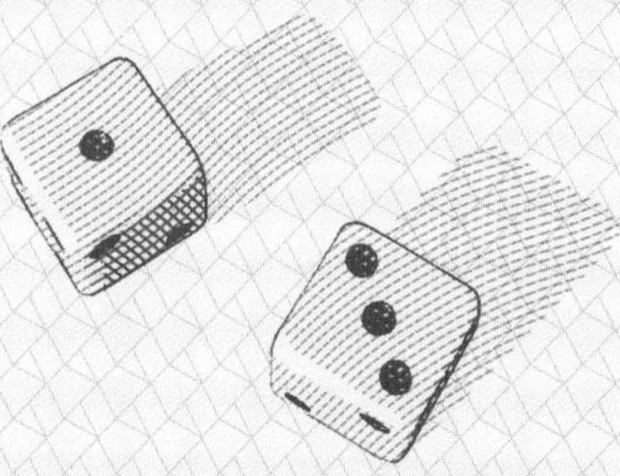

A thing is worth only
what someone else will pay for it.
SENECA

Assets & Markets

From a financial perspective, everything is a potential asset that can be bought and sold on a market. Finance is obsessed with prices, indexes, and rates. But financial markets—such as those for stocks, currencies, insurance, real estate, infrastructure, remittances, and investment banking services—produce more than prices. Distributing wealth and power, they produce space. With finance you can trade people and their skills, and even sell things you do not have.

Markets at a Glance

Annual maximum
Start
End
Annual minimum

Rising
Falling

Stock market indexes provide a window into the makeup of the world economy and its dynamics.

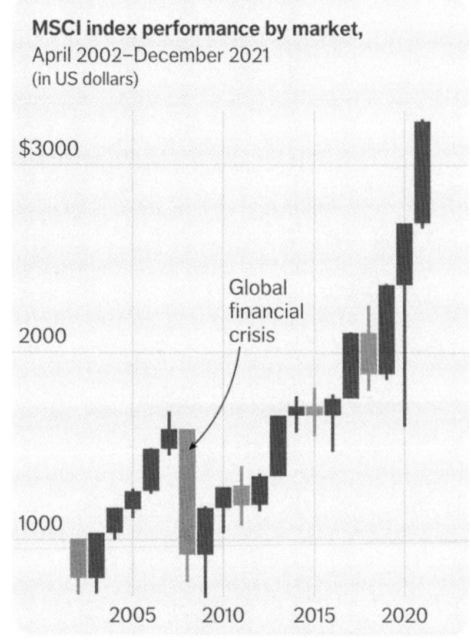

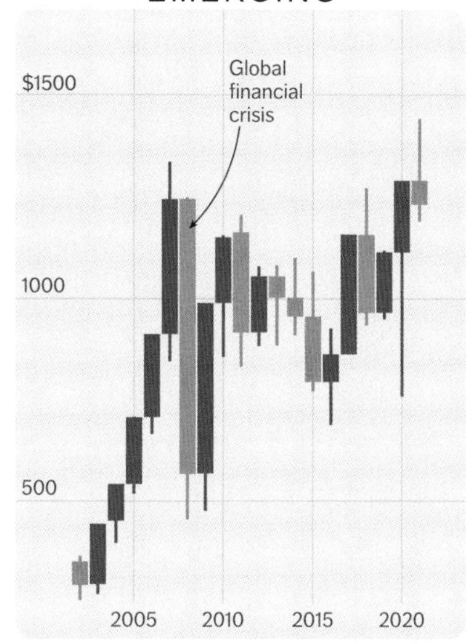

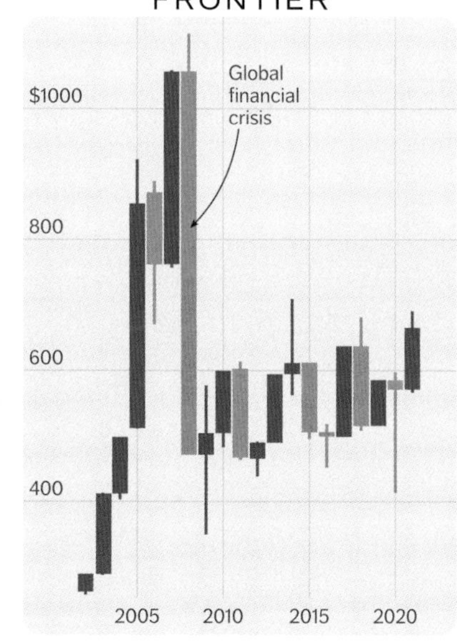

STOCK MARKET INDEXES track bundles of the most valuable stocks listed in a particular country. As a single number, an index provides a convenient shorthand for capturing what is happening in that country's financial markets. Names of indexes like the S&P 500, Nikkei 225, or FTSE 100 regularly appear in headlines of the business press. But what do they mean? And what can you learn from them?

A stock market index's market capitalization tells you the combined value of all companies in that index, typically covering the country's top 25 to 500 most valuable publicly traded companies. You can't buy a share in an index, and purchasing a single share of every company in an index is complex and expensive. However, financial products—called passive exchange-traded funds—mimic the movements of indexes through owning a portfolio of shares from the index in proportion to the market value of those shares. Passive funds can track aggregate movements across industries, countries, and markets and are often used as benchmarks for the performance of actively managed funds where investors pick the stocks.

Traders use groupings of advanced, emerging, and frontier markets from Morgan Stanley Capital International (MSCI) to gauge the global economy. This classification reflects the perceived stability, security, and risk associated with investing in stocks in a country. The candlestick charts to the right show the impact of the 2008 global financial crisis on each market group and the rate of their recoveries. Advanced markets recovered quickly, surpassing their 2007 peaks by 2014 and more than doubling in value thereafter. Emerging markets lost more and took until 2020 to reach their precrisis levels. Frontier markets suffered the largest losses in 2008 and never dug out of the hole. The sectoral structure of stock markets may explain why.

The stock market recovery of the past decade was driven by technology companies, the biggest sector in large, advanced markets such as the Netherlands, Hong Kong, and above all, the US (see donut charts). This sector (shown in turquoise) also dominates in some emerging markets such as Taiwan and South Korea and is significant in others, including China, India, and South Africa, but is typically smaller in frontier markets. By contrast, the biggest sector in many emerging and frontier markets is finance (light green), a relatively poor performer since 2008.

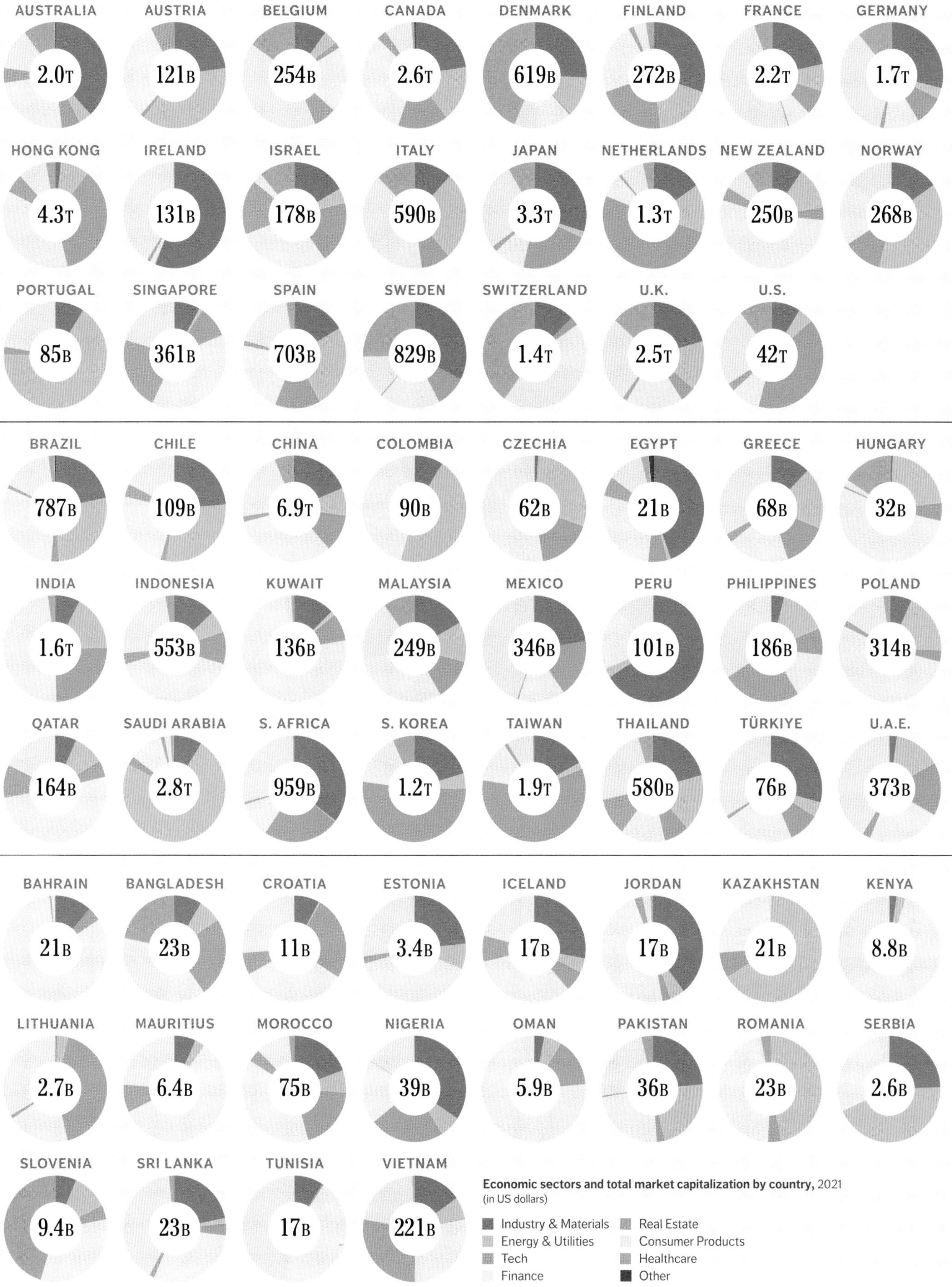

AUSTRALIA 2.0T
AUSTRIA 121B
BELGIUM 254B
CANADA 2.6T
DENMARK 619B
FINLAND 272B
FRANCE 2.2T
GERMANY 1.7T
HONG KONG 4.3T
IRELAND 131B
ISRAEL 178B
ITALY 590B
JAPAN 3.3T
NETHERLANDS 1.3T
NEW ZEALAND 250B
NORWAY 268B
PORTUGAL 85B
SINGAPORE 361B
SPAIN 703B
SWEDEN 829B
SWITZERLAND 1.4T
U.K. 2.5T
U.S. 42T

BRAZIL 787B
CHILE 109B
CHINA 6.9T
COLOMBIA 90B
CZECHIA 62B
EGYPT 21B
GREECE 68B
HUNGARY 32B
INDIA 1.6T
INDONESIA 553B
KUWAIT 136B
MALAYSIA 249B
MEXICO 346B
PERU 101B
PHILIPPINES 186B
POLAND 314B
QATAR 164B
SAUDI ARABIA 2.8T
S. AFRICA 959B
S. KOREA 1.2T
TAIWAN 1.9T
THAILAND 580B
TÜRKIYE 76B
U.A.E. 373B

BAHRAIN 21B
BANGLADESH 23B
CROATIA 11B
ESTONIA 3.4B
ICELAND 17B
JORDAN 17B
KAZAKHSTAN 21B
KENYA 8.8B
LITHUANIA 2.7B
MAURITIUS 6.4B
MOROCCO 75B
NIGERIA 39B
OMAN 5.9B
PAKISTAN 36B
ROMANIA 23B
SERBIA 2.6B
SLOVENIA 9.4B
SRI LANKA 23B
TUNISIA 17B
VIETNAM 221B

Economic sectors and total market capitalization by country, 2021
(in US dollars)

- Industry & Materials
- Energy & Utilities
- Tech
- Finance
- Real Estate
- Consumer Products
- Healthcare
- Other

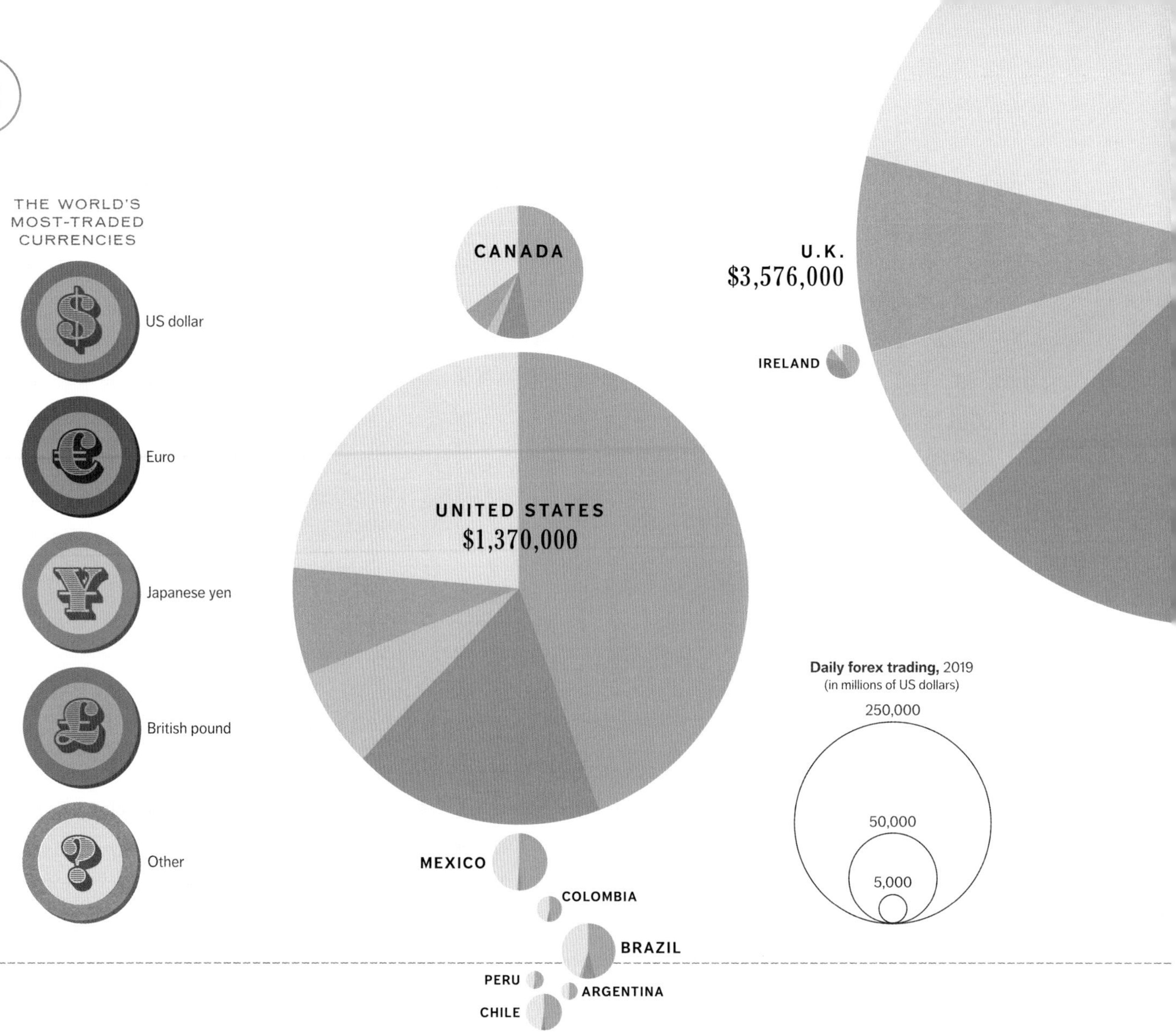

THE WORLD'S MOST-TRADED CURRENCIES
US dollar
Euro
Japanese yen
British pound
Other
CANADA
U.K.
$3,576,000
IRELAND
UNITED STATES
$1,370,000
Daily forex trading, 2019
(in millions of US dollars)
250,000
50,000
5,000
MEXICO
COLOMBIA
BRAZIL
PERU
ARGENTINA
CHILE

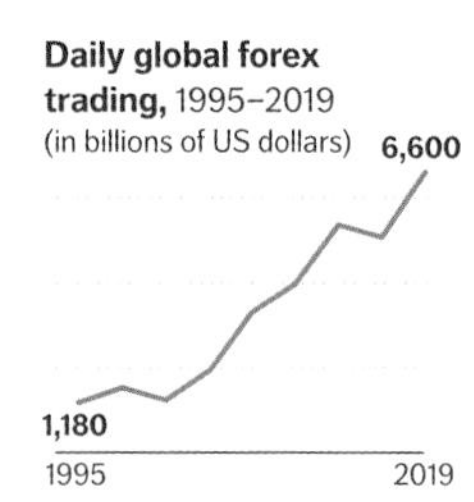

Unchanging Currencies

Daily global forex trading, 1995–2019
(in billions of US dollars)
6,600
1,180
1995
2019

The market for currencies has grown faster than the real economy, but it's been remarkably stable in terms of what currencies are traded and where.

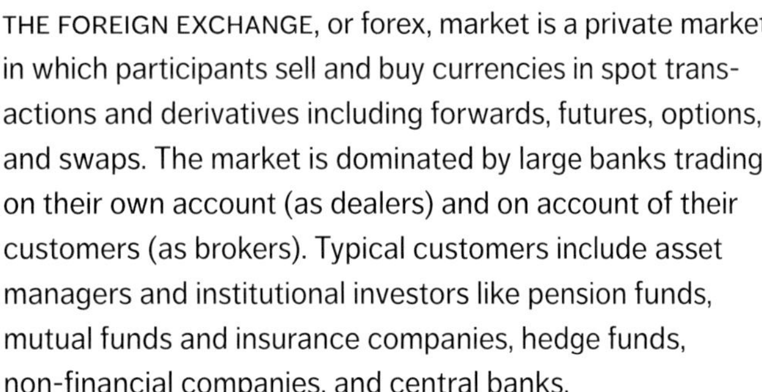

THE FOREIGN EXCHANGE, or forex, market is a private market in which participants sell and buy currencies in spot transactions and derivatives including forwards, futures, options, and swaps. The market is dominated by large banks trading on their own account (as dealers) and on account of their customers (as brokers). Typical customers include asset managers and institutional investors like pension funds, mutual funds and insurance companies, hedge funds, non-financial companies, and central banks.

The forex market is as old as currencies themselves, but a new era began in the 1970s when the US took the dollar off the gold standard and let its value "float." Most major currencies followed suit, with their prices driven by transactions on the forex market. As the line chart shows, trading increased nearly sixfold between 1995 and 2019, due in large part to the activity of hedge funds and the digitization of trading. By 2019, daily forex turnover worldwide was twenty-seven times bigger than daily GDP and ninety-six times bigger than daily merchandise trade. This demonstrates that only a fraction of forex trading is related to production or

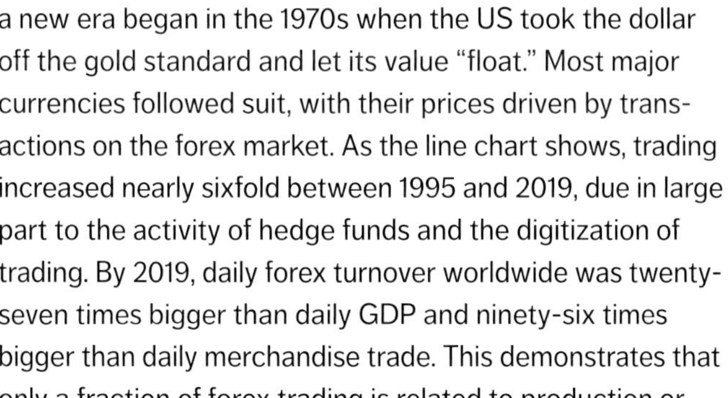

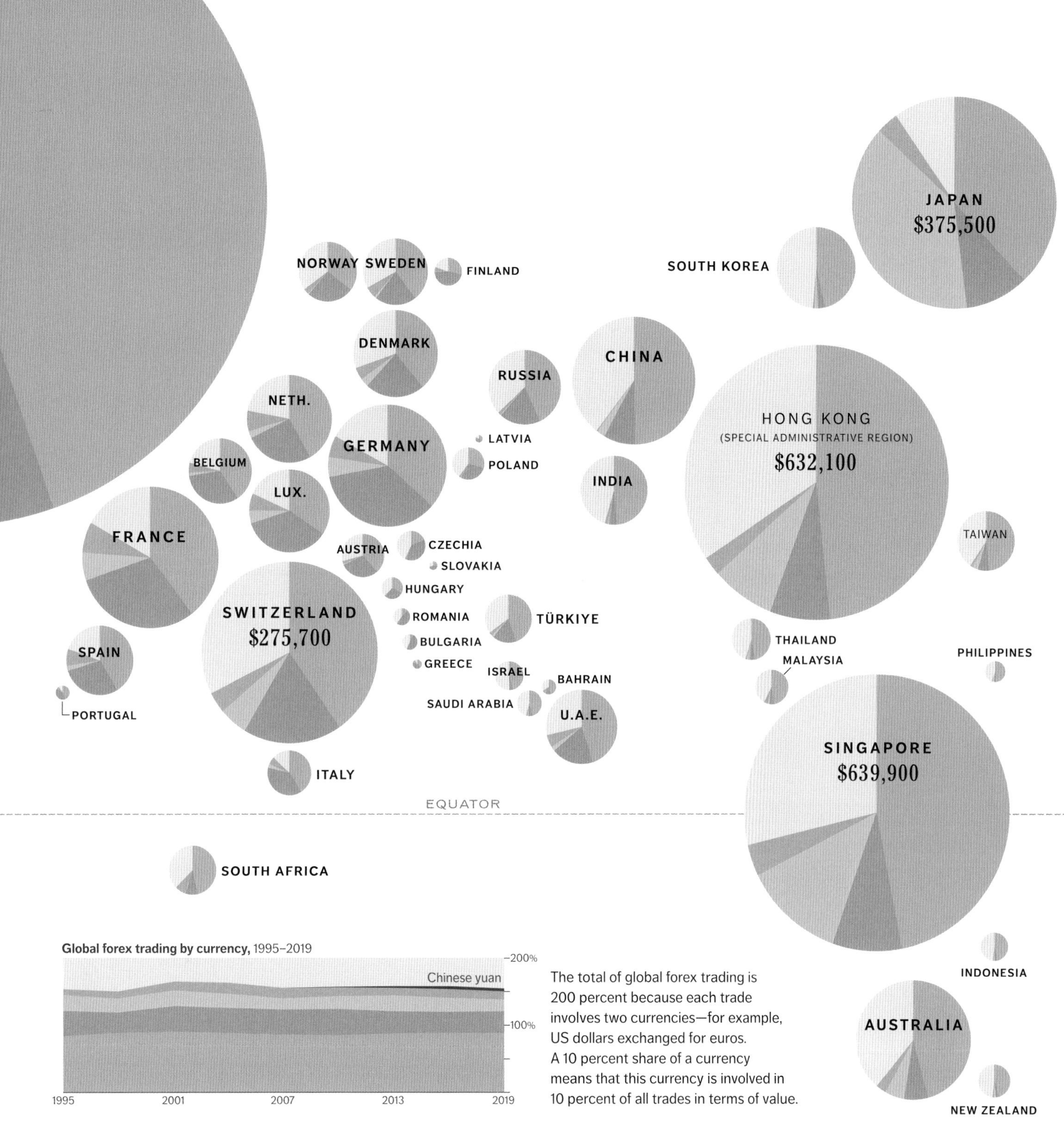

The total of global forex trading is 200 percent because each trade involves two currencies—for example, US dollars exchanged for euros. A 10 percent share of a currency means that this currency is involved in 10 percent of all trades in terms of value.

trade in goods. The bulk of it serves other financial activities such as investment, hedging, and speculation.

Forex trading is highly concentrated (see pie charts). The UK is the global center, accounting for 43 percent of turnover in 2019, with almost all trading conducted in London. It is hard to think of any other economic activity in which a single city is so dominant. Almost all major currencies have their biggest trading center in London, not in their home economy. The US, with New York as its trading center, comes second, with a 17 percent share in 2019.

The composition of forex trading by currency is also highly concentrated and remarkably stable (see stacked area chart). The US dollar has been involved in 80 percent of trades since at least 1995. The euro comes second but has deteriorated slightly since the eurozone crisis. Japan's yen and the British pound come third and fourth. Recently the Chinese yuan has inserted a wedge in the structure of forex trading. However, the size of the Chinese economy notwithstanding, the limited openness of Chinese financial markets limits the ability of its yuan to challenge the dollar.

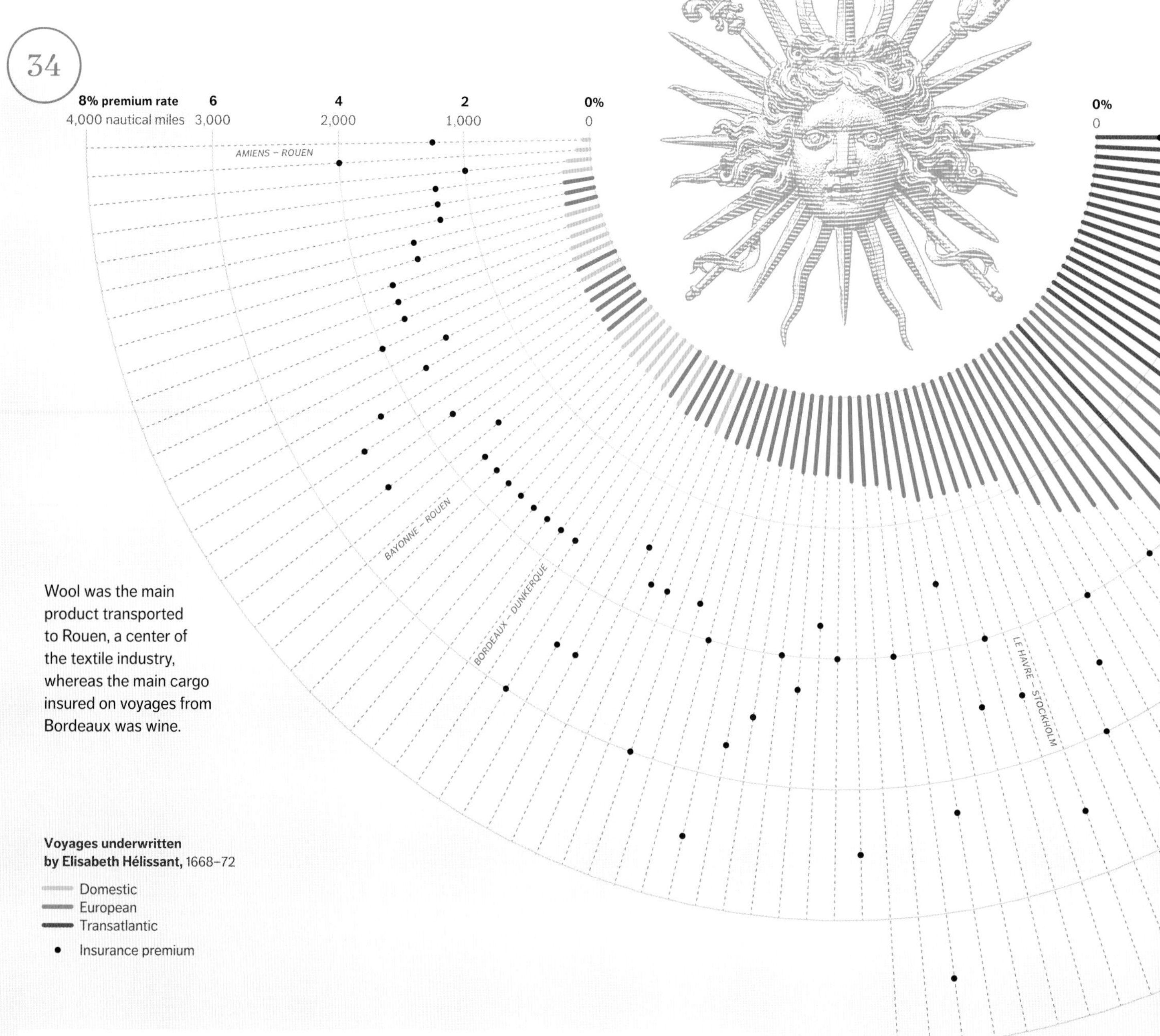

Wool was the main product transported to Rouen, a center of the textile industry, whereas the main cargo insured on voyages from Bordeaux was wine.

Voyages underwritten by Elisabeth Hélissant, 1668–72

- Domestic
- European
- Transatlantic
- Insurance premium

Pooling Risk in Paris

In 1672, during the Dutch War, Elisabeth Hélissant insured a ship sailing from Le Havre to Stockholm to bring provisions to Charles XI, the king of Sweden, a French ally against the Dutch.

The market for insuring marine risks was designed to promote trade, empower the French state, and enrich Parisian elites.

SHIPOWNERS HAVE ALWAYS faced huge risks. A ship can be grounded, flooded, hijacked, wrecked, burned, delayed, or sunk in war. Therefore, for maritime trade to be viable, shipowners need insurance.

Enter Jean-Baptiste Colbert. Eighteen years before Edward Lloyd opened the famous coffeehouse that would one day become the insurance giant Lloyd's of London, Colbert, France's first minister of state under the Sun King, Louis XIV, established a Royal Insurance Chamber in Paris in 1668, a major step in the history of insurance.

The chamber functioned as both a club for private insurers and a place to meet with merchants and mariners. The insurers underwrote voyages by promising to pay for losses of cargo and damage to vessels. High-risk voyages were underwritten by many insurers. Nearly four hundred voyages were insured this way within the first year. Over time, the chamber codified its practices, standardized policy forms, developed arbitration procedures, and created a register of ships and transactions.

One of the first insurers active in the Chamber was

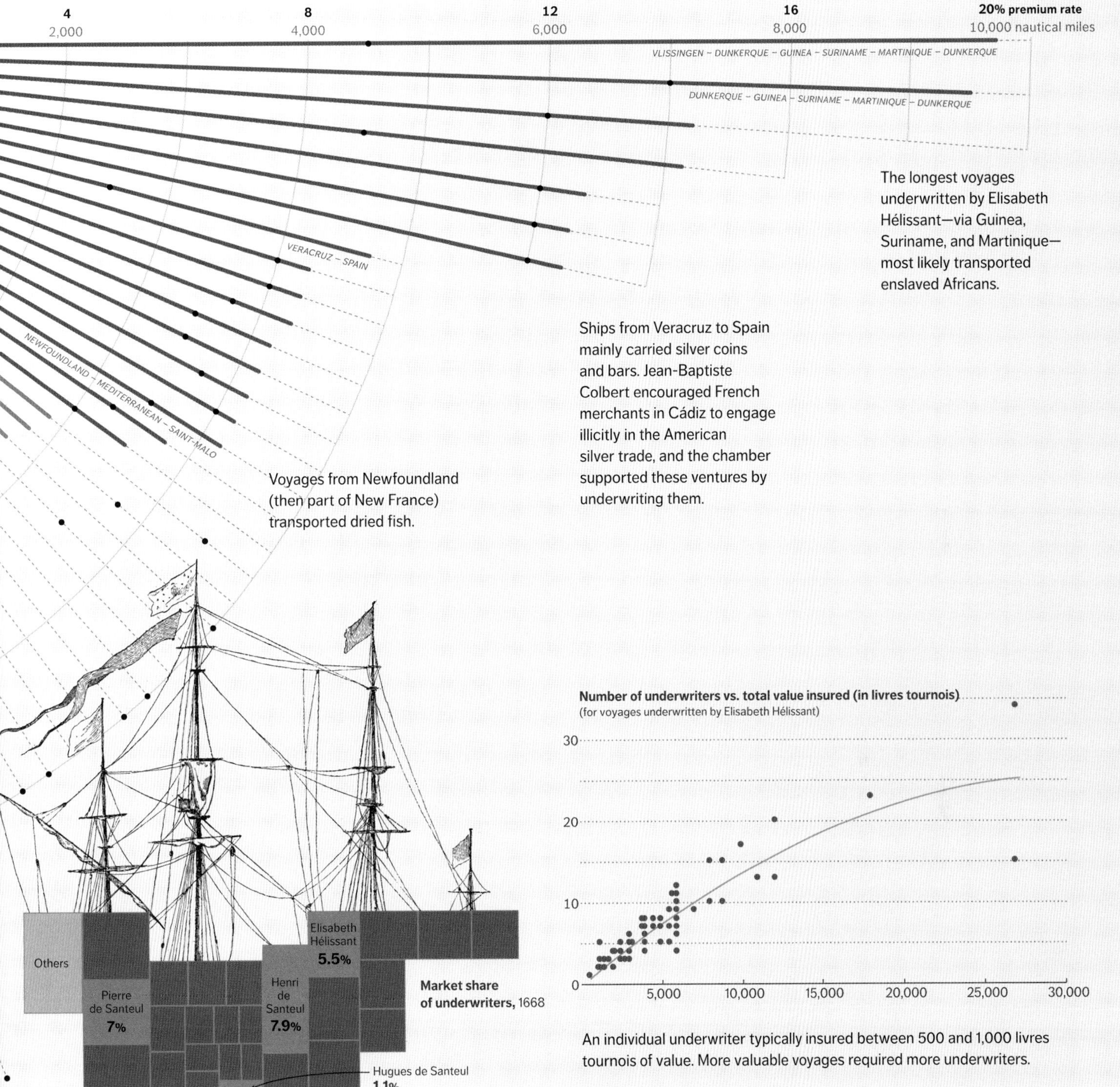

Hugues de Santeul, a wealthy merchant (along with his brothers Henri and Pierre). When he died, his wife Elisabeth Hélissant took over and quickly became one of France's leading insurers. She insured all kinds of cargo, including salt bound for the Netherlands and sugar from the Caribbean. The sunburst above shows eighty-six of the voyages she insured, from shortest to longest; black dots indicate her varying premium rates. Hélissant charged the lowest rates for short domestic voyages, higher rates for European voyages, and the highest for transatlantic voyages. Premiums also depended on factors such as the quality of the ship, the captain, and seasonal risks. Altogether Hélissant collected 3,188 *livres tournois* in premiums, a sum that would now exceed a million US dollars.

Marine risk underwriting promoted the French colonial empire, centralized power, and concentrated wealth. Paris, with its club of underwriters, became the center of France's insurance industry instead of port cities like Marseille or Rouen. In the hands of Parisian elites, insurance activity supported their wealth and power for generations.

Boomtown

International investment can make property prices soar and leave locals priced out.

INVESTING IN PROPERTY OVERSEAS can be an alluring prospect for rich individuals looking to stash their wealth. As a globalized asset, luxury housing functions as a safety-deposit box because houses are tangible, relatively easy to buy and sell, hold their value quite well, and stay put. For investors from politically unstable or oppressive countries, real estate can also be a refuge.

Vancouver has become a prime location for overseas, particularly Asian, investors this century, and the demand has led to a rapid rise in house prices across the Canadian city. In 2000, the average price was nearly six times the

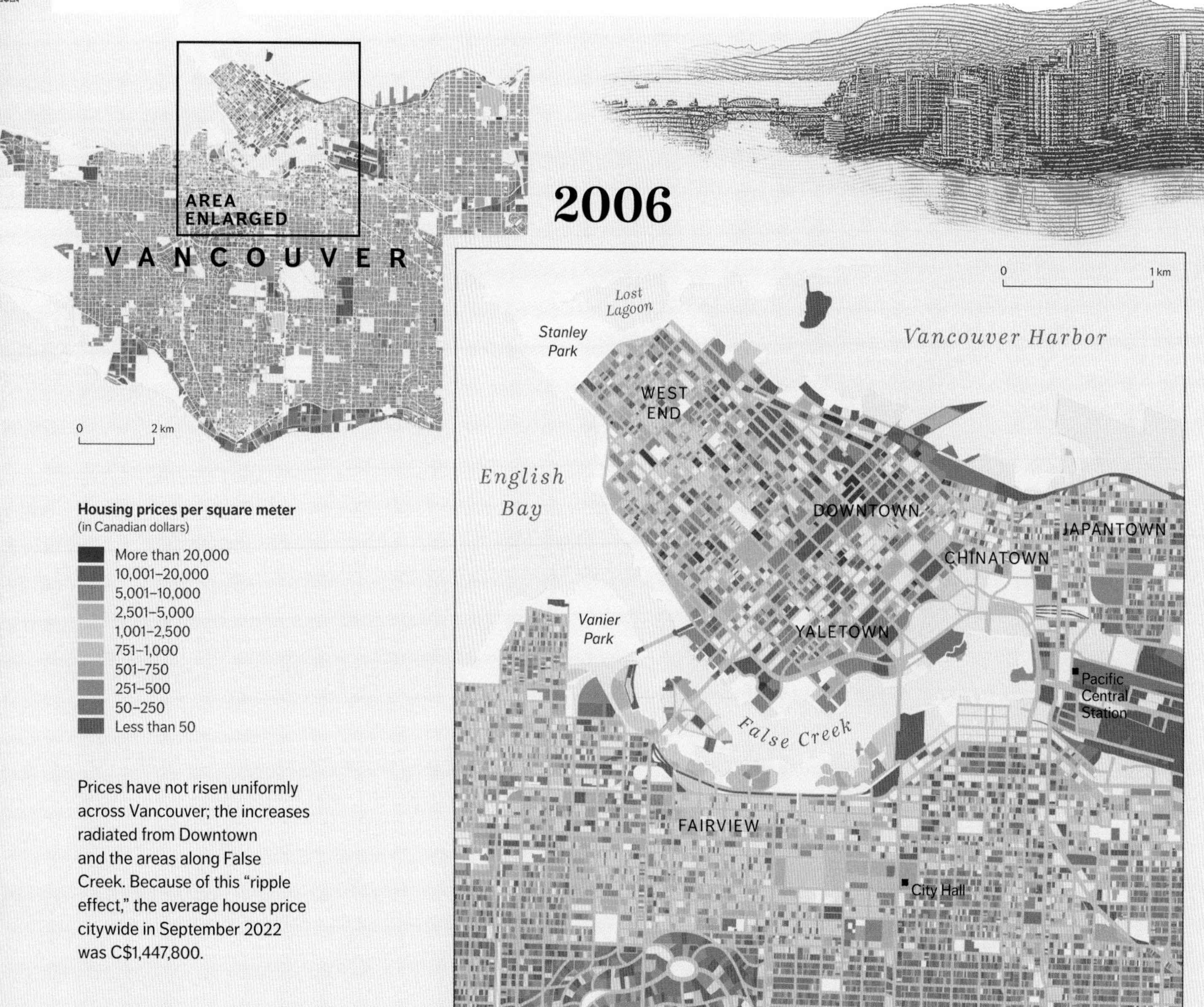

Prices have not risen uniformly across Vancouver; the increases radiated from Downtown and the areas along False Creek. Because of this "ripple effect," the average house price citywide in September 2022 was C$1,447,800.

average yearly income; by 2018, it was twelve times as much.

Rising house prices are not unique to Vancouver. Indeed, house prices have risen faster than incomes in most countries over the past decade. What sets Vancouver apart is that house price growth there has been primarily driven by immense overseas investment, leading to house prices becoming decoupled from the local and national economy. Prices have risen across the city and across all property types, not just for the luxury houses favored by investors. Red areas on our maps show particularly high spikes in the West End, Yaletown, and Downtown.

Proving the link between house prices and overseas investment is tricky. Properties can be rented out to local residents, lived in by family members while the primary breadwinner continues to live and work in their home country, or owned through corporate structures that provide both tax advantages and anonymity. However, the fall in house price growth in Vancouver following the introduction of the foreign buyers tax in August 2016 and the speculation and vacancy tax in February 2018 (see chart) indicates that prior house price growth was likely driven by money from overseas investment.

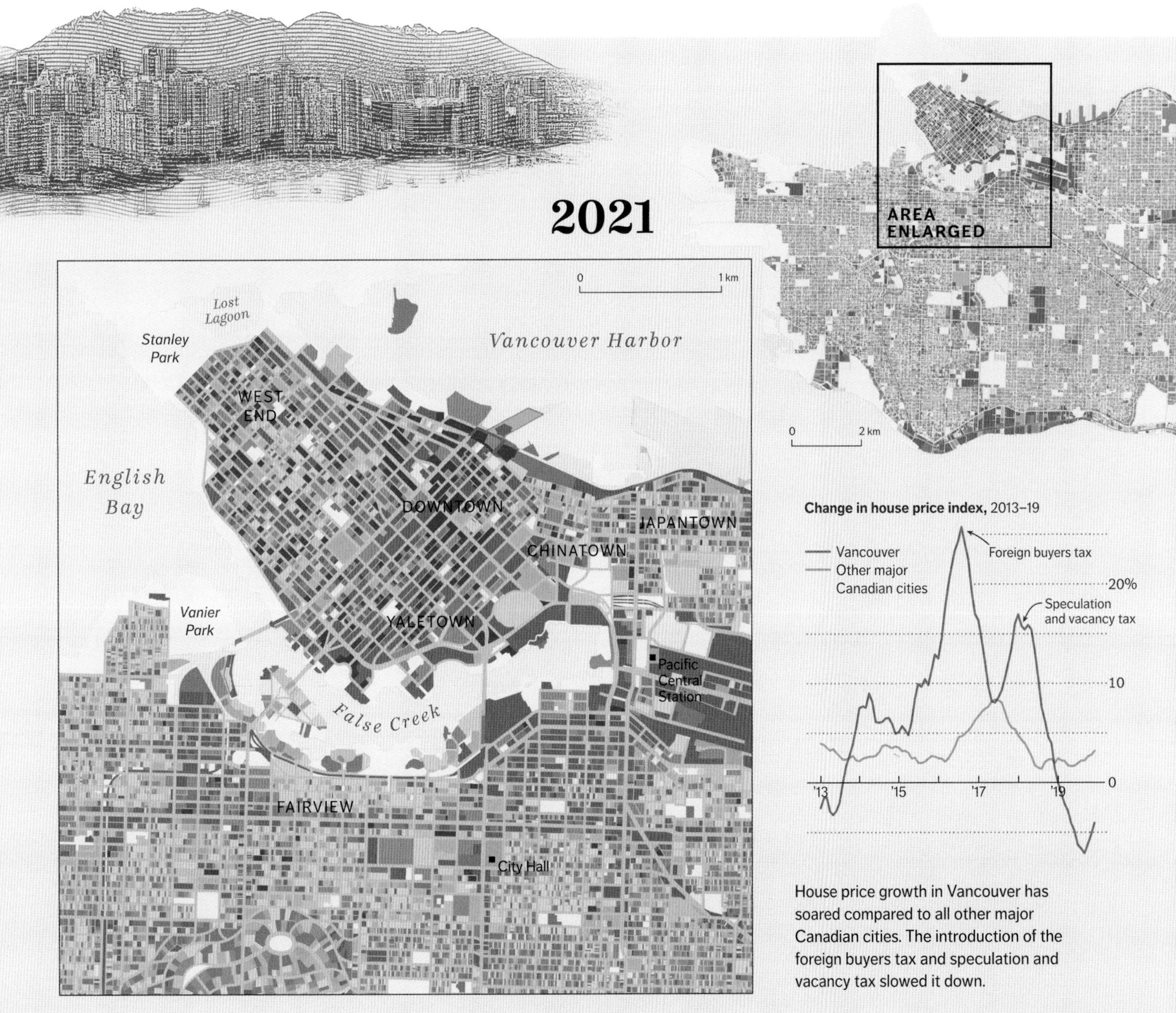

House price growth in Vancouver has soared compared to all other major Canadian cities. The introduction of the foreign buyers tax and speculation and vacancy tax slowed it down.

EUROPE
£200 AS YOU PASS
EXCHANGE
HEATHROW
AIRPORT
UK
£6 billion
in assets
SOUTHERN
WATER
UK
£7 billion
in assets
NATIONAL
GRID
UK
£15 billion
in annual revenue
EUROTUNNEL
UK-FRANCE
£11 billion
in enterprise value
FRENCH
OLL ROADS
FRANCE
€48 billion
annual revenue

TORONTO
407 TOLL ROAD
CANADA
C$6 billion
in assets
AMTRAK
US
US$18 billion
in assets
TEXAS CENTRAL
RAILWAY
US
US$20 billion
project cost
CANCÚN
AIRPORT
MEXICO
MXN 6 billion
in annual revenue
ROUTE 68
TOLL ROAD
CHILE
CLP 87 billion
in annual revenue

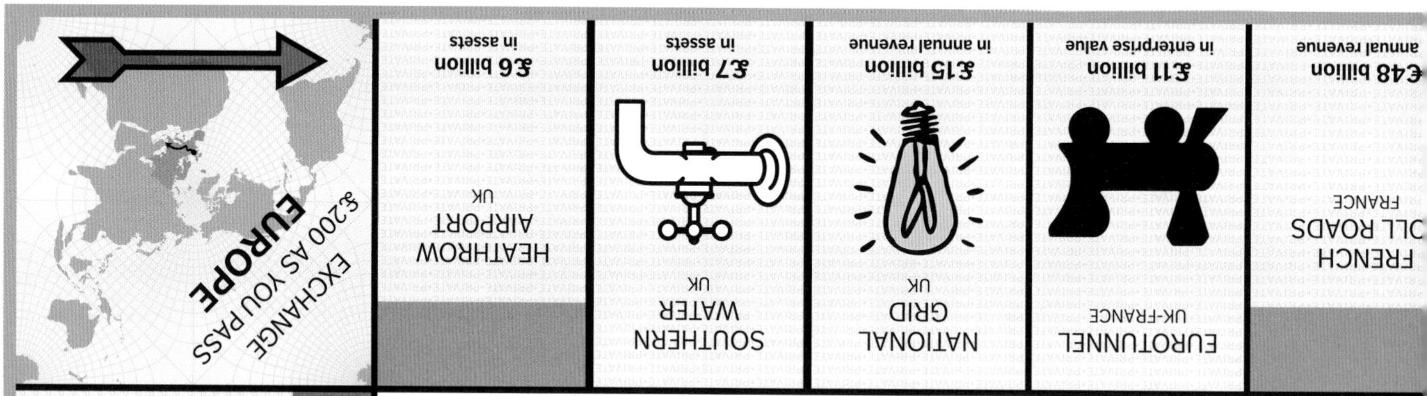

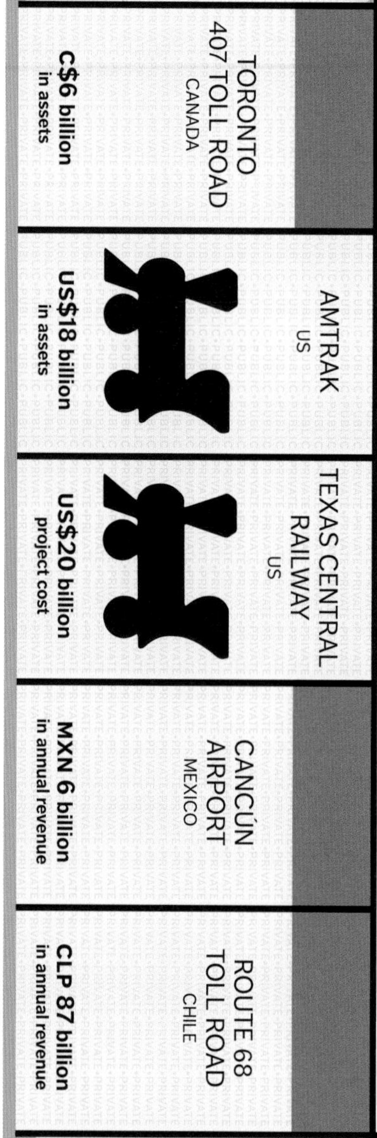

Infrastructure Monopoly

Financing infrastructure has become a global game of privatization and globalization. Investors and taxpayers roll the dice.

THROUGHOUT THE TWENTIETH CENTURY governments were responsible for financing, construction, and management of infrastructure assets like water and electricity networks, roads, and airports. In the late 1980s, however, the UK government pioneered infrastructure privatization, followed by Australia in the early 1990s. The World Bank and the International Monetary Fund promoted this shift to private ownership—or public-private partnerships across emerging economies and developing countries—often by making loans to governments conditional on privatization. The sellout of infrastructure accelerated in the late 1990s as more private investors considered owning infrastructure assets. Such assets are attractive because they're relatively safe investments that offer long-term returns, which are particularly important to investors with long-term liabilities—for example, pension funds. In the process of privatization, infrastructure has changed from a local or national asset to part of the global financial market.

We've visualized this market as a Monopoly board with infrastructure properties colored by continent and their ownership type noted in green. As you circle the globe, you will pass airports in Frankfurt, Abidjan, Bangkok, and Auckland; toll roads in France, Southern Africa, Canada, and Chile; electricity networks in the UK and Australia; and a power station in India. For each privatized project on our board, there are hundreds of similar examples in the world.

THE AMERICAS
AUCKLAND
INTERNATIONAL
AIRPORT
NEW ZEALAND
NZ$11 billion
market value
AUSNET
SERVICES
AUSTRALIA
A$4 billion
purchase price
CITYLINK
TOLL ROAD
AUSTRALIA
A$2 billion
project cost
MELBOURNE
WATER
AUSTRALIA
NOT FOR SALE?
MELBOURNE
AIRPORT
AUSTRALIA
A$1 billion
purchase price

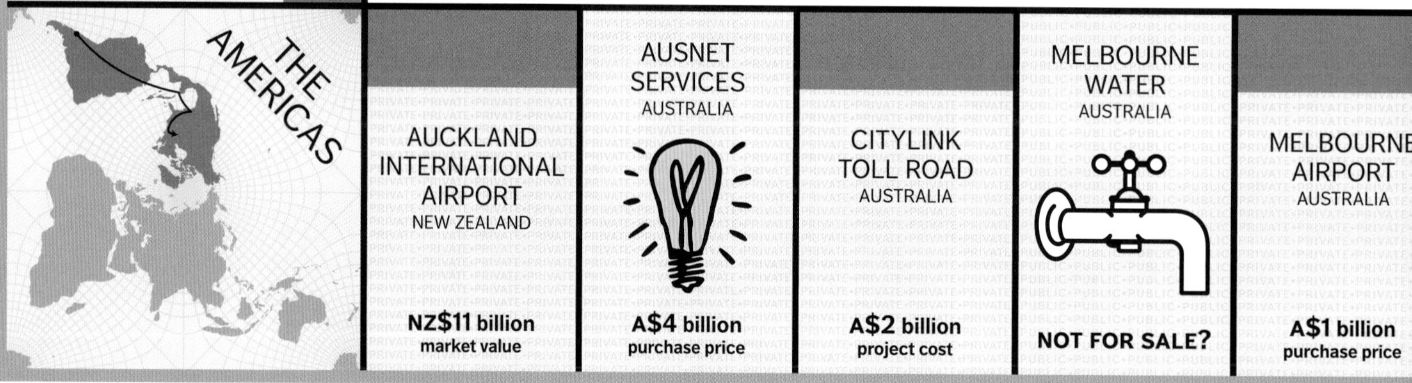

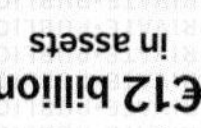

FRANKFURT AIRPORT
GERMANY
€12 billion
in assets

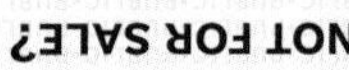

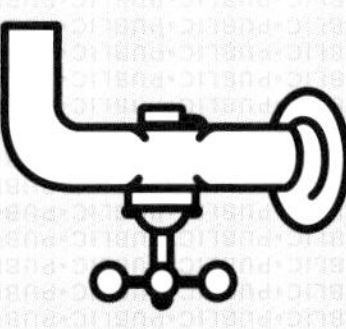

WASSER-VERSORGUNG
SWITZERLAND
NOT FOR SALE?

ZÜRICH AIRPORT
SWITZERLAND
CHF 6 billion
in enterprise value

CHANCE

SOFIA AIRPORT
BULGARIA
€1 billion
project value

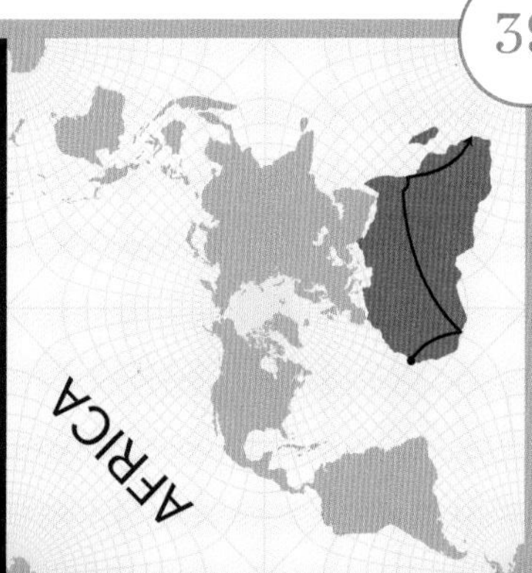

AUTOROUTE DE L'AVENIR
SENEGAL
CFA 92 billion
project cost

ABIDJAN AIRPORT
COTE D'IVOIRE
CFA 1 billion
in capital

LAKE TURKANA WIND POWER
KENYA
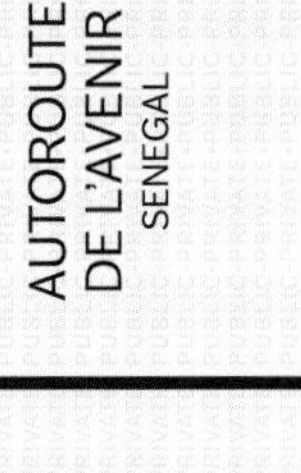
KES 95 billion
project cost

NAIROBI–MOMBASA RAILWAY
KENYA
US$3 billion
loan from China

PRETORIA–MAPUTO N4 TOLL ROUTE
SOUTH AFRICA & MOZAMBIQUE
ZAR 3 billion
in capital

GLOBAL PORTFOLIO

FRAPORT AG

Revenues, 2020 (in millions of euros)

Initially set up to manage Frankfurt Airport in Germany, Fraport now owns an international portfolio of airports.

City	Revenue	Change from 2019
Xi'an	174	−35%
St. Petersburg	127	−57%
Greek regional airports	185	−60%
Ljubljana	17	−63%
Fortaleza & Porto Alegre	88	−69%
Antalya	110	−73%
Burgas & Varna	15	−76%

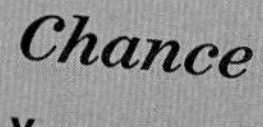

Chance

Your railway company underperforms and gets re-nationalized. Go back to EUROPE.

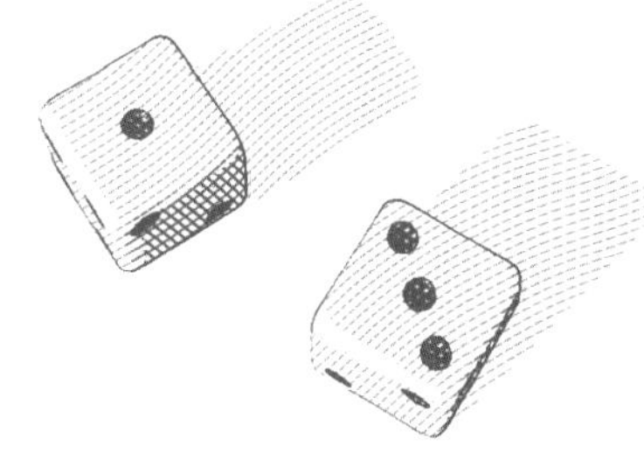

Proponents of infrastructure privatization claim it improves efficiency and relieves taxpayers of billion-dollar burdens, but it is a risky game. Taxpayers often have no or little choice in who supplies their electricity or water. Monopolistic markets allow private companies to price gouge and cut corners. With this in mind, we're fortunate that water infrastructure is rarely for sale. In 2021, Southern Water, a creation of the 1989 water privatization in England and Wales, pleaded guilty to 6,971 unpermitted sewage discharges that polluted protected rivers and coastal waters. In privatizing infrastructure, society is gambling with its own future.

TOKAIDO SHINKANSEN
JAPAN

¥ 9,603 billion
in assets

HONG KONG MASS TRANSIT
CHINA

HK$263 billion
in assets

SUVARNABHUMI AIRPORT
THAILAND
THB 174 billion
in assets

DELHI JAL BOARD
INDIA
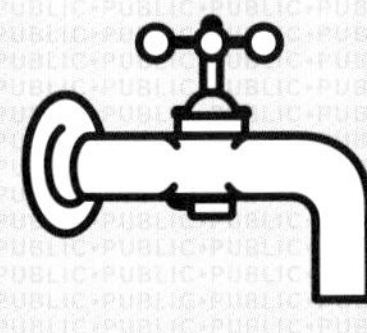
NOT FOR SALE?

INDIRA GANDHI INTERNATIONAL AIRPORT
INDIA
INR 1.5 billion
purchase price

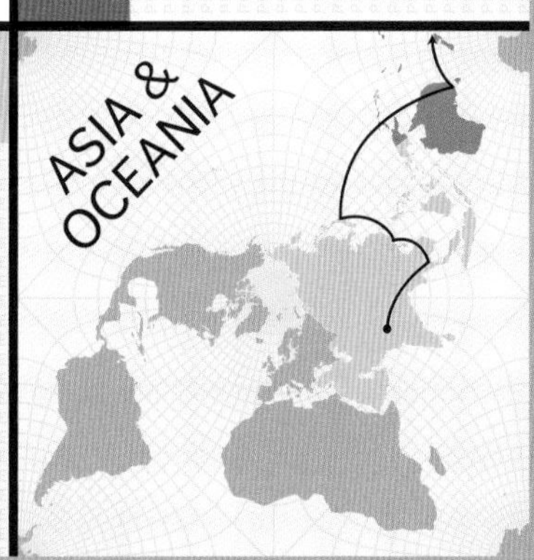

For Few Eyes Only

Much art bought by high-net-worth individuals disappears into dark vaults, away from any public or private display.

WHAT WOULD YOU DO with a spare million? For pleasure and prestige, why not buy a small Picasso? Then head to London or New York, the two largest art marketplaces in the world—or possibly Hong Kong, Asia's capital for the art market. In 2020, auction companies reported sales worth a total of US$20.8 billion, with the US, UK, and China as the leading auction locations.

Investing in art would diversify your portfolio. Artworks, especially higher-end oil paintings, might generate superior returns to gold or real estate and outperform traditional investments like bonds. The information illustrated below

can help you and your wealth manager decide what to buy.

For a few dollars more, you might consider using a luxury free port to store your Picasso. Designed in the nineteenth century to facilitate trading, free ports provide bounded spaces of national exception: by virtue of law, owners don't have to pay any tax or duty as long as their properties—technically in transit—remain stored inside. Free ports store art to hide wealth away from the taxman, sometimes enabling money laundering. The Geneva Freeport, the oldest of its kind, reportedly stores around 1.2 million artworks. With only 380,000 pieces of art, the Louvre pales in comparison. Or how about Singapore? It ticks all the boxes: a location within a duty-free, special economic zone; proximity to an international airport with a terminal for private jets; and an established, politically stable financial center in a rising art-market hub with lenient legislation on art trafficking. This 22,000-square-meter free port operates as both a fortress and a gallery. Private viewing suites and storage vaults are protected by biometric recognition, armed guards, security cameras, vibration-detection technology, nitrogen fire extinguishers, seven-ton doors, three-meter walls, and barbed wire. A perfect place for art, is it not?

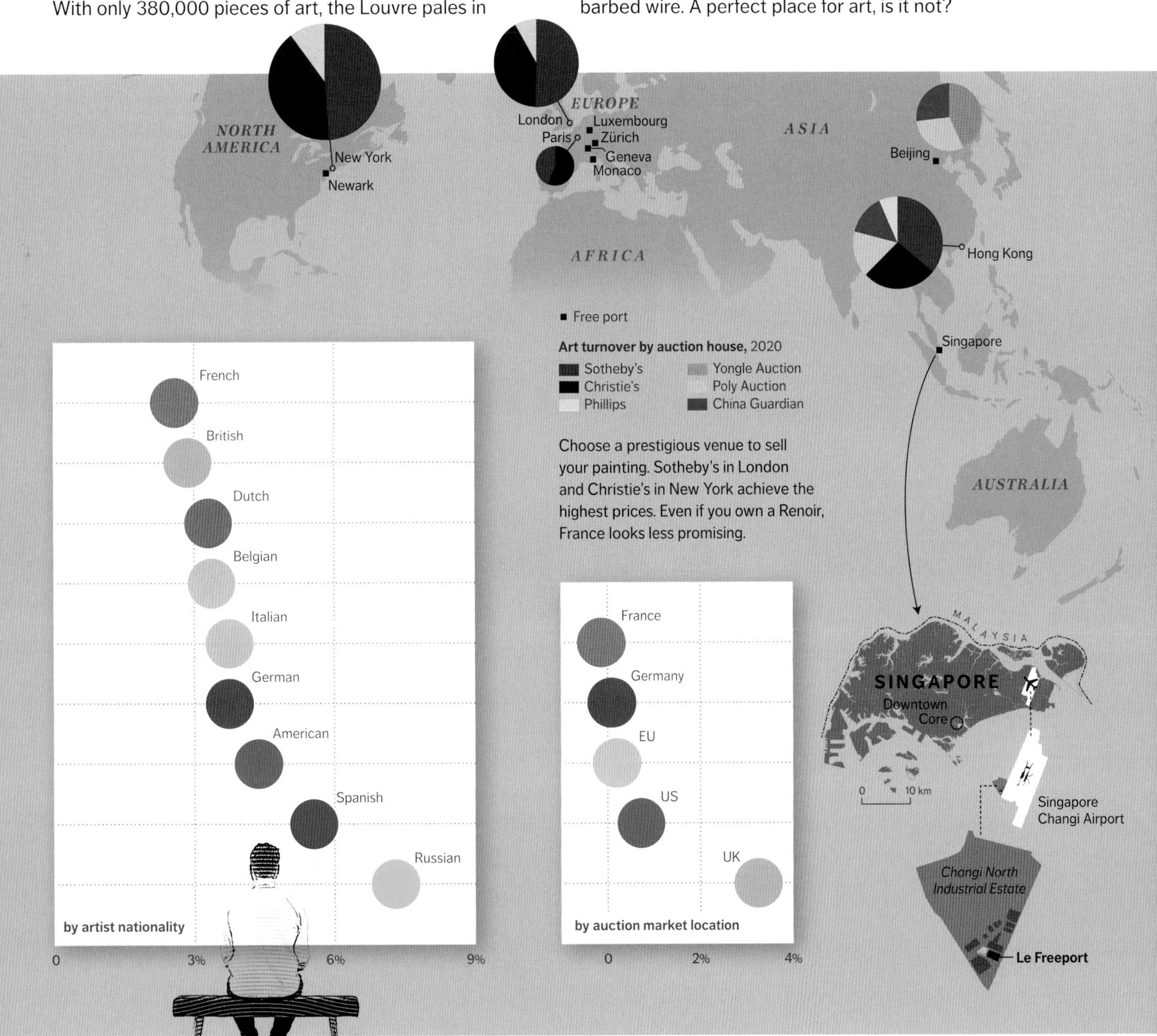

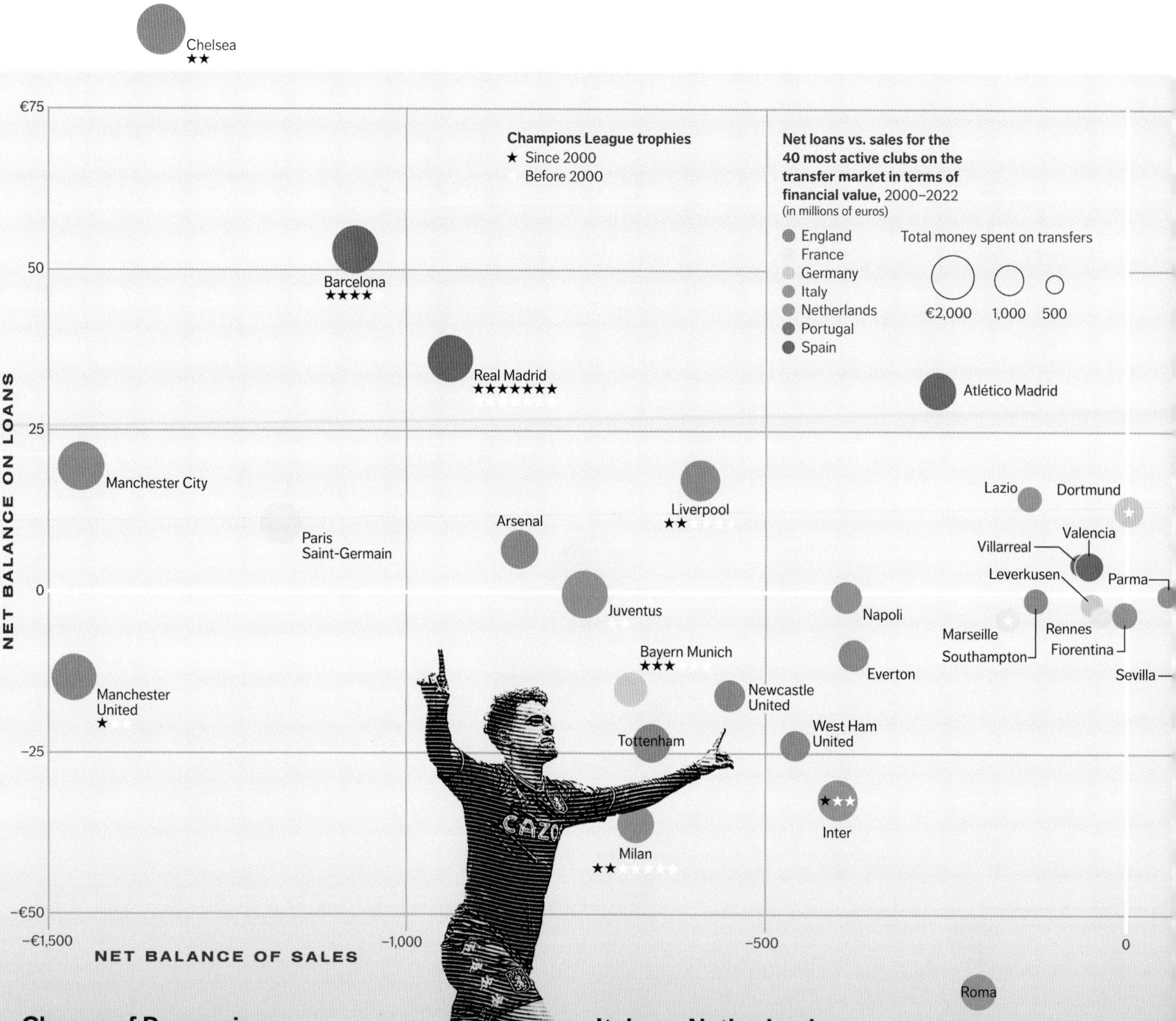

Net loans vs. sales for the 40 most active clubs on the transfer market in terms of financial value, 2000–2022
(in millions of euros)

England
France
Germany
Italy
Netherlands
Portugal
Spain

Total money spent on transfers
€2,000 1,000 500

Champions League trophies
★ Since 2000
Before 2000

NET BALANCE ON LOANS
€75
50
25
0
-25
-€50

NET BALANCE OF SALES
–€1,500
-1,000
-500
0

Barcelona ★★★★
Real Madrid ★★★★★★★
Atlético Madrid
Manchester City
Paris Saint-Germain
Arsenal
Liverpool ★★
Lazio
Dortmund
Valencia
Villarreal
Leverkusen
Parma
Juventus
Napoli
Marseille
Rennes
Southampton
Fiorentina
Sevilla
Bayern Munich ★★★
Everton
Manchester United ★
Newcastle United
West Ham United
Tottenham
Inter ★
Milan ★★
Roma

Change of Possession

Starting in Brazil, Philippe Coutinho played in five major European leagues. He was sold four times and lent three times, including a €135 million transfer to Barcelona.

Transfers of Philippe Coutinho, 2008–22
(in millions of euros)

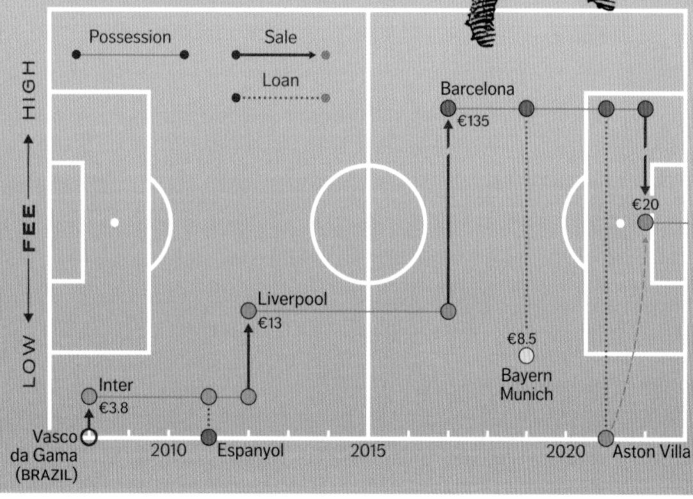

Possession
Sale
Loan
LOW ← FEE → HIGH
Vasco da Gama (BRAZIL)
Inter €3.8
Espanyol
Liverpool €13
Barcelona €135
€8.5 Bayern Munich
€20
Aston Villa
2010
2015
2020

Italy vs. Netherlands

Since the 1995 Bosman ruling, which turned football into a global transfer market, loans have gained popularity as a means to transfer players. In Italian clubs, many of which are struggling financially, loans far exceed sales. FIFA plans to regulate this growing market.

Percentage of transfers financed with loans, 1992–2022

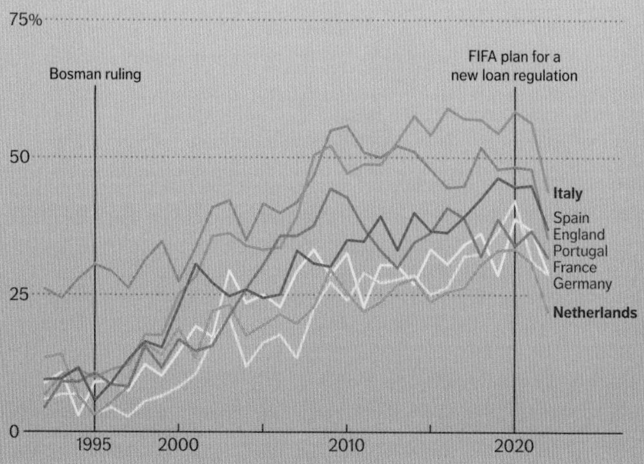

75%
50
25
0
1995
2000
2010
2020
Bosman ruling
FIFA plan for a new loan regulation
Italy
Spain
England
Portugal
France
Germany
Netherlands

A Widening Lead

Between 2000–2010 and 2011–22 the median sale price rose by 90 percent in the top clubs of the main European leagues and by 53 percent in other clubs.

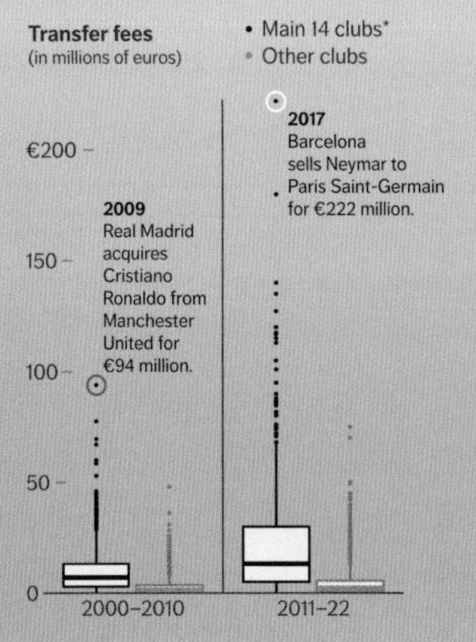

The Beautiful Game

To be crowned champions, clubs use the best players and creative financial management.

"FOOTBALL IS NOW ALL ABOUT MONEY," mourned the three-time Ballon d'Or winner Johan Cruyff, who reigned over European football in the early 1970s with Ajax Amsterdam. Now a globalized industry, football is played on spreadsheets as well as the pitch. Over the past few decades, the transfer market has experienced a spectacular rise in fees. Top players have become incredibly expensive, widening financial inequalities between elite clubs and the rest.

Because transfers account for a large share of a club's expenses and income, clubs manage players as financial assets, trading them to optimize club budgets as market values fluctuate depending on players' age, talent, performance, and marketing power. While clubs like Benfica, Udinese, or Lille share a "buy low, sell high" strategy to make a profit from selling players, others, particularly in the English Premier League, spend lavishly and accumulate debt to recruit high-profile footballers. For example, Manchester City, a club backed by Abu Dhabi–based investors, spent €2,300 million on acquiring players from 2000 to 2021. Among the eighty clubs competing in the Champions League, only a few financial powerhouses grasp the ultimate trophy. Since Porto's victory in 2004, only nine clubs have won the final. All rank among the top fifteen spenders.

As transfer fees increased, player loans became a popular form of financial management among football executives. On one hand, loans allow clubs to sign a promising or experienced player at a fraction of the cost. On the other, loans can reduce expenses. Barcelona, for example, took Philippe Coutinho's high salary off their books by loaning him to Bayern Munich and then Aston Villa (see far left). These temporary transfers also enable clubs to develop the skills, experience, and market value of young players by offering them more playing time. Chelsea is notorious for creating a profitable business model by swapping an army of loan players every year. Loans also help dodge regulatory bullets. Having bought Neymar for a record €222 million in 2017, Paris Saint-Germain would have been punished for purchasing Kylian Mbappé the same year. The Financial Fair Play Regulations set up by the Union of European Football Associations require clubs to limit their losses. But with Mbappé first joining on a €45 million loan-to-buy deal, delaying the eventual transfer payments to the following year, the club argued they played by the rules. Expensive players might offer Paris Saint-Germain their first Champions League trophy one day. For now, financial management brings on the magic.

Migrating Money

Remittances have become a major part of livelihoods and the global financial system.

HUNDREDS OF BILLIONS of US dollars are sent between countries each year in the form of remittance payments. These are often payments from foreign workers to relatives in their home country. Recipients can use the money to help meet their basic needs, access healthcare, start new businesses, or pay for education and vocational training. Remittances reached record heights in 2019, with over $554 billion sent between countries worldwide.

For many developing countries, these cross-border flows of money have become an important mechanism for poverty alleviation and economic development. In some cases, developing countries receive more money in remittances than they do through foreign direct investment and overseas aid. As the darker areas on our map show, remittance payments made up a substantial share of GDP for low- and middle-income countries in 2019. Those most reliant on remittances were broadly spread across the Americas, Eastern Europe, Africa, and Asia. Haiti and South Sudan were the most dependent countries, with remittances making up over 30 percent of their GDP.

So where is the money coming from? While remittance payments are truly global, they exhibit an exclusive and uneven geography. This is because remittances depend on migration, and not everyone is able to migrate. Arrows on the map mark some of the world's most important remittance corridors and are scaled by the total amount of money sent between two countries. These corridors often mirror colonial legacies and geopolitical ties. For example, the value of remittances between the US and Mexico topped $30 billion in 2017.

Considering that remittance payments have been leveraged as an important part of global development strategies, their uneven geography raises questions around financial inclusion and exclusion and unsustainable forms of dependency. If countries promote remittance payments as a form of development, how do they intend to support households incapable of migration? For those who do migrate, how do they ensure their safety and human rights abroad? Despite these challenges, remittances remain an essential source of income for billions of people. As existing corridors grow and new ones emerge, the key task will be ensuring that remittances translate into fair, equitable, and sustainable development for those most in need.

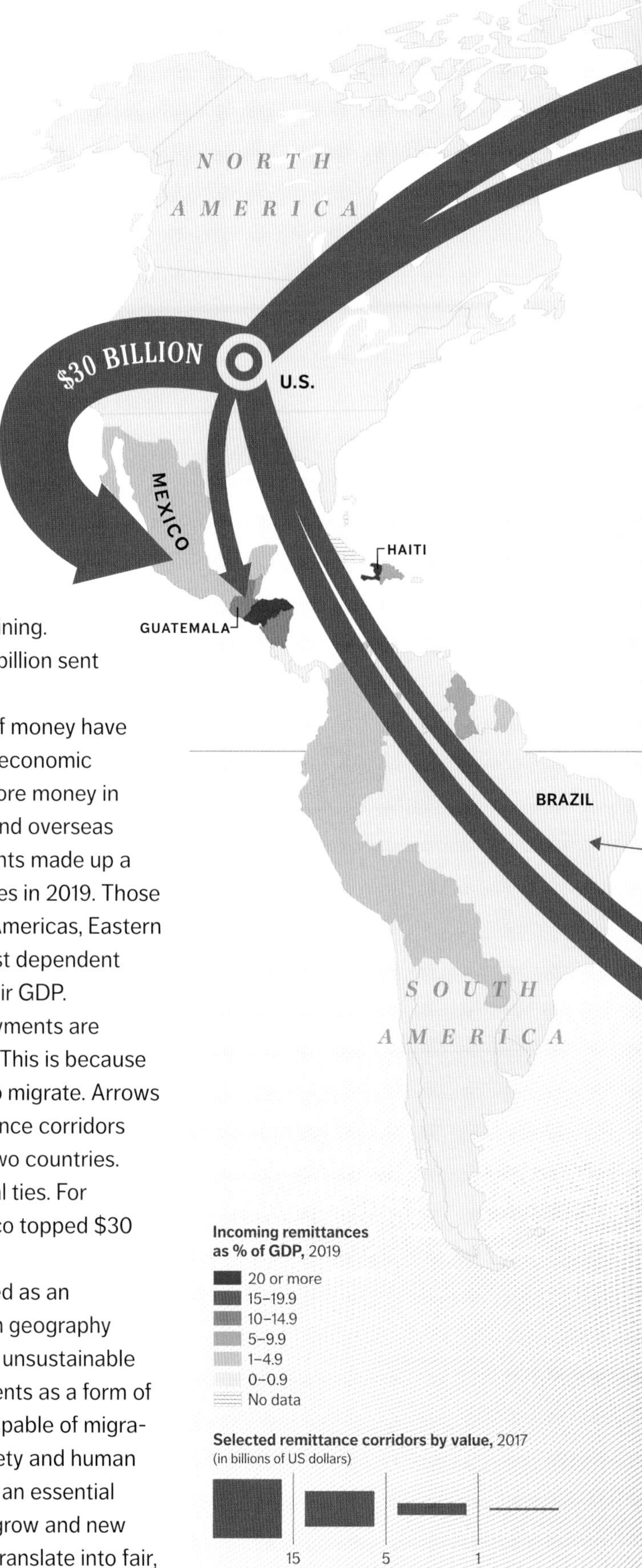

RUSSIA
U.K.
EUROPE
UKRAINE
ASIA
FRANCE
JAPAN
CHINA
ALGERIA
EGYPT
SAUDI ARABIA
U.A.E.
INDIA
AFRICA
SENEGAL
NIGERIA
SOUTH SUDAN
VIETNAM
PHILIPPINES
EQUATOR
KENYA
INDONESIA
AUSTRALIA

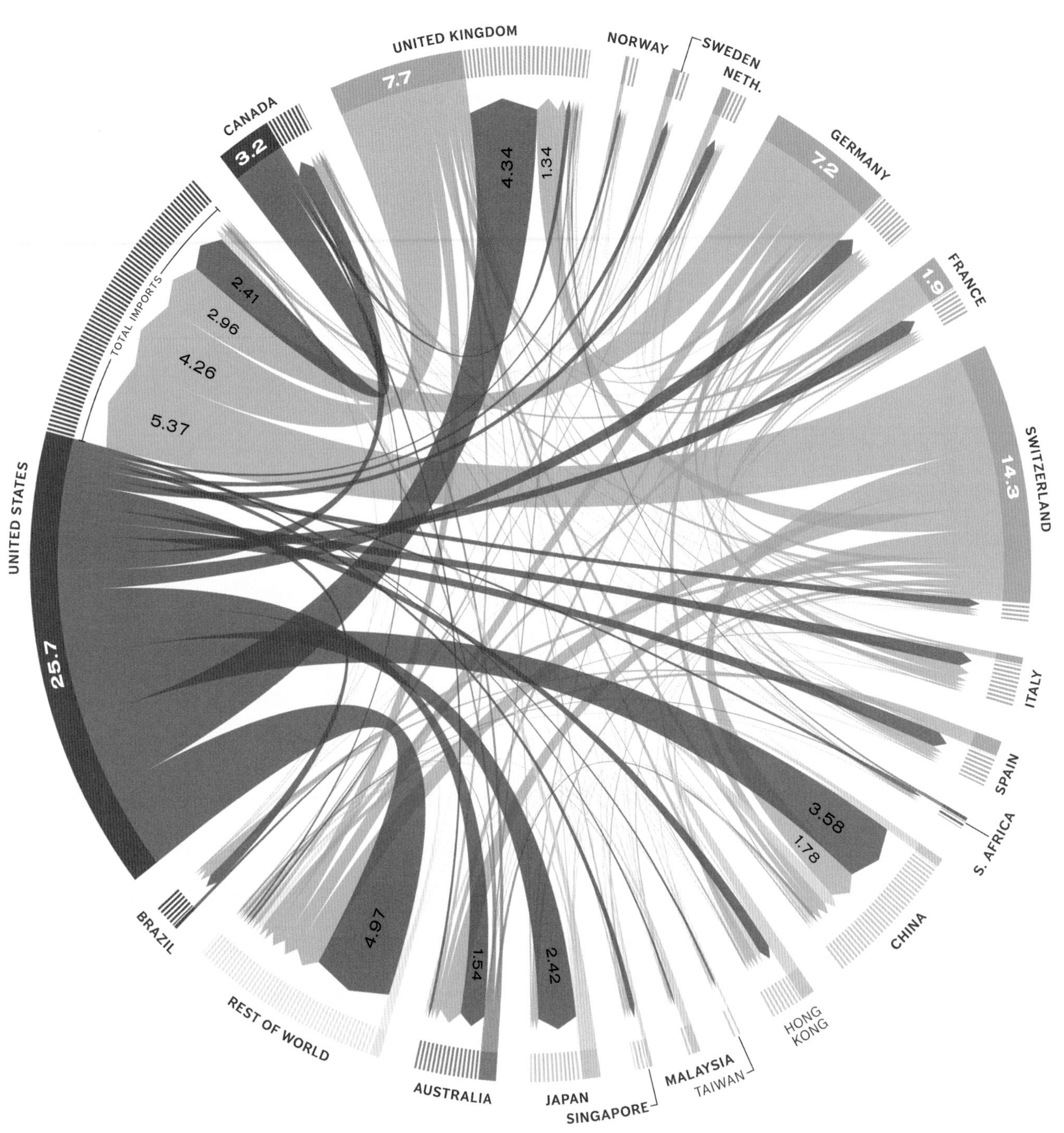

2008–2015

Top 20 exporters of equity securities underwriting services (in billions of US dollars)

Africa Americas Asia Europe Australia

Each arrow flows from an exporter to an importer.
Before the 2008 global financial crisis, the US was the biggest exporter of equity securities underwriting services. In the years after, it has only strengthened its position.

Persistent Patterns

Despite the widespread panics and recessions that followed, the 2008 global financial crisis did little to change the map of international trade in financial services.

PRIOR TO THE GLOBAL FINANCIAL CRISIS, the world of international finance was dominated by the US, which served as the leading exporter of investment banking services to all major overseas markets. As shown in the chord diagrams to the right, the US exported an estimated $22.4 billion in equity securities underwriting services, followed by Switzerland ($15.5 billion) and the UK ($6.2 billion). While aggregate exports of Switzerland and the UK were high, they had few significant trading partners apart from the US.

Despite the impression that the 2008 global financial crisis shook the world of finance to its foundations, our comparison of patterns of international trade in financial services before and after the financial crisis reveals a great deal of stability. The large chord diagram for 2008–15 reveals that the US not only maintained its network of international trading partners, but it also increased its exports to an estimated $25.7 billion, while those of Switzerland fell to $14.3 billion. This pattern of sustained US dominance is further corroborated by a more granular analysis of key importers of financial services. Between 2008 and 2015, the UK imported an estimated $4.34 billion in equity securities underwriting services from the US but only imported an estimated $1.34 billion from Switzerland. Similar import patterns can be observed for China, Japan, and Australia, where the US dominated with exports totaling $3.58, $2.42, and $1.54 billion, respectively.

These patterns of stability reflect the persistent power of leading investment banks, which are responsible for the bulk of international trade of equity underwriting services. While Lehman Brothers went bankrupt in 2008, other US banks like J.P. Morgan, Goldman Sachs, Morgan Stanley, and Bank of America maintained the US dominance in global markets. The US government helped them by providing emergency funding during the financial crisis. Leading European banks, such as the Swiss UBS and Credit Suisse, German Deutsche Bank, and British Barclays, recovered too, also with the help of their central banks and governments, though they never regained positions that would make them think of challenging the US banks in global markets. Meanwhile, rising Asian banks, such as the Japanese Mitsubishi UFJ, operate mainly within Asian markets. Growing companies around the world that seek truly global investment banking services continue to rely on European and, mainly, US banks, which offer global expertise and unparalleled networks.

2000–2007

Top 3 exporters of equity securities underwriting services

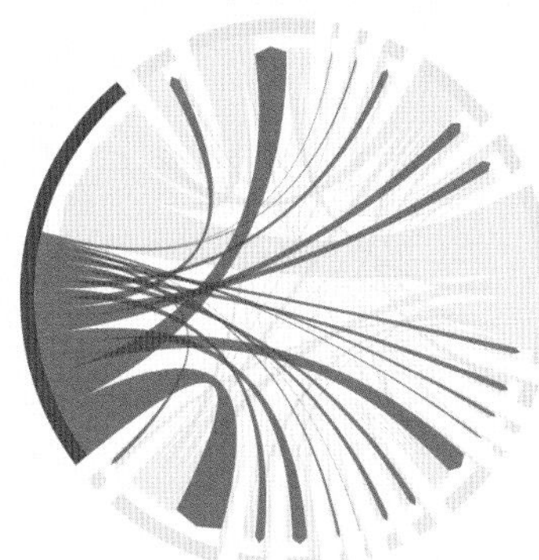

US EXPORTS: **$22.4 BILLION**

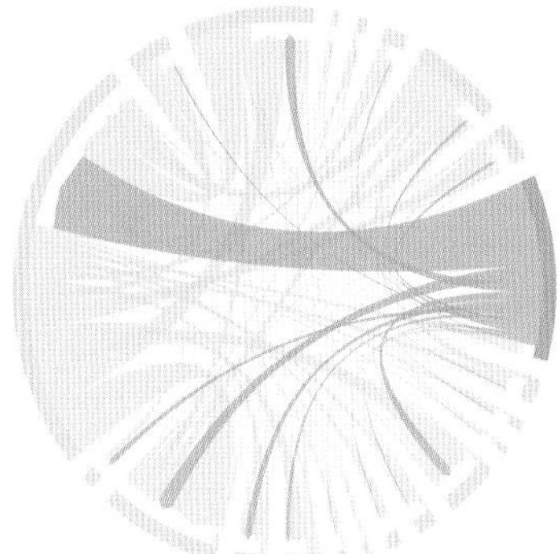

SWITZERLAND: **$15.5 BILLION**

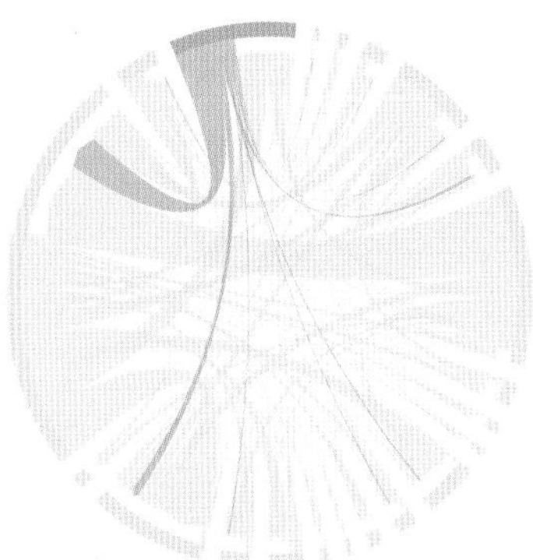

UK: **$6.2 BILLION**

The US dominates the export and import of financial services. Even Switzerland and the UK export more to the US than to any other country.

A Cautionary Tale

Short selling is an investment strategy that allows you to sell something you do not own. There's just one catch.

IF IT IS HARD TO IMAGINE selling something you do not own, perhaps a metaphor will help. Picture a sorcerer at a medieval market. We'll call him the Wizard of Wall Street. The wizard is searching for a stock he can borrow that he expects will depreciate, say, a basket of soon-to-be-obsolete wooden tops. If all goes according to his nefarious plan, the wizard will sell them back to the market immediately, wait for demand to crater, and then repurchase the tops at a lower price before returning them to his broker on a predetermined date. Easy money, right? However, if the price of those tops were to rise unexpectedly, our short-selling wizard would be exposed to unlimited losses.

Our imaginary tale depicted below became all too real

in January 2021, when the US-based video game retailer GameStop—“Gemma’s Tops” in our story—was shorted by some of Wall Street’s biggest hedge funds. Following several public posts by high-profile short sellers who expected GameStop’s shares to decline, momentum gathered on Twitter and the subreddit /r/WallStreetBets. Soon, everyday investors—the birds and Reddit bots below—were racing to digital platforms such as Robinhood to purchase GameStop shares with the aim of inflating the share price, inflicting damage on the hedge funds, and making a profit for themselves. As a result, GameStop’s share price reached a record $347.51 on January 27—over twenty times its valuation at the start of the month. As the short period closed out, hedge funds lost billions of dollars—Melvin Capital alone suffered a $4.5 billion decline in their total assets. The Wizard of Wall Street had been beaten at his own game.

While this epic fail shows the dangers of short selling, we must not forget the geographical impacts. When investors short a stock, they send a signal to the market that they believe the stock is overpriced. This may encourage shareholders to sell, which may reduce the company’s value, change how it operates, or influence where it chooses to locate its labor. For all the dreams of legendary profits or defeating Goliath, consequences of short selling are grounded in the real world.

GameStop stock price
January 4–27, 2021
(in US dollars)

3

Investors have much to learn from academics, and certainly not just from economists. . . . Now it is the turn of geographers.
JOHN AUTHERS

Investors & Investments

Mapping the long history and broad geography of investments offers powerful lessons for investors. While most investments remain local or domestic, global investment has accelerated. Everyone is affected by it, whether through the way they shop or how they save for retirement. At the same time, globalization of investment has made the rich richer, increasing inequality. It is also a powerful tool of foreign policy.

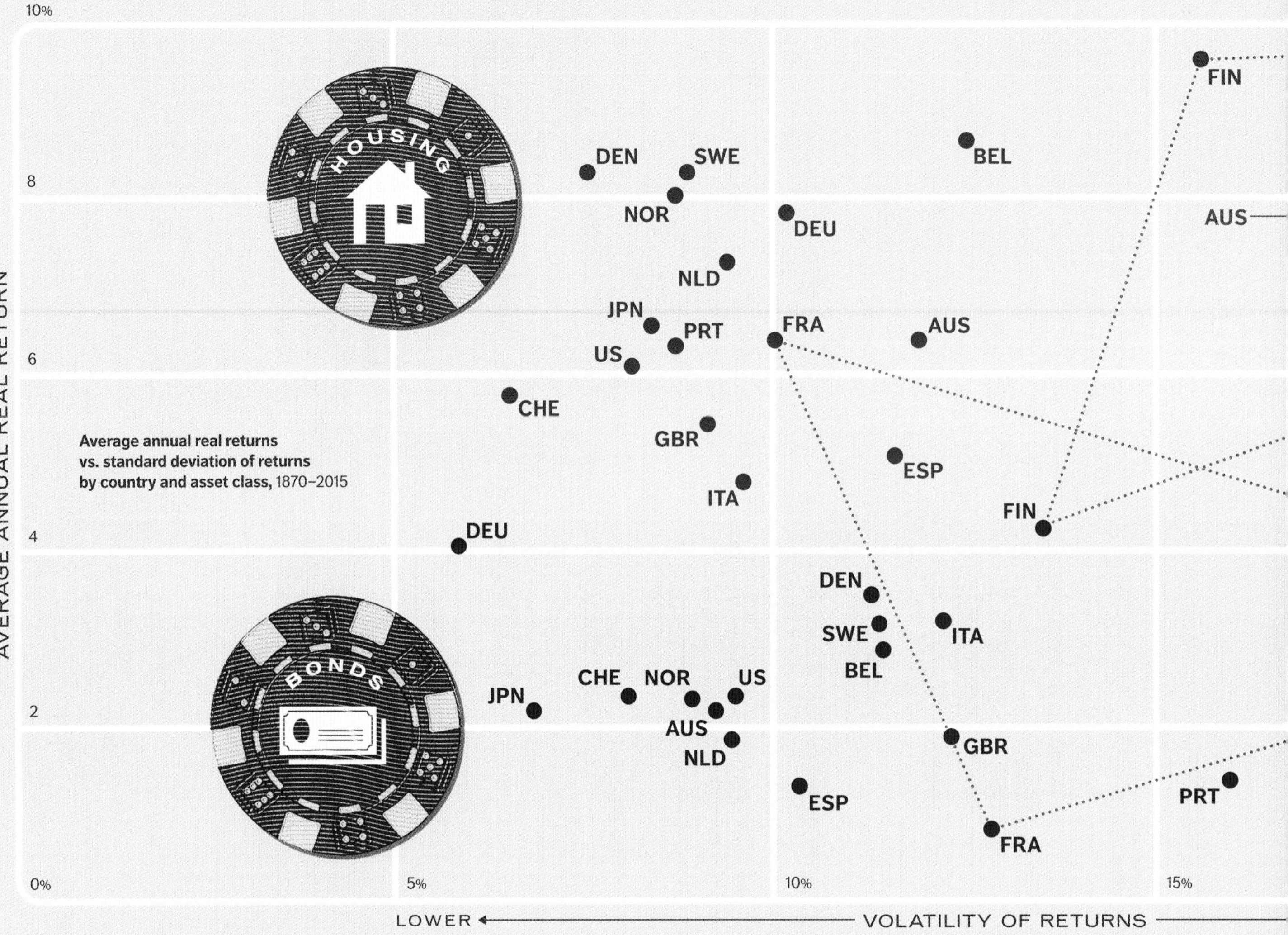

The Safest Bets

Historically, equity offers higher returns and risk than bonds, while housing offers equity-like returns and bond-like risk.

WHAT IS THE BEST INVESTMENT in the world? The answer depends on where, when, and whom you ask. In general investors are looking for the ratio of return to risk that suits their risk appetite. The calculation of return must include capital gains, based on the changing price of an asset and income in the form of a dividend (for equity), interest (for bonds), and rent (for housing). Risk is usually calculated as the standard deviation of returns over a series of periods. This tells you how much the returns in each period differ from the long-term average.

The dots above denote the total returns and risks for listed equity, government bonds, and housing in sixteen countries for the period of 1870–2015. This chart is based on a dataset on international investment performance with the longest historical coverage available. It does not cover assets such as commercial real estate, agricultural land, corporate bonds, deposits, or precious metals. However, listed equity, government bonds, and housing account for the majority of investable assets in advanced economies. These three asset classes are the main choices available to most investors.

The average international real return from equity (green) has been close to a handsome 7 percent per year, but it has been quite volatile. Nearly a quarter of all years witnessed

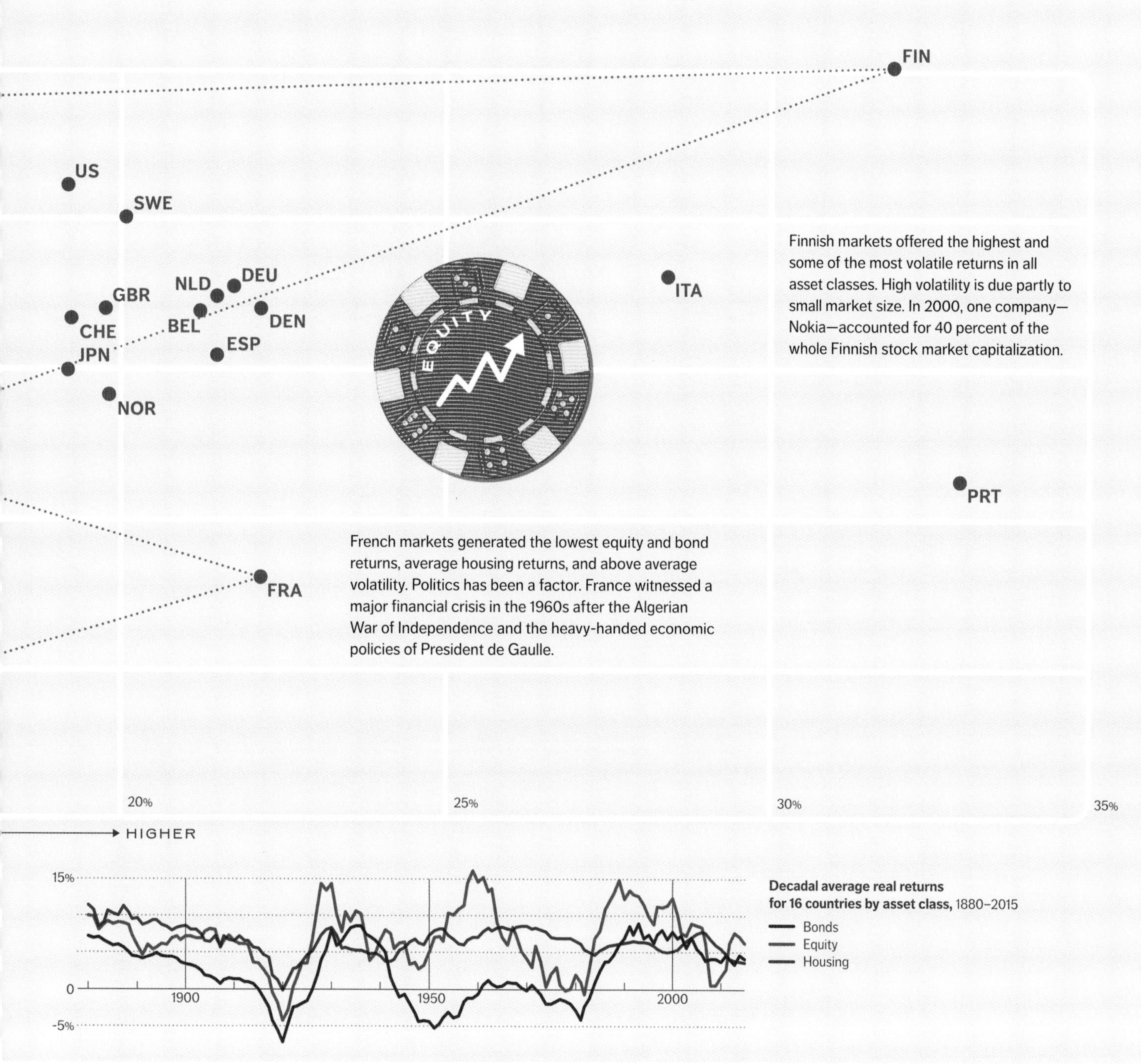

negative real returns on equity, with the biggest dips on our line chart driven by world wars, macroeconomic instability in the 1970s, and recurrent financial crises. Bonds (blue) exhibited lower swings but at the expense of much lower returns, close to only 2.4 percent per year. What stands out is housing (red), with average real return also close to 7 percent and risk level similar to that for bonds. Returns on housing have outperformed those on equity for most years, due mainly to the stable and reliable nature of rent. This should not surprise those of us who rent and rarely experience a decrease in the amount we pay a landlord.

Investment returns vary geographically. Historically Finland offered the highest returns and high volatility in all three asset classes. Other Nordic countries (Denmark, Norway, and Sweden) also saw high returns on housing with much lower risks. The US offered high returns on equity despite a relatively low risk. On the other side, France and Portugal produced particularly unattractive return-risk profiles for equity and bonds. Post–World War II nationalizations lowered returns in France, while decades of civil strife hampered markets in Portugal. In all sixteen countries, though, the return-to-risk ratio for housing was higher than that for equity or bonds. Getting on the property ladder makes a lot of financial sense.

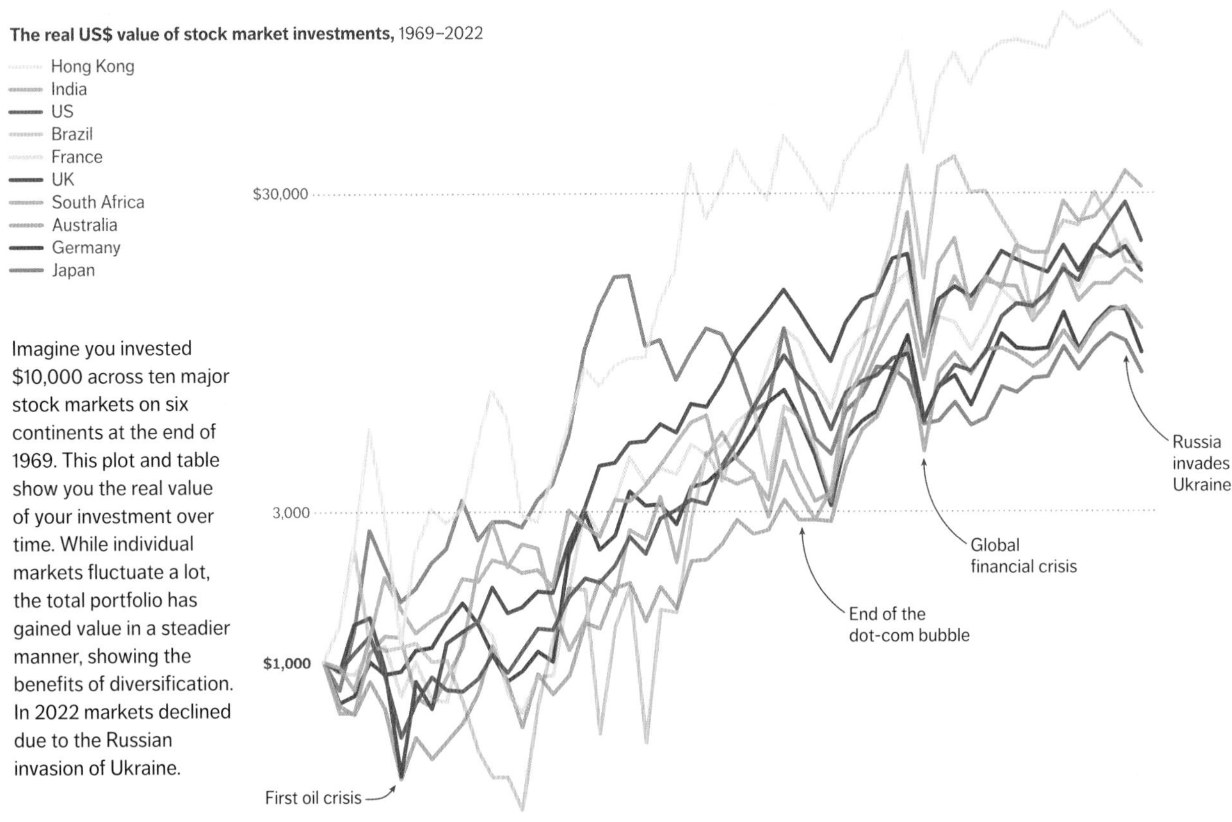

Imagine you invested $10,000 across ten major stock markets on six continents at the end of 1969. This plot and table show you the real value of your investment over time. While individual markets fluctuate a lot, the total portfolio has gained value in a steadier manner, showing the benefits of diversification. In 2022 markets declined due to the Russian invasion of Ukraine.

	1969	1979	1989	1999	2009	2019	2022
Hong Kong	1,000	4,890	9,039	45,527	67,589	104,527	87,484
India	1,000	1,802	3,200	5,860	17,868	25,315	31,241
US	1,000	891	2,464	9,255	7,370	20,067	21,075
Brazil	1,000	525	1,720	6,389	36,436	30,178	17,963
France	1,000	1,357	4,445	11,259	12,224	18,613	17,474
UK	1,000	1,349	4,889	14,859	13,797	20,553	16,974
South Africa	1,000	1,997	2,621	4,300	12,520	15,426	15,727
Australia	1,000	800	1,770	3,246	8,115	11,358	11,272
Germany	1,000	1,316	3,438	7,174	7,317	11,549	9,454
Japan	1,000	2,422	16,410	11,225	5,721	9,686	8,166
Total	$10,000	$17,350	$49,995	$119,096	$188,957	$267,271	$236,830

The plot to the right shows how correlated equity market returns have been over time. We see a major growth between the late 1980s and the global financial crisis of 2008. Growing similarities among stock market performances reduce the benefits of diversification.

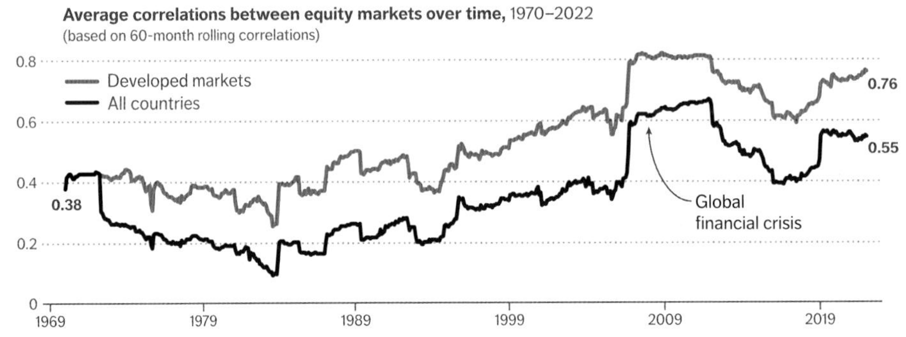

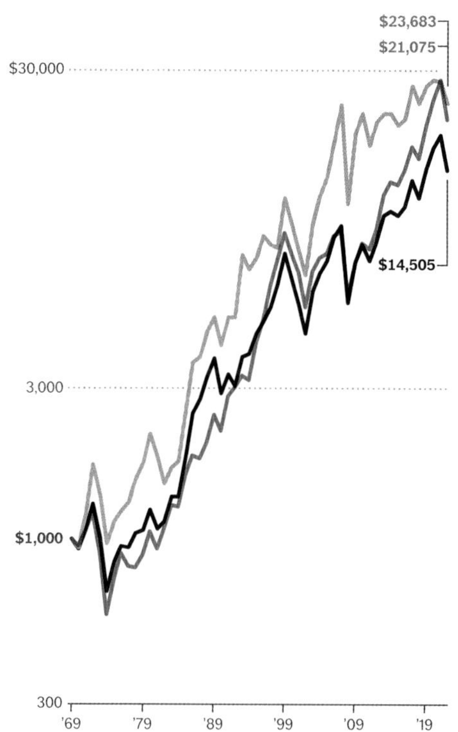

The plot above compares the performance of a $1,000 investment in the US stock market (orange) with a portfolio of $100 investments in each of the ten markets on the left (gray) and a world portfolio based on thirty-five markets (black). Between 1969 and 2022, a US investment returned nearly 50 percent more than a portfolio allocated more globally.

Data source: Elroy Dimson, Paul Marsh, and Mike Staunton. 2023. The Dimson-Marsh-Staunton Global Investment Returns Database 2023 (the "DMS Database"), Morningstar Inc.

The Only Free Lunch in Finance?

Geographical diversification can smooth investment returns and reduce risk, but its benefits are decreasing as stock markets move increasingly in tandem.

IN 1894 THE AMERICAN WRITER Mark Twain said, "Behold the fool saith, 'Put not all thine eggs in the one basket'—which is but a manner of saying, 'Scatter your money and your attention'; but the wise man saith, 'Put all your eggs in the one basket and—watch that basket.'" While few investors know this quote, most seem to heed Twain's advice and concentrate their portfolios on few investments, typically within their domestic market.

Financial science, however, contradicts Twain's wisdom. As Harry Markowitz demonstrated in 1952, portfolio diversification—investing across a larger number of uncorrelated or weakly correlated assets—offers an opportunity to increase returns while at the same time lowering the risk of the portfolio as a whole. Markowitz referred to diversification as "the only free lunch in finance." Building on his work, Bruno Solnik in 1974 demonstrated major benefits of international diversification with investments allocated across countries. For his contribution, Markowitz was awarded the Nobel Memorial Prize in Economic Sciences in 1990.

Long before Markowitz's theoretical model of portfolio selection, the geographical distribution of capital and its benefits were visualized by Polish-British entrepreneur Henry Lowenfeld in his 1909 book *Investment: An Exact Science*. Inspired by Lowenfeld, our table and top chart on the left page show the performance of an investment spread across ten large equity markets on six continents between 1969 and 2022. While individual stock markets fluctuate a lot, limited correlation between them produces the benefit of diversification. An investment of US$10,000 allocated across these ten markets at the end of 1969 would be worth $236,830 fifty-three years later after accounting for inflation.

The performance of the US equity market, however, offers a puzzle for proponents of geographical diversification. Since 2009, it has outperformed other markets to an extent that outweighed the benefits of diversification. This reflects the power of the US economy, its capital market, and currency. Another factor that limits the absolute benefits of geographical diversification over time is international capital market integration. As our plot in the lower left shows, the correlations among equity markets have grown significantly, particularly for developed markets. We may need to give Mark Twain some credit after all.

Home Bias

Proximity shapes the geography of investments.

IF YOU HAD A MILLION US DOLLARS to invest in any set of companies in the world, what would your portfolio look like? Would you choose US tech giants like Apple and Tesla, or would you prefer investing in firms from your home country? According to modern portfolio theory, the distribution of your investments should reflect each country's proportion of the world market portfolio, resulting in a globally diversified set of equity investments. In other words, if your home country's equity accounts for only 5 percent of the world's market portfolio, then 95 percent of the value of your investments should be allocated to foreign companies.

However, investors do not follow this fundamental prescription of mainstream financial economics. According to International Monetary Fund data on the geographical breakdown of equity investments, portfolios across the world exhibit a high degree of home bias. Investors tend to overinvest in financial assets from their own country or from countries close to it. The reasons for such behavior are diverse. Some countries have regulations that encourage domestic investment and discourage international diversification in order to keep capital at home, people tend to invest in what they are familiar with, and proximate investments can be cheaper to make. Also, as the old Danish adage at right suggests, local investments can be easier to monitor.

Our heatmap shows the geographical distribution of equity investments for seventy-four countries in 2022. The vertical axis lists investment origins; the horizontal axis, investment destinations. The darkest squares lie on a diagonal, revealing the prevalence and magnitude of home bias. Other dark squares are often near the diagonal, marking investments in countries close to home. For instance, EU investors prefer to buy stocks from other member states, particularly those in the Eurozone. Elsewhere, Namibians invest a lot in South Africa and New Zealanders invest in Australia, whereas Singaporeans prefer opportunities in China, India, South Korea, and Japan. Four markets seem popular with both proximate and faraway investors: the US, Luxembourg, Ireland, and the Cayman Islands. Investing in US companies means investing in US dollars—the most popular as well as a relatively stable and safe currency. As such, the US is by far the largest equity market in the world, and its largest companies have the most global visibility, attracting investors from most rows on our plot. By contrast, Luxembourg, Ireland, and the Cayman Islands offer diversified investment funds based on tax, legal, and regulatory flexibility. To international investors, they're homes away from home.

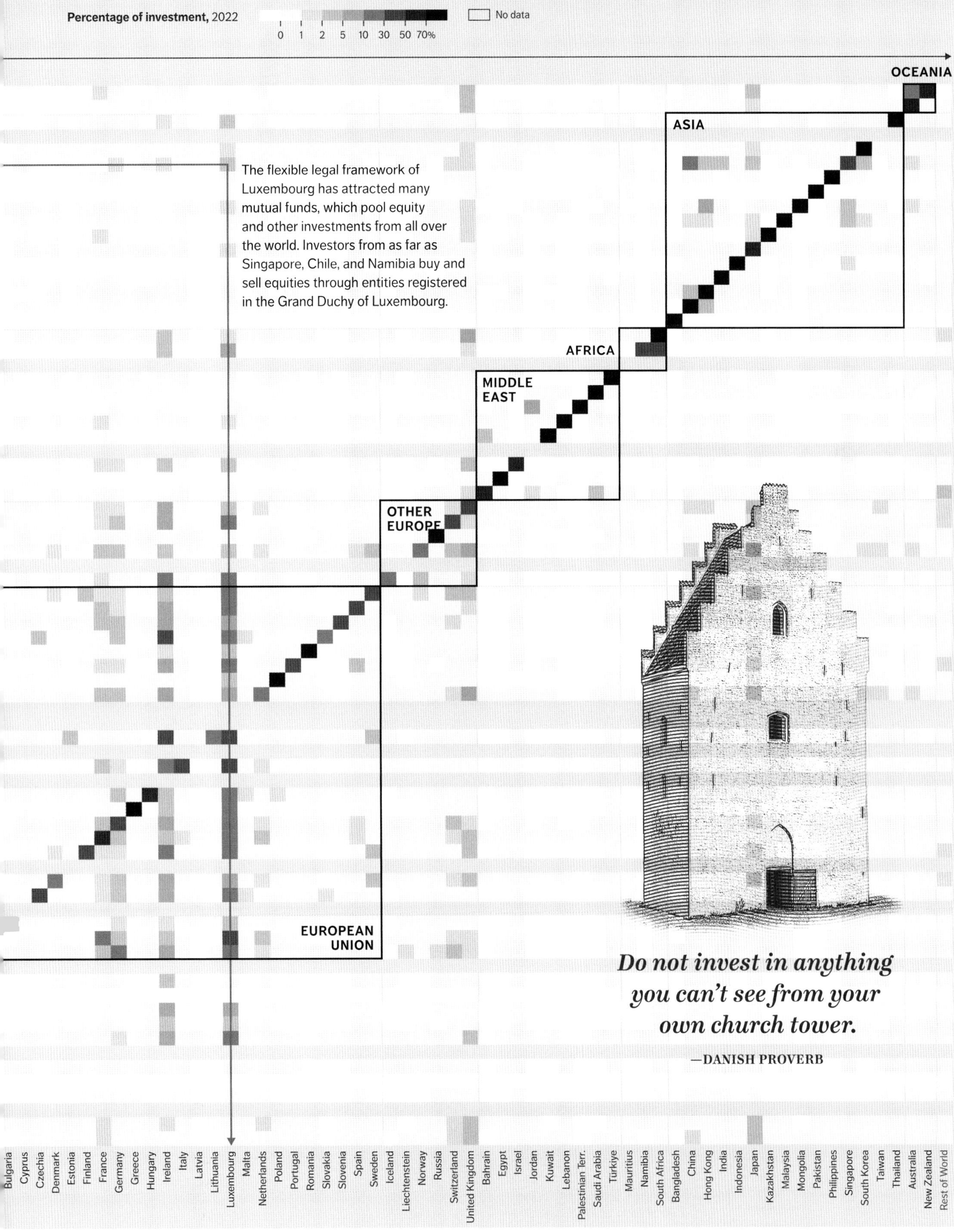

Percentage of investment, 2022

0 1 2 5 10 30 50 70%

No data

OCEANIA

ASIA

The flexible legal framework of Luxembourg has attracted many mutual funds, which pool equity and other investments from all over the world. Investors from as far as Singapore, Chile, and Namibia buy and sell equities through entities registered in the Grand Duchy of Luxembourg.

AFRICA

MIDDLE EAST

OTHER EUROPE

EUROPEAN UNION

Bulgaria Cyprus Czechia Denmark Estonia Finland France Germany Greece Hungary Ireland Italy Latvia Lithuania Luxembourg Malta Netherlands Poland Portugal Romania Slovakia Slovenia Spain Sweden Iceland Liechtenstein Norway Russia Switzerland United Kingdom Bahrain Egypt Israel Jordan Kuwait Lebanon Palestinian Terr. Saudi Arabia Türkiye Mauritius Namibia South Africa Bangladesh China Hong Kong India Indonesia Japan Kazakhstan Malaysia Mongolia Pakistan Philippines Singapore South Korea Taiwan Thailand Australia New Zealand Rest of World

Do not invest in anything you can't see from your own church tower.

—DANISH PROVERB

The Rideshare Race

Both Uber and Didi successfully navigated their way to becoming multibillion-dollar businesses.

COMPANIES WITH HIGH GROWTH POTENTIAL that aren't yet profitable rely on external financing to succeed. However, the enormous risk start-ups face, particularly during their first few years of operation, makes them unlikely to secure sufficient bank loans. Venture capitalists help to fill this gap. They manage the risk associated with early-stage companies by investing only a small amount of money at first and making additional funding rounds conditional on meeting certain goals. Once companies establish themselves, they can obtain much larger pots of funding from private equity investors who specialize in the scale-up phase of company development.

We can chart the role of venture capital and private equity in business growth with data from Uber and Didi. Both companies operate a ridesharing platform through their mobile applications. Both initially suffered heavy losses from operations despite being market leaders in the US and China, respectively. And in order to withstand these losses and support their aggressive expansions, both had to rely on billions of US dollars in funding from a range of sources. On the imaginary city grid below, we plot their funding journeys from Zero Boulevard to Twenty Billion Street and ultimately the New York Stock Exchange. Early on, funding came from frequent stops at venture capital investors (marked with pink pins) before private equity firms (green) and banks (blue) helped both companies cross the Cashflow River and go public. At Uber's initial public offering at the New York Stock Exchange in May 2019, its stockholders sold $8.1 billion of equity at $45 per share, valuing the company at $82 billion. Didi followed suit, listing on the New York Stock Exchange in July 2021 and achieving a market value of close to $70 billion.

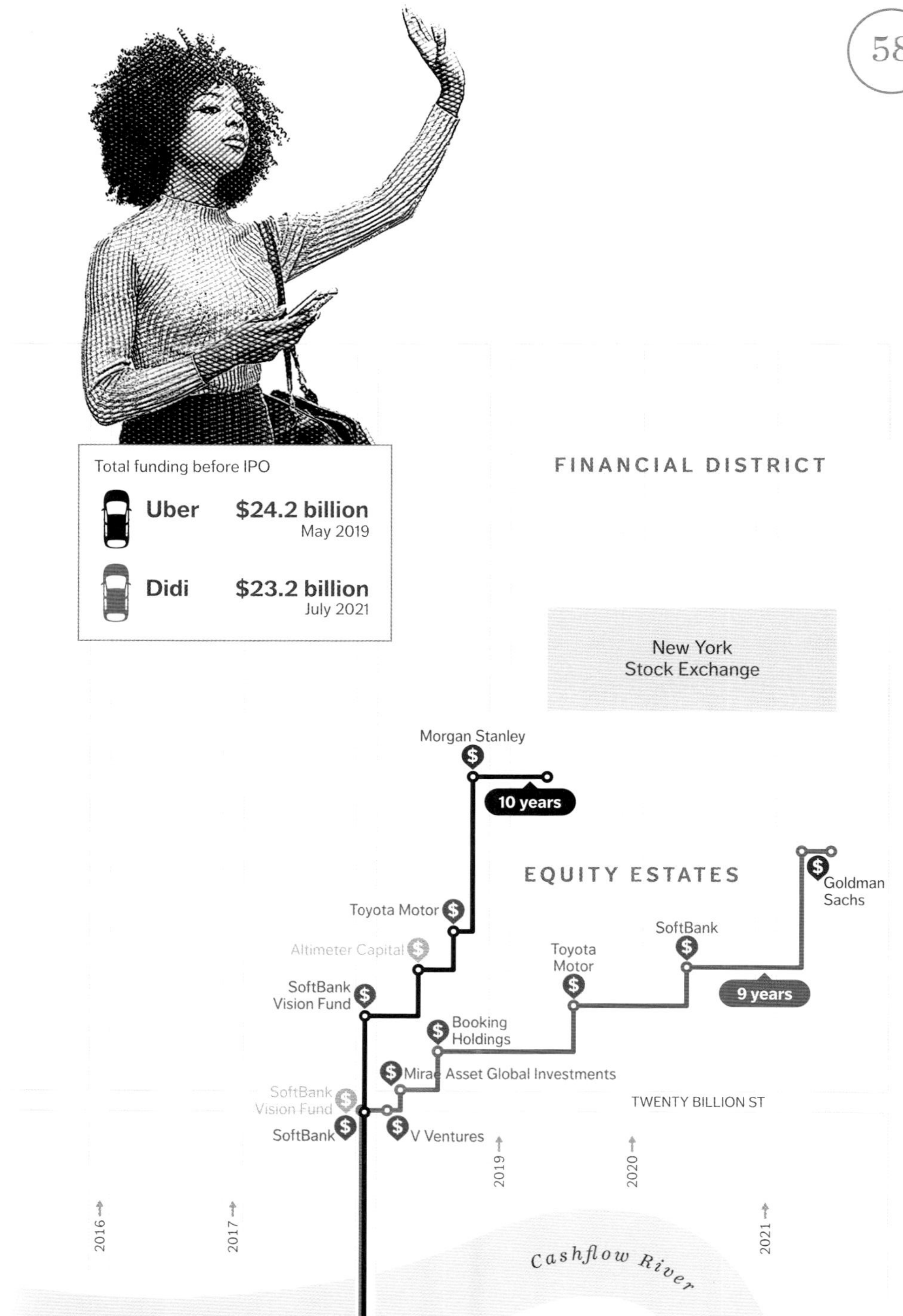

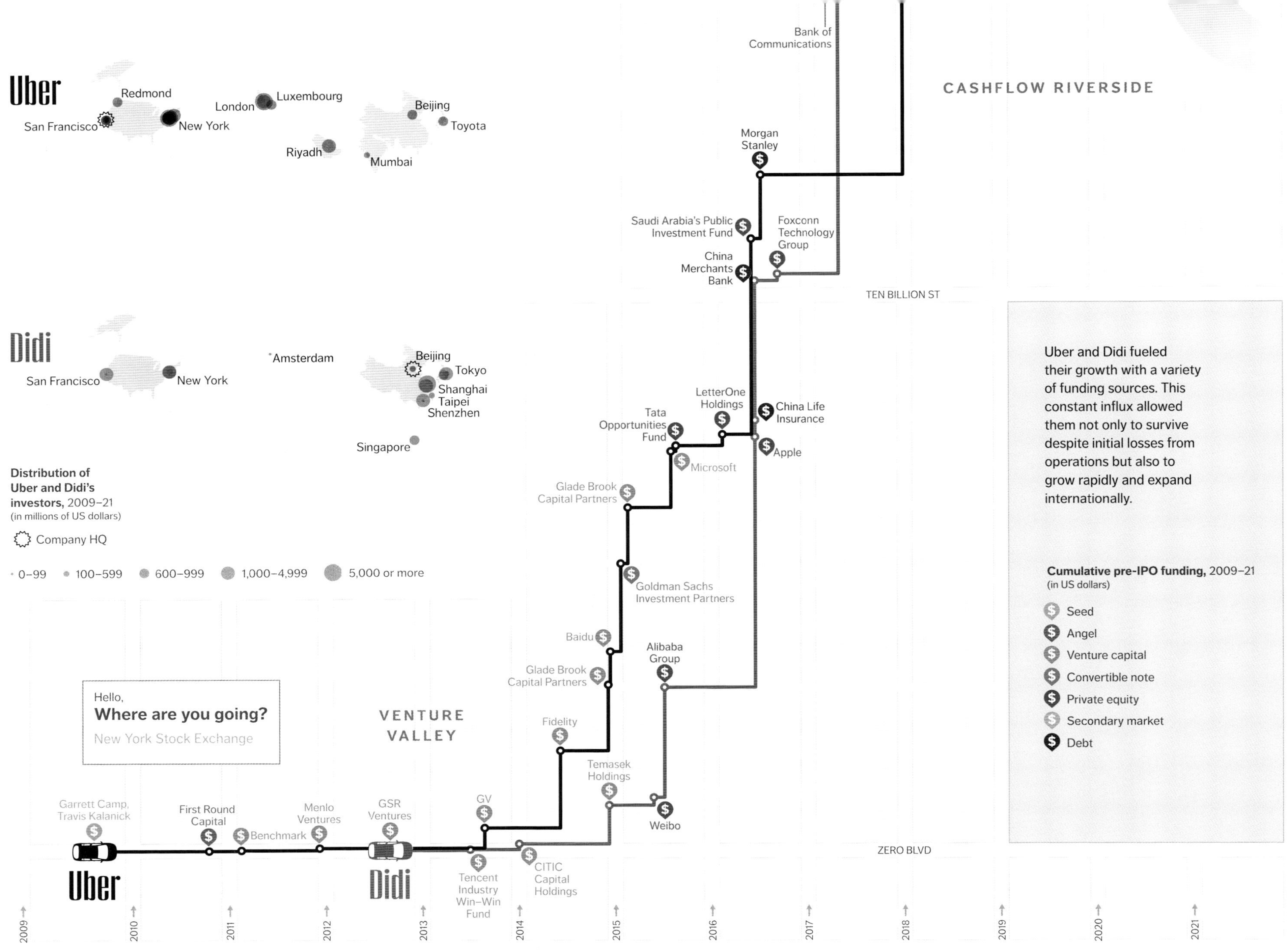

Uber and Didi fueled their growth with a variety of funding sources. This constant influx allowed them not only to survive despite initial losses from operations but also to grow rapidly and expand internationally.

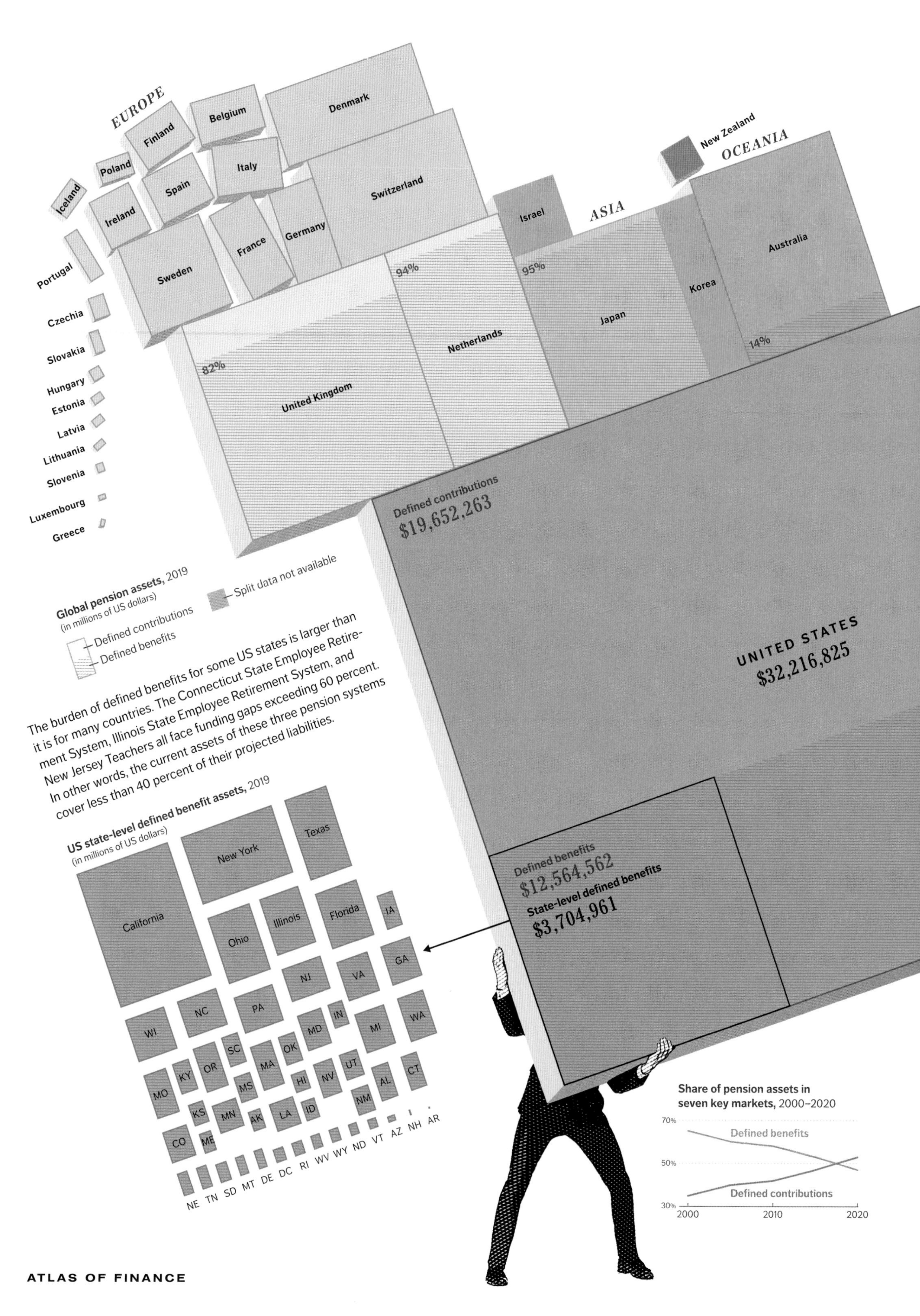

EUROPE
Iceland
Poland
Finland
Belgium
Denmark
Ireland
Spain
Italy
Switzerland
Portugal
Sweden
France
Germany
Czechia
Slovakia
Hungary
Estonia
Latvia
Lithuania
Slovenia
Luxembourg
Greece
82%
United Kingdom
94%
Netherlands
ASIA
Israel
95%
Japan
Korea
New Zealand
OCEANIA
Australia
14%
Defined contributions
$19,652,263
UNITED STATES
$32,216,825
Defined benefits
$12,564,562
State-level defined benefits
$3,704,961
Global pension assets, 2019
(in millions of US dollars)
Split data not available
Defined contributions
Defined benefits
The burden of defined benefits for some US states is larger than it is for many countries. The Connecticut State Employee Retirement System, Illinois State Employee Retirement System, and New Jersey Teachers all face funding gaps exceeding 60 percent. In other words, the current assets of these three pension systems cover less than 40 percent of their projected liabilities.
US state-level defined benefit assets, 2019
(in millions of US dollars)
California
New York
Texas
Ohio
Illinois
Florida
IA
GA
NJ
VA
WI
NC
PA
IN
MD
MI
WA
MO
KY
OR
SC
MS
MA
OK
HI
NV
UT
AL
CT
KS
MN
AK
LA
ID
NM
CO
ME
NE
TN
SD
MT
DE
DC
RI
WV
WY
ND
VT
AZ
NH
AR
Share of pension assets in seven key markets, 2000–2020
70%
50%
30%
Defined benefits
Defined contributions
2000
2010
2020

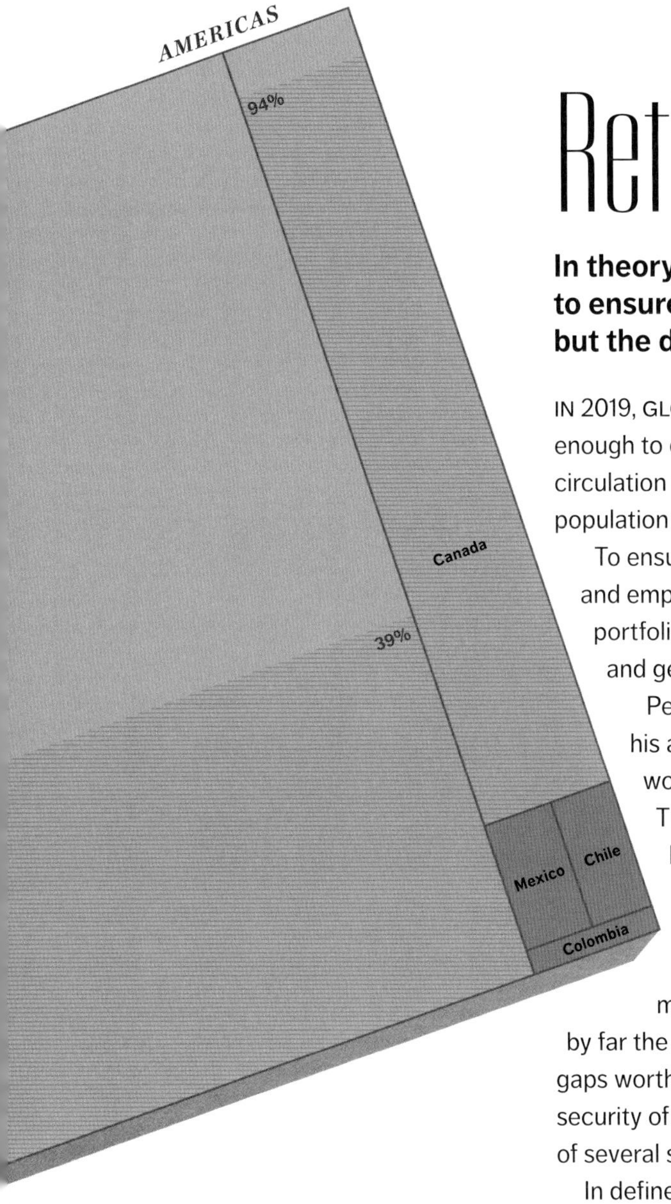

AMERICAS
94%
Canada
39%
Mexico
Chile
Colombia

Retirement (In)security

In theory, pension funds are an ingenious mechanism to ensure individuals' subsistence after retirement, but the devil is in the details.

IN 2019, GLOBAL PENSION ASSETS amounted to more than US$50 trillion, enough to own more than a quarter of the debt and equity securities in circulation that year. Yet close to 90 percent of the world's working-age population was still excluded from adequate pension coverage.

To ensure retirement security, pension systems generally collect employer and employee contributions and invest them into broadly diversified portfolios of financial securities, with the objective of protecting capital and generating a return on investment.

Pension systems have existed for millennia. To foster the loyalty of his army, the Roman emperor Augustus offered his soldiers a pension worth twelve times their annual salary for sixteen years of service. This system, which guarantees a set retirement income, is also known as a prefunded, or defined, benefit plan. While it helps employers attract and retain employees and provides a high standard of retirement security, it is also very expensive to run. Augustus is said to have spent half of Rome's tax revenues to pay military personnel and fund his pension promises. Today the US is by far the largest provider of prefunded pensions. Yet US states face funding gaps worth more than a trillion dollars. This situation is putting the retirement security of millions of Americans at risk and could precipitate the bankruptcy of several states.

In defined contribution pension systems, future benefits are not guaranteed and depend on investment earnings. As such, the burden of uncertainty inherent to financial market investments is borne by the participants of defined contribution schemes—that is, future retirees. Defined contribution plans became favored by employees because they could be transferred from one employer to the next—a trend that gathered momentum as structural shifts in industrial makeup and labor markets increased workers' mobility. The shift from defined benefit to defined contribution systems has also been motivated by employers (states and companies alike), who find the former increasingly burdensome. As a result, the social contract between generations present in defined benefit schemes is being replaced by individual risk-bearing subject to the vagaries of international financial markets. What if markets collapse just when you are about to retire?

Fearing the fate of Emperor Augustus, employers in the public and private sectors have been shifting their pension systems from defined benefits to defined contributions. On the line chart to the left, we see a consistent increase in the share of assets managed by defined contribution systems. Specifically, over the past twenty years this share has increased by 18 percent to reach 53 percent in 2020.

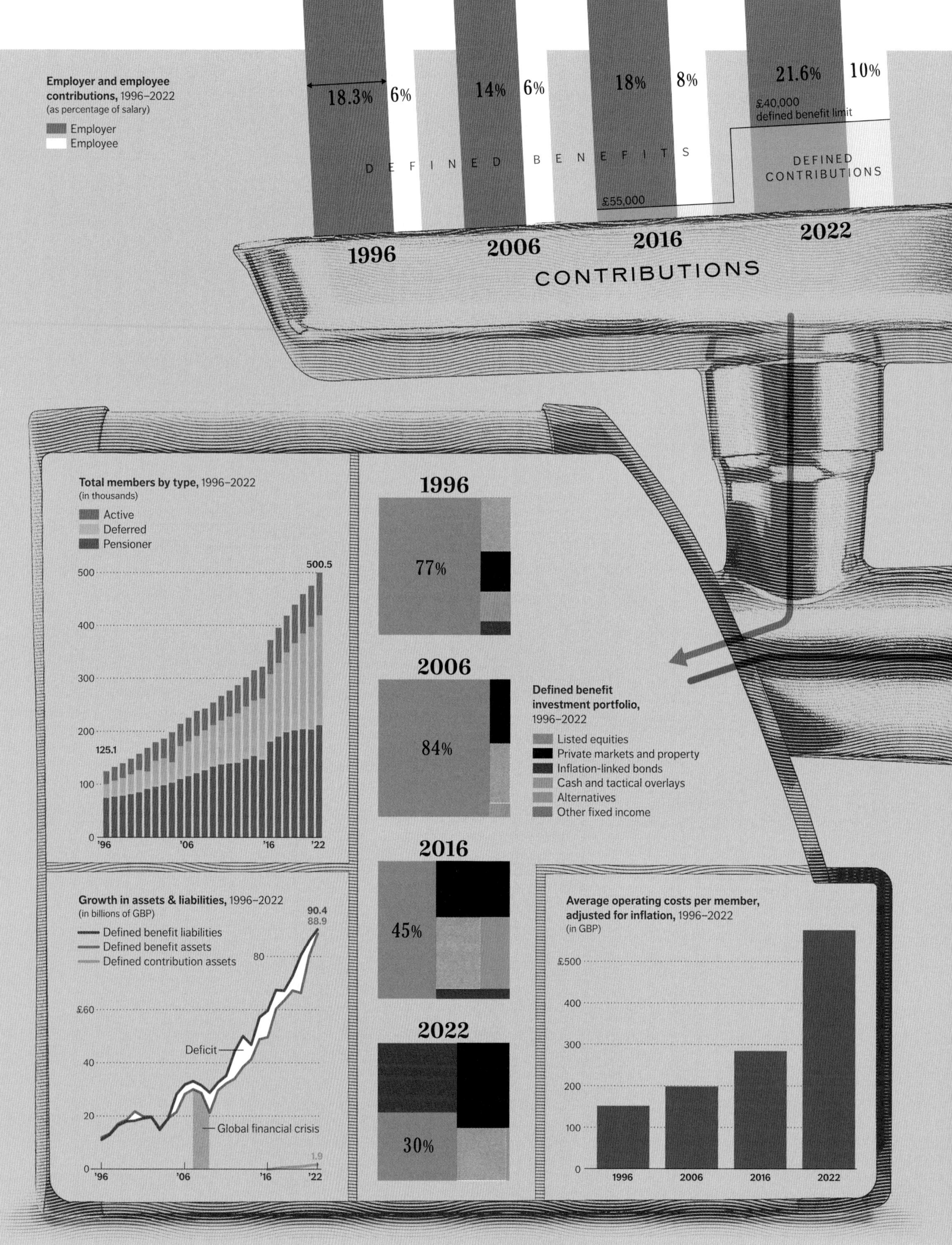
Employer and employee contributions, 1996–2022
(as percentage of salary)
Employer
Employee
18.3%
6%
14%
6%
18%
8%
21.6%
10%
£40,000
defined benefit limit
DEFINED BENEFITS
DEFINED CONTRIBUTIONS
£55,000
1996
2006
2016
2022
CONTRIBUTIONS
Total members by type, 1996–2022
(in thousands)
Active
Deferred
Pensioner
500.5
125.1
500
400
300
200
100
0
'96
'06
'16
'22
1996
77%
2006
84%
2016
45%
2022
30%
Defined benefit investment portfolio, 1996–2022
Listed equities
Private markets and property
Inflation-linked bonds
Cash and tactical overlays
Alternatives
Other fixed income
Growth in assets & liabilities, 1996–2022
(in billions of GBP)
Defined benefit liabilities
Defined benefit assets
Defined contribution assets
90.4
88.9
80
£60
40
20
0
Deficit
Global financial crisis
1.9
'96
'06
'16
'22
Average operating costs per member, adjusted for inflation, 1996–2022
(in GBP)
£500
400
300
200
100
0
1996
2006
2016
2022

The Pension Grinder

Members of the Universities Superannuation Scheme in the UK see their contributions growing and their expected pensions shrinking.

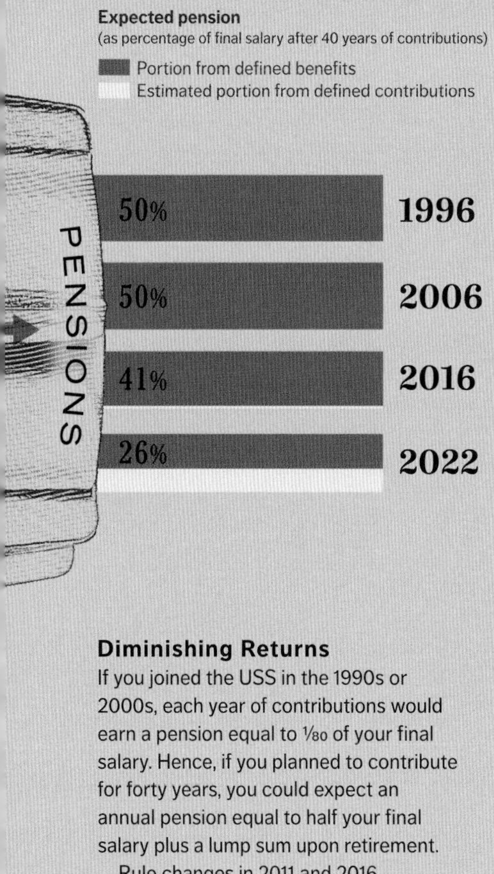

ARE YOU LUCKY ENOUGH to have a private pension that pays out retirement income based on your lifetime earnings or, even better, your final salary? In such defined benefit (DB) pension schemes, an intergenerational pooling of age cohorts allows, in theory, a mix of relatively riskier and safer assets to yield returns that will keep up with future benefits. This promise of a fixed pension benefit has come under pressure due to intervening developments in the financial markets. Notably, the 2008 global financial crisis and the regulatory response to it drove DB schemes to reduce risk in investment portfolios by increasing bond allocations, which in a low-interest-rate environment has reduced returns and increased costs to employers and plan members.

The UK's largest private DB plan, the Universities Superannuation Scheme (USS), is a case in point. It was created in 1974 to replace a defined contribution (DC) scheme in place since 1913, where only contributions were known and pensions were undetermined. One of the few DB schemes still open to new members, USS, which we have visualized here as a machine whose inner workings are rarely seen, underwent major shifts between 1996 and 2022.

The red-and-white strips entering the grinder show that contributions as a percentage of pay have increased significantly for both employers (red) and employees (white), with an increasing share of contributions going to the DC part of the scheme. This is in response to developments highlighted on graphs inside the grinder. Starting in the upper left, the number of pensioners and deferred members—who receive or expect benefits but no longer contribute—has grown faster than that of active contributing members. The line graph below shows that after a short-lived surplus in the late 1990s, liabilities have grown faster than assets. Meanwhile, the stack of multicolored squares chronicles how listed equities (light brown) have shrunk as a percentage of the investment portfolio in favor of private equity and property (black) as well as bonds (red). The chart in the lower right corner reveals increasing operating costs. Finally, the brown strips exiting the grinder represent how, upon retirement, expected DB pension benefits have been almost halved and replaced partly with risky and uncertain investment returns from DCs (paler strips). Intergenerational fairness and risk-sharing are no longer de rigueur. Instead, current members must stomach the reality of higher contributions and the prospects of diminished future pensions.

Diminishing Returns

If you joined the USS in the 1990s or 2000s, each year of contributions would earn a pension equal to 1/80 of your final salary. Hence, if you planned to contribute for forty years, you could expect an annual pension equal to half your final salary plus a lump sum upon retirement.

Rule changes in 2011 and 2016 meant that the expected DB pension of someone contributing for forty years declined to just over 40 percent of their final salary. In addition, if your annual salary exceeded £55,000 (plus inflation), contributions based on the excess would feed a DC rather than the DB part of your pension. Since 2022, the DB portion has reduced further, while the uncertain DC portion has enlarged. Now, each year of contributions earns only 1/85 of your career average salary.

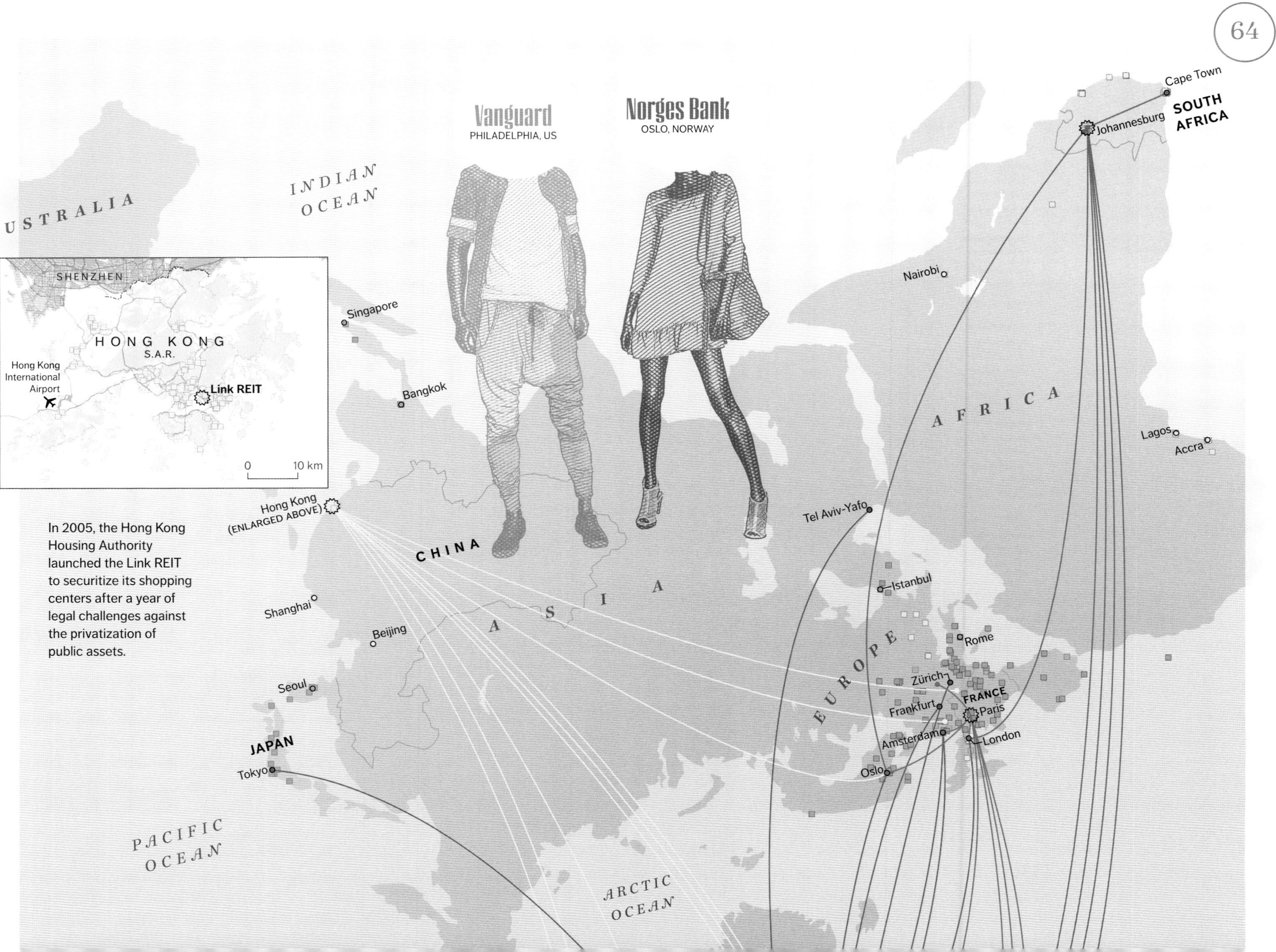

In 2005, the Hong Kong Housing Authority launched the Link REIT to securitize its shopping centers after a year of legal challenges against the privatization of public assets.

Who Owns the Mall?

Around the world, malls link financial investors and consumers.

PEOPLE GO TO A MALL for shopping or just to hang out with friends. Meanwhile, some investors shop for malls. While you try on a new pair of jeans, the mall itself could change owners.

Real estate investment trusts (REITs) specialize in acquiring, developing, and managing real estate, including malls, in order to generate profits by collecting rents from retailers. To maximize profits they minimize vacancy rates and capitalize on the malls' attractiveness. Focusing their activities on metropolitan (and particularly suburban) areas, Simon Property Group, the largest of its kind, has malls all over our map (red squares). Paris-based Klépierre has conquered the European market (purple), while Link REIT owns an empire of malls in Asia, mostly in Hong Kong (gold, see inset). Johannesburg-based REITs Growthpoint and Hyprop have developed networks across Africa and Eastern Europe (blue).

REITs have shareholders, who offer funding and participate in profits. These can be asset management firms like Vanguard, BlackRock, or Austin-based Dimension Fund Advisors. Pension funds and sovereign wealth funds have also shown an appetite for REITs. Norges Bank, the central bank managing the Government Pension Fund Global for Norway, has diversified holdings in Link, Simon Property Group, Growthpoint, Hyprop, and Klépierre.

Every time you go to a mall to buy a movie ticket or ice cream, your money enters a complex global circulation connecting consumers and retail stores to REITs and eventually their investors. Profit from every Ghanian cedi paid in a mall in Accra connects the city to New York via Johannesburg. Profit from pesos spent in Mexican malls arrives in Oslo via Indianapolis. The global spread of REITs has turned malls into financial assets and everyone who uses them, even if only for socializing, into actors in global financial networks.

Headquartered in Indianapolis, where the two Simon brothers originally built their first malls, Simon Property Group is a public company listed on the New York Stock Exchange. The firm owns more than 230 malls scattered across North America and select European and Asian cities, for a total portfolio of 190 km² of commercial properties—equivalent to about 26,000 football pitches.

Investors and mall locations
(as of September 2021)

INVESTOR — MALL — REIT
HQ
Hyprop & Growthpoint
Klépierre
Link REIT
Simon Property Group

0 — 2,000 km

BlackRock and Vanguard are the largest asset management firms in the world. They invest in REITs through multiple specialized and diversified funds. In 2021, BlackRock's and Vanguard's assets under management were valued at US$9 trillion and $7 trillion, respectively.

An Inverted World

Fortunes of the ultrarich have grown so fast that the world's 166 richest people now own more wealth than the poorest 50 percent.

GLOBAL WEALTH HAS GROWN at a highly unequal rate since 1995. For most of the world's adult population, wealth has grown around 3 to 4 percent a year, as shown on the yellow segment of our graph on the far right. For the richest 1 percent (the purple and red segments), wealth has grown as fast as 9.3 percent. Cumulatively this means the top 1 percent took 38 percent of all additional global wealth in the past twenty-five years, while the bottom 50 percent accrued only 2 percent.

This pyramidal distribution of wealth exists both within and between countries. The bottom tier (less than $10,000 in wealth) represents over half the world's population, predominantly in countries of the Global South. Within these lower-income countries, most of the population never exceeds this level of wealth. However, even in higher-income developed countries, poverty, unemployment, youth, and old age keep much of the population in the lowest tier.

North America and Europe have the dominant share of millionaires, accounting for 70 percent of this group, followed by the Asia-Pacific region (excluding China and India) at 17 percent. The unequal distribution of wealth is not only between the top 1 percent and the rest but within the top 1 percent itself. Compare the light purple tier here with its darker tip. Those with more than $10 million make up 3 percent of the top 1 percent but account for 36 percent of this group's total wealth.

The faster growth of the wealth of the richest reflects the fact that money can be "put to work" and multiplied. Invested in stocks, bonds, and real estate, this wealth brings in returns, which continue to grow the fortunes of the rich. By contrast, poorer households rely primarily on a monthly income to cover living expenses, with little leftover for savings or investments. Moreover, assets that they may own, such as cars, tend to lose value over time.

Inequality fractures society and turns it upside down. It is also unsustainable. With a typically lavish lifestyle and conspicuous consumption, an average person in the top 1 percent of the global wealth pyramid is responsible for seventeen times more carbon emissions than an average citizen of the world. Addressing the growing inequality will require more taxation on those with the most wealth and highest incomes, redistribution of wealth, and clamping down on tax avoidance and evasion through tax havens. We must act now or our societies will turn into plutocracies.

World's adult population by wealth range and their share of global wealth
(in US dollars)

Wealth data are from 2020 except for those worth more than $1 million. Their data are from 2021.

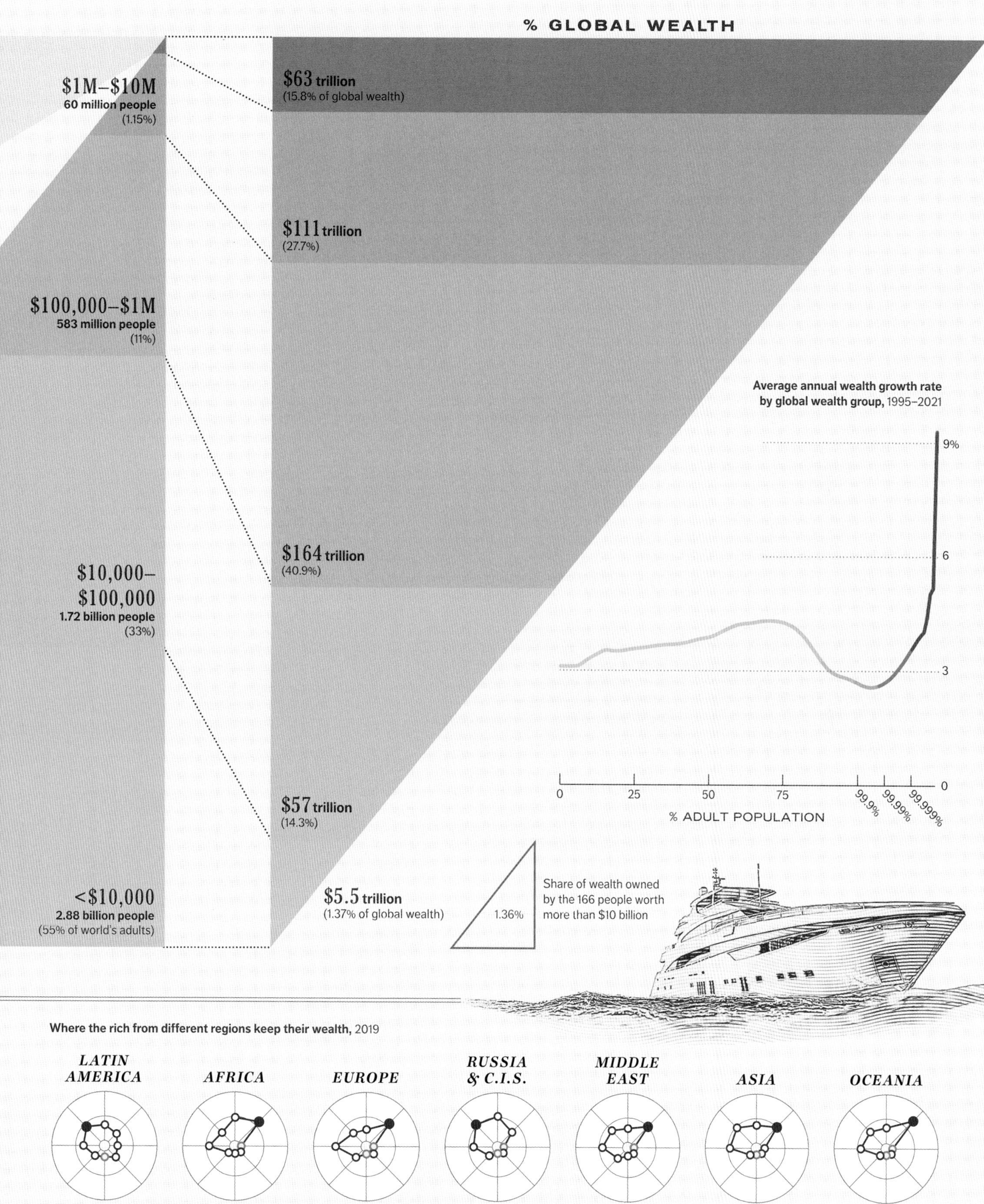
% GLOBAL WEALTH
$1M–$10M
60 million people
(1.15%)
$63 trillion
(15.8% of global wealth)
$111 trillion
(27.7%)
$100,000–$1M
583 million people
(11%)
Average annual wealth growth rate by global wealth group, 1995–2021
9%
6
3
0
0
25
50
75
99.9%
99.99%
99.999%
% ADULT POPULATION
$10,000–$100,000
1.72 billion people
(33%)
$164 trillion
(40.9%)
$57 trillion
(14.3%)
<$10,000
2.88 billion people
(55% of world's adults)
$5.5 trillion
(1.37% of global wealth)
1.36%
Share of wealth owned by the 166 people worth more than $10 billion
Where the rich from different regions keep their wealth, 2019
LATIN AMERICA
AFRICA
EUROPE
RUSSIA & C.I.S.
MIDDLE EAST
ASIA
OCEANIA
Equities and bonds are the favorite wealth stores, but cash and investment properties help the rich keep money safe and accessible.

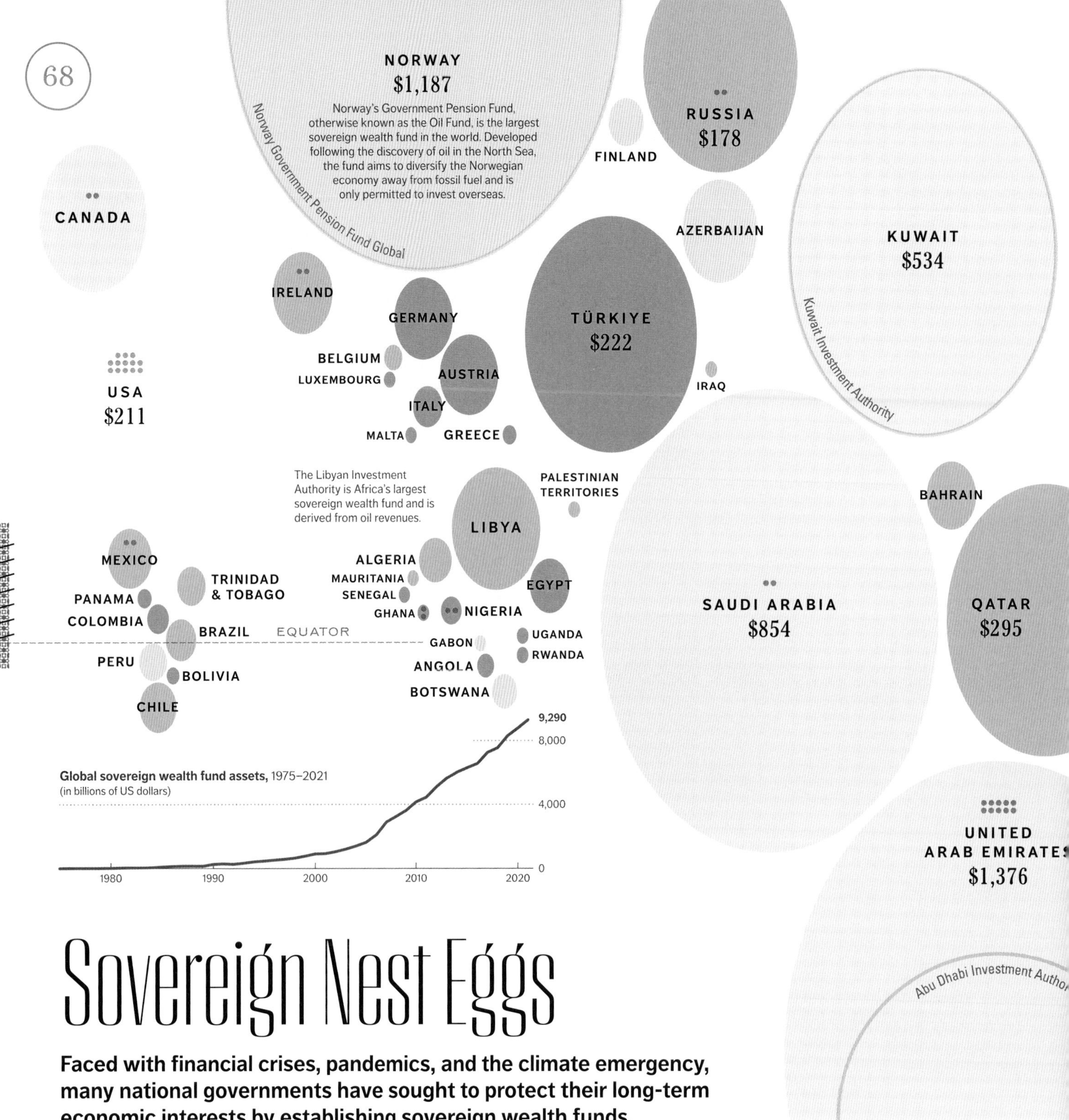

Sovereign Nest Eggs

Faced with financial crises, pandemics, and the climate emergency, many national governments have sought to protect their long-term economic interests by establishing sovereign wealth funds.

FOR DECADES, governments have been hatching plans to diversify their economies, build resilience, and safeguard the prosperity of future generations. Whether the result of oil and gas revenues or foreign exchange reserves, sovereign wealth funds are a unique type of investment vehicle operated by governments and created through fiscal surpluses. While they allow governments to act like private investors spreading investments around the world, not every country has the luxury of spare change.

On our map of the top 100 sovereign wealth funds in 2020, the size of each country's oval corresponds to the amount of assets under management. China and the UAE have the largest nest eggs at US$1,703 billion and US$1,376 billion, respectively, and both operate more than one fund. The single largest fund, the Government Pension Fund of Norway, manages over US$1,187 billion in assets.

Our map also shows that sovereign wealth funds are nothing new. The color of each country represents the age of its first fund. The oldest (in white) is the Permanent School Fund in the US, which the State of Texas created in

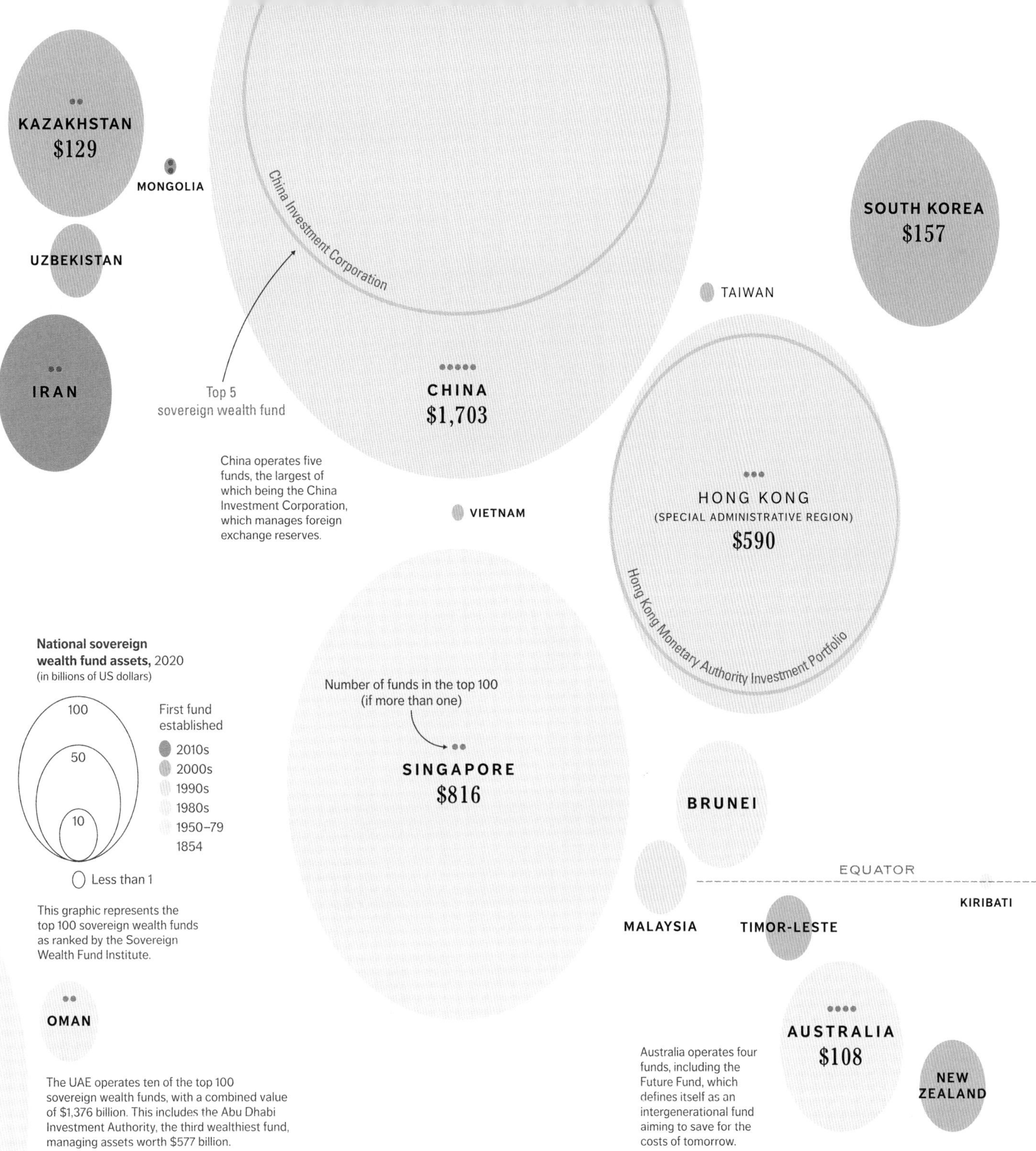

1854 to support education. The prevalence of orange and red eggs reveals the rapid growth of sovereign wealth funds in the twenty-first century as governments scramble to take advantage of international investment opportunities. Many Asian countries hatched and expanded their nest eggs after the painful experiences of the Asian financial crisis of 1997–98 in order to lessen their dependence on foreign money.

While the COVID-19 pandemic created challenges for investors all over the world, the sovereign wealth fund model is yet to crack. Governments continue to invest, and the funds' role in the global economy grows. The UK does not have a nest egg of its own, but it has become a popular destination for investment by other countries' funds, particularly from the Gulf States. Pay to see your beloved Newcastle United play at St. James Park? Saudi Arabia benefits. Treat your partner to designer clothes from Harrods? Qatar gains. Escape for some sun via Etihad Airways? The UAE wins. The UK is no exception. Money from sovereign wealth funds is being whisked all over the world.

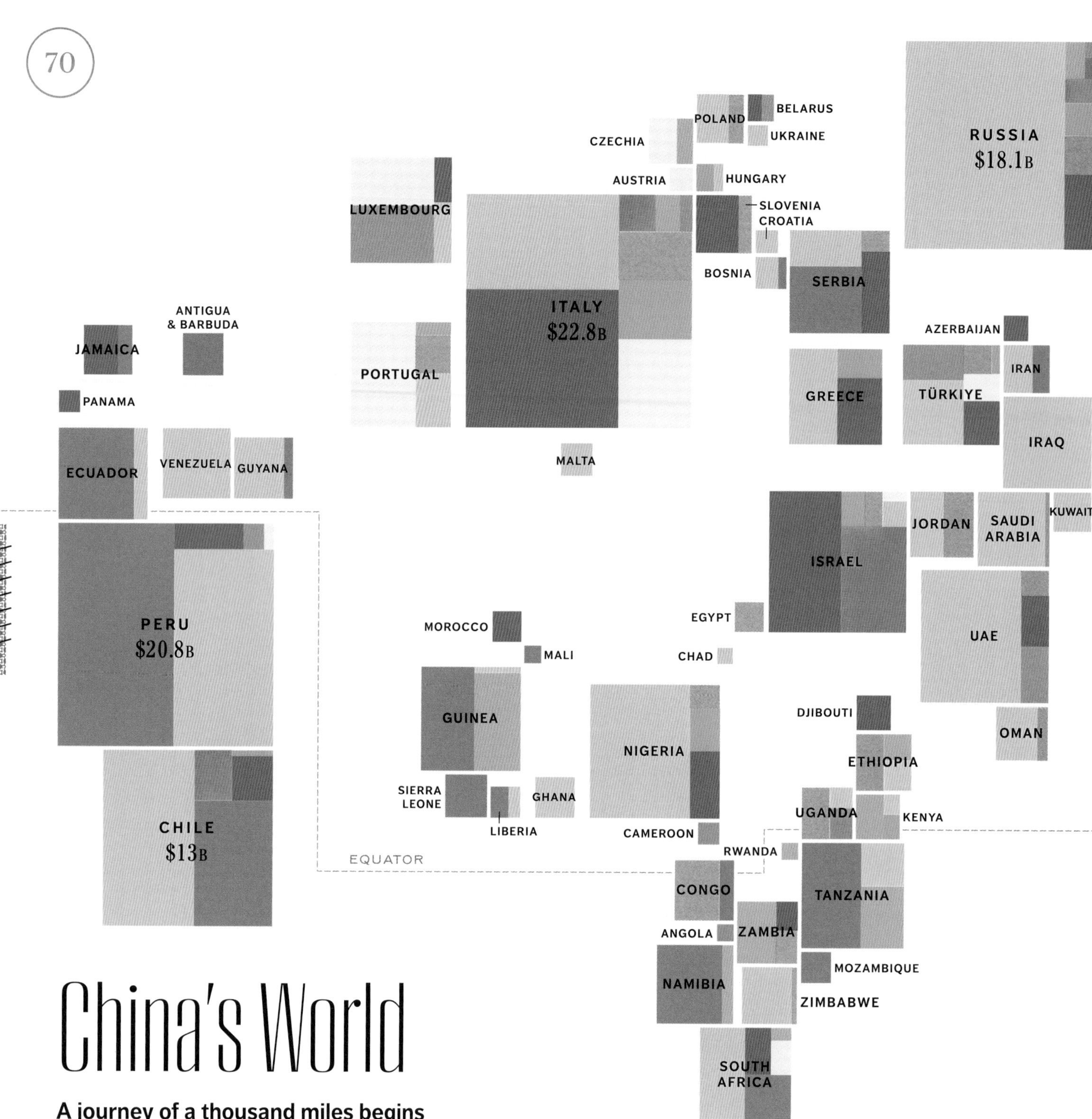

China's World

A journey of a thousand miles begins with a single step.

AS YOUR TRAIN DEPARTS from Furi-Lebu Railway Station in Addis Ababa you could be forgiven for feeling surprised. After all, you did not necessarily expect a Chinese train conductor and Mandarin signposts in Ethiopia. The duration of your trip to Djibouti's Red Sea port is yet another surprise, as what would have taken over three days by road now takes less than twelve hours in an air-conditioned carriage. The cause of your surprise? China's Belt and Road Initiative.

Launched in 2013 by President Xi Jinping and announced during a visit to Kazakhstan, the Belt and Road Initiative has become the trademark of Chinese foreign policy. Based on state-backed cross-border investment, it reimagines and extends the ancient Silk Road by developing overland and maritime economic routes that deepen the political and economic ties between China and the rest of the world. While infrastructure development is central to the initiative, its official priorities are much broader and aim to promote policy coordination, infrastructure connectivity, unimpeded trade, financial integration, and deeper cultural connections between China and participating countries.

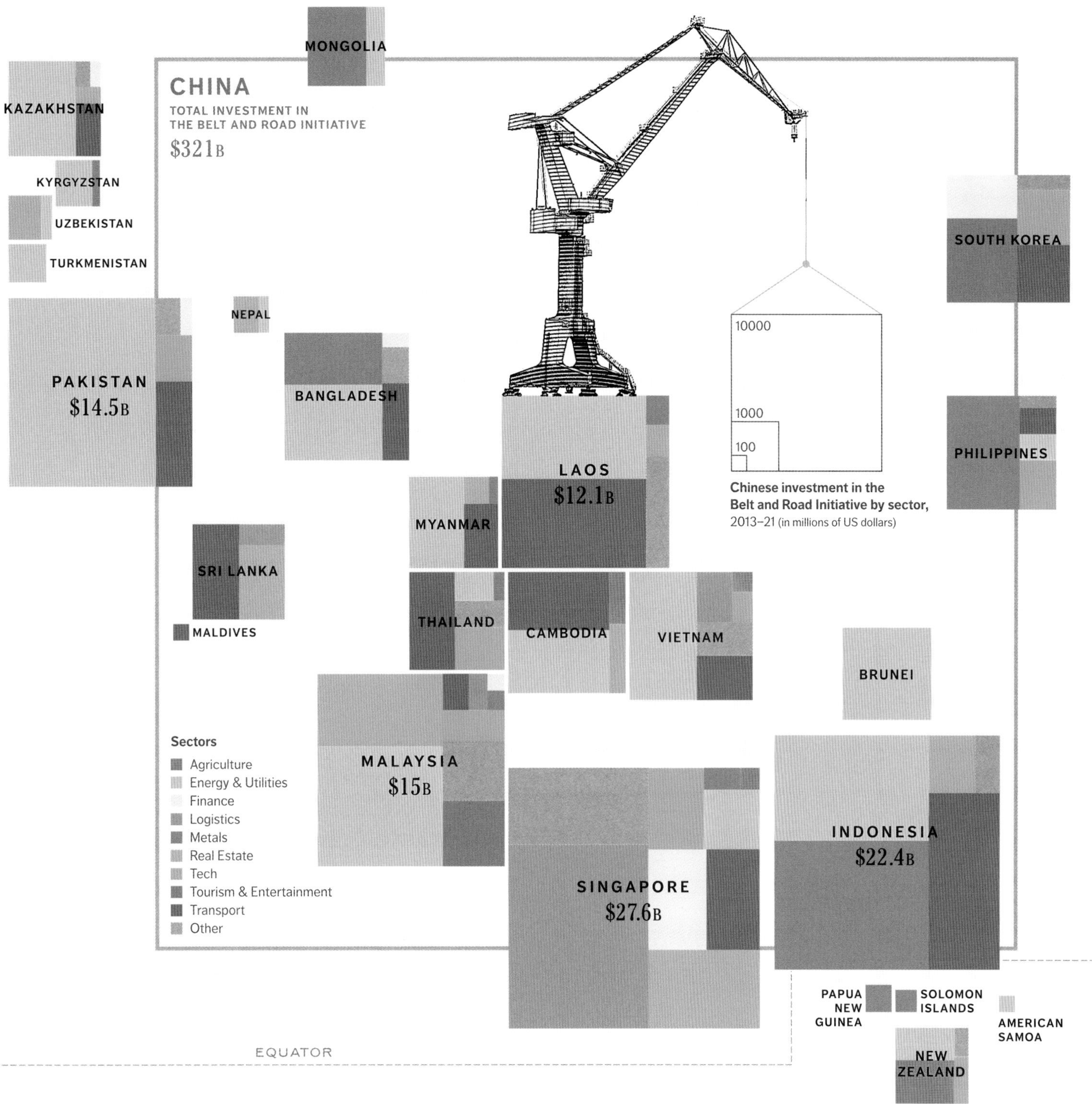

Chinese investment in the Belt and Road Initiative by sector, 2013–21 (in millions of US dollars)

Our map suggests that China's world means business. Revealing the size and sectoral focus of investments, the boxes show how China has invested over US$321 billion across eighty-two countries since 2013, with Singapore ($27.6 billion), Indonesia ($22.4 billion), and Italy ($22.8 billion) receiving the most money. China has also funded railways in Nigeria, lithium mines in Chile, online gaming in Israel, and nuclear power plants in Malaysia.

Characterized by significant investments in energy and utilities (gold), metals (brown), and real estate (dark green), China's Belt and Road Initiative is clearly much more than the construction of roads and bridges. With China's spatial and sectoral foci expanding, so too are geopolitical tensions. Italy's prominent participation reminds us that Venice was the key terminus of the historical Silk Road. But as Italy is a G7 member, its participation is also controversial. Western governments view the Belt and Road Initiative as a new form of globalization, replacing free-market logic with state-led intervention. Irrespective of where you stand on the debate, the money keeps flowing and China's world keeps spinning.

2:28

The amount of money in the world is not limited—it's infinite.
PAUL MCKENNA

Intermediation & Technology

The history of financial intermediation is a story of innovation. Its starting point is the creation of money by financial institutions. Over time people have invented new ways of raising money and insuring themselves against financial losses. In recent decades, digitalization has unleashed a race to measure the financial risk of everything and everyone, to trade at the speed of light, and to put financial instruments in everyone's hands. Though increasingly intangible, financial intermediation has tangible social and environmental costs.

The Rainmakers

Contrary to common perception, bank credit is created out of thin air.

DESPITE CONVENTIONAL RHETORIC, commercial banks do not lend money and are not financial intermediaries. Lending typically involves something that exists beforehand. You lend some cash to a friend, who promises to repay you next week. Under similar financial mechanics, a loan shark lends money to a gambler to play in a casino.

Commercial banks do not do that. When providing credit, they do not pass anybody's money around. They create money as if it fell from the sky. For this to happen, what is required are not savings piled in the vaults of

Where Does Credit Come From?

The Myth

Individuals hand their savings to the bank, which uses them to create loans.

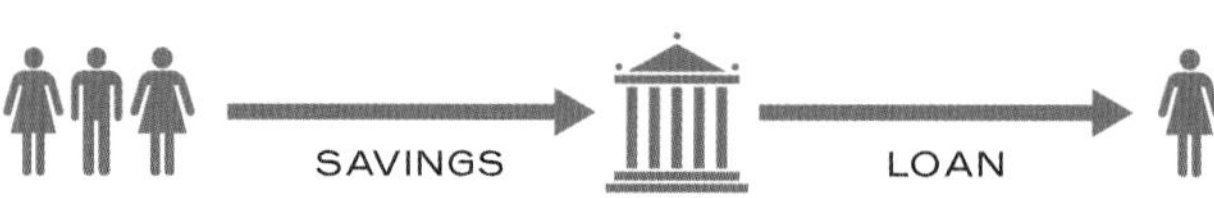

The Reality

The bank creates credit money. Individuals and businesses use this money for consumption or investment and save what is left.

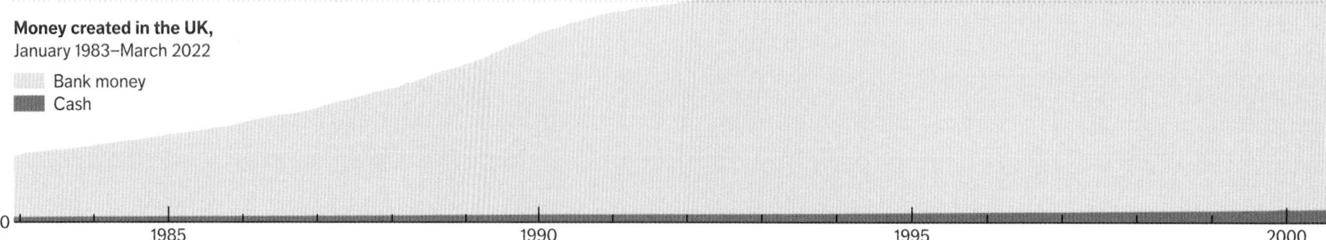

the bank but trust between the bank and the borrower. The bank trusts the borrower to repay the loan, while the borrower trusts the bank to provide cash upon demand. To be able to fulfill its promise, the bank needs to access a central bank's reserves, a form of interbank money the central bank also creates out of nothing. The interest rate on reserves is the main policy tool in the hands of the central bank. To be sure, a commercial bank will always welcome deposits from its customers, not as a precondition for providing credit, but as an additional source of low-cost liquidity.

Trust is by nature forward-looking. The real driving forces in credit creation are thus the expectations of the borrower and the bank. Conversely, the actual constraints are the profitability and solvency considerations of the bank, the demand for credit from households and firms, and the limitations set by banking regulations.

The chart below shows how trillions of pounds' worth of money has been created by banks in the UK, while the amount of cash has remained tiny. Times of crisis are particularly "rainy." Steep increases during the 2008 global financial crisis and the COVID-19 pandemic are the result of stimulus from the central bank.

Savings and credit are not correlated. Rather than savings driving credit growth, evidence shows a much weaker relationship that can even turn negative.

Cornering the Market

Initial public offerings often offer extraordinary profits, which market players with privileged access tend to skim.

IN THE DAYS BEFORE Royal Mail went public in 2013, its underwriters gave an exclusive low-price offer of 330 pence per share to a handpicked set of initial investors, two-thirds of which were institutions such as banks and funds. Individual investors and Royal Mail's 167,000 employees, meanwhile, got much smaller slices of the pie chart.

As shown on the graph to the right, the opening price for a share of Royal Mail on the first day of public trading was 451p. At the closing bell, it was worth four pence more, earning those lucky few who invested at 330p a return of 37.9 percent. But how much of it was luck?

While selling shares at the initial public offering (IPO) to select investors below the eventual market price may seem illegal, it is a common practice. Known as IPO underpricing, it is meant to boost demand and to make the stock's first-day performance headline news. Royal Mail's IPO was underwritten by a syndicate of investment banks led by Goldman Sachs and UBS, who decided who got shares and who didn't. As the market for IPO underwriting services is heavily concentrated, particularly in smaller and developing economies (see below), large issuers like Royal Mail have only a few banks to turn to. Investors, in turn, only need to have relationships with a handful of banks to receive these exclusive and lucrative investment opportunities. In exchange, they reward the banks by paying them for other services such as trading and research. If this seems like a crony way to run capital markets, perhaps that's because it is.

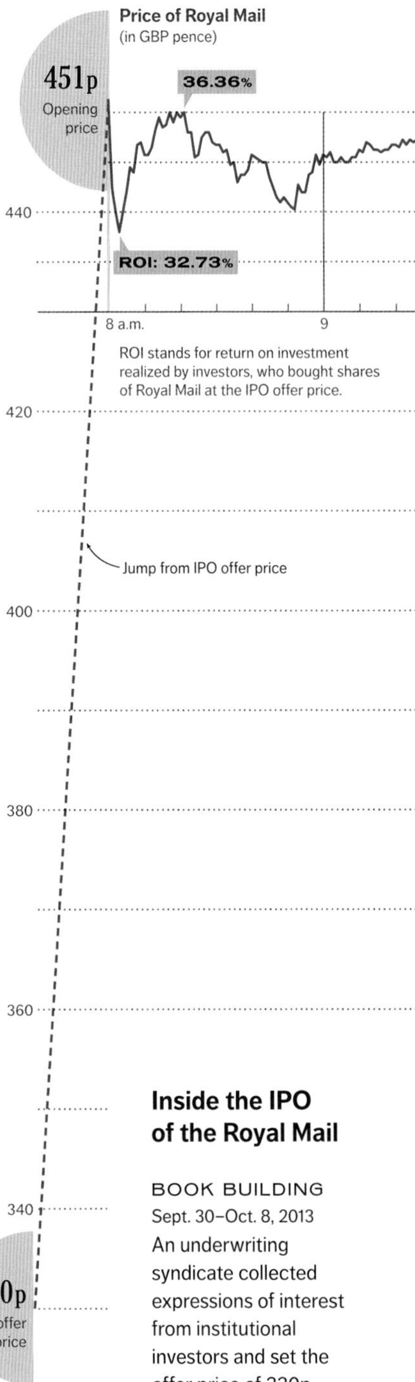

Market share of the top five IPO underwriters by country, 2000–2015

Africa · Americas · Asia · Europe · Oceania

ECUADOR, UGANDA, PALESTINE, GABON, KYRGYZSTAN, BARBADOS, LIECHTENSTEIN, MAURITIUS, DOMINICAN REPUBLIC, LATVIA, RWANDA, SLOVAKIA, CENTRAL AFRICAN REP., DEM. REP. OF THE CONGO, IRAQ, MADAGASCAR, BOTSWANA, TOGO, LEBANON, JAMAICA, TRINIDAD & TOBAGO, SYRIA, QATAR, JORDAN, URUGUAY, MONGOLIA, ESTONIA, PAPUA NEW GUINEA, GHANA, LAOS, KENYA, SLOVENIA, CROATIA, TUNISIA, ZIMBABWE, CAMBODIA, OMAN, VIETNAM, PANAMA, BAHAMAS, KUWAIT, ICELAND, TANZANIA, SRI LANKA, ZAMBIA, GEORGIA, MONACO, BAHRAIN, JAPAN, MOROCCO, KAZAKHSTAN, LITHUANIA, NEW ZEALAND

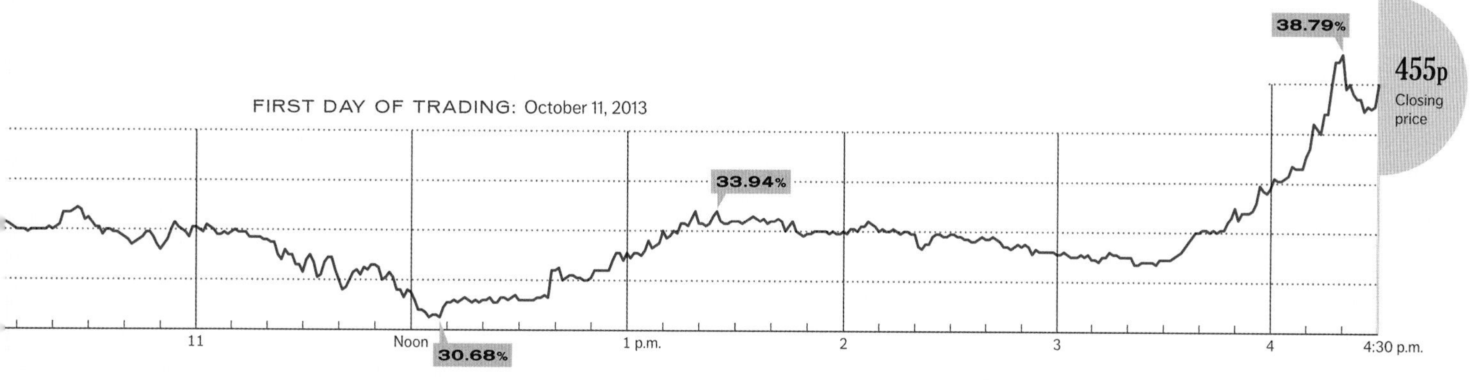

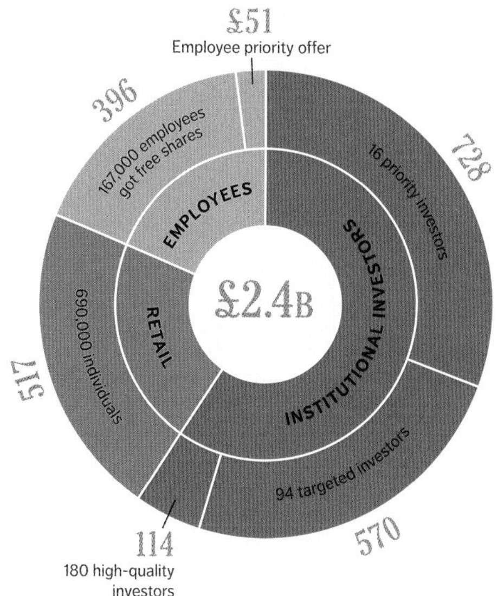

ALLOCATION

Oct. 8–11, 2013

Most shares were allocated to a select group of institutional investors (see pie chart). Royal Mail's 167,000 employees were given 16 percent of the shares, valued at £396 million, or over £2,000 per full-time employee.

EGYPT
BRAZIL
CYPRUS
ARGENTINA
CHILE
PERU
SWITZERLAND
PHILIPPINES
CZECHIA
BANGLADESH
BULGARIA
COLOMBIA
MACAU S.A.R.
LUXEMBOURG
PAKISTAN
MALAYSIA
UKRAINE
IRELAND
GERMANY
ROMANIA
SWEDEN
BELGIUM
NETHERLANDS
FINLAND
MEXICO
CANADA
AUSTRALIA
AUSTRIA
SINGAPORE
ITALY
UNITED STATES
RUSSIA
NORWAY
FRANCE
DENMARK
NIGERIA
SPAIN
TÜRKIYE
SOUTH AFRICA
THAILAND
UNITED ARAB EMIRATES
GREECE
UNITED KINGDOM
INDIA
PORTUGAL
INDONESIA
TAIWAN
POLAND
ISRAEL
HONG KONG S.A.R.
SOUTH KOREA
CHINA

–100%
–75
–50
–25
–0
MARKET SHARE

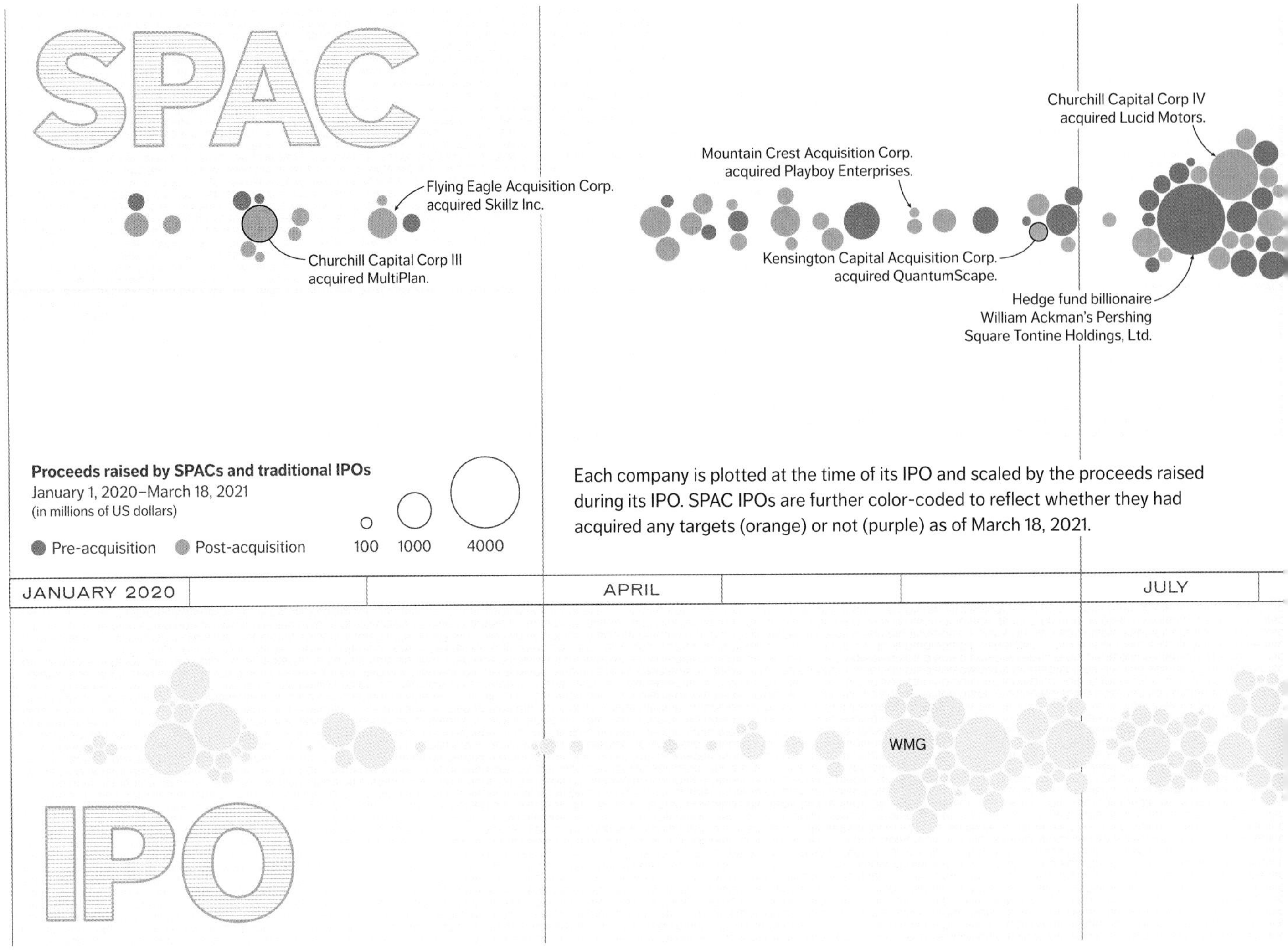

What the SPAC?

Special purpose acquisition companies were the hottest fad in finance. Now questions about regulatory issues and their investment risk abound.

TYPICALLY, operating companies with a proven track record of sustained profits go through an initial public offering (IPO)—a process of being vetted by investment bankers, auditors, and lawyers—before their shares are offered to the general public. The year 2020 wasn't a typical year. While waves of COVID-19 swept the globe, investors saw waves of special purpose acquisition companies, or SPACs, entering the market. These are companies established specifically to raise money through IPOs to acquire other companies at a later date. The bubble chart above displays SPACs and traditional IPOs listed on the New York Stock Exchange and NASDAQ from January 2020 until March 2021. As the clusters on the right reveal, US-based SPACs raised far more through their IPOs in the first quarter of 2021 than traditional IPOs.

Despite the increasing popularity of SPACs, the risks faced by investors are still not fully understood. In a traditional IPO, potential investors are presented with a prospectus that details the issuer's financial history, scope of operations, and other information relevant to its future prospects. In contrast, SPACs do not have a record of

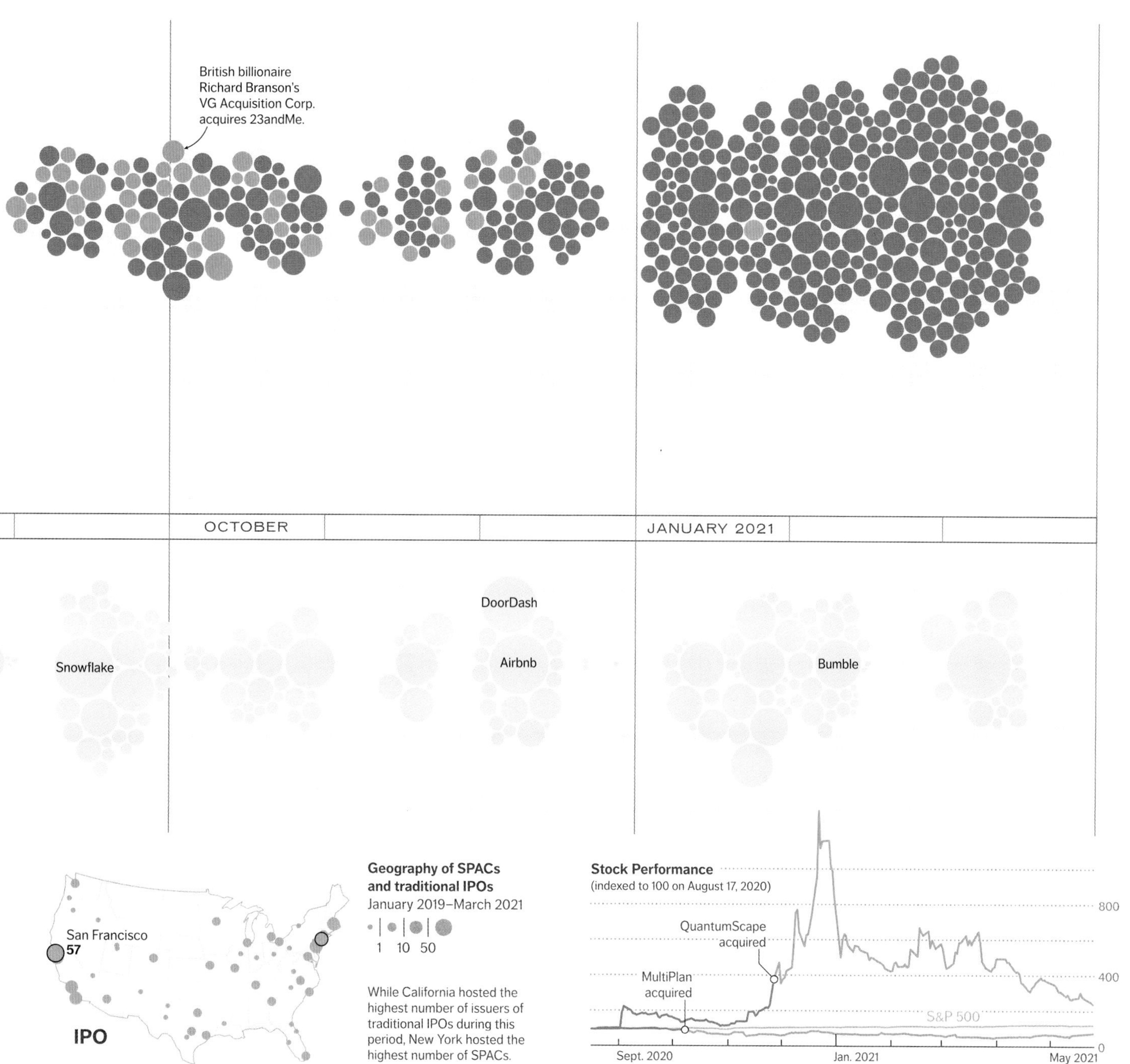

operations or financial history, and the specific companies they will acquire are often not known at the time of their IPOs. So those who invest in them generally go in blind and bet on the success of the subsequent acquisition. Because the share price of a SPAC reflects the value of companies it acquires, investors lose money if a SPAC overpays for its acquisitions. For example, take the fates of MultiPlan and QuantumScape. In February 2020, a SPAC called Churchill Capital Corp III initially offered their shares for $10. So did Kensington Capital Acquisition Corp. a few months later. Come October, Churchill completed its acquisition of MultiPlan, a health care services provider, and took on its name; Kensington did the same with battery manufacturer QuantumScape in November. Following acquisition, shares of MultiPlan bottomed out, while shares of QuantumScape skyrocketed at first but then declined (see line chart). Both companies have since been sued by investors for providing misleading information about their planned acquisitions. In 2022, the US Securities and Exchange Commission imposed new regulations on SPACs to improve investor protection.

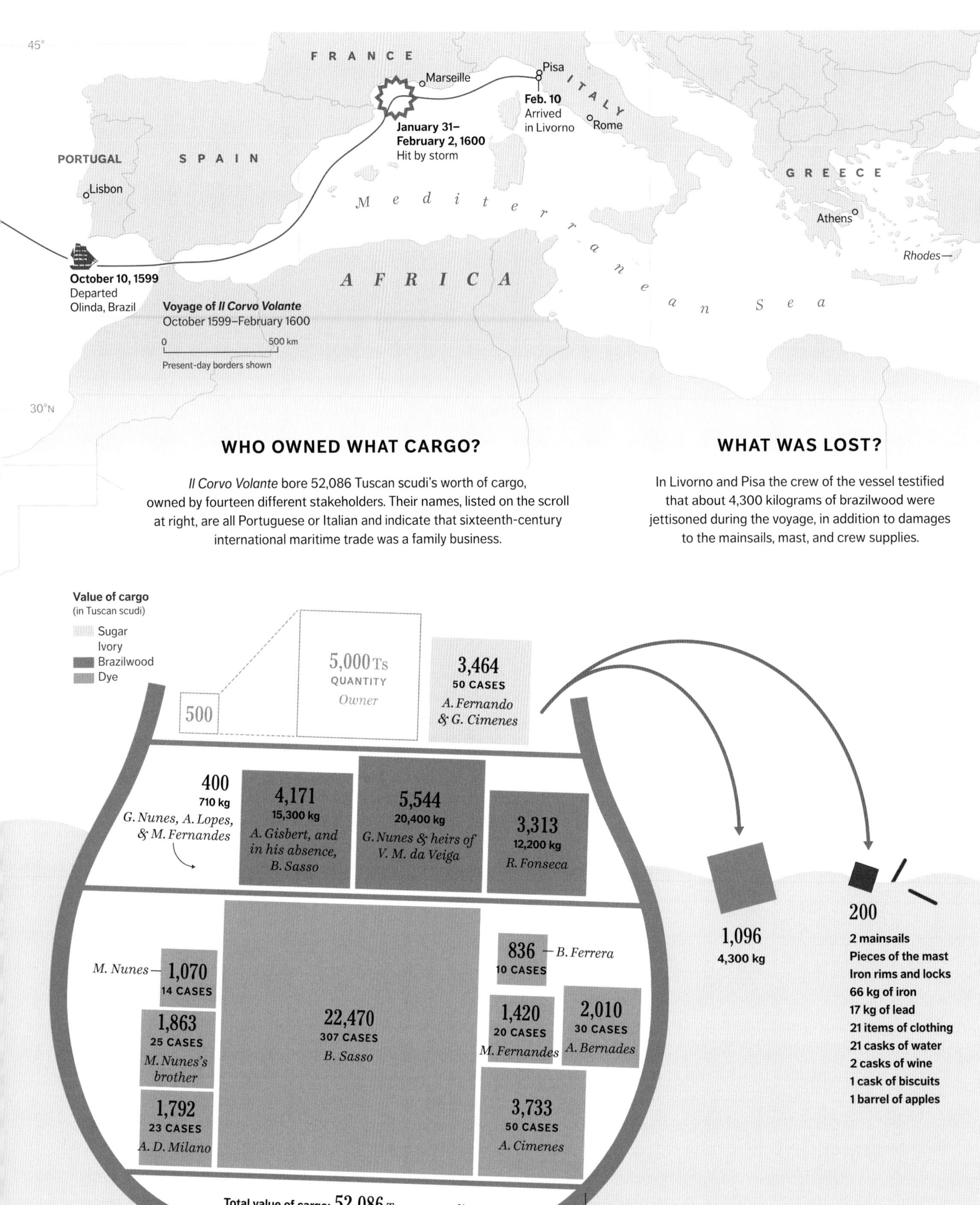

WHO OWNED WHAT CARGO?

Il Corvo Volante bore 52,086 Tuscan scudi's worth of cargo, owned by fourteen different stakeholders. Their names, listed on the scroll at right, are all Portuguese or Italian and indicate that sixteenth-century international maritime trade was a family business.

WHAT WAS LOST?

In Livorno and Pisa the crew of the vessel testified that about 4,300 kilograms of brazilwood were jettisoned during the voyage, in addition to damages to the mainsails, mast, and crew supplies.

Calcuation of general average for *Il Corvo Volante*, February 12, 1600 (in Tuscan scudi)

IL TESTIMONIALE	
Gio. Nunes, Andrea Lopes, & Manuel Fernandes	10.4
Basto Ferrera	21.7
Marco Nunes	27.7
M. Fernandes	36.8
Arrighes Dies Milano	46.5
Marco Nunes's brother	48.3
Arrighes Bernades	52.1
Il Corvo Volante	71.3
Rodrigho Fonseca	85.9
Antonio Fernando & Gaspar Cimenes	89.8
Andrea Cimenes	96.8
Arrigho Gisbert, and in his absence, Bernardo Sasso	108.1
Gio. Nunes & the heirs of Vasco Martines da Veiga	143.7
Bernardo Sasso	582.5

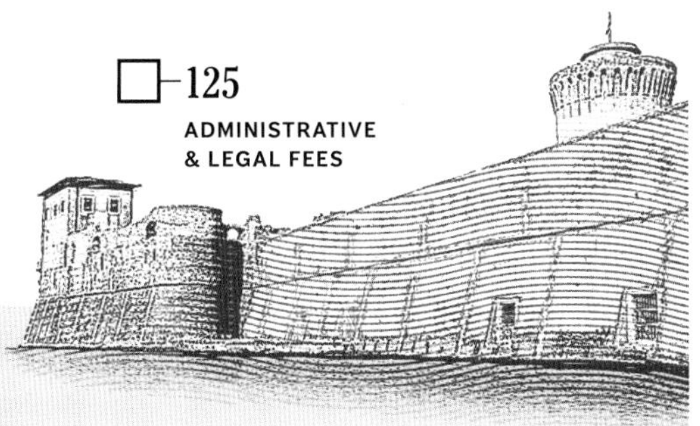

$$\frac{\text{damages} + \text{fees}}{\text{cargo} + \text{vessel}} = \frac{1{,}421}{54{,}836} = 2.59\%$$

WHO BEARS THE LOSSES?

Two merchants in Pisa were selected by the Consuls of the Sea to perform the general average calculations. They divided the combined losses from the jettisoned cargo, the damage to the vessel, and the administrative costs by the total value of the venture to establish the contributing share of each constituent party. For the general average of *Il Corvo Volante*, each party paid 2.59% of the value of their cargo.

Maritime Risk Sharing

General average is an ancient financial tradition that continues to facilitate maritime trade.

ON OCTOBER 10, 1599, the sailing vessel *Il Corvo Volante* left Olinda, Brazil, for Europe loaded with sugar, wood, dye, and other merchandise. Its final destination was the Tuscan port of Livorno, with an intermediate stop in Lisbon, Portugal. For unknown reasons the vessel never stopped in Lisbon. What we do know from surviving records is that in late January 1600, a strong storm pummeled the ship off the coast of France, ripping two mainsails and snapping the ship's mast. After two days of unrelenting seas, Captain Martino Erman, of Antwerp, and his crew decided to throw some cargo overboard in order to help them stay afloat. Eight days later, the so-called "Flying Crow" limped into Livorno.

Who was to be held responsible for the lost cargo? Could the owners of the jettisoned goods claim them back from the captain? Fortunately for Captain Erman, under the rule of Grand Duke Ferdinando I de' Medici, there was a maritime principle in Tuscany known as "general average" that permitted the crew to sacrifice cargo in an emergency to save the ship and the rest of the venture. Compensation for losses would then be shared among the voyage's stakeholders in proportion to the value of their total cargo. Thus for *Il Corvo Volante,* those with the most to lose—such as Bernardo Sasso and his 307 cases of dye—would pay the lion's share of the losses.

Following Tuscan protocol, upon arrival in Livorno, Captain Erman wrote a report of the events that led to the ship's damages and lost cargo. Then he went to Pisa, where an administrative body called the Consuls of the Sea calculated each party's contribution to the general average. According to the consuls' final *testimoniale*, the stakeholders split 1,421 Tuscan scudi's worth of damages and administrative fees (see table).

The origins of general average date back to ancient Greece and the customary legal practices of maritime traders in the port of Rhodes. In the sixth century CE those customs entered Roman civil law as a set of regulations governing commercial trade known as Rhodian Sea Law. The principle was first codified globally by the York-Antwerp Rules in 1890 and is still widely used in international trade and inscribed in maritime laws. Combining money, law, and accounting, general average complements insurance in safeguarding business activity from the perilous nature of maritime trade. Without an equitable mechanism for measuring and spreading losses, such voyages would not be viable.

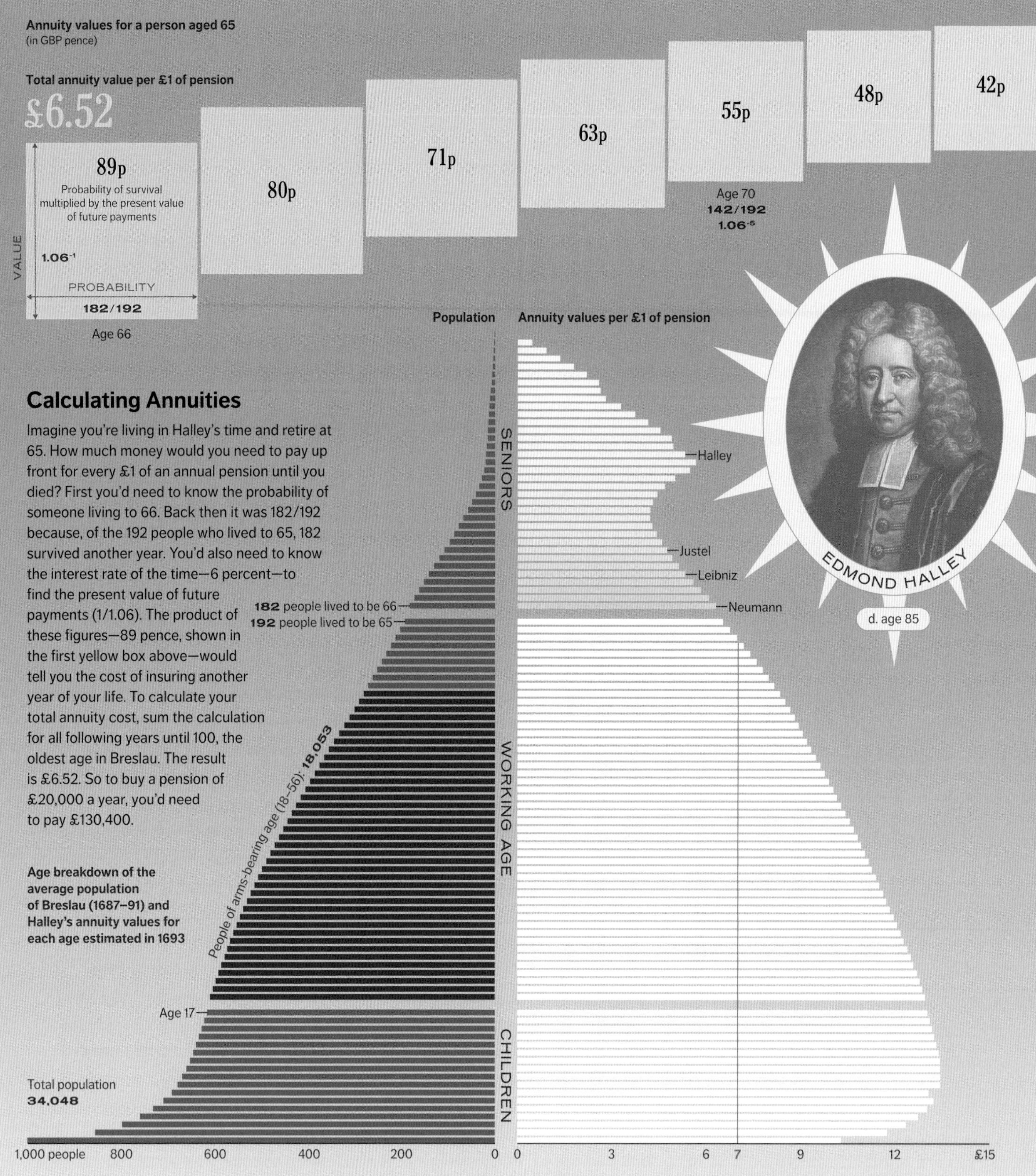

Calculating Annuities

Imagine you're living in Halley's time and retire at 65. How much money would you need to pay up front for every £1 of an annual pension until you died? First you'd need to know the probability of someone living to 66. Back then it was 182/192 because, of the 192 people who lived to 65, 182 survived another year. You'd also need to know the interest rate of the time—6 percent—to find the present value of future payments (1/1.06). The product of these figures—89 pence, shown in the first yellow box above—would tell you the cost of insuring another year of your life. To calculate your total annuity cost, sum the calculation for all following years until 100, the oldest age in Breslau. The result is £6.52. So to buy a pension of £20,000 a year, you'd need to pay £130,400.

Age breakdown of the average population of Breslau (1687–91) and Halley's annuity values for each age estimated in 1693

A Stable Population . . .

While earlier data on births and deaths existed for London and Dublin, large uncounted migration flows in these cities made estimations of survival odds unreliable. In Breslau, almost everyone born in the city died there, so Halley could use Neumann's data with confidence.

. . . for Predicting Longevity

Due to high child mortality in the seventeenth century, the value of annuities peaked at ages 9 and 10. The value then fell until the age of 77, at which point it increased again as the number of deaths slowed. Mortality should not slow down at this age, but in the small Breslau sample it did.

18 14 11 9 7 5 4 3 2 1 <1p

Age 85
19/192
1.06^{-20}

Age 95
6/192
1.06^{-30}

Halley's Calculation

The great astronomer stumbled upon data that helped to revolutionize insurance and relate finance to demographics.

HOW MUCH WOULD YOU PAY now for the right to receive a given amount of money each year for the rest of your life? Or in the parlance of the insurance industry: What is the present value of an annuity? This question at the heart of finance was not answered until the end of the seventeenth century.

Caspar Neumann, a pastor in late seventeenth-century Breslau (Wrocław in today's Poland) hated astrological superstitions, including one about death being particularly imminent in the sixty-third year of human life. To rebut it, he collected data on births and deaths in Breslau from 1687 to 1691 and sent them to a leading German scientist and court librarian to the elector of Hanover, Gottfried von Leibniz. Leibniz forwarded the data to Henri Justel, a royal librarian in London, who presented them to the Royal Society. Edmond Halley, a fellow of the Royal Society famous for his contributions to astronomy, then analyzed them and published pathbreaking results in 1693.

At the time, England was fighting the Nine Years' War against France. Halley started his paper using the Breslau population to calculate the proportion of men able to bear arms. He simply divided the number of people aged 18–56 by the total population (18,053/34,048) and then by two (assuming a similar number of men and women). His quotient of 0.265 is very close to the proportion you'd get today using population data of the US (0.24).

The core contribution of Halley's paper—estimating the value of annuities—was also related to the war. The English government was raising money for the war by selling annuities to the public with a fixed price of seven times the annual payment irrespective of the buyer's age, mainly because they sold well at this price and other countries were doing the same. As the red line on our chart shows, £7 was far too cheap. For children aged 5 to 17, an annuity of £1 should have cost over £13; its value should have fallen below £7 only for people aged 63 and above. The government continued this unsustainable activity for another century, catering to vested interests and placing a huge burden on the future finances of the country.

Halley's calculation, which he claimed "took the pains to compute," laid the foundations of actuarial science and clarified the connection between demographics and finance. It showed the value of data collection as well as the power of abstraction. Halley took down-to-earth data on the passage of life and turned it into a formula of astronomical significance.

The Quantified Consumer

Credit-scoring algorithms try to predict the future, renewing inequalities of the past.

GETTING A MORTGAGE, finding a job, accessing a student loan, renting an apartment: credit scores determine life choices in the United States. Credit scores measure credit-worthiness—how likely you are to repay money on time. Since they were first introduced by Fair, Isaac, and Company in 1989, FICO scores have become the gold standard. The higher your score, the lower your risk of default. Any late or missed payment negatively affects your score, which can directly affect your life. Subprime borrowers—nearly one in three US consumers—have a harder time getting loans and are charged higher interest rates.

To calculate and update scores, credit bureaus like Equifax or TransUnion collect digital traces of people's financial history and behavior. This huge volume of data is fed to algorithms that compare and rank customers, assigning them an individual score. In the age of machine learning, scoring algorithms have become increasingly sophisticated. But critics have found racial and social biases in the ways data are harnessed, analyzed, and used, turning a seemingly fair and unbiased technology into a data-driven engine for perpetuating inequalities of wealth and opportunity.

Credit scoring sorts people into groups of "good" and "bad" consumers. While this ostensibly renders structural categories such as race or gender invisible, it penalizes several million people, particularly minorities and recent immigrants, who do not have a credit score, or have a very low one, due to "thin" records. More than one in five Black consumers have FICO scores of 620 or lower, versus one in nineteen white people.

Mapping the share of population with subprime scores reveals territorial inequities of debt born of centuries of slavery, segregation, and poverty. Counties with a large proportion of Black, Native, or Hispanic communities have larger shares of subprime scores. No wonder, then, that the subprime loans that precipitated the 2008 global financial crisis disproportionately focused on racially and ethnically marginalized people and places.

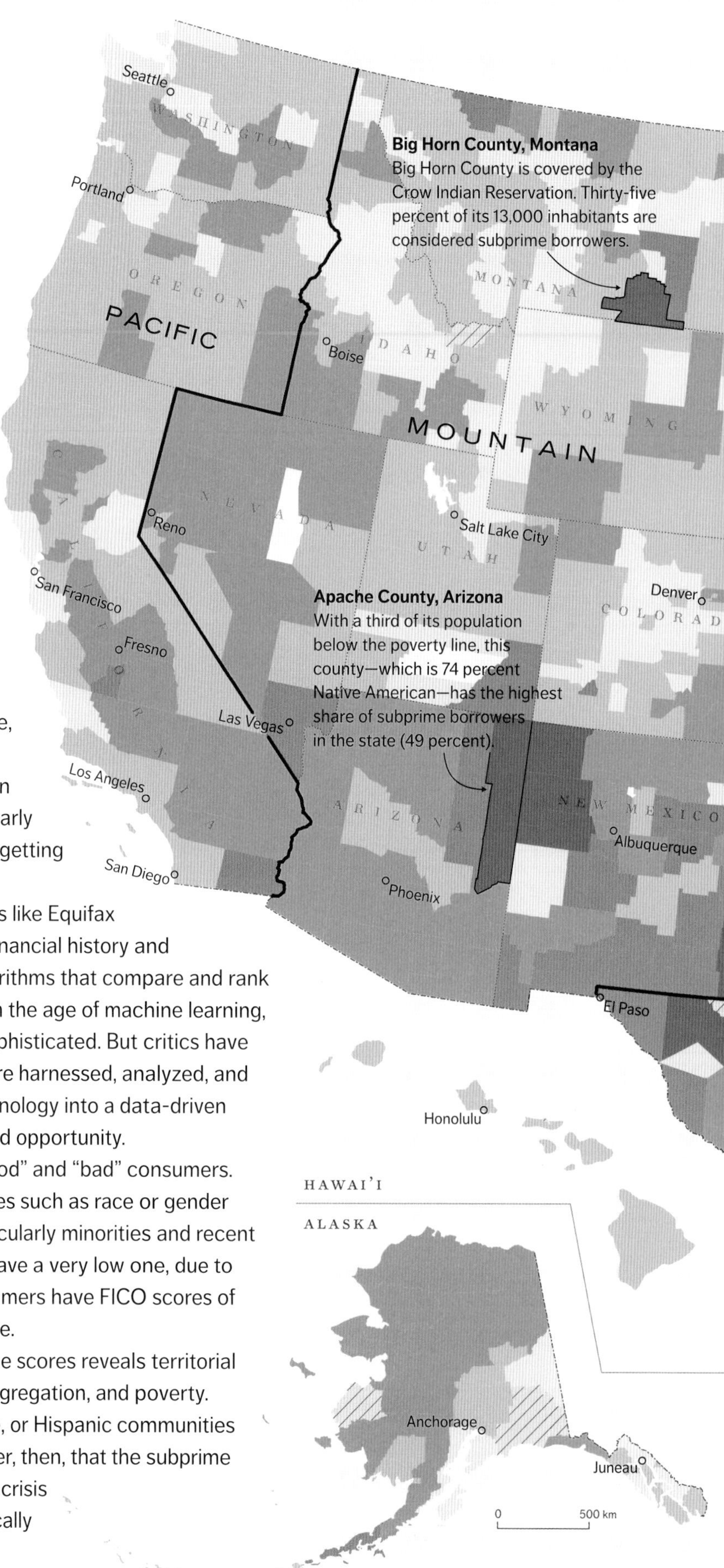

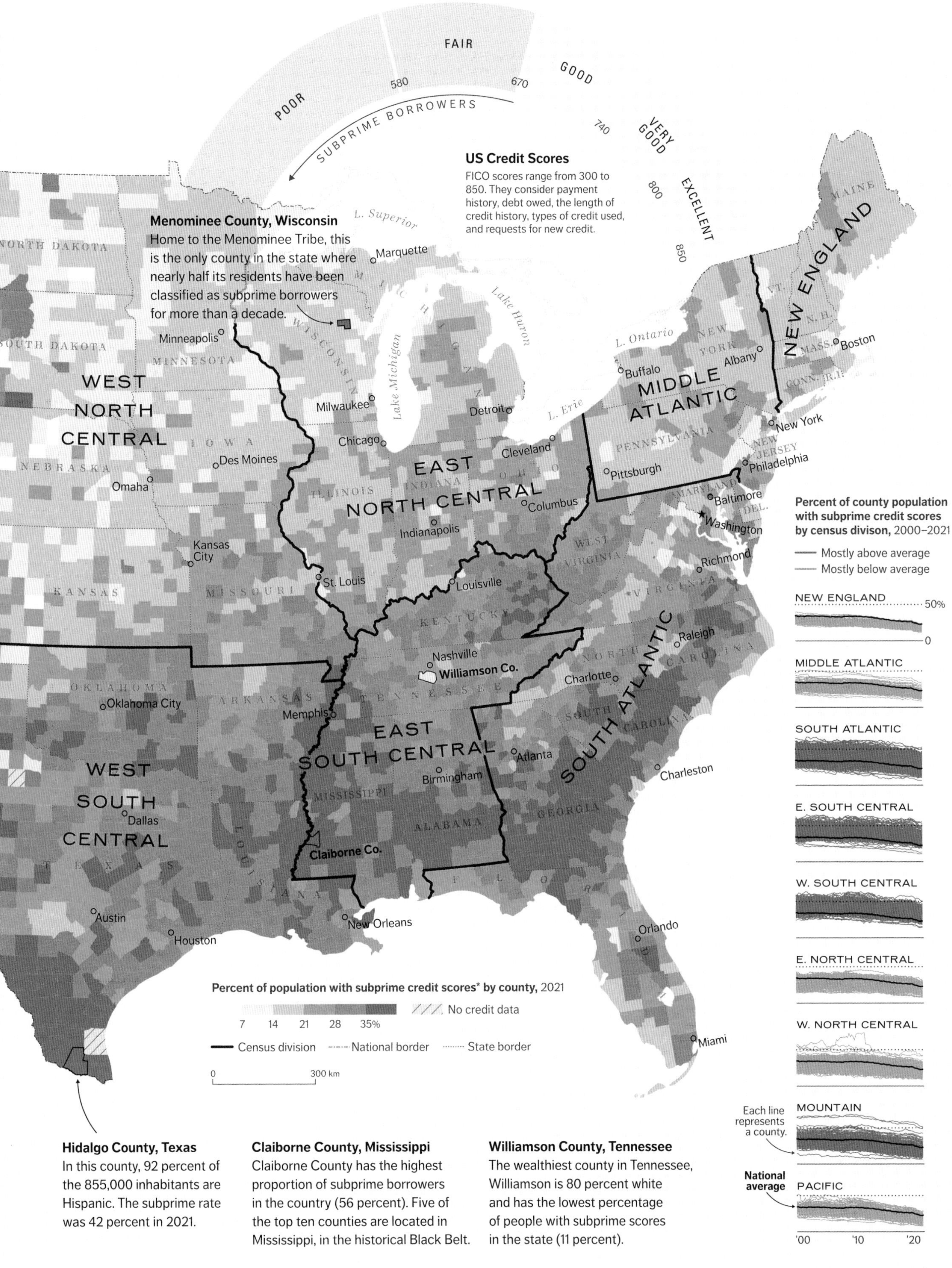

*For this map, researchers considered subprime to be scores lower than 660.

A Need for Speed

Finance seeks ever faster technologies to take advantage of market movements.

A FUTURES CONTRACT locks you into buying a stock at a set price at a specified date in the future. You can use one to hedge against or speculate on price fluctuations. In fact, futures were first developed to hedge on future grain harvests. So, unlike stocks, which are traded mainly in New York, futures are still mainly traded in Chicago, the gateway to North America's agricultural region.

As trading floors began to digitize in the 1980s, traders noticed that prices for stock index futures in Chicago tended to change before prices of the underlying stocks on New York markets. The so-called futures lead traders exploited

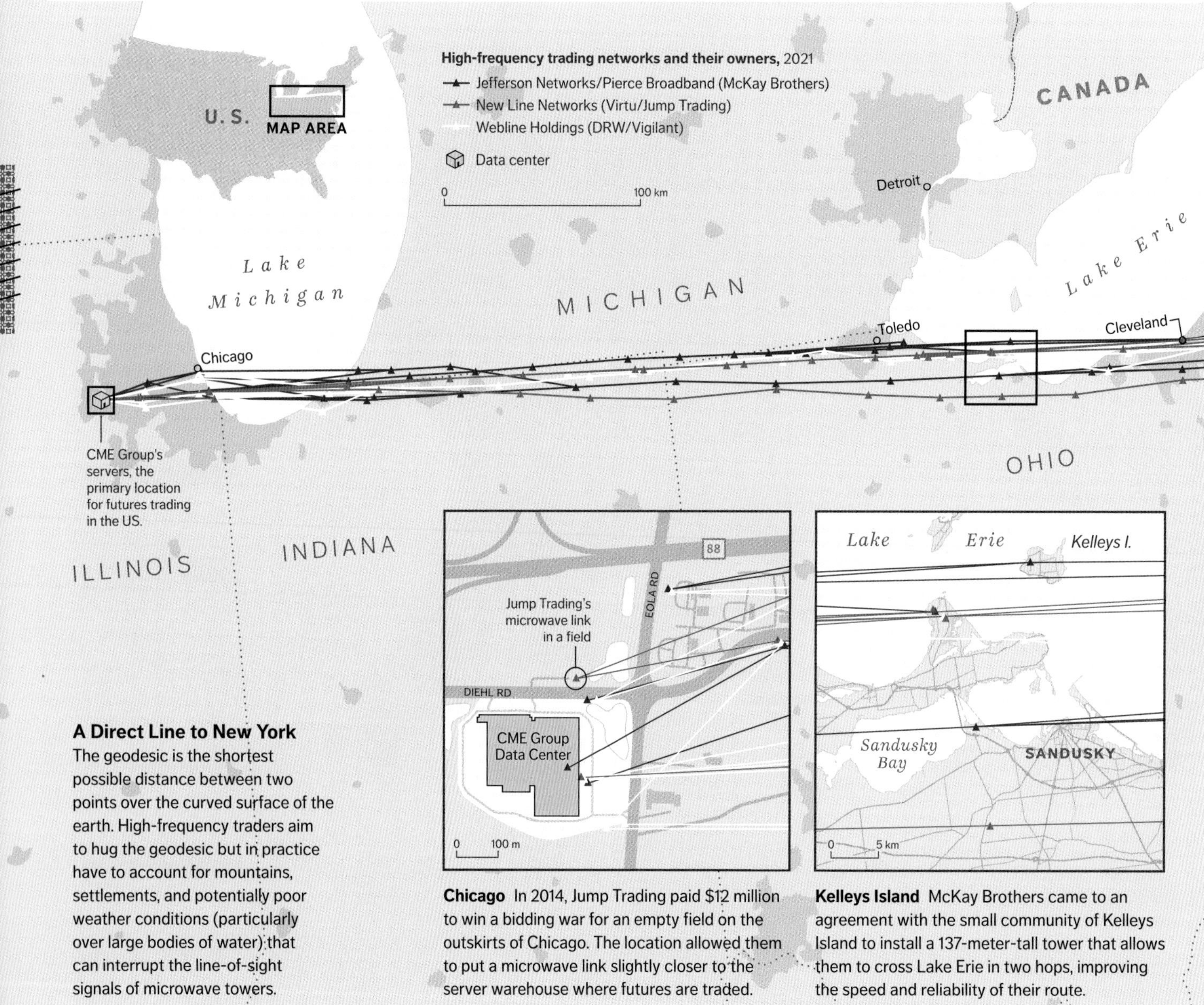

A Direct Line to New York The geodesic is the shortest possible distance between two points over the curved surface of the earth. High-frequency traders aim to hug the geodesic but in practice have to account for mountains, settlements, and potentially poor weather conditions (particularly over large bodies of water) that can interrupt the line-of-sight signals of microwave towers.

Chicago In 2014, Jump Trading paid $12 million to win a bidding war for an empty field on the outskirts of Chicago. The location allowed them to put a microwave link slightly closer to the server warehouse where futures are traded.

Kelleys Island McKay Brothers came to an agreement with the small community of Kelleys Island to install a 137-meter-tall tower that allows them to cross Lake Erie in two hops, improving the speed and reliability of their route.

this tendency and used information from Chicago futures to trade on stocks in New York, netting an easy profit.

Back then, a futures lead could be minutes. It soon fell to seconds as traders raced to be the fastest. By the mid-1990s, the reaction speeds of human traders were surpassed by the rise of automated trading. With busy trading floors replaced by computers, leads were down to microseconds and determined by internet speeds and computer code (see chart).

In 2010, Spread Networks spent $300–$500 million US dollars to lay a custom fiber-optic cable along the shortest possible line, or geodesic, between Chicago and New York. Using the new line at a reported cost of $176,000 a month per user gave automated high-frequency traders (HFT) an edge of a few microseconds over their rivals.

Fiber-optic cables have now been surpassed by microwave towers which, still hugging the geodesic, require a clear line of sight to work. Three competing firms—McKay Brothers, Virtu/Jump Trading, and DRW/Vigilant—each now maintain their own infrastructure of towers that can pass signals between Chicago and New York at nearly the speed of light.

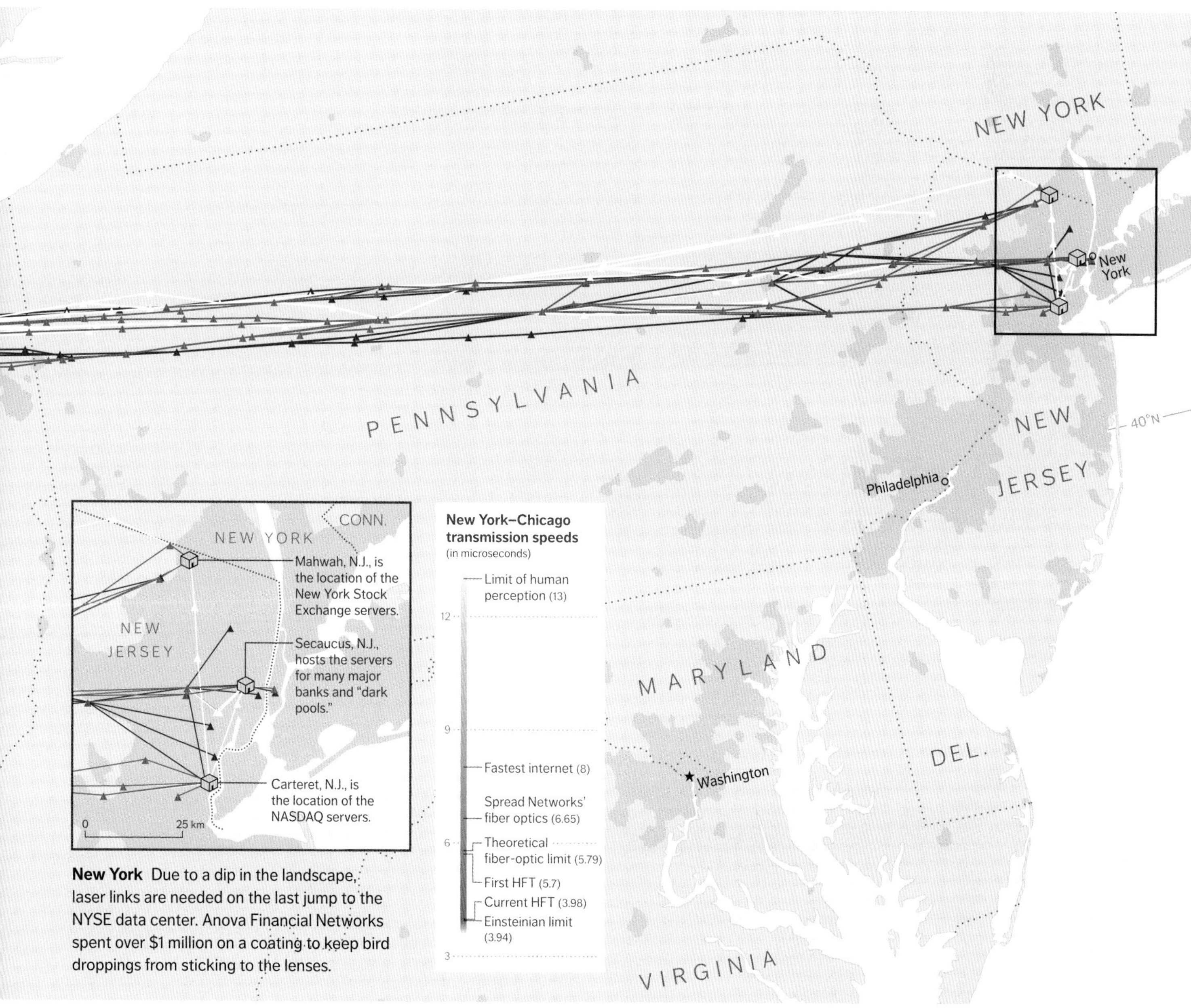

New York Due to a dip in the landscape, laser links are needed on the last jump to the NYSE data center. Anova Financial Networks spent over $1 million on a coating to keep bird droppings from sticking to the lenses.

Defying convention, financial services are now accessible in Kenya through an intricate network of kiosks, cellular and electronics shops, pharmacies, salons, grocery stores, cafes, bars, restaurants, and other businesses that offer mobile money deposits and withdrawals in addition to their primary business.

Smartphone Finance

Since the late 2000s, the smartphone has become the new workhorse of finance, surpassing the use of ATMs in some countries.

THE FIRST AUTOMATED TELLER MACHINE (ATM) was unveiled in 1967, and it revolutionized the way people accessed their money. In the aftermath of the 2008 global financial crisis, Paul Volcker, a former chair of the Federal Reserve of the United States, referred to the ATM as the "only useful innovation in banking for the past twenty years." Concurrently, the end of the global financial crisis marked the beginning of a financial technology (fintech) revolution. Smartphones are now more commonly used than ATMs in a number of countries, including Kenya, where the first money transfer service based on mobile phones, M-Pesa, was launched by Vodafone and Safaricom in 2007. As indicated in the chart in the lower right, the amount of money transferred through smartphones in Kenya in December 2020 was about ten times larger than the amount withdrawn from ATMs.

What makes smartphones particularly appealing is their widespread availability in developing countries, where the traditional financial infrastructure of bank branches and ATMs is thinnest. Consequently, a financial infrastructure that relies on the smartphone as its workhorse is able to bring financial services to previously unbanked consumers, including those living in rural areas that were never attractive enough for banks to open branches in. Mobile money agents are an important part of this new infrastructure. Unlike the business model of dedicated bank branches, mobile money agents can operate either as stand-alone businesses or as a secondary business activity for one of the many primary business types displayed on the phone screen to the left. Depositing and withdrawing cash is now as easy as stopping by a pharmacy or hair salon.

As a result, the number of mobile money agents in Kenya has exploded since 2007 (see maps). In 2007 most mobile money agents were primarily in and around Nairobi. Eight years later, their services were widely available across Kenya's biggest cities including Nakuru, Eldoret, Kisumu, Mombasa, and Lamu as well as along the coast and major roads. M-Pesa now competes with other mobile payment companies in Kenya and has expanded into several other African countries and Afghanistan. Globally, smartphone finance represents the first-ever access to finance for millions of people and improves financial inclusion. Its popularity has only increased since the COVID-19 pandemic. Why risk your health if finance can be found at your fingertips?

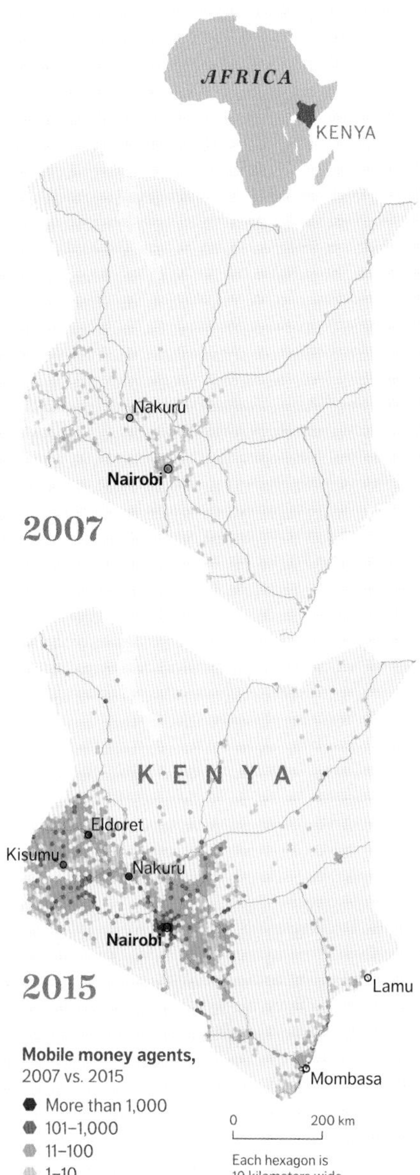

Between 2007 and 2015, the number of mobile money agents grew rapidly within Kenya's urban centers as well as in many rural and sparsely populated areas.

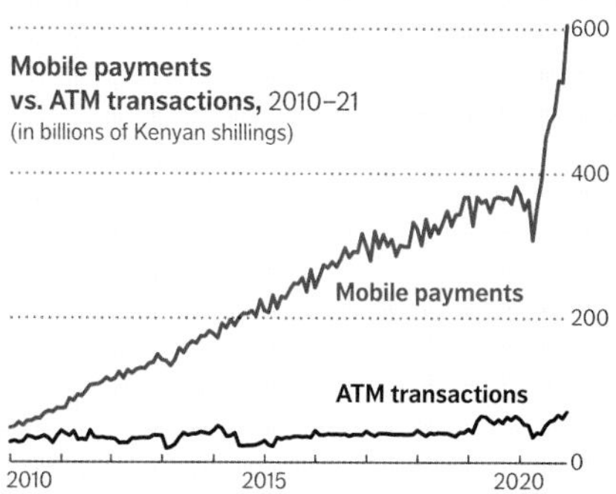

The volume of mobile payments surged from Ksh 48 billion in January 2010 to 606 billion in December 2020, far surpassing ATM transactions for the same month.

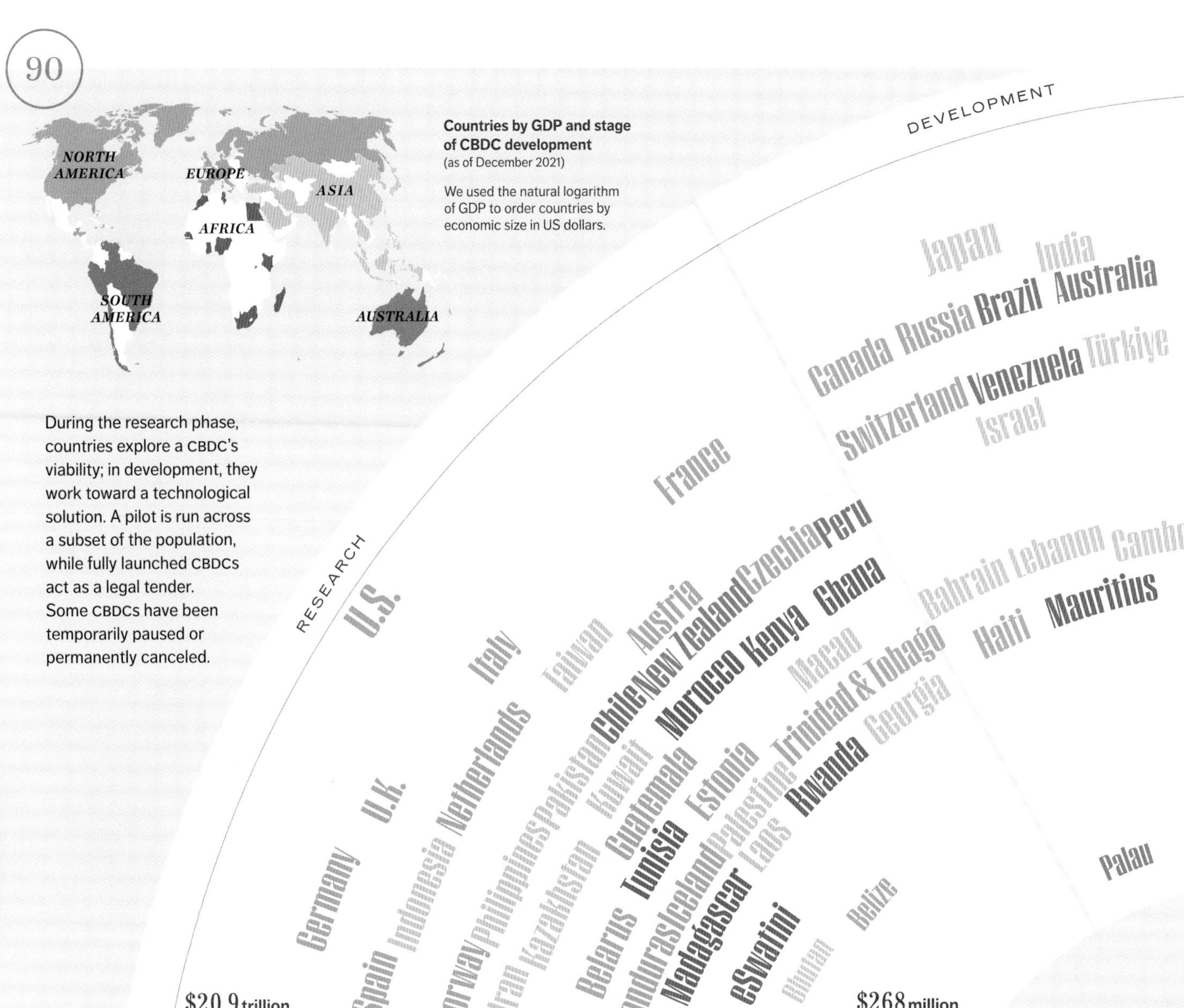

Countries by GDP and stage of CBDC development
(as of December 2021)

We used the natural logarithm of GDP to order countries by economic size in US dollars.

During the research phase, countries explore a CBDC's viability; in development, they work toward a technological solution. A pilot is run across a subset of the population, while fully launched CBDCs act as a legal tender. Some CBDCs have been temporarily paused or permanently canceled.

Central Bank Digital Currencies

Following the meteoric rise of cryptocurrencies, countries around the world have begun planning and launching their own digital currencies.

WHILE THE WORLD'S FINANCIAL SUPERPOWERS lag behind, developing countries are leading the way in developing central bank digital currencies (CBDCs). On the fan chart above, we list nearly eighty countries that had worked on CBDCs as of December 2021. And it was not just research and development. In October 2020 the Bahamas became the first country to adopt its CBDC as legal tender. A year later, the Central Bank of Nigeria launched the first CBDC outside of the Caribbean. China, whose CBDC pilot is the largest in scale worldwide, operates digital yuan across more than a dozen major cities; as of July 2021, 70.85 million transactions had been executed with an aggregate value of US$5.2 billion. India launched a pilot of the digital rupee for the wholesale segment for nine banks including the State Bank of India, India's top lender, in the last quarter of 2022. In contrast the US, UK, France, Germany, Italy, and a number of other countries with large GDPs are taking a more cautious approach and are currently researching their options for implementing a CBDC.

CBDC, also called digital fiat currency or digital base money, is the digital form of fiat money, a currency

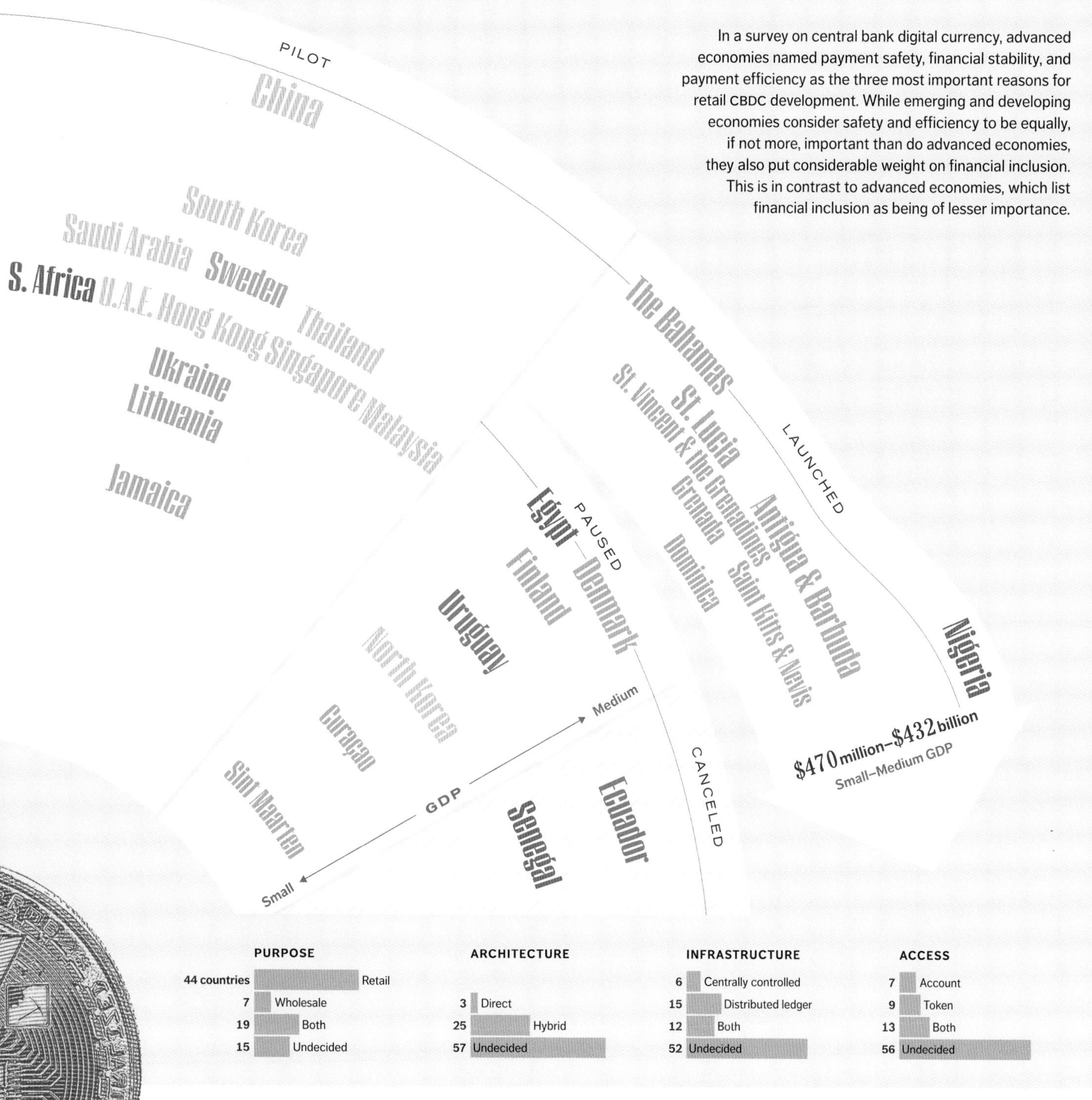

In a survey on central bank digital currency, advanced economies named payment safety, financial stability, and payment efficiency as the three most important reasons for retail CBDC development. While emerging and developing economies consider safety and efficiency to be equally, if not more, important than do advanced economies, they also put considerable weight on financial inclusion. This is in contrast to advanced economies, which list financial inclusion as being of lesser importance.

established as money by government regulation, monetary authority, or law. CBDCs share many of the advantages of cryptocurrencies while avoiding their shortcomings, such as high energy use and lack of accountability. However, CBDCs allow central banks unprecedented access to data on financial transactions, raising privacy concerns. As the bar charts show, most CBDCs focus on retail transactions among consumers and businesses rather than wholesale transactions among banks. The dominant form of CBDC architecture currently is a hybrid model, which relies on financial intermediation by commercial banks. In contrast to leading cryptocurrencies, the infrastructure of most CBDCs does not rely solely on a distributed ledger but instead uses a centrally controlled database. Users can access CBDCs through either an account linked to their identity or an anonymous token.

The future of fiat currencies is looking increasingly digital, and it may be closer than you think. According to a 2020 survey by the Bank of International Settlements, about 20 percent of central banks were likely to launch a CBDC sometime in the next six years.

Powering Bitcoin

Bitcoin is the world's first and largest cryptocurrency, but its instability and energy use raise questions.

THERE WAS GREAT HOPE for cryptocurrency when Satoshi Nakamoto established Bitcoin in 2009. Two breakthroughs came the following year. First, Bitcoin developer Laszlo Hanyecz bought two pizzas, the first goods purchased with the new currency. Then Silk Road, a black-market online marketplace, decided to use Bitcoin as a method of payment. Things were looking up. Then in 2013, the People's Bank of China banned the use of Bitcoin by financial institutions, and in 2014, Mt. Gox, then the world's leading cryptocurrency exchange, collapsed following a security breach. Despite these setbacks, Bitcoin's value continued to grow, peaking at just under US$20,000 in December 2017 (see graph). Just over a year later, the price fell to $3,177, causing widespread disenchantment. Bitcoin then skyrocketed to a new maximum of $62,000 in March 2021. With this price, the total value of Bitcoin was comparable to the market capitalization of Microsoft, Amazon, or Alphabet, some of the world's largest companies.

Bitcoin relies on blockchain technology and a distributed ledger to verify transactions. Crucially, it does not require a central counterparty to manage its payment network. Instead, vast amounts of computing power pooled across a world of "Bitcoin miners" operate and secure the network. In principle, anyone can become a Bitcoin miner. In practice, much of the computing power that supports Bitcoin's blockchain comes from businesses of various sizes that specialize in Bitcoin mining and operate purpose-made computers, or "mining rigs." The majority of Bitcoin mining used to happen in Chinese provinces with relatively cheap energy (see right) until the activity was banned by the People's Bank of China in 2021.

Notwithstanding Bitcoin's numerous successes, including falling transaction costs, the security of its blockchain, and its increasing adoption, the energy use of Bitcoin's blockchain is comparable to the usage of entire countries like Belgium or Chile. This is due mainly to the energy-intensive nature of Bitcoin's proof-of-work algorithm used to validate transactions. A single transaction uses roughly 707.6 kilowatt-hours of electrical energy —equivalent to the power consumed by an average US household over twenty-four days. This raises concerns about the environmental impact of cryptocurrencies and blockchain technology more broadly. Bitcoin may seem intangible, but its creation and maintenance are anything but. Financial innovation does not power itself.

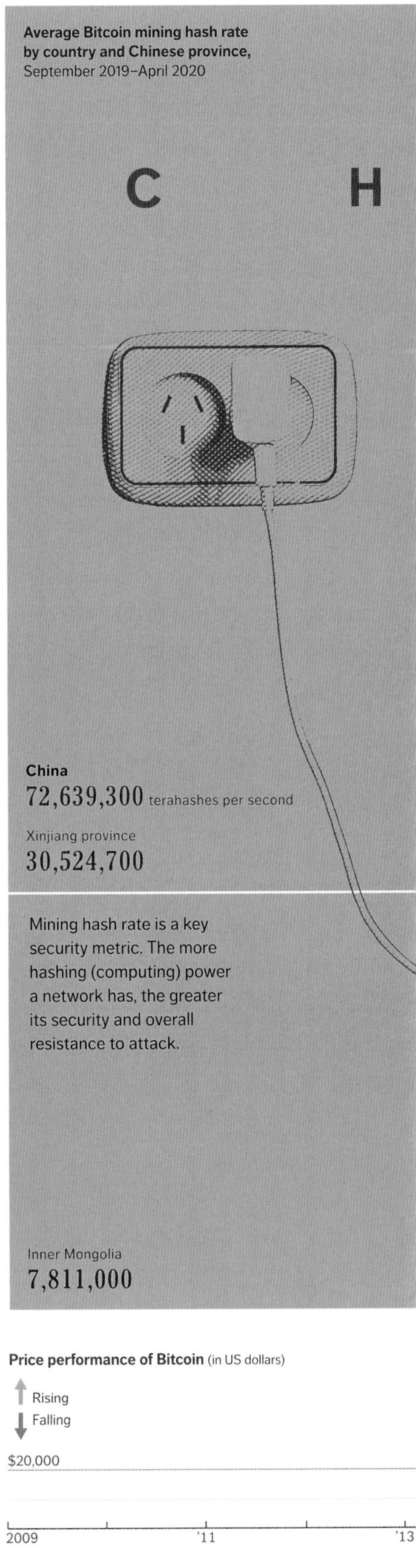

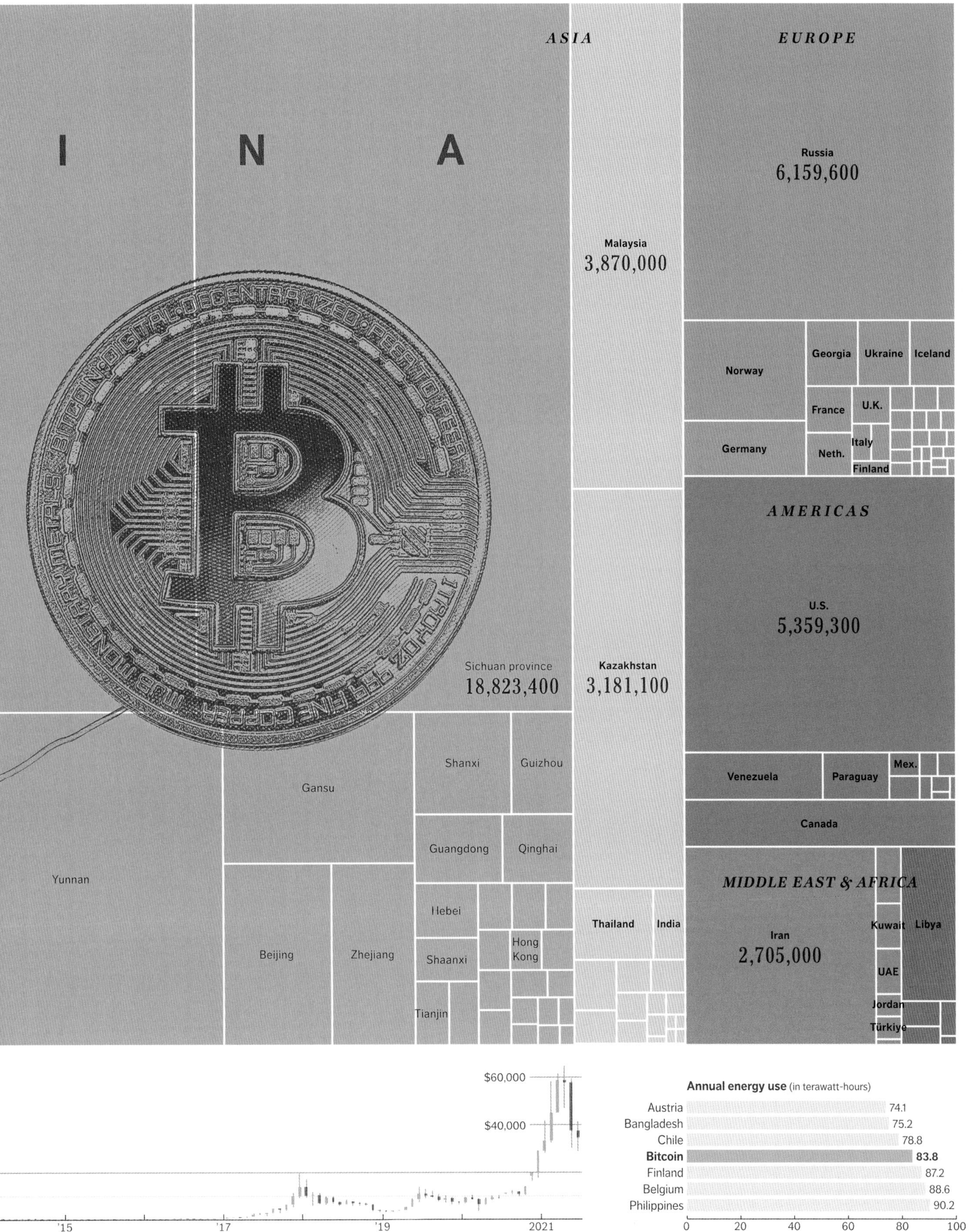
ASIA
EUROPE
I N A
Russia
6,159,600
Malaysia
3,870,000
Norway
Georgia
Ukraine
Iceland
France
U.K.
Germany
Neth.
Italy
Finland
AMERICAS
U.S.
5,359,300
Sichuan province
18,823,400
Kazakhstan
3,181,100
Venezuela
Paraguay
Mex.
Shanxi
Guizhou
Gansu
Canada
Guangdong
Qinghai
Yunnan
MIDDLE EAST & AFRICA
Hebei
Thailand
India
Kuwait
Libya
Iran
2,705,000
Beijing
Zhejiang
Shaanxi
Hong Kong
UAE
Tianjin
Jordan
Türkiye
$60,000
$40,000
'15
'17
'19
2021
Annual energy use (in terawatt-hours)
Austria 74.1
Bangladesh 75.2
Chile 78.8
Bitcoin 83.8
Finland 87.2
Belgium 88.6
Philippines 90.2
0
20
40
60
80
100

5

Cities & Centers

Financial centers epitomize the geographical nature of finance. They compete and collaborate with each other, shaping the fates of cities, urban networks, and the rest of the world in the process. To function, they host a wide variety of financial and other business services. To succeed, they need to be open and often take this to the extreme, focusing on the needs of super-rich foreigners. Financial centers evolve incessantly by adjusting themselves to different cultures, technologies, and political changes.

Nothing happens until something moves.

ALBERT EINSTEIN

Venice to London

The history of Europe's financial centers is a story of places that connected people, money, and ideas.

HOW DOES A CITY become an international financial center? The history of Europe shows that it takes a long time. As economies grew through industry, trade, and often war, leading cities accumulated people, wealth, and ideas. But having a big, wealthy, urban population was insufficient; of the cities on our map, only London ever held the status of Europe's most populous. To become an international financial center, you also needed cross-border connections. All leading centers below save Florence were seaports, and many were full of expats. Bruges welcomed Italian bankers. Later, Antwerp offered more freedom and resources to

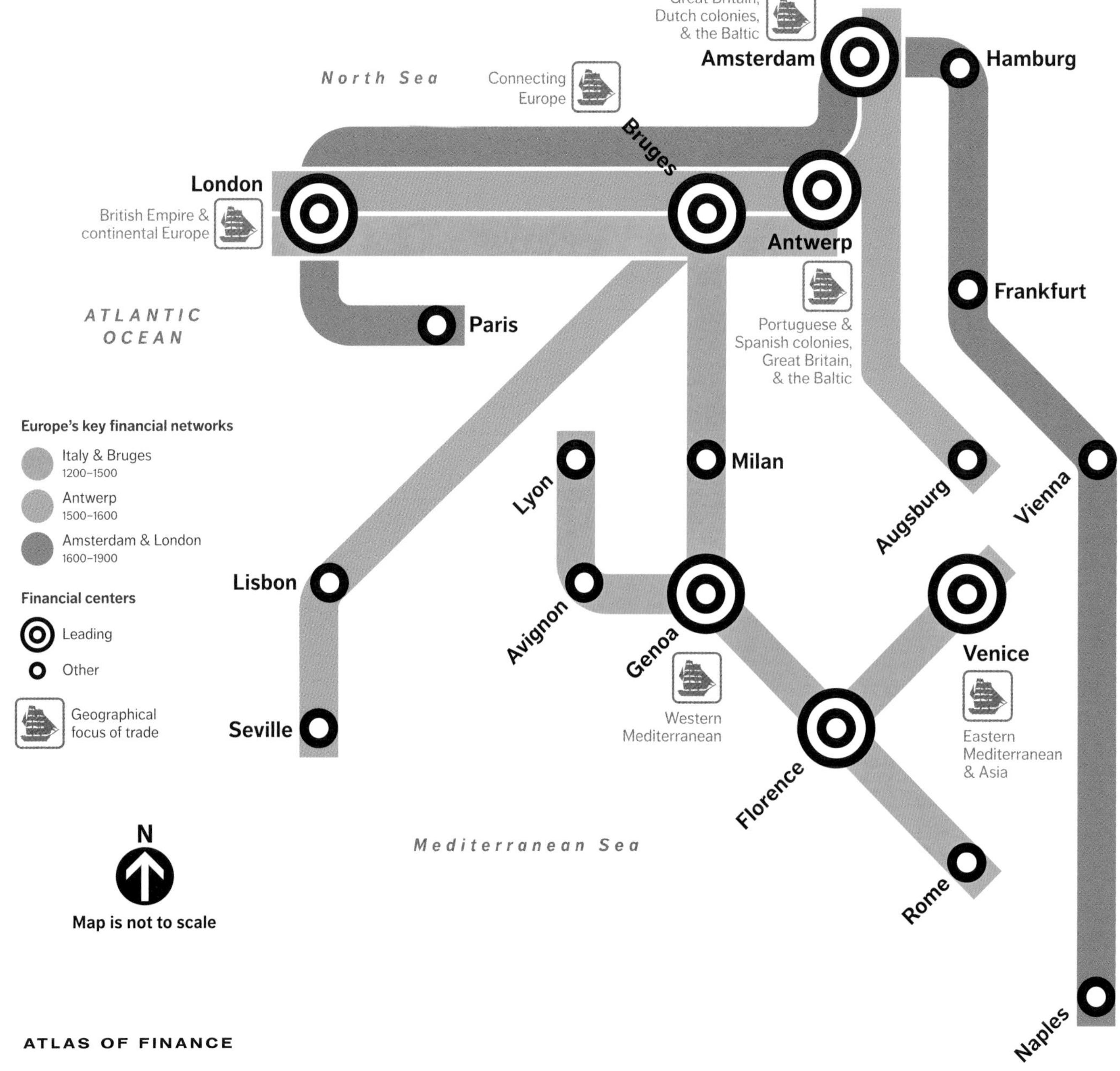

bankers than the imperial cities of Portugal and Spain. Such openness helps innovation. Fibonacci's use of Hindu-Arabic numerals revolutionized financial education, with Florence as its leading center; the idea of government bonds spread from Venice and Genoa; and the Royal Exchange in London imitated the operations of the Amsterdam Stock Exchange, which was modeled after the New Exchange in Antwerp, which was inspired by Beurs Square in Bruges and the Rialto Bridge in Venice. New centers do not replace predecessors as much as they build on their ideas and resources, attracting their capital, talent, and customers.

Major political and economic events also shaped the succession of financial powers. Our transit map shows how Italian cities (gold) ruled supreme when trade focused on the Mediterranean and Asia; how Turkish dominance in the Middle East and the emerging Atlantic trade moved the financial center of gravity to northwestern Europe (blue) in the late fifteenth century; and how both the Spanish invasion of Antwerp in 1585 and the French attack on the Dutch Republic in 1795 helped to propel the center toward Amsterdam and London, respectively (mauve). Would it take another war to dislodge it?

A Short History of Europe's Financial Centers

1202
Abacus schools open in Florence, boosting financial skills.

1204
Venice gains territory in the eastern Mediterranean, controls Asian trade.

1277
Genoa's merchant fleet opens trade with Bruges.

1300–1343
The Peruzzi family of Florence develops a bank with branches in Bruges, Antwerp, and London.

1397–1470
The Medici family of Florence develops a bank with branches in Avignon, Bruges, London, Lyons, Milan, Rome, and Venice.

1454
Turkish capture of Constantinople ends Italian control of Asian trade.

1492–1500
The Habsburgs damage Bruges after a failed revolt; silt in the Zwin channel cuts off access to the sea.

1494
The Medici Bank goes bankrupt.

1500s
Portuguese traders move from Bruges to Antwerp.

1500s
Jewish bankers, expelled from Spain and Portugal, move here.

1500s
Fugger and Welser families from Augsburg open bank offices here.

1531
New Exchange, a dedicated financial exchange building, opens.

1540s
Dona Gracia runs the House of Mendes—the leading bank in Europe—from here and helps many Jews escape the Inquisition.

1560s
Thomas Gresham works here before returning to London to set up the Royal Exchange, modeled after the New Exchange.

1585
Spanish occupation of Antwerp

1590s
Jewish bankers leave for Amsterdam.

1602
Dutch East India Co. and Amsterdam Stock Exchange founded.

1694
Bank of England created, modeled after the Bank of Amsterdam.

1734
Hope & Co. founded in Amsterdam, becoming the leading European bank of the century.

1774
The world's first investment fund is created in Amsterdam.

1794
Henry Hope, the leading banker of the eighteenth century, moves from Amsterdam to London.

1795
France attacks the Dutch Republic.

1799–1820
The Rothschilds from Frankfurt set up their main bank office in London and open branches in Paris, Naples, and Vienna.

1818
The Schroders from Hamburg start an investment bank in London.

GDP per capita, 1000–1870
(in thousands of 1990 international dollars)

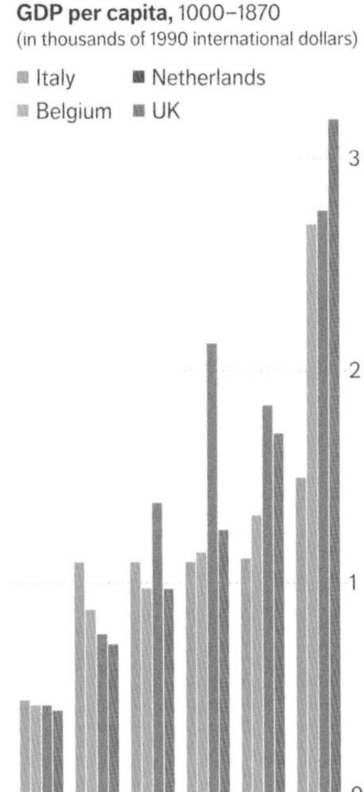

The historical GDP per capita of four countries demonstrates the mutual relationship between the evolution of financial centers and the development of surrounding economies. By 1500, Italy was the most prosperous part of Europe, followed by Belgium. Both were eventually surpassed, first by the Netherlands and then by the UK.

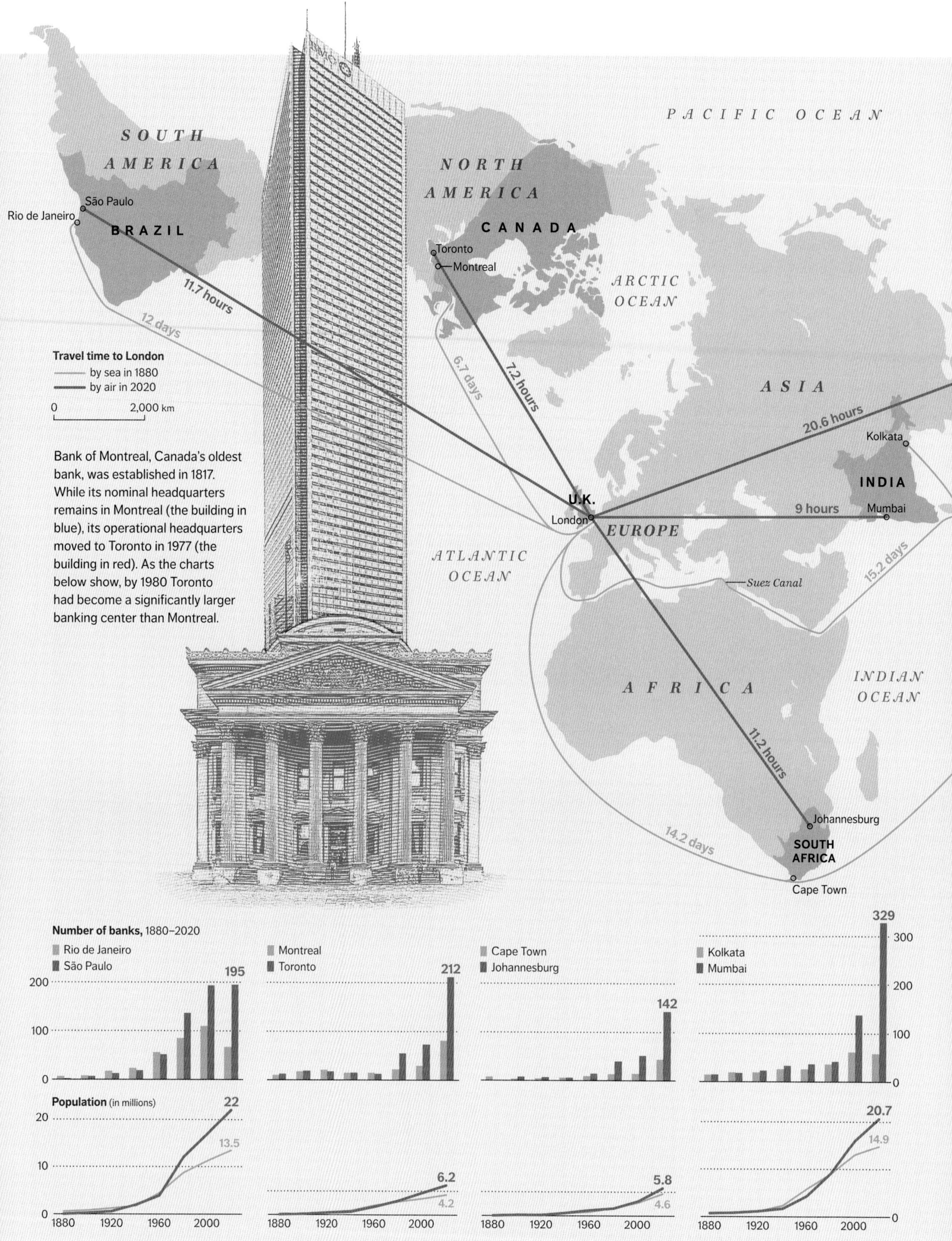

Bank of Montreal, Canada's oldest bank, was established in 1817. While its nominal headquarters remains in Montreal (the building in blue), its operational headquarters moved to Toronto in 1977 (the building in red). As the charts below show, by 1980 Toronto had become a significantly larger banking center than Montreal.

Sydney
Melbourne
AUSTRALIA
28 days

Taking the Lead

The telegraph, the rise of air travel, and financial globalization contributed to the shift of leading financial centers in several countries.

IN MOST COUNTRIES the leading financial center is the capital city, which is typically also the country's population and economic center. Think of London, Paris, Warsaw, Mexico City, Tokyo, and countless other examples. In some countries, however, such as Australia, Brazil, Canada, India, and South Africa, multiple cities have competed for this role. Sydney, São Paulo, Toronto, Mumbai, and Johannesburg are now their leading financial centers, respectively. But in the late nineteenth century this position belonged to Rio de Janeiro in Brazil and Cape Town in South Africa, while in Australia, Sydney was on par with Melbourne; in Canada, Montreal rivaled Toronto; and in India, Kolkata kept pace with Mumbai.

As the graphs show, the leading financial centers of these countries today (red) surged ahead of their competitors (blue) in the past forty to fifty years. Specific reasons differ from country to country. Melbourne lost capital-city status in 1927. Rio did so in 1960. In Canada, the growing US economy favored a closer and less Eurocentric Toronto, with Quebec separatism aggravating Montreal's loss of business. The end of the British Empire in India made Kolkata—headquarters of the British East India Company—less dominant. And in South Africa the shift from Dutch to British influence, combined with the gold rush and mining boom in Witwatersrand, made Cape Town less central.

Other factors working against Melbourne, Rio, Montreal, and Cape Town were use of the telegraph and a shift from sea to air transport during the twentieth century. Both made physical distance less important. When urgent financial information traveled with people by sea—and when London was by far the most important global financial center—a shorter travel time to London was a major advantage (see map). To profit from new information, you had to be in the city closer to London.

But the new financial centers also did some things right. With conditions of financial liberalization and globalization, these cities attracted large numbers of domestic and foreign banks, becoming the gateways of their countries for foreign business. In the process, their populations and economies grew larger too, triggering agglomeration economies wherein one activity attracts another. Bigger customer bases attract more banks, which in turn attract other financial and business services, increasing employment and the availability of credit, which then attracts more people. And on it goes.

Despite Melbourne's loss of leadership as a banking center, its population and economy largely kept pace with those of Sydney. While a clear majority of foreign banks chose Sydney as their gateway to Australia, Melbourne continues to host major domestic banks—such as ANZ and NAB—and remains the center of Australia's pension fund industry.

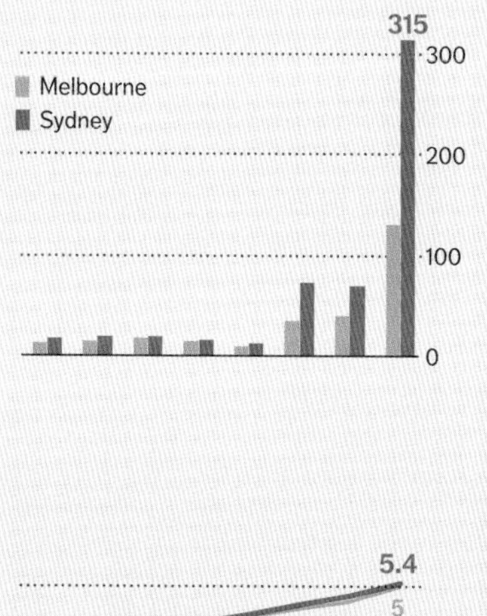

Financial Centers

Financial and business services benefit from each other's company, forming clusters within financial centers.

TO BE A FINANCIAL CENTER you need more than banks. Top financial centers like New York and London are also home to accounting firms, asset managers, hedge funds, private equity firms, real estate firms, and increasingly fintech companies pioneering the latest digital technologies. Completing the spectrum of organizations on our maps of these two financial centers are corporate law firms, financial exchanges, central

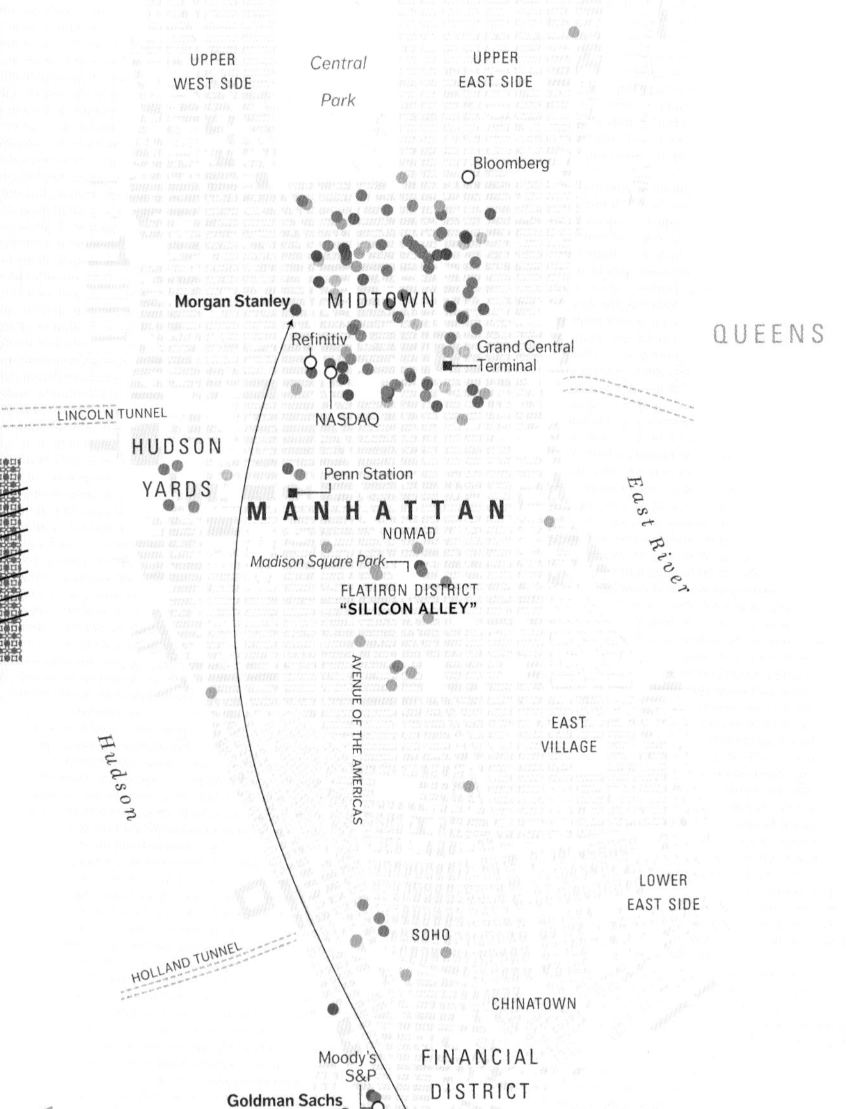

Types of financial and business services, 2022

- Accounting
- Consulting
- Banks
- Fintech
- Corporate law
- Asset management
- Insurance
- Hedge funds & private equity
- Real estate
- Other

Financial District

The district follows the boundaries of New Amsterdam, a Dutch settlement and trading post established in 1624 at the tip of Manhattan. Trading in financial instruments followed, culminating in the opening of the New York Stock Exchange in 1792. The Erie Canal made Wall Street the epicenter of American finance for nearly two centuries until the 9/11 terrorist attacks accelerated an outflow of financial firms.

Silicon Alley

The Flatiron District attracted tech firms during the dot-com boom of the late 1990s. With proximity to financial expertise, the area—as well as NoMad, south and north of Madison Square Park—has since become home to fintech firms, including Betterment and the American operations of Wise. While employing relatively few people, fintech is crucial to financial innovation.

Midtown

Throughout the nineteenth and early twentieth centuries, New York City expanded north, with train stations linking the city with the rest of the country. Recently, Midtown became a bigger center of finance than the Financial District. The Midtown section of 6th Avenue (Avenue of the Americas) itself hosts the headquarters of more leading financial and business services firms than the whole Financial District.

Hudson Yards

When the financial sector was booming in the mid-2000s, developers embarked on a major project in Hudson Yards. Morgan Stanley was to become the anchor tenant, but it pulled out of the project after the global financial crisis, as did Goldman Sachs. By early 2021 the area had attracted a few financial and business services firms, including the private equity giant KKR and the consultancy BCG.

banks, rating agencies, and financial media companies. Colored dots indicate the locations of leading firms in each of these sectors.

Financial firms in both cities are highly concentrated, and their concentrations tell histories. In London, the financial district expanded from the City to the West End, over to Canary Wharf, and is now growing along the South Bank. In New York, the financial epicenter began downtown in the Financial District before moving to Midtown Manhattan, with more recent clusters forming in the Flatiron District and Hudson Yards. You can also trace such histories by following individual firms. The famous investment bank Goldman Sachs has moved their headquarters in New York many times but always within a short walk to Wall Street. Since becoming one of the first US banks to establish a branch in London, Goldman Sachs has stayed within the City's walls. In contrast, Morgan Stanley has changed neighborhoods in both cities.

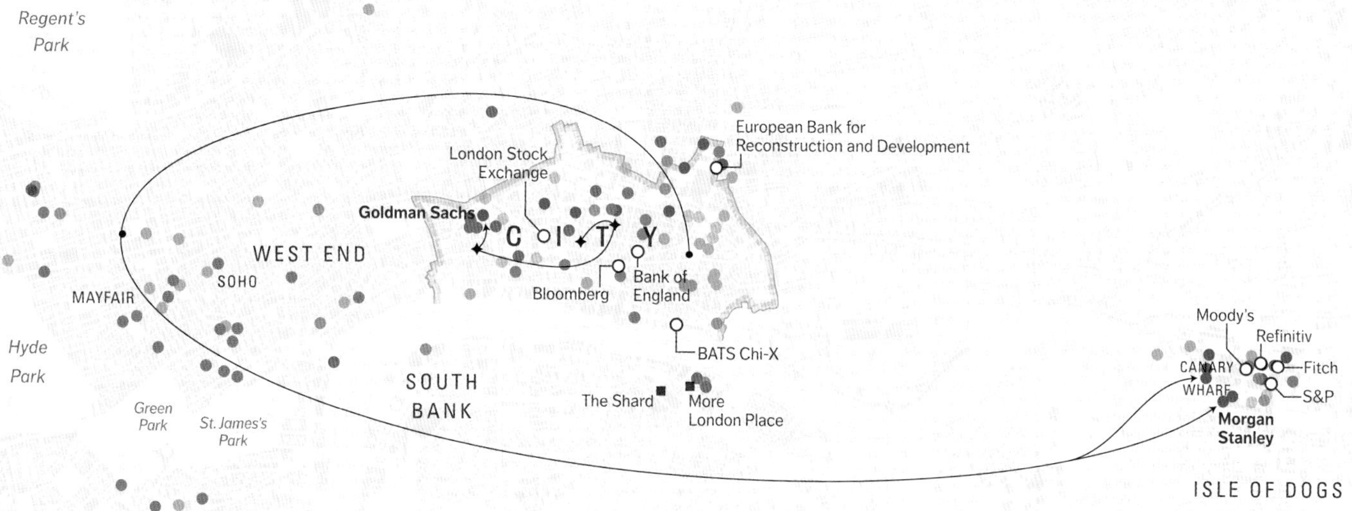

The City of London
The Square Mile has been a commercial center since its establishment by the Romans in the first century CE. Its rise as a financial center took off in the sixteenth and seventeenth centuries with the establishment of the Royal Exchange and nearby coffeehouses, where news of the world circulated and informed financial trading. Today over 200,000 people are employed here in financial and business services.

West End
London's West End, particularly Mayfair, has been the destination of wealthy Londoners ever since the Great Fire of 1666 devastated the City. With time the area became home to firms for which proximity to wealth matters most, including leading private equity firms, hedge funds, and real estate developers. It has also attracted consulting and advertising firms, who enjoy the creative environment of Soho.

Canary Wharf
By 1980, London's docklands had closed because the Thames was too narrow for container ships. The area was revived in the 1990s to satisfy the needs of a globalizing financial sector. Here you'll find the headquarters of HSBC and Barclays, and the European headquarters of Citibank, Credit Suisse, J.P. Morgan, and Morgan Stanley, with total employment in financial and business services exceeding 100,000.

South Bank
With growing demand for space, developers have set their eyes on the other side of the Thames. Vis-à-vis the City, the Shard became the tallest building in the UK when it opened in 2012 as a home to many financial and business services firms. Its neighbor, More London Place, houses approximately 20,000 professionals, most in the global headquarters of the accountancy and consulting firms PwC and EY.

Historical office locations
✦ Goldman Sachs
1869–2009 in New York
1970–2019 in London
• Morgan Stanley
1935–95 in New York
1977–91 in London

0 1 km

GLOBAL INVESTMENT BANKING NETWORK

1993

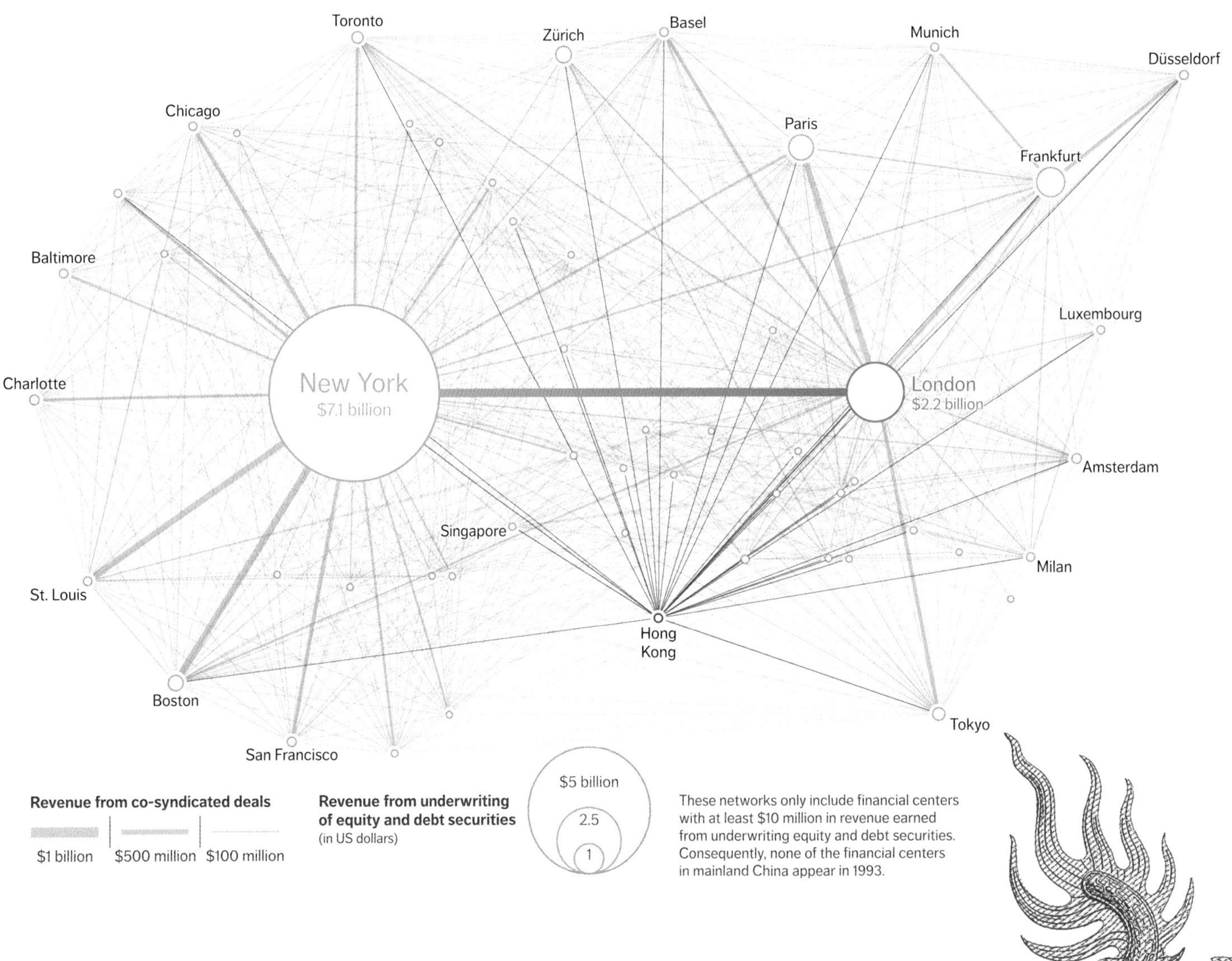

Rising Dragon

In less than twenty-five years, Chinese financial centers have gone from having bit parts to major roles in the global investment banking network.

WITH CHINA CURRENTLY on track to become the world's largest economy, will Chinese financial centers challenge the dominance of New York and London in international finance? As we show in the diagrams above, the structure of global investment banking networks is far from fixed.

In 1993, the only Chinese center with at least US$10 million in underwriting revenue was Hong Kong, which had syndication ties with investment banks in New York, London, Singapore, Tokyo, and Zürich among others. Mainland Chinese cities were just beginning to develop their stock exchanges and had not yet been integrated into the world's investment banking networks. By 2016, the picture had changed completely. Six of the top twenty financial centers are now in China, and they have outgrown many second-tier European and American financial centers, including Luxembourg, Amsterdam, Munich, Milan, Chicago, and San Francisco. As indicated in the line chart (right), Chinese financial centers have been growing at a faster pace than New York and London. However, in terms of deal value across the global banking network (above), the New

GLOBAL INVESTMENT BANKING NETWORK

2016

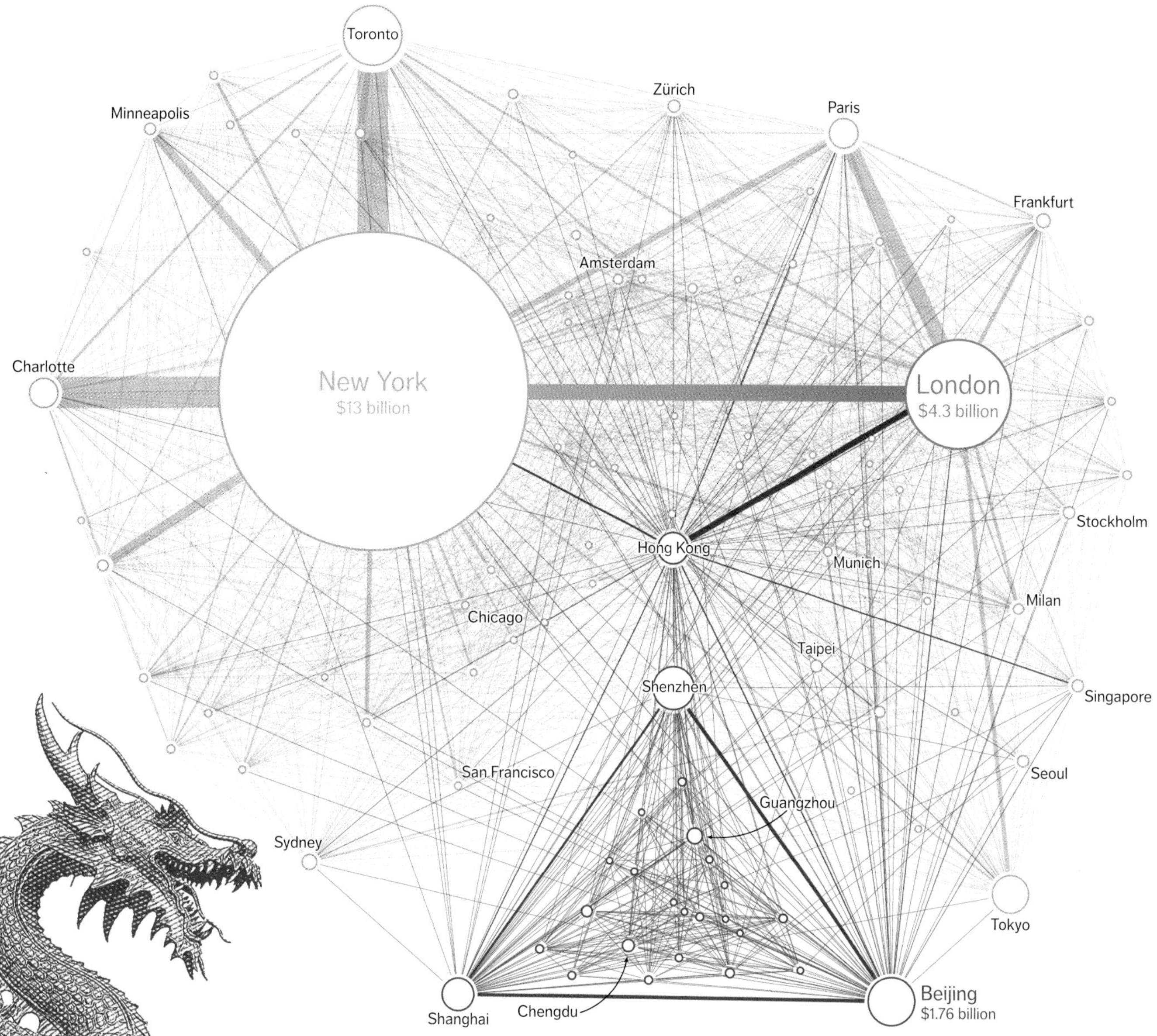

Toronto
Minneapolis
Zürich
Paris
Frankfurt
Amsterdam
Charlotte
New York
$13 billion
London
$4.3 billion
Stockholm
Hong Kong
Munich
Milan
Chicago
Taipei
Shenzhen
Singapore
Seoul
San Francisco
Guangzhou
Sydney
Tokyo
Shanghai
Chengdu
Beijing
$1.76 billion

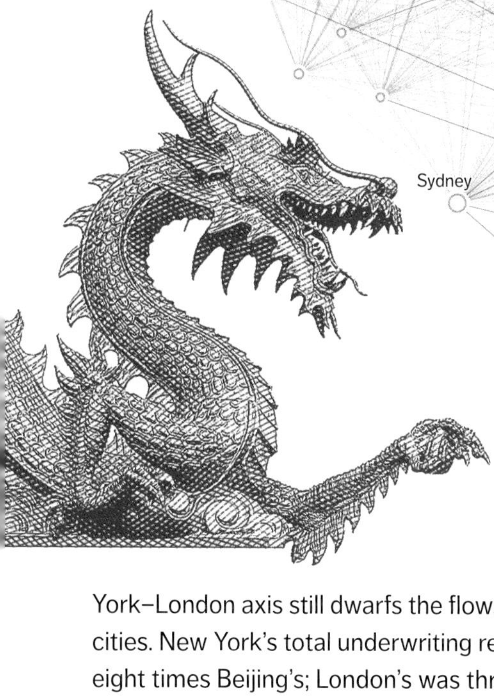

York–London axis still dwarfs the flows to and from Chinese cities. New York's total underwriting revenue in 2016 was eight times Beijing's; London's was three times as much. In fact, you'd have to combine the underwriting revenue from China's four largest financial centers (Beijing, Shanghai, Shenzhen, Hong Kong) to equal London's. Even then, the combined figure would be but a fraction of New York's total—at least for now. Collaborating tightly with each other, the rising dragons of Chinese finance still depend on Hong Kong for their global connections.

Revenue from underwriting of equity and debt securities, 1993–2016
(log_{10} of millions of 2010 US dollars)

New York
London
10,000
1,000
100
10
1
Hong Kong
Shanghai
Shenzhen
Beijing
1990
2000
2010
Largest to smallest
Beijing
Shenzhen
Shanghai
Hong Kong
Guangzhou
Chengdu

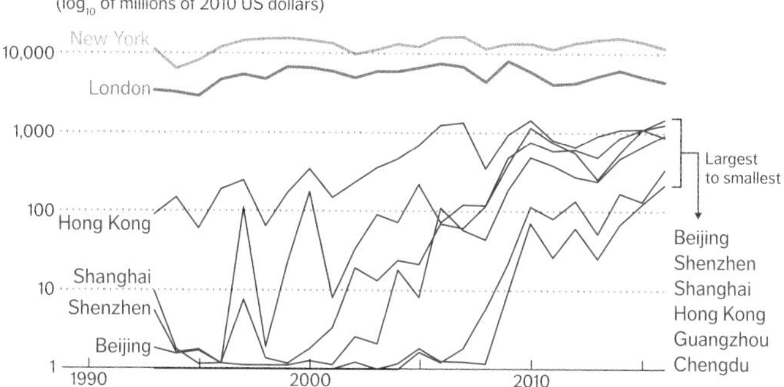

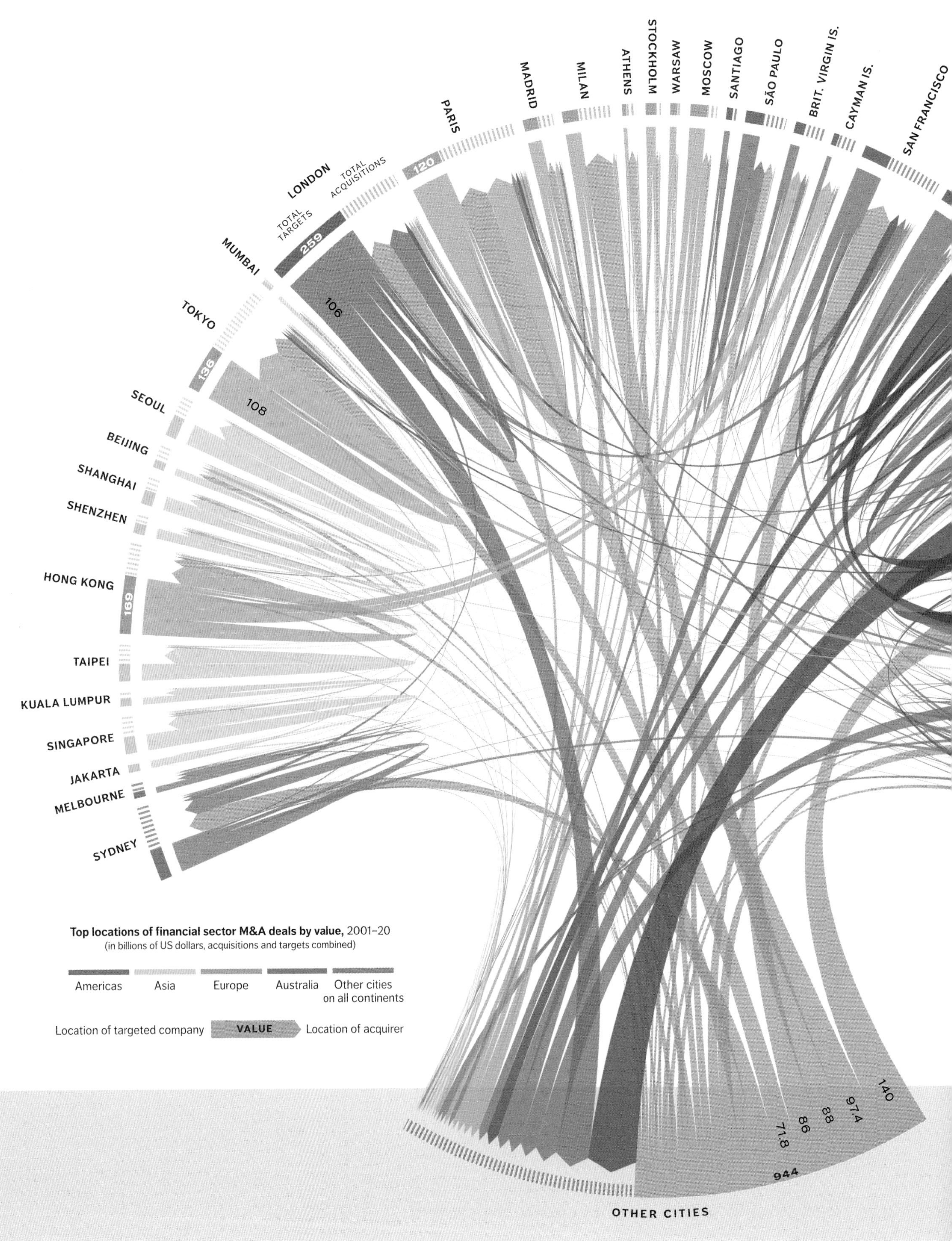

LONDON
TOTAL TARGETS
TOTAL ACQUISITIONS
259
106
MUMBAI
TOKYO
136
108
SEOUL
BEIJING
SHANGHAI
SHENZHEN
HONG KONG
169
TAIPEI
KUALA LUMPUR
SINGAPORE
JAKARTA
MELBOURNE
SYDNEY
PARIS
120
MADRID
MILAN
ATHENS
STOCKHOLM
WARSAW
MOSCOW
SANTIAGO
SÃO PAULO
BRIT. VIRGIN IS.
CAYMAN IS.
SAN FRANCISCO
140
97.4
88
86
71.8
944
OTHER CITIES
Top locations of financial sector M&A deals by value, 2001–20
(in billions of US dollars, acquisitions and targets combined)
Americas
Asia
Europe
Australia
Other cities on all continents
Location of targeted company
VALUE
Location of acquirer

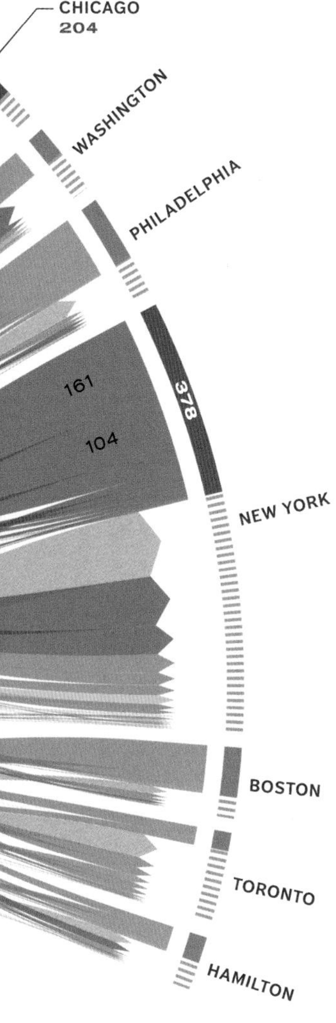

Mushrooming Mergers

Mergers and acquisitions are shooting up across the financial world, but they are not as global as you might expect.

WHY WASTE TIME AND MONEY outmaneuvering competitors when you can simply acquire them? Clearly, financial firms have applied this logic, as mergers and acquisitions (M&As) have risen sharply over the past two decades. An M&A is a transaction in which an acquirer firm buys a target firm. They occur as firms seek to access foreign markets, generate financial synergies, and capture new talent, technology, and intellectual property. Far from only increasing the footprint of the firm, M&As also provide opportunities to the financial centers on both sides of the transaction.

M&As cultivate urban growth. They attract money, people, and ideas through forging deeper connections between cities. By hosting acquirer firms, financial centers can enrich the breadth and depth of their financial ecosystem while capturing greater levels of decision-making power. By hosting target firms, financial centers receive new investments and generate closer collaborative ties with other cities. However, while M&As can be a force of growth, they can also be a force of destruction. In some cases, targeted firms lose their autonomy. Offices close; workers relocate.

Regardless of these outcomes, financial firms from some cities are better at acquiring competitors than others. Based exclusively on financial-sector deals valued at or above US$10 million, our diagram reveals the flows of M&A investment across leading financial centers between 2001 and 2020. New York, London, Chicago, Hong Kong, Paris, and Tokyo have hosted M&A acquirers and targets with the largest values. While financial firms in New York, Paris, and Tokyo are mostly on the acquirer side, those from London, Chicago, and Hong Kong are typically targets. Enormous levels of activity in the US, Europe, and Asia—and the significance of offshore financial centers like Hamilton (Bermuda) and the British Virgin Islands—contrast with scarce activity in Latin America and Africa.

While cross-border flows keep some financial centers global and interconnected, our diagram shows that U-shaped domestic and intra-city deals are much more common. M&As within New York, Paris, and Tokyo feature among the top ten acquirer–target pairs globally. Because language, culture, and national regulatory frameworks play important roles in any merger, financial firms are more likely to acquire competitors from their own country—a bias that makes global finance less global and more divided by national borders. Put simply, geography matters.

Total value of M&A deals by continent, 2001–20
(in billions of US dollars)

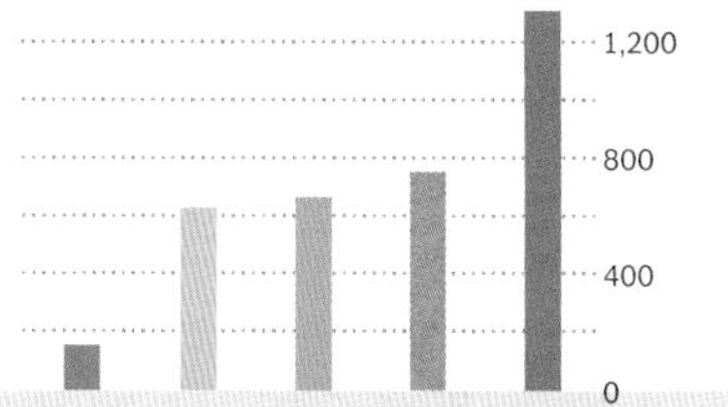

There have been thousands of mergers and acquisitions in the financial sector this century, especially in the Americas.

Colindale I.
Hampstead Reef
WEST SEA
Hampstead Bay
Wembley I.
1, 2, and 3 Cornwall Terrace were bought for £120 million by a member of the Qatari royal family, who own many properties across London—including the Shard—through offshore shell companies.
St. John's Wood
Regent's Cove
Silicon Spit
Wormwood Deep
1–3 Cornwall Terrace
OFFSHORE LONDON
Mayfair Ridge
City Channel
East End
Ealing Broadway I.
Shepherd's Atoll
Hyde Lagoon
3 Carlton Gardens
Chelsea Beach
Mount Belgravia
111 properties within the smallest contour
Eaton Square
Elephant & Castle
Hammersmith I.
Thames Trench
Vauxhall Sandbar
Fulham Point
To U.S.
Wandsworth I.
Putney I.
Gulf of Lambeth
Overseas sales and purchases of properties per 20m², 2008–18
0.6
Offshore property
0.05
Borough boundary
0
0
2 km
In 2019, the CEO and owner of the American hedge fund Citadel broke the post-Brexit blues of ultra-luxury property by paying £95 million for 3 Carlton Gardens, the most expensive property sold in the UK since 2011.
Wimbledon Seamount

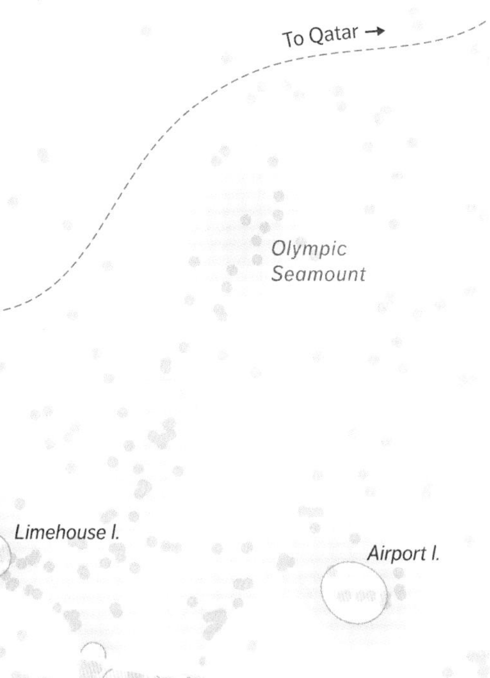

Islands of Wealth

For the rich, London is paradise, a sunny archipelago of expensive properties registered in offshore jurisdictions and tax havens.

JUST AS CORPORATIONS take advantage of complex multinational structures to avoid taxes, so too do wealthy individuals. The very rich do not hold their money in one bank or savings account; they spread it across a range of investments and financial holdings, such as desirable real estate.

As a global financial center, London is a hotspot for shell games. Our map shows sales and purchases of London properties by non-UK companies. Most overseas sales between 2008 and 2018 involved properties in Mayfair, Belgravia, Chelsea, and St. John's Wood, neighborhoods we've depicted here as topographic landmarks on the central island of "Offshore London." Orange areas had the most overseas sales; light blue had the least. Purchases on the outer islands, such as Elephant and Castle, were likely investment properties in new redevelopment schemes.

London is not only a place to stash wealth, it is also where many rich people choose to live. In 2018, London had approximately 4,944 ultra-high-net-worth individuals—each worth more than US$30 million—the world's largest concentration of such people. Often, they do not track the details of how their wealth is held themselves, instead employing professional wealth managers, lawyers, and accountants to maximize their investments and minimize their tax burden. For the super-rich, this extends to having "family offices" whose mandate is to manage their employer's money. These operate like private hedge funds, often out of anonymous-looking and well-appointed buildings in Mayfair.

One way to structure the ownership of property to minimize or avoid tax is to "envelop" it through a company in an offshore tax haven. Not all overseas companies that own domestic properties in London are enveloping their holdings, but the majority are. Of the properties on our map, 40 percent are owned by companies in the British Virgin Islands; 31 percent are based in Guernsey, Jersey, or the Isle of Man; and 18 percent are based in other offshore locations. Only 11 percent are owned by companies in locations that do not specialize in low tax and secrecy. Furthermore, the sole purpose of these companies is often to hold property, with 37 percent of companies mapped involved in only one transaction and 89 percent in fewer than ten. In addition to tax benefits, companies in many of these jurisdictions bestow anonymity on the ultimate owner through "closed registers" that prevent further scrutiny. Regulation and transparency would shed much-needed sunlight on these shady islands.

Eaton Square, one of London's most desirable and expensive streets, has been dubbed "Red Square" because of its popularity with Russian oligarchs, including Roman Abramovich and Oleg Deripaska.

To Russia →

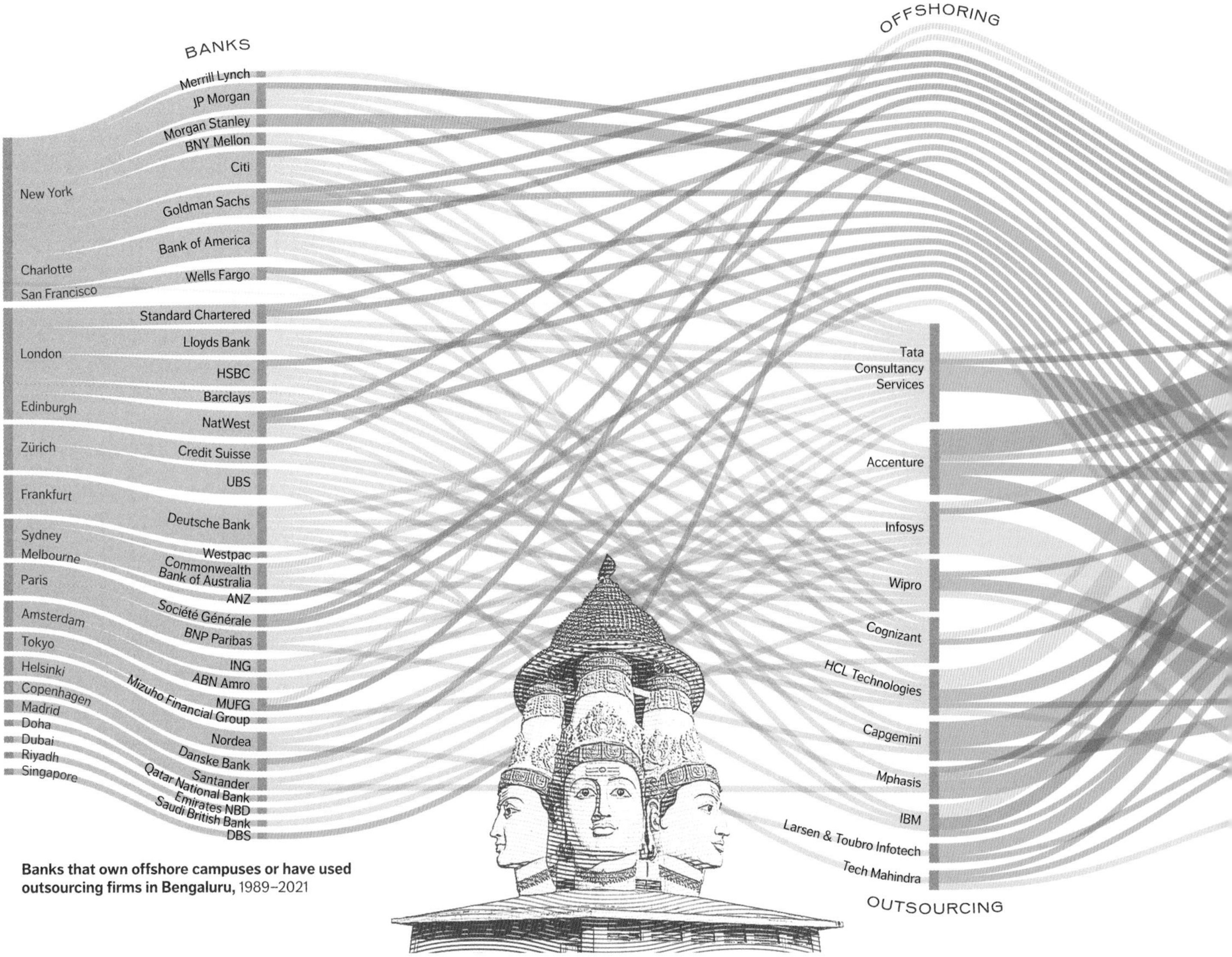

OFFSHORING

BANKS

Merrill Lynch
JP Morgan
Morgan Stanley
BNY Mellon
Citi
Goldman Sachs
Bank of America
Wells Fargo
Standard Chartered
Lloyds Bank
HSBC
Barclays
NatWest
Credit Suisse
UBS
Deutsche Bank
Westpac
Commonwealth Bank of Australia
ANZ
Société Générale
BNP Paribas
ING
ABN Amro
MUFG
Mizuho Financial Group
Nordea
Danske Bank
Santander
Qatar National Bank
Emirates NBD
Saudi British Bank
DBS

New York
Charlotte
San Francisco
London
Edinburgh
Zürich
Frankfurt
Sydney
Melbourne
Paris
Amsterdam
Tokyo
Helsinki
Copenhagen
Madrid
Doha
Dubai
Riyadh
Singapore

Tata Consultancy Services
Accenture
Infosys
Wipro
Cognizant
HCL Technologies
Capgemini
Mphasis
IBM
Larsen & Toubro Infotech
Tech Mahindra

OUTSOURCING

Banks that own offshore campuses or have used outsourcing firms in Bengaluru, 1989–2021

All Roads Lead to Bengaluru

As finance went digital, Bengaluru emerged as a global IT center.

INFORMATION TECHNOLOGIES profoundly reshaped the geography of finance. Since the late 1980s, many leading banks have relocated business tasks to cities abroad where real estate and labor are cheaper, a process known as offshoring. Melbourne-based ANZ was one of the first banks to open an office in Bengaluru, India. Back then, offshoring mostly concerned low-value, high-volume, back-office tasks that could be conducted remotely, such as data management, invoicing, accounting, or server maintenance.

Simultaneously, as finance gradually transformed into a more tech-driven industry, banks outsourced core tasks such as data analytics, market modeling, or customer management to third-party providers (gray flows above). Take Infosys. In 1993, the Bengaluru-based firm launched Bancs 2000, the first web-enabled banking solution. Known today as Finacle, it caters to 200 corporate clients across 100 countries, serving more than a billion individual customers. Indian firms such as Wipro or Tata Consultancy Services also became outsourcing giants, providing banks with cloud computing, cybersecurity solutions, and research consulting. Supported by this demand from the financial industry, export-oriented information technology

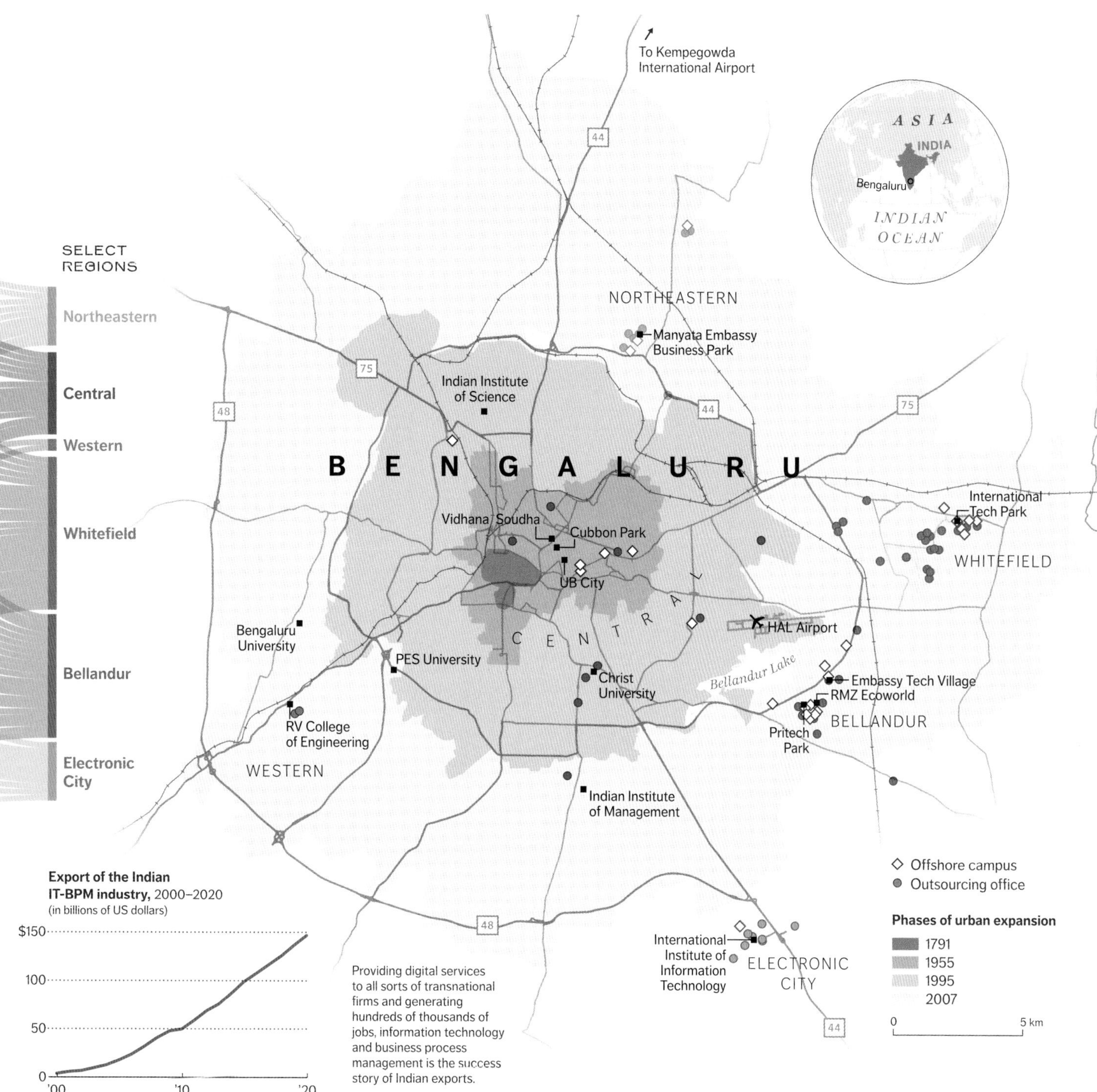

Providing digital services to all sorts of transnational firms and generating hundreds of thousands of jobs, information technology and business process management is the success story of Indian exports.

and business process management (IT-BPM) became a thriving sector in India, recording steady growth in terms of revenues and creating thousands of jobs (see chart).

This changing division of labor turned Bengaluru into the capital of the outsourcing and offshoring networks. Major banks such as Goldman Sachs and Société Générale opened their own units here in the early 2000s. Outsourcing firms, both Indian and foreign (e.g., Capgemini, IBM), developed myriad offices to service their clients headquartered in Zürich or Dubai. With plenty of prestigious universities and engineering schools, Bengaluru provides banks and outsourcing firms with an exceptional pool of talent accustomed to working at the intersection of tech and finance.

Unbundling the value chain in the financial sector accelerated Bengaluru's urban sprawl, as campuses mushroomed in a chain of techno-parks, where firms locate their branches to benefit from tax rebates. New urban clusters consequently appeared on the outskirts of the city, such as in Whitefield or Electronic City, where the daily work of thousands of employees and the circulation of data connect Bengaluru's campuses to the skyscrapers of the major financial centers.

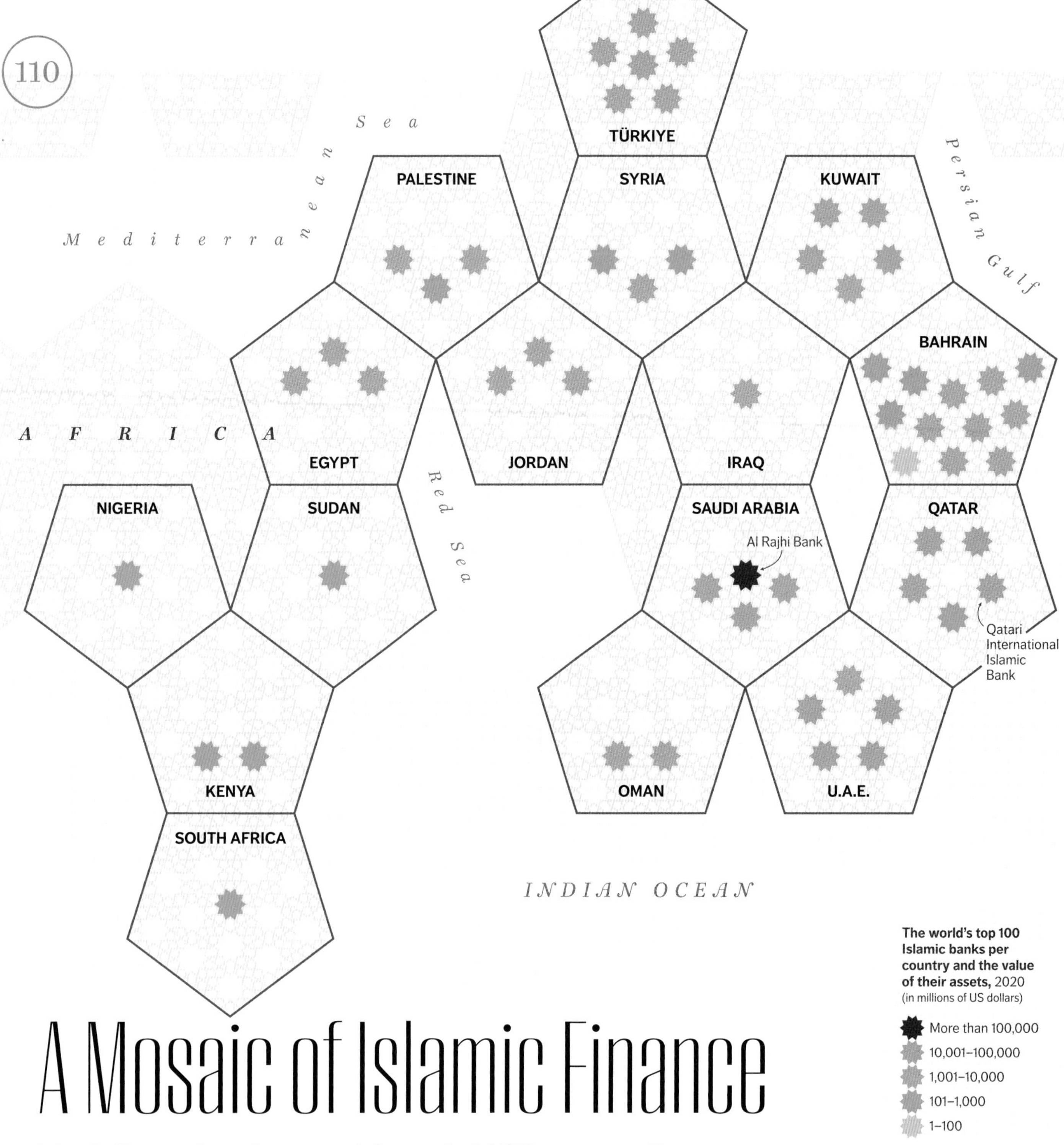

A Mosaic of Islamic Finance

Islamic finance is no longer a niche market. With new growth comes the extension of its geographical footprint.

ISLAMIC FINANCE refers to financial products, services, and institutions that comply with Sharia. Derived from the Quran, the central religious scripture of Islam, and the Sunnah, a social model based on the life and practices of the Prophet Muhammad, Islamic finance operates differently than Western finance. It is governed by three overarching principles. The first is the forbiddance of interest payments, or *riba*. These are seen as an unjust and unproductive form of usury. The second, *gharar*, refers to restrictions around speculative and risky financial transactions and instruments such as short selling and derivatives. The third, *maysir*, prohibits all forms of gambling and forbids investment in areas deemed to be haram under the Quran and Sunnah, such as alcohol and pork. These principles have spawned a range of financial products and services, including insurance (*takaful*), bonds (*sukuk*), and leasing (*ijarah*). Investors in sukuk bonds, for example, become owners of the issuer's assets that generate profit instead of receiving interest.

Islamic finance rose to prominence in the 1970s when Middle Eastern countries amassed huge amounts of

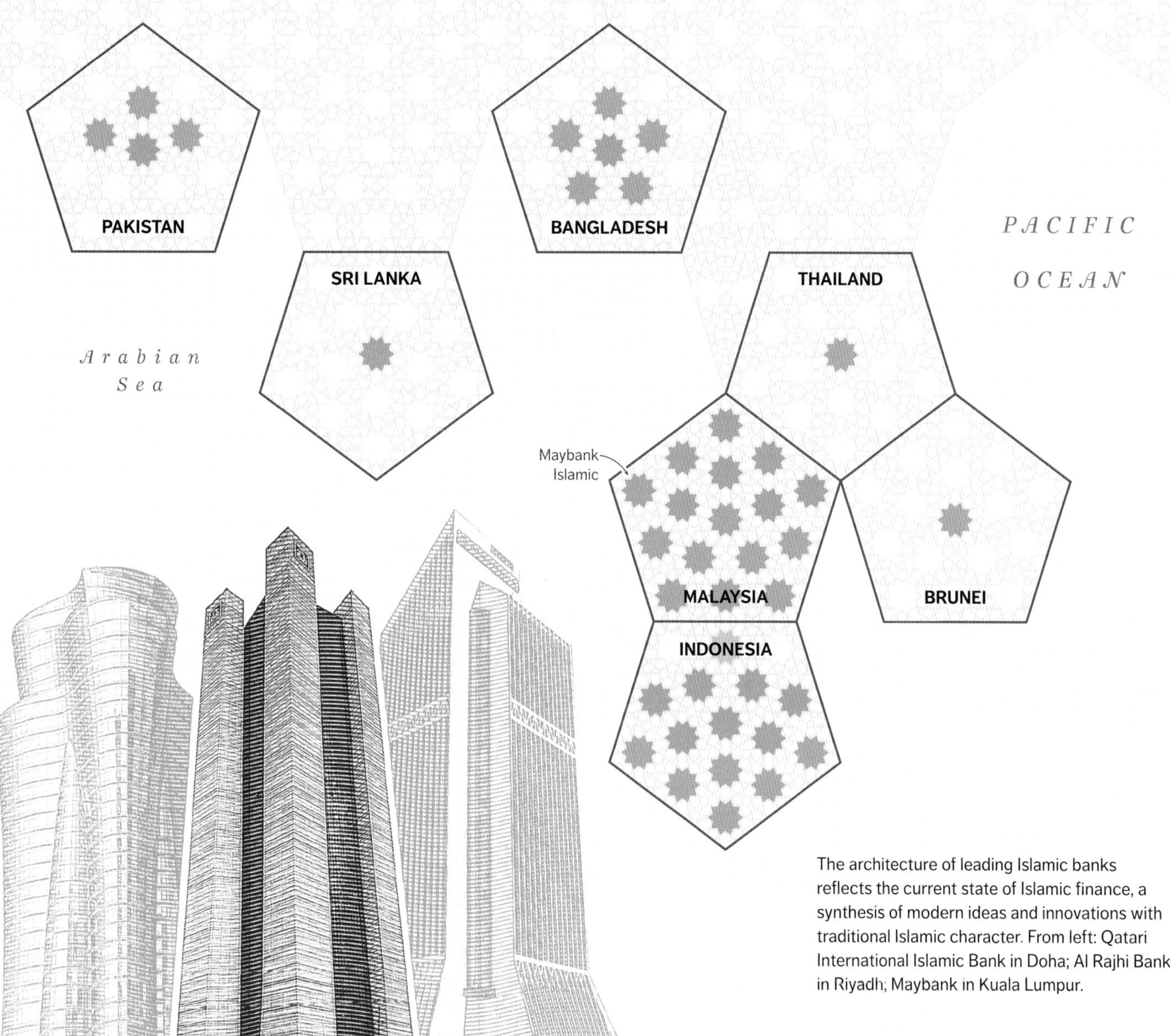

The architecture of leading Islamic banks reflects the current state of Islamic finance, a synthesis of modern ideas and innovations with traditional Islamic character. From left: Qatari International Islamic Bank in Doha; Al Rajhi Bank in Riyadh; Maybank in Kuala Lumpur.

money through the production of oil. Sharia-compliant finance supported the development of these countries. Globalization has since facilitated its expansion into a wide range of Islamic and non-Islamic countries. Our map shows the distribution of the top one hundred Islamic banks colored according to the value of their Sharia-compliant assets. As expected, many are located in the Middle East, with Saudi Arabia, Qatar, UAE, Bahrain, and Kuwait housing thirty-one of the top one hundred banks. Al Rajhi Bank in Riyadh, Saudi Arabia, is ranked the highest (dark blue), with Sharia-compliant assets of US$111,338 million. However, the country with the most banks and the highest asset value is Malaysia, making Kuala Lumpur the largest Islamic banking center. As of 2019, Malaysia was also the country with the largest number of Islamic scholars, the leaders who determine what is religiously acceptable in Islamic finance.

With Islamic finance expected to grow from $2.9 trillion of assets in 2020 to $3.7 trillion by 2024, and with Western banks offering more of their own Sharia-compliant services, Islamic finance will likely reach new frontiers.

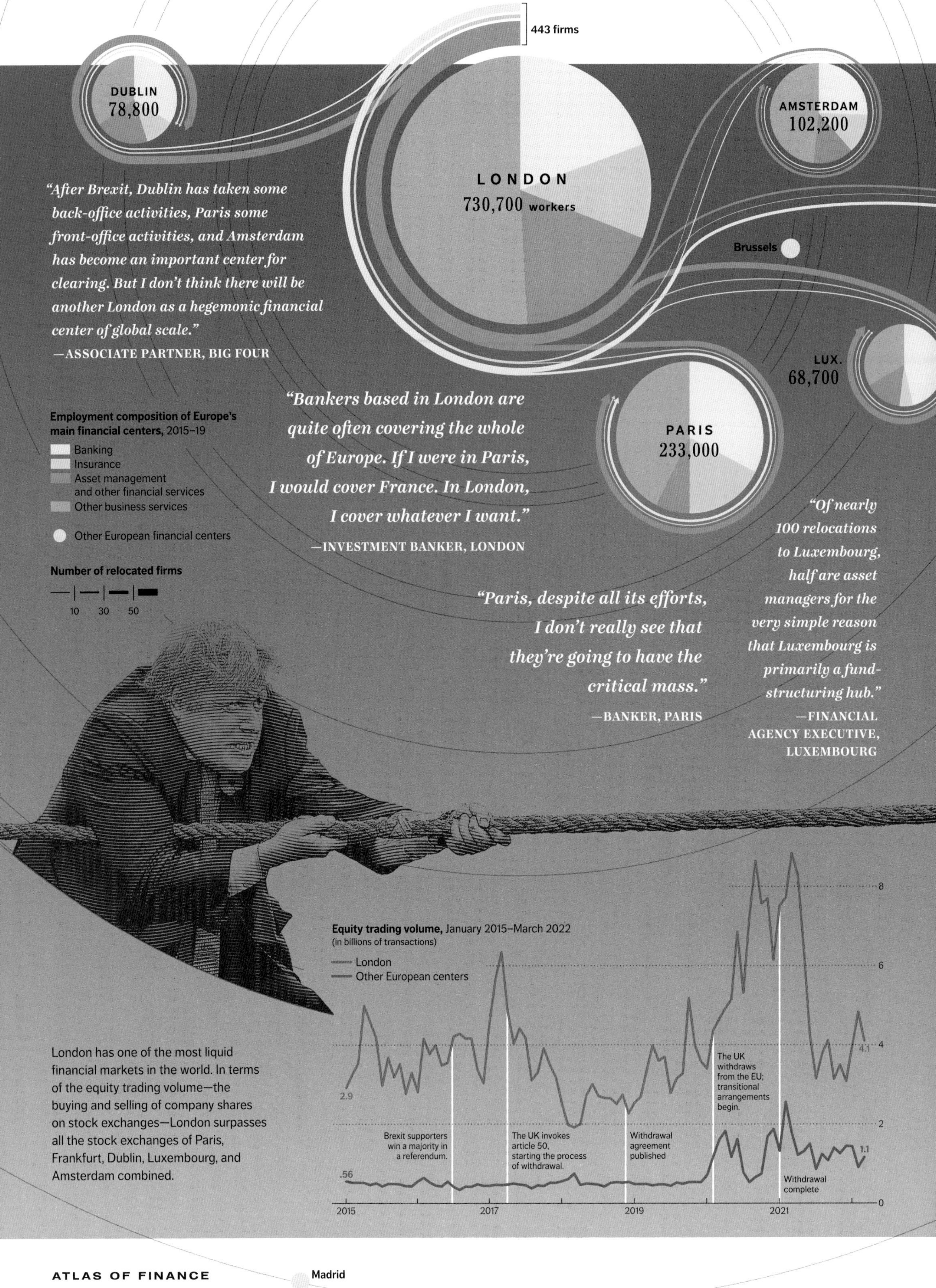

London has one of the most liquid financial markets in the world. In terms of the equity trading volume—the buying and selling of company shares on stock exchanges—London surpasses all the stock exchanges of Paris, Frankfurt, Dublin, Luxembourg, and Amsterdam combined.

London's Pull

Despite the uncertain future of the UK after Brexit, London remains the most powerful financial center in Europe.

ON JUNE 23, 2016, the UK held a referendum on its membership in the European Union in which 52 percent of voters opted to leave. And so, after forty-three years of cooperation with its European partners, the UK entered a new era. Facing uncertainty, some commentators expected major job losses as well as an exodus from London, where thousands of financial firms were soon to be deprived of direct access to the EU single market. Was the unrivaled gravity center of the European financial system about to vanish into a black hole?

As of April 2021, 443 firms had relocated part of their business activity to continental Europe. Rather than realign the financial cosmos, the distribution of these relocations only seems to have reinforced a historical structure of European finance, with London orbited by a few specialized and complementary financial centers, all within a ninety-minute flight from London (see pie charts). Banks shipped some of their staff to Paris and Frankfurt, both traditional hubs for the banking sector, while asset management firms and equity funds went to Dublin and Luxembourg. With an established focus on trading, Amsterdam appealed to firms providing trading and other business services. Cities further away attracted even fewer relocations.

Despite these relocations, London still dwarfs its satellites in terms of trading volumes (see line chart). And in interviews we conducted, members of the financial industry continued to view London as the main financial center of Europe and the must-go destination when business calls (see quotes). In fact, six years after the vote, 90 percent of euro-denominated interest rate derivatives were still cleared on the London Stock Exchange. Brexit reinforced the existing division of labor between Europe's financial centers without dissolving the London-centric geography of the overall system. The size and global connections of London's markets; its concentration of firms, clients, suppliers, and expertise; the role of the British sterling as a global reserve currency; and the power of British common law constitute competitive advantages unmatched by any other city in Europe.

Brexit is an unfinished process. UK-based financial and business services firms may have lost the right to trade seamlessly in the European Union, but they still have access to its markets because the EU recognizes UK laws and regulations as sufficiently similar to theirs. For now, finance remains an empire on which London's sun never sets.

"There's an idea that London is a planet on its own, that it's starting to diverge from the rest of the solar system. We need to combat that."
—BORIS JOHNSON, 2014

Fintech start-ups and scale-ups typically rely on external financing to support their growth. The cohort of fintech start-ups that spawned after the global financial crisis initially only attracted limited seed funding. However, as they demonstrated the viability of their business models, much larger pots of investment capital became available. Venture capital and private equity investment into fintech peaked at $38.2 billion in 2018, nearly forty times higher than its value in 2007.

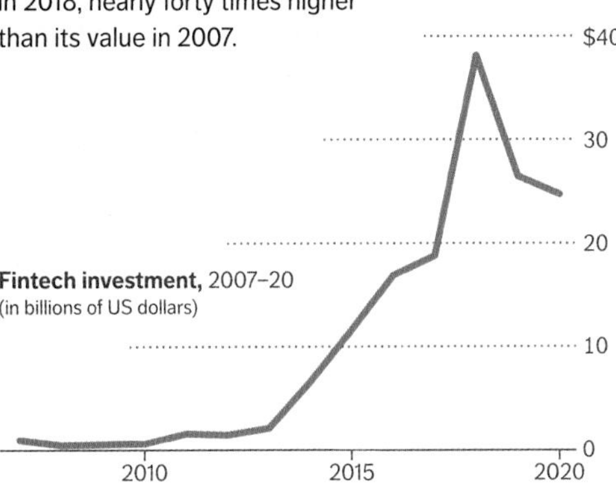

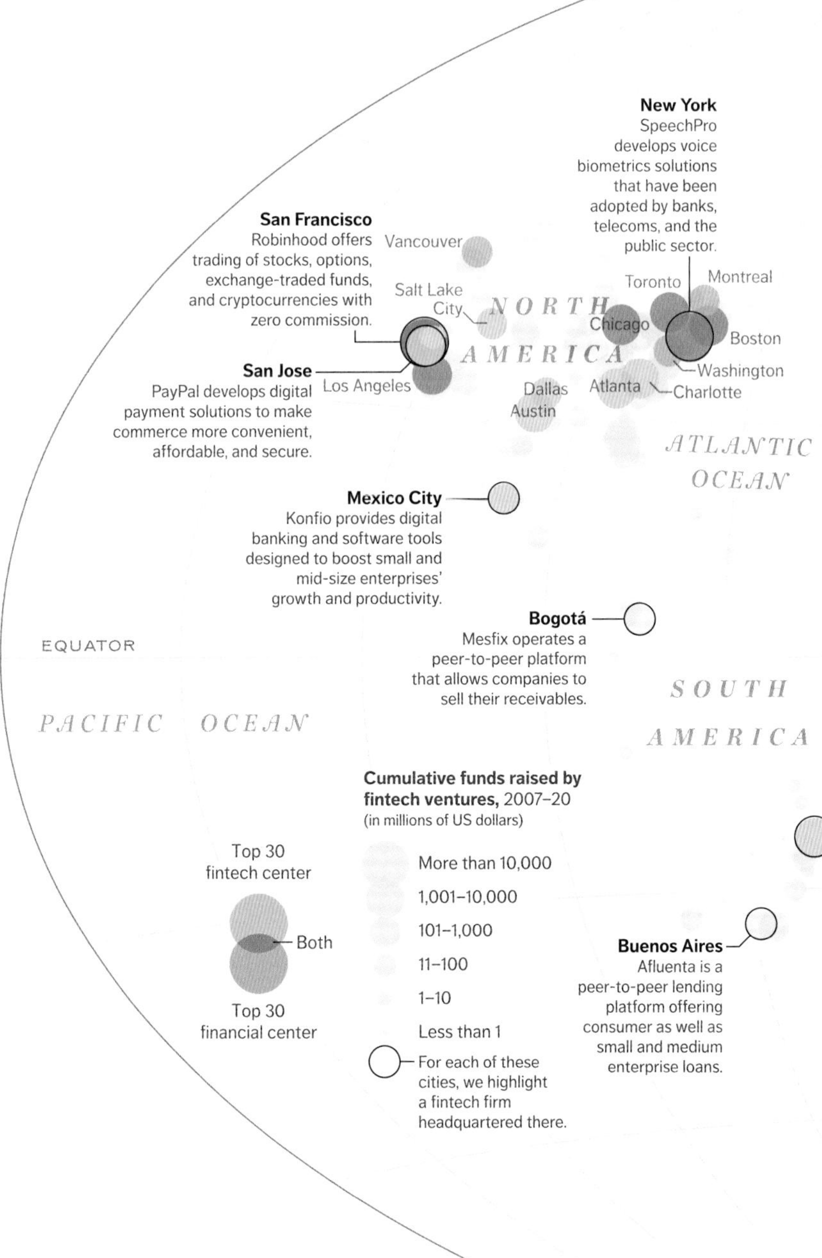

Fintech Planet

The world of finance is undergoing a widespread technological change that does not stem only from established financial centers.

POWERED BY ADVANCES in data science and computing power, a new wave of financial innovations, or fintech, is changing the way the world does business. Since the 1990s, there has been a rapid accumulation of published patents related to payments, investment, data analytics, fraud detection, and insurance (see far right). This process has accelerated rapidly since the start of the millennium. However, it took the global financial crisis and the resulting disenchantment with established financial institutions for investors to see the viability of fintech start-ups (see above). These innovative companies have connected with younger generations of consumers who wish to access financial services in a convenient and cheap manner, mostly on their phones. And in developing economies, they're providing financial services to hundreds of millions of unbanked and underbanked consumers.

Crucially, the rise of fintech firms is not limited to the leading financial centers. Emerging information technology clusters are hotspots too. This is understandable, as much of the expertise required to support fintech firms lies in the

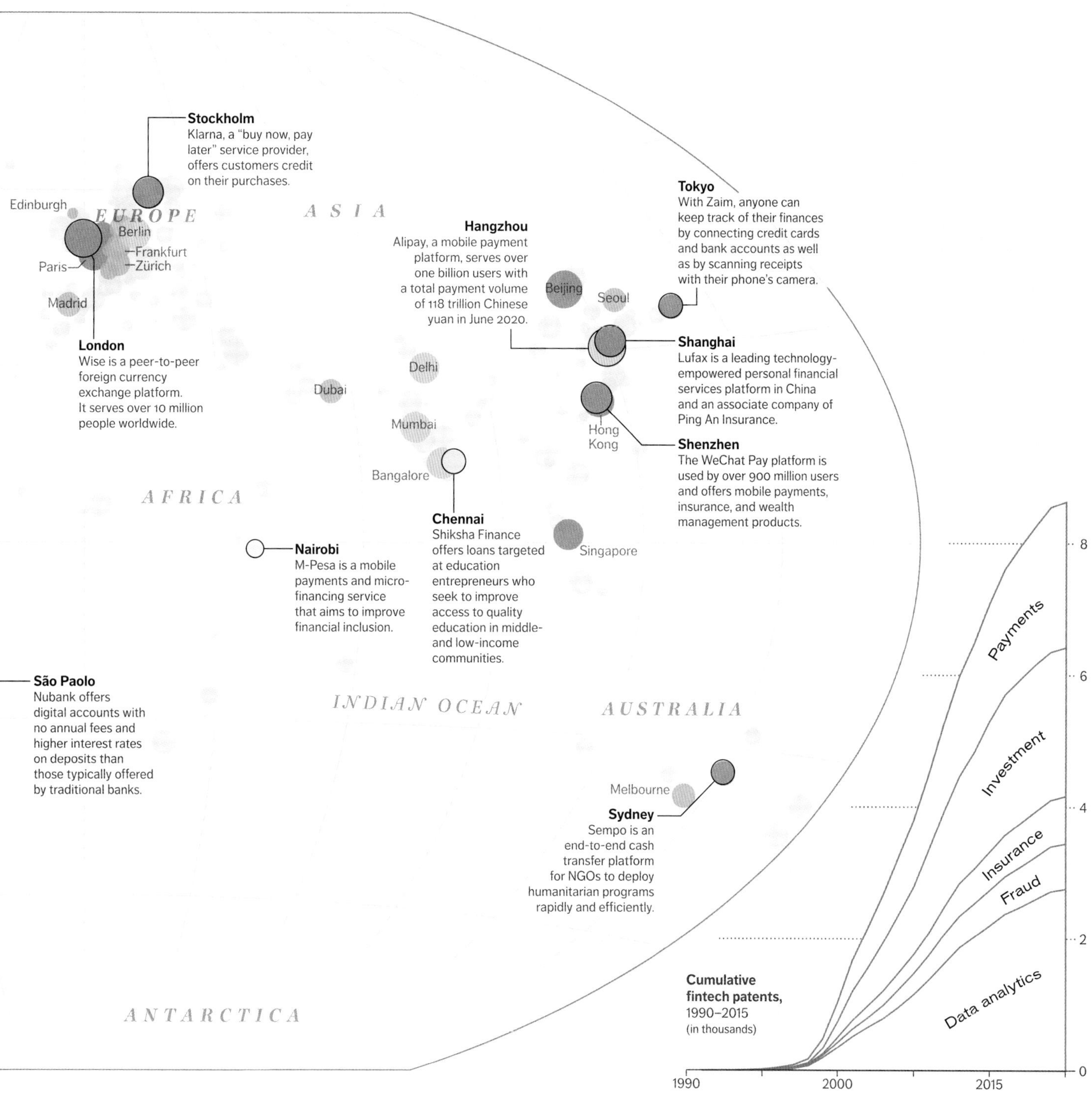

hands of computer scientists rather than financiers. On the map above we have highlighted the top thirty financial centers in pink and the top thirty fintech centers in gold; some cities (in brown) made both lists. Cities are sized by the amount of funds raised by fintech ventures there. With US$27.4 and $21.2 billion, respectively, San Francisco (brown) and Hangzhou (gold) secured more venture capital and private equity investment into fintech than the world's top financial centers, London ($13.5 billion) and New York ($10 billion), in the 2007–20 period.

In Europe, Stockholm ($2.7 billion) and Berlin ($2.5 billion) emerge as the second and third largest centers of fintech investment, ahead of Paris ($1.1 billion) and Amsterdam ($0.9 billion). In India, Delhi ($4.5 billion) and Bangalore ($2.2 billion) are ahead of Mumbai ($1.1 billion). In Latin America, São Paulo ($2.5 billion) and Mexico City ($0.8 billion) lead. Fintech makes the map of global finance more diverse but does not necessarily revolutionize it. Just as it creates new hubs of finance, it adds to the activity of established centers.

ΞΕΣΗΚΩΘΕΙΤΕ
6

What we learn from history is that people don't learn from history.
WARREN BUFFETT

Bubbles & Crises

Financial crises are as old as finance. Their explanations are controversial, with fundamental macroeconomic factors competing with plain greed and complacency. A single individual acting fraudulently or recklessly can bring down the largest financial institution. Their impacts on local livelihoods can be devastating and highly uneven and unjust. Typically, the most vulnerable places and people pay the price rather than those who brewed and perpetrated the crises.

A World of Crises

The history of capitalism is peppered with financial crises, but their type and frequency vary from region to region.

FINANCIAL CRISES are inseparable from the expansion of capitalism. Its inherently fickle nature ensures that normal periods of growth and prosperity will eventually turn into sudden episodes of instability. Triggered by bank failures, currency crashes, or debt defaults, nearly a thousand crises have marked the world in the past four centuries. We've mapped them here by country and colored them by type; hatched dots are crises that occurred before 1950.

In the early stages of capitalism, traditional monarchies like the kingdoms of France and Spain financed their wars and trade explorations with borrowed money. Often the appetite for power led to an unsustainable buildup of debt,

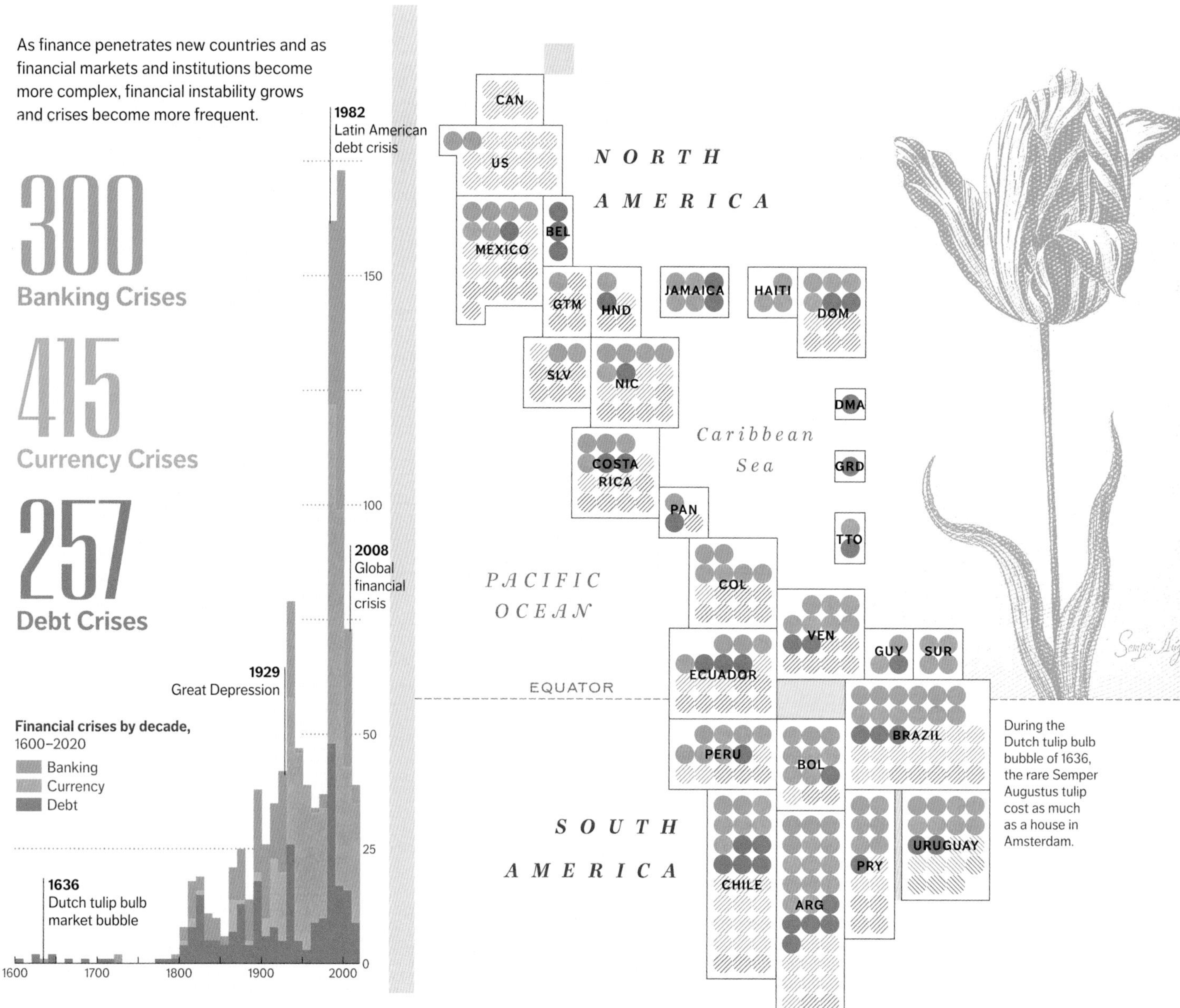

During the Dutch tulip bulb bubble of 1636, the rare Semper Augustus tulip cost as much as a house in Amsterdam.

posing significant risks to the viability of state finances. Later, as the world became more interconnected through international trade, speculation over the price of a currency became common and often led to abrupt devaluations.

Financial crises are widespread, but their frequency varies from region to region. The Global South has been affected by more instability and crises than the Global North. Debt defaults, speculative currency attacks, inflationary spirals, and severe bank runs—accompanied by political and social instability—are frequent phenomena in the Global South. For example, during the rise of national independence movements in the 1800s, Latin America was the epicenter of multiple global debt crises.

Within the Global North, financial crises are not evenly distributed; their extent and effects depend on each country's financial system. The US and UK, arguably two of the most advanced financial markets in the world, have experienced a number of notable banking crises. On the other end of the spectrum, Switzerland and Luxembourg have only had one or two. Their relatively resilient financial systems have developed appropriate mechanisms and regulatory environments to cope with the eruptions of financial instability, at least thus far.

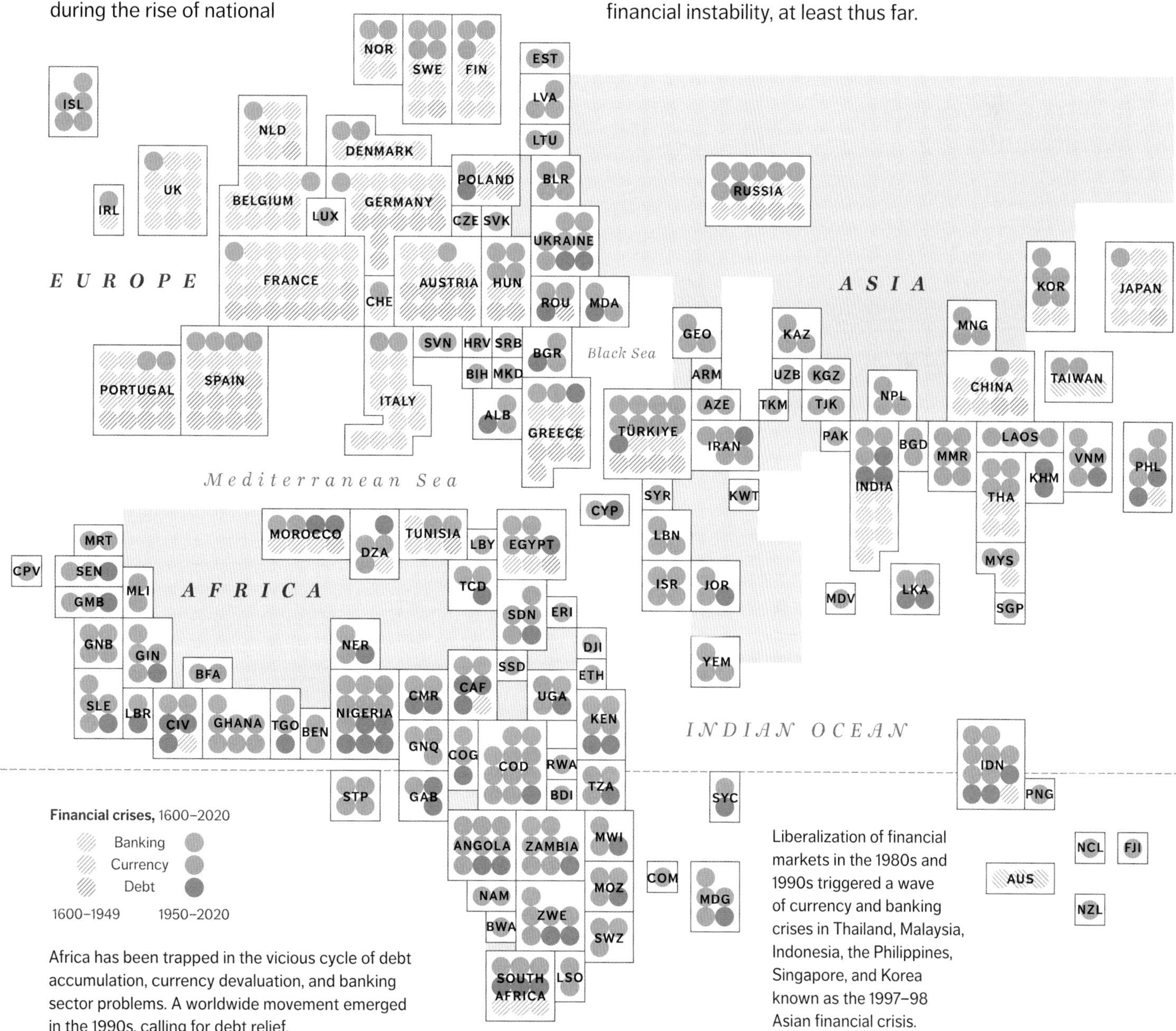

Africa has been trapped in the vicious cycle of debt accumulation, currency devaluation, and banking sector problems. A worldwide movement emerged in the 1990s, calling for debt relief.

Liberalization of financial markets in the 1980s and 1990s triggered a wave of currency and banking crises in Thailand, Malaysia, Indonesia, the Philippines, Singapore, and Korea known as the 1997–98 Asian financial crisis.

A HYPOTHETICAL DEBATE

Monetarism

A rise in US interest rates spurs monetary tightening in global financial markets.

My dear friends, have you ever wondered what triggers a financial crisis? *Take the Asian financial crisis of 1997–98. When the US raised interest rates from 3.05% in 1994 to 5.5% in 1997 to avoid overheating its economy, investors started questioning their positions in East Asia, shifting capital away from the region. This sudden withdrawal called into doubt the viability of the Asian economies. Of the factors that can trigger a crisis,* ***it seems to me that money supply matters most.***

Anna Schwartz
1915–2012

Debt-Deflation

Unsustainable debt buildup eventually leads to asset price deflation.

I do not necessarily disagree with you, but monetarism doesn't explain why the crisis spread to countries like Singapore and Hong Kong, which—unlike Thailand, Indonesia, and the Philippines—had high trade surpluses and foreign exchange reserves. This was a typical debt-deflation crisis. Those countries liberalized their markets in the 1990s and allowed highly mobile international capital to invest in almost everything. ***When the market sentiment changed slightly, short-term investors flew away, triggering a chain reaction*** *of falling asset prices, indebtedness, economic losses and bankruptcies.*

Irving Fisher
1867–1947

Financial Instability Hypothesis

The dynamics of financial instability are linked to a regular business cycle.

Yes! But this is not the full story. Financial crises are not random. ***Capitalism creates cycles of economic expansions and contractions.*** *What happened in Asia was a classic "Minsky moment." After a long period of prolonged economic prosperity, during which optimism about East Asian economies led to unsustainable debt-financed asset bubbles, economies moved from stable financial relations (hedge financing) to unstable ones (speculation and Ponzi schemes). The asset bubbles finally burst and generated a debt-deflation cycle.*

Hyman Minsky
1919–1996

Herd Behavior
The imitative behavior of investors causes a financial crisis to spread.

Wait a second. How do you explain the fact that a speculative attack against Thailand triggered a crisis that spread to seven other Asian countries and later, Russia, Brazil and the US? I'll tell you how: herd behavior. Humans imitate each other. Given the interconnectedness of global financial markets, ***any decision made in one economy prompts financial actors in other economies to make similar decisions.***

Daniel Kahneman
1934–

Theories of Instability

What caused the 1997 Asian financial crisis? Depends on who you ask.

IMAGINE A TABLE strewn with research papers and heavy books, all adorned with words like *foundations, finance,* and *macroeconomics*. The headline of an orange-ish newspaper reads, "Turmoil in Asian Markets: Recession Follows Months of Financial Distress." If four leading economists from the past century were gathered around this table and we asked how a currency devaluation in Thailand could trigger a chain reaction of financial distress and business failures across Southeast Asia, Brazil, and Russia, here's what they might say:

Anna Schwartz—the monetarist of the group—would emphasize the causal link between money supply and economic activity, arguing that financial instability results from policy errors made by monetary authorities in their effort to control money supply. Too much money in the economy and prices start to rise, causing inflation; too little and the economy shrinks.

Irving Fisher would note the destabilizing effects of high debt and deflation on economic performance. Having experienced the disaster of the 1930s' Great Depression firsthand, he argues in his debt-deflation theory that when highly indebted individuals and businesses try to get rid of their debts, they unintentionally trigger deflation (falling prices), which in turn increases the real burden of debt. Eventually, indebtedness and deflation lead to economic losses, business and household bankruptcies, and a general pessimism about the future of the economy.

Hyman Minsky would likely concur, while stressing his financial instability hypothesis, which reasons that, over periods of prolonged prosperity, businesses and individuals are encouraged to increase their borrowing, while financial institutions increase their lending. Such optimism leads to unsustainable debt-financed asset bubbles, with the economy moving from stable financial relations to unstable ones. The asset bubbles eventually burst, generating debt-deflation cycles, financial distress, and economic losses.

Daniel Kahneman, the founding father of behavioral economics, would cut through the conversation to remind everyone of herd behavior: the tendency of individuals to imitate the behavior of others. In the context of financial markets, he says, investors are herding when they synchronize their investment decisions with other investors, generating a feedback mechanism that intensifies market volatility.

If we invited Asian economists to the table, they would stress the role of fickle foreign financial flows fueling the boom and aggravating the bust.

The Big One

A single rogue trader armed with risky financial instruments can cause a disaster of seismic proportions.

AT THE CLIMAX of the film *Rogue Trader,* we see a Barings Bank broker named Nick Leeson, star of their Singapore office, in bed with his girlfriend. The phone rings. On the other end of the line, a friend urges him to turn on the news. Leeson's face goes pale. An earthquake has devastated the Japanese city of Kobe, killing more than six thousand people. Leeson clutches his forehead as he realizes a bet he placed the previous day is about to bring down one of the oldest banks in the world.

To understand the real events that inspired the film, you need to understand Leeson's gamble. Derivatives allow betting on the price movements of bonds, stocks, and other financial assets—usually with borrowed money—without ever acquiring the underlying assets. For years, Leeson had been using Barings's money to make unauthorized trades on futures and option contracts. Futures and option contracts are types of financial derivatives that amplify speculators' returns. Seventeen days before the Kobe quake, his losses were around £208 million (see innermost ripple at right). In an attempt to limit them, Leeson tried what's known as a "short straddle." He sold a large amount of both put and call options, financial contracts that allow one to sell (put) and buy (call) assets with a predetermined price and date. If volatility in Singapore's and Japan's stock markets had been low, Leeson would have collected high premiums as profits. Instead, the earth shook and so did global markets (see chart). Seeing the writing on the wall, Leeson fled the country on February 23, 1995. By the time Barings ceased operations three days later, its losses had climbed to more than £900 million!

But who was the real culprit of this disaster? As reckless as Leeson was, the truth is, Barings didn't fail because of an earthquake or one rogue trader. The fault lines were far deeper. Instead point a finger at the underlying financial system that rewards aggressive and speculative trading behavior. The same poor management and regulatory processes that permitted a renegade employee to hide huge losses also inflated financial risks hidden beneath the highly complex structure of financial derivatives.

Founded in 1762 in London, Barings was one of the oldest and largest banks in the world. It had financed Napoleon's wars and hundreds of miles of railways in Argentina. But even a bank that big couldn't withstand a bad day at the office.

Leeson's escape route
February 23–March 2, 1995

On February 23, Leeson and his wife fled from Singapore. From the Regent Hotel in Kuala Lumpur, he sent a fax to Barings with his resignation. A few days later they flew to Brunei and then to Bangkok, where they bought a plane ticket for Frankfurt via Abu Dhabi. In Frankfurt, they were eventually captured by the Germany authorities.

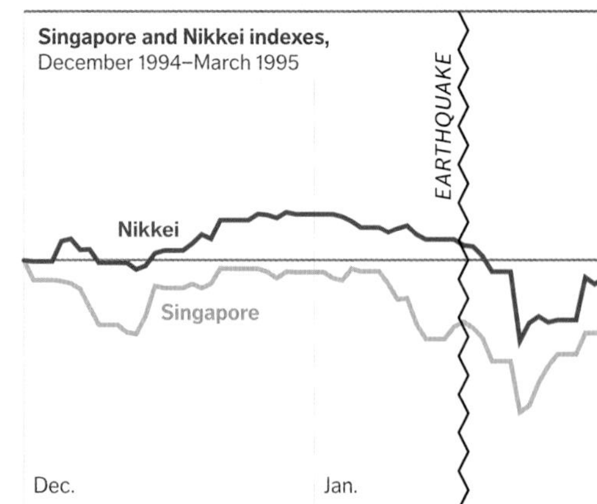

Singapore and Nikkei indexes,
December 1994–March 1995

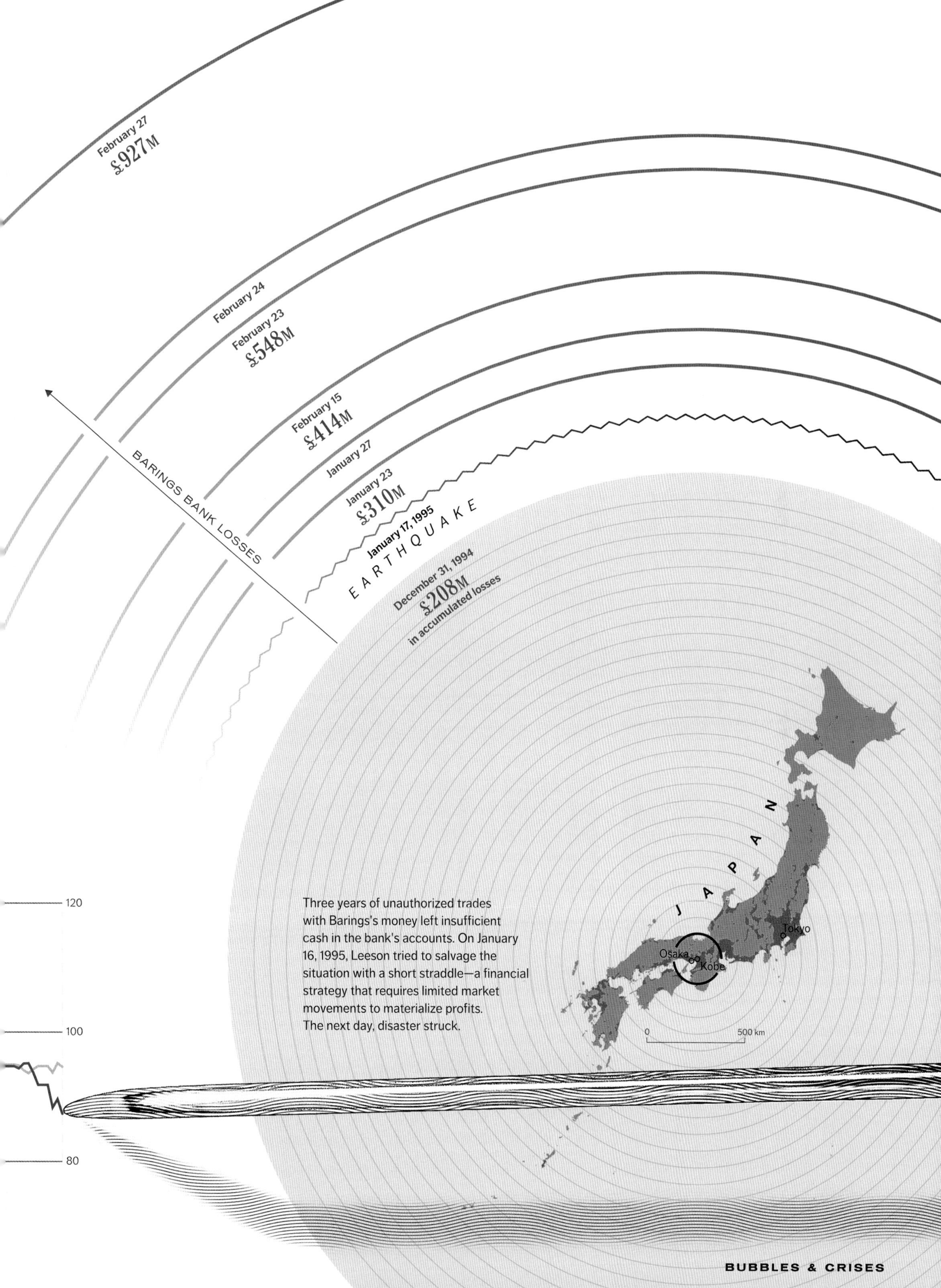

Three years of unauthorized trades with Barings's money left insufficient cash in the bank's accounts. On January 16, 1995, Leeson tried to salvage the situation with a short straddle—a financial strategy that requires limited market movements to materialize profits. The next day, disaster struck.

THE NEW YORK TIMES
January 6, 2002

Fixing Argentina

Whose job is it?

NEW YORK – On the day he was designated Argentina's fifth president in two weeks, Eduardo Duhalde cautioned his countrymen not to try to fix blame for the country's chaos. Then he did just that. . . . Regardless of how long he lasts in office, Mr. Duhalde has already raised questions sure to complicate American relations with Argentina and perhaps other Latin countries.

THE ECONOMIST
January 5, 2002

Flirting with anarchy

Needed: a government and a policy

LONDON – Many Argentines are fed up beyond measure with what they see as a corrupt and self-serving political system. Austerity and corruption make an explosive cocktail. There is a risk that Argentina will slide towards mob rule. What can stop that awful prospect? The first requirement is a competent and legitimate government. . . . The second requirement is a new economic plan.

THE WALL STREET JOURNAL
January 9, 2002

How Argentina got into this mess

NEW YORK – It is fashionable now to blame Argentina's problems on the free market. The country's latest president, old-school Peronist and unabashed protectionist Eduardo Duhalde, has joined the anti-market chorus by vowing to break with the "failed economic model" of the past decade. But Argentina's tragic crack-up occurred not because pro-market reforms went too far, but because they did not go nearly far enough.

PAGINA 12
December 6, 2001

The middle finger of the IMF

There will be no disbursement and the program will come down. Argentina without help!

BUENOS AIRES – After ten years of putting Argentina as the exemplary student, last night the Monetary Fund said enough is enough. In a statement released in Washington minutes after Finance Minister Domingo Cavallo (right) said at a press conference that the negotiations were going "very well" and that work was continuing "side by side," the organization announced that it would not disburse fresh funds to Argentina. . . . the refusal of the IMF to transfer that money, as a result of the breach of the Zero Deficit, places Argentina on the brink of default.

LA NACIÓN
January 11, 2002

IMF concerned about Argentine political instability

BUENOS AIRES – In reality, the IMF is not sympathetic to Argentina's new plan and wants the government to comply with Washington's long-standing demands: fiscal order and paths to sustainable growth.

O GLOBO
January 6, 2002

Bush takes a hard line on emerging economies

US position towards Argentina, called "tough love," is a warning to other countries.

RIO DE JANEIRO – The US government is using the Argentine crisis as a practical example of how it intends to conduct its new policy from now on—already dubbed "tough love"—to tackle financial instability in developing countries. The idea is to demonstrate, both to the governments of those nations and to American investors, that the White House and the Treasury Department no longer intend to play the role of guarantor.

A — The Asian financial crisis moves to Latin America; Argentina enters a recession.

B — The president announces a US$40 billion assistance package with the support of the IMF; borrowing costs rise.

Bank runs begin with over $1.3 billion in withdrawals.

C — Riots begin in major cities; 28 people die. The president and his finance minister resign.

D — New floating-exchange-rate regime. The dollar ends as an official circulating currency; peso devalues by 60 percent within a month.

E — Inflation peaks at 10 percent in April.

1998 — 1999 — 2000 — 2001 — 2002

President de la Rúa resigns from office and leaves the presidential palace in a helicopter.

Financial Crises Making Headlines

The media report on financial events, but they can also influence them.

IN THE EARLY 1990S Argentina was living an economic miracle. High growth rates, low inflation, fiscal discipline, capital inflows, and pro-market reforms signaled a new era of prosperity. Financial markets and mainstream media praised the decisiveness of its policymakers. Argentina, they said, was the new model economy for emerging countries. History would prove otherwise.

As the Asian financial crisis of 1997–98 undermined investors' confidence in emerging markets, Argentina slipped into a spiral of devaluation, over-indebtedness, and economic contraction. In late 2001, the Argentine peso collapsed in value. Inflation and borrowing costs soared (see charts). In an attempt to avoid a general run on the country's banks, the Argentine finance minister Domingo Cavallo imposed a limit on cash withdrawals on December 1, triggering a wave of social unrest, rioting, and deadly protests. A few days later, he and the president of Argentina, Fernando de la Rúa, resigned from office. Argentina was on the brink of collapse. The scene of President de la Rúa fleeing the presidential palace in a helicopter dominated headlines around the world.

Take a look at the reaction of Western and local media and you'll see two completely different worldviews. The three excerpts from Western media (top row) depict the crisis as one of disorder. The centrist *Economist* noted that Argentina was "flirting with anarchy" and advised its readership that there was only one way to overcome the crisis: "legitimate government . . . and a new economic plan." This depiction was common across the political spectrum, with the left-leaning *New York Times* wondering "whose job is it" to fix Argentina, and the conservative *Wall Street Journal* attacking President Duhalde for his anti-market political ideas. Contrast that with Latin American media (bottom row), which put the blame on US economic policy and disastrous crisis management by the International Monetary Fund (IMF). *Pagina 12* revealed how the IMF fooled Cavallo during negotiations about the disbursement of funds. *La Nación* implied that the IMF's ultimate goal was to impose the US economic agenda, whereas Brazilian *O Globo* viewed President Bush's harsh position against Argentina as a warning to other countries.

Reviewing newspaper archives is a valuable method of historical financial analysis. Journalists can reflect popular sentiment but also influence it according to the political interests and inclinations of their editors and funders. Who pays for newspapers matters.

ARGENTINA'S ECONOMY

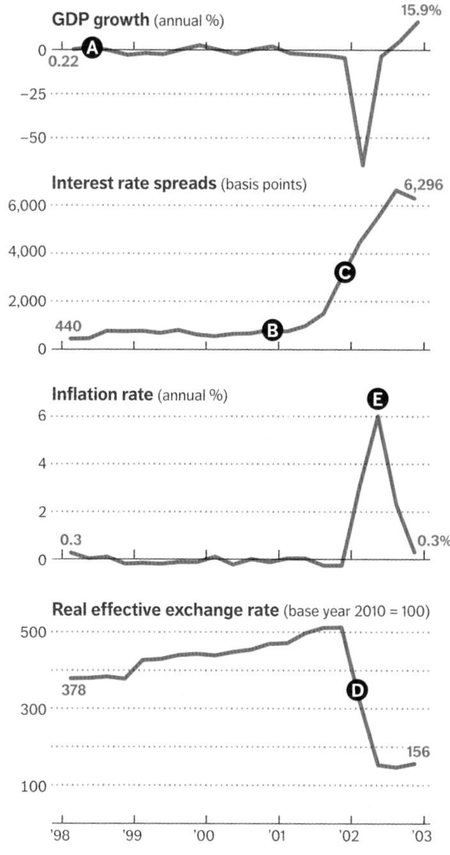

Calling Time on Northern Rock

A building society that turned into a bank became a fallen angel of the North, shattering Newcastle-upon-Tyne's prospects of becoming a major financial center.

ON SEPTEMBER 14, 2007, news broke that Northern Rock, a bank headquartered in the northeast of England, was in crisis. Customers lined the streets of Newcastle-upon-Tyne in the thousands, racing to withdraw their savings and triggering the first run on a British bank in over 150 years. The city was in a panic. Decisions made a decade earlier help explain why.

The countdown to disaster began in 1997, when Northern Rock transitioned from a building society to a private bank. The bank adopted a new model that relied on lending money from wholesale international financial markets to provide mortgages. In 1999, Northern Rock created its own offshore special-purpose vehicle in Guernsey to issue mortgage-backed securities. With cheap debt freely available, growth was good. Customers were offered "Together" mortgages, allowing them to borrow 125 percent of a house's value. While debt papered over the cracks of an unsustainable business model, Northern Rock was the pride of the northeast. A successful financial services firm heralded the region's transition away from the nightmares of deindustrialization. It seemed to defy the received wisdom that a large successful British bank could grow only in London.

Fewer constraints and more borrowing allowed Northern Rock to grow rapidly, but it left the bank highly leveraged and exposed when the credit crisis struck in 2007. Banks stopped lending to one another, and the debt tap ran dry. The second the media announced that Northern Rock sought emergency funds from the Bank of England, customers wanted out. With fewer deposits and no debt to fund mortgages, Northern Rock crumbled. The UK government announced measures to protect customers' savings before nationalizing the bank in 2008 and eventually selling off parts to Virgin Money in 2012.

The shockwaves of Northern Rock's collapse were felt far beyond the pockets of its shareholders. Nearly two decades of constant growth had supported Newcastle-upon-Tyne in its attempts to become a regional financial center capable of competing with the likes of London. Nationalization and the layoffs of nearly two thousand employees ended this ambition. Having lost its only major financial services firm, the region found its problems compounded by the global financial crisis and government-led austerity measures. When it comes to being a financial center, Newcastle-upon-Tyne is still stuck between a rock and a hard place.

Turning Points

1965 Two building societies merge to form the Northern Rock Building Society.

1997 Northern Rock goes public on the London Stock Exchange. Labour Chancellor Gordon Brown says, "I am satisfied that the new monetary policy arrangements will deliver long-term price stability and prevent a return to the cycle of boom and bust."

2000 Northern Rock enters the Financial Times Stock Exchange 100 Index (FTSE 100).

2007 Following demutualization, Northern Rock's assets grow at an annual rate of 23.2%. News breaks of Northern Rock seeking emergency support from the Bank of England. Customers rush to withdraw money from the bank. In October, the UK government announces a plan to protect up to 100 percent of customers' first £35,000 worth of savings.

2008 Shares are suspended and Northern Rock is placed under "temporary" nationalization. Northern Rock announces a first round of layoffs (1,300 jobs) and losses of £585 million for the first half of the year.

2010 Northern Rock cuts 650 more jobs.

2012 Virgin Money acquires Northern Rock for £747 million. The demise of Northern Rock takes a toll on North East England's economy, with the region still in recession and financial sector employment at its lowest levels for over a decade.

2015 Cerberus Capital Management acquires Northern Rock's riskier mortgage assets, which were not acquired by Virgin and had remained under public ownership.

2020 Regional GDP growth remains low, and there are approximately 10,000 fewer jobs in the financial services sector when compared to precrisis levels.

After Northern Rock shares plunged in September 2007, worried savers queued up to withdraw their savings.

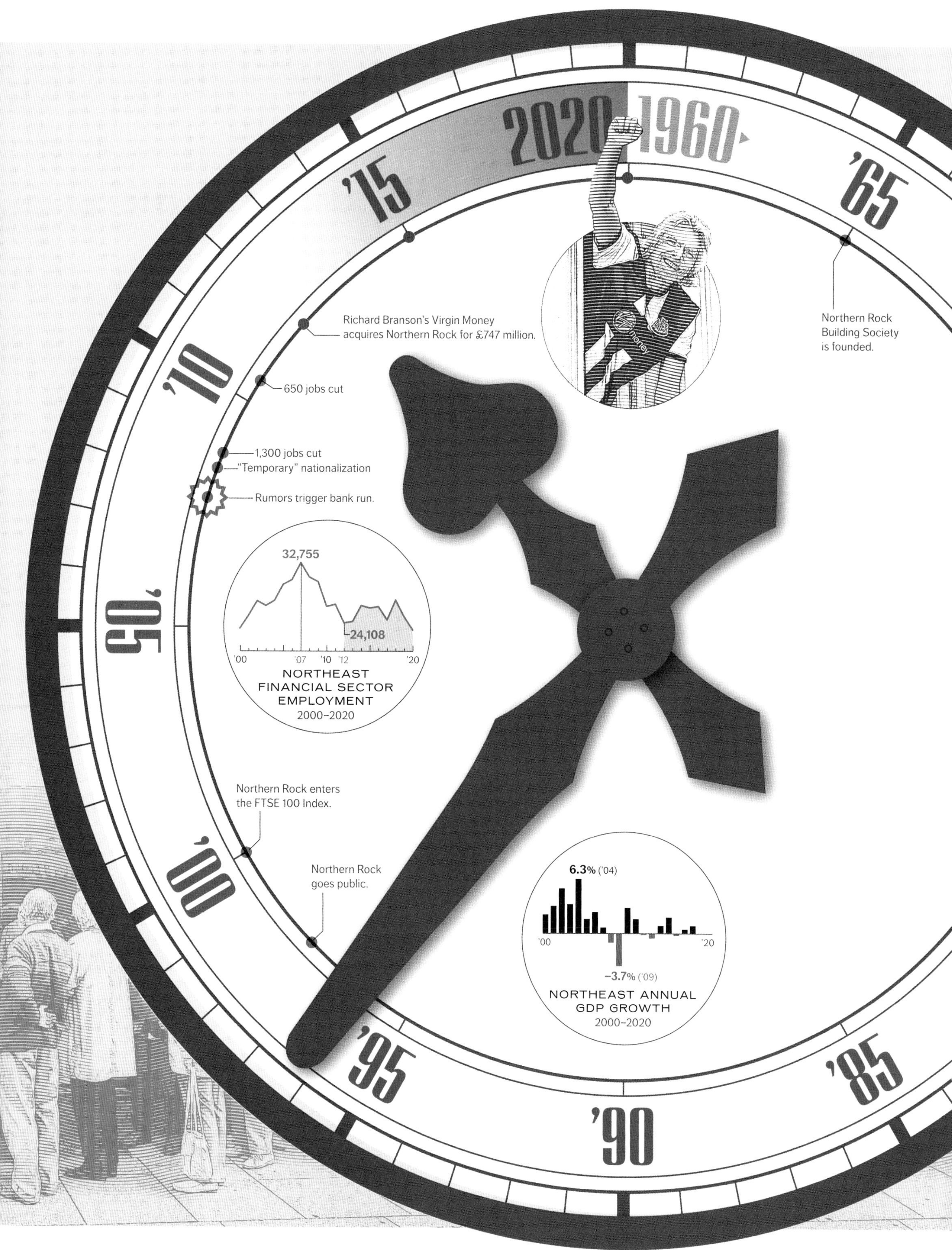
2020
1960
'15
'65
'10
'05
'00
'95
'90
'85
Richard Branson's Virgin Money acquires Northern Rock for £747 million.
Northern Rock Building Society is founded.
650 jobs cut
1,300 jobs cut
"Temporary" nationalization
Rumors trigger bank run.
32,755
24,108
'00
'07
'10
'12
'20
NORTHEAST FINANCIAL SECTOR EMPLOYMENT
2000–2020
Northern Rock enters the FTSE 100 Index.
Northern Rock goes public.
6.3% ('04)
'00
'20
−3.7% ('09)
NORTHEAST ANNUAL GDP GROWTH
2000–2020

When Financial Innovation Blew Up the US Economy

Fueled by soaring house prices and mounting mortgage debt, the US economy crashed in 2007, leading to a geographically uneven recession.

SECURITIZATION is one of the most common practices of financial "innovation." A bank packages a set of loans and sells them to a third party. The advantages for the selling bank are clear: instant profit from the transaction and the removal of credit risk from its own accounts. The receiving party pools together loans of various risk levels from different banks and creates new financial products (securities) backed by loan repayments. The securities are then sold to investors, marketed as safe products underpinned by diversified assets and offering attractive returns.

Securitization gained ground in the US in the 1990s and reached unprecedented heights in the 2000s, predominantly via mortgage loans. Enjoying a lucrative and seemingly safe lending practice, retail banks had a strong incentive to stretch their lending as much as possible. Once they ran out of borrowers with good credit history, they started offering mortgages to lower-income groups, known as subprime borrowers. Investment banks eagerly bought these mortgages to convert them into mortgage-backed securities and sold them to investors at a profit. Meanwhile,

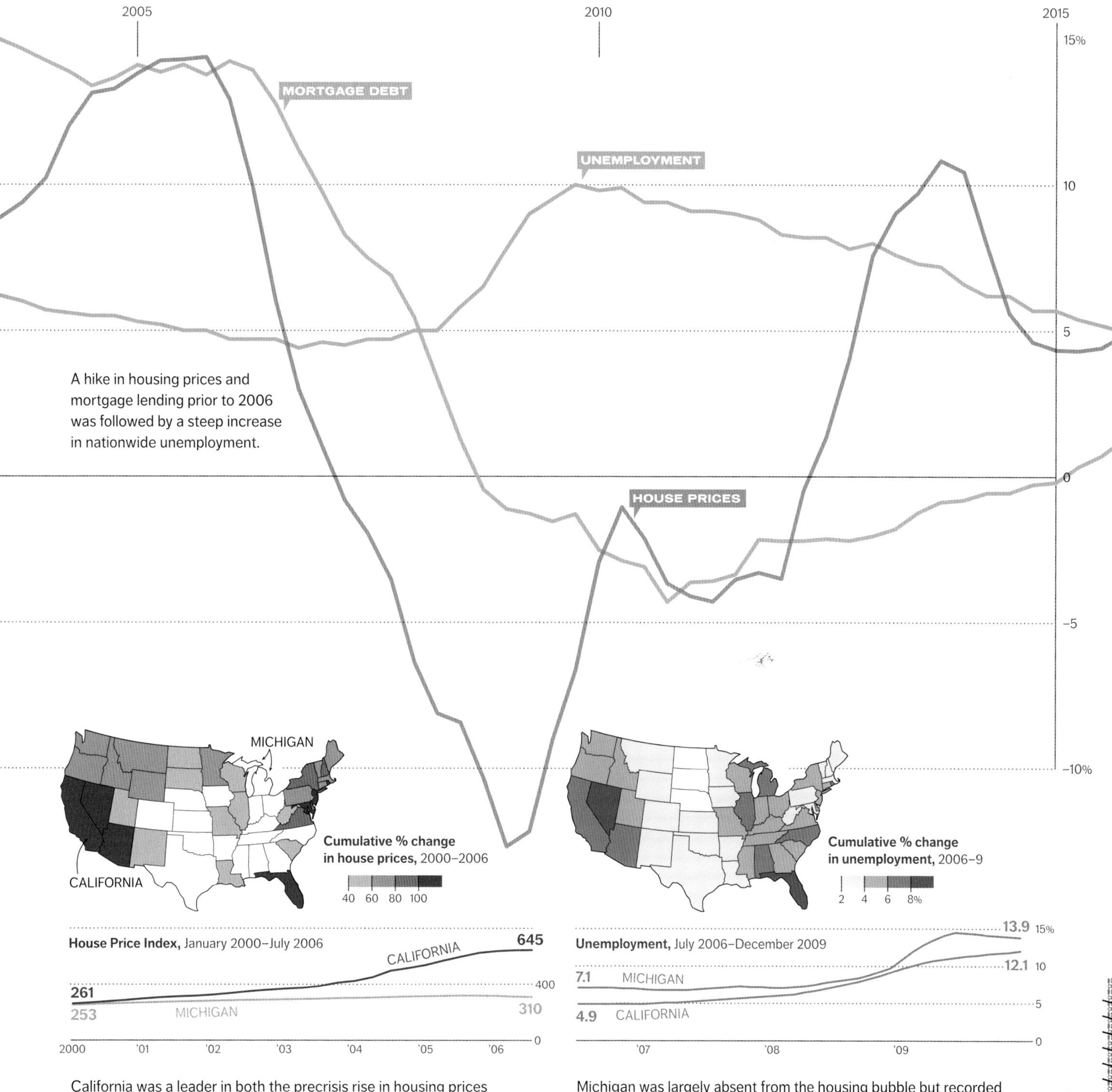

California was a leader in both the precrisis rise in housing prices and the postcrisis jump in unemployment.

Michigan was largely absent from the housing bubble but recorded a steep increase in unemployment once the crisis broke out.

financial regulators in the US relaxed prior banking regulations, such as the separation between retail and investment banking, allowing lending volumes and securitization to grow even further.

Following a decline in house prices in the second half of 2006, a soaring number of low-income borrowers became unable to refinance their loans. The simultaneous outbreak of defaults in many parts of the US shook the confidence in mortgage-backed securities. Pooling large volumes of loans may have been adequate for eliminating the risk of localized defaults, but it did little to tackle the risk of large-scale default across the country. The collapsing value of mortgage-backed securities damaged those who had invested heavily in them, in the US and globally. US banks themselves were among the biggest investors.

As the maps above show, the US subprime crisis spread unevenly throughout the country and contributed to the growing inequality between regions. The next time you hear about the latest financial innovation, buyer beware. In finance, the borderline between innovation and fraud is thin.

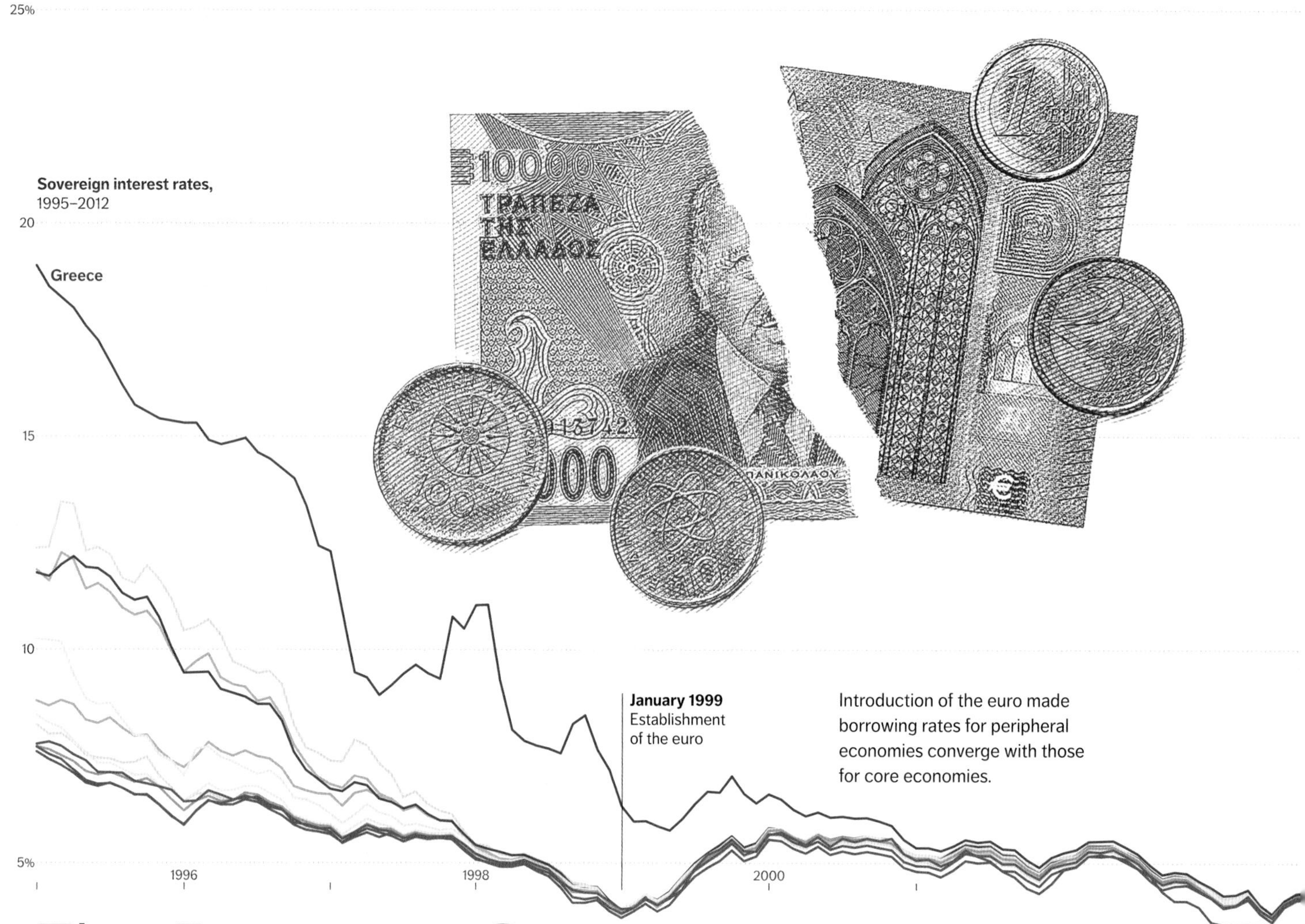

Sovereign interest rates, 1995–2012

25%

20

Greece

15

10

January 1999
Establishment of the euro

Introduction of the euro made borrowing rates for peripheral economies converge with those for core economies.

5%

1996

1998

2000

2002

The Eurozone Crisis

The European crisis of 2010 exposed the divide of the monetary union into a surplus-led core and a debt-led periphery and brought peripheral countries close to bankruptcy.

THE MAJOR IDEA behind the establishment of the European Union (EU) was to create a pan-European market in which member countries would be able to trade freely with one another. The establishment of the eurozone in 1999 pushed integration a step further. The euro allowed the initial participating countries to trade in the same currency. Previously, a Spanish importer of cars from Germany would have to convert Spanish pesetas into deutsche marks, and uncertainty about the exchange rates would impede trade. The euro removed this uncertainty.

The stability introduced by the euro also enabled EU countries with traditionally volatile currencies, such as Greece and Spain, to enjoy significantly lower borrowing costs than before. A French bank, for example, would now charge a lower interest rate for lending to a bank or an enterprise in Greece, given that Greece was no longer using a currency that was at risk of a sudden loss in value.

Faced with lower interest rates, peripheral European countries increased their foreign borrowing, albeit with different sectors in the lead. In Spain and Ireland, for example, borrowing was led by the private sector. In Ireland, mortgage debt alone rose from 32 percent of GDP in 2002 to 61 percent in 2009. In contrast, Greek debt was predominantly driven by the public sector.

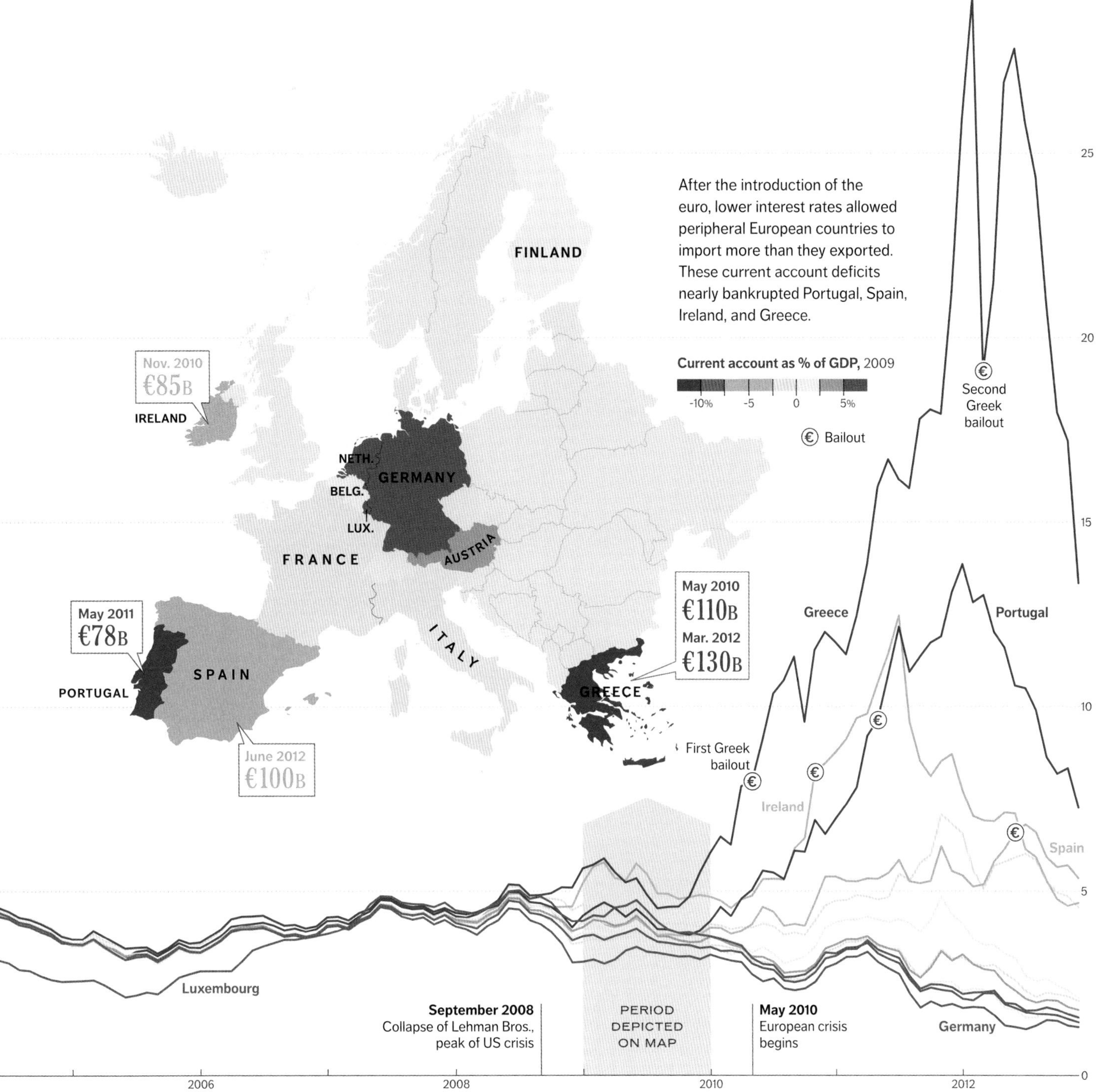

Cheap borrowing enabled these countries to import more than they exported, creating what's known as a current account deficit (see redder countries on the map). Meanwhile, core countries, such as Germany and the Netherlands, experienced sustained trade surpluses (shown in blue).

Over the course of the 2000s, these dynamics furthered the geographical division of the eurozone between core and periphery. Growth in peripheral economies relied on uninterrupted access to credit; that in the core economies depended on exports toward the periphery and, consequently, the continuing indebtedness of the latter.

By 2010, this imbalanced model of growth and interdependence was coming to a halt. Greece, whose fundamental economic indicators were weakest, was the first to face skyrocketing borrowing costs and looming bankruptcy. Other countries of the European periphery followed suit. Between 2010 and 2012, Greece, Spain, Portugal, and Ireland received billions of euros in bailouts from what came to be called the "Troika" (the International Monetary Fund, the European Central Bank, and the European Commission). The eurozone survived, but the structural imbalance between surpluses in the core and deficits in the periphery persists.

Flow of bailout funds, 2010–14
(in billions of euros)

INCOMING

131 **European Financial Stability Facility (EFSF)**

This is the financial assistance vehicle of the eurozone, established in 2010 to handle bailouts for Greece, Ireland, and Portugal. Backed by the European Commission and the European Central Bank, the EFSF funding followed that from individual eurozone countries.

52.9 **Eurozone countries**

32 **International Monetary Fund (IMF)**

Between 2010 and 2014, 215.9 billion euros were lent to Greece, finding their way almost exclusively to creditors rather than to the country's real economy and its society.

Solvency over Solidarity

Designed by the "Troika" with the supposed purpose of supporting Greece through the crisis, bailout funds were actually mostly used for repaying original creditors and rescuing failing banks.

GREECE FOUND ITSELF on the verge of bankruptcy in 2010. In response, the so-called Troika (European Commission, European Central Bank, and International Monetary Fund) designed a bailout package of 110 billion euros, almost half the size of Greece's entire economy (Greece's GDP for that year was €226 billion). The conditionalities attached to this megaloan involved a fire sale of Greek public assets (e.g., electricity and water utilities), structural reforms (e.g., flexibility for firms in hiring and firing), and cuts in public pensions and salaries.

In May 2010 the IMF forecasted a temporary decline of Greek GDP for 2010 and 2011, about 6.5 percent in total (following a decline of 4 percent in 2009), and a robust recovery thereafter. Contrary to these predictions, the bailout conditionalities kept the country close to a state of default, forcing the Troika to issue another megaloan of €130 billion in 2012. By the end of 2013, at the peak of the crisis, Greek GDP losses had accumulated to 29.5 percent in total. In the same year, national unemployment reached 27.5 percent. As the map shows, the crisis was particularly acute in the country's

The Greek crisis of 2010–13 was ten times more severe than the US crisis of 2007–9 in terms of GDP contraction. It was also three times more damaging than the US crisis in terms of unemployment.

most populous regions. In Attica for example, the region that includes Athens, unemployment increased more than fivefold, from 3.3 percent in 2009 to 19.7 percent in 2013.

While the bailouts were conducted in the name of "solidarity with the Greek people," their main purpose was to repay creditors, 70 percent of whom were foreign banks and foreign institutional investors, with French and German banks in the lead. The outgoing arrows above show that 94 percent of the funds loaned to Greece between 2010 and 2014 were ultimately used either to repay the country's original creditors (by repaying maturing debt and interest, debt buy-back, and debt restructuring) or to support failing Greek banks, in many cases also foreign owned. Hardly any of the funds made it to the real economy (orange arrow).

Forgiveness of debts has been practiced since the origins of finance in Mesopotamia but is rarely practiced in modern times. Economists claim a lenient treatment of borrowers by lenders makes the former behave less responsibly and be more likely to default. But how responsible is it for governments to save banks rather than struggling communities?

Toxic Loans

Structured loans have intoxicated hundreds of French municipalities and brought them to the edge of bankruptcy.

FROM SCHOOLS TO TRANSPORT, local governments require capital to finance their activities and investments. They obtain central government funding and collect taxes, but often these are not enough. This makes municipal finance a lucrative market for banks. Loans link the everyday life of a city, town, or village to the unpredictable fate of financial markets, sometimes with disastrous consequences. In the 2010s, no fewer than 1,500 local French governments were in critical condition, as an epidemic of toxic loans contaminated local budgets, from small ski resorts nested in the French Alps, through regions and departments, to major metropolitan councils.

In 2005, the Franco-Belgian bank Dexia started to aggressively market new types of loans structured in sequential tranches: fixed, low interest rates for the first years and variable interest rates thereafter, determined by money markets, including the euro–Swiss franc exchange rate. Should that rate decrease, interest rates would go up (see page 136). At the time, such a scenario seemed unlikely. Scores of local governments across rural and urban areas subscribed to these loans, helping Dexia become a global leader of the municipal bond market, with a 42 percent market share in France. Meanwhile, asymptomatic local budgets had become dependent on international financial market volatility beyond their control.

The situation deteriorated rapidly through a chain reaction. From 2007, the market turmoil of the subprime crisis and the sovereign debt crisis activated the variable-interest-rate virus hidden inside the second tranche. In 2011, toxic local government debt culminated at a total of €18.83 billion across the country. Afflicted by unsustainable debt, infected municipalities took Dexia to court for fraudulent practices. Dexia, hit hard by the financial crisis, was dissolved by the French, Belgian, and Luxembourg governments.

At the local level, the prognosis was grim. Feverish municipalities faced skyrocketing interest rates varying from 12.5 percent to 81 percent, putting vital infrastructure and services such as schools, roads, and waste man agement in jeopardy and leading to budget cuts for cultural and urban renovation projects. Rather than canceling the debts owed to Dexia, the French government decided to renegotiate the terms of the loans with municipalities. Their residents have since experienced the long-lasting financial sequelae of toxic loans, enduring higher local taxes, lack of public investments, and declining quality of local services.

BEFORE

2005

Paris's suburbs

The inner band of suburbs surrounding Paris (Bagnolet, Aubervilliers, Ivry-sur-Seine, and Pantin) were characterized by the early and compulsive use of toxic loans.

Asnières-sur-Seine, Île-de-France

POPULATION: 84,000

In 2012, the mayor of Asnières-sur-Seine announced a debt strike, refusing to pay the interest generated by the new rate: "Otherwise, it means no more staff in schools and no more daycare centers."

Lyon, Auvergne-Rhône-Alpes

POPULATION: 1.3 MILLION

The city council, the department, the social housing syndicate, the syndicate for public transport, and the public and university hospitals—nearly all layers of public services and local government were contaminated with a total of €570 million in toxic debt.

Saint-Étienne, Auvergne-Rhône-Alpes

POPULATION: 173,000

With fifteen toxic loans, Saint-Étienne, one of the most indebted cities in France, was on the front line of the legal cases. The last toxic loan was settled in 2021. The toxic loan crisis cost a total of €40 million for the city and its taxpayers, with a 3 percent increase in local taxes.

Turn the page to see the spread of the variable-interest-rate virus.

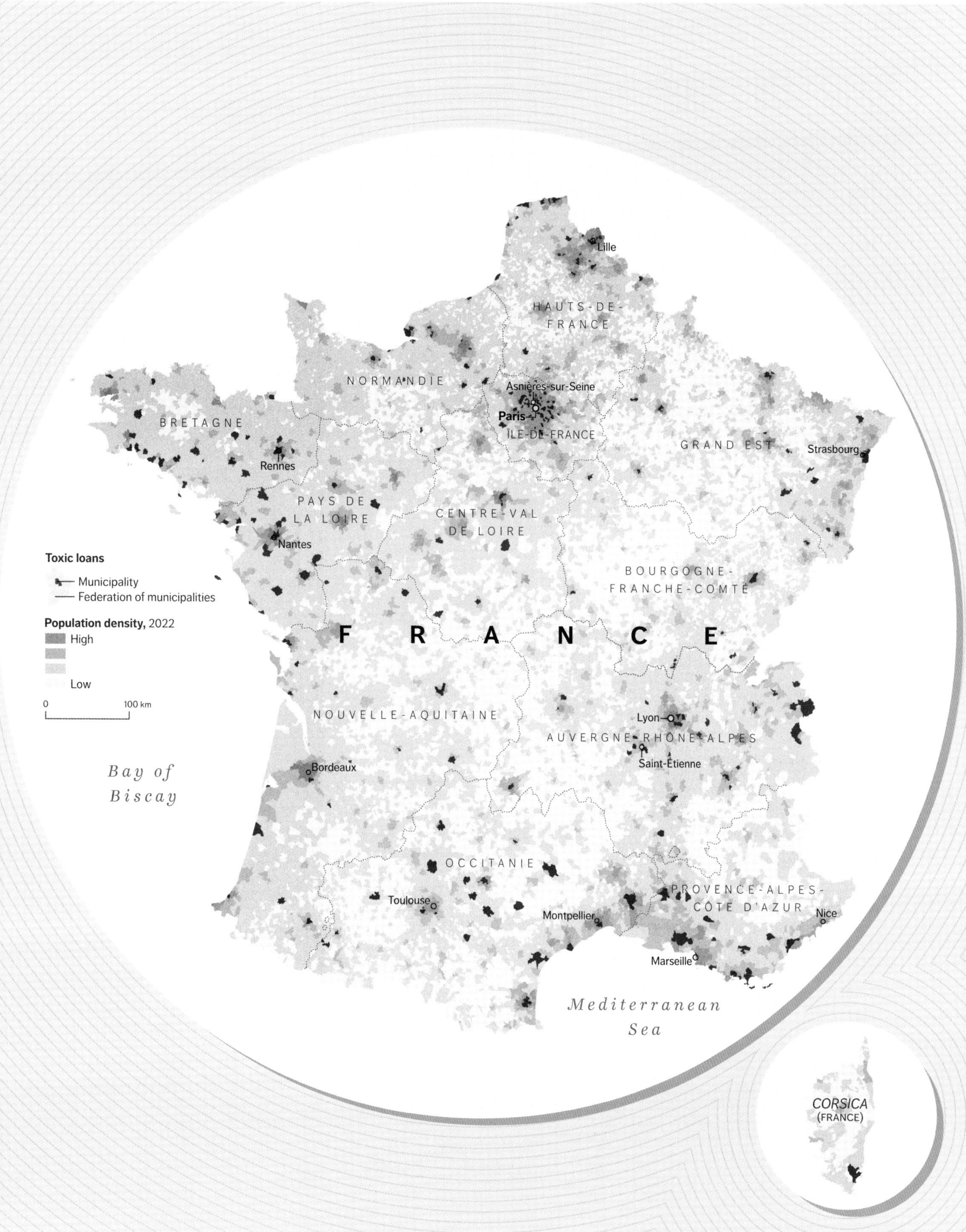
Lille
HAUTS-DE-FRANCE
NORMANDIE
Asnières-sur-Seine
Paris
ÎLE-DE-FRANCE
BRETAGNE
Rennes
GRAND EST
Strasbourg
PAYS DE LA LOIRE
CENTRE-VAL DE LOIRE
Nantes
Toxic loans
Municipality
Federation of municipalities
BOURGOGNE-FRANCHE-COMTÉ
Population density, 2022
High
Low
F R A N C E
0
100 km
NOUVELLE-AQUITAINE
Lyon
AUVERGNE-RHÔNE-ALPES
Saint-Étienne
Bay of Biscay
Bordeaux
OCCITANIE
PROVENCE-ALPES-CÔTE D'AZUR
Toulouse
Montpellier
Nice
Marseille
Mediterranean Sea
CORSICA (FRANCE)

Signs of Infection

A Political Pattern

Many local government officials behaved opportunistically, taking potentially toxic loans to announce new investments before elections. Small municipalities often lacked the expertise to understand the risk associated with the loans.

Number of new municipal authorities with toxic loans, 1995–2011

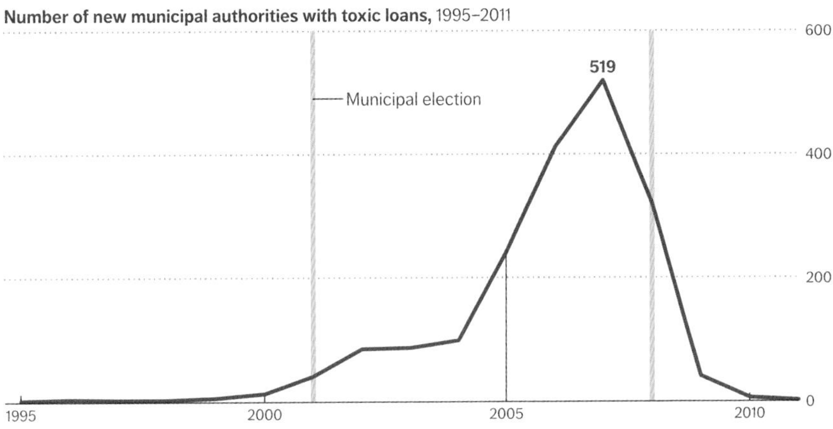

A Formula for Disaster

According to the loan formula and contract, as long as the euro–Swiss franc exchange rate remains above 1.44, total interest due remains the same. Below that exchange rate, interest rate rises proportionally, increasing the debt burden.

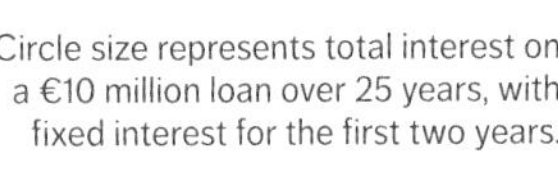
Circle size represents total interest on a €10 million loan over 25 years, with fixed interest for the first two years.

Loan interest rate vs. euro–Swiss franc exchange rate

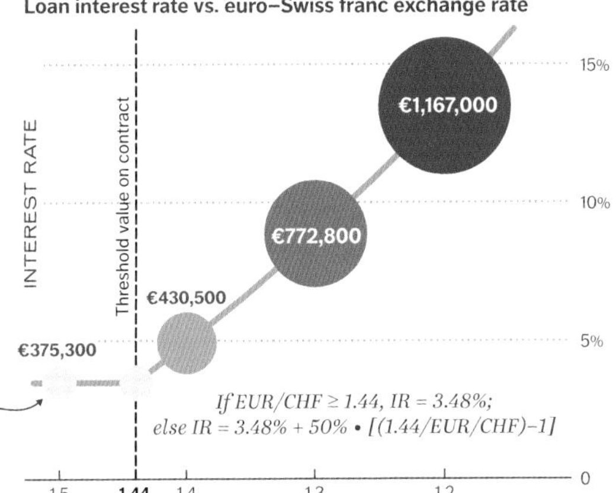

An Unprecedented Crash

The US subprime crisis and subsequent eurozone crisis caused an appreciation of the Swiss franc. Following the Swiss Central Bank's decision to cancel the floor rate in 2015, additional interest costs for French local entities surged by a total of €2 billion.

Euro–Swiss franc exchange rate, 1999–2022

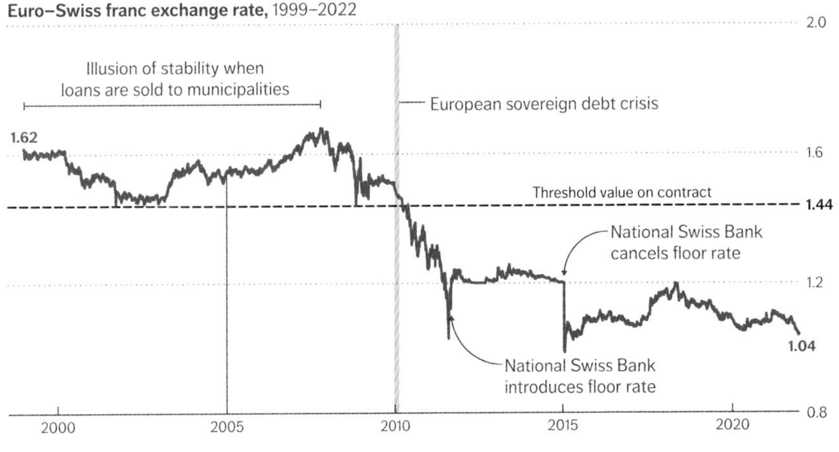

AFTER

2005

Trégastel, Bretagne

POPULATION: 2,400

With two toxic loans taken in 2007, the town had to pay €290,000 in additional interest in 2011. A down-town renovation project and the repair of 30 km of roads were postponed. The budget for festivals and children's holiday activities was reduced from €40,000 to zero. The local librarian was replaced by volunteers. "I was not elected to raise taxes and to have those taxes go directly into banks," declared the mayor in 2012.

Saint-Cast-le-Guildo, Bretagne

POPULATION: 3,200

The twenty-four-year loan obtained in 2009 offered a one-year fixed interest rate of 3.99%, with annual interest totaling €147,000. In 2011, the rate went up to 14.5% and annual interest to €523,000. The municipality interrupted the renovation of its waste-treatment basin and froze urban projects for youth.

Angoulême, Nouvelle-Aquitaine

POPULATION: 41,000

The city took three loans in 2006–7. Additional interest costs rose by nearly €1 million in 2011, delaying all urban renovation projects. As a municipal employee confessed to the press, "The first thing people do when arriving in the morning is to check rates on the internet."

Dax, Nouvelle-Aquitaine

POPULATION: 21,000

When facing escalating interest on a loan taken in 2007, the city increased local taxes in 2015, did not replace retiring civil servants, and offered fewer summer jobs.

Sassenage, Auvergne-Rhône-Alpes

POPULATION: 11,000

In August 2012, the interest rate for a €4 million loan from 2007 escalated to 23.49%, seven times the original rate. The mayor refused to pay the €636,000 of interest due to Dexia and took the bank to court. Despite a long fight, the city eventually lost the legal battle in 2021.

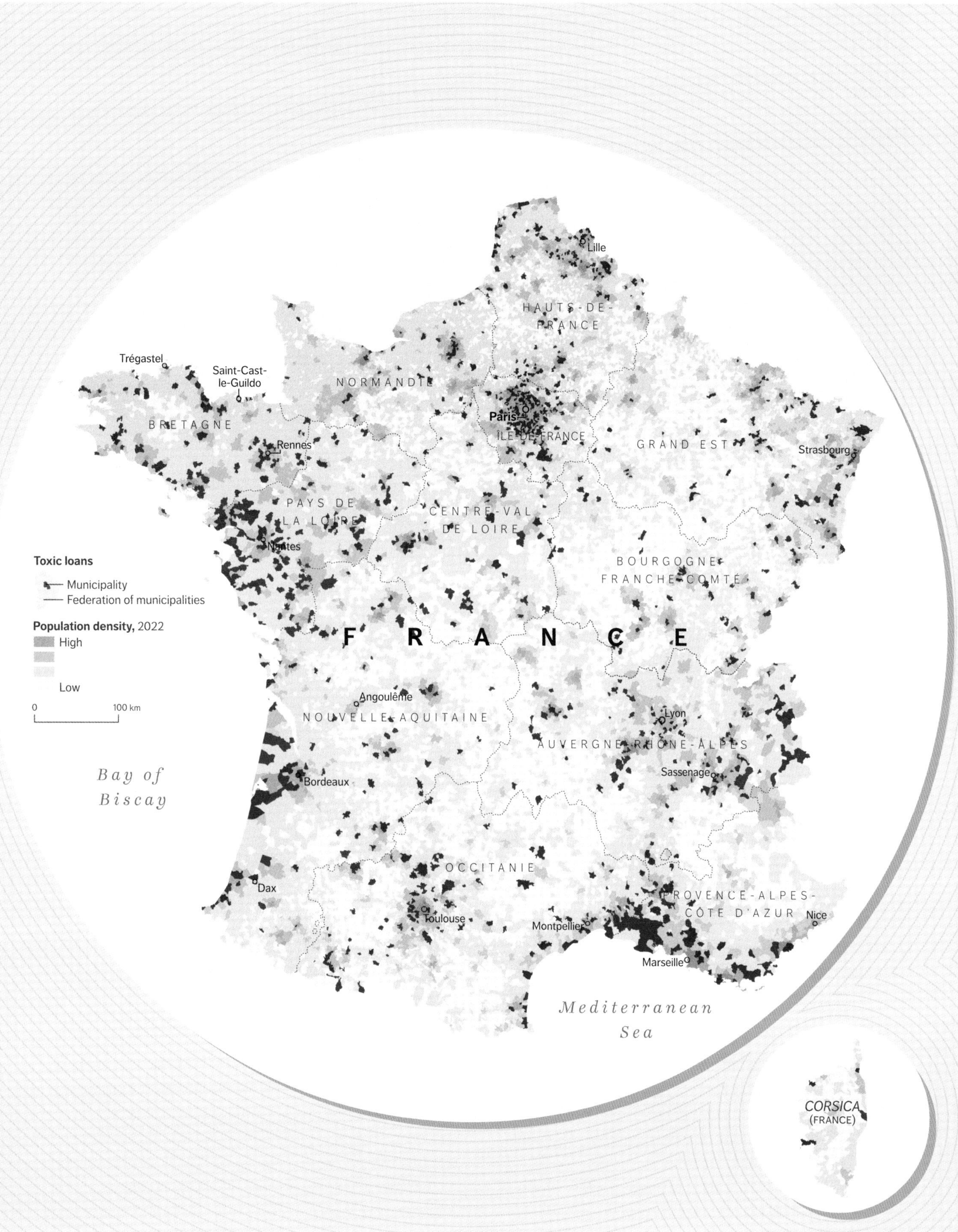
Toxic loans
Municipality
Federation of municipalities
Population density, 2022
High
Low
0
100 km
FRANCE
Lille
HAUTS-DE-FRANCE
NORMANDIE
Trégastel
Saint-Cast-le-Guildo
BRETAGNE
Rennes
Paris
ÎLE-DE-FRANCE
GRAND EST
Strasbourg
PAYS DE LA LOIRE
CENTRE-VAL DE LOIRE
Nantes
BOURGOGNE-FRANCHE-COMTÉ
Angoulême
NOUVELLE-AQUITAINE
Lyon
AUVERGNE-RHÔNE-ALPES
Sassenage
Bay of Biscay
Bordeaux
OCCITANIE
Dax
Toulouse
Montpellier
PROVENCE-ALPES-CÔTE D'AZUR
Nice
Marseille
Mediterranean Sea
CORSICA (FRANCE)

A Holiday Heist To hide their theft, the hackers made clever use of national holidays, which delayed communication between banks.

THE HACK
For months the hackers have been lurking inside the Bank of Bangladesh's network, patiently watching from their servers in Cairo. On Thursday, February 4, 2016, they launch their attack, sending thirty-five SWIFT transfer orders from the bank totaling US$951 million.

THE TRANSFERS
The SWIFT network routes these transfers through the Federal Reserve Bank of New York, as there is no direct link between the Bank of Bangladesh and the hacker-controlled accounts. Thirty orders are blocked automatically because they contain *Jupiter*, the name of a Greek shipping company under US sanctions.

THE PURSUIT
The five remaining transactions for over $101 million are processed automatically overnight with SWIFT routing them via another round of intermediary banks. On Friday, the Fed notices the number of unusually large, blocked requests and tries to contact the Bank of Bangladesh, but no one responds as it is a national bank holiday in Bangladesh. Later, Deutsche Bank blocks one transfer due to a typo, but $81 million lands in hacker-controlled RCBC bank accounts in the Philippines. By Monday, the Bank of Bangladesh is trying to recover the missing money, but due to the Chinese New Year holiday, RCBC acts too slowly to freeze the accounts.

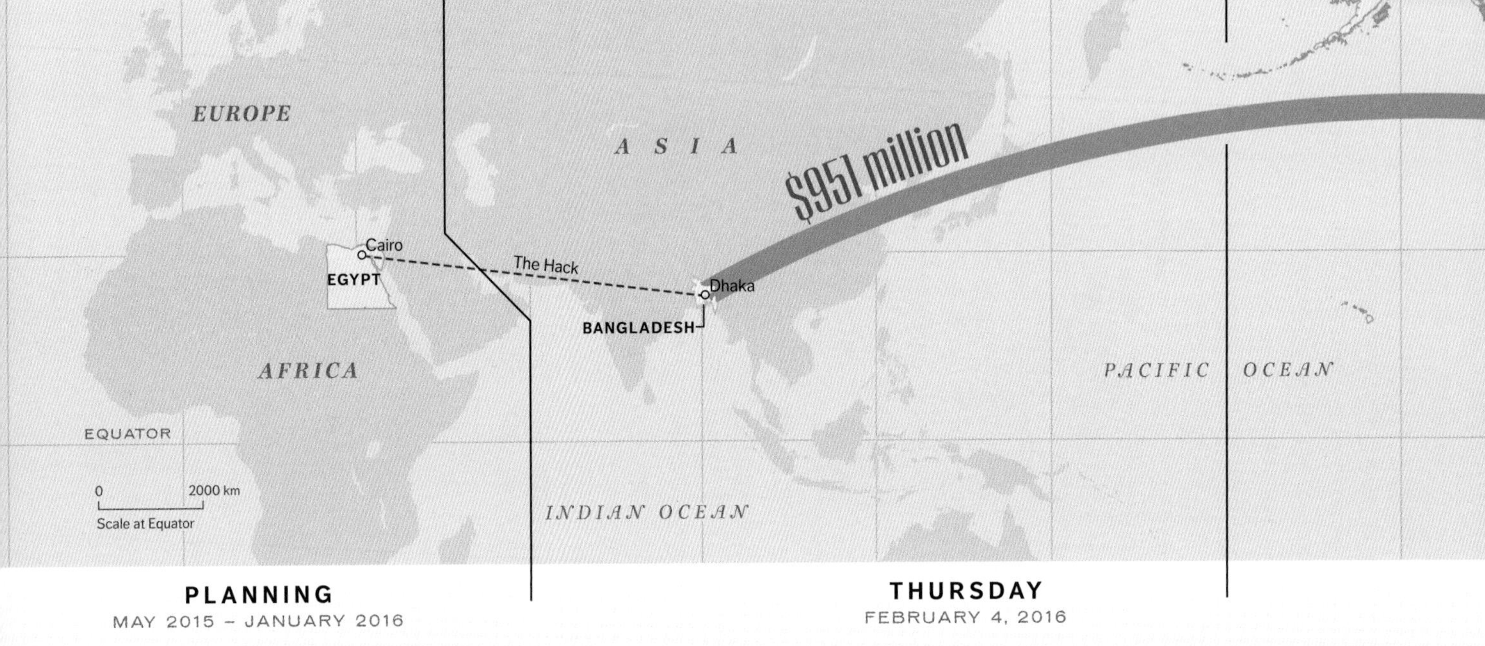

How to Rob a Bank

The theft of US$81 million makes the Bangladesh Bank robbery one of the biggest heists of all time, but the hackers behind it could have made off with far more if it wasn't for a few simple mistakes.

SWIFT CODES
BANK OF BANGLADESH
BBHOBDDHXXX
FEDERAL RESERVE BANK OF NEW YORK
FRNYUS33FX1

A MODERN BANK HEIST doesn't involve guns, safes, and hostages. It's all about breaking into computer networks and getting the money out before it's locked down. In 2016 a group of hackers gained access to the Central Bank of Bangladesh's network and monitored its day-to-day operations from servers in Cairo for months while planning the world's most ambitious heist.

Understanding how this heist worked requires understanding the plumbing of international banking. The main pipes are the SWIFT network, a cooperative headquartered in Brussels that has facilitated international transfers between banks for over fifty years. Billions of messages zip across the network every year. What the hackers realized was that banks only transfer money directly if they have a current account with each other. Many banks only have such relationships with banks in a few other countries and therefore rely on passing money via SWIFT until it reaches its ultimate destination. Known as "correspondence banking," this chain of international accounts is how money moves across borders. By using SWIFT and taking advantage

THE GETAWAY
As soon as the funds reach mysterious RCBC accounts in Manila, casino junket operators—working with the hackers—launder them through Filipino casinos during the Chinese New Year celebrations, one of the busiest gambling days of the year.

Transaction flows, February 4–13, 2016

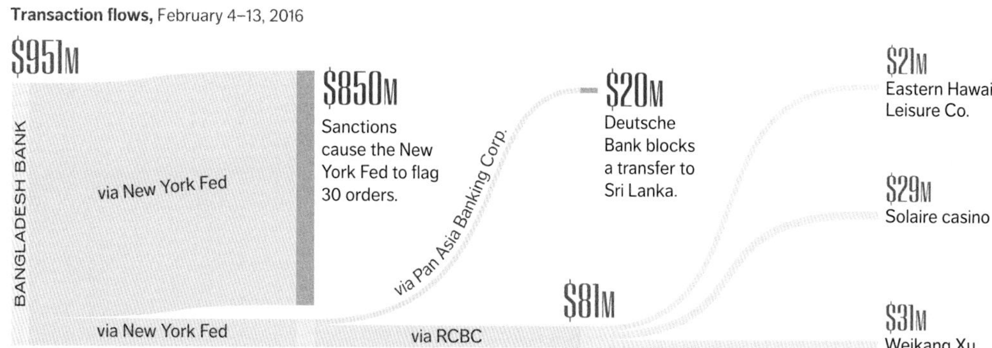

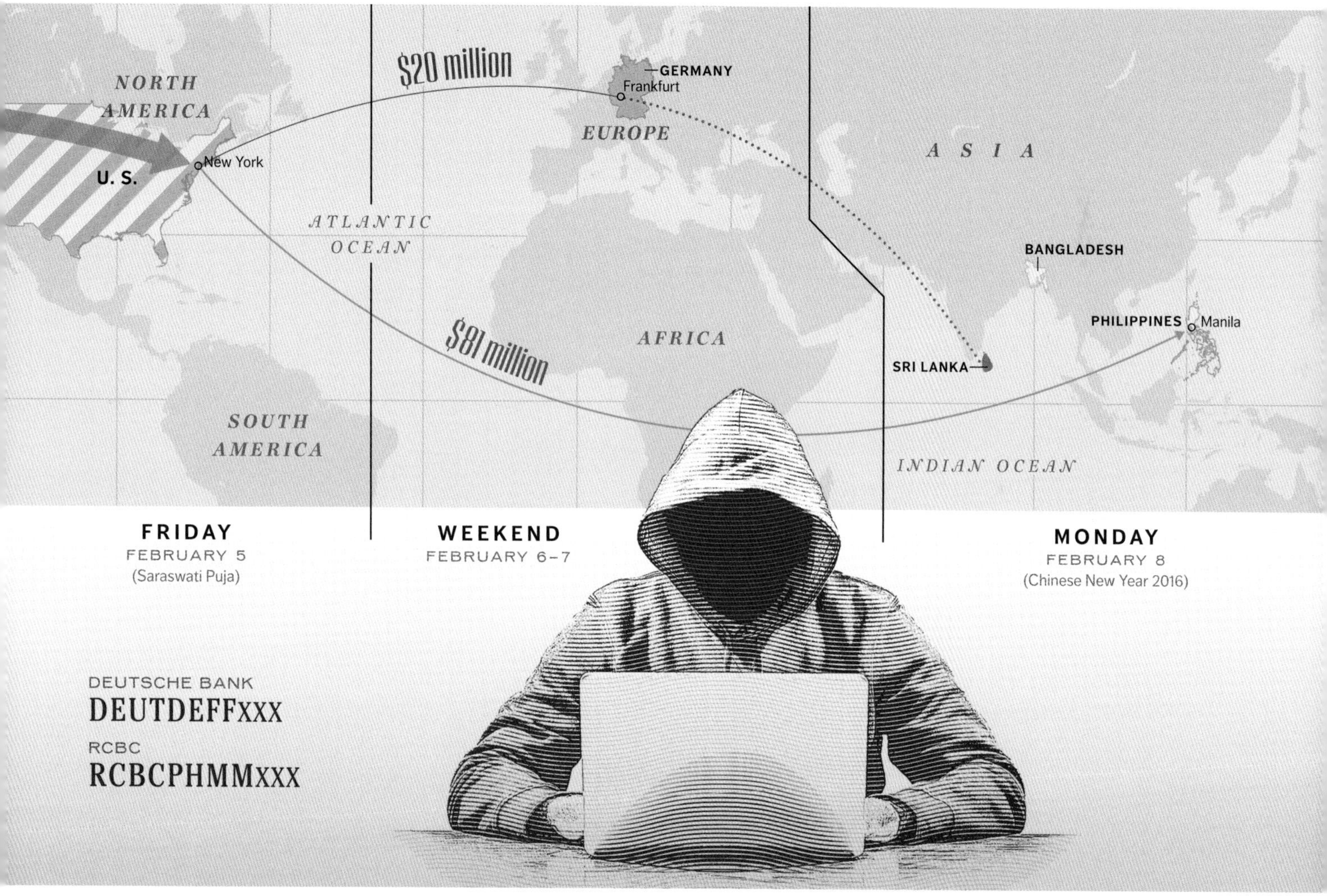

of national holidays and weekends, the hackers could withdraw the money before the banks could catch them.

Crucially, and to the hackers' advantage, the SWIFT network is based on a system of trust. Security protocols and decades of reliable performance mean that banks in the network trust each other. It was only the bad luck of a single typo and having a target bank account that shared the word *Jupiter* with a company under sanctions that stopped the hackers from making off with nearly one billion US dollars.

Who was behind the hack? The hackers' identities have never been fully confirmed, although there is widespread suspicion that a North Korean hacking group was responsible. The only person to be prosecuted for the heist was an RCBC branch manager, Maia Santos-Deguito, who was convicted on eight counts of money laundering for facilitating a very swift withdrawal of the stolen money.

Cybercrime in finance is bound to happen whenever hackers get ahead of cybersecurity specialists. At worst it may even be the source of a future global financial crisis.

Unexpected things happen more often than those you hope for.
PLAUTUS

Regulation & Governance

To limit its destructive potential, finance must be, and is, heavily regulated, with central banks and international organizations leading the charge. Regulation, however, tends to react to problems rather than prevent them. It is also shaped heavily by the legacies of colonialism, which concentrate financial regulatory power in rich countries and places like London, New York, and Washington. The governance of global finance is dominated by white males, with little democratic scrutiny.

Warning Signs

Financial risk management and its regulation have made progress, but they cannot address the fundamental uncertainty prevalent in increasingly complex financial markets.

FINANCIAL ASSETS come in many forms: a house, a pension fund account, or just physical cash in one's pocket. All are subject to risk. House prices can fall, pension fund investments can lose value, and inflation can make cash worthless. One is well advised to consider these risks before investing. The same applies to financial institutions with large and complex portfolios of bonds, stocks, and derivatives. To manage financial risks, we first need to be able to measure them.

One method is to calculate a worst-case scenario. Value-at-risk (VaR) is the worst loss that can happen under normal market conditions over a specified time horizon and at a specified confidence level. For example, a one-day VaR of US$50 million at the 95 percent confidence level means that a firm expects to lose more than $50 million on only one out of twenty trading days. Firms use VaR to estimate how large their financial reserves need to be to protect against these losses. In practice, VaR is estimated using combinations of historical data, mathematical models, and computer simulations.

Invented in 1993, VaR was intended as a practical indicator for companies to communicate risk but quickly became widespread and was endorsed by regulators. In 1996, the Basel Committee on Banking Supervision, located at the Bank for International Settlements in Switzerland, required commercial banks globally to base their reserves on an estimated ten-day VaR at the 99 percent confidence level. The main drawback of the VaR formula, however, is that it neglects high-impact, low-probability events. In other words, it does not account for what happens in abnormal market conditions. VaR calculations do not consider whether the worst possible outcome, outside the 99 percent probability range, would be just slightly worse than the VaR or catastrophic.

Many financial firms have collapsed despite measuring and managing financial risk and creating reserves based on VaR. So after the 2008 global financial crisis, expected shortfall (ES) began to replace VaR as the new standard for regulation. ES focuses on calculating the expected loss if VaR is exceeded. The scarcity of data on extreme events, however, makes ES difficult to calculate. Whatever data, models, and technologies are used, we can be sure that uncertainty will continue to defy attempts to manage financial risks. As the scale and complexity of global finance grows, so will the shock and reach of financial crises.

Vital Events in Regulation and Deregulation

1973 The US takes the dollar off the gold standard; other currencies follow. Exchange rates are henceforth determined by fluctuating and volatile markets.

1974 Basel Committee on Banking Supervision (BCBS) is established.

1980 The US Securities and Exchanges Commission upgrades capital requirements due to exchange rate volatility. These are based on what is essentially a **value-at-risk**, as they require firms to hold enough capital to cover, with 95 percent confidence, losses that might be incurred during the time it would take to liquidate a troubled securities firm, assumed as thirty days.

1988 BCBS implements Basel I, a set of rules with a minimum ratio of capital to risk-weighted assets of 8 percent.

1993 J.P. Morgan researcher Till Guldimann publishes the first known use of the term *value-at-risk* in a report on derivatives.

1996 BCBS amends Basel I to include a VaR requirement. Daily 99 percent VaR is now the standard for credit-related risk. Banks are advised to do their own calculations, with regulators checking them.

1999 The mathematician-engineer duo of Stanislav Uryasev and Tyrrell Rockafellar introduce conditional VaR, later called **expected shortfall,** in a scientific paper.

2009 BCBS introduces stressed VaR, a VaR calculation that uses a stressed historical period, similar to the way ES focuses on worst-case scenarios.

2013 In Basel III, the BCBS replaces the 99% VaR with an ES with a 97.5% confidence interval.

2017 Basel IV requires banks to hold even more capital to cover larger losses.

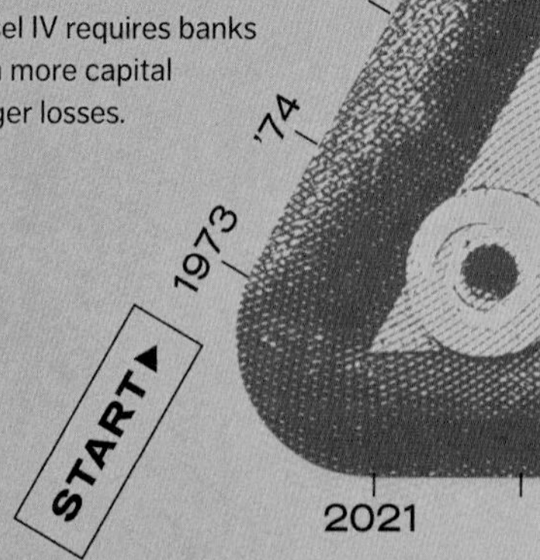

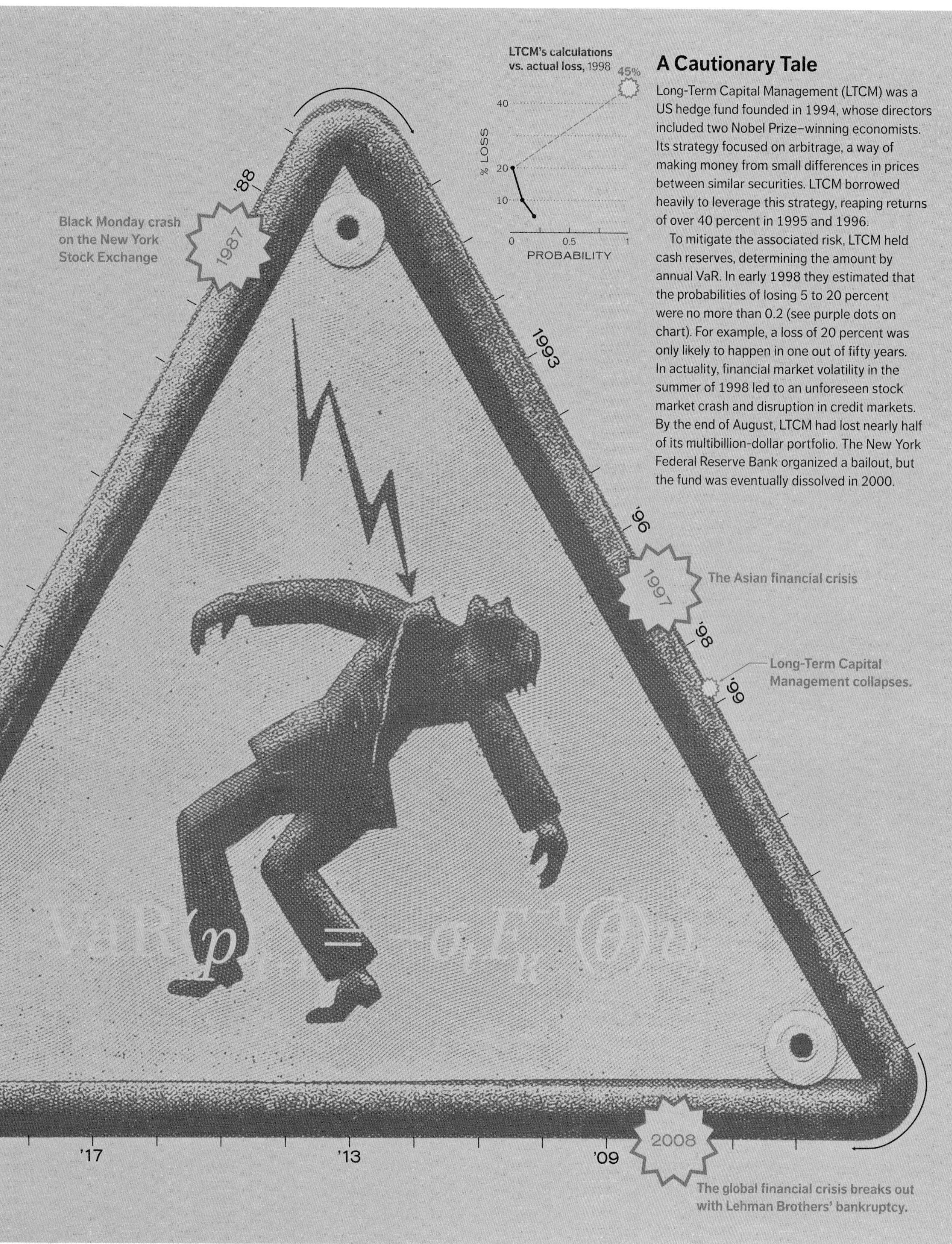

A Cautionary Tale

Long-Term Capital Management (LTCM) was a US hedge fund founded in 1994, whose directors included two Nobel Prize–winning economists. Its strategy focused on arbitrage, a way of making money from small differences in prices between similar securities. LTCM borrowed heavily to leverage this strategy, reaping returns of over 40 percent in 1995 and 1996.

To mitigate the associated risk, LTCM held cash reserves, determining the amount by annual VaR. In early 1998 they estimated that the probabilities of losing 5 to 20 percent were no more than 0.2 (see purple dots on chart). For example, a loss of 20 percent was only likely to happen in one out of fifty years. In actuality, financial market volatility in the summer of 1998 led to an unforeseen stock market crash and disruption in credit markets. By the end of August, LTCM had lost nearly half of its multibillion-dollar portfolio. The New York Federal Reserve Bank organized a bailout, but the fund was eventually dissolved in 2000.

[G]local Governance

Despite what their names imply, the International Monetary Fund and the World Bank are in effect governed by the world's wealthiest nations, most notably the United States.

THE INTERNATIONAL MONETARY FUND (IMF) and the World Bank are the closest the world has to institutions of global financial governance. Both were born out of the post–World War II political and economic arrangement, and both are headquartered in Washington, DC, a short walk from the White House and other buildings of the US federal government. According to the IMF's website, its mission is to promote international financial stability and monetary cooperation and to facilitate trade and employment. Likewise, the World Bank strives to end extreme poverty and promote shared prosperity.

Currently, both institutions count close to 190 members, from large countries, such as the US and China, to smaller ones, like Tuvalu and Palau. The condition for joining the World Bank is prior membership in the IMF.

Both the IMF and the World Bank portray themselves as accountable to their members. This might give the impression that member states all have an equal voice (one country, one vote), similar in logic to the US Senate, or a proportionate voice, based on population size, as in the US House of Representatives. In truth, IMF and World Bank voting rights are adjusted, predominantly based on economic size. This means that rich countries are overrepresented relative to their shares of the global population. The slope-graphs to the right reveal these imbalances. Inclines indicate countries with more sway than population share; declines indicate those with less.

By design, the US has always been the most influential member in both the IMF and the World Bank. At the end of 2021, it held 16.51 percent of total IMF votes, more than three times its population share (4.48 percent). This means that the US can block any major changes in the fund's Articles of Agreement, which require 85 percent of votes for approval.

While the voices of large developing countries have strengthened in recent years, representation elsewhere in the world remains uneven. China's voting share in the fund is 6.08 percent, about a third of its population share (18.91 percent). Even more extreme is India's underrepresentation, with a voting share less than a sixth of its share in population (2.63 percent vs. 17.57 percent, respectively). Or consider Africa. The voting share of the entire continent is 6.2 percent, comparable to Germany's 5.32 percent despite representing more than a billion more people. An update of global financial governance is long overdue.

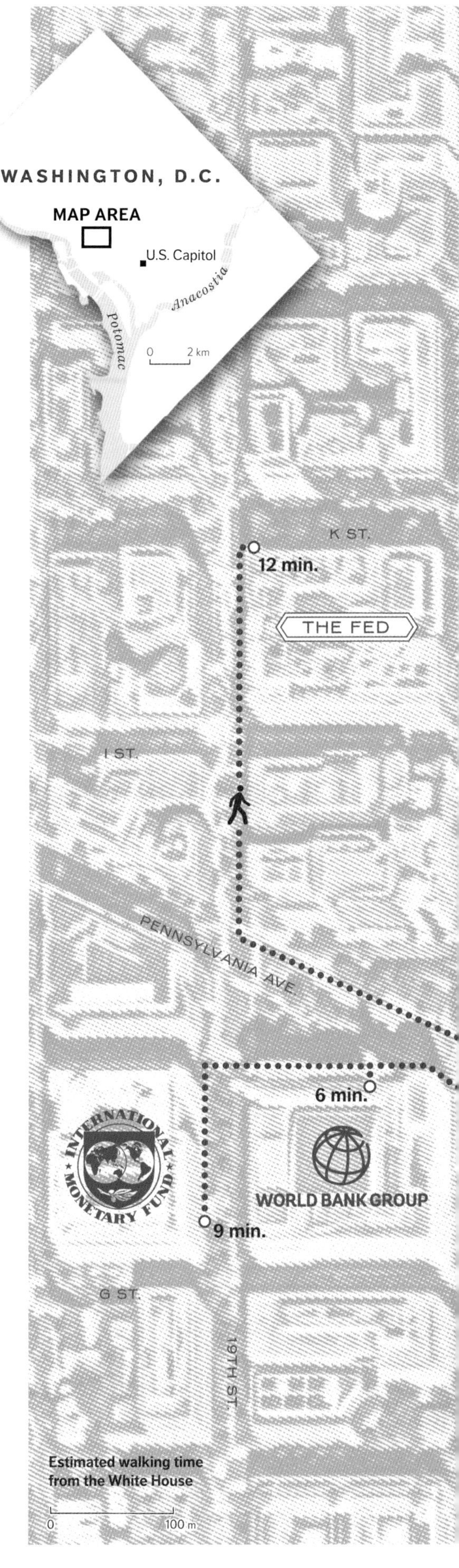

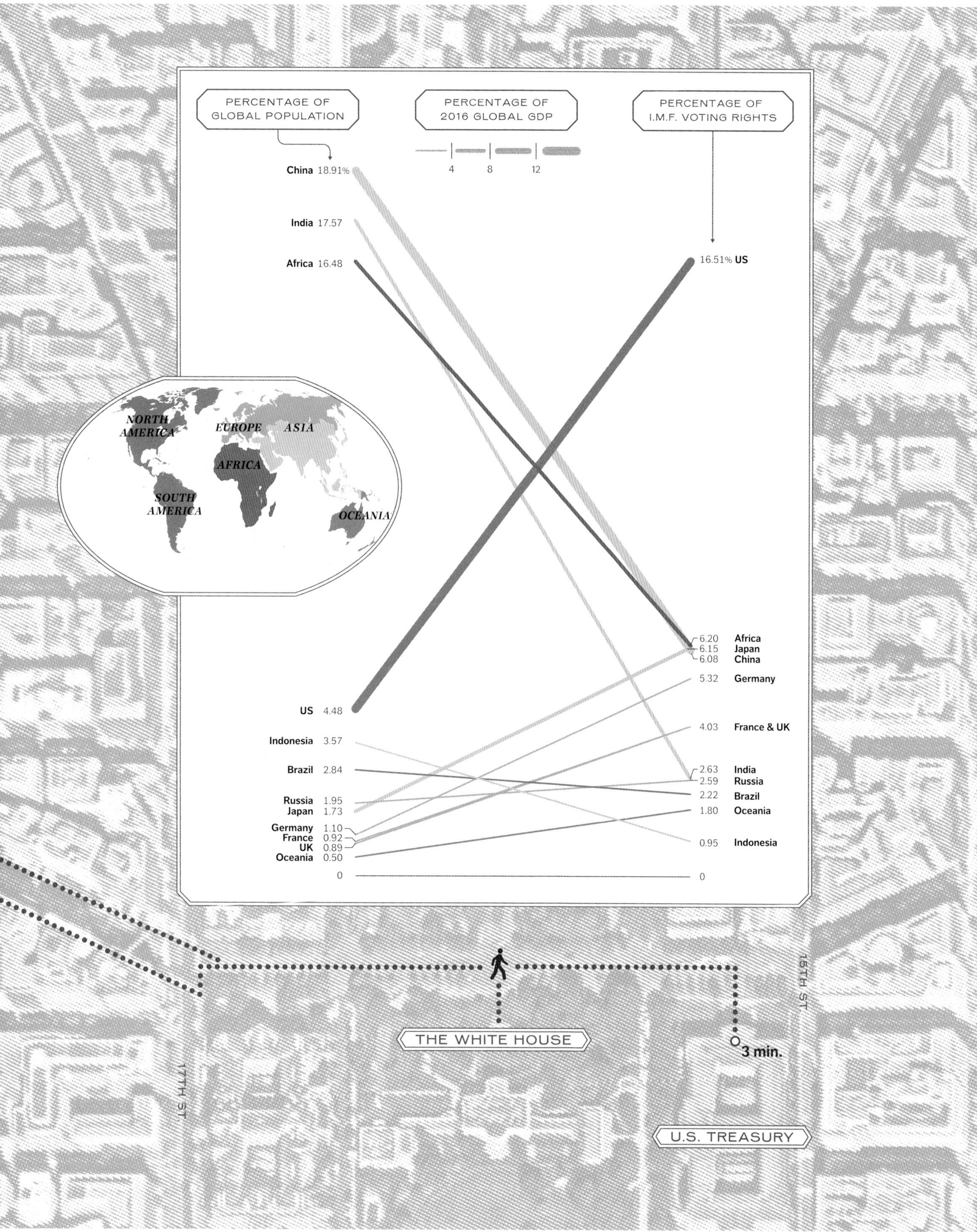
PERCENTAGE OF GLOBAL POPULATION
PERCENTAGE OF 2016 GLOBAL GDP
PERCENTAGE OF I.M.F. VOTING RIGHTS
4
8
12
China 18.91%
India 17.57
Africa 16.48
US 4.48
Indonesia 3.57
Brazil 2.84
Russia 1.95
Japan 1.73
Germany 1.10
France 0.92
UK 0.89
Oceania 0.50
0
16.51% US
6.20 Africa
6.15 Japan
6.08 China
5.32 Germany
4.03 France & UK
2.63 India
2.59 Russia
2.22 Brazil
1.80 Oceania
0.95 Indonesia
0
NORTH AMERICA
EUROPE
ASIA
AFRICA
SOUTH AMERICA
OCEANIA
THE WHITE HOUSE
3 min.
15TH ST.
17TH ST.
U.S. TREASURY

Banks of Banks

Central banking, key to the functioning of modern economies, is a product of the historical and geographical context.

CENTRAL BANKS are the pillars of economic governance. Each country has one. They provide official currency to the economy, lend money to the government, set interest rates, manage foreign exchange and gold reserves, supervise banks, and control inflation. In the US, for example, the central bank is also mandated to maximize employment.

The first banking institutions with official status as lenders of the local government emerged in the early fifteenth century in Barcelona and Genoa. One could describe them as proto-central banks. At the national level, the first central bank was established in Sweden in 1668, followed by England, Spain, and France. Many central banks, like

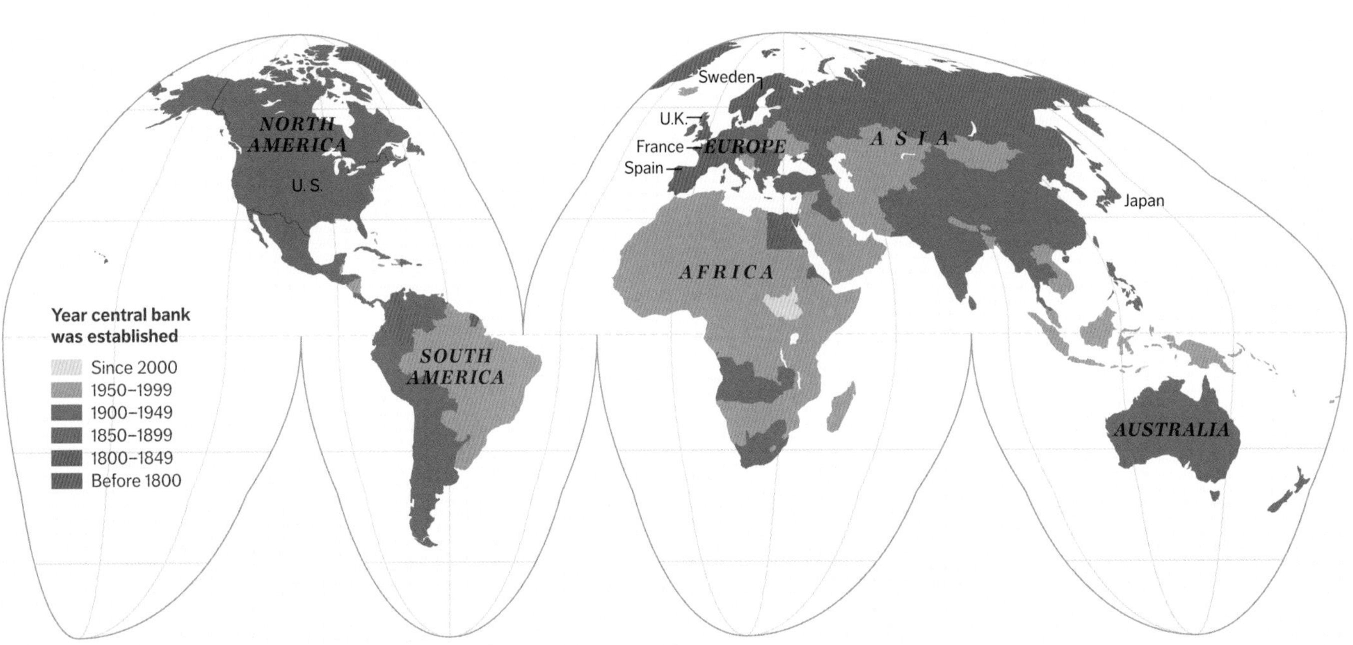

Number of central banks established per decade

1401
The *Taula de canvi,* or "table of change," in Barcelona becomes the first bank to function as the official lender of a government. Genoa's Casa di San Giorgio follows in 1404.

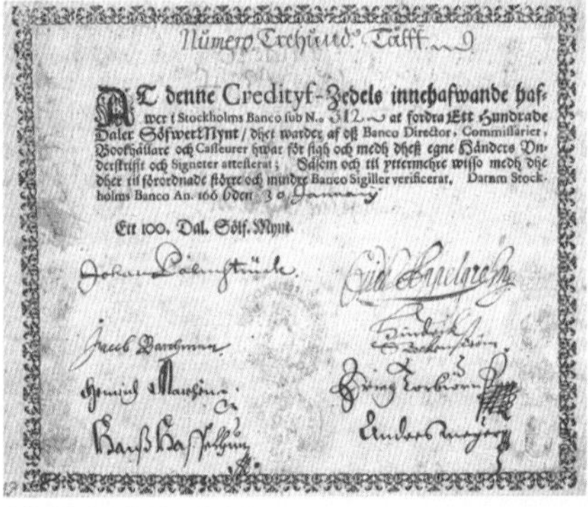

1666
Stockholms Banco prints the first banknote in Europe (left). Two years later, the bank is folded into the world's first central bank: Riksens Ständers Bank, which means "Bank of the Parliament."

1694
In the midst of King William III's war with France, the Bank of England becomes the official lender of the English government.

Sweden England

1400 1500 1600 1700

those in France and England, were originally established as private banks and nationalized later.

The genesis of central banks and their subsequently expanding functions had more to do with historical and geographical context than any economic theory. The Bank of England was founded during King William III's war with France. The US Federal Reserve was founded in 1913 as a response to a series of financial panics in preceding years and as a means to curtail the power of private bankers. Following World War II, a wave of new central banks came along as colonies gained independence and the Soviet Union collapsed (see timeline). In 1999, the European Central Bank was founded as the next step of European integration, introducing the euro as the common currency for eleven European economies.

The biggest central banking invention of the twenty-first century to date is quantitative easing (QE), whereby a central bank injects money directly into the financial system by buying bonds and other assets from banks and financial institutions in order to increase the amount of money available for lending and investment. QE was used on a massive scale in response to the US subprime and eurozone crises as well as the COVID-19 pandemic (see line chart), raising the power of central banks to new heights.

Bank of England logo

1800
By Napoleon's decree, Banque de France is formed from a coalition of French bankers.

1844
The Bank of England Act grants the bank exclusive right to issue banknotes and to regulate England's banking system, thus turning the bank into the first central bank in the contemporary sense of the term.

1889
In one of the first instances of rescuing a "too-big-to-fail" bank, Banque de France bails out Comptoir d'Escompte, one of the largest banks in France at the time. The rescue effort also guarantees deposits and restructures the bank, while judges impose heavy fines on the failing bank's board members.

1913
The US establishes the Federal Reserve as the lender of last resort for commercial banks, following a series of financial panics.

Post–World War II
Dozens of central banks are founded in the decades after the Second World War, as colonies gain independence and the Soviet Union eventually collapses.

1990
The Bank of New Zealand becomes the first to implement "inflation targeting," a monetary policy designed to achieve a specific rate of price inflation.

1999
Eleven member states of the European Union agree to replace their national currencies with a common currency, the euro.

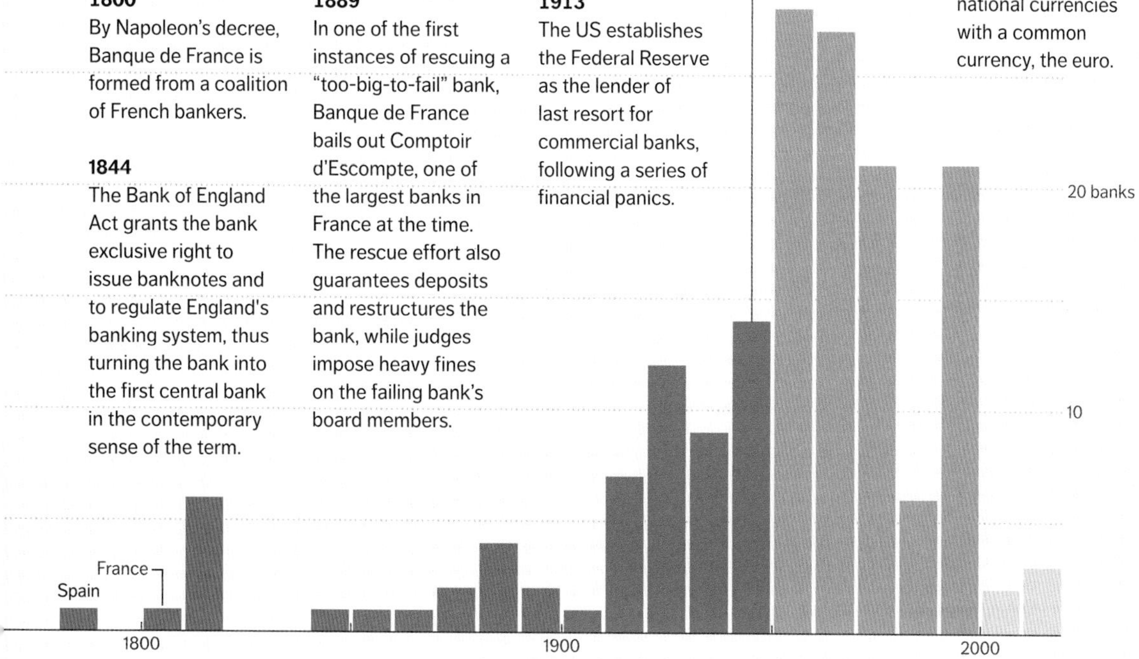

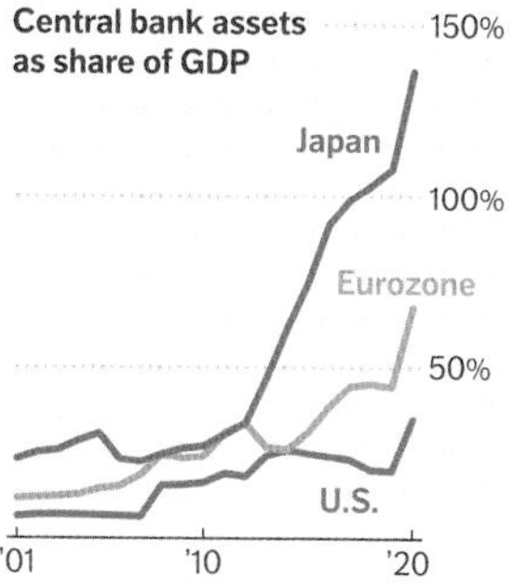

Spain
France
1800
1900
2000
10
20 banks

Central bank assets as share of GDP
150%
100%
50%
Japan
Eurozone
U.S.
'01
'10
'20

2001
With interest rates near zero, the Bank of Japan pioneers QE to stimulate a stagnant economy. By buying assets from the financial system through QE, central banks grow their own assets. In Japan, these have far exceeded the annual output of the whole economy. As assets and influence of central banks rise, questions arise about their accountability.

Legal Dominion

English common law continues to rule global finance through the legacy of colonialism and the reach of Anglo-American law firms and London's Commercial Court.

FROM SMALL CONSUMER LOANS and house purchases to complex derivative deals and corporate mergers, financial transactions involve legal contracts. As such, finance cannot exist without law. English common law is by far the most influential set of legal practices in global finance. Its proponents attribute its influence to its principles of predictability, flexibility, and fairness. Common law is grounded in the rule of law and a strong independent judiciary. Unlike civil law, which is based on codified statutes (lists of what is allowed), common law (a.k.a., case law) is based on precedent. This makes it better suited to financial innovation. For instance, both common and civil law endorse the freedom to devise and enter into contracts, but the types of contracts and property rights allowed under civil law are less flexible. Common law gives private lawyers more freedom to fashion the law.

Originating in eleventh-century England, English common law spread around the world through the British Empire and leading international law firms. Financial globalization has since expanded its reach. All red-tinted countries on our map have some connection to common law. In 2019, the top ten law firms in the world (based on revenue) had headquarters in London or the US and operated in dozens of countries. As a further reflection of the power of English common law, every year hundreds of corporations and other litigants use the Commercial Court in the City of London to resolve commercial disputes. Underlined countries on the map sent the most litigants between April 2020 and April 2021, a record year for the court despite the pandemic. The Singapore International Commercial Court, established in 2015 and based on common law, has been trying to serve a similar role in Asia. The principles and power of English common law have led many courts, and whole financial centers in non–common law countries including China, to adopt it to attract legal, financial, and other business.

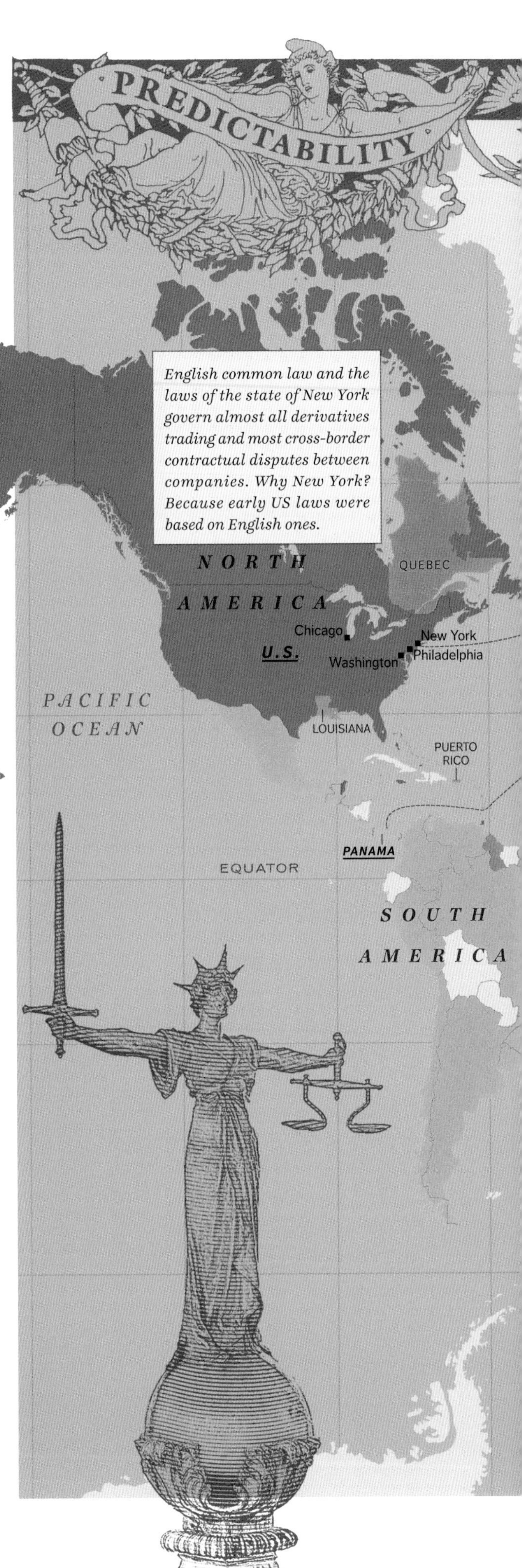

FLEXIBILITY
FAIRNESS
Founded by Samuel Denton in London in 1788, Dentons merged with the Chinese firm Dacheng (大成) in 2015. With a main office in Beijing as well as in London and Washington, Dentons was the only law firm in the world's top ten in 2019 that could not be described as purely Anglo-American. In 2023, however, Dentons separated from Dacheng, citing changes in Chinese regulations as the key reason.
RUSSIA
EUROPE
SCOTLAND
U.K.
London
GER.
UKRAINE
Astana
KAZAKHSTAN
SWITZ.
ITALY
ASIA
Beijing
CHINA
JAPAN
CYPRUS
Shanghai
PACIFIC OCEAN
U.A.E.
Dubai
Doha
Abu Dhabi
INDIA
Shenzhen
HONG KONG S.A.R.
AFRICA
SINGAPORE
EQUATOR
INDIAN OCEAN
AUSTRALIA
ATLANTIC OCEAN
SOUTH AFRICA
Prevalence of English Common Law, 2021
In use
Mixed with other laws
At least one office of the top 10 law firms
None
COUNTRY
London
Top 10 nationalities of litigants most often appearing in London's Commercial Court, April 2020–March 2021
Financial centers in non–common law countries that use English common law
Headquarters of at least one of the world's top 10 law firms (based on 2019 revenue)
0
2000 km
Scale at Equator
Almost all former British colonies inherited English common law. Many mixed common law with local customary laws and civil-law influences of other colonial powers, such as the Dutch in South Africa.
ANTARCTICA

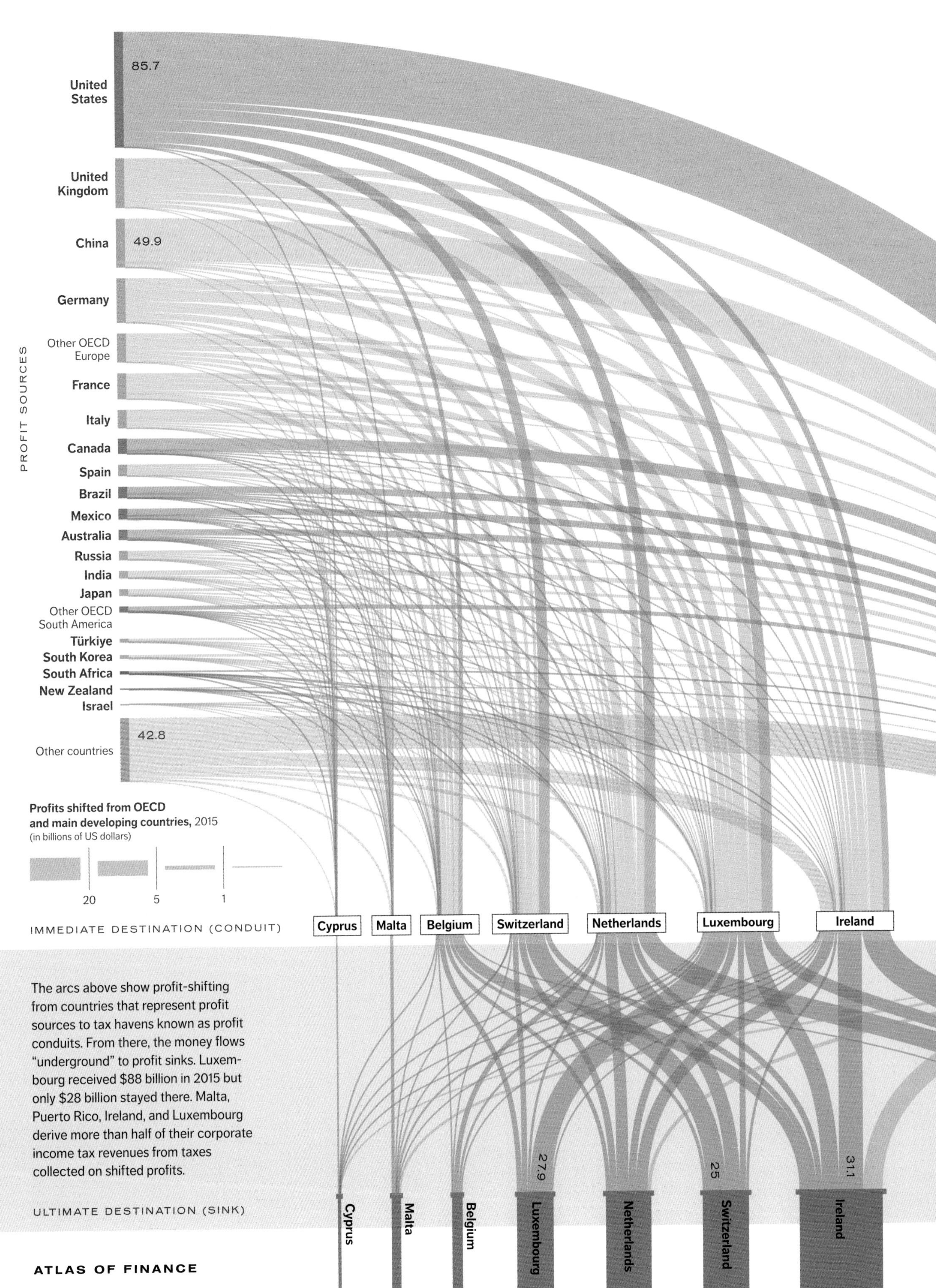

The arcs above show profit-shifting from countries that represent profit sources to tax havens known as profit conduits. From there, the money flows "underground" to profit sinks. Luxembourg received $88 billion in 2015 but only $28 billion stayed there. Malta, Puerto Rico, Ireland, and Luxembourg derive more than half of their corporate income tax revenues from taxes collected on shifted profits.

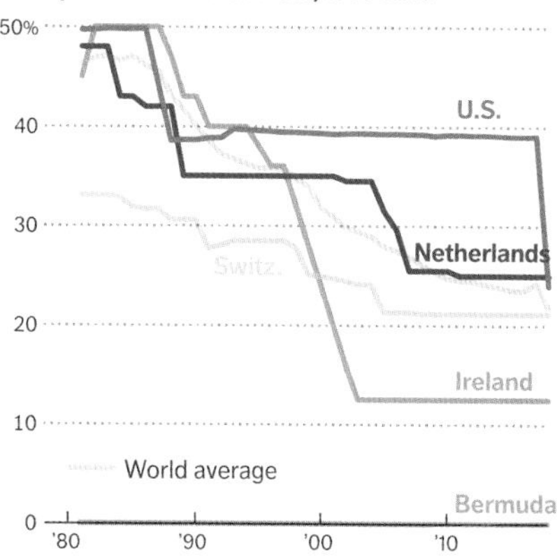

The US Tax Cuts and Jobs Act of 2017 created a single corporate income tax rate of 21 percent.

Offshore Plumbing

Tax havens aren't all tropical islands. In fact, seven rich European countries siphon a considerable share of corporate profits.

IN 2018, CORPORATIONS SHIFTED 800 billion US dollars' worth of profits to tax havens. Tax havens enable multinational firms to shift profits to jurisdictions offering opacity and low-to-zero corporate tax rates. Here we show profit-shifting as a system of flows from profit sources through immediate conduits to sinks. Sources are countries where companies operate and generate profits. Conduits are intermediate destinations, where profits are booked, typically through a web of corporate subsidiaries and offshore entities. Sinks are ultimate destinations, where the shifted profits are subject to low-to-zero taxation. The deeper we go into this "offshore plumbing," the more opaque it becomes. As the plot illustrates, European profits (blue) are shifted mainly through and to European jurisdictions, while Asian profits (gold) primarily flow through and to Singapore, Bermuda, the Cayman Islands, and other tax havens. The pumping of profits from the Americas (purple) relies on both European and Caribbean conduits and sinks.

In 2020, US and European Union authorities cracked down on the tax-evading scheme known as the "Double Irish with a Dutch Sandwich," which allowed US corporations to drastically reduce their taxable income. Through subsidiaries located in Ireland and the Netherlands, tech giants like Google and Apple took advantage of lower taxes and legal loopholes to channel profits from the European and Middle East consumer markets toward offshore entities headquartered in Bermuda, where the corporate income tax rate is zero. In 2017, Google reported $23 billion revenue on this small island, where neither production nor sales take place. To design these sophisticated schemes, multinationals seek advice from financial and business services firms such as Baker McKenzie.

Since 1985, the global average corporate tax rate has fallen by half, to 24 percent, as countries, rather than cooperating to achieve tax justice, have competed to attract foreign profits (see line chart). This race to the bottom has drained significant revenue from national budgets. For every dollar tax havens have gained in tax by attracting profits, countries of origin have lost five dollars of tax. In 2018, the US, UK, and China lost $50 billion, $23 billion, and $18 billion of corporate tax, respectively. In 2021, 136 countries agreed on a deal to introduce a minimum corporate tax rate of 15 percent. Corporations and their advisors will surely devise new schemes to avoid and evade it.

Singapore, Bermuda, Cayman Islands, and other tax havens*

*ANDORRA, ANGUILLA, ANTIGUA AND BARBUDA, ARUBA, THE BAHAMAS, BAHRAIN, BARBADOS, BELIZE, BRITISH VIRGIN ISLANDS, GIBRALTAR, GRENADA, GUERNSEY, HONG KONG, ISLE OF MAN, JERSEY, LEBANON, LIECHTENSTEIN, MACAU, MARSHALL ISLANDS, MAURITIUS, MONACO, NETHERLANDS ANTILLES, PANAMA, PUERTO RICO, SAMOA, SEYCHELLES, ST. KITTS AND NEVIS, ST. LUCIA, ST. VINCENT & GRENADINES, TURKS AND CAICOS, VANUATU

35.6

Singapore, Bermuda, Cayman Islands, and other tax havens*

The World's Laundromats

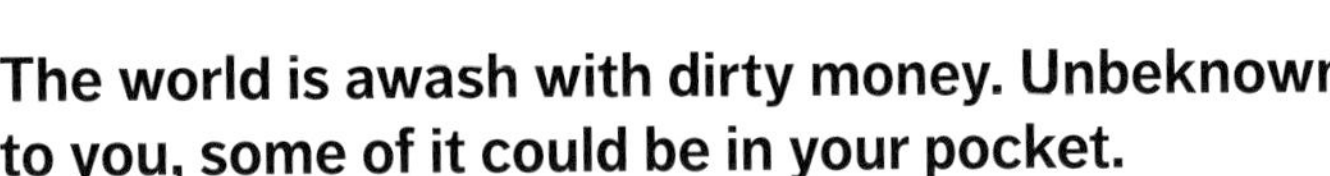

The world is awash with dirty money. Unbeknown to you, some of it could be in your pocket.

THE TERM *MONEY LAUNDERING* is said to have originated with Al Capone, one of America's most notorious gangsters, who used funds from illegal activity to buy laundromats, thereby attaching the money to a legitimate business. Whether or not this legend is true, the term remains. Laundering refers to any manner of rinsing illegal cash through the financial system.

While many methods exist, the normal cycle has three stages: placement, when dirty money enters the financial system through legitimate cash businesses or currency exchanges; layering, when the origins of this money are obscured through intricate and repeated webs of transactions or transfers; and integration, when the money can finally be reabsorbed by the criminal through wages, profits, loans, or shareholder dividends.

Money laundering happens anywhere and everywhere. While its inherent nature makes it difficult to detect, the UN estimates that laundered money equates to 2 to 5 percent of global GDP each year. This money evades all types of taxation, propping up illegal economies that linger in the shadows of national sovereignty. Governments invest heavily in anti–money laundering initiatives to investigate, expose, and criminalize activities, but stopping the cycle is easier said than done. Some countries are more effective than others.

Our circular bar chart shows how countries perform across four key indicators from the Financial Secrecy Index, a politically neutral tool developed by the Tax Justice Network to rank countries on their compliance with international regulations. The higher the score, the greater the financial secrecy and the lower the compliance with anti–money laundering standards. Across these four indicators, Norway is the most compliant and Moldova the least. The variation among countries is stark, creating opportunities for money launderers to use this geography to their advantage.

Almost paradoxically, more compliance does not always translate into less money laundering. For example, despite the UK being one of the most transparent countries, London is often described as the world's laundromat. As a center of financial innovation, many of its bankers, lawyers, and accountants know how to bypass anti–money laundering regulations. Criminals are constantly developing new ways to launder their money, and regulatory loopholes and developments in digital finance help them stay one step ahead. While regulators play catch-up, the global machine keeps spinning.

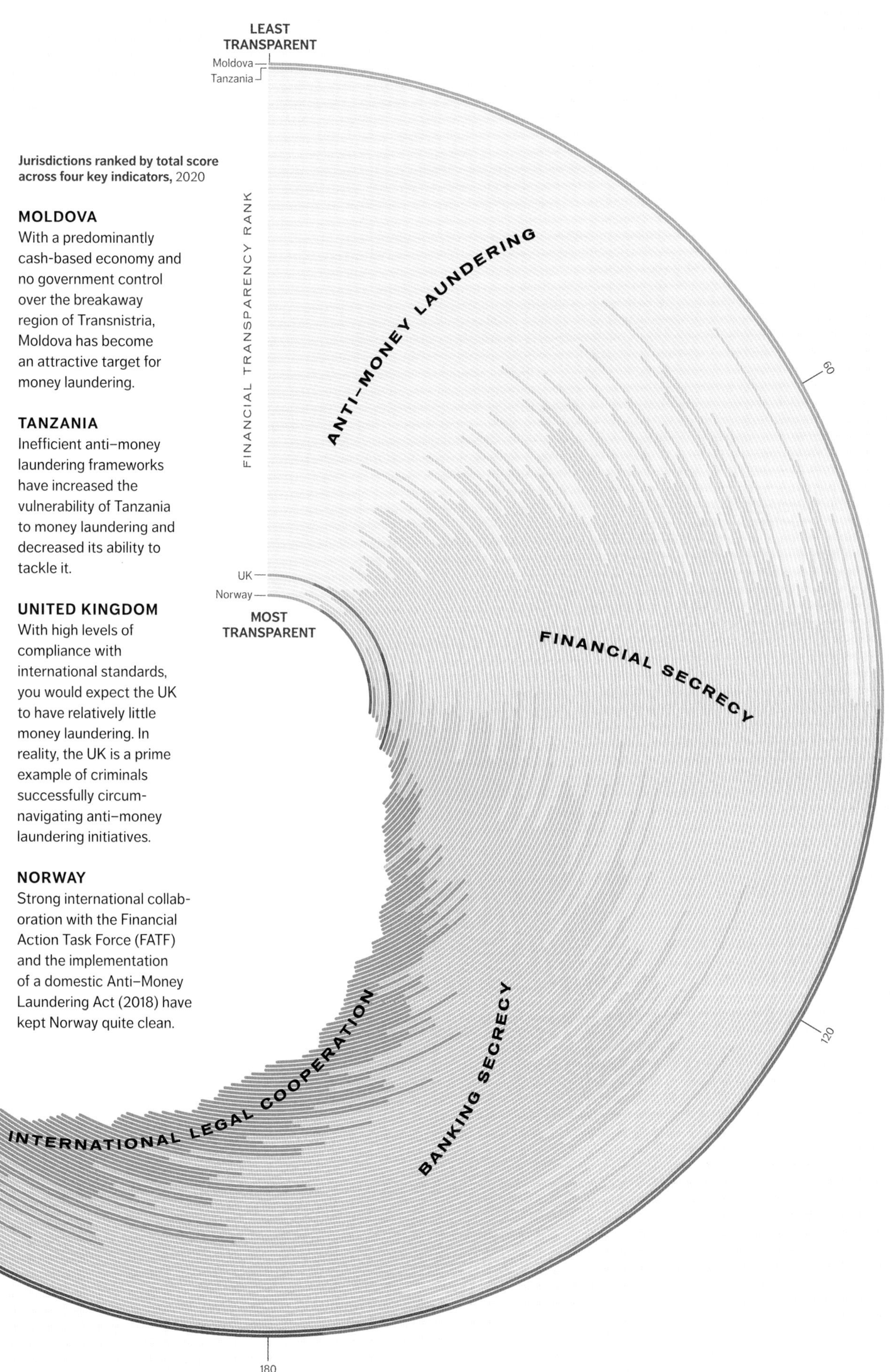

Jurisdictions ranked by total score across four key indicators, 2020

MOLDOVA
With a predominantly cash-based economy and no government control over the breakaway region of Transnistria, Moldova has become an attractive target for money laundering.

TANZANIA
Inefficient anti–money laundering frameworks have increased the vulnerability of Tanzania to money laundering and decreased its ability to tackle it.

UNITED KINGDOM
With high levels of compliance with international standards, you would expect the UK to have relatively little money laundering. In reality, the UK is a prime example of criminals successfully circum-navigating anti–money laundering initiatives.

NORWAY
Strong international collab-oration with the Financial Action Task Force (FATF) and the implementation of a domestic Anti–Money Laundering Act (2018) have kept Norway quite clean.

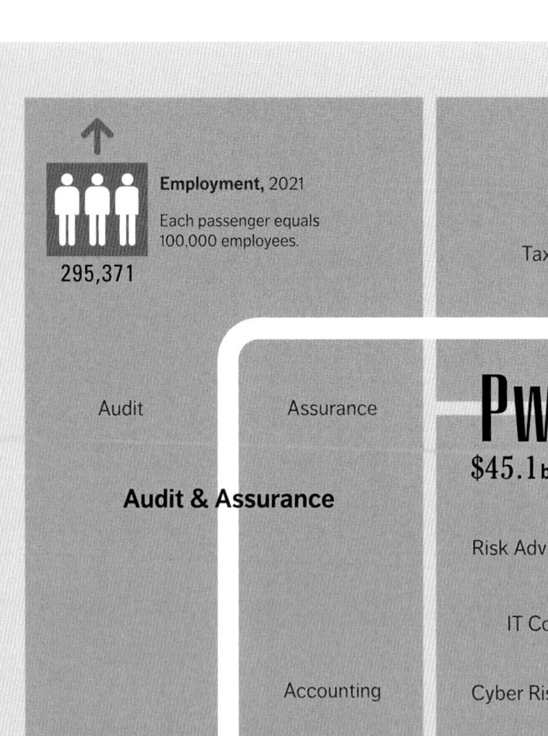

Colored boxes represent each firm's 2021 gross revenue from three core services.

Tax Planning **Tax & Legal** Legal Advisory

Gross revenue, 2011–21

733 offices
684 cities
128 countries

Oligopoly Food Court

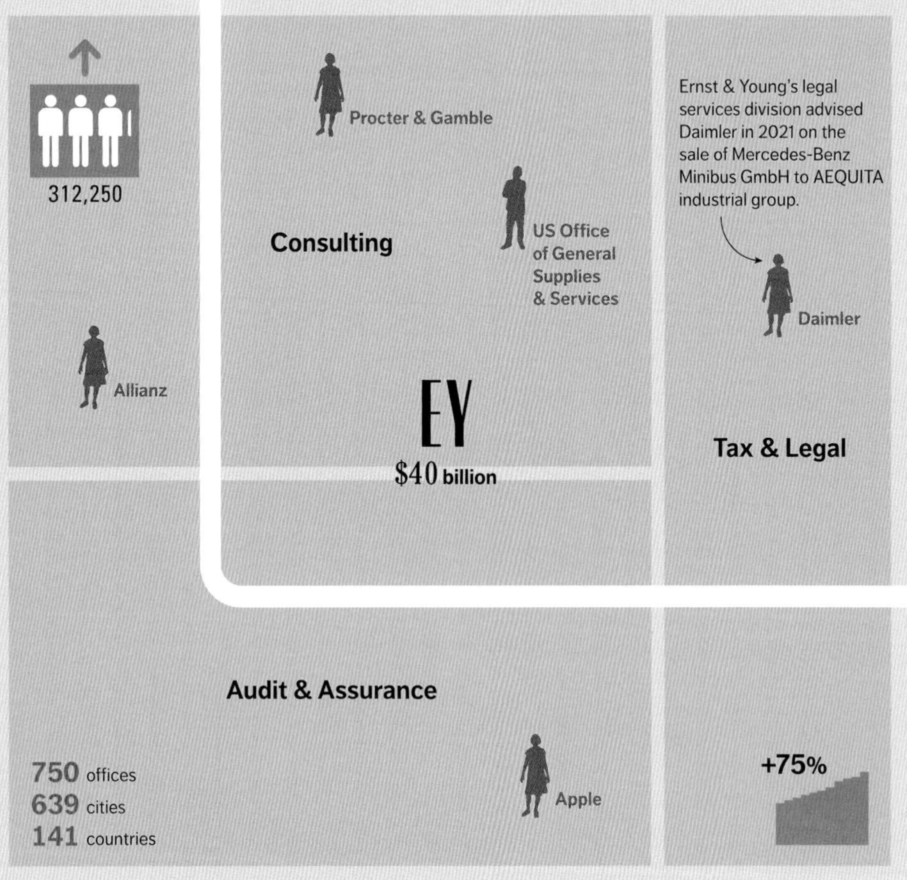

Ernst & Young's legal services division advised Daimler in 2021 on the sale of Mercedes-Benz Minibus GmbH to AEQUITA industrial group.

Daimler

Tax & Legal

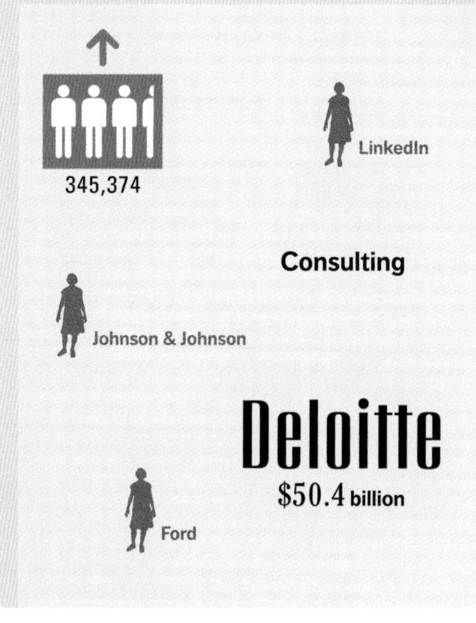

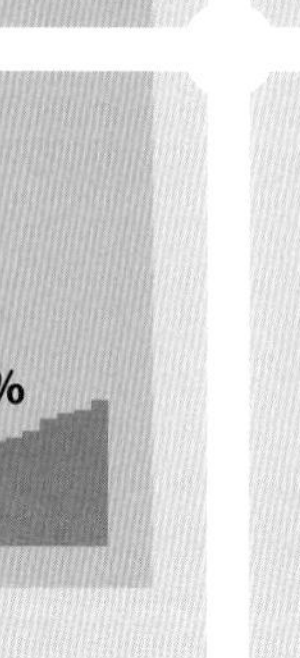

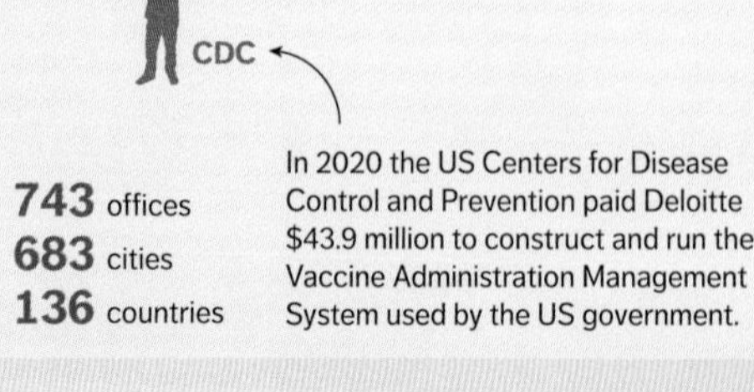

In 2020 the US Centers for Disease Control and Prevention paid Deloitte $43.9 million to construct and run the Vaccine Administration Management System used by the US government.

The Global Financial Services Megastores

At the center of the financial and business services sector, four firms of Anglo-American origin render any services their clients can imagine.

A HANDFUL OF ICONIC department store names signify the emergence of modern-age consumerism: Galeries Lafayette in France, Selfridges in the UK, El Corte Inglés in Spain. Whereas these corporate names specialize in selling consumer goods, Deloitte, PwC, EY, and KPMG—also known as the Big Four—serve the needs of businesses all around the world.

The roots of the Big Four go back to nineteenth-century, small-scale Anglo-American accountancy firms that served emerging multinational businesses. Over time they expanded their services beyond traditional auditing and accounting by adding tax and law consulting, corporate strategy, IT transformation, and financial advisory. (See the red box for a full list.)

As a result, the Big Four today resemble megastores of financial and business services dedicated to corporate customers, governments, and public-sector entities. Their long list of clients reflects their business success: they audit Pepsi, AstraZeneca, and Morgan Stanley; offer legal advice to Glencore, Volkswagen, and Daimler; and provide consulting for P&G, Amazon, and the European Commission.

The scale of business operations, performance, and workforce is impressive. With combined revenues of almost US$170 billion in 2021 and a workforce of over a million employees (see elevator icons), the Big Four's economy can be compared to that of a small country. Combined, they generate more revenues than the GDPs of countries like Luxembourg, Hungary, and Slovakia, while their immense network of 2,911 offices in 137 countries ensures 24/7 business support for their customers in every corner of the world, including all leading financial centers and tax havens.

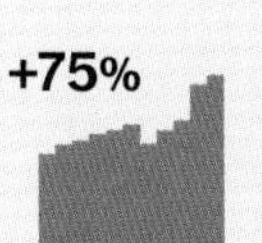

The power wielded by the Big Four raises the issue of responsibility. Dominating the audit market for large companies, they act as an oligopoly. Through their expertise and networks, they lobby governments and regulators, often setting the agenda of public debates. Many of their former employees end up leading governments and regulatory agencies. How should we evaluate their overall impact? Maybe we need an independent audit of the auditors.

Judging from Afar

With offices in just a handful of global financial centers, credit rating agencies act as gatekeepers of global finance.

CREDIT RATING AGENCIES (CRAs) are some of the most influential institutions in contemporary capitalism. They judge creditworthiness of private and public entities that want to borrow money (including firms, banks, and governments) and prescribe policy recommendations for maintaining and improving ratings, which are followed closely by investors. Effectively, they act as the gatekeepers of global finance.

Although there are dozens of CRAs around the world, only three are truly global: Standard & Poor's, Moody's, and Fitch. Together they control close to 95 percent of the

New York

The headquarters of Moody's leads rating assessments of countries in the Americas as well as others, including Egypt, India, and Lebanon.

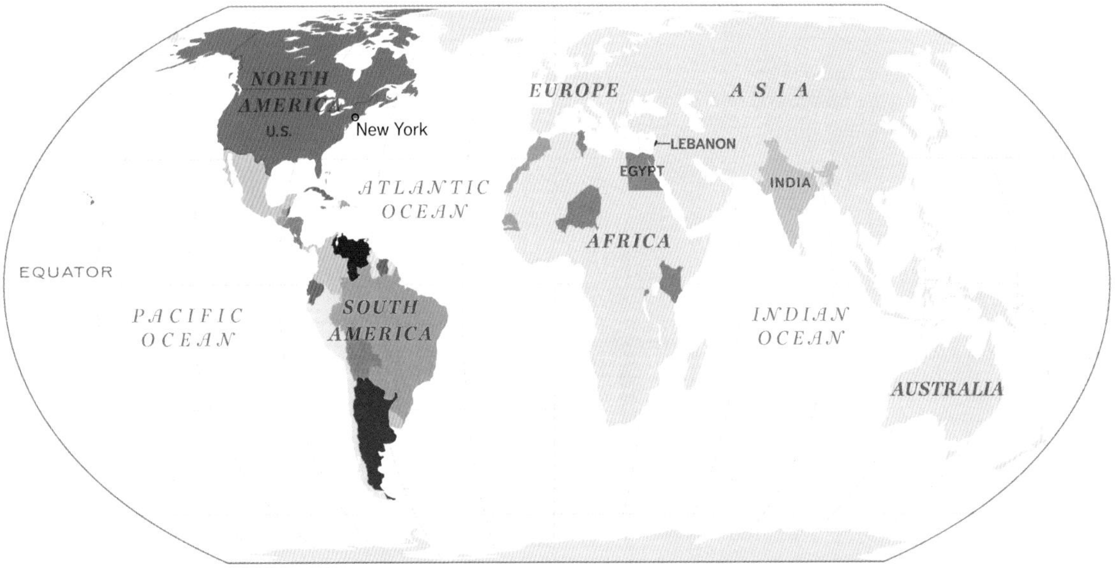

Moody's sovereign credit ratings by location of lead analyst
(at the end of 2020)

- Aaa
- Aa
- A
- Baa
- Ba
- B
- Caa
- Ca
- C

London

The London office assesses numerous countries around the world, including Russia and Türkiye. In Europe, it focuses on non-EU economies.

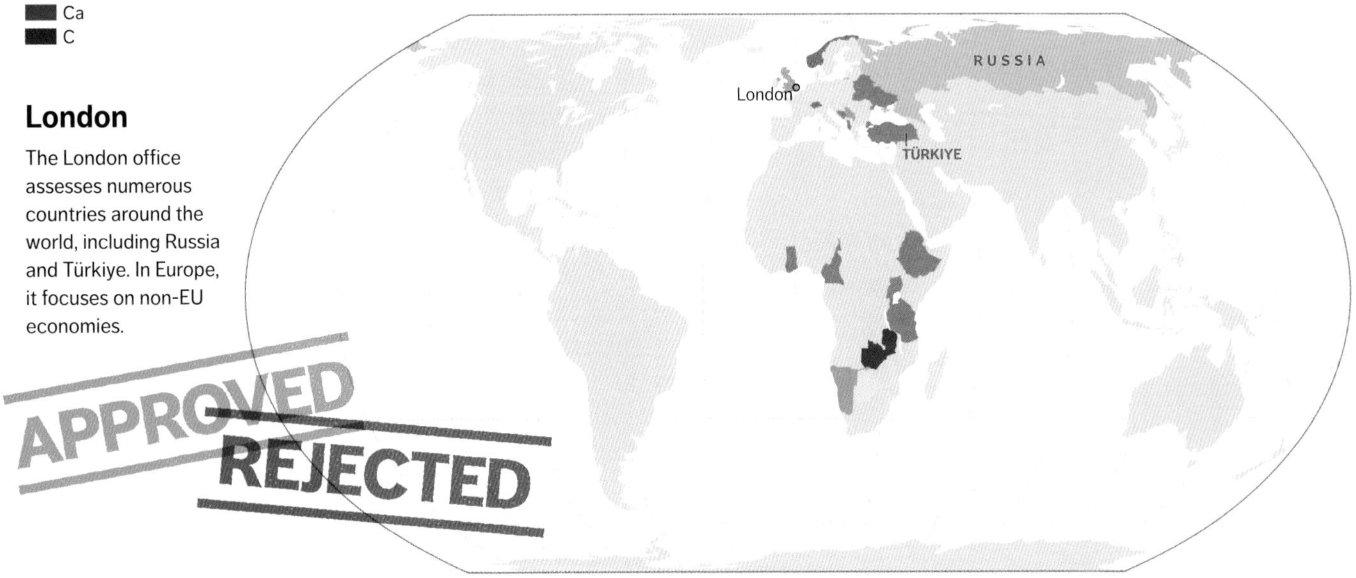

ratings market and rate anything that can be rated, from simple bonds to complex financial products to national governments (known as sovereign ratings). All are headquartered in New York City. Moody's, the oldest of all, was founded there in 1909, initially for providing ratings for bonds of US railroad companies.

Lead analysts of rating agencies tend to be located in just a few global financial centers. As we show on the four maps below, Moody's sovereign ratings in Latin America are led by analysts based in New York; those in continental Europe by analysts located in Paris and Frankfurt; Asian ratings are designed mostly in Singapore and Dubai; and Africa is divided among analysts from New York, Paris, and London as well as Singapore and Dubai.

CRAs have attracted much criticism. One is that they are paid by the very firms and organizations that are being rated. In the run-up to the US subprime crisis of 2007–8, banks were training CRAs to evaluate their own complex financial products, further undermining the impartiality of ratings. CRAs are biased in their judgments. They give higher ratings to countries close to them, with the US in the lead. Being judged from afar is a disadvantage.

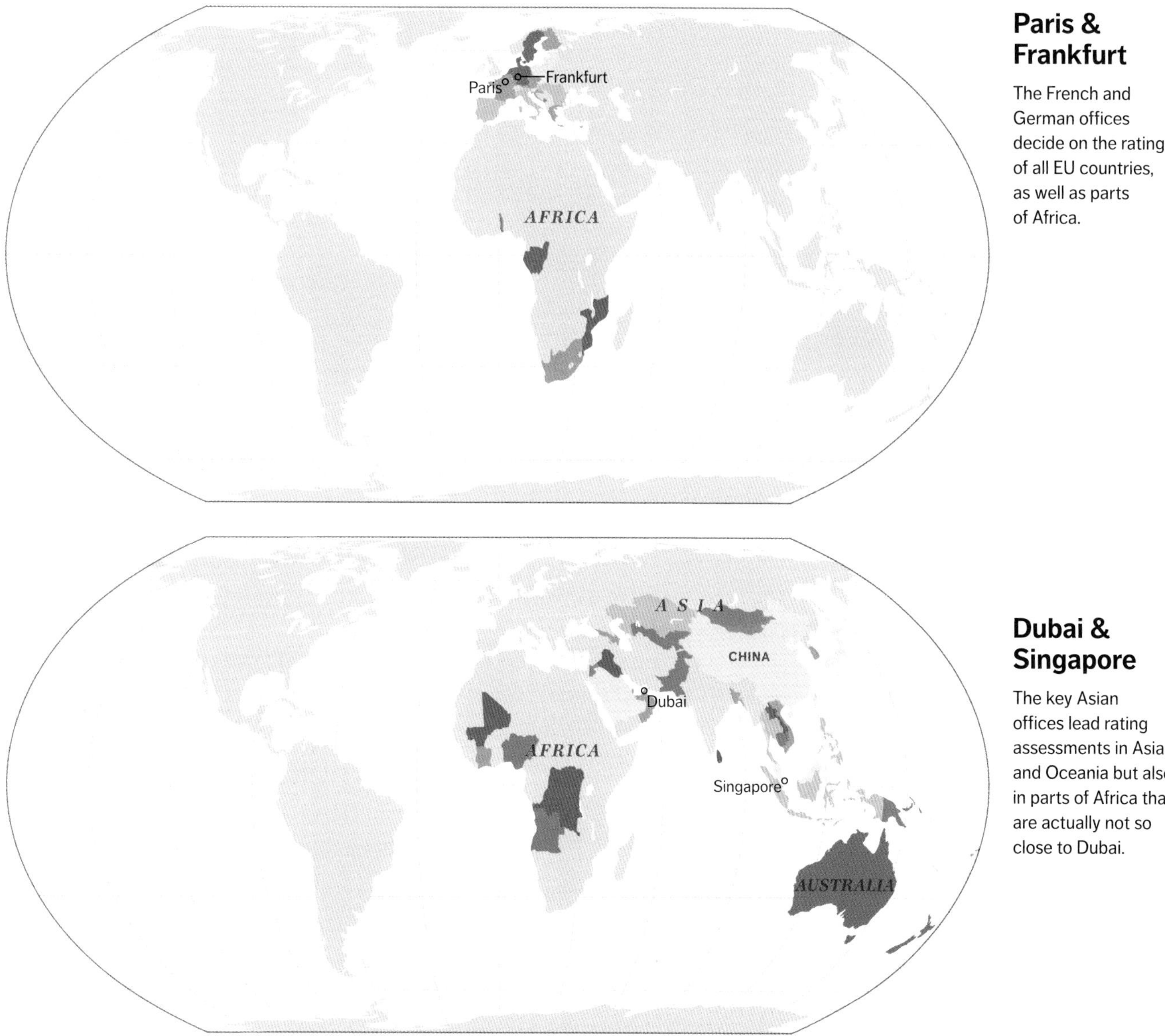

Paris & Frankfurt

The French and German offices decide on the ratings of all EU countries, as well as parts of Africa.

Dubai & Singapore

The key Asian offices lead rating assessments in Asia and Oceania but also in parts of Africa that are actually not so close to Dubai.

Change at the Top

Men have held almost all leadership positions in financial and business services, but in recent years that glass ceiling has finally begun to crack.

GENDER INEQUALITY remains shockingly pervasive in financial and business services, a reflection of poor diversity in the industry in general. Out of the world's top 275 companies in this sector (comprising the hundred largest banks and twenty-five largest companies from insurance, asset management, real estate, accounting, law, consulting, and fintech sectors each), only eighteen (6.5 percent) had female CEOs (or holders of equivalent titles) as of March 2021. All the female CEOs worked for US or European companies (headquartered in Germany, France, Ireland, Norway, Sweden, or the UK), while the leadership of the world's top financial and business services firms in the rest of the world remained exclusively male, including thirty-one Chinese, fourteen Japanese, eight Indian, and eight Canadian firms.

Male dominance varies by sector. It is lowest in asset management (80 percent), with 88 percent in law, and over 90 percent in real estate, accounting, insurance, banking, and consulting; fintech was 100 percent male. The combination of male-dominated financial and technological cultures embedded in the fintech sector seems to make the glass ceiling even more difficult to break. This is a major issue considering the fast growth of fintech globally and its claims of transforming finance. What offers hope is that female CEO appointments have become more common. Thirteen out of the eighteen female CEOs in leading firms assumed their positions after the start of 2019; Debra Cafaro, who has been CEO of Ventas since 1999, is an exception. Appointments to the helms of intergovernmental and governmental financial organizations are also encouraging. Christine Lagarde became the first woman to lead the International Monetary Fund in 2011 (followed by Kristalina Georgieva in 2019) and the first woman to chair the European Central Bank in 2019. Janet Yellen became the first female chair of the Federal Reserve (the US central bank) in 2014 and the country's first female Secretary of the Treasury in 2021.

Turn the page to meet the women running financial and business services firms east of the Americas. None of the sixty-nine Asia-Pacific–headquartered financial and business services firms in the world's top 275 has a female CEO. It seems that the fast growth of the sector in this part of the world has not empowered female leadership. To improve the diversity of finance, radical change is needed at the top.

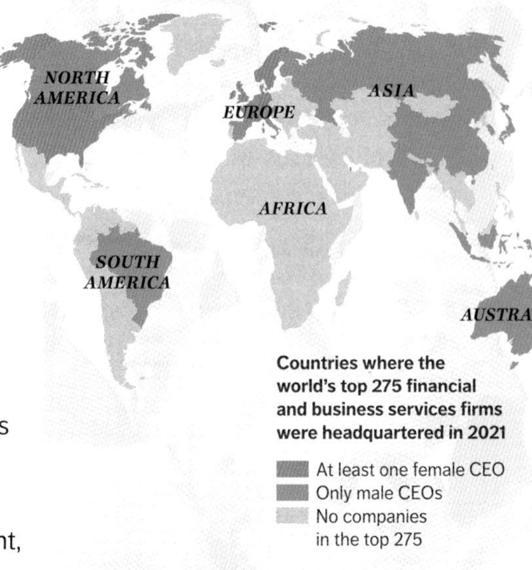

Countries where the world's top 275 financial and business services firms were headquartered in 2021

- At least one female CEO
- Only male CEOs
- No companies in the top 275

THE LEADERS

Debra Cafaro

Ventas

SECTOR
Real Estate

YEAR APPOINTED
1999

When Cafaro joined Ventas in 1999, the company was in dire straits. It is now a Fortune 1000 corporation. She credits her family and love of sports for her strong work ethic.

Jennifer Johnson

Franklin Templeton

SECTOR
Asset Management

YEAR APPOINTED
2020

With over thirty years of experience, Johnson has won awards for leadership and performance and also for enhancing customer service practices in asset and fund management.

Barbara Becker

Gibson, Dunn & Crutcher (Chair, Managing Partner)

SECTOR
Law

YEAR APPOINTED
2021

Made managing partner of a law firm at the age of 31, Becker is an advocate for executive involvement in the recruitment process.

Forenames of the CEOs from the top 275 companies in financial and business services, as of March 31, 2021

Scott Jamie Thomas Eric David
James David Michel Hugh Robert
Arvind Jane Peter William Mario
Mauricio Steven Ted Barry Daniel
Martine Dan Laurence Joseph
David Kevin Thasunda Neil

Cyrus
Tom Anne
Manny Owen
David Rich Jean
Barry Eugène
Vivek

NEW YORK CITY

THE AMERICAS

David Bruce
Baharat Roy George
Brian Victor Darryl
Devin
William Eric

CANADA

Andrew
Brian Charles
Jeremy Michael David Shankh Jami Mortimer
Jennifer Charles Hamid Dave Mark Wayne John William William
Nate John Chuck Warren Jon Debra Michael Steven James Horacio
Michael Alfredo Anthony
Milton Timothy Richard
Ron Charles Stephen Joseph
Antonio Martin Brian
Barbara Emmanuel Peter
Kelly
Sumit Timothy Richard
Brian

UNITED STATES

João Fausto
Octavio David
Gabriel

BRAZIL

Jami McKeon

Morgan Lewis (Chair)

SECTOR

Law

YEAR APPOINTED

2014

McKeon has rapidly expanded client reach into new regions, particularly East Asia. She is an advocate of diversity in law.

Jane Fraser

Citigroup

SECTOR

Banking

YEAR APPOINTED

2021

The first female CEO in the firm's history, Fraser is a published author on globalization in finance. She speaks frequently about maintaining a career while being a mother.

Martine Ferland

Mercer LLC

SECTOR

Consulting

YEAR APPOINTED

2019

An advocate for improved opportunities for the LGBTQ+ community, Ferland is passionate about inclusion, sustainability, and technology to improve productivity.

Thasunda Brown

TIAA

SECTOR

Asset Management

YEAR APPOINTED

2021

The second Black woman to lead a Fortune 500 company, Brown also heads a foundation named after her parents that empowers individuals who help their communities.

Anne Richards

Fidelity International

SECTOR

Asset Management

YEAR APPOINTED

2018

Richards is a chartered engineer and worked at CERN. She was appointed Dame Commander of the Order of the British Empire for services to women, education, and science.

Jean Hynes

Wellington Mgmt.

SECTOR

Asset Management

YEAR APPOINTED

2021

With a background in biotechnology and the pharmaceutical industry, Hynes is known for fostering a culture of focusing on the long term and putting the client first.

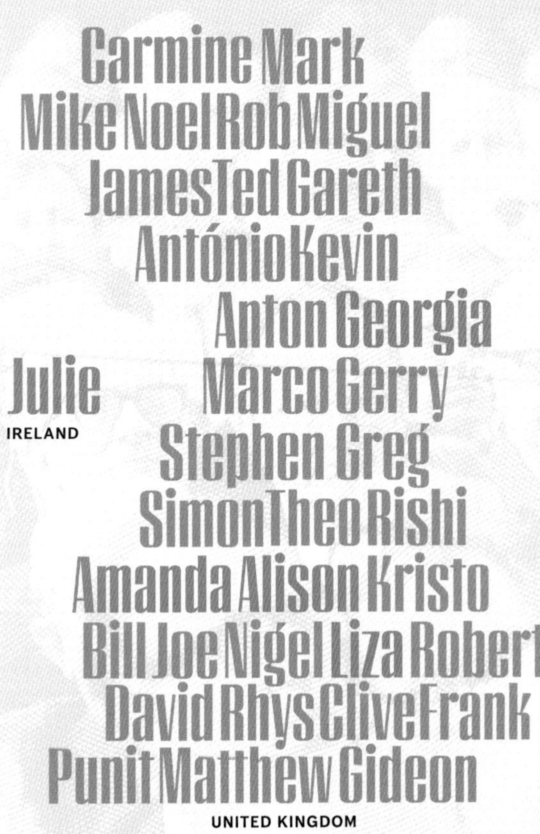

EUROPE

Sebastian
Johan Frank
Carina
FINLAND
Kjerstin
NORWAY
Fredrik
Jens
SWEDEN
Chris
DENMARK
Uwe
William
Steven Robert
Lard Wiebe
NETHERLANDS
Valentin Christian
Christian Matthias
Manfred Cornelius
Rainer Sirma
Stephan Oliver
GERMANY
Wayne Marc
Johan
BELGIUM
Phillippe
Méka Christophe
Jean-Laurent Daniel
Frédéric Yves Aiman
Laurent Antoine Phil
Philippe Thomas
FRANCE
Kay Mario Heinz
Thomas Ralph
SWITZERLAND
Bernd
AUSTRIA
Andrea
Caarlo
Philippe
ITALY
José Jaime
Gonzalo
Onur
SPAIN

Forenames of the CEOs from the top 275 companies in financial and business services, as of March 31, 2021

Julie Sweet

Accenture

SECTOR

Consulting

YEAR APPOINTED

2019

Under Sweet, the first female CEO of the firm, Accenture is working toward equal representation of men and women on their staff by 2025.

Amanda Blanc

Aviva

SECTOR

Insurance

YEAR APPOINTED

2020

Hailing from a background in Wales, Blanc has been the first woman to hold many positions, including chair of the Insurance Fraud Bureau. She is also an accomplished musician.

Liza Robbins

Kreston Global

SECTOR

Accounting

YEAR APPOINTED

2018

Educated in Hong Kong, Robbins considers herself a change agent. Under her leadership, the firm has expanded from 70 countries to over 110.

Alison Rose

NatWest Group

SECTOR

Banking

YEAR APPOINTED

2019

An advocate for diversity, Rose was commissioned by the UK to report on the barriers women face to starting their own businesses. She has also won many fintech awards.

Georgia Dawson

Freshfields Bruckhaus Deringer (Sr. Partner)

SECTOR

Law

YEAR APPOINTED

2020

Dawson has set diversity targets for Freshfields with the intent to change attitudes toward diversity within major law firms.

Herman
RUSSIA

Jin
Shu Guang
Wanchun
Jianguo Ke
Siqing Xinshuang Franklin
Elliott Hengxuan Shengqiang Wei
Dazhi Guohua Ji Shaoxian Gregory
Bingzhu Eric Renyan Yuchen Jin Deqi
Kai Wangchun Yonglin Yiping
Huiyu George
CHINA

Ok-dong
Jun-hak
Jung-tai Yin
Kwang-seok
Jong-won
KOREA

Seiji Junichi
Akio Norito
Makoto
Fumio Tatsufumi
Kentro Kazuto
Tetsuya Masahiro
Masahiro Tetsuo
Hiroshi
JAPAN

Abdulla
QATAR

Vijay
Yashish
Harshvardhan
Vipin Rajesh
Ashwini
Bhavish
Salil
INDIA

Ee Cheong
Piyush Samuel
Anthony
SINGAPORE

ASIA-PACIFIC

Andre
INDONESIA

Matt
Ross
Shayne Peter
AUSTRALIA

Méka Brunel

Gecina

SECTOR
Real Estate

YEAR APPOINTED
2017

With a background in civil engineering, Brunel has contributed to public policy as well as business. She also chairs the French Green Building Council.

Sirma Boshnakova

Allianz Group

SECTOR
Asset Management

YEAR APPOINTED
2019

Boshnakova has held top positions in the pharmaceutical and insurance industries as well as in consulting. She is passionate about supporting future generations.

Kjerstin Braathen

DNB ASA

SECTOR
Banking

YEAR APPOINTED
2019

Braathen has over twenty years of experience at DNB, with clients in shipping and offshore logistics. She formerly worked at an aluminium company, chartering gas tankers.

Carina Åkerström

Handelsbanken

SECTOR
Banking

YEAR APPOINTED
2019

With a background in law, Åkerström broke a 150-year-old rule by becoming the first female CEO of the bank. She joined the bank in 1986.

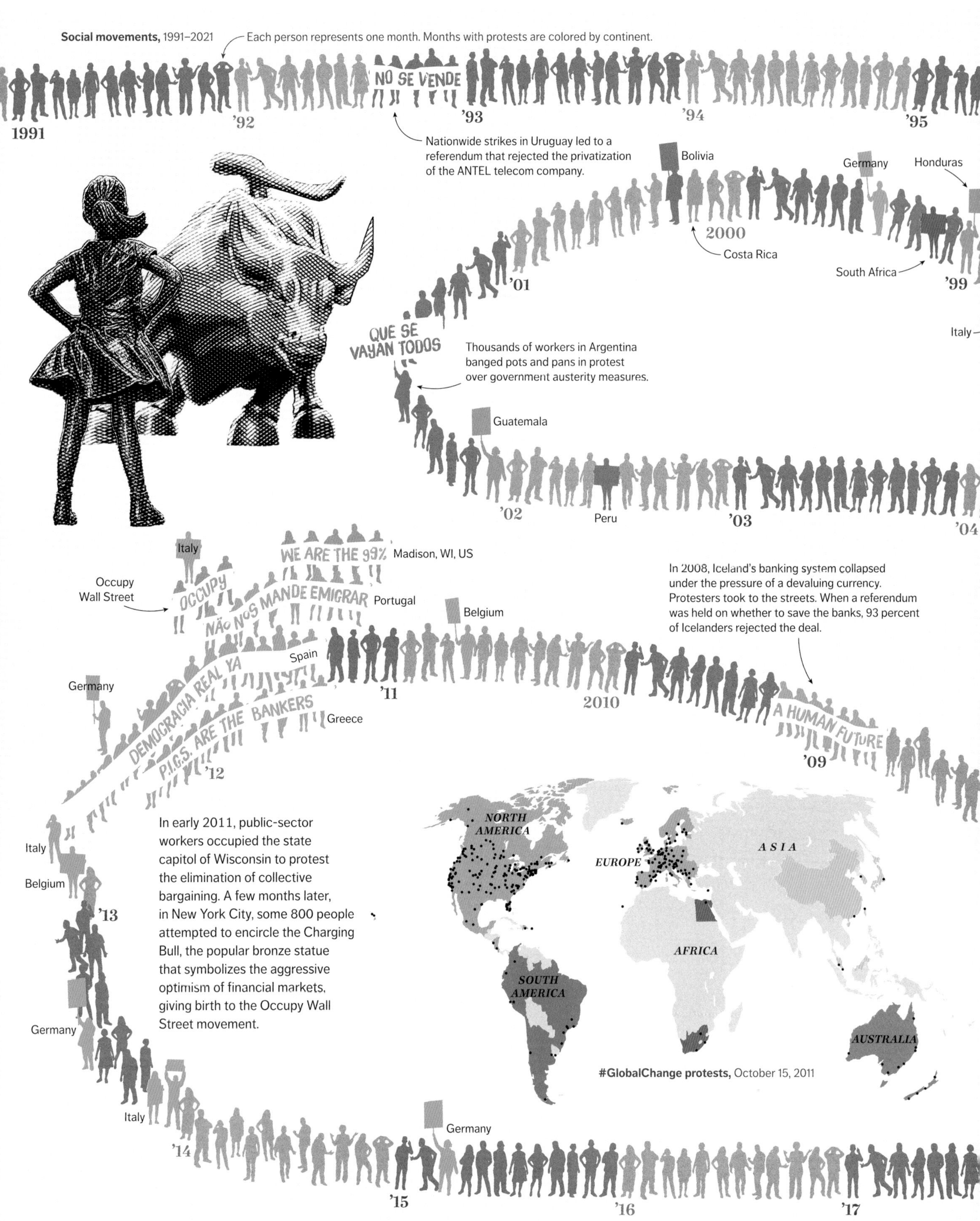
Social movements, 1991–2021
Each person represents one month. Months with protests are colored by continent.
1991
'92
NO SE VENDE
'93
'94
'95
Nationwide strikes in Uruguay led to a referendum that rejected the privatization of the ANTEL telecom company.
Bolivia
Germany
Honduras
2000
Costa Rica
South Africa
'99
'01
QUE SE VAYAN TODOS
Thousands of workers in Argentina banged pots and pans in protest over government austerity measures.
Italy
Guatemala
'02
Peru
'03
'04
Italy
WE ARE THE 99%
Madison, WI, US
Occupy Wall Street
OCCUPY
NÃO NOS MANDE EMIGRAR
Portugal
Belgium
In 2008, Iceland's banking system collapsed under the pressure of a devaluing currency. Protesters took to the streets. When a referendum was held on whether to save the banks, 93 percent of Icelanders rejected the deal.
Spain
Germany
DEMOCRACIA REAL YA
'11
2010
P.I.G.S. ARE THE BANKERS
Greece
A HUMAN FUTURE
'12
'09
In early 2011, public-sector workers occupied the state capitol of Wisconsin to protest the elimination of collective bargaining. A few months later, in New York City, some 800 people attempted to encircle the Charging Bull, the popular bronze statue that symbolizes the aggressive optimism of financial markets, giving birth to the Occupy Wall Street movement.
Italy
Belgium
'13
NORTH AMERICA
EUROPE
ASIA
AFRICA
SOUTH AMERICA
AUSTRALIA
Germany
#GlobalChange protests, October 15, 2011
Italy
'14
Germany
'15
'16
'17

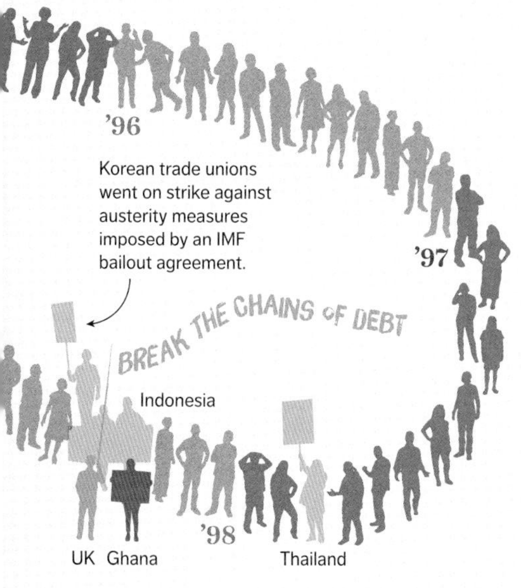

People's Power?

Three years after the global financial crisis crippled the world economy, millions of people hit the streets demanding social justice and true democracy.

ON OCTOBER 15, 2011, more than three hundred demonstrations took place around the world under the banner United for #GlobalChange to protest corporate greed, political corruption, and austerity measures. These protests highlighted a divide between "politics from below" and "politics of finance." The latter describes a system of *bankocracy* and *debtocracy*, with financial institutions influencing public policymaking and debt accumulation becoming an instrument of politico-economic control. The former represents voices of the people and popular movements who question the logic of capitalist markets and are fighting for a democratic, fair, and equitable economic order.

The events of 2011 were not historically unique. They follow a long line of social uprisings of people against the excesses of corporate power and international financial institutions. In 1998, at the G7 summit in Birmingham, 70,000 people formed a ten-kilometer human chain, calling for debt relief for poor countries, shouting, "Break the chains of debt!" A few years later, Norway actually canceled part of the debt it was owed by underdeveloped countries. In 1998, Koreans went on strike for months against IMF-imposed austerity measures and wage cuts, leading to the introduction of the first publicly financed safety-net program. In Latin America, the guinea pig of neoliberal policies for decades, social resistance has paved the way for alternative forms of economic organization and development, which, despite their problems and deficiencies, lifted millions from poverty and socioeconomic exclusion. Critics say that such movements often lack a clear agenda amid a chaotic combination of anti-capitalist slogans. History indicates mixed results. Micah White, the codirector of *Adbusters*—the magazine that circulated the idea for Occupy Wall Street—said, "The Occupy movement was a constructive failure," as it did not end the influence of money in politics. However, like movements before and after it, it managed to make the issues of income inequality and social justice more central to economic and political debates.

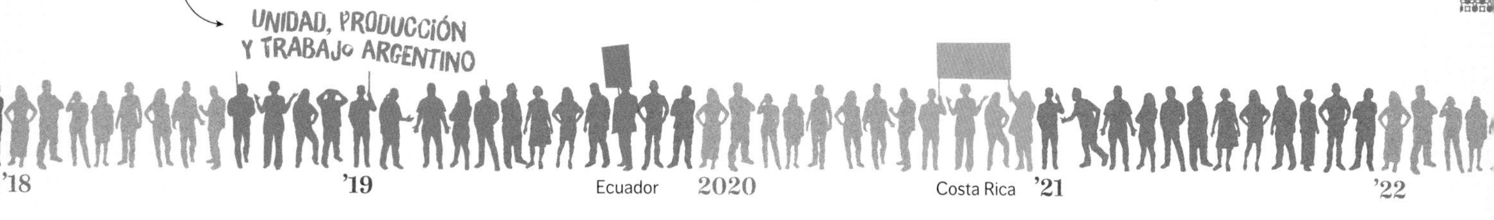

8

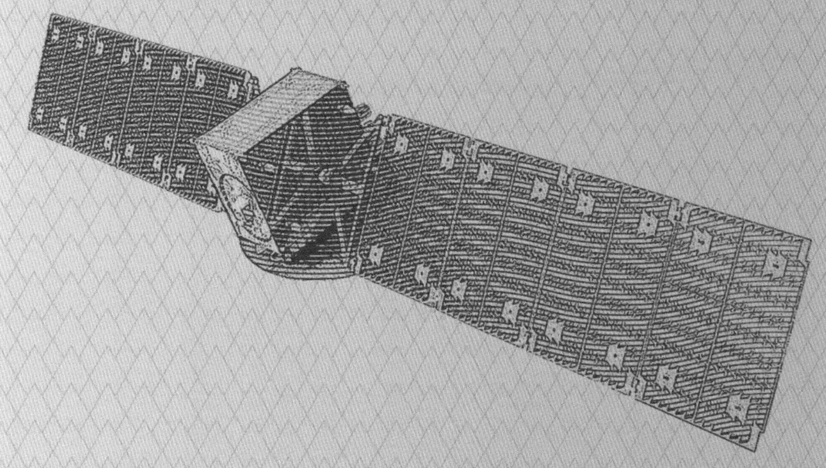

While money may well grow on trees,
trees and the natural environment are more important.
ANNABELLE MOONEY

Society & Environment

Access to money shapes society, and its use requires financial literacy. Blocking the access of whole countries to global finance has been used increasingly as a weapon in international politics. As money shapes human relationships with the environment, it will be decisive for developing new energy systems, the mitigation of and adaptation to the environmental crisis, and human activities beyond planet Earth. Finance is already in space.

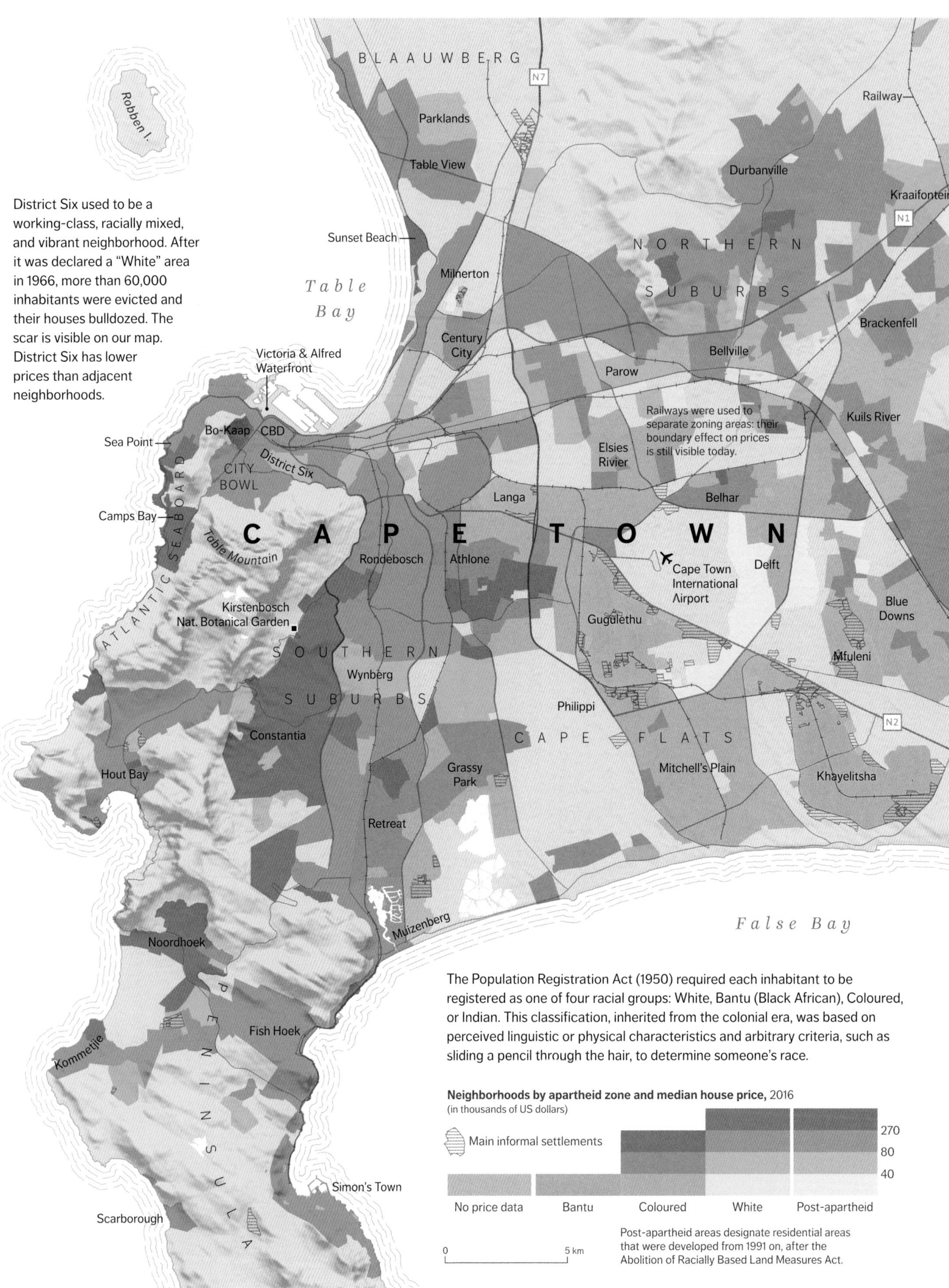

District Six used to be a working-class, racially mixed, and vibrant neighborhood. After it was declared a "White" area in 1966, more than 60,000 inhabitants were evicted and their houses bulldozed. The scar is visible on our map. District Six has lower prices than adjacent neighborhoods.

The Population Registration Act (1950) required each inhabitant to be registered as one of four racial groups: White, Bantu (Black African), Coloured, or Indian. This classification, inherited from the colonial era, was based on perceived linguistic or physical characteristics and arbitrary criteria, such as sliding a pencil through the hair, to determine someone's race.

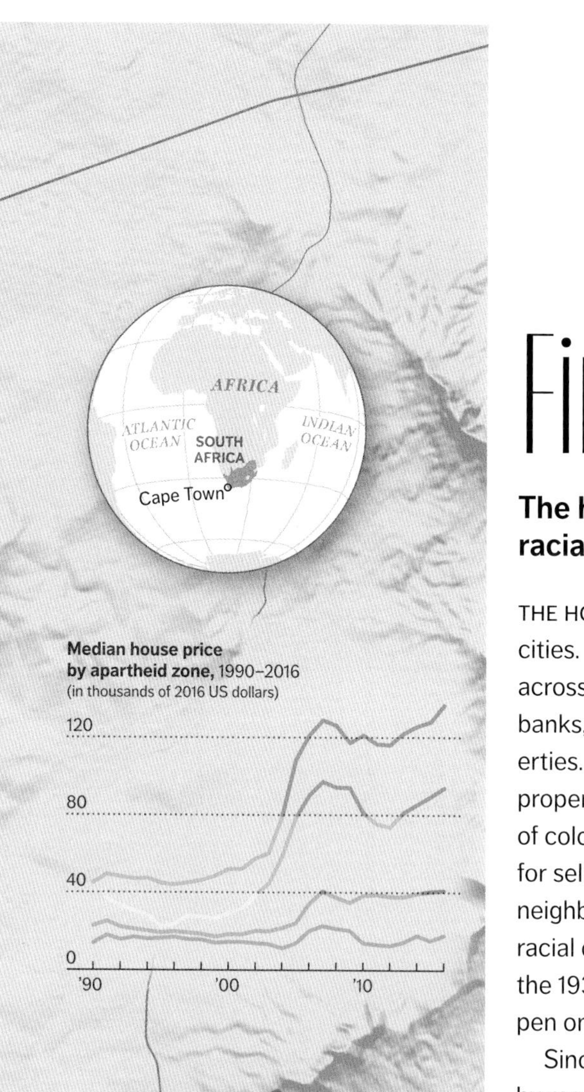

Finance and Inequality

The housing market reflects, produces, and maintains racial inequalities and segregation.

THE HOUSING MARKET plays a major role in shaping the uneven structures of cities. People have unequal incomes and assets, and house prices sort people across urban space. The real estate industry, led by agents and mortgage banks, claims professional authority and objectivity in the valuation of properties. Research, however, demonstrates that if all characteristics, such as property size and amenities, are taken into account, housing in communities of color remains significantly undervalued, which reduces access to wealth for sellers and access to mortgage credit for buyers. This bias, whereby some neighborhoods are considered risky and undesirable based on their social and racial composition, harks back to the practices of "redlining," first identified in the 1930s' US, when government institutions and mortgage lenders used red pen on maps to demarcate areas of perceived lending risk.

Since its colonial foundation in 1652, Cape Town has been segregated by race and class by public authorities and the real estate industry. During apartheid, the Group Areas Act (1950) systematized racial inequalities and segregation by strictly regulating the housing market through zoning. People were only allowed to own and rent in areas classified for their racial group. While banks and public institutions promoted homeownership and quality housing in "White" areas, which enjoyed better services and access to natural amenities, people classified as "Coloured" or "Bantu" were confronted with the removal, and sometimes destruction, of their property and forced to live in the sandy Cape Flats (see map). Until the mid-1980s, people classified as Bantu were even denied property ownership rights in urban areas, while those classified as Coloured were eligible to obtain mortgages only in designated areas, such as Mitchell's Plain.

Despite three decades of democracy, the racial engineering of colonialism and apartheid remain visible in the spatial structures of the housing market. In fact, racial gaps in housing values increased during the property boom of the early 2000s (see chart). In Bantu townships a typical house price has hardly changed since 1990. In White areas it has nearly tripled, allowing property owners to accumulate wealth.

Microfinance

Microfinance has the potential to help people escape poverty, but in some cases debt turns dreams into nightmares.

IN 1976, ECONOMICS PROFESSOR Muhammad Yunus conducted a small experiment in the Bangladeshi village of Jobra. His idea was simple: lend small amounts of interest-free money to women there to improve their lives—roughly the equivalent of US$27 each. In so doing, he hoped to "liberate people's dreams and help the poorest of the poor to achieve dignity." It worked. The women used the money to better themselves and their families and repaid the debt in full. Modern microfinance was born.

Central to global development strategies, microfinance involves lending money to low-income people who have otherwise been excluded from traditional financial services. It has revolutionized foreign and domestic aid programs around the world, as governments view it as a key tool for alleviating poverty. While coverage is uneven, India is the world's biggest market with the largest number of borrowers.

The two dominant microfinance models in India are microfinance institutions (MFIs) and women's self-help groups (SHGs). MFIs lend to individuals with similar socioeconomic backgrounds as well as to groups, where social guarantees replace the need for collateral or guarantors. The SHG model works similarly, but exclusively, for women who form a group, pool their savings together, begin lending internally, and by doing so gain eligibility for microloans from local banks.

Our map of India shows the distribution of MFI headquarters across cities and the number of SHGs per 1,000 women for each state. Some cities host high numbers of MFIs, such as Kolkata and Chennai, and some states have higher ratios of SHGs to women, such as Meghalaya and Odisha. Booming microfinance in Bangladesh influenced its development in neighboring Indian states. In many states, like Odisha, the government actively supports SHGs.

The stories around the map bring this geography to life, revealing the complexities of microfinance in India. While both models can empower people, there are inescapable problems attached to overindebtedness, predatory lending, and fraudulent activities. The success of microfinance depends on both who you are and where you are.

Number of self-help groups per 1,000 women by state, 2020

Number of microfinance institutions headquartered by city, 2019

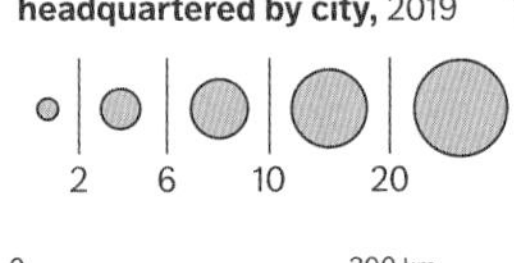

Arabian Sea

GUJARAT

Yavatmal, Maharashtra
Easy access to finance through SHGs and MFIs can lead to social problems. Investigative journalists have shown how a spate of suicides by farmers in Yavatmal and surrounding areas over the past decade have been driven by overindebtedness. These cases, and many others across India, emphasize the need for effective debt regulation and relief by public institutions.

Kerala
The COVID-19 pandemic forced many businesses opened through microfinance to close permanently, leaving their owners without an income and unable to repay their debt. While the pandemic exposed problems of overindebtedness, SHGs have been at the forefront of addressing its impacts. With over four million members, the Kudumbashree network of SHGs in Kerala has supported the government by operating around 1,300 community kitchens, while also delivering essential items to those isolating in quarantine.

70°E

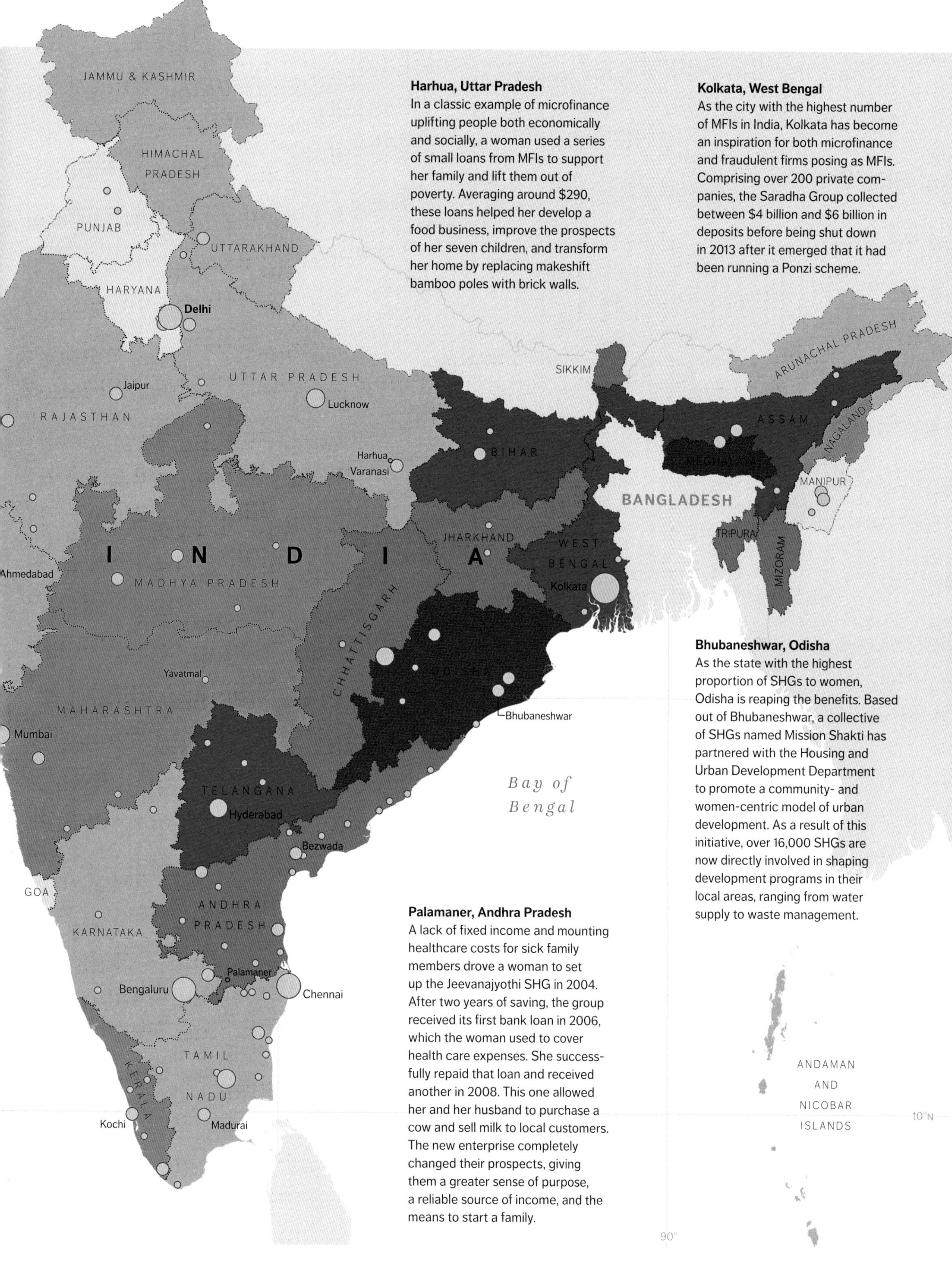

JAMMU & KASHMIR
HIMACHAL PRADESH
PUNJAB
UTTARAKHAND
HARYANA
Delhi
UTTAR PRADESH
Jaipur
Lucknow
RAJASTHAN
Harhua
Varanasi
BIHAR
SIKKIM
ARUNACHAL PRADESH
ASSAM
MEGHALAYA
NAGALAND
MANIPUR
BANGLADESH
TRIPURA
MIZORAM
JHARKHAND
WEST BENGAL
Kolkata
I N D I A
Ahmedabad
MADHYA PRADESH
CHHATTISGARH
ODISHA
Bhubaneshwar
Yavatmal
MAHARASHTRA
Mumbai
TELANGANA
Hyderabad
Bezwada
Bay of Bengal
GOA
ANDHRA PRADESH
KARNATAKA
Palamaner
Bengaluru
Chennai
TAMIL NADU
KERALA
Kochi
Madurai
ANDAMAN AND NICOBAR ISLANDS
10°N
90°
Harhua, Uttar Pradesh
In a classic example of microfinance uplifting people both economically and socially, a woman used a series of small loans from MFIs to support her family and lift them out of poverty. Averaging around $290, these loans helped her develop a food business, improve the prospects of her seven children, and transform her home by replacing makeshift bamboo poles with brick walls.
Kolkata, West Bengal
As the city with the highest number of MFIs in India, Kolkata has become an inspiration for both microfinance and fraudulent firms posing as MFIs. Comprising over 200 private companies, the Saradha Group collected between $4 billion and $6 billion in deposits before being shut down in 2013 after it emerged that it had been running a Ponzi scheme.
Bhubaneshwar, Odisha
As the state with the highest proportion of SHGs to women, Odisha is reaping the benefits. Based out of Bhubaneshwar, a collective of SHGs named Mission Shakti has partnered with the Housing and Urban Development Department to promote a community- and women-centric model of urban development. As a result of this initiative, over 16,000 SHGs are now directly involved in shaping development programs in their local areas, ranging from water supply to waste management.
Palamaner, Andhra Pradesh
A lack of fixed income and mounting healthcare costs for sick family members drove a woman to set up the Jeevanajyothi SHG in 2004. After two years of saving, the group received its first bank loan in 2006, which the woman used to cover health care expenses. She successfully repaid that loan and received another in 2008. This one allowed her and her husband to purchase a cow and sell milk to local customers. The new enterprise completely changed their prospects, giving them a greater sense of purpose, a reliable source of income, and the means to start a family.

Learning Money

According to a global survey, most of the world's adults do not have a grasp of basic financial concepts.

FINANCIAL LITERACY refers to the ability of individuals to understand fundamental concepts of finance that enable them to make sound financial decisions. In 2014, the S&P Global Financial Literacy Survey conducted over 150,000 interviews in more than 140 countries to assess how financial literacy varies across regions, countries, and gender. The results indicated that poorer and less developed countries exhibit lower financial literacy rates than wealthier and more developed countries.

To show this relationship, we've plotted financial literacy rates by country against their Human Development Index, an aggregate measure of human development considering health, knowledge, and material standard of living. The positive relationship is unsurprising. Human development, particularly education, helps financial literacy. However, the relationship is not straightforward. In Europe, for example, Italy has a much lower rate of financial literacy than Hungary, despite having a higher level of human development. The contrast between Africa and Asia is particularly intriguing. While most African countries (in red) lag behind in human development, they perform far better than most Asian countries (gold) in financial literacy. Factors that may explain this difference include earlier and wider implementation of financial education programs in Africa compared to Asia as well as faster and deeper penetration of digital money services, such as M-Pesa in Kenya. Huge disparities in financial literacy also exist within continents. Compare the 71 percent financial literacy rate in Denmark, Norway, and Sweden to the 14 percent in Albania.

In terms of gender, the difference in financial literacy rates is striking. Only 31.9 percent of the world's adult population can be considered financially literate: 29 percent of adult women and 35 percent of adult men. As the bar graph in the bottom right-hand corner shows, this gender gap in financial literacy is found in all regions and almost every country, reflecting the many social and economic barriers faced by women. Of course, financial literacy is hard to measure precisely, and the four questions asked in the S&P survey may appear controversial and biased. One could argue that someone with little savings would do better by putting that money into one business or investment and watching it carefully rather than by diversifying and spreading their attention.

Since you are reading an atlas of finance, chances are you are financially literate. Why not take the quiz yourself to be sure?

Are You Financially Literate?

RISK DIVERSIFICATION

Suppose you have some money. Is it safer to put your money into one business or investment or to put your money into multiple businesses or investments?

a) one business or investment
b) multiple businesses or investments
c) don't know
d) refused to answer

Answers at the bottom of the page.

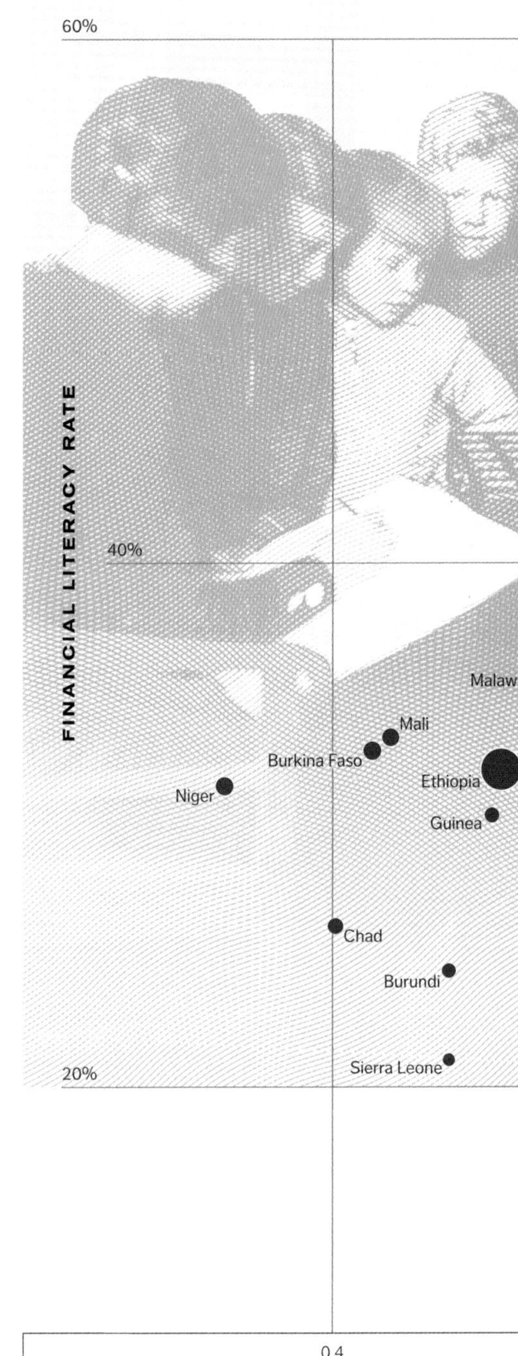

The survey defined a person as financially literate if they correctly answered at least three out of these four questions:

INFLATION

Suppose over the next ten years the prices of the things you buy double. If your income also doubles, will you be able to buy less than you can buy today, the same as you can buy today, or more than you can buy today?

a) less
b) the same
c) more
d) don't know
e) refused to answer

NUMERACY (INTEREST)

Suppose you need to borrow 100 US dollars. Which is the lower amount to pay back: 105 US dollars or 100 US dollars plus three percent?

a) $105
b) $100 plus 3%
c) don't know
d) refused to answer

COMPOUND INTEREST

Suppose you put money in the bank for two years and the bank agrees to add 15 percent per year to your account. Will the bank add more money to your account the second year than it did the first year, or will it add the same amount of money both years?

a) more
b) the same
c) don't know
d) refused to answer

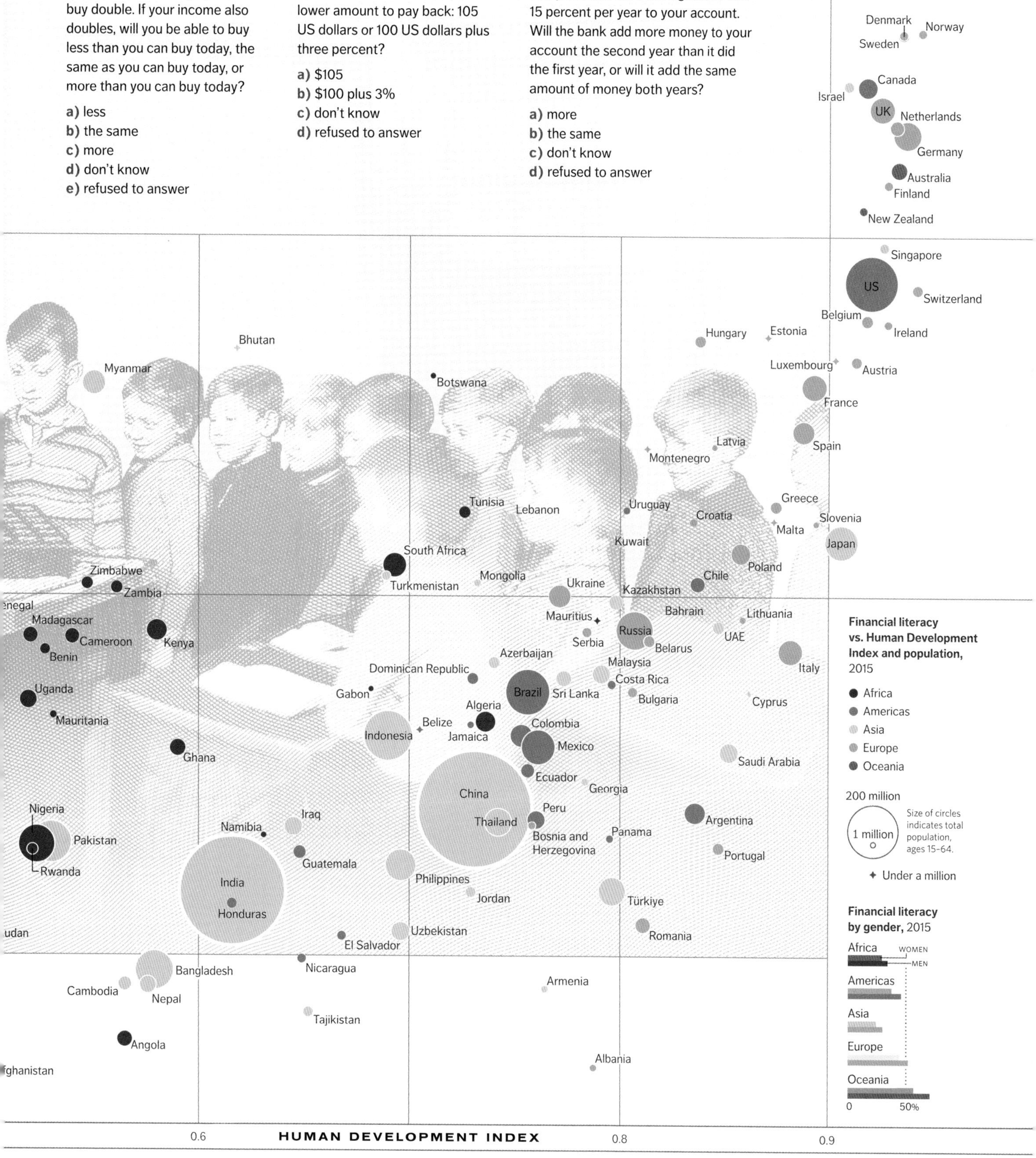

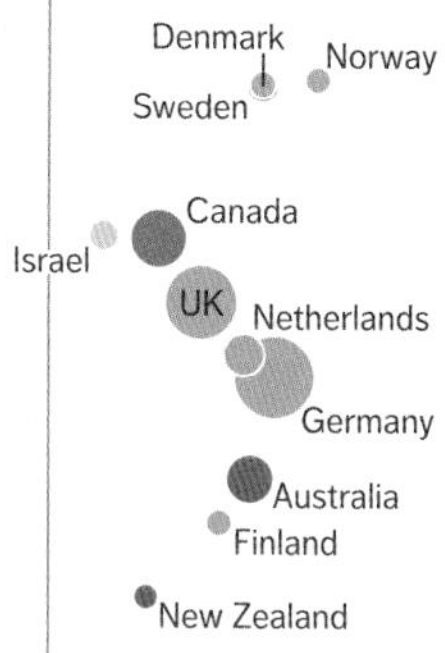

ANSWERS: B, B, A

Weaponizing Finance

Money is power. In the twenty-first century, financial sanctions have become the weapon of choice.

ECONOMIC WARFARE has always been part of human civilization. Centuries ago, fleets of ships enforced trade embargoes through naval blockades. Now, governments and bankers use financial sanctions to undermine rival countries. Taking several different forms, these measures prevent governments from accessing capital markets, restrict businesses from procuring foreign financial services, terminate international banking relationships, freeze

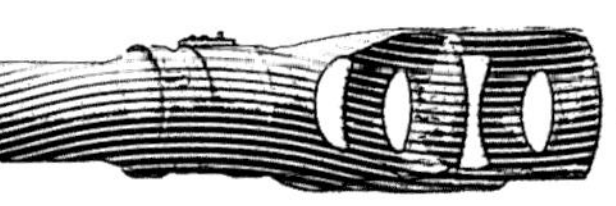

overseas assets, and exclude access to global financial infrastructures such as SWIFT (the Society for Worldwide Interbank Financial Telecommunication).

Not all governments have these weapons in their arsenal. Financial sanctions are about power, and only those countries that are more influential in the regulation of global finance can punish those that are less influential. This creates an uneven geography of sanctioned and sanctioning countries, whereby governments leading the way in expanding global financial integration can limit and exclude access for those governments lagging behind.

Our stream graph shows the geographical distribution of active financial sanctions from 1950 to 2019, colored by region. Given the dominance of the West in global finance, it is no surprise that the US, the European Union, Norway, and Canada implement the most financial sanctions, although the UN as a whole has become a common sanctioner. In contrast, the most sanctioned countries are Myanmar, Cambodia, Pakistan, Syria, and Iran. The regional geography of financial sanctions evolves over time, shifting with major geopolitical events such as the Cold War and the War on Terror. While our timeline provides some answers as to why countries have been sanctioned, it is impossible to fully isolate causation. Countries disagree on war, democracy, human rights, and an endless set of political, economic, and social issues.

As the globalization and financialization of the economy has increased the impact of sanctions, their use has exploded. In a deeply interconnected, globalized economy, excluding countries from critical financial networks creates new and expensive challenges. The technologization and digitalization of finance also makes these sanctions easier to implement, monitor, and evaluate. As finance becomes ever more important to the global economy, financial sanctions will increasingly be conscripted into service.

Top Sanctioners

1950–69

- 28 US
- 4 France
- 3 Soviet Union
- 3 UK
- 2 Japan

Number of active financial sanctions by region of sanctioned countries, 1950–2019

4

September 1962
The US and Germany sanction Egypt as it militarily intervenes in the Yemeni civil war.

October 1962
The US increases sanctions against Cuba following the Cuban missile crisis.

June 1967
Arab-Israeli War

June 1950
Korean War starts

November 1955
Vietnam War starts

1950

Most Sanctioned

1950–69

- 6 Egypt
- 3 Rhodesia
- 3 Cuba
- 2 Algeria, China, Laos, North Korea, Peru, Tunisia (tie)

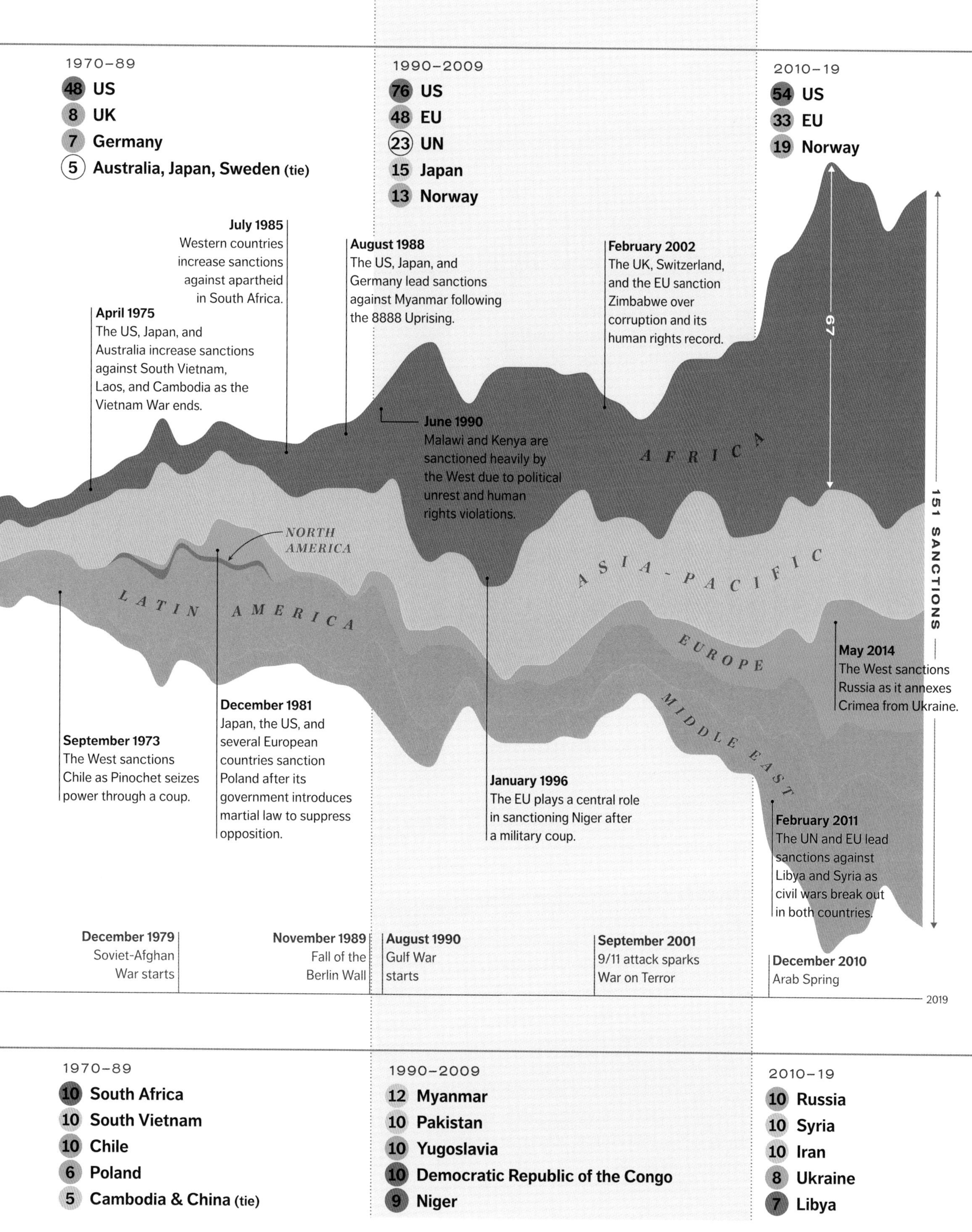

1970–89
48 US
8 UK
7 Germany
5 Australia, Japan, Sweden (tie)
1990–2009
76 US
48 EU
23 UN
15 Japan
13 Norway
2010–19
54 US
33 EU
19 Norway
July 1985
Western countries increase sanctions against apartheid in South Africa.
August 1988
The US, Japan, and Germany lead sanctions against Myanmar following the 8888 Uprising.
February 2002
The UK, Switzerland, and the EU sanction Zimbabwe over corruption and its human rights record.
April 1975
The US, Japan, and Australia increase sanctions against South Vietnam, Laos, and Cambodia as the Vietnam War ends.
67
June 1990
Malawi and Kenya are sanctioned heavily by the West due to political unrest and human rights violations.
AFRICA
151 SANCTIONS
NORTH AMERICA
ASIA-PACIFIC
LATIN AMERICA
EUROPE
May 2014
The West sanctions Russia as it annexes Crimea from Ukraine.
MIDDLE EAST
December 1981
Japan, the US, and several European countries sanction Poland after its government introduces martial law to suppress opposition.
September 1973
The West sanctions Chile as Pinochet seizes power through a coup.
January 1996
The EU plays a central role in sanctioning Niger after a military coup.
February 2011
The UN and EU lead sanctions against Libya and Syria as civil wars break out in both countries.
December 1979
Soviet-Afghan War starts
November 1989
Fall of the Berlin Wall
August 1990
Gulf War starts
September 2001
9/11 attack sparks War on Terror
December 2010
Arab Spring
2019
1970–89
10 South Africa
10 South Vietnam
10 Chile
6 Poland
5 Cambodia & China (tie)
1990–2009
12 Myanmar
10 Pakistan
10 Yugoslavia
10 Democratic Republic of the Congo
9 Niger
2010–19
10 Russia
10 Syria
10 Iran
8 Ukraine
7 Libya

Mining the Future

The shift to storing energy in batteries intensifies the need for minerals, their trading, and associated financial instruments.

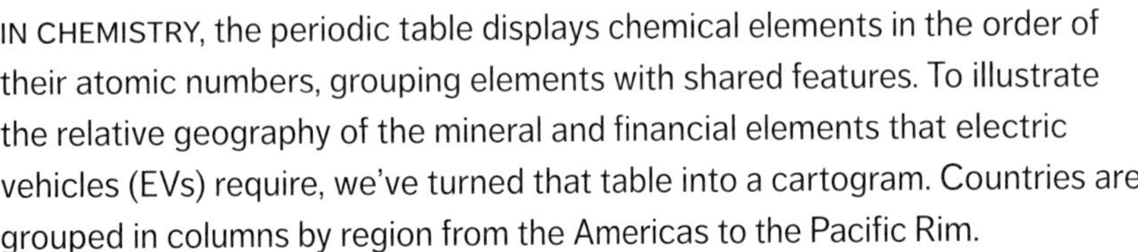

IN CHEMISTRY, the periodic table displays chemical elements in the order of their atomic numbers, grouping elements with shared features. To illustrate the relative geography of the mineral and financial elements that electric vehicles (EVs) require, we've turned that table into a cartogram. Countries are grouped in columns by region from the Americas to the Pacific Rim.

The geography of the mineral and metal deposits used in rechargeable batteries is rather fixed. The heatmaps in the top right show mineral reserves and the largest producers of the key ingredients for lithium-ion EV batteries; the main table shows data on their global trade. These maps reveal that overall mineral production for EV batteries is more geographically concentrated than for fossil fuels. Countries with larger land areas such as Australia, Brazil, Canada, China, and the US are well resourced, while the oil- and gas-rich Middle East hardly features. Global reliance on exports from a handful of developing countries however—lithium from Chile and cobalt from the Democratic Republic of the Congo—has led to local environmental damage and human rights abuses.

In Europe, we see the contrast between empty mineral boxes and Europe's active role in the financial and trade networks. The London Metal Exchange (LME), the world's largest metals exchange, holds a vital position in setting prices and facilitating physical delivery of cobalt, copper, and nickel. Countries with LME-approved warehouses have a higher share of global trade, as commodity traders on the LME play a central role in directing trade from producers to end users, such as battery and car manufacturers concentrated in Asia. Recently, exchanges in London and New York have introduced lithium and cobalt futures contracts. Joining copper and nickel futures, these contracts offer speculative trading opportunities, but crucially they also help producers identify prices and participants in the battery supply chain hedge input costs and manage risk.

When you plug in your car, you are also plugging into the global mineral and financial networks.

Exports and imports of six EV minerals by country, 2020

NORTH AMERICA	SOUTH AMERICA	WEST COAST OF AFRICA	CENTRAL AFRICA	EAST AFRICA
6.1 1.8 Ca CANADA		Ma MOROCCO		
1.3 6.2 Us UNITED STATES (LME warehouse, $)	.09 .09 Br BRAZIL	Ci CÔTE D'IVOIRE	10 Cd DEM. REP. OF THE CONGO	1.1 Tz TANZANIA
Mx MEXICO	Pe PERU	Gh GHANA	19 Zm ZAMBIA	.06 Mz MOZAMBIQUE
Cu CUBA	8.7 Cl CHILE	.04 Ga GABON	Zw ZIMBABWE	.06 Mg MADAGASCAR
.06 Do DOMINICAN REPUBLIC	.42 Ar ARGENTINA	4.5 4.1 Na NAMIBIA	3.4 Za SOUTH AFRICA	

Who Extracts Them?

Many reserves are mined by global companies such as London-headquartered Rio Tinto and Melbourne-headquartered BHP.

Where Are the Minerals of the Electric Economy?

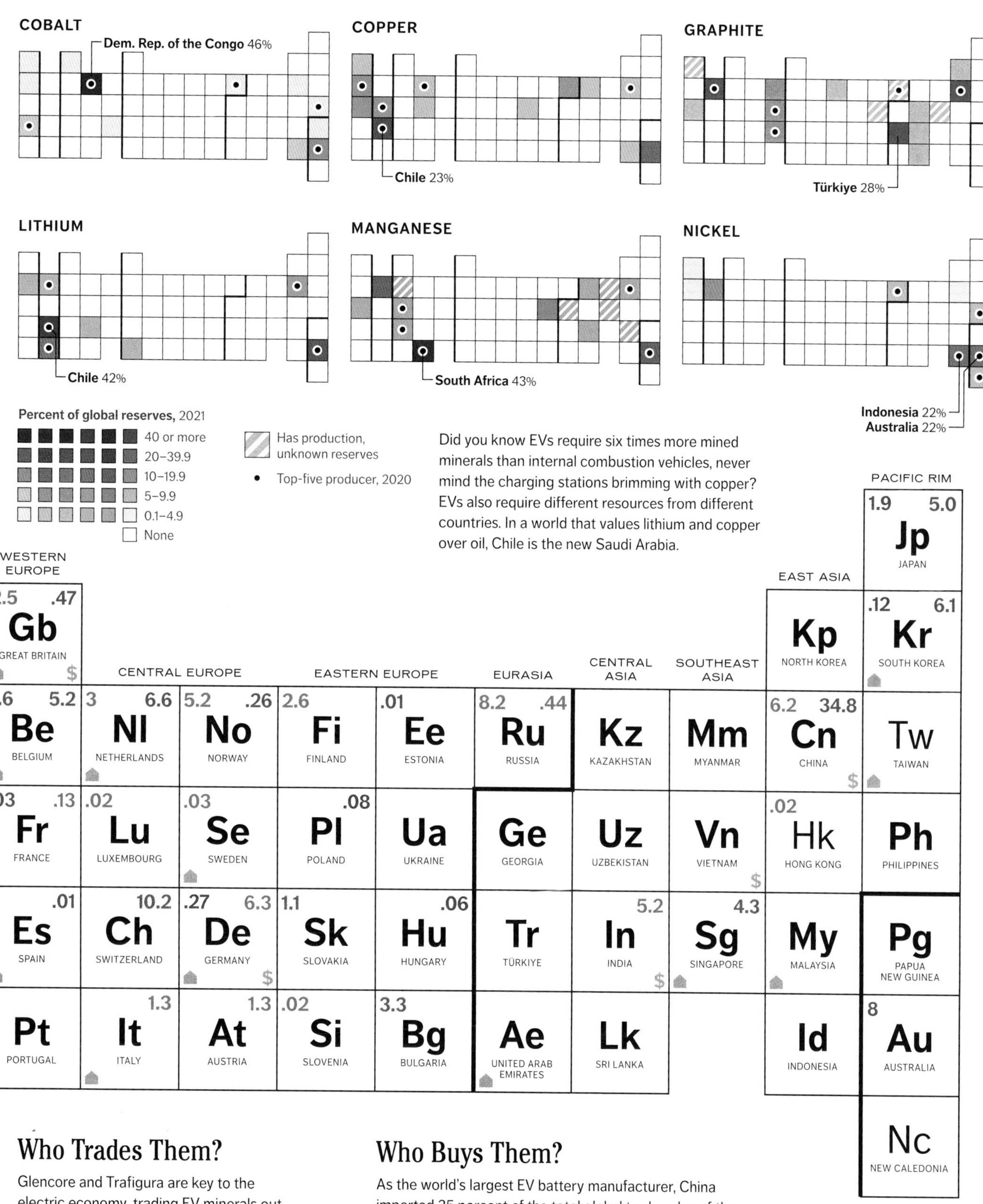

Who Trades Them?

Glencore and Trafigura are key to the electric economy, trading EV minerals out of their headquarters in Switzerland.

Who Buys Them?

As the world's largest EV battery manufacturer, China imported 35 percent of the total global trade value of the six minerals in 2020, despite mining all of them at home.

A Drop in the Ocean?

By investing in the quality of our seas and oceans, blue-bond holders can help nurture ecosystems vital to life on Earth.

IN WINTER, do you daydream about warm summer days and a refreshing dip in the sea? Like so many, summer visitors to the Baltic Sea look forward to a plunge. Many are now encountering a green, slimy sludge instead.

In July, cropland runoff and rising temperatures bring algal blooms to the Baltic, one of the planet's most polluted seas. Fishermen worry about their catch, hoteliers and restaurateurs brace for a drop in tourism, and swimmers tiptoe around the goo. The problem extends far beyond the shoreline. As shown on the map, a green layer swirling across the entire sea was visible from space in 2019.

Our largest ecosystem is the ocean, covering 71 percent of Earth's surface. Marine ecosystems provide the livelihood of three billion people and in 2010 generated an annual economic value of US$1.5 trillion. Despite their importance, they are among the most endangered habitats on the planet. Taking a blue-tinged page out of the popular Green Bond Principles handbook, the blue bond is a new debt instrument that can assist in funding coastal preservation needs, such as stormwater collection and sewage treatment. Blue-bond investors no longer discount Earth's natural capital—the elements of nature that produce economic benefits for people.

The first blue bond was issued in the Seychelles in 2018. Then the Nordic Investment Bank issued one to clean up the Baltic. Scandinavian investors were keen to invest. After their first bond was twice over-subscribed in 2019, the bank issued a second bond in 2020. The proceeds of the Nordic-Baltic Blue Bonds have so far funded thirteen projects to reduce nitrogen and phosphorus discharge, to protect sensitive marine environments, and to minimize raw agricultural runoff during the climate's increasingly heavy downpours. Still, managing the nutrient discharge from around the coastal areas of the Baltic remains an upstream battle. The countries with the most cropland have made the fewest reductions. If these are monumental tasks in a small sea, can blue bonds become a watershed moment, or will they remain just a drop in the global ocean?

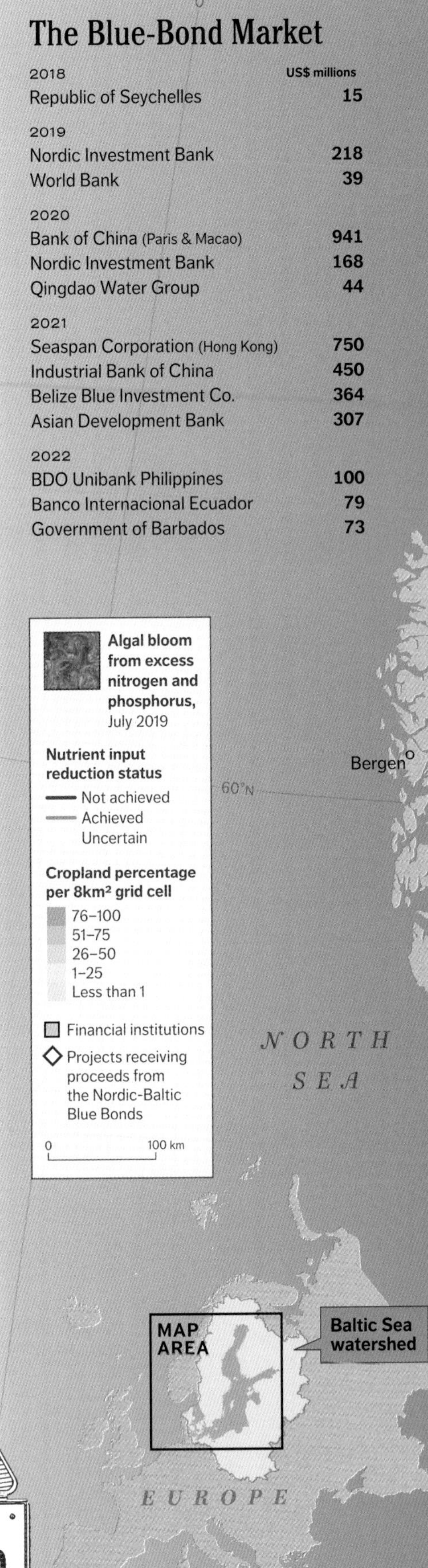

The Blue-Bond Market

	US$ millions
2018	
Republic of Seychelles	15
2019	
Nordic Investment Bank	218
World Bank	39
2020	
Bank of China (Paris & Macao)	941
Nordic Investment Bank	168
Qingdao Water Group	44
2021	
Seaspan Corporation (Hong Kong)	750
Industrial Bank of China	450
Belize Blue Investment Co.	364
Asian Development Bank	307
2022	
BDO Unibank Philippines	100
Banco Internacional Ecuador	79
Government of Barbados	73

ARCTIC CIRCLE
NORWAY
SWEDEN
FINLAND
RUSSIA
Luleå received a €19.5 million loan for the construction of a second bio-waste digester to convert methane into biofuel, a new sewage pipeline, and the expansion of a drinking water plant.
Lule
Luleå
Gulf of Bothnia
Baltic Sea watershed
Lake Ladoga
Espoo received a €115 million loan for its Blominmäki sewage plant to reduce nitrogen discharge by 300 tons per year. Built underground, it will reduce odor and noise impacts on the neighborhood.
Tampere
Petersburg
Nordic Investment Bank
Mäntsälä
Turku
Helsinki
Espoo
Gulf of Finland
Hamar
Vorma
Lännheden
Tallinn
Nasdaq Nordic Sustainable Market
Oslo
ESTONIA
Lake Peipus
Stockholm received a €22.4 million loan to secure drinking water and adapt stormwater collection to reduce discharge into the ecosystem.
Stockholm
Tallinn received a €17.6 million loan to adapt its sewage network to reduce the risk of sewer overflows discharging into the Baltic.
Vänern
Tanum
Vättern
Skagerrak
Göta älv
Gotland I.
LATVIA
Riga
Daugava
Göteborg
Varberg
Aalborg
Kattegat
Halmstad
BALTIC SEA
LITHUANIA
Århus
København
Malmö
Neman
Vilnius
DENMARK
Odense
RUSSIA
Kaliningrad
BELARUS
Gdańsk
Hrodna
POLAND
Białystok
Hamburg
Vistula
Oder
Bydgoszcz
GERMANY

How to Grow a Tree
The green circles represent a hypothetical user's activity over ninety days through various types of activities. Points are logged primarily via QR codes. Walking somewhere? Log one point for every sixty steps. Paying in-store using Alipay to avoid paper receipts? That's five points per payment. Ordering food at a restaurant using a QR code? Seven points. Points add up quickly with a growing number of low-carbon actions available to users. In 2016–19 all users reduced their carbon emissions by 7.9 million tons, the equivalent of total emissions over this period by countries like Iceland or Namibia.

Low-carbon actions available to users	2017	2022	Cumulative carbon emission reduction of all users, 2016–19
Green travel	4	5	5,412,700
Energy-efficient appliances	0	15	2,121,300
Travel reduction	5	14	385,200
Recycling	1	13	8,100
Paper/plastic reduction	2	16	1,800
Total	12	63	7,929,100 tons

Users choose from seventeen different tree species. Point redemptions match the absorption level: a virtual saxaul tree requires 17,900 points to be planted since a real one absorbs 17,900 grams of carbon dioxide in its lifetime.

The Alipay Ant Forest

Financial technology can facilitate land restoration in a digital society.

PICTURE ROWS OF SEEDLINGS perfectly spaced in a vast desert. Half a bucket of water brought in by truck is poured over each, the minimum needed for this "guardian of the desert" to survive. Once grown, these saxaul trees —scientifically known as *Haloxylon ammodendron*—can prevent sand from blowing away, reducing dust storms.

In northern China, 326 million of these gnarled plants took root in just five years through an app launched in 2016 by the Chinese fintech company Ant Group. The Ant Forest mini app is a virtual tree-growing game within Alipay, China's largest mobile and online payment system. As depicted above, users are encouraged to grow a virtual tree by collecting green energy points for less carbon-intensive activities such as walking, driving electric vehicles, recycling, buying energy-rated appliances, or opting for electronic rather than paper receipts. When you collect enough points, your emission reductions are redeemed for a real tree planted on your behalf, with you choosing the tree species and location. The map shows that the most active users, connecting to "their" trees via webcams and satellite

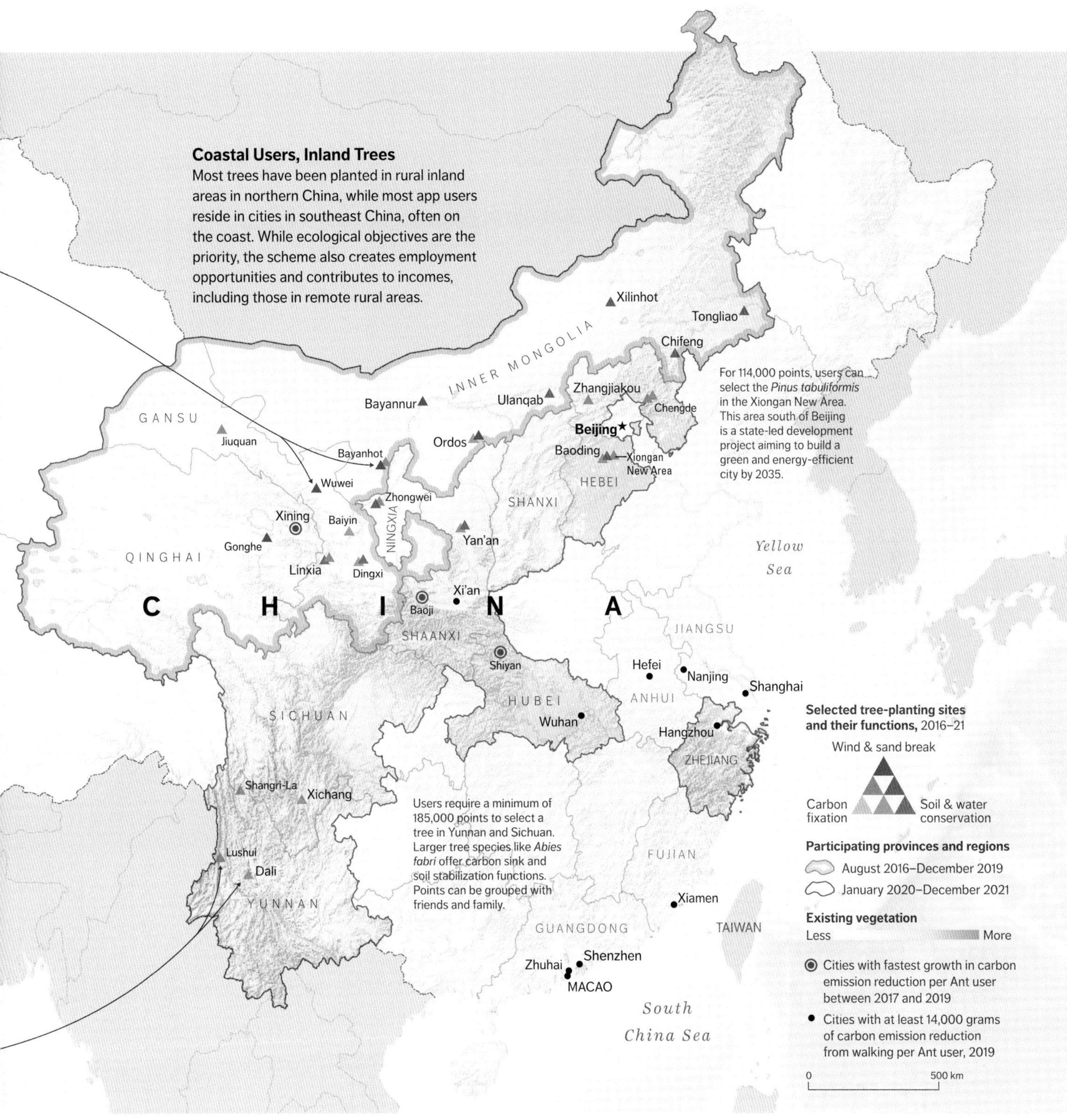

images, come from southeastern cities. The first 122 million trees were planted before 2020 to tackle desertification in Inner Mongolia, Gansu, and Qinghai. The program has since expanded geographically, and new carbon emission reduction activities were added. It is now the largest private tree-planting initiative in the world: 600 million Alipay users have participated, and 2,650 square kilometers—an area the size of Hong Kong or Luxembourg—has been planted.

Rather than donating trees as a charitable act, Ant Group chose to engage with consumers and encourage behavioral changes. This has made Alipay the world's largest digital platform gathering data on people's willingness to reduce their carbon footprints. By offering microsolutions to global problems, fintech can help mobilize individuals to improve environmental conditions and socioeconomic development. This potentially positive effect has received attention, most notably from the United Nations, which awarded Ant Forest the UN Champions of the Earth prize in 2019—making Ant Group the first financial company to receive this global environmental award.

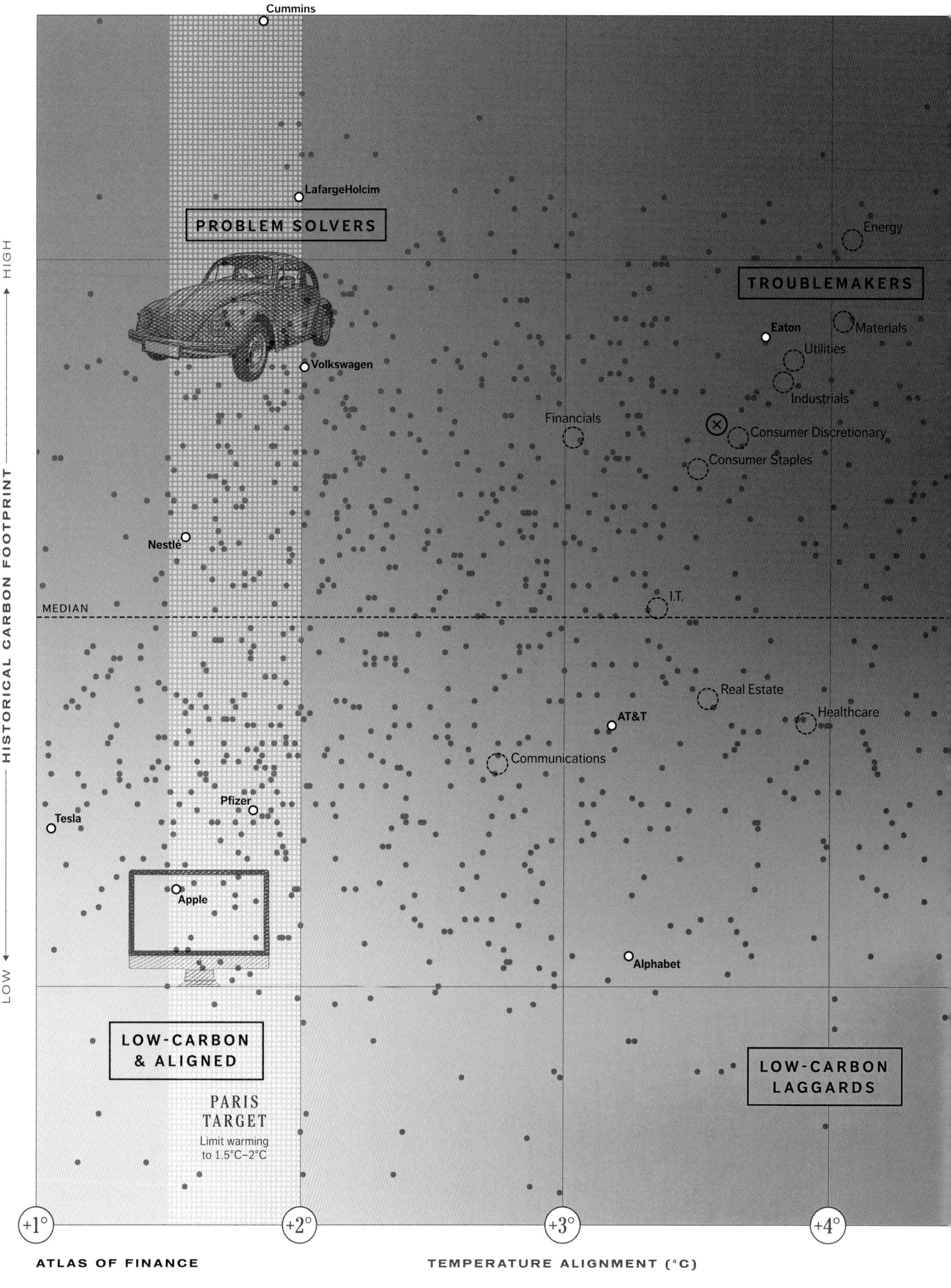

HISTORICAL CARBON FOOTPRINT

LOW ← → HIGH

Cummins

LafargeHolcim

PROBLEM SOLVERS

Energy

TROUBLEMAKERS

Eaton

Materials

Utilities

Volkswagen

Industrials

Financials

Consumer Discretionary

Consumer Staples

Nestlé

MEDIAN

I.T.

Real Estate

Healthcare

AT&T

Communications

Pfizer

Tesla

Apple

Alphabet

LOW-CARBON & ALIGNED

LOW-CARBON LAGGARDS

PARIS TARGET

Limit warming to 1.5°C–2°C

+1° +2° +3° +4°

TEMPERATURE ALIGNMENT (°C)

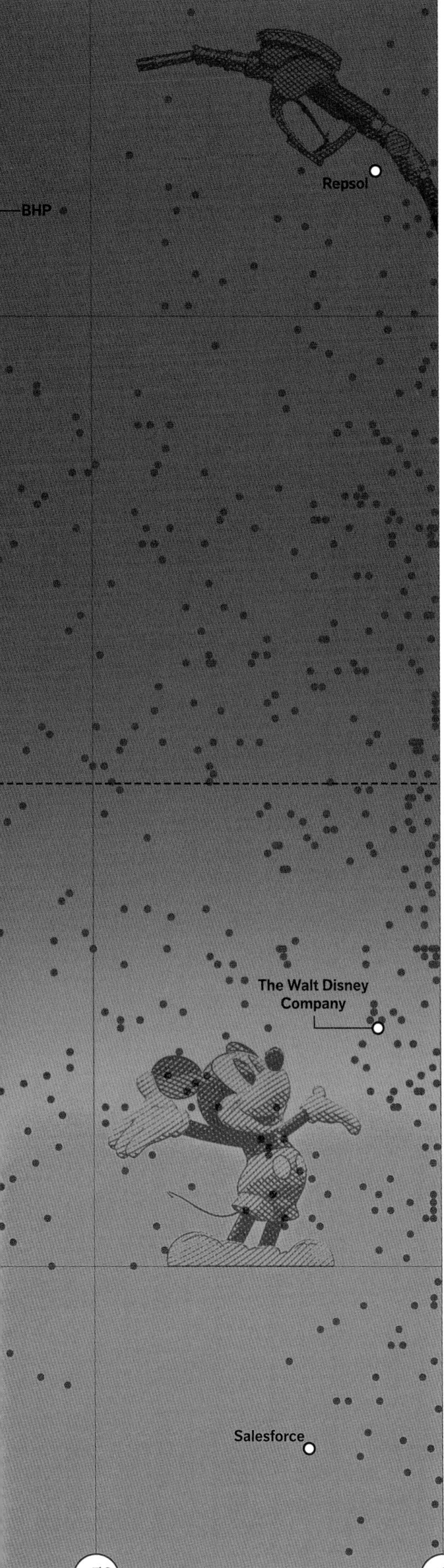

Historical carbon footprint and future global temperature alignment for 1,559 developed-market listed companies, 2021

• **Company**  Sector ⊗ Index average

Is Your Portfolio on Fire?

Investors are increasingly aware of climate-related financial risks and opportunities. Temperature alignment data offers an innovative way to measure and manage them.

EARTH IS ON A WARMING TRAJECTORY with catastrophic environmental and socioeconomic consequences. Here we look at how investors can assess their investment portfolio's alignment with the Paris Agreement, which aims to keep global warming to well below 2°C, and preferably 1.5°C. The carbon footprint of a company (how big its historical emissions are) offers a useful starting point but, on its own, does not constitute a robust decision-making tool. Different geography-sector pairs of the economy have very different carbon budgets. For instance, an Asian cement manufacturer produces vastly larger amounts of carbon per US$1,000 of revenue than a European media company. Yet the world cannot function with media companies only.

Temperature alignment data offers an innovative, forward-looking way to compare the emissions of a company, sector, or portfolio with a fair Paris-aligned carbon budget (here calculated for the period 2015 to 2050). Should this budget be overshot, the "company's temperature" (its contribution to global warming) would overshoot the objectives of the Paris Agreement. Consequently, the company could be considered as more exposed to risks of lost consumer appeal, stranded assets, and compliance, being effectively misaligned with the Paris Agreement. Those risks are most material if the company also has a large carbon footprint.

This scatterplot shows the temperature alignment and carbon footprint of 1,559 large and mid-sized companies. The biggest climate-related investment risks and opportunities lie with the heavy emitters in the upper part of the graph. "Problem Solvers" like the vehicle manufacturer Volkswagen are taking radical steps to decarbonize their business models, while "Troublemakers" like the energy company Repsol are not addressing the problem. Financial companies fall in between with their surprisingly large average carbon footprints, linked to the emissions they finance in the real economy. In the bottom half of the plot, "Low-Carbon Laggards" seem under little pressure and complacent but should also make more effort to become "Low-Carbon & Aligned."

Whether you are a big or small investor, you can take action. Do people managing your and other people's money use their voice as shareholders and do enough to make companies move to the left on this graph?

Data Source: Lombard Odier Asset Management

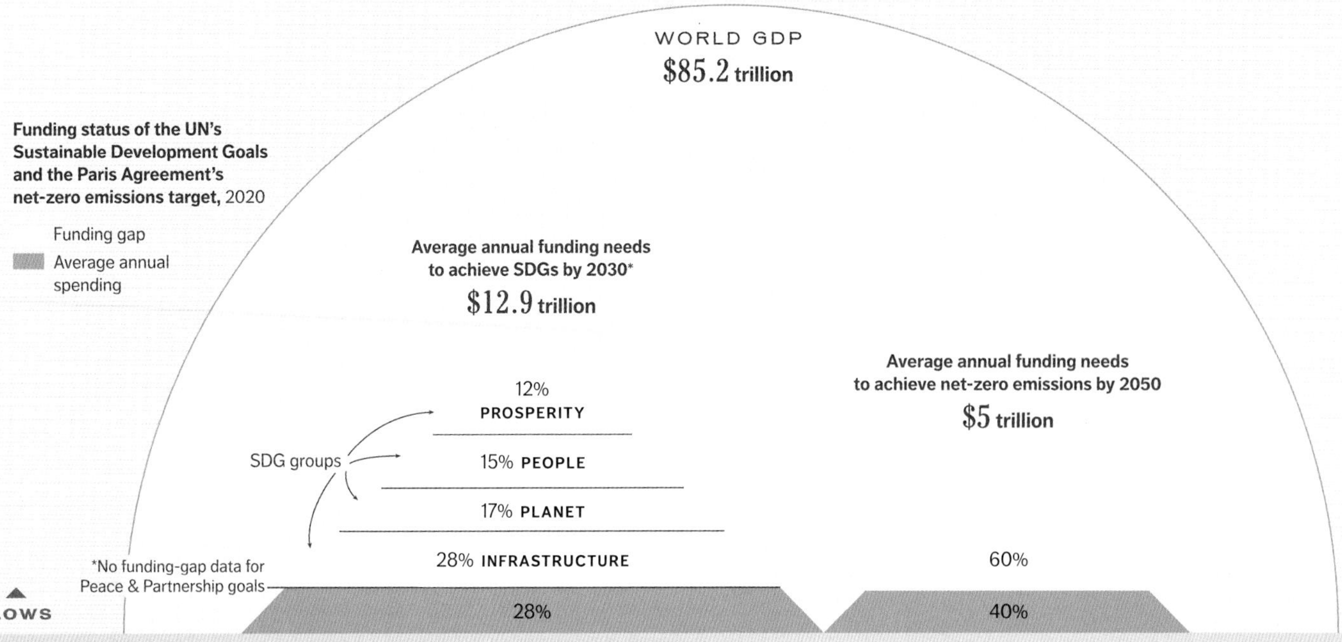

WORLD GDP
$85.2 trillion

Funding status of the UN's Sustainable Development Goals and the Paris Agreement's net-zero emissions target, 2020

Funding gap
Average annual spending

Average annual funding needs to achieve SDGs by 2030*
$12.9 trillion

12% **PROSPERITY**

15% **PEOPLE**

17% **PLANET**

28% **INFRASTRUCTURE**

28%

SDG groups

*No funding-gap data for Peace & Partnership goals

Average annual funding needs to achieve net-zero emissions by 2050
$5 trillion

60%

40%

FLOWS

ASSETS

Annual assets **and** spending **by SDG group** (rounded to nearest US$ half-billion)	European Investment Bank	World Bank Group	Asian Dev. Bank	Inter-American Dev. Bank	European Bank for Reconstruction and Dev.	African Dev. Bank Group	Islamic Dev. Bank	Council of Europe Dev. Bank	Asian Infrastructure Investment Bank	New Dev. Bank
Assets	$626.5 billion	571	222	140	76.5	47	32.5	29	22.5	12
PROSPERITY	103.0	1,165.0	5.5	3.0	5.5	1.0	0.5	< 0.5	—	1.0
PEOPLE	21.5	6.0	1.5	1.0	< 0.5	1.0	0.5	< 0.5	—	0.5
PLANET	43.0	3.0	1.0	1.0	5.0	< 0.5	—	< 0.5	1.0	< 0.5
INFRASTRUCTURE	107.0	16.5	12.0	5.0	314.0	2.5	1.0	< 0.5	3.5	4.0
PEACE & PARTNERSHIP	2.5	22.5	4.5	2.5	107.0	< 0.5	< 0.5	—	—	< 0.5
TOTAL	$277.0	1,213.0	24.5	12.0	431.5	5.0	2.0	0.5	4.5	6.0

The total amount of credit generated by the global financial system in 2021 was $194 trillion; the total value of financial assets in the world economy was $404 trillion.

TOTAL GLOBAL CREDIT
$194 trillion

TOTAL GLOBAL FINANCIAL ASSETS
$404 trillion

Sustainable Development Goals

PROSPERITY
- No poverty
- Gender equality
- Decent work and economic growth
- Reduced inequalities

PEOPLE
- Zero hunger
- Good health and well-being
- Quality education

PLANET
- Responsible consumption and production
- Climate action
- Life below water
- Life on land

INFRASTRUCTURE
- Clean water and sanitation
- Affordable and clean energy
- Industry, innovation, and infrastructure
- Sustainable cities and communities

PEACE & PARTNERSHIP
- Peace, justice, and strong institutions
- Partnership for the goals

Lofty Goals

Reaching UN Sustainable Development Goals and net-zero emissions requires a transformation of the global financial system.

IN 2015, ALL UN MEMBER STATES adopted the 2030 Agenda for Sustainable Development, a plan for addressing universal economic, social, and environmental challenges. The plan's seventeen Sustainable Development Goals (SDGs) range from eradicating poverty and promoting gender equality, education, and decent work to building sustainable cities, promoting peace and justice, and protecting the environment.

These lofty goals don't come cheap, though. In 2020, the total funding needed each year to achieve all seventeen by 2030 was estimated at $US 12.9 trillion, a sum we've depicted as a large peak on the horizon. So far, the mountaintop seems out of reach. The white snowcap represents how far we are falling short every year. If we add that $9.2 trillion to the $3 trillion annual funding shortfall for reaching net-zero emissions by 2050 (see the smaller peak), we see just how much easier sustainability is said than done.

The total shortfall in funding SDG and net-zero emission targets tells us more when we put it in context. In 2020, the global GDP was $85.2 trillion. Directing a fifth of it toward SDGs and a net-zero economy should be possible. With the annual investment needed representing less than 10 percent of total global credit and less than 5 percent of total global financial assets outstanding in 2021, there's enough money. The question is whether there's enough will.

Critical mediators on the path to these SDGs and net-zero emission targets are development banks. They are specialized institutions that finance public- and private-sector development projects by raising money from financial markets using government guarantees. Most development banks are nationally or regionally based and owned by governments. In 2020, there were more than five hundred development banks worldwide with an annual financing of approximately $2.2 trillion and total assets exceeding $18 trillion. Forty-seven are the result of multilateral cooperation of international bodies (World Bank, IMF, EU) and national governments. The ten largest multilateral development banks in terms of total assets spent $2 trillion on investment projects targeting SDGs, with the World Bank Group, the European Bank for Reconstruction and Development, and the European Investment Bank spending the lion's share (see green totals in the table). This is a fraction of what our economies and societies need to move closer to living in a sustainable and equitable world. On our way to reaching these goals, we have hardly left base camp.

Space Investors

Observational satellites per country, 2021

- 385 United States
- 222 China
- 50 European Space Agency
- 31 Japan
- 22 Russia
- 22 Argentina
- 14 Other

2,000 km above the Earth

LOW ORBIT

400 km

Gaofen
This series of satellites (*Gaofen* means "high resolution") is operated by China's National Space Administration and used to monitor environmental and agricultural risks.

Where Is Money Going?

Having penetrated every nook and cranny of Earth, finance looks set to conquer outer space.

SPACE INVESTMENT has truly blasted off, with more money being spent every year to launch satellites into space. While some satellites are being used by scientists to explore distant galaxies and uncover secrets about the origins of the universe, others have their lenses focused a lot closer to home. The financial world has noticed (see bar chart). Financial firms are getting satellite projects off the ground, and some are beginning to use these eyes in the sky to their own advantage.

The integration of geospatial data with financial products, services, and analysis is transforming the global financial system. Combining satellite imagery and artificial intelligence, spatial finance allows insurance companies to monitor environmental risks, helps real estate companies to identify new investment opportunities, and empowers transnational corporations to map supply chains and improve logistics. Accurate, granular, and real-time data is propelling finance to even greater heights.

Based on data collected from the Union of Concerned Scientists, our visual shows the altitudinal distribution of

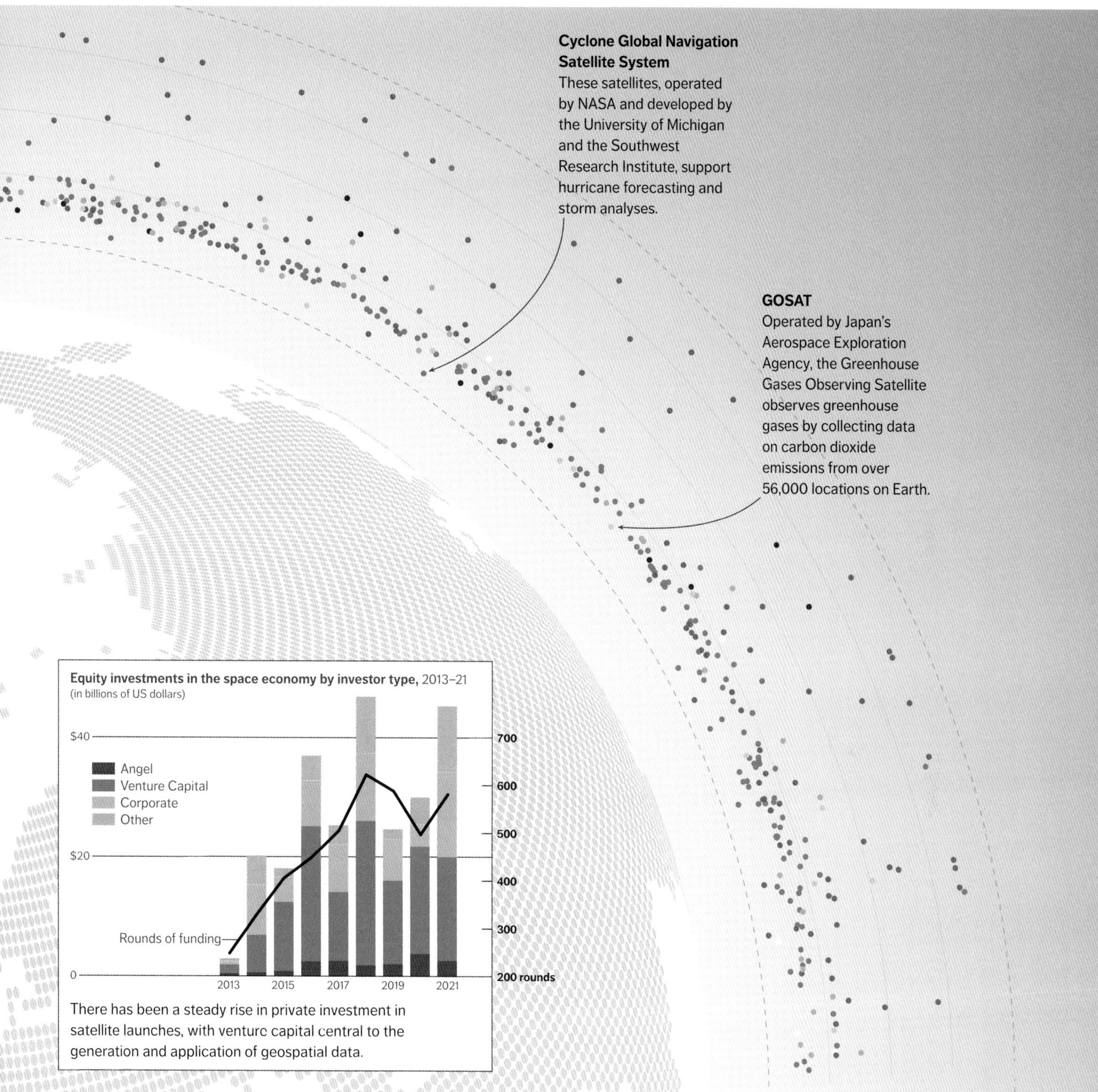

There has been a steady rise in private investment in satellite launches, with venture capital central to the generation and application of geospatial data.

observation satellites over Earth. The bulk of these satellites operate at low orbit, which requires less energy for placement and provides better conditions for communications. These satellites capture images and transmit them back to Earth, forming the foundations of geospatial data.

While the actors using this data are diverse—from central banks and regulators to hedge funds and cryptocurrency investors—the geography of satellite ownership is less so. The US and China eclipse the rest of the world, with public and private organizations from these countries owning over 80 percent of all satellites. In this sense, investment in space looks as increasingly bipolar as the global financial system.

As the opportunities presented by spatial finance continue to grow, the geography of satellite ownership may expand as more firms from around the world strive to integrate geospatial data into their activities. The ascent of humanity from clay foundations to possible colonization of other planets has been and will be linked to the ascent of finance. But can we collaborate and repurpose finance to harness its power to save our planet and humanity?

Notes & References

Introduction: Demystifying Finance

NOTES

The paraphrased statement of Max Weber's on money as a weapon comes from Roth and Wittich (1968).

The Mudrooroo quote comes from Odyssey Traveller (2021); information on the Uranopolis coin is from Marotta (n.d.).

For discussion of Fra Mauro and his map, see Falchetta (2006); on Abraham Ortelius, see Pye (2021); on Joan Blaeu, see Brotton (2013). For a discussion about *The Great Mirror of Folly,* see Goetzmann et al. (2013). For information about the CityNet project, see CityNet (n.d.).

REFERENCES

Brotton, Jerry. 2013. *A History of the World in Twelve Maps.* London: Penguin.

CityNet. n.d. Cities in Global Financial Networks: Financial and Business Services in the 21st Century [website]. *https://www.citynet21.org/*

Falchetta, Piero. 2006. *Fra Mauro's World Map.* Turnhout: Brepols.

Goetzmann, William, Catherine Labio, K. Geert Rouwenhorst, Timothy Young, and Robert Shiller. 2013. *The Great Mirror of Folly: Finance, Culture, and the Crash of 1720.* New Haven, CT: Yale University Press.

Marotta, Michael E. n.d. "Globes on Ancient Coins." 1-World Globes. *https://www.1worldglobes.com/globes-on-ancient-coins/*

Odyssey Traveller. 2021. "Ancient Aboriginal Trade Routes of Australia." Updated February 2021. *https://www.odysseytraveller.com/articles/ancient-aboriginal-trade-routes-of-australia/*

Pye, Michael. 2021. *Antwerp: The Glory Years.* London: Allen Lane.

Roth, Guenter, and Claus Wittich. 1968. *Max Weber: Economy and Society.* New York: Bedminster Press.

Chapter 1: History & Geography

NOTE

The quote is from: Levitt, Steven D. 2012. "If All the Economists Were Laid End to End, Would They Reach a Conclusion?" *Freakonomics,* January 9, *https://freakonomics.com/2012/01/if-all-the-economists-were-laid-end-to-end-would-they-reach-a-conclusion/*

Clay Foundations

NOTES

The main source of the spread is Nissen, Damerow, and Englund (1993). We are grateful to Dr. Paul Collins of Oxford University for recommending the book to us. For the measurement system of Mesopotamia, we also consulted Englund (2001).

The Sumerian proverb "Enlil's temple is a summation of accounts. The temple manager is its overseer" is from Black et al. (1998–).

The base map for the location of the Sumer civilization in ancient Mesopotamia is adapted from Goran tek-en (2014). For the ancient river courses and shoreline, we consulted Morozova (2005), Jotheri et al. (2016), and Iacobucci et al. (2023).

For information on ancient Mesopotamia and the Sumer economy in the text, we consulted Algaze (2012), Nissen (2003), and Podany (2022).

REFERENCES

Algaze, Guillermo. 2012. "The End of Prehistory and the Uruk Period." In *The Sumerian World,* edited by Harriet Crawford, 68–94. London: Routledge.

Black, J. A., G. Cunningham, E. Fluckiger-Hawker, E. Robson, and G. Zólyomi. 1998–2006. *The Electronic Text Corpus of Sumerian Literature.* Oxford. *http://www-etcsl.orient.ox.ac.uk/*

Englund, R. K. 2001. "Grain Accounting Practices in Archaic Mesopotamia." In *Changing Views on Ancient Near Eastern Mathematics,* edited by J. Høyrup and P. Damerov, 1–35. Berlin: Dietrich Reimer Verlag. *https://cdli.ucla.edu/staff/englund/publications/englund2001b.pdf*

Goran tek-en. 2014. Map of Mesopotamia. *https://commons.wikimedia.org/wiki/File:N-Mesopotamia_and_Syria_english.svg*

Iacobucci, Giulia, Francesco Troiani, Salvatore Milli, and Davide Nadali. 2023. "Geomorphology of the Lower Mesopotamian Plain at Tell Zurghul Archaeological Site." *Journal of Maps* 19 (1): 1–14. *https://doi.org/10.1080/17445647.2022.2112772*

Jotheri, Jaafar, Mark B. Allen, and Tony J. Wilkinson. 2016. "Holocene Avulsions of the Euphrates River in the Najaf Area of Western Mesopotamia: Impacts on Human Settlement Patterns." *Geoarchaeology* 31 (3): 175–93. *https://doi.org/10.1002/gea.21548*

Morozova, Galina S. 2005. "A Review of Holocene Avulsions of the Tigris and Euphrates Rivers and Possible Effects on the Evolution of Civilizations in Lower Mesopotamia." *Geoarchaeology* 20 (4): 401–23. *https://doi.org/10.1002/gea.20057*

Nissen, Hans J. 2003. "Uruk and the Formation of the City." In *Art of the First Cities: The Third Millennium B.C. from the Mediterranean to the Indus,* edited by J. Aruz, 11–20. New York: Metropolitan Museum of Art.

Nissen, Hans J., Peter Damerow, and Robert K. Englund. 1993. *Archaic Bookkeeping: Early Writing and Techniques of Economic Administration in the Ancient Near East.* Chicago: University of Chicago Press.

Podany, Amanda H. 2022. *Weavers, Scribes, and Kings: A New History of the Ancient Near East.* Oxford: Oxford University Press.

Metallic Money

NOTES

The main source of data is Cribb et al. (1999). For countries not covered by it, additional information was collected from the following sources:

Montenegro—Central Bank of Montenegro (n.d.)
Slovenia—Šmit and Šemrov (2006)
Latvia—Baltic Coins (2013)
Estonia—Leimus and Tvauri (2021)
Lithuania—Pinigų Muziejus (2015)
Armenia—Central Bank of Armenia (n.d.)
Azerbaijan—Central Bank of Azerbaijan (n.d.)
East Timor—Wikipedia (n.d.)

The main text and coin captions were also informed by Eagleton and Williams (2011) and Hockenhull (2015).

REFERENCES

Baltic Coins. 2013. "Riga Coins." Facebook, March 24. https://pt-br.facebook.com/BalticCoins/photos/riga-coinsthe-first-documents-confirming-coin-minting-in-riga-are-from-1211-when/588476021163736/

Central Bank of Armenia. n.d. "History of Money Circulation in Armenia from the First Mentions up to the Creation of Transcaucasian Commissariat in 1917." https://www.cba.am/en/SitePages/achmoneycyclefirstmention.aspx

Central Bank of Azerbaijan. n.d. "History of National Money Tokens." https://www.cbar.az/page-168/history-of-national-currency

Central Bank of Montenegro. n.d. "Money in Montenegro through History." https://www.cbcg.me/en/currency/money-museum/money-in-montenegro-through-history

Cribb, Joe, Barrie Cook, and Ian Carradice. 1999. *The Coin Atlas: A Comprehensive View of the Coins of the World throughout History.* Cartography by John Flower. London: Little, Brown and Company.

Eagleton, Catherine, and Jonathan Williams, with Joe Cribb and Elizabeth Errington. 2011. *Money: A History,* 3rd ed. London: British Museum Press.

Hockenhull, Thomas, ed. 2015. *Symbols of Power: The Coins That Changed the World.* London: British Museum Press.

Leimus, Ivar, and Andres Tvauri. 2021. "Coins and Tokens from a 15th-Century Landfill in the Kalamaja Suburb of Tallin." *Estonian Journal of Archeology* 25 (2): 140–59. https://doi.org/10.3176/arch.2021.2.03

Pinigų Muziejus. 2015, August 22. "History of Mints in Lithuania." https://www.pinigumuziejus.lt/en/news/history-of-mints-in-lithuania

Šmit, Žiga, and Andrej Šemrov. 2006. "Early Medieval Coinage in the Territory of Slovenia." *Nuclear Instruments and Methods in Physics Research Section B: Beam Interactions with Materials and Atoms* 252 (2): 290–98. https://doi.org/10.1016/j.nimb.2006.08.014

Wikipedia. n.d. "Portuguese Timorese Pataca." https://en.wikipedia.org/wiki/Portuguese_Timorese_pataca

Sequere Pecuniam

NOTE

The main source of data is the Coin Hoards of the Roman Empire dataset. We are grateful to Professor Chris Howgego of Oxford University for recommending the dataset. The mainland and sea routes come from ORBIS. Additional sources consulted for the main text are Cribb et al. (1999), Eagleton and Williams (2011), Hockenhull (2015), and Howgego (1995, 2013).

REFERENCES

Coin Hoards of the Roman Empire [dataset]. University of Oxford. https://chre.ashmus.ox.ac.uk/

Cribb, Joe, Barrie Cook, and Ian Carradice. 1999. *The Coin Atlas: A Comprehensive View of the Coins of the World throughout History.* Cartography by John Flower. London: Little, Brown and Company.

Eagleton, Catherine, and Jonathan Williams, with Joe Cribb and Elizabeth Errington. 2011. *Money: A History.* 3rd ed. London: British Museum Press.

Hockenhull, Thomas, ed. 2015. *Symbols of Power: The Coins That Changed the World.* London: British Museum Press.

Howgego, Christopher. 1995. *Ancient History from Coins.* London: Routledge.

——. 2013. "The Monetization of Temperate Europe." *Journal of Roman Studies* 103: 16–45. http://www.jstor.org/stable/43286778

ORBIS: The Stanford Geospatial Network Model of the Roman World. Designed and executed by Walter Scheidel and Elijah Meeks. https://orbis.stanford.edu/

Yuan and Its Ancestors

NOTES

The main sources of information on ancient Chinese finance are Goetzmann (2016), Horesh (2013), Vivier (2008), and Glahn (2005).

The quotes in the main text are from the following sources:

"If you grasp three coins . . . and to pacify the world."—the ancient Chinese text Guanzi, quoted in Goetzmann (2016, 158).

"How the Great Kaan Causeth . . . Money Over All His Country." —*The Travels of Marco Polo,* as translated and edited by Yule (1903).

The story on the loan contract from Turfan mentioned in the caption on silk is based on Hansen (2005).

For additional information on ancient money in Korea, we consulted Craig (1955); in Japan, Bramsen (1880); and in Southeast Asia, Heng (2006).

REFERENCES

Bramsen, William. 1880. *The Coins of Japan.* Yokohama: Kelly & Co.

Craig, Alan D. 1955. *The Coins of Korea and an Outline of Early Chinese Coinage.* New York: Ishi Press.

Glahn, Richard von. 2005. *The Origins of Paper Money in China.* Edited by William N. Goetzmann and Geert K. Rouwenhorst. Oxford: Oxford University Press.

Goetzmann, William N. 2016. *Money Changes Everything: How Finance Made Civilization Possible.* Princeton, NJ: Princeton University Press.

Hansen, Valerie. 2005. "How Business Was Conducted on the Chinese Silk Road during the Tang Dynasty, 618–907." In *The Origins of Value: The Financial Innovations That Created Modern Capital Markets,* edited by William N. Goetzmann and Geert K. Rouwenhorst, 43–65. Oxford: Oxford University Press.

Heng, Derek Thiam Soon. 2006. "Export Commodity and Regional Currency: The Role of Chinese Copper Coins in the Melaka Straits, Tenth to Fourteenth Centuries." *Journal of Southeast Asian Studies* 37 (2): 179–203. http://www.jstor.org/stable/20072706

Horesh, Niv. 2013. *Chinese Money in Global Context: Historic Junctures between 600 BCE and 2012.* Stanford, CA: Stanford University Press.

Vivier, Brian Thomas. 2008. *Chinese Foreign Trade, 960–1276.* Dissertation completed at Yale University. https://www.proquest.com/openview/58577c-57589cf8f175dbfe1361a7c993/1?pq-origsite=gscholar&cbl=18750

Yule, Henry. 1903. "How the Great Kaan Causeth the Bark of Trees, Made into Something like Paper, to Pass for Money Over All His Country." In *The Book of Ser Marco Polo: A Venetian Concerning Kingdoms and Marvels of the East.* Vol. 1, edited by Colonel Sir Henry Yule. London: John Murray. Excerpted by Columbia University, Asia for Educators. http://afe.easia.columbia.edu/mongols/figures/figu_polo.htm

Treasury of the World

NOTES

Data on flows to and from Potosí, as well as the main routes on the map and the timeline (both in the text and under the bar plot), is based on Lane (2019). The quote at the end of the text is also drawn from that source: "If Potosí was an environmental disaster and a moral tarpit, it was also a monument to human ingenuity and survival" (Lane 2019, 14).

Data on Potosí silver production during 1545–1823 is from Garner and TePaske (2011).

Additional sources consulted for the main text are Schottenhammer (2020) and Barragán Romano (2016).

REFERENCES

Barragán Romano, Rossana. 2016. "Dynamics of Continuity and Change: Shifts in Labour Relations in the Potosí Mines (1680–1812)." *International Review of Social History* 61 (S24): 93–114. https://doi.org/10.1017/S0020859016000511

Garner, Richard, and John Jay TePaske. 2011. Peru Silver [dataset]. https://www.insidemydesk.com/hdd.html

Lane, K. 2019. *Potosí: The Silver City That Changed the World.* Oakland: University of California Press.

Schottenhammer, Angela. 2020. "East Asia's Other New World, China and the Viceroyalty of Peru: A Neglected Aspect of Early Modern Maritime History." *Medieval History Journal* 23 (2): 181–239. https://doi.org/10.1177/0971945819895895

Who Paid for This?

NOTE

The main sources of the data and ideas for the text are Mullen (2021, 2022) and Mullen and Newman (2018).

REFERENCES

Mullen, Stephen. 2021. "British Universities and Transatlantic Slavery: The University of Glasgow Case." *History Workshop Journal* 91 (1): 210–33. https://doi.org/10.1093/hwj/dbaa035

——. 2022. *Glasgow, Slavery and Atlantic Commerce: An Audit of Historic Connections and Modern Legacies.* Glasgow: Glasgow City Council. https://www.glasgow.gov.uk/index.aspx?articleid=29117

Mullen, Stephen, and Simon Newman. 2018. *Slavery, Abolition and the University of Glasgow. Report and Recommendations of the University of Glasgow History of Slavery Steering Committee.* Glasgow: University of Glasgow. https://www.gla.ac.uk/media/media_607547_en.pdf

Adam Smith, Financial Geographer

NOTES

All quotes are from the 1976 reprint of Smith (1776).

On the image:
"At Amsterdam . . . of the bank": p. 486.
"Amidst all the revolutions . . . of the bank": p. 486.

In the text:
"fortune, probity, and prudence of a particular banker": p. 292.
"Daedalian wings of paper money": p. 321.

Other key sources for the text are Roncaglia (2005), Ross (1995), and Ioannou and Wójcik (2022).

REFERENCES

Ioannou, Stefanos, and Dariusz Wójcik. 2022. "Was Adam Smith an Economic Geographer?" *GeoJournal* 87 (6): 5425–34. https://doi.org/10.1007/s10708-021-10499-y

Roncaglia, Alessandro. 2005. *The Wealth of Ideas: A History of Economic Thought.* Cambridge: Cambridge University Press.

Ross, Ian Simpson. 1995. *The Life of Adam Smith.* Oxford: Oxford University Press.

Smith, Adam. 1776. *An Inquiry into the Nature and Causes of the Wealth of Nations.* Reprinted 1976. Indianapolis: Liberty Fund. Page references are to the 1976 edition.

Money in a World of Contradictions

NOTES

Quotes in the text are from the 1969 reprint of Marx and Engels (1848):
"mere money relation": p. 16.
"centralization of money . . . banks and bankers": p. 49.

Quotes on the image are from the 1990 reprint of Marx (1867):
"In a system . . . social need": pp. 621–22.
"In this paper world . . . concentrated": p. 622.
"The rural depositor . . . slightest control": p. 631.

Other key sources for the text are Brunhoff (1998), Harvey (2006), Itoh and Lapavitsas (1999), and Roncaglia (2005, pp. 244–77).

REFERENCES

Brunhoff, Suzanne de. 1998. "Money, Interest and Finance in Marx's Capital." In *Marxian Economics: A Reappraisal,* edited by Riccardo Bellofiore, 176–88. London: Palgrave Macmillan UK. https://doi.org/10.1007/978-1-349-26118-5_11

Harvey, David. 2006. *Limits to Capital.* London: Verso.

Itoh, Makoto, and Costas Lapavitsas. 1999. *Political Economy of Money and Finance.* New York: Palgrave Macmillan.

Marx, Karl. 1867. *Capital.* Vol. 3. Reprinted in 1990. London: Penguin Books. Page references are to the 1990 edition.

Marx, Karl, and Friedrich Engels. 1848. *Manifesto of the Communist Party*. In *Marx/Engels Selected Works,* vol. 1. Moscow: Progress Publishers, 1969. https://www.marxists.org/archive/marx/works/download/pdf/Manifesto.pdf.

Roncaglia, Alessandro. 2005. *The Wealth of Ideas: A History of Economic Thought.* Cambridge: Cambridge University Press.

Finance as a Beauty Contest

NOTES

Quotes on the image are from Keynes (1936):
"The outstanding fact . . . sometimes to nothing": pp. 149–50.
"The social object . . . to the other fellow": p. 155.
"When he purchases . . . whirlpool of speculation": p. 159.

Other key sources for the text are Chick (1983) and Skidelsky (2003).

REFERENCES

Chick, Victoria. 1983. *Macroeconomics after Keynes.* London: Philip Allan.

Keynes, John Maynard. 1936. *The General Theory of Employment, Interest and Money.* Reprinted in 1973. Cambridge: Cambridge University Press. Page references are to the 1973 edition.

Skidelsky, Robert. 2003. *John Maynard Keynes, 1883–1946.* London: Penguin Books.

Made in the USA

NOTES

Data on the papers on finance published by region is from a search on March 31, 2021, of SJR: Scimago Journal and Country Rank, with *finance* selected as the subject category.

Data on the authors of the 100 most cited papers on finance was sourced from the Web of Science, as of March 31, 2021. Data on male and female authors was added based on the first names and pronouns used on the internet.

The top ten most cited journals in finance were identified according to Google Scholar h5-index as of March 31, 2021, and include (from the most to the least cited): *Journal of Financial Economics, Journal of Finance, Review of Financial Studies, Journal of Banking & Finance, Journal of Corporate Finance, Journal of Accounting and Economics, Journal of Financial and Quantitative Analysis, Review of Finance, International Review of Financial Analysis, Journal of International Money and Finance.* Names and affiliations of editors-in-chief were collected from the official websites of journals. Data on male and female authors was added based on the first names and pronouns used on their professional websites.

Data on the winners of the Nobel Memorial Prize in Economic Sciences is from the official Nobel Prize website (Nobel Prize, n.d.). The official justification for each prize was studied to identify laureates recognized for contributions to broadly defined financial economics. Other data on the winners, including birthplaces and universities where they obtained their PhDs, was collected from the individual Wikipedia pages of the laureates.

REFERENCES

Nobel Prize. n.d. *https://www.nobelprize.org/prizes/lists/all-nobel-prizes/*

SJR. "Scimago Journal & Country Rank." *https://www.scimagojr.com/countryrank.php*

Chapter 2: Assets & Markets

NOTE

The quote from Seneca, a Roman philosopher who lived from approximately 4 BCE to 65 CE, is from: "From the Vault: Origin of the Market Approach." *BVWire,* issue #193-5. *https://www.bvresources.com/articles/bvwire/from-the-vault-origin-of-the-market-approach*

Markets at a Glance

NOTES

Data was collected from datasets by Refinitiv (*https://www.refinitiv.com/en*) and MSCI (*https://www.msci.com/*). Indexes were selected based on the Refinitiv Eikon country page—i.e., the first piece of financial information a trader would see when looking up each individual country. Sector classification was based on the Refinitiv TRBC (the Refinitiv Business Classification) codes. Some sectors were combined to aid data visualization; these include "Consumer Cyclicals" and "Consumer Non-Cyclicals" combined into "Consumer Products," "Industrials" and "Basic Materials" into "Industrials & Materials," and "Energy" and "Utilities" into "Utilities & Energy."

The market capitalization figure for each country is the sum of market capitalizations for each company listed in the index. These figures therefore reflect some of the variation in how each index is composed, for which there is not global standardization. For example, Vietnam's index contains over 400 companies, many of which remain partially owned by the state—leading to the disproportionally large market capitalization of US$221 billion. By contrast, Italy's index has only forty companies, as fewer companies are listed due to the importance of small and family-owned businesses to the Italian economy—resulting in a comparatively small market capitalization of $590 billion. When considering the whole economy, outside index-listed companies, Italy's economy by gross domestic product (GDP) is the ninth largest in the world, and Vietnam's the forty-fifth.

Country indexes: Australia AXJO, Austria ATX, Bahrain BHSEASI, Bangladesh DS30, Belgium BFX, Brazil BVSP, Canada GSPTSE, Chile SPIPSA, China CSI 300, Colombia COLCAP, Croatia CRBEX, Czechia PX, Denmark OMXC25CAP, Egypt EGX 30, Estonia OMXTGI, Finland OMXH25, France FCHI, Germany GDAXI, Greece ATG, Hong Kong HSI, Hungary BUX, Iceland OMXIPI, India BSESN, Indonesia JKSE, Ireland ISEQ, Israel TA-35, Italy IT40, Japan NIKKEI 225, Jordan AMGNRLX, Kazakhstan KASE, Kenya NSE20, Kuwait BKA, Lithuania OMXVGI, Malaysia KLSE, Mauritius SEMDEX, Mexico MXX, Morocco MASI, Netherlands AEX, New Zealand NZX50, Nigeria NGSE, Norway OBX, Oman MSX30, Pakistan KSE, Peru SPBLPGPT, Philippines PSI, Poland WIG, Portugal PSI 20, Qatar QSI, Romania BETI, Saudi Arabia TASI, Serbia BELEX15, Singapore STI, Slovenia SBITOP, South Africa JTOPI, South Korea KOPSI, Spain IBEX, Sri Lanka CSE, Sweden OMXS30, Switzerland SSMI, Taiwan TWII, Thailand SETI, Tunisia TUNINDEX20, Türkiye XUO30, United Arab Emirates ADI, United Kingdom FTSE 100, United States SPX, Vietnam VNI

Unchanging Currencies

NOTES

All data on forex trading is based on Bank for International Settlements (BIS, 2019). For countries not presented on the main map, no data is available, but given the methodology of the BIS, forex trading in these countries can be assumed to be smaller than it is in any country for which data is available.

Data on daily global forex trading by country, presented in the main map, is available on a net-gross basis, while data for daily global forex trading is available on a net-net basis. Net-net basis means that data is adjusted for local and cross-border inter-dealer double-counting. Net-gross basis means that it is adjusted only for local inter-dealer double-counting. Hence the total calculated on a net-gross basis is larger than that calculated on a net-net basis, US$8,301,000 million versus $6,600,000 million, respectively.

For the main text we also consulted Wójcik et al. (2017).

REFERENCES

BIS. 2019. "Triennial Central Bank Survey of Foreign Exchange and Over-the-Counter Derivatives Markets." Basel, Switzerland. *https://www.bis.org/statistics/rpfx19.htm*

Wójcik, Dariusz, Duncan MacDonald-Korth, and Simon X. Zhao. 2017. "The Political–Economic Geography of Foreign Exchange Trading." *Journal of Economic Geography* 17 (2): 267–86. *https://doi.org/10.1093/jeg/lbw014*

Pooling Risk in Paris

NOTE

For this spread we used data from the online database AveTransRisk (n.d.), which was created by the European Research Council (ERC)–funded research project Average-Transaction Costs and Risk Management during the First Globalization (Sixteenth–Eighteenth Centuries). Hosted by the Centre for Maritime Historical Studies of the University of Exeter, the database provides historical information about insurance policies from the sixteenth to the eighteenth centuries in Europe, concentrating on Italy (Livorno, Pisa, Florence, and Genoa), France, and Spain. In particular, we used information about the insurance policies that were signed in the first year of operation (1668) of the French Royal Insurance Chamber (Chambre générale des assurances et grosses aventures). The information includes the origin and destination of the trade route, the ports visited during the voyage, the premium rate, and the value of the cargo, as well as the number and names of the underwriters. From the 363 insurance policies that were signed in that year, we selected the 86 that were underwritten by Elisabeth Hélissant. For calculating the distance of each journey in nautical miles, we used an online distance calculator.

REFERENCES

AveTransRisk. n.d. Average-Transactions Costs and Risk Management during the First Globalization (Sixteenth–Eighteenth Centuries) [database]. Centre for Maritime Historical Studies, University of Exeter. http://humanities-research.exeter.ac.uk/avetransrisk/

Wade, Lewis. 2023. *Privilege, Economy and State in Old Regime France.* Woodbridge: The Boydell Press.

Boomtown

NOTES

Data for the maps of Vancouver comes from the City of Vancouver's Open Data Portal: Property Tax Data 2006, Property Tax Data 2021, and Property Parcels Polygons. Data for change in the House Price Index in the line plot comes from Teranet and National Bank of Canada's House Price Index. Data for average Vancouver house price, referred to in the caption below the legend, comes from RPS: Real Property Solutions (n.d.).

Other key sources for the main text are Fernandez et al. (2016), Gordon (2020, 2022), Grigoryeva and Ley (2019), and International Monetary Fund (n.d.).

REFERENCES

City of Vancouver. n.d. "Open Data Portal." https://opendata.vancouver.ca/pages/home/

Fernandez, Rodrigo, Annelore Hofman, and Manuel B. Aalbers. 2016. "London and New York as a Safe Deposit Box for the Transnational Wealth Elite." *Environment and Planning A: Economy and Space* 48 (12): 2443–61. https://doi.org/10.1177/0308518X16659479

Gordon, Joshua C. 2020. "Reconnecting the Housing Market to the Labour Market: Foreign Ownership and Housing Affordability in Urban Canada." *Canadian Public Policy* 46 (1): 1–22. https://doi.org/10.3138/cpp.2019-009

——. 2022. "Solving Puzzles in the Canadian Housing Market: Foreign Ownership and De-Coupling in Toronto and Vancouver." *Housing Studies* 37 (7): 1250–73. https://doi.org/10.1080/02673037.2020.1842340

Grigoryeva, Idaliya, and David Ley. 2019. "The Price Ripple Effect in the Vancouver Housing Market." *Urban Geography* 40 (8): 1168–90. https://doi.org/10.1080/02723638.2019.1567202.

International Monetary Fund. n.d. "Global Housing Watch." Updated September 22, 2022. https://www.imf.org/external/research/housing/index.htm

RPS: Real Property Solutions. 2022. "RPS House Price Index—Public Release: September 2022." https://www.rpsrealsolutions.com/house-price-index/house-price-index (data for 2022 has been removed from the site).

Teranet and National Bank of Canada. n.d. "House Price Index." https://housepriceindex.ca/#maps=c11

Infrastructure Monopoly

NOTES

While there are broader and narrower definitions of infrastructure, we focused on transport and utilities and collected a diverse set of examples from six continents.

Monetary data on infrastructure companies, assets, and projects at the bottom of each space on the Monopoly board is shown in local currency. The values presented refer to various financial categories: market values and purchase prices of companies and enterprises, their annual revenues, project costs and values, assets, capital, and loans used to finance a project. All data refers to historical prices (based on sources) without conversion to current values, with all figures rounded to the nearest billion in the local currency. We followed the sources rather than trying to bring all data to the same common denominator. The latter would be fraught with difficulty, and given the heterogeneity of infrastructure investments and the local currency denomination of many transactions, it would also be potentially misleading.

Private, public-private, and *public* categories depicted in the background of each game-board space refer to the ownership of each company, asset, or project established on the basis of the sources listed below. *Public* refers to state ownership, irrespective of the level of government, from local to national.

Data on the global portfolio of Fraport AG inside the gameboard comes from Fraport (2021).

Sources of data for individual game-board spaces (clockwise):

Heathrow Airport—Heathrow (2021)
Southern Water—Southern Water (2021)
National Grid—National Grid (2020)
Eurotunnel—Getlink SE (2020)
French Toll Roads—Vinci (2021)
Frankfurt Airport—Fraport (2021)
Wasserversorgung—City of Zürich (2023)
Zürich Airport—Zürich Airport (2021)
Sofia Airport—Petrova (2021)
Autoroute de l'Avenir—Eiffage (n.d.)
Abidjan Airport—Egis (n.d.)
Lake Turkana Wind Power—*The EastAfrican* (2014)
Nairobi-Mombasa Railway—*Business Daily* (2014)
Pretoria-Maputo N4 Toll Route—N4 Toll Route (n.d.)
Indira Gandhi International Airport—Ministry of Civil Aviation, India (2006)
Delhi Jal Board—Government of Delhi (n.d.)
Suvarnabhumi Airport—Airports of Thailand PLC (2021)
Hong Kong Mass Transit—MTR (2021)
Tokaido Shinkansen—Central Japan Railway Company (2021)
Melbourne Airport—Australia Pacific Airports Corporation (1998)
Melbourne Water—Melbourne Water (n.d.)
CityLink Toll Road—Institution of Engineers Australia (2002)
AusNet Services—S&P Global (1995)
Auckland International Airport—Auckland Airport (n.d.) and NZX (2023)
Route 68 Toll Road—BNamericas (1998)
Cancun Airport—Aviation Pros (2002)
Texas Central Railway—Baddour (2015)
Amtrak—Amtrak (2018)
Toronto 407 Toll Road—407 International Inc. (2021)

Other key sources consulted for the main text are Berg et al. (2002) and Torrance (2008).

REFERENCES

407 International Inc. 2021. *407 International Inc.: Consolidated Financial Statements,* December 31, 2020. https://407etr.com/documents/major-financial-filings/74%20-%20Q4%202020%20-%20Consolidated%20Financial%20Statements%20-%20407%20International%20-%20December%2031%202020.pdf

Airports of Thailand PLC. 2021. *Annual Report 2020.* https://investor.airportthai.co.th/ar.html

Amtrak. 2018. *Amtrak FY2018 Company Profile.* https://www.amtrak.com/content/dam/projects/dotcom/english/public/documents/corporate/nationalfactsheets/Amtrak-Corporate-Profile-FY2018-0319.pdf

Auckland Airport. n.d. "Investors." https://corporate.aucklandairport.co.nz/investors

Australia Pacific Airports Corporation. 1998. *Australia Pacific Airports Corporation Annual Report 1997–8.* https://web.archive.org/web/20080724032806/http:/www.melbourneairport.com.au/downloads/pdfs/Annual%20Report%2097-98.pdf

Aviation Pros. 2002. "Bienvenidos a Cancun: Privatization Stimulates Expansion at Cancun International Airport." October 8. https://www.aviationpros.com/home/article/10387289/bienvenidos-a-cancun-privatization-stimulates-expansion-at-cancun-international-airport

Baddour, Dylan. 2015. "Texas High Speed Rail Passes Major Milestone with First Fundraising Announcement." *Houston Chronicle,* July 22. https://www.chron.com/news/transportation/article/Texas-high-speed-rail-passes-major-milestone-with-6400089.php

Berg, Stanford V., Michael G. Pollitt, and Masatsugu Tsuji, eds. 2002. *Private Initiatives in Infrastructure: Priorities, Incentives and Performance.* Cheltenham, UK: Edward Elgar.

BNamericas. 1998. "Rutas del Pacific Wins Chile Route 68 Concession." February 20. https://www.bnamericas.com/en/news/Rutas_del_Pacifico_Wins_Chile_Route_68_Concession

Business Daily. 2014. "Truckers Lose Out under Railway Financing Deal." February 23. https://www.businessdailyafrica.com/Truckers-lose-out-in-China-bank-railway-funding-deal/-/539546/2218808/-/n6kkyq/-/index.html

Central Japan Railway Company. 2021. *Central Japan Railway Company Annual Report 2020.* https://global.jr-central.co.jp/en/company/ir/annualreport/_pdf/annualreport2020.pdf

City of Zürich. 2023. "Wasserversorgung." https://www.stadt-zuerich.ch/dib/de/index/wasserversorgung.html

The EastAfrican. 2014. "$250m for Lake Turkana Wind Power Project." June 14. https://www.theeastafrican.co.ke/business/-250m-for-Lake-Turkana-wind-power-project-/-/2560/2348230/-/itepg9z/-/index.html

Egis. n.d. "Abidjan Airport Concession." https://www.egis-group.com/projects/abidjan-international-airport-cote-d-ivoire

Eiffage. n.d. "Construction de l'Autoroute de l'Avenir au Sénégal." https://www.eiffage.com/groupe/projets-ouvrages-et-realisations-eiffage/construction-de-l-autoroute-de-l-avenir-au-senegal

Fraport. 2021. *Annual Report 2020.* https://www.fraport.com/en/investors/publications-events.html

Getlink SE. 2020. *Universal Registration Document 2020.* https://www.getlinkgroup.com/content/uploads/2021/03/2020-universal-registration-document-getlink-se.pdf

Government of Delhi. n.d. "Delhi Jal Board." http://delhijalboard.nic.in/home/delhi-jal-board-djb

Heathrow. 2021. *Annual Report and Financial Statements 2020.* https://www.heathrow.com/content/dam/heathrow/web/common/documents/company/investor/reports-and-presentations/annual-accounts/finance/Heathrow-Finance-plc-31-December-2020.pdf

The Institution of Engineers Australia. 2002. "Journey and Arrival: The Story of the Melbourne CityLink." http://businessoutlook.com.au/exfiles/docs/Melbourne_CityLink_Book.pdf

Melbourne Water. n.d. [website] https://www.melbournewater.com.au/

Ministry of Civil Aviation, India. 2006. *Operation, Management and Development Agreement between Airports Authority of India and Delhi International Airport Private Limited for Delhi Airport.* April 4. https://www.civilaviation.gov.in/sites/default/files/moca_000971.pdf

MTR. 2021. *Annual Report 2020 MTR Corporation Limited.* http://www.mtr.com.hk/en/corporate/investor/2020frpt.html

N4 Toll Route. n.d. Global Infrastructure Hub. https://cdn.gihub.org/umbraco/media/3722/gi-hub-cross-border-case-study_n4-toll-route.pdf

National Grid. 2020. *Annual Report and Accounts 2019/20.* https://www.nationalgrid.com/document/138741/download

NZX. 2023. "AIA." https://www.nzx.com/instruments/AIA

Petrova, Aleksia. 2021. "Sofia Airport Concessionaire Confirms to Invest 460 mln Euro Despite Crisis." SeeNews, March 22. https://seenews.com/news/sofia-airport-concessionaire-confirms-pledge-to-invest-460-mln-euro-despite-crisis-735280

Southern Water. 2021. *Annual Report and Financial Statements for the Year Ended 31 March 2021.* https://southernwater.annualreport2021.com/media/unml5lxq/30055_southern-water-ar2021_full.pdf

S&P Global. 1995. "Texas Utilities Co. to Buy Australia's Eastern Energy." *Journal of Commerce Online,* November 6. https://www.joc.com/texas-utilities-co-buy-australias-eastern-energy_19951106.html

Torrance, Morag. 2008. "The Rise of a Global Infrastructure Market through Relational Investing." *Economic Geography* 85 (1): 75–97. https://doi.org/10.1111/j.1944-8287.2008.01004.x

Vinci. 2021. *Report on the Financial Statements 2020.* https://www.vinci.com/publi/vinci/vinci-report_on_the_financial_statements_2020.pdf

Zürich Airport. 2021. "Key Financial Data." https://report.flughafen-zuerich.ch/2020/ar/en/key-financial-data/

For Few Eyes Only

NOTES

Data for the average annualized rate of return is based on Li et al. (2022).

The geographical shapes of the Changi Airport, the Changi North Industrial Estate, and the Singapore freeport were obtained by digitizing aerial pictures accessed on Google Maps in July 2021.

Figures on auction houses are from Artprice (2021) and McAndrew (2021).

Due to the lack of exact figures for Chinese auction houses, the total auction turnover for Poly Auction and China Guardian were split equally between Beijing and Hong Kong.

Dates for art movements are from the Metropolitan Museum of Art (n.d.).

For the main text we also used Goetzmann et al. (2011), Renneboog and Spaenjers (2013), and Spaenjers et al. (2015).

For more discussion on the case of freeports, see Carver (2015), Helgadóttir (2020), Offshoreart.co et al. (2020), Zarobell (2020a; 2020b), and Weeks (2020).

REFERENCES

Artprice. 2021. "The Art Market in 2020." Artprice.com by Art Market. https://www.artprice.com/artprice-reports/the-art-market-in-2020

Carver, Jordan. 2015. "On Art Storage and Tax Evasion." *Thresholds* 43 (January): 188–225. https://doi.org/10.1162/thld_a_00068

Goetzmann, William N., Luc Renneboog, and Christophe Spaenjers. 2011. "Art and Money." *American Economic Review* 101 (3): 222–26. https://doi.org/10.1257/aer.101.3.222

Helgadóttir, Oddný. 2020. "The New Luxury Freeports: Offshore Storage, Tax Avoidance, and 'Invisible' Art." *Environment and Planning A: Economy and Space* 55 (4): 1020–40. https://doi.org/10.1177/0308518X20972712

Li, Yuexin, Marshall Xiaoyin Ma, and Luc Renneboog. 2022. "Pricing Art and the Art of Pricing: On Returns and Risk in Art Auction Markets." *European Financial Management* 28 (5): 1139–98. https://doi.org/10.1111/eufm.12348

McAndrew, Clare. 2021. *The Art Market 2021.* An Art Basel & UBS Report. Basel, Switzerland. https://d2u3kfwd92fzu7.cloudfront.net/The-Art-Market_2021.pdf

Metropolitan Museum of Art. n.d. "Heilbrunn Timeline of Art History." https://www.metmuseum.org/toah/chronology

Offshoreart.co, Kathleen Ditzig, and Robin Lynch. 2020. "Art On/Offshore: The Singapore Freeport and Narrative Economics that Frame the Southeast Asian Art Market." *Southeast of Now: Directions in Contemporary and Modern Art in Asia* 4 (2): 161–201. https://doi.org/10.1353/sen.2020.0009

Renneboog, Luc, and Christophe Spaenjers. 2013. "Buying Beauty: On Prices and Returns in the Art Market." *Management Science* 59 (1): 36–53. https://doi.org/10.1287/mnsc.1120.1580

Spaenjers, Christophe, William N. Goetzmann, and Elena Mamonova. 2015. "The Economics of Aesthetics and Record Prices for Art since 1701." *Explorations in Economic History* 57 (July): 79–94. https://doi.org/10.1016/j.eeh.2015.03.003

Weeks, Samuel. 2020. "A Freeport Comes to Luxembourg, or, Why Those Wishing to Hide Assets Purchase Fine Art." *Arts* 9 (3): 87. https://doi.org/10.3390/arts9030087

Zarobell, John. 2020a. "Freeports and the Hidden Value of Art." *Arts* 9 (4): 117. https://doi.org/10.3390/arts9040117

——. 2020b. "Interview with Yves Bouvier." *Arts* 9 (3): 97. https://doi.org/10.3390/arts9030097

The Beautiful Game

NOTES

Data on transfers is from the specialized website Transfermarkt and was sourced in September 2022 from a GitHub repository accessible online at https://github.com/ewenme/transfers

The opening quote in the main text, "Football is now all about money," is from McRae (2014).

Other sources for the main text are Aarons (2021), Ahmed and Burn-Murdoch (2019), Bond et al. (2020), Marcotti (2021), Neri et al. (2021), Poli et al. (2019), Prendergast and Gibson (2022), Richau et al. (2021), and Rohde and Breuer (2016).

REFERENCES

Aarons, Ed. 2021. "How Loans Have Risen to Dominate the Covid-Affected Transfer Market." *Guardian,* September 9. https://www.theguardian.com/football/2021/sep/09/how-loans-have-risen-to-dominate-the-covid-affected-transfer-market

Ahmed, Murad, and John Burn-Murdoch. 2019. "How Player Loans Are Reshaping European Football's Transfer Market." *Financial Times,* August 30. https://www.ft.com/content/9bd82b30-caf2-11e9-a1f4-3669401ba76f

Bond, Alexander John, Paul Widdop, and Daniel Parnell. 2020. "Topological Network Properties of the European Football Loan System." *European Sport Management Quarterly* 20 (5): 655–78. https://doi.org/10.1080/16184742.2019.1673460

Marcotti, Gabriele. 2021. "Udinese Turned 125 This Week and Are an Example of How Small Clubs Can Compete. Just Ask Giampaolo Pozzo." ESPN, December 2. https://www.espn.co.uk/football/blog-marcottis-musings/story/4537022/udinese-turned-125-this-week-and-are-an-example-of-how-small-clubs-can-compete-just-ask-giampaolo-pozzo

McRae, Donald. 2014. "Interview—Johan Cruyff: 'Everyone Can Play Football but Those Values Are Being Lost. We Have to Bring Them Back.'" *Guardian,* September 12. https://www.theguardian.com/football/2014/sep/12/johan-cruyff-louis-van-gaal-manchester-united

Neri, Lorenzo, Antonella Russo, Marco di Domizio, and Giambattista Rossi. 2021. "Football Players and Asset Manipulation: The Management of Football Transfers in Italian Series A." *European Sport Management Quarterly,* June, 1–21. https://doi.org/10.1080/16184742.2021.1939397

Poli, Raffaele, Loïc Ravenel, and Roger Besson. 2019. "Financial Analysis of the Transfer Market in the Big-5 European Leagues (2010–2019)." CIES Football Observatory. https://football-observatory.com/IMG/pdf/mr47en.pdf

Prendergast, Gareth, and Luke Gibson. 2022. "A Qualitative Exploration of the Use of Player Loans to Supplement the Talent Development Process of Professional Footballers in the Under 23 Age Group of English Football Academies." *Journal of Sports Sciences* 40 (4): 422–30. https://doi.org/10.1080/02640414.2021.1996985

Richau, Lukas, Florian Follert, Monika Frenger, and Eike Emrich. 2021. "The Sky Is the Limit?! Evaluating the Existence of a Speculative Bubble in European Football." *Journal of Business Economics* 91 (6): 765–96. https://doi.org/10.1007/s11573-020-01015-8

Rohde, Marc, and Christoph Breuer. 2016. "Europe's Elite Football: Financial Growth, Sporting Success, Transfer Investment, and Private Majority Investors." *International Journal of Financial Studies* 4 (2): 12. https://doi.org/10.3390/ijfs4020012

Migrating Money

NOTES

Data on incoming remittances as a percent of GDP is from World Bank (2019). Data on selected remittance corridors by value is from Pew Research Center (2019).

Other sources used in the main text are Abduvaliev and Bustillo (2020) and Cazachevici et al. (2020).

REFERENCES

Abduvaliev, Mubinzhon, and Ricardo Bustillo. 2020. "Impact of Remittances on Economic Growth and Poverty Reduction amongst CIS Countries." *Post-Communist Economies* 32 (4): 525–46. https://doi.org/10.1080/14631377.2019.1678094

Cazachevici, Alina, Tomas Havranek, and Roman Horvath. 2020. "Remittances and Economic Growth: A Meta-Analysis." *World Development* 134 (October): 105021. https://doi.org/10.1016/j.worlddev.2020.105021

Pew Research Center. 2019. "Remittance Flows by Country 2017." https://www.pewresearch.org/global/interactives/remittance-flows-by-country/. The page has since been updated with more recent data.

World Bank. 2019. "Migration and Remittances." https://www.worldbank.org/en/topic/labormarkets/brief/migration-and-remittances. This brief is no longer available on the website.

Persistent Patterns

NOTE

We used estimates on international trade flows of equity securities underwriting services from Milsom et al. (2020). Their estimates are based on data from the Dealogic Equity Capital Market (ECM) database and concern revenues earned from underwriting equity securities. Revenues are reported in current US dollars (nominal). The dataset covers 91,511 issues of equity securities offerings during the 2000–2015 period. These can be divided into 23,136 initial public offerings (IPOs), 58,454 follow-on offerings, and 9,921 convertible debt securities. The key parties for each transaction are the underwriter(s) and the issuer. In order to aggregate individual revenue flows to a country-dyadic level, the country of the underwriter(s) (exporting country/countries) and the country of the issuer (importing country) were identified for each transaction. They adopted two conventions. First, exporting and importing countries were assigned based on the headquarters of operations for the underwriter(s) and the issuer, respectively—i.e., where their de facto head office is located—rather than where each company is registered for tax or legal purposes. Second, if the underwriter directly involved in a transaction is a subsidiary company, the exporting country was determined by the nationality of its parent company, in line with international trade statistics conventions.

The 91,511 offerings in this dataset were linked to 46,408 clients and 7,326 underwriter subsidiaries controlled by 4,287 parent companies. Data on revenue earned from underwriting equity securities in Dealogic's ECM database is either directly reported by underwriters or is estimated by Dealogic. Revenue data is directly disclosed for 45.1 percent of transactions by the underwriters involved in them and undisclosed for the remaining 54.9 percent of transactions. However, Dealogic's ECM database offers proprietary estimates of revenue earned for 47.7 percent of transactions. We therefore have a combination of disclosed and estimated fees available for 92.8 percent of transactions. Finally, 7.2 percent of transactions do not have disclosed or estimated revenue data available and were therefore omitted from our sample.

REFERENCE

Milsom, Luke, Vladimír Pažitka, Isabelle Roland, and Dariusz Wójcik. 2020. "Gravity in International Finance: Evidence from Fees on Equity Transactions." CEP Discussion Paper no. 1703, London, Centre for Economic Performance. *https://cep.lse.ac.uk/pubs/download/dp1703.pdf*

A Cautionary Tale

NOTES

All data on the share price of GameStop is from Yahoo Finance (n.d.).

The statement in the main text that the record-high share price of $347.51 for GameStop was over 20 times the valuation at the start of the month is based on dividing 347 by 17, GameStop's share price on January 1, 2021.

The statement in the main text about the billions of dollars lost by hedge funds is based on Nagarajan (2021).

More information on GameStop and short-selling reports can be found in Fitzgerald (2021).

REFERENCES

Fitzgerald, Maggie. 2021. "Citron Research, Short Seller Caught up in GameStop, Is Pivoting." CNBC. January 29. *https://www.cnbc.com/2021/01/29/citron-research-short-seller-caught-up-in-gamestop-squeeze-pivoting-to-finding-long-opportunities.html*

Nagarajan, Shalini. 2021. "2 of the Biggest Hedge Fund Victims of GameStop's Short-Squeeze Suffered More Losses in May, Report Says." *Market Insider.* January 11. *https://markets.businessinsider.com/news/stocks/gamestop-short-squeeze-melvin-capital-light-street-losses-meme-stocks-2021-6*

Yahoo Finance. n.d. GameStop Corporation (GME). *https://finance.yahoo.com/quote/GME/?guccounter=1*

Chapter 3: Investors & Investments

NOTE

The quote is from: Authers, John. 2015. "Why New York Takes Biggest Slice of Asset Pie." *Financial Times,* August 19, p. 28. *https://www.ft.com/content/68125644-455a-11e5-b3b2-1672f710807b*

The Safest Bets

NOTE

The main source of the data and ideas for the text is Jordá et al. (2019). Volatility of returns in the main plot is measured as the standard deviation of annual real returns, 1870–2015. Average annual real returns for the sixteen countries in the line plot were calculated by weighting the annual real returns of individual countries by their gross domestic product (GDP) in a given year. To smooth the results, we used a ten-year moving average. The plot starts in 1880 as the first year for which the decadal moving average can be calculated, given that the data series starts in 1870.

REFERENCE

Jordà, Òscar, Katharina Knoll, Dmitry Kuvshinov, Moritz Schularick, and Alan M. Taylor. 2019. "The Rate of Return on Everything, 1870–2015." *Quarterly Journal of Economics* 134 (3): 1225–98. *https://doi.org/10.1093/qje/qjz012*

The Only Free Lunch in Finance?

NOTES

The main data was sourced from Dimson, Marsh, and Staunton (2023). For a presentation and discussion of the data, see, for example, Credit Suisse Research Institute (2022).

The idea for visualizing the data was inspired by Henry Lowenfeld's (1909) book discussed in Goetzmann (2016).

Other references mentioned in the text are Markowitz (1952) and Solnik (1974).

Mark Twain's quotes are from *http://www.twainquotes.com/Wisdom.html*

REFERENCES

Credit Suisse Research Institute. 2022. *Credit Suisse Global Investment Returns Yearbook: 2022 Summary Edition.* *https://www.credit-suisse.com/media/assets/corporate/docs/about-us/research/publications/credit-suisse-global-investment-returns-yearbook-2022-summary-edition.pdf*

Dimson, Elroy, Paul Marsh, and Mike Staunton. 2023. The Dimson-Marsh-Staunton Global Investment Returns Database 2023 (the "DMS Database"), Morningstar Inc.

Goetzmann, William N. 2016. *Money Changes Everything: How Finance Made Civilization Possible.* Princeton, NJ: Princeton University Press.

Lowenfeld, Henry. 1909. *Investment, an Exact Science.* London: Financial Review of Reviews.

Markowitz, Harry. 1952. "Portfolio Selection." *Journal of Finance* 7 (1): 77–91. *https://doi.org/10.1111/j.1540-6261.1952.tb01525.x*

Solnik, Bruno H. 1974. "Why Not Diversify Internationally Rather than Domestically?" *Financial Analysts Journal* 30 (4): 48–52, 54. *http://www.jstor.org/stable/4529718*

Home Bias

NOTES

For the plot we used the IMF (2022), which provides data on international (cross-border) portfolio allocation for a set of countries, distinguishing between home countries (holders of assets) and target countries (issuers of assets). To complement it with data on domestic equity holdings, we used data on the market capitalization of listed domestic companies from the World Bank (2022), the World Federation of Exchanges (2022) and Global Financial Data (2022).

The "Rest of World" category features only on the horizontal axis as it captures data for countries that are investment destinations for which we do not have data on where their own investments go.

REFERENCES

Global Financial Data (GFD). 2022. "Stock Market Capitalization." Global Financial Data (GFD) Finaeon. *https://globalfinancialdata.com/gfd-finaeon-overview*

International Monetary Fund. 2022. "Coordinated Portfolio Investment Survey (CPIS)." IMF Data. *https://data.imf.org/?sk=b981b4e3-4e58-[illegible]7e-9b90-9de0c3367363*

World Bank. 2022. "Market Capitalization of Listed Domestic Companies (Current US$)." World Bank. *https://data.worldbank.org/indicator/CM.MKT.LCAP.CD*

World Federation of Exchanges. 2022. "Market Capitalization." World Federation of Exchanges. *https://statistics.world-exchanges.org/*

The Rideshare Race

NOTES

To construct the step chart illustrating Uber's and Didi's journeys to their respective IPOs, we used data on various sources of pre-IPO funding obtained from Crunchbase (2021). At each funding round we display the name of the investor (or a lead investor if there are multiple) and a type of funding. To calculate the value of cumulative funding at each round, we added up all the previous funding rounds, irrespective of funding type.

The types of funding that we used are defined as follows by Crunchbase (2021). Seed rounds are among the first rounds of funding a company will receive, generally while the company is young and working to gain traction. Round sizes range between US$10K and $2M, though larger seed rounds have become more common in recent years. An angel round is typically a small round designed to get a new company off the ground. Investors in an angel round include individual angel investors, angel investor groups, friends, and family. A seed round typically comes after an angel round, if applicable, and before a company's Series A round. Venture capital funding is provided by institutional investors specializing in investing into companies at early stages of development.

The term *venture funding* refers to an investment that comes from a venture capital firm and describes Series A, Series B, and later rounds. In the Crunchbase database, venture capital funding is divided into series A–J. We combined all these series of venture capital funding into a single funding type, which we refer to as "venture capital." A private equity round is led by a private equity firm or a hedge fund and is a late-stage round. It is a less risky investment because the company is more firmly established, and the rounds are typically upwards of US$50M. A convertible note is a funding mechanism used in between rounds to help companies hold over until they want to raise their next round of funding. When they raise the next round, this note "converts" with a discount at the price of the new round. For example, you will typically see convertible notes after a company raises a Series A round but does not yet want to raise a Series B round. A secondary market transaction is a fundraising event in which one investor purchases shares of stock in a company from other, existing shareholders rather than from the company directly. These transactions often occur when a private company becomes highly valuable and early-stage investors or employees want to earn a profit on their investment. They are rarely announced or publicized. In a debt round, an investor lends money to a company, and the company promises to repay the debt with added interest.

In the main text we also used information about Uber's and Didi's IPOs from Driebusch and Farrell (2019) and Wang et al. (2021).

REFERENCES

Crunchbase. 2021. "Glossary of Funding Types." https://support.crunchbase.com/hc/en-us/articles/115010458467-Glossary-of-Funding-Types

Driebusch, Corrie, and Maureen Farrell. 2019. "Uber's High-Profile IPO Upsets with Weak Debut." *Wall Street Journal,* May 10. https://www.wsj.com/articles/uber-stumbles-in-trading-debut-11557503554

Wang, Echo, Anirban Sen, and Scott Murdoch. 2021. "China's Didi Raises $4.4 Bln in Upsized U.S. IPO." Reuters, June 30. https://www.reuters.com/business/chinas-didi-raises-4-billion-us-ipo-source-2021-06-29/

Retirement (In)security

NOTE

National statistics on pension assets are from OECD Pension Statistics (2019). Subnational statistics on pension assets (US states) are based on data from Center for Retirement Research (n.d.). All data on defined benefit and defined contribution pension assets is from Thinking Ahead Institute (2020). The main text is also based on Clark and Monk (2017) and Urban (2019).

REFERENCES

Center for Retirement Research at Boston College, MissionSquare Research Institute, and National Association of State Retirement Administrators. n.d. Public Plans Data. 2001–20. https://publicplansdata.org/public-plans-database/. Website currently displays an updated date range.

Clark, Gordon L., and Ashby H. B. Monk. 2017. *Institutional Investors in Global Markets.* Vol. 1. Oxford: Oxford University Press. https://doi.org/10.1093/oso/9780198793212.001.0001

OECD. 2019. "OECD Pension Statistics." https://www.oecd-ilibrary.org/finance-and-investment/data/oecd-pensions-statistics_pension-data-en

Thinking Ahead Institute. 2020. "Global Pension Assets Study 2020." https://www.thinkingaheadinstitute.org/research-papers/global-pension-assets-study-2020/

Urban, Michael A. 2019. "Placing the Production of Investment Returns: An Economic Geography of Asset Management in Public Pension Plans." *Economic Geography* 95 (5): 494–518. https://doi.org/10.1080/00130095.2019.1649090

The Pension Grinder

NOTES

The data is based on twenty-seven annual reports available on the Universities Superannuation Scheme website in August 2022 (USS 2022a). The funding ratios reported did, in some instances, change from year to year based on the auditor and actuarial statements. The most recent percent or value for any given year was used; for example, for the DB liabilities value for 2017, a reference from the 2020 report was used rather than the value given in the 2018 report. In instances where funding ratios were given as a percent and not a value, an estimate was made of the annual value based on over- or underfunding of the assets.

In the 2022 investment portfolio depicted inside the grinder, the USS allocation to "cash and tactical overlays" included a –27.4 percent exposure, which translates to borrowing cash/leveraging the portfolio, to buy more inflation-linked bonds. To keep the investment boxes at 100 percent, we divided all asset classes by 1.27; i.e., actual equities exposure was 37.8 percent, not 30 percent.

For expected pensions, note that all USS members receive a lump sum upon retirement, which has not been specified in the visual.

The main text is also based on Otuska (2021), Platanakis and Sutcliffe (2016), Staton (2021), and Universities Superannuation Scheme (2022b).

REFERENCES

Otsuka, Michael. 2021. "Does the Universities Superannuation Scheme Provide a Model of Reciprocity between Generations?" *LSE Public Policy Review* 2 (1): 1–6. https://doi.org/10.31389/lseppr.42

Platanakis, Emmanouil, and Charles Sutcliffe. 2016. "Pension Scheme Redesign and Wealth Redistribution between the Members and Sponsor: The USS Rule Change in October 2011." *Insurance: Mathematics and Economics* 69 (July): 14–28. https://doi.org/10.1016/j.insmatheco.2016.04.001

Staton, Bethan. 2021. "Lecturers at 58 UK Universities Strike over Pensions and Pay." *Financial Times,* December 1. https://www.ft.com/content/1caeea0f-c145-4bf0-89b9-bd28e6afc2ef

Universities Superannuation Scheme (USS). 2022a. "Annual Reports and Accounts: 1996–2022." https://www.uss.co.uk/about-us/report-and-accounts

——. 2022b. "USS Statement in Response to Recent Media Coverage on Liability-Driven Investment (LDI) Strategies." https://www.uss.co.uk/news-and-views/latest-news/2022/10/10102022_uss-statement-in-response-to-recent-media-coverage-on-ldi-strategies

Who Owns the Mall?

NOTES

Data was hand-collected from March to September 2021. For each REIT, we retrieved its list of malls from their corporate website then geocoded each property using Google Maps' application programming interface (API). The list of shareholders was sourced from the websites Fintel and MarketScreener, which provide data on financial markets. We focused on the main institutional shareholders. We selected five REITs based on their market size and geographical diversity. For the values of assets under management we used Mackenzie (2021) and Vanguard (2021).

Other sources used for the text are Aalbers (2019), Aveline-Dubach (2016), Brounen and Koning (2012), Gotham (2006), and Theurillat et al. (2010).

REFERENCES

Aalbers, Manuel B. 2019. "Financial Geography II: Financial Geographies of Housing and Real Estate." *Progress in Human Geography* 43 (2): 376–87. *https://doi.org/10.1177/0309132518819503*

Aveline-Dubach, Natacha. 2016. "Embedment of 'Liquid' Capital into the Built Environment: The Case of REIT Investment in Hong Kong." *Issues & Studies* 52 (4): 1640001. *https://doi.org/10.1142/S1013251116400014*

Brounen, Dirk, and Sjoerd de Koning. 2012. "50 Years of Real Estate Investment Trusts: An International Examination of the Rise and Performance of REITs." *Journal of Real Estate Literature* 20 (2): 197–223. *https://doi.org/10.1080/10835547.2014.12090324*

Gotham, Kevin Fox. 2006. "The Secondary Circuit of Capital Reconsidered: Globalization and the U.S. Real Estate Sector." *American Journal of Sociology* 112 (1): 231–75. *https://doi.org/10.1086/502695*

Mackenzie, Michael. 2021. "BlackRock Assets under Management Surge to Record $9tn." *Financial Times,* April 15. *https://www.ft.com/content/e49180b1-2158-4adf-85d6-0eb4766f4d5f*

Theurillat, Thierry, Jose Corpataux, and Olivier Crevoisier. 2010. "Property Sector Financialization: The Case of Swiss Pension Funds (1992–2005)." *European Planning Studies* 18 (2): 189–212. *https://doi.org/10.1080/09654310903491507*

Vanguard. 2021. "Fast Facts about Vanguard." *https://about.vanguard.com/who-we-are/fast-facts/*

An Inverted World

NOTES

Data on wealth greater than $1M is from Chancel et al. (2022); data on wealth less than $1M is from Davies et al. (2021); data on invested wealth is from Knight Frank (2019).

Other sources are Piketty (2014) and Milanovic (2016).

REFERENCES

Chancel, Lucas, Thomas Piketty, Emmanuel Saez, and Gabriel Zucman. 2022. *World Inequality Report 2022.* Paris: World Inequality Lab. *https://wir2022.wid.world/www-site/uploads/2021/12/WorldInequalityReport2022_Full_Report.pdf*

Davies, D., R. Lluberas, and A. Shorrock. 2021. *Global Wealth Report 2021.* Credit Suisse. *https://www.credit-suisse.com/media/assets/corporate/docs/about-us/research/publications/global-wealth-report-2021-en.pdf*

Knight Frank Research. 2019. *The Wealth Report: The Global Perspective on Prime Property and Investment.* *https://content.knightfrank.com/resources/knightfrank.com.my/pdfs/the-wealth-report-2019.pdf*

Milanovic, B. 2016. *Global Inequality: A New Approach for the Age of Globalization.* Cambridge, MA: Harvard University Press.

Piketty, Thomas. 2014. *Capital in the Twenty-First Century.* Cambridge, MA: Harvard University Press.

Sovereign Nest Eggs

NOTES

All data on the top 100 sovereign wealth funds in 2020, their assets under management, and year of inception is from Ouni et al. (2020) and the Sovereign Wealth Fund Institute (2020a).

All data in the secondary figure that shows the growth of global assets over time is from the Sovereign Wealth Fund Institute (2020b).

Sources for specific information in the main text are as follows:

"The oldest (in white) is the Permanent School Fund in the US, which the State of Texas created in 1854 to support education." —Texas Education Agency (2022)

"Pay to see your beloved Newcastle United play at St. James Park? Saudi Arabia benefits."—Reuters (2021)

"Treat your partner to designer clothes from Harrods? Qatar gains."—Ormsby (2010)

"Escape for some sun via Etihad Airways? The UAE wins." —Etihad Aviation Group (2020)

More information on the Australian Future Fund is available from "About Us" on the Future Fund website at *https://www.futurefund.gov.au/about-us*

More information on the China Investment Corporation is available from "Who We Are" on the China Investment Corporation website at *http://www.china-inv.cn/en/*

More information on the Libyan Investment Authority is available from "About Us" on the Libyan Investment Authority website at *https://lia.ly/en/about-us/*

More information on Norway's Government Pension Fund is available from "About the Fund" on the Norges Bank website at *https://www.nbim.no/en/the-fund/about-the-fund/*

More information on the Abu Dhabi Investment Authority is available from "Purpose" on the Abu Dhabi Investment Authority website at *https://www.adia.ae/en/purpose*

The text is also based on Alhashel (2015) and Megginson and Fotak (2015).

REFERENCES

Alhashel, Bader. 2015. "Sovereign Wealth Funds: A Literature Review." *Journal of Economics and Business* 78 (March): 1–13. *https://doi.org/10.1016/j.jeconbus.2014.10.001*

Etihad Aviation Group. 2020. "Leadership." *https://www.etihadaviationgroup.com/en-ae/about/leadership*

Megginson, William L., and Veljko Fotak. 2015. "Rise of the Fiduciary State: A Survey of Sovereign Wealth Fund Research." *Journal of Economic Surveys* 29 (4): 733–78. *https://doi.org/10.1111/joes.12125*

Ormsby, Avril. 2010. "Qatar Investor Buys UK Department Store Harrods." Reuters, May 8. *https://www.reuters.com/article/us-harrods-idUSTRE6470V520100508*

Ouni, Zeineb, Prosper Bernard, and Michel Plaisent. 2020. "Sovereign Wealth Funds Empirical Studies: A Critical View." *Journal of Economics Studies and Research* 2020: 434738. *https://doi.org/10.5171/2020.434738*

Reuters. 2021. "Saudi Arabia-Led Consortium Completes Takeover of Newcastle United." Reuters, October 7. *https://www.reuters.com/lifestyle/sports/saudi-arabia-led-consortium-completes-takeover-newcastle-united-2021-10-07/*

Sovereign Wealth Fund Institute. 2020a. "Rankings by Total Assets." *https://www.swfinstitute.org/fund-rankings/sovereign-wealth-fund*

———. 2020b. "What Is a Sovereign Wealth Fund?" *https://www.swfinstitute.org/research/sovereign-wealth-fund*

Texas Education Agency. 2022. "Texas Permanent School Fund." *https://tea.texas.gov/finance-and-grants/texas-permanent-school-fund*

China's World

NOTES

All data on the Belt and Road Initiative is from the American Enterprise Institute (2021).

More information on the Addis Ababa–Djibouti railway is available from Muller (2019). More on the aims, priorities, and history of the Belt and Road Initiative is available from the State Council of the People's Republic of China (2022). For more discussion on the Belt and Road Initiative, see Huang (2016), Lai et al. (2020), and Lu et al. (2018).

REFERENCES

American Enterprise Institute. 2021. "China Global Investment Tracker." *https://www.aei.org/china-global-investment-tracker/*

Huang, Yiping. 2016. "Understanding China's Belt & Road Initiative: Motivation, Framework and Assessment." *China Economic Review* 40 (September): 314–21. *https://doi.org/10.1016/j.chieco.2016.07.007*

Lai, Karen P. Y., Shaun Lin, and James D. Sidaway. 2020. "Financing the Belt and Road Initiative (BRI): Research Agendas beyond the 'Debt-Trap' Discourse." *Eurasian Geography and Economics* 61 (2): 109–24. *https://doi.org/10.1080/15387216.2020.1726787*

Lu, Hui, Charlene Rohr, Marco Hafner, and Anna Knack. 2018. "China Belt and Road Initiative: Measuring the Impact of Improving Transport Connectivity on International Trade in the Region—a Proof-of-Concept Study." Cambridge, MA: RAND Corporation.

Muller, Nicholas. 2019. "The Chinese Railways Remolding East Africa." *Diplomat,* January 25. *https://thediplomat.com/2019/01/the-chinese-railways-remolding-east-africa/*

State Council of the People's Republic of China. 2022. "Action Plan on the Belt and Road Initiative." *http://english.www.gov.cn/archive/publications/2015/03/30/content_281475080249035.htm*

Chapter 4: Intermediation & Technology

NOTE

The quote is from: McKenna, Paul. 2007. *I Can Make You Rich.* London: Bantam Press, p. 40.

The Rainmakers

NOTES

Data in the main chart is from Bank of England (2023). For "bank money," we used monetary aggregate M4.

For savings and credit in the UK chart, we used the IMF's *World Economic Outlook* (*https://www.imf.org/en/Publications/WEO*) and the World Bank's World Development Indicators (*https://databank.worldbank.org/source/world-development-indicators*).

For additional information, see Fontana (2009), McLeay et al. (2014), Jakab and Kumhof (2015), and Deutsche Bundesbank Eurosystem (2017).

REFERENCES

Bank of England. 2023. "Further Details about M4 Data." Updated January 31, 2023. *https://www.bankofengland.co.uk/statistics/details/further-details-about-m4-data*

Deutsche Bundesbank Eurosystem. 2017. "How Money Is Created." *https://www.bundesbank.de/en/tasks/topics/how-money-is-created-667392*

Fontana, Giusseppe. 2009. *Money, Uncertainty and Time.* London: Routledge.

Jakab, Zoltan, and Michael Kumhof. 2015. "Banks Are Not Intermediaries of Loanable Funds—and Why This Matters." Working Paper no. 529, Bank of England, London. *https://www.bankofengland.co.uk/-/media/boe/files/working-paper/2015/banks-are-not-intermediaries-of-loanable-funds-and-why-this-matters.pdf?la=en&hash=D6ACD5F0AC55064A95F295C-5C290DA58AF4B03B5*

McLeay, Michael, Amar Radia, and Ryland Thomas. 2014. "Money Creation in the Modern Economy." *Bank of England Quarterly Bulletin* (Q1): 14–27. *https://www.bankofengland.co.uk/-/media/boe/files/quarterly-bulletin/2014/money-creation-in-the-modern-economy*

Cornering the Market

NOTES

Data and information on Royal Mail's IPO are based on stock price data sourced from Bloomberg and the UK National Audit Office (2014) report on the privatization of Royal Mail.

We measured the market share of IPO underwriters by sourcing all IPOs issued between 2000 and 2015 from the Dealogic Equity Capital Market database. We then calculated market shares of aggregate IPO deal value country by country for IPO underwriters, using the operational headquarters of issuers to group individual IPOs into countries.

Further information on IPO underpricing and rent extraction by investment banks can be found in Liu and Ritter (2011), Nimalendran et al. (2007), Pažitka et al. (2021), and Reuter (2006).

REFERENCES

Liu, Xiaoding, and Jay R. Ritter. 2011. "Local Underwriter Oligopolies and IPO Underpricing." *Journal of Financial Economics* 102 (3): 579–601. *https://doi.org/10.1016/j.jfineco.2011.01.009*

Nimalendran, M., J. Ritter, and D. Zhang. 2007. "Do Today's Trades Affect Tomorrow's IPO Allocations?" *Journal of Financial Economics* 84 (1): 87–109. *https://doi.org/10.1016/j.jfineco.2006.01.007*

Pažitka, Vladimír, David Bassens, Michiel van Meeteren, and Dariusz Wójcik. 2021. "The Advanced Producer Services Complex as an Obligatory Passage Point: Evidence from Rent Extraction by Investment Banks." *Competition & Change* 26 (1): 53–74. *https://doi.org/10.1177/10245294211992253*

Reuter, Jonathan. 2006. "Are IPO Allocations for Sale? Evidence from Mutual Funds." *Journal of Finance* 61 (5): 2289–324. *https://doi.org/10.1111/j.1540-6261.2006.01058.x*

UK National Audit Office (NAO). 2014. "The Privatisation of Royal Mail." *https://www.nao.org.uk/wp-content/uploads/2014/04/The-privatisation-of-royal-mail.pdf*

What the SPAC?

NOTES

We used data on initial public offerings (IPOs) sourced from the Refinitiv Eikon database for the maps, bubble charts, and comparisons of money raised by SPACs and traditional IPOs. We included all IPOs of US companies for which there were data on proceeds available and which were listed either on the New York Stock Exchange or NASDAQ in the period January 2019–March 2021. We used only a subset of this data for the bubble chart, covering IPOs listed in the period January 2020–March 2021. To apportion IPOs to US states, we used the operational headquarters of issuers. We divided IPOs into two categories: (1) SPACs—special purpose acquisition companies (these transactions are identified by an indicator variable available in the Refinitiv Eikon database)—and (2) traditional IPOs, which constitute the remainder of the IPOs in our dataset. For each SPAC included in our dataset, we searched for mergers and acquisitions (M&As) in the Refinitiv Eikon database to identify any acquisition targets.

In the line chart we show the stock price performance of two SPACs, namely Kensington Capital Acquisition Corp. and Churchill Capital Corp III, which acquired QuantumScape and MultiPlan, respectively. We also include the S&P 500 index for comparison. We sourced the data on the stock prices of Kensington Capital Acquisition Corp. (renamed to QuantumScape post-acquisition) and Churchill Capital Corp III (renamed to MultiPlan post-acquisition) and S&P 500 index values from Bloomberg. Information on lawsuits involving MultiPlan and QuantumScape comes from Frankel (2022) and Wille (2022), respectively.

REFERENCES

Frankel, Alison. 2022. "Multiplan SPAC's Bid to Kill Shareholder Suit? Blame Muddy Waters." Reuters, February 23. *https://www.reuters.com/legal/transactional/multiplan-spacs-bid-kill-shareholder-suit-blame-muddy-waters-2022-02-23/*

Wille, Jacklyn. 2022. "QuantumScape Must Face Investor Suit Over Electric Car Batteries." *Bloomberg Law*, January 18. *https://news.bloomberglaw.com/litigation/quantumscape-must-face-investor-suit-over-electric-car-batteries*

Maritime Risk Sharing

NOTES

All the accounting data and the details about the journey of the vessel *Il Corvo Volante* are from the online database AveTransRisk (n.d.), which is part of the research project Average-Transaction Costs and Risk Management during the First Globalization (Sixteenth–Eighteenth Centuries) funded by the European Research Council (ERC).

For more about the general average principle, see Bolanca et al. (2017), Constable (1994), Dreijer (2020), Fusaro et al. (2016), and Harris (2020). For more on Rhodian Sea Law, see Britannica (2012) and Kruit (2015).

REFERENCES

AveTransRisk. n.d. "Average-Transaction Costs and Risk Management during the First Globalization." University of Exeter. *http://humanities-research.exeter.ac.uk/avetransrisk/*

Bolanca, Dragan, Vilma Pezelj, and Petra Amizic. 2017. "General Average—An Ancient Institution of Maritime Law Section III: Private Law." *Ius Romanum* 2017 (2): 390–401. *http://iusromanum.info/wp-content/uploads/2020/10/2_2017_UNIVERSUM_OFF_OFF-f.pdf*

Britannica. 2012. "Rhodian Sea Law, Byzantine Law." Updated July 29, 2012. *https://www.britannica.com/event/Rhodian-Sea-Law*

Constable, Olivia Remie. 1994. "The Problem of Jettison in Medieval Mediterranean Maritime Law." *Journal of Medieval History* 20 (3): 207–20. *https://doi.org/10.1016/0304-4181(94)90001-9*

Dreijer, Gijs. 2020. "Maritime Averages and the Complexity of Risk Management in Sixteenth-Century Antwerp." *TSEG/Low Countries Journal of Social and Economic History* 17 (2): 31. *https://doi.org/10.18352/tseg.1101*

Fusaro, Maria, Richard J. Blakemore, Benedetta Crivelli, Kate J. Ekama, Tijl Vanneste, Jan Lucassen, Matthias van Rossum, Yoshihiko Okabe, Per Hallén, and Patrick M. Kane. 2016. "Entrepreneurs at Sea: Trading Practices, Legal Opportunities and Early Modern Globalization." *International Journal of Maritime History* 28 (4): 774–86. *https://doi.org/10.1177/0843871416667413*

Harris, Ron. 2020. "General Average and All the Rest: The Law and Economics of Early Modern Maritime Risk Mitigation." *SSRN*, November 29. *https://doi.org/10.2139/ssrn.3739491*

Kruit, J. A. 2015. "General Average—General Principle plus Varying Practical Application Equals Uniformity?" *Journal of International Maritime Law* 21 (3): 190–202. *https://www.vantraa.nl/media/1416/jolien-kruit-general-average-general-principle-plus-varying-practical-application-equals-uniformity-jiml-21-2015.pdf*

Halley's Calculation

NOTES

For the population data in the bar chart (ages 1–84), we used the reconstruction by Ciecka (2008). We complemented this with data from Bellhouse (2011) for the ages 85–100. The annuity values were calculated based on the formula presented in Bellhouse (2011).

The original article by Edmond Halley (1693) was published in *Philosophical Transactions of the Royal Society of London.*

The dates of the birth and death of Edmond Halley, Henri Justel, Gottfried von Leibniz, and Caspar Neumann and their biographical details were based on Cotter (1981), Eggen (2023), Look and Belaval (2023), and Wikipedia (2023a, 2023b).

REFERENCES

Bellhouse, David R. 2011. "A New Look at Halley's Life Table." *Journal of the Royal Statistical Society: Series A (Statistics in Society)* 174 (3): 823–32. *https://doi.org/10.1111/j.1467-985X.2010.00684.x*

Ciecka, J. E. 2008. "Edmond Halley's Life Table and Its Uses." *Journal of Legal Economics* 15 (1): 65–74. *https://fac.comtech.depaul.edu/jciecka/Halley.pdf*

Cotter, Charles H. 1981. "Biography: Captain Edmond Halley R.N., F.R.S." *Notes and Records: The Royal Society Journal of the History of Science* 36: 61–77. *https://royalsocietypublishing.org/doi/pdf/10.1098/rsnr.1981.0004*

Eggen, Olin Jeuck. 2023. "Edmond Halley: British Scientist." Britannica. Updated January 10, 2023. *https://www.britannica.com/biography/Edmond-Halley*

Halley, Edmond. 1693. "VI. An Estimate of the Degrees of the Mortality of Mankind; Drawn from Curious Tables of the Births and Funerals at the City of Breslaw; with an Attempt to Ascertain the Price of Annuities upon Lives." *Philosophical Transactions of the Royal Society of London* 17 (196): 596–610. *https://doi.org/10.1098/rstl.1693.0007*

Look and Belaval. 2023. "Gottfried Wilhelm Leibniz. German Philosopher and Mathematician." Britannica. *https://www.britannica.com/biography/Gottfried-Wilhelm-Leibniz*

Wikipedia. 2023a. "Caspar Neumann." Updated May 20, 2023. *https://en.wikipedia.org/wiki/Caspar_Neumann*

——. 2023b. "Henri Justel." Updated May 20, 2023. *https://en.wikipedia.org/wiki/Henri_Justel*

The Quantified Consumer

NOTES

Data on subprime-credit population by county for the map was sourced from Equifax and Federal Reserve Bank of New York (2022). To obtain the national average on a longitudinal basis, we calculated the weighted mean of the subprime population, using the adult population of each county as a denominator. Historical data on county population was sourced from Manson et al. (2021). Data on median household income and demographics comes from the 2019 American Community Survey, accessed through the "Tidycensus" R package, which was also used to download geographical boundaries for US counties (Walker and Herman 2022).

In the text, "nearly one in three US consumers" is based on Stolba (2021).

"More than one in five Black consumers have FICO scores of 620 or lower, versus one in nineteen white people" is based on Campisi (2021). The statement "it penalizes several million people" is based on Karger (2007) and Brevoort et al. (2016).

Information regarding FICO scores and the development of scoring methods in the US comes from Marron (2009). To further explore the geography and social structures of credit scoring and subprime lending in the US, see Darden and Wyly (2010), Fuster et al. (2022), Krippner (2017), Ludwig (2015), Poon (2009), Singletary (2020), Wainwright (2009), and Wyly et al. (2009).

REFERENCES

Brevoort, Kenneth P., Philipp Grimm, and Michelle Kambara. 2016. "Credit Invisibles and the Unscored." *Cityscape* 18 (2): 9–34. *http://www.jstor.org/stable/26328254*

Campisi, Natalie. 2021. "From Inherent Racial Bias to Incorrect Data—The Problems with Current Credit Scoring Models." *Forbes Advisor,* February 26. *https://www.forbes.com/advisor/credit-cards/from-inherent-racial-bias-to-incorrect-data-the-problems-with-current-credit-scoring-models/*

Darden, Joe T., and Elvin Wyly. 2010. "Cartographic Editorial—Mapping the Racial/Ethnic Topography of Subprime Inequality in Urban America." *Urban Geography* 31 (4): 425–33. *https://doi.org/10.2747/0272-3638.31.4.425*

Equifax and Federal Reserve Bank of New York. 2022. "Equifax Subprime Credit Population." FRED, Federal Reserve Bank of St. Louis. *https://fred.stlouisfed.org/tags/series?t=equifax%3Bsubprime*

Fuster, Andreas, Paul Goldsmith-Pinkham, Tarun Ramodarai, and Ansgar Walther. 2022. "Predictably Unequal? The Effects of Machine Learning on Credit Markets." *Journal of Finance* 77 (1): 5–47. *https://doi.org/10.1111/jofi.13090*

Karger, Howard Jacob. 2007. "The 'Poverty Tax' and America's Low-Income Households." *Families in Society: The Journal of Contemporary Social Services* 88 (3): 413–17. *https://doi.org/10.1606/1044-3894.3650*

Krippner, Greta R. 2017. "Democracy of Credit: Ownership and the Politics of Credit Access in Late Twentieth-Century America." *American Journal of Sociology* 123 (1): 1–47. *https://doi.org/10.1086/692274*

Ludwig, Sarah. 2015. "Credit Scores in America Perpetuate Racial Injustice. Here's How." *Guardian,* October 13. *https://www.theguardian.com/commentisfree/2015/oct/13/your-credit-score-is-racist-heres-why*

Manson, Steven, Jonathan Schroeder, David van Riper, Tracy Kugler, and Steven Ruggles. 2021. IPUMS National Historical Geographic Information System: Version 16.0. [database]. Minneapolis: IPUMS. *https://doi.org/http://doi.org/10.18128/D050.V16.0*

Marron, Donncha. 2009. *Consumer Credit in the United States.* New York: Palgrave Macmillan US. *https://doi.org/10.1057/9780230101517.*

Poon, Martha. 2009. "From New Deal Institutions to Capital Markets: Commercial Consumer Risk Scores and the Making of Subprime Mortgage Finance." *Accounting, Organizations and Society* 34 (5): 654–74. *https://doi.org/10.1016/j.aos.2009.02.003*

Singletary, Michelle. 2020. "Credit Scores Are Supposed to Be Race-Neutral. That's Impossible," *Washington Post,* October 16. *https://www.washingtonpost.com/business/2020/10/16/how-race-affects-your-credit-score/*

Stolba, Stefan Lembo. 2021. "Fewer Subprime Consumers Across U.S. in 2021." *https://www.experian.com/blogs/ask-experian/research/subprime-study/*

Wainwright, Thomas A. 2009. "The Geographies of Securitisation and Credit Scoring." PhD diss., University of Nottingham. *http://eprints.nottingham.ac.uk/10949/*

Walker, Kyle, and Matt Herman. 2022. "Tidycensus." R package. *https://walker-data.com/tidycensus/*

Wyly, Elvin, Markus Moos, Daniel Hammel, and Emanuel Kabahzi. 2009. "Cartographies of Race and Class: Mapping the Class-Monopoly Rents of American Subprime Mortgage Capital." *International Journal of Urban and Regional Research* 33 (2): 332–54. *https://doi.org/10.1111/j.1468-2427.2009.00870.x*

A Need for Speed

NOTES

Data is from the Federal Communications Commission (2021). Jefferson Networks and Pierce Broadband are companies owned by McKay Brothers, which their FCC licenses are filed under. McKay Brothers operates the high-frequency trading (HFT) network and sells access for HFT firms to trade on them. New Line Networks is jointly owned by Virtu (after buying the HFT firm Getco) and Jump Trading. Webline Holdings is owned by the HFT firm Vigilant, which is owned by the larger DRW group.

In the main text, the statement "In 2010, Spread Networks spent $300–$500 million US dollars" is based on Lewis (2015).

In the caption for Chicago, the statement "In 2014, Jump Trading paid $12 million" is based on Louis (2017).

The statements "McKay Brothers came to an agreement," in the caption for Kelleys Island, and "Anova Financial Networks spent over $1 million," in the caption for New York, are based on MacKenzie (2021).

For more information on HFT, see Louis (2017) and MacKenzie (2021).

REFERENCES

Federal Communications Commission. 2021. "Universal Licensing System." Updated August 26, 2021. *https://www.fcc.gov/wireless/universal-licensing-system*

Lewis, M. 2015. *Flash Boys: A Wall Street Revolt.* New York: W. W. Norton.

Louis, Brian. 2017. "Trading Fortunes Depend on a Mysterious Antenna in an Empty Field." Bloomberg, May 12. *https://www.bloomberg.com/news/articles/2017-05-12/mysterious-antennas-outside-cme-reveal-traders-furious-land-war?leadSource=uverify%20wall*

MacKenzie, D. 2021. *Trading at the Speed of Light: How Ultra-Fast Algorithms Are Transforming Financial Markets.* Princeton, NJ: Princeton University Press.

Smartphone Finance

NOTES

We used GPS coordinates of mobile money agents and their primary business activities from the Bill and Melinda Gates Foundation et al. (2015).

In the main text, "In the aftermath of the 2008 global financial crisis, Paul Volcker, a former chair of the Federal Reserve of the United States, referred to the ATM as the 'only useful innovation in banking for the past twenty years'" is based on Shepherd-Barron (2017).

"What makes smartphones particularly appealing is their widespread availability in developing countries, where the traditional financial infrastructure of bank branches and ATMs is thinnest" is based on Aron and Muellbauer (2019).

REFERENCES

Aron, Janine, and John Muellbauer. 2019. "The Economics of Mobile Money: Harnessing the Transformative Power of Technology to Benefit the Global Poor." Policy report, Oxford Martin School, University of Oxford. *https://www.oxfordmartin.ox.ac.uk/publications/mobile-money/*

Bill and Melinda Gates Foundation, Central Bank of Kenya, and FSD Kenya. 2015. "FinAccess Geospatial Mapping 2015." Edited by Brand Fusion. Harvard Dataverse. *https://doi.org/10.7910/DVN/SG589T*

Shepherd-Barron, James. 2017. "Meet the True Star of Financial Innovation—the Humble ATM." *Financial Times,* June 22. *https://www.ft.com/content/052f9310-5738-11e7-80b6-9bfa4c1f83d2*

Central Bank Digital Currencies

NOTES

For the fan chart, we used data on stages of CBDC development collated by the Atlantic Council (n.d.). We excluded the territories of Montserrat and Anguilla as well as the eurozone from the original dataset prepared by the Atlantic Council. We complemented this data with the USD-denominated value of GDP for each country sourced from the World Bank's World Development Indicators database (*https://databank.worldbank.org/source/world-development-indicators*) and used the natural logarithm of GDP to order countries by economic size.

In the bar charts, we present data on the technological design of CBDCs collated by the Atlantic Council (n.d.) from the Bank of International Settlements, International Monetary Fund, and John Kiff database. The many countries that are still in the early stages of research on CBDCs and have not yet published some elements of their design are marked as "undecided."

In the main text, "CBDC, also called digital fiat currency or digital base money, is the digital form of fiat money, a currency established as money by government regulation, monetary authority, or law" is based on Prasad (2021). "In October 2020 the Bahamas became the first country in the world to adopt its CBDC as legal tender" is based on Bharathan (2020). "A year later, the Central Bank of Nigeria launched the first CBDC outside of the Caribbean" is based on Ree (2021).

"China, whose CBDC pilot is the largest in scale worldwide . . . 70.85 million transactions had been executed with an aggregate value of US$5.2 billion" is based on Working Group (2021). "According to a 2020 survey by the Bank of International Settlements, about 20 percent of central banks were likely to launch a CBDC sometime in the next six years" is based on Boar and Wehrli (2021).

The statement in the caption in the top right corner, "In a survey on central bank digital currency, advanced economies . . . ," is based on Boar and Wehrli (2021).

REFERENCES

Atlantic Council. n.d. "Central Bank Digital Currency Tracker." *https://www.atlanticcouncil.org/cbdctracker/*

Bharathan, Vipin. 2020. "Central Bank Digital Currency: The First Nationwide CBDC in the World Has Been Launched by the Bahamas." *Forbes*, October 21. *https://www.forbes.com/sites/vipinbharathan/2020/10/21/central-bank-digital-currency-the-first-nationwide-cbdc-in-the-world-has-been-launched-by-the-bahamas/?sh=323a8c50506e*

Boar, Codruta, and Andreas Wehrli. 2021. "Ready, Steady, Go?—Results of the Third BIS Survey on Central Bank Digital Currency." BIS Papers, no. 114, Bank for International Settlements, Basel, Switzerland. *https://www.bis.org/publ/bppdf/bispap114.pdf*

Prasad, Eswar. 2021. *The Future of Money: How the Digital Revolution Is Transforming Currencies and Finance.* Cambridge, MA: Harvard University Press.

Ree, Jack. 2021. "Five Observations on Nigeria's Central Bank Digital Currency." *IMF News*, November 16. *https://www.imf.org/en/News/Articles/2021/11/15/na111621-five-observations-on-nigerias-central-bank-digital-currency*

Working Group on E-CNY Research and Development of the People's Bank of China. 2021. "Progress of Research & Development of E-CNY in China." *http://www.pbc.gov.cn/en/3688110/3688172/4157443/4293696/2021071614584691871.pdf*

Powering Bitcoin

NOTES

We calculated average Bitcoin mining hash rate by country (or Chinese province) by using estimates of percentage shares of Bitcoin mining obtained from the Cambridge Centre for Alternative Finance (*https://ccaf.io/cbeci/mining_map*) and multiplying them by the average hash rate for the entire Bitcoin network for the same period (September 2019–April 2020) obtained from *blockchain.com*.

In the main text, "A single transaction uses roughly 707.6 kilowatt-hours . . . over twenty-four days" is based on Ponciano (2021).

For an additional discussion of Bitcoin's environmental impact and its use in illegal activities, see Foley et al. (2019), Foteinis (2018), and Stoll et al. (2019).

REFERENCES

Foley, Sean, Jonathan R. Karlsen, and Tālis J. Putniņš. 2019. "Sex, Drugs, and Bitcoin: How Much Illegal Activity Is Financed through Cryptocurrencies?" *Review of Financial Studies* 32 (5): 1798–1853. *https://doi.org/10.1093/rfs/hhz015*

Foteinis, Spyros. 2018. "Bitcoin's Alarming Carbon Footprint." *Nature* 554 (7691): 169. *https://doi.org/10.1038/d41586-018-01625-x*

Ponciano, Jonathan. 2021. "Bill Gates Sounds Alarm on Bitcoin's Energy Consumption—Here's Why Crypto Is Bad for Climate Change." *Forbes*, March 9. *https://www.forbes.com/sites/jonathanponciano/2021/03/09/bill-gates-bitcoin-crypto-climate-change/?sh=70d65c836822*

Stoll, Christian, Lena Klaaßen, and Ulrich Gallersdörfer. 2019. "The Carbon Footprint of Bitcoin." *Joule* 3 (7): 1647–61. *https://doi.org/10.1016/j.joule.2019.05.012*

Chapter 5: Cities & Centers

NOTE

The quote is from: Quotefancy. n.d. "Albert Einstein Quotes." *https://quotefancy.com/quote/762857/Albert-Einstein-Nothing-happens-until-something-moves-When-something-vibrates-the*

Venice to London

NOTES

The map and the short history are based on Cassis (2006), Goetzmann (2016), Pye (2021), Roover (1963), and Spufford (2006).

Data on GDP per capita is from Maddison (2007).

Other sources that inform the text are Carlos and Neal (2011), Flandreau et al. (2009), Mosselar (2018), and Roover (1944).

REFERENCES

Carlos, Ann M., and Larry Neal. 2011. "Amsterdam and London as Financial Centers in the Eighteenth Century." *Financial History Review* 18 (1): 21–46. *https://doi.org/10.1017/S0968565010000338*

Cassis, Y. 2006. *Capitals of Capital: A History of International Financial Centers, 1780–2005.* Cambridge: Cambridge University Press.

Flandreau, M., C. Galimard, C. Jobst, and P. Nogues-Marco. 2009. "Monetary Geography before the Industrial Revolution." *Cambridge Journal of Regions, Economy and Society* 2 (2): 149–71. *https://doi.org/10.1093/cjres/rsp009*

Goetzmann, William N. 2016. *Money Changes Everything: How Finance Made Civilization Possible.* Princeton, NJ: Princeton University Press.

Maddison, Angus. 2007. *Contours of the World Economy 1–2030 AD: Essays in Macro-Economic History.* Oxford: Oxford University Press.

Mosselar, Jan Sytze. 2018. *A Concise Financial History of Europe.* Rotterdam: Robeco.

Pye, Michael. 2021. *Antwerp: The Glory Years.* London: Allen Lane.

Roover, Raymond de. 1963. *The Rise and Decline of the Medici Bank, 1397–1494.* Cambridge, MA: Harvard University Press.

——. 1944. "Early Accounting Problems of Foreign Exchange." *Accounting Review* 19 (4): 381–407. http://www.jstor.org/stable/240200

Spufford, Peter. 2006. "From Antwerp and Amsterdam to London: The Decline of Financial Centres in Europe." *De Economist* 154 (2): 143–75. https://doi.org/10.1007/s10645-006-9000-7

Taking the Lead

NOTES

Data on the number of banks present in each city was collected by the CityNet project (2022). The data includes both domestic and foreign banks. Each bank counts once irrespective of the number of branches in a given city. The data was collected from the Banking Almanac (a.k.a. Bankers Almanac) from 1880 onwards. For 2020 we used SWIFTBIC (2023).

Data on the population of each city was also collected by the CityNet project (2022) based on historical and contemporary statistical sources.

Data on travel times by air in 2020 was based on the flight time calculator at https://flighttimecalculator.org, while that on travel by sea and rail (when necessary for inland destinations) in 1880 was based on "Mass Migration as a Travel Business" at https://www.business-of-migration.com/data/other-data/vessel-size-and-speed-1873-1913/

Additional sources that informed the text are Bain (2007), Cassis (2006), Contel and Wójcik (2019), Polèse and Shearmur (2009), and Porteous (1995).

REFERENCES

Bain, J. 2007. *A Financial Tale of Two Cities: Sydney and Melbourne's Remarkable Contest for Commercial Supremacy.* Sydney: New South Publishing.

Cassis, Y. 2006. *Capitals of Capital: A History of International Financial Centers, 1780–2005.* Cambridge: Cambridge University Press.

CityNet. n.d. Cities in Global Financial Networks: Financial and Business Services in the 21st Century [website]. https://www.citynet21.org/

Contel, Fabio Betioli, and Dariusz Wójcik. 2019. "Brazil's Financial Centers in the Twenty-First Century: Hierarchy, Specialization, and Concentration." *Professional Geographer* 71 (4): 681–91. https://doi.org/10.1080/00330124.2019.1578980

Polèse, Mario, and Richard Shearmur. 2009. "Culture, Language, and the Location of High-Order Service Functions: The Case of Montreal and Toronto." *Economic Geography* 80 (4): 329–50. https://doi.org/10.1111/j.1944-8287.2004.tb00241.x

Porteous, David J. 1995. *The Geography of Finance: Spatial Dimensions of Intermediary Behaviour.* Aldershot, UK: Avebury.

SWIFTBIC. 2023. [Website]. Updated July 27, 2023. https://www.swiftbic.com/countries-with-A.html

Financial Centers

NOTES

The CityNet project (2022) collected data on the location of the ten largest companies (domestic or foreign) in eleven groups of financial and business services: accounting, consulting, banks, fintech, corporate law, asset management, insurance, hedge funds, private equity, real estate, and other (exchanges, central banks, rating agencies, and financial media companies). When the exact size and ranking of firms (based on revenues, assets, or employment) was not available to select exactly ten firms, the number was extended to include all leading companies. This resulted in a total of 142 locations in New York and 130 in London.

Other sources consulted are Campbell (1977), Cohen (2011), Beard (2008), Ellis (2001), Goldman Sachs (n.d.), Kynaston (2002), Morgan Stanley (n.d.), and Prokesh (1990).

REFERENCES

Beard, P. 2008. *Blue Blood and Mutiny: The Fight for the Soul of Morgan Stanley*. New York: HarperCollins.

Campbell, M. 1977. "Morgan Stanley Opens in London." *Financial Times,* April 19.

CityNet. n.d. Cities in Global Financial Networks: Financial and Business Services in the 21st Century [website]. https://www.citynet21.org/

Cohen, W. D. 2011. *Money and Power: How Goldman Sachs Came to Rule the World.* New York: Penguin.

Ellis, C. 2001. *Wall Street People: True Stories of Today's Masters and Moghuls.* New York: Wiley.

Goldman Sachs. n.d. "History." https://www.goldmansachs.com/our-firm/history/

Kynaston, D. 2002. *The City of London.* Vol. 4. London: Pimlico.

Morgan Stanley. n.d. "Our History." https://ourhistory.morganstanley.com/stories/new-horizons-with-new-challenges/story-1977-london?linkId=116685253

Prokesh, S. 1990. "London Betting on Itself and on Canary Wharf." *New York Times,* November 13.

Rising Dragon

NOTE

The data on size of financial centers, network ties among them, and the evolution of underwriting revenue is from the analysis of Dealogic data by Pažitka et al. (2021). To measure the size of financial centers, we used fees earned from underwriting of equity and debt securities offerings. We initially sampled all capital market deals available in Dealogic Equity Capital Market (ECM) and Debt Capital Market (DCM) databases for the period 1993–2016. This yielded 584,680 deals in total, 100,777 for ECM and 483,903 for DCM. For each deal, we identified the issuer as well as the underwriting syndicate members at the bank subsidiary level. Our dataset contained 15,032 bank subsidiaries and 91,879 issuers and featured 1,727,111 market interactions among them. The revenue data available in the Dealogic ECM and DCM databases is apportioned among individual banks conditional on their role and share of the securities underwritten and is representative of the revenue earned by banks from deals with given industrial, geographical, and size characteristics. Dealogic employs a designated data science team to manage their data on apportioning revenue to individual banks, and their models are periodically calibrated to provide estimates of revenue earned from individual deals with a 5 percent margin of error. To allocate bank subsidiaries to financial centers, we hand-collected data on the addresses of their operational headquarters from a variety of sources, including Orbis, Amadeus, FAME, Bloomberg, Nexis UK, and corporate websites. This allowed us to obtain addresses of 12,827 bank subsidiaries, while we could not identify 2,205. These typically relate to very small subsidiaries with typically fewer than five deals and without a traceable online footprint. The resulting missing data problem is negligible, given that 1,716,394 of 1,727,111 (99.4 percent) of market interactions in our dataset are covered by bank subsidiaries for which we have data on headquarters location. This allowed us to cover 540 financial centers between 1993 and 2016. In the network visualizations displayed in this spread we only show financial centers with at least US$10 million in revenue in the given year. We obtained values of network ties among financial centers by weighting syndication ties among securities underwriters by the fees earned from a given deal and aggregating these value-weighted ties by city dyad.

REFERENCE

Pažitka, Vladimír, Michael Urban, and Dariusz Wójcik. 2021. "Connectivity and Growth: Financial Centres in Investment Banking Networks." *Environment and Planning A: Economy and Space* 53 (7): 1789–1809. https://doi.org/10.1177/0308518X211026318

Mushrooming Mergers

NOTES

Data on financial sector mergers and acquisitions is available from Bureau van Dijk's Zephyr database (2020).

For more information on mergers and acquisitions, see Keenan et al. (2022), Wójcik et al. (2022), and Zademach and Rodríguez-Pose (2009).

REFERENCES

Bureau van Dijk. 2020. "M&A Deals & Rumours Data." Zephyr database. https://www.bvdinfo.com/en-us/our-products/data/greenfield-investment-and-ma/zephyr

Keenan, Liam, Timothy Monteath, and Dariusz Wójcik. 2022. "Financial Discipline through Inter-Sectoral Mergers and Acquisitions: Exploring the Convergence of Global Production Networks and the Global Financial Network." *Environment and Planning A: Economy and Space* 54 (8): 1532–50. https://doi.org/10.1177/0308518X221115739

Wójcik, Dariusz, Liam Keenan, Vladimír Pažitka, Michael Urban, and Wei Wu. 2022. "The Changing Landscape of International Financial Centers in the Twenty-First Century: Cross-Border Mergers and Acquisitions in the Global Financial Network." *Economic Geography* 98 (2): 97–118. https://doi.org/10.1080/00130095.2021.2010535

Zademach, Hans-Martin, and Andrés Rodríguez-Pose. 2009. "Cross-Border M&As and the Changing Economic Geography of Europe." *European Planning Studies* 17 (5): 765–89. https://doi.org/10.1080/09654310902778276

Islands of Wealth

NOTES

Data is from the Land Registry, Overseas Company Ownership Data, and the Energy Performance of Buildings Data from the Department for Communities and Local Government. For more on the history, use, and processing of this data, see Monteath (2021). For an in-depth look at London, the ultrarich, and offshore finance, see Atkinson (2021). For more on family offices, see Glucksberg and Burrows (2016).

In the main text, "London had approximately 4,944 ultra-high-net-worth individuals" is based on Shirley (2019). The statement "bestow anonymity on the ultimate owner through 'closed registers'" is based on Transparency International (2015).

REFERENCES

Atkinson, Rowland. 2021. *Alpha City: How London Was Captured by the Super-Rich.* London: Verso.

Glucksberg, Luna, and Roger Burrows. 2016. "Family Offices and the Contemporary Infrastructures of Dynastic Wealth." *Sociologica* 10 (2). https://doi.org/10.2383/85289

Monteath, Timothy. 2021. "The Information Infrastructure of Land Registration in England: A Sociology of Real Estate at the Intersection of Elites, Markets and Statistics." PhD thesis, London School of Economics and Political Science. https://doi.org/10.21953/LSE.00004293

Shirley, Andrew, ed. 2019. *The Wealth Report: The Global Perspective on Prime Property and Investment.* 13th ed. Knight Frank. https://content.knightfrank.com/resources/knightfrank.com.my/pdfs/the-wealth-report-2019.pdf

Transparency International. 2015. "Corruption on Your Doorstep: How Corrupt Capital Is Used to Buy Property in the UK." https://www.transparency.org.uk/sites/default/files/pdf/publications/2016CorruptionOnYourDoorstepWeb.pdf

All Roads Lead to Bengaluru

NOTES

To select a sample of representative firms in financial services, we used the 2016 list of firms compiled by the Globalization and World Cities Research Network (GaWC) and available at https://www.lboro.ac.uk/gawc/datasets/da28.html

The location of campuses in Bengaluru and the list of customers for outsourcing companies were hand-collected through online searches and then geolocated. To improve the readability of the plot, Bengaluru was divided into six neighborhoods, using existing denominations (Whitefield, Bellandur, Electronic City) or geographical locations (Northeastern, Western, Central).

The data for the phases of urban expansion is from Deb et al. (2020).

The data for the export of the IT-BPM industry was sourced from the annual reports of the National Association of Software and Service Companies, accessible at https://nasscom.in/knowledge-centre/publications

In the main text, "Melbourne-based ANZ was one of the first banks to open an office in Bengaluru" is based on Heitzman (1999). "It caters to 200 corporate clients across 100 countries, serving more than a billion individual customers" is based on Srivats (2019).

To further understand how offshoring has affected the spatial division of labor in finance, and how it both relates to and differs from outsourcing, see Kleibert (2020), Massini and Miozzo (2012), and Peck (2017).

To learn more about the trajectory of Bengaluru as an IT capital, read Aranya (2008), Didelon (2003), Madon (1997), and Parthasarathy (2004).

REFERENCES

Aranya, Rolee. 2008. "Location Theory in Reverse? Location for Global Production in the IT Industry of Bangalore." *Environment and Planning A: Economy and Space* 40 (2): 446–63. https://doi.org/10.1068/a38416

Deb, Amartya, Jaya Dhindaw, and Robin King. 2020. "Metropolitan Bangalore: Crossing Boundaries to Integrate Core and Periphery." In *Greater than Parts: A Metropolitan Opportunity,* vol. 2, edited by Shagun Mehrota, Lincoln L. Lewis, Mariana Orloff, and Beth Olberding, Washington, DC: World Bank.

Didelon, Clarisse. 2003. "Bangalore, Ville des Nouvelles Technologies." *Mappemonde* 70 (2): 35–40. https://doi.org/10.3406/mappe.2003.1833

Heitzman, James. 1999. "Corporate Strategy and Planning in the Science City: Bangalore as 'Silicon Valley.'" *Economic and Political Weekly* 34 (5): 2–11. http://www.jstor.org/stable/4407603

Kleibert, Jana M. 2020. "Unbundling Value Chains in Finance." In *The Routledge Handbook of Financial Geography,* edited by Janelle Knox-Hayes and Dariusz Wójcik, 1st ed., 421–39. New York: Routledge. https://doi.org/10.4324/9781351119061-23

Madon, Shirin. 1997. "Information-Based Global Economy and Socio-economic Development: The Case of Bangalore." *Information Society* 13 (3): 227–44. https://doi.org/10.1080/019722497129115

Massini, Silvia, and Marcela Miozzo. 2012. "Outsourcing and Offshoring of Business Services: Challenges to Theory, Management and Geography of Innovation." *Regional Studies* 46 (9): 1219–42. https://doi.org/10.1080/00343404.2010.509128

Parthasarathy, Balaji. 2004. "India's Silicon Valley or Silicon Valley's India? Socially Embedding the Computer Software Industry in Bangalore." *International Journal of Urban and Regional Research* 28 (3): 664–85. https://doi.org/10.1111/j.0309-1317.2004.00542.x

Peck, Jamie. 2017. *Offshore: Exploring the Worlds of Global Outsourcing.* Oxford: Oxford University Press.

Srivats, K. R. 2019. "More Banks Will Soon Enter the Platform Business: Rajashekara Maiya." *Hindu Businessline,* September 9. https://www.thehindubusinessline.com/money-and-banking/more-banks-will-soon-enter-the-platform-business-rajashekara-maiya/article29354495.ece

A Mosaic of Islamic Finance

NOTES

Data on the top 100 Islamic banks is from Asian Banker in 2020.

In the main text, the statement "with Saudi Arabia, Qatar, UAE, Bahrain, and Kuwait housing 31 of the top 100" was calculated by summing the banks in each country (Saudi Arabia = 4; Qatar = 5; UAE = 5; Bahrain = 12; Kuwait = 5). "With Islamic finance expected to grow from $2.9 trillion of assets in 2020 to $3.7 trillion by 2024" is based on ICD-REFINITIV (2020). "As of 2019, Malaysia was also the country with the largest number of Islamic scholars" is based on Statista (2021).

For more discussion on the principles, services, history, and geography of Islamic finance, see Bassens et al. (2010) and Pollard and Samers (2007).

REFERENCES

Asian Banker. n.d. "Largest Banks Rankings: 2020." https://www.theasianbanker.com/ab500/2018-2019/largest-islamic-banks

Bassens, David, Ben Derudder, and Frank Witlox. 2010. "Searching for the Mecca of Finance: Islamic Financial Services and the World City Network." *Area* 42 (1): 35–46. http://www.jstor.org/stable/27801437.

ICD-REFINITIV. 2020. "Islamic Finance Development Report 2020." https://icd-ps.org/uploads/files/ICD-Refinitiv IFDI Report 20201607502893_2100.pdf

Pollard, Jane, and Michael Samers. 2007. "Islamic Banking and Finance: Postcolonial Political Economy and the Decentring of Economic Geography." *Transactions of the Institute of British Geographers* 32 (3): 313–30. http://www.jstor.org/stable/4626252

Statista. 2021. "Worldwide: Leading Countries for Shariah Scholars by 2019." https://www.statista.com/statistics/1092291/worldwide-leading-countries-of-shariah-scholars/

London's Pull

NOTE

Data on the number of firms reallocating part of their business activity and personnel from London to the other European financial centers was retrieved from Hamre and Wright (2021). The employment data on the sectoral composition of financial centers comes from Panitz and Glückler (2022), whereas for the equity trading volumes of London's and other EU exchanges, we used data from Global Financial Data (2022). The quotes from industry professionals come from a pool of over 200 interviews carried out from 2016 to 2019 by researchers of the CityNet project (2022).

REFERENCES

CityNet. n.d. Cities in Global Financial Networks: Financial and Business Services in the 21st Century [website]. https://www.citynet21.org/

Global Financial Data. 2022. "Stock Market Capitalization." Global Financial Data (GFD) Finaeon. https://globalfinancialdata.com/gfd-finaeon-overview

Hamre, Eivid Friis, and William Wright. 2021. "Brexit & the City: The Impact So Far: An Updated Analysis of How the Banking & Finance Industry Has Responded to Brexit—And Who Is Moving What to Where." New Financial. https://newfinancial.org/brexit-the-city-the-impact-so-far/

Panitz, Robert, and Johannes Glückler. 2022. "Relocation Decisions in Uncertain Times: Brexit and Financial Services." *Economic Geography* 98 (2): 119–44. https://doi.org/10.1080/00130095.2021.2009336

Fintech Planet

NOTES

We constructed cumulative funds raised by fintech companies by aggregating venture capital and private equity funding rounds raised between 2007 and 2020 by the city of headquarters of the funded organization, using data obtained from Crunchbase. For selected cities we have included an example of a notable fintech company or a platform. Data on fintech investment shown in a chart is an aggregation of this data for the whole world. We have identified the top thirty fintech centers using this data on cumulative funds raised by fintech companies between 2007 and 2020 and simply selected the thirty cities with the highest value of cumulative funds raised. We have identified the top thirty financial centers using the Global Financial Centres Index 30 (Z/Yen, 2021). The chart showing cumulative fintech patents is based on a categorization of patents obtained from the European Patent Office and the United States Patent and Trademark Office (Caragea et al., 2020).

For a detailed discussion of the emergence of fintech, see Arner et al. (2016), Cojoianu et al. (2021), and Goldstein (2019).

REFERENCES

Arner, D. W., J. N. J. E. Barberis, and R. P. Buckley. 2016. "The Evolution of Fintech: A New Post-Crisis Paradigm?" *Georgetown Journal of International Law* 47 (4): 1345–93. https://papers.ssrn.com/sol3/papers.cfm?abstract_id=2676553

Caragea, Doina, Mark Chen, Theodor Cojoianu, Mihai Dobri, Kyle Glandt, and George Mihaila. 2020. "Identifying FinTech Innovations Using BERT." In 2020 IEEE International Conference on Big Data (Big Data), 1117–26. https://doi.org/10.1109/BigData50022.2020.9378169

Cojoianu, Theodor Florian, Gordon L. Clark, Andreas G. F. Hoepner, Vladimir Pažitka, and Dariusz Wójcik. 2021. "Fin vs. Tech: Are Trust and Knowledge Creation Key Ingredients in Fintech Start-up Emergence and Financing?" *Small Business Economics* 57: 1715–31. https://doi.org/10.1007/s11187-020-00367-3

Goldstein, Itay, Wei Jiang, and G. Andrew Karolyi. 2019. "To FinTech and Beyond." *Review of Financial Studies* 32 (5): 1647–61. https://doi.org/10.1093/rfs/hhz025

Z/Yen. 2021. "The Global Financial Centres Index 30." London. https://www.longfinance.net/media/documents/GFCI_30_Report_2021.09.24_v1.0.pdf

Chapter 6: Bubbles & Crises

NOTE

The quote is from: Quotefancy. 2023. "Warren Buffett Quotes." https://quotefancy.com/quote/931421/Warren-Buffett-What-we-learn-from-history-is-that-people-don-t-learn-from-history

A World of Crises

NOTES

For the banking, currency, and debt crises after 1970, we used data from Laeven and Valencia (2018, 30–33). For the banking, currency, and debt crises before 1970, we used data from the following tables and figures in Reinhart and Rogoff (2009):

Table 6.1 1. "The early external defaults: Europe, 1300–1799" (p. 87). *https://carmenreinhart.com/wp-content/uploads/2020/02/175_data2.xlsx*

Figure 6.1. "Spain: Defaults and loans to the Crown, 1601–1679" (p. 89). *https://carmenreinhart.com/wp-content/uploads/2020/02/151_data1.xlsx*

Table 6.2. "External default and rescheduling: Africa, Europe, and Latin America, nineteenth century" (p. 91). *https://carmenreinhart.com/wp-content/uploads/2020/02/176_data3.1.xlsx*

Table 6.3. "Default and rescheduling: Africa and Asia, twentieth century to 2008" (p. 95). *https://carmenreinhart.com/wp-content/uploads/2020/02/178_data4.xlsx*

Table 6.4. "Default and rescheduling: Europe and Latin America, twentieth century to 2008" (p. 96). *https://carmenreinhart.com/wp-content/uploads/2020/02/179_data5.xlsx*

Figure 10.1. "Capital mobility and the incidence of banking crises: All countries, 1800–2008" (p. 156). *https://carmenreinhart.com/wp-content/uploads/2020/04/126_data1.xlsx*

Figure 12.3. "Currency crashes: The share of countries with annual depreciation rates greater than 15 percent, 1800–2008" (p. 190). *https://carmenreinhart.com/wp-content/uploads/2020/04/114_data3.xlsx*

The database produced by Laeven and Valencia (2018, 30–33) reports financial crises for 165 countries, covering the period from 1970 to 2017. Whereas their study focuses primarily on systemic banking crises, they complement their database with information on currency and sovereign debt crises. A systemic banking crisis, according to Laeven and Valencia, is defined as an event that leads to either a significant financial distress or a significant banking policy intervention. More specifically, they consider a significant financial distress to be (1) a rate of nonperforming loans per total bank loans over 20 percent or bank closures involving over 20 percent of the banking system's assets, and/or (2) fiscal restructuring that costs more than 5 percent of gross domestic product (GDP). Likewise, policy interventions that denote the presence of a systemic banking crisis are (1) deposit freezes and/or banking holidays, (2) significant bank nationalizations, (3) extensive liquidity support, (4) significant bank guarantees, and (5) significant asset purchases (p. 5). They define a currency crisis, on the other hand, as either a nominal depreciation of more than 30 percent of the national currency compared to the US dollar or a depreciation that is 10 percent higher than the depreciation rate of the previous year. For sovereign debt crises, Laeven and Valencia gathered information from various sources on sovereign debt default episodes and debt restructurings (p. 10).

Reinhart and Rogoff (2009) begin their analysis with the sovereign default of England in 1340 and continue their meticulous report of financial crises to the US subprime crisis of 2007–8. They distinguish between sovereign default episodes, banking crises, currency crashes, and inflationary events. For sovereign debt crises, the authors search for outright defaults on payments of debt obligations or cases of debt restructuring, based on historical studies. For currency crises, they set the depreciation threshold to 15 percent versus the US dollar or any other historically relevant anchor currency. For identifying a banking crisis, they use a definition that includes the presence of a bank run that initiates a process of "closure, merging, or takeover by the public sector of one or more financial institutions" (p. 11) or large-scale government assistance. For consistency and comparability with the study of Laeven and Valencia (2018), we included only the financial crises before 1970. Furthermore, we considered only single financial episodes in our analysis rather than the whole period in which a country was experiencing a particular type of financial crisis. For example, if a country experienced three years of continuous depreciation in its currency, we counted this as one event. Lastly, we excluded from the dataset the inflationary crisis episodes (which are not covered in Laeven and Valencia's study), and we applied a 30 percent, rather than a 15 percent, threshold for currency crises.

REFERENCES

Laeven, Luc, and Fabian Valencia. 2018. "Systemic Banking Crises Revisited." IMF Working Paper WP/18/206, Washington, DC.

Reinhart, Carmen M., and Kenneth S. Rogoff. 2009. *This Time Is Different: Eight Centuries of Financial Folly.* Princeton, NJ: Princeton University Press.

Theories of Instability

NOTES

To present the four most important theoretical approaches to financial instability (monetarism, debt-deflation theory, the financial instability hypothesis, and herd behavior), we constructed an imaginary debate about the root causes of the Asian financial crisis of 1997–98, involving four famous economists, each representing one theory. These are Anna Schwartz (1915–2012), Irving Fisher (1867–1947), Hyman Minsky (1919–1996), and Daniel Kahneman (1934–). Although the debate in this spread is imaginary, it reflects real theoretical controversies about the role of financial markets, their impact on economies and societies, and the root causes of distress, instability, and eventually crisis.

For the map we relied on PBS coverage of the 1997–98 Asian financial crisis (PBS, n.d.). The percentage fall of stock market indexes in the region was calculated using data from Global Financial Data (2022).

For more information about monetarism, see Friedman and Schwartz (1963). On debt-deflation theory, see Fisher (1933). On Minsky's ideas, see Burger (1969), Minsky (1968, 1994), and Wray (2011). On herd behavior, see Kahneman and Tversky (1974) and Kahneman (2011).

REFERENCES

Burger, Albert E. 1969. "A Historical Analysis of the Credit Crunch of 1966." Federal Reserve Bank of St. Louis *Review* (September): 13–30. *https://doi.org/10.20955/r.51.13-30.hfp*

Fisher, Irving. 1933. "The Debt-Deflation Theory of Great Depressions." *Econometrica* 1 (4): 337. *https://doi.org/10.2307/1907327*

Friedman, Milton, and Anna Jacobsen Schwartz. 1963. *A Monetary History of the United States, 1867–1960.* Princeton, NJ: Princeton University Press. *http://www.jstor.org/stable/j.ctt7s1vp.*

Global Financial Data. 2022. "Stock Market Capitalization." Global Financial Data (GFD) Finaeon. *https://globalfinancialdata.com/gfd-finaeon-overview*

Kahneman, Daniel. 2011. *Thinking, Fast and Slow.* London: Allen Lane.

Kahneman, Daniel, and Amos Tversky. 1974. "Judgment under Uncertainty." *Science* 185: 1124–31. *https://www.science.org/doi/10.1126/science.185.4157.1124*

Minsky, Hyman. 1968. "The Crunch of 1966—Model for New Financial Crises?" *Trans-Action* 5 (4): 44–51. *https://doi.org/10.1007/BF03180468*

Minsky, Hyman Philip. 1994. "Financial Instability Hypothesis." In *The Elgar Companion to Radical Political Economy,* edited by Philip Arestis and Malcom Sawyer, 153–58. Aldershot: Edward Elgar.

PBS. n.d. "Timeline of the Panic." *Frontline. https://www.pbs.org/wgbh/pages/frontline/shows/crash/etc/cron.html*

Wray, Randall. 2011. "Minsky Crisis." Working Paper no. 659, Levy Economics Institute of Bard College, Annandale-on-Hudson, NY.

The Big One

NOTE

For the events that led to the demise of Barings Bank, including the financial losses, we used Bhalla (1995), Board of Banking Supervision (1995), and Lim and Tan (1995). Data on the Singapore and Nikkei indexes was retrieved from Global Financial Data (2022).

REFERENCES

Bhalla, A. S. 1995. "Collapse of Barings Bank: Case of Market Failure." *Economic and Political Weekly* 30 (13): 658–62. http://www.jstor.org/stable/4402560

Board of Banking Supervision. 1995. *Report of the Board of Banking Supervision Inquiry into the Circumstances of the Collapse of Barings.* London: HMSO. https://www.gov.uk/government/publications/report-into-the-collapse-of-barings-bank

Global Financial Data. 2022. "Stock Market Indices." Global Financial Data (GFD) Finaeon. https://globalfinancialdata.com/gfd-finaeon-overview

Lim, C. S. M., and N. K. N. Tan. 1995. *The Report of the Inspectors Appointed by the Minister of Finance.* Singapore: Ministry of Finance.

Financial Crises Making Headlines

NOTE

For the unfolding of the Argentine crisis, we relied on Hornbeck (2003). Data on GDP growth, interest rate spreads, and real effective exchange rate were retrieved from Global Financial Data (2022). The interest rate spreads are measured in basis points and reflect the difference in interest rates of government bonds between Argentina and the US (treasury bills). The effective exchange rate is an index with 2010 as the base year. For inflation data we used the database of the Argentine Central Bank (Banco Central de la República Argentina, n.d.). All economic data are on a quarterly basis.

REFERENCES

Banco Central de la República Argentina. n.d. Monthly Inflation. https://www.bcra.gob.ar/PublicacionesEstadisticas/Principales_variables_datos_i.asp?serie=7931&detalle=Monthly%20Inflation%A0(%%20change)

Global Financial Data. 2022. "Stock Market Capitalization." Global Financial Data (GFD) Finaeon. https://globalfinancialdata.com/gfd-finaeon-overview

Hornbeck, J. F. 2003. *The Financial Crisis in Argentina.* CRS Report for Congress, Congressional Research Service, Library of Congress, Washington, DC. https://digital.library.unt.edu/ark:/67531/metacrs7071/m1/1/high_res_d/RS21072_2003Jun05.pdf

Calling Time on Northern Rock

NOTES

Data on the turning points and timeline of Northern Rock is based on BBC (2008a, 2008b, 2010); Eley, Moore, and Powley (2012), *Guardian* (2008a, 2008b), and *Independent* (2008).

Data on regional GDP growth rates is from the Office for National Statistics. https://www.ons.gov.uk/economy/grossdomesticproductgdp/bulletins/regionaleconomicactivitybygrossdomesticproductuk/1998to2019

Data on financial sector employment is from Nomis through the Office for National Statistics. https://www.nomisweb.co.uk/

In the main text, "With cheap debt freely available, growth was good. Customers were offered 'Together' mortgages, allowing them to borrow 125 percent of a house's value" is based on BBC (2008a).

For more discussion on the case of Northern Rock, see Marshall et al. (2012) and Dawley et al. (2014).

REFERENCES

BBC. 2008a. "Northern Rock Ends 125% Mortgages." February 21. http://news.bbc.co.uk/1/hi/business/7256903.stm

——. 2008b. "Timeline: Northern Rock Bank Crisis." August 5. http://news.bbc.co.uk/1/hi/business/7007076.stm

——. 2010. "Northern Rock to Cut 650 Jobs by Year End." June 8. https://www.bbc.co.uk/news/10266501

Dawley, Stuart, Neill Marshall, Andy Pike, Jane Pollard, and John Tomaney. 2014. "Continuity and Evolution in an Old Industrial Region: The Labour Market Dynamics of the Rise and Fall of Northern Rock." *Regional Studies* 48 (1): 154–72. https://doi.org/10.1080/00343404.2012.669473

Eley, Jonathan, Elaine Moore, and Tanya Powley. 2012. "Rock Collapse Left Many in a Hard Place." *Financial Times,* September 14. http://ig-legacy.ft.com/content/2abdeb34-fda8-11e1-8e36-00144feabdc0#axzz7JXZy7Qib

Guardian. 2008a. "Northern Rock to Make 800 Compulsory Redundancies." July 31. https://www.theguardian.com/business/2008/jul/31/northernrock.creditcrunch

——. 2008b. "Timeline: The Northern Rock Crisis." March 26. https://www.theguardian.com/business/2008/mar/26/northernrock

Independent. 2008. "Northern Rock: The Timeline." March 26. https://www.independent.co.uk/news/business/news/northern-rock-the-timeline-800709.html

Marshall, J. N., A. Pike, J. S. Pollard, J. Tomaney, S. Dawley, and J. Gray. 2012. "Placing the Run on Northern Rock." *Journal of Economic Geography* 12 (1): 157–81. https://doi.org/10.1093/jeg/lbq055

When Financial Innovation Blew Up the US Economy

NOTE

All data was retrieved from Federal Reserve Bank of St. Louis (2021). The S&P/Case-Shiller U.S. National Home Price Index was used for calculating the annual growth rate of house prices at the national level. Data from the Households and Nonprofit Organizations; One-to-Four-Family Residential Mortgages table was used for calculating the annual growth rate of mortgage debt. The All-Transactions House Price Index was used for calculating the annual growth of house prices at the state level. The unemployment rate describes the number of people aged sixteen and over actively searching for a job, as a percentage of the total labor force. The rate is seasonally adjusted. For more information and discussion about the causes of the US crisis, see Aalbers (2009), Ashton (2009), Dymski (2010), and Martin (2011).

REFERENCES

Aalbers, Manuel B. 2009. "Geographies of the Financial Crisis." *Area* 41 (1): 34–42. https://doi.org/10.1111/j.1475-4762.2008.00877.x

Ashton, Philip. 2009. "An Appetite for Yield: The Anatomy of the Subprime Mortgage Crisis." *Environment and Planning A: Economy and Space* 41 (6): 1420–41. https://doi.org/10.1068/a40328

Dymski, G. A. 2010. "Why the Subprime Crisis Is Different: A Minskyian Approach." *Cambridge Journal of Economics* 34 (2): 239–55. https://doi.org/10.1093/cje/bep054

Federal Reserve Bank of St. Louis. 2021. "Federal Reserve Economic Data." Economic Research. https://fred.stlouisfed.org/

Martin, R. 2011. "The Local Geographies of the Financial Crisis: From the Housing Bubble to Economic Recession and Beyond." *Journal of Economic Geography* 11 (4): 587–618. https://doi.org/10.1093/jeg/lbq024

The Eurozone Crisis

NOTES

Troika refers to the European Commission, the European Central Bank, and the International Monetary Fund. The bailout sums in the map correspond to the amounts agreed upon between the respective countries and the Troika. These differ from the actual sums disbursed during these bailout programs. European Commission (2021) provides details of each bailout program.

Data on current account balances was retrieved from Eurostat (2021a), series code Balance of Payments—International Transactions (BPM6). Sovereign interest rates were also downloaded from Eurostat (2021b), series code EMU Convergence Criterion Bond Yields. As defined by Eurostat, "Maastricht criterion bond yields are long-term interest rates, used as a convergence criterion for the European Monetary Union, based on the Maastricht Treaty. . . . The Maastricht Treaty EMU convergence criterion series relates to interest rates for long-term government bonds denominated in national currencies. Selection guidelines require data to be based on central government bond yields on the secondary market, gross of tax, with a residual maturity of around ten years" (Eurostat 2021b).

For further information and discussion on the eurozone crisis, see Bellofiore (2013), Hein and Dodig (2014), and Lapavitsas et al. (2010).

REFERENCES

Bellofiore, R. 2013. "'Two or Three Things I Know about Her': Europe in the Global Crisis and Heterodox Economics." *Cambridge Journal of Economics* 37 (3): 497–512. *https://doi.org/10.1093/cje/bet002*

European Commission. 2021. "EU Financial Assistance." *https://ec.europa.eu/info/business-economy-euro/economic-and-fiscal-policy-coordination/financial-assistance-eu_en*

Eurostat. 2021a. "Balance of Payments—International Transactions (BPM6) (Bop_6)." *https://ec.europa.eu/eurostat/cache/metadata/en/bop_6_esms.htm*

——. 2021b. "Maastricht Criterion Interest Rates (Irt_lt_mcby)." *https://ec.europa.eu/eurostat/cache/metadata/en/irt_lt_mcby_esms.htm*

Hein, Eckhard, and Nina Dodig. 2014. "Financialisation, Distribution, Growth and Crises: Long-Run Tendencies." IPE Working Papers 35/2014. *https://econpapers.repec.org/RePEc:zbw:ipewps:352014*

Lapavitsas, Costas, A. Kaltenbrunner, Giorgos Lambrinidis, D. Lindo, J. Meadway, J. Michell, J. P. Painceira, et al. 2010. "The Eurozone between Austerity and Default." Research on Money and Finance occasional report, September. *https://www.researchgate.net/publication/265451569_The_Eurozone_Between_Austerity_and_Default*

Solvency over Solidarity

NOTES

Calculation of all incoming and outgoing money flows is based on Bortz (2019), which provides a comprehensive breakdown of the first two bailout programs of Greece (granted in 2010 and 2012). Bortz's analysis is based on data originally provided by the European Commission and the European Central Bank.

The rest of the empirical analysis was conducted as part of CityNet (2022) research. Specifically, we retrieved regional unemployment data for Greece from Eurostat (2021), series *lfst_r_lfu2ltu*. The series corresponds to long-run unemployment, defined as unemployment for twelve months or more. The regional breakdown is based on NUTS2 (Nomenclature of Territorial Units for Statistics) regions. For the purposes of this map, we calculated the cumulative change in long-run unemployment for the period 2009–13.

We also retrieved national unemployment and GDP data for Greece and the US from Eurostat (2021) and the Federal Reserve Bank of St. Louis (2021), respectively. Eurostat's codes for the unemployment and GDP series we used are *une_rt_a* and *nama_10_gdp*, respectively; the Fed's codes for its unemployment and GDP series are *UNRATE* and *GDPCA*, respectively. We manually calculated GDP growth rates.

For further reading on the Greek crisis, see Laskos and Tsakalotos (2013) and Varoufakis (2011). Other references that support our data analysis are Arslanalp and Takahiro (2012), European Commission (2014), and International Monetary Fund (2010).

REFERENCES

Arslanalp, Serkan, and Tsuda Takahiro. 2012. "Tracking Global Demand for Advanced Economy Sovereign Debt." IMF Working Paper no. 12/284, Washington, DC. *https://www.imf.org/-/media/Websites/IMF/imported-full-text-pdf/external/pubs/ft/wp/2012/_wp12284.ashx*

Bortz, Pablo G. 2019. "The Destiny of the First Two Greek 'Rescue' Packages: A Survey." *International Journal of Political Economy* 48 (1): 76–99. *https://doi.org/10.1080/08911916.2018.1564493*

CityNet. n.d. Cities in Global Financial Networks: Financial and Business Services in the 21st Century [website]. *https://www.citynet21.org/*

European Commission. 2014. "The Second Economic Adjustment Programme for Greece: Fourth Review—April 2014." European Economy: Occasional Papers 192, Brussels, Belgium.

Eurostat. 2021. "Long-Term Unemployment (12 Months and More) by Sex, Age, Educational Attainment Level and NUTS 2 Regions (%)." *http://appsso.eurostat.ec.europa.eu/nui/show.do?dataset=lfst_r_lfu2ltu&lang=en*

Federal Reserve Bank of St. Louis. 2021. Federal Reserve Economic Data [database]. *https://fred.stlouisfed.org/*

International Monetary Fund. 2010. "Greece: Staff Report on Request for Stand-By Arrangement." IMF Staff Country Reports, Washington, DC. *https://www.imf.org/en/Publications/CR/Issues/2016/12/31/Greece-Staff-Report-on-Request-for-Stand-By-Arrangement-23839*

Laskos, Christos, and Euclid Tsakalotos. 2013. *Crucible of Resistance: Greece, the Eurozone and the World Economic Crisis.* London: Pluto Press.

Varoufakis, Yanis. 2011. *The Global Minotaur: America, the True Origins of the Financial Crisis and the Future of the World Economy.* London: Zed Books.

Toxic Loans

NOTES

In the text, "interest rates varying from 12.5 percent to 81 percent" is based on Oldani (2019).

Data on toxic bonds presented on the maps was sourced from Ferlazzo (2018b). Each bond was then geolocated at the entity level, using historical shapefiles of public administrative boundaries, available at *https://www.data.gouv.fr/fr/*

The population-density layer on the maps is from Institut National de la Statistique et des Études Économiques (2022).

In the "Formula for Disaster" graph, total interest to pay on a €10 million, twenty-five-year loan with two initial years of fixed interest was calculated using the "FinancialMath" R package (Penn and Schmidt, 2016).

For the information depicted in the captions for selected localities, we used the following sources:

Angoulême—Bastien (2011) and Karroum (2011)
Asnières-sur-Seine—Laurent (2012)
Dax—Denis (2015)
Lyon—Sautot (2012)
Saint-Cast-le-Guildo—Bendali (2012)
Saint-Étienne—Gallo Triouleyre (2021)
Sassenage—Pavard (2021)
Trégastel—Monin (2013) and Laurent (2012)

To further explore the crisis of toxic debt in France and the role of Dexia, see Bartolone and Gorges (2011), Ferlazzo (2018a, 2021), and Sauvagnat and Vallee (2021).

REFERENCES

Bartolone, Claude, and Jean-Pierre Gorges. 2011. "Rapport fait au nom de la commission d'enquête sur les produits financiers à risque souscrits par les acteurs publics locaux." *https://www.assemblee-nationale.fr/13/rap-enq/r4030.asp*

Bastien, Daniel. 2011. "Emprunts toxiques: le cauchemar d'angoulême." *Les Echos,* November 23. *https://www.lesechos.fr/2011/11/emprunts-toxiques-le-cauchemar-dangouleme-1091887*

Bendali, Linda. 2012. "Les villes en faillite." *Envoyé spécial,* France 2.

Denis, Frédéric. 2015. "Les impôts locaux augmentent d'un point à Dax en 2015." *Ici,* April 10. *https://www.francebleu.fr/infos/economie-social/les-impots-locaux-augmentent-d-un-point-dax-en-2015-1428658499*

Ferlazzo, Edoardo. 2018a. "La financiarisation des gouvernements locaux: Retour sur la gestion de la crise des emprunts « toxiques » par les collectivités locales, l'État et les banques privées." *Actes de la recherche en sciences sociales* 221–22 (1–2): 100–119. *https://doi.org/10.3917/arss.221.0100*

——. 2018b. "La forme financiarisée de la relation de crédit des collectivités locales françaises. De la crise à l'institutionnalisation." Thesis, Université de recherche Paris Sciences et Lettres, Paris. *http://www.theses.fr/2018PSLEH142/document*

——. 2021. "Dexia, ou la faillite d'une régulation du crédit local par le marché." *Revue de la régulation* 30 (Spring). *https://doi.org/10.4000/regulation.18900*

Gallo Triouleyre, Stéphanie. 2021. "Comment Saint-Etienne s'est désengagée de son dernier emprunt toxique." *La Tribune,* June 24. *https://region-aura.latribune.fr/territoire/politique-publique/2021-06-24/comment-saint-etienne-s-est-desengagee-de-son-dernier-emprunt-toxique-887591.html*

Institut National de la Statistique et des Études Économiques (INSEE). 2022. "La grille communale de densité à 4 niveaux." *https://www.insee.fr/fr/information/2114627*

Karroum, Ismaël. 2011. "Angoulême au bord de la cessation de paiement." *Charente Libre,* August 10. *https://www.charentelibre.fr/politique/philippe-lavaud/angouleme-au-bord-de-la-cessation-de-paiement-6483550.php*

Laurent, Lionel. 2012. "French Towns Launch Debt Strike over 'Toxic' Dexia Loans." Reuters, October 12. *https://www.reuters.com/article/uk-france-dexia-mayors-idUKBRE89B0SI20121012*

Monin, Christine. 2013. "Les banques ont ruiné ma ville." *Le Parisien,* March 25. *https://www.leparisien.fr/week-end/les-banques-ont-ruine-ma-ville-25-03-2013-2669723.php*

Oldani, Chiara. 2019. "On the Perils of Structured Loans Financing in France and Italy." *Global Policy* 10 (3): 391–96. *https://doi.org/10.1111/1758-5899.12686*

Pavard, Manuel. 2021. "Emprunts toxiques: la Ville de Sassenage finalement déboutée par la cour d'appel, la fin d'une longue bataille judiciaire." Place Gre'Net. October 27. *https://www.placegrenet.fr/2021/10/27/emprunts-toxiques-la-ville-de-sassenage-finalement-deboutee-par-la-cour-dappel-la-fin-dune-longue-bataille-judiciaire/549610*

Penn, Kameron, and Jack Schmidt. 2016. "Financial mathematics for actuaries." "FinancialMath" R package, Version 0.1.1, December. *https://CRAN.R-project.org/package=FinancialMath*

Sautot, Emmauelle. 2012. "Tous pourris. . . par les prêts toxiques." Lyon Capitale, no. 713. *https://www.lyoncapitale.fr/wp-content/uploads/2012/07/260154-ez-LC-713-p.-32-33.png*

Sauvagnat, Julien, and Boris Vallee. 2021. "The Effects of Local Government Financial Distress: Evidence from Toxic Loans." SSRN, February 9. *https://doi.org/10.2139/ssrn.3782619*

How to Rob a Bank

NOTES

For the events of the Bangladesh bank robbery, and amounts involved, we used Hammer (2018) and Kehrli (2017).

In the main text, the statement "there is widespread suspicion that a North Korean hacking group was responsible" is based on Frinkle (2017) and Cockery and Goldstein (2017). "Maia Santos-Deguito, who was convicted on eight counts of money laundering" is based on Lema (2019).

REFERENCES

Cockery, M., and M. Goldstein. 2017. "North Korea Said to Be Target of Inquiry Over $81 Million Cyberheist." *New York Times,* March 22. *https://www.nytimes.com/2017/03/22/business/dealbook/north-korea-said-to-be-target-of-inquiry-over-81-million-cyberheist.html*

Frinkle, Jim. 2017. "Cyber Security Firm: More Evidence North Korea Linked to Bangladesh Heist." Reuters, April 3. *https://www.reuters.com/article/us-cyber-heist-bangladesh-northkorea-idUSKBN175214*

Hammer, Joshua. 2018. "The Billion-Dollar Bank Job." *New York Times Magazine,* May 3. 43–48. *https://www.nytimes.com/interactive/2018/05/03/magazine/money-issue-bangladesh-billion-dollar-bank-heist.html*

Kehrli, Jerome. 2017. "Deciphering the Bangladesh Bank Heist." Niceideas.ch (blog). November 15. *https://www.niceideas.ch/roller2/badtrash/entry/deciphering-the-bengladesh-bank-heist*

Lema, Karen. 2019. "Philippine Court Orders Jail for Former Bank Manager over Bangladesh Central Bank Heist." Reuters, January 10. *https://www.reuters.com/article/us-cyber-heist-philippines-idUSKCN1P40AG*

Chapter 7: Regulation & Governance

NOTE

The quote from Plautus, a comic dramatist from ancient Rome, is from: Oxford Reference. n.d. "Unexpected Always Happens." *https://www.oxfordreference.com/display/10.1093/oi/authority.20110803110638310;jsessionid=E6162A281F2214BF72662CB4188F16B3*

Warning Signs

NOTES

The history of the BCBS in the timeline is based on the Bank of International Settlements (n.d.) and the history of VaR on Holton (2002). The formula in the background is based on Danielsson et al. (2016, 89), formula A.1.

The cautionary tale about the case of LTCM is based on Jorion (2000) and Lowenstein (2000).

The statement "reaping returns of over 40 percent in 1995 and 1996" is based on Jorion (2000).

"In early 1998 they estimated that the probabilities of losing 5 to 20 percent were no more than 0.2. For example, a loss of 20 percent was only likely to happen in one out of fifty years" is based on Lowenstein (2000), which provides a detailed history of LTCM's rise and collapse.

REFERENCES

Bank of International Settlements. n.d. "History of the Basel Committee." *https://www.bis.org/bcbs/history.htm*

Danielsson, Jon, Kevin R. James, Marcela Valenzuela, and Ilknur Zer. 2016. "Model Risk of Risk Models." *Journal of Financial Stability* 23 (April): 79–91. https://doi.org/10.1016/j.jfs.2016.02.002

Holton, Glyn A. 2002. "History of Value-at-Risk: 1922–1998." Working Paper, Contingency Analysis, Boston, MA. http://stat.wharton.upenn.edu/~steele/Courses/434/434Context/RiskManagement/VaRHistlory.pdf

Jorion, Philippe. 2000. "Risk Management Lessons from Long-Term Capital Management." *European Financial Management* 6 (3): 277–300. https://doi.org/10.1111/1468-036X.00125

Lowenstein, Roger. 2000. *When Genius Failed: The Rise and Fall of Long-Term Capital Management.* New York: Random House.

(G)local Governance

NOTE

We used the IMF website for retrieving data on countries' voting shares in the governance of the fund (2023). For data on GDP and population we used IMF's World Economic Outlook (2021). Our estimates of walking distances between various buildings in Washington, DC, are based on Google Maps. For data and further information, see World Bank (2022, n.d.) and International Monetary Fund (2010, 2020, 2022, 2023).

REFERENCES

International Monetary Fund. 2001. "World Economic Outlook. Managing Divergent Recoveries." Washington, DC: IMF https://www.imf.org/en/Publications/WEO/Issues/2021/03/23/world-economic-outlook-april-2021

——. 2010. "IMF Board of Governors Approves Major Quota and Governance Reforms." Press release, December 16. https://www.imf.org/en/News/Articles/2015/09/14/01/49/pr10477

——. 2020. "Articles of Agreement of the International Monetary Fund." March. https://www.imf.org/external/pubs/ft/aa/index.htm

——. 2022. "What Is the IMF?" Updated April 2022. https://www.imf.org/en/About/Factsheets/IMF-at-a-Glance

——. 2023. "IMF Members' Quotas and Voting Power, and IMF Board of Governors." Updated July 31, 2023. Data included here was collected from the site in 2021. https://www.imf.org/en/About/executive-board/members-quotas

World Bank. 2022. "Member Countries." Updated December 19, 2022. https://www.worldbank.org/en/about/leadership/members

——. n.d. "Who We Are." https://www.worldbank.org/en/who-we-are

Bank of Banks

NOTES

Data on the years of establishment of central banks was collected from the websites of individual central banks. Data on central bank assets and GDP is from the International Monetary Fund (2021).

The first eleven countries to become members of the eurozone, as mentioned in the caption to 1999 on the timeline, include Austria, Belgium, Finland, France, Germany, Italy, Ireland, Luxembourg, Netherlands, Spain, and Portugal. Greece joined in 2001. The euro started circulating as physical currency in these twelve countries on January 1, 2002.

For the history of central banking we used Bordo and Siklos (2018), Cassis (2006), Federal Reserve Bank of St. Louis (n.d.), Goodhart (2018), Hautcoeur et al. (2014), Roberds and Velde (2014), and Siklos (2020). For a discussion of current political controversies on central banks' policies, see Ioannou et al. (2019).

REFERENCES

Bordo, Michael D., and Pierre L. Siklos. 2018. "Central Banks: Evolution and Innovation in Historical Perspective." In *Sveriges Riksbank and the History of Central Banking,* edited by R. Edvinsson, T. Jacobson, and D. Waldenström, 26–89. Cambridge: Cambridge University Press. https://doi.org/10.1017/9781108140430.002

Cassis, Y. 2006. *Capitals of Capital: A History of International Financial Centers, 1780–2005.* Cambridge: Cambridge University Press.

Federal Reserve Bank of St. Louis. n.d. "In Plain English—Making Sense of the Federal Reserve." https://www.stlouisfed.org/in-plain-english

Goodhart, Charles. 2018. "The Bank of England, 1694–2017." In *Sveriges Riksbank and the History of Central Banking,* edited by R. Edvinsson, T. Jacobson, and D. Waldenström, 143–71. Cambridge: Cambridge University Press. http://eprints.lse.ac.uk/89064/

Hautcoeur, Pierre-Cyrille, Angelo Riva, and Eugene N. White. 2014. "Floating a 'Lifeboat': The Banque de France and the Crisis of 1889." NBER Working Paper 20083. https://www.nber.org/papers/w20083

International Monetary Fund. 2021. International Financial Statistics. https://data.imf.org/?sk=4c514d48-b6ba-49ed-8ab9-52b0c1a0179b

Ioannou, Stefanos, Dariusz Wójcik, and Gary Dymski. 2019. "Too-Big-To-Fail: Why Megabanks Have Not Become Smaller since the Global Financial Crisis?" *Review of Political Economy* 31 (3): 356–81. https://doi.org/10.1080/09538259.2019.1674001

Roberds, William, and François R. Velde. 2014. "The Descent of Central Banks (1400–1815)." Paper written for the Norges Bank 2014 conference "Of the Uses of Central Banks: Lessons from History." https://www.norges-bank.no/contentassets/3fba8b3a3432407d929ae9218db1ffc4/11_roberds_and_velde2014.pdf

Siklos, Pierre. 2020. *The Changing Face of Central Banking. Evolutionary Trends since World War II.* Cambridge: Cambridge University Press.

Legal Dominion

NOTES

Data on the prevalence of English common law was based on GlobaLex (2023).

The top ten law firms were identified based on 2020 revenues, as reported on Law.com (2021). Data on their headquarters and office locations was collected manually from corporate websites in September 2021.

For information on the recent split of Dentons with the Chinese law firm Dacheng, see Thomas (2023).

Data on the home countries of litigants most often appearing in London's Commercial Court was based on Portland (2022).

Data on financial centers in non-common law countries that use English common law was based on the following:

Abu Dhabi—Sovereign (n.d.)
Astana—Norton Rose Fulbright (2018)
Doha—Dahdal and Botchway (2020)
Dubai—Allen (2020)
Shanghai—Great Britain China Centre (2014)
Shenzhen—Erie (2020)

The main text was also based on Pistor (2019). For the role of Singapore, see, for example, Norton Rose Fulbright (2015).

REFERENCES

Allen, Jason Grant. 2020. "A Common Law Archipelago." Blackstone Chambers, October 15. https://www.blackstonechambers.com/news/common-law-archipelago/

Dahdal, Andrew, and Francis Botchway. 2020. "A Decade of Development: The Civil and Commercial Court of the Qatar Financial Centre." *Arab Law Quarterly* 34: 59–73. doi:10.1163/15730255-12341045

Erie, M. A. 2020. "The New Legal Hubs: The Emergent Landscape of International Commercial Dispute Resolution." *Virginia Journal of International Law* 60 (2): 226–96. https://www.matthewserie.com/publications.html

GlobaLex. 2023. "International Law Research, Comparative Law Research, Foreign Law Research." Updated June 2023. https://www.nyulawglobal.org/globalex/index.html?open=FLR

Great Britain China Centre. 2014. "Debate on Free Trade Zone Policy." November 14. https://www.gbcc.org.uk/news-events/2014/debate-on-free-trade-zone-policy

Law.com. 2021. "The 2020 Global 200." https://www.law.com/international-edition/2020/09/21/the-2020-global-200-ranked-by-revenue/?slreturn=20221012062506

Norton Rose Fulbright. 2015. "The Singapore International Commercial Court: A Challenge to Arbitration?" November. https://www.nortonrosefulbright.com/en-gb/knowledge/publications/f65079aa/the-singapore-international-commercial-court-a-challenge-to-arbitration

——. 2018. "Inauguration of Astana's International Financial Centre." April. https://www.nortonrosefulbright.com/en/knowledge/publications/db1c0753/inauguration-of-astanas-international-financial-centre

Pistor, K. 2019. *The Code of Capital: How the Law Creates Wealth and Inequality.* Princeton, NJ: Princeton University Press.

Portland. 2022. *Commercial Courts Report 2021.* https://portland-communications.com/publications/commercial-courts-report-2021/

Sovereign. n.d. "ADGM Free Zone." https://www.sovereigngroup.com/abu-dhabi/corporate-services/adgm-free-zone/

Thomas, David. 2023. "Law Firm Dentons Splits with China's Dacheng as Counter-espionage Law Takes Hold." Reuters, August 9. https://www.reuters.com/legal/legalindustry/law-firm-dentons-splits-with-chinas-dacheng-counter-espionage-law-takes-hold-2023-08-08/

Offshore Plumbing

NOTES

The spread is inspired by Tørsløv et al. (2023), and the data is also reported on https://missingprofits.world/. Data used for the Sankey plot comes from the replication archive tables available at https://gabriel-zucman.eu/missingprofits/. Data for the upper section comes from Table C4; data for the lower section comes from Table C4x. Historical data for corporate tax rates was sourced from the raw data.

In the main text, the statement "In 2017, Google reported $23 billion revenue" is based on missingprofits.world (2022). The statement "such as Baker McKenzie" is based on Bowers (2017) and Freedberg et al. (2021). "In 2018, the US, UK, and China lost $50 billion, $23 billion, and $18 billion of corporate tax, respectively" is based on data available at https://missingprofits.world/. "In 2021, 136 countries agreed" is based on Giles et al. (2021).

To further explore the role of tax havens and the design of tax evasion schemes, see Garcia-Bernardo et al. (2017), Haberly and Wójcik (2015), Hines (2010), Dyreng et al. (2017), Jones et al. (2018), Kleinbard (2022), Phillips (2018), Zucman (2014), and Saez and Zucman (2019).

REFERENCES

Bowers, Simon. 2017. "Apple's Secret Offshore Island Hop Revealed by Paradise Papers Leak." ICIJ: International Consortium of Investigative Journalists, November 6. https://www.icij.org/investigations/paradise-papers/apples-secret-offshore-island-hop-revealed-by-paradise-papers-leak-icij/

Dyreng, Scott D., Michelle Hanlon, Edward L. Maydew, and Jacob R. Thornock. 2017. "Changes in Corporate Effective Tax Rates over the Past 25 Years." *Journal of Financial Economics* 124 (3): 441–63. https://doi.org/10.1016/j.jfineco.2017.04.001

Freedberg, Sydney P., Agustin Armendariz, and Jesús Escudero. 2021. "How America's Biggest Law Firm Drives Global Wealth into Tax Havens." ICIJ: International Consortium of Investigative Journalists, October 4. https://www.icij.org/investigations/pandora-papers/baker-mckenzie-global-law-firm-offshore-tax-dodging/

Garcia-Bernardo, Javier, Jan Fichtner, Frank W. Takes, and Eelke M. Heemskerk. 2017. "Uncovering Offshore Financial Centers: Conduits and Sinks in the Global Corporate Ownership Network." *Scientific Reports* 7 (1): 6246. doi:10.1038/s41598-017-06322-9

Giles, Chris, Emma Agyemang, and Aime Williams. 2021. "136 Nations Agree to Biggest Corporate Tax Deal in a Century." *Financial Times,* October 8. https://www.ft.com/content/5dc4e2d5-d7bd-4000-bf94-088f17e21936

Haberly, Daniel, and Dariusz Wójcik. 2015. "Tax Havens and the Production of Offshore FDI: An Empirical Analysis." *Journal of Economic Geography* 15 (1): 75–101. https://doi.org/10.1093/jeg/lbu003

Hines, James R. 2010. "Treasure Islands." *Journal of Economic Perspectives* 24 (4): 103–26. https://doi.org/10.1257/jep.24.4.103

Jones, Chris, Yama Temouri, and Alex Cobham. 2018. "Tax Haven Networks and the Role of the Big 4 Accountancy Firms." *Journal of World Business* 53 (2): 177–93. https://doi.org/10.1016/j.jwb.2017.10.004

Kleinbard, Edward D. 2022. "Stateless Income." *Florida Tax Review* 11 (9). https://doi.org/10.5744/ftr.2011.1009

missingprofits.world. 2022. "Close to 40% of Multinational Profits Are Shifted to Tax Havens Each Year." https://missingprofits.world/

Phillips, Tim. 2018. "The Missing Profits of Nations." *VoxTalks Economics* [podcast]. September 21. https://audioboom.com/posts/7009349-the-missing-profits-of-nations

Saez, Emmanuel, and Gabriel Zucman. 2019. *The Triumph of Injustice: How the Rich Dodge Taxes and How to Make Them Pay.* New York: W. W. Norton.

Tørsløv, Thomas, Ludvig Wier, and Gabriel Zucman. 2023. "The Missing Profits of Nations." *Review of Economic Studies* 90 (3): 1499–1534. https://doi.org/10.1093/restud/rdac049

Zucman, Gabriel. 2014. "Taxing across Borders: Tracking Personal Wealth and Corporate Profits." *Journal of Economic Perspectives* 28 (4): 121–48. https://doi.org/10.1257/jep.28.4.121

The World's Laundromats

NOTES

All data on anti–money laundering, financial secrecy, banking secrecy, and international legal cooperation is available from the Tax Justice Network (2020).

In the main text, "The term *money laundering* is said to have originated with Al Capone" is based on Debczak and Thompson (2021). "While many methods exist, the normal cycle has three stages" is based on the Financial Action Task Force (n.d.). "While its inherent nature makes it difficult to detect, the UN estimates that laundered money equates to 2 to 5 percent of global GDP each year" is based on the United Nations (n.d.). "For example, despite the UK being one of the most transparent countries, London is often described as the world's laundromat" is based on Thomas et al. (2022).

More information on money laundering in Norway is available from the OECD (2014), on Moldova from the Organized Crime and Corruption Reporting Project (n.d.), on Tanzania from Mniwasa (2019), and on money laundering in the UK from the National Crime Agency (n.d.). On change in financial secrecy, see Janský et al. (2023).

REFERENCES

Debczak, Michele, and Austin Thompson. 2021. "The Myth of How Al Capone Gave Us the Term 'Money Laundering.'" *Mental Floss,* June 18. *https://www.mentalfloss.com/article/502449/myth-how-al-capone-gave-us-term-money-laundering*

Financial Action Task Force—GAFI. n.d. "Financial Action Task Force (FATF)." *https://www.fatf-gafi.org/*

Janský, Petr, Miroslav Palanský, and Dariusz Wójcik. 2023. "Shallow and Uneven Progress towards Global Financial Transparency: Evidence from the Financial Secrecy Index." *Geoforum* 141: 103728. *https://doi.org/10.1016/j.geoforum.2023.103728*

Mniwasa, Eugene E. 2019. "Money Laundering Control in Tanzania." *Journal of Money Laundering Control* 22 (4): 796–835. *https://doi.org/10.1108/JMLC-10-2018-0064*

National Crime Agency. n.d. "Money Laundering and Illicit Finance." *https://www.nationalcrimeagency.gov.uk/what-we-do/crime-threats/money-laundering-and-illicit-finance*

Organisation for Economic Co-operation and Development (OECD). 2014. "Norway Has Some Good Measures to Combat Money Laundering and Terrorist Financing, but Significant Weaknesses Undermine Overall Effectiveness, Says FATF." December 18. *https://web-archive.oecd.org/2014-12-18/333640-norway-significant-weaknesses-undermine-overall-effectiveness-to-combat-money-laundering-and-terrorist-financing.htm*

Organized Crime and Corruption Reporting Project. n.d. "Moldova Laundromat." *https://www.occrp.org/en/component/tags/tag/moldova-laundromat*

Tax Justice Network. 2020. "Financial Secrecy Index 2020 Reports Progress on Global Transparency—but Backsliding from US, Cayman and UK Prompts Call for Sanctions." February 18. *https://taxjustice.net/press/financial-secrecy-index-2020-reports-progress-on-global-transparency-but-backsliding-from-us-cayman-and-uk-prompts-call-for-sanctions/*

Thomas, Daniel, Laura Hughes, George Hammond, Stephen Morris, and Kate Beioley. 2022. "The 'London Laundromat': Will Britain Wean Itself off Russian Money?" *Financial Times,* March 4. *https://www.ft.com/content/cfb74ef3-13d2-492a-b8da-c70b6340ccdd*

United Nations. n.d. "Money Laundering." UN Office on Drugs and Crime. *https://www.unodc.org/unodc/en/money-laundering/overview.html*

The Global Financial Services Megastores

NOTE

The quantitative data used in this spread was hand-collected from corporate websites and annual reports (Deloitte, PwC, EY, KPMG), news articles, and special reports from various sources as part of the CityNet project (2022). Details about specific business services provided by the Big Four firms to private- and public-sector clients were found in ProPublica (n.d.a; n.d.b), PepsiCo. (2021), and Ernst & Young (n.d.).

REFERENCES

CityNet. n.d. Cities in Global Financial Networks: Financial and Business Services in the 21st Century [website]. *https://www.citynet21.org/*

Ernst & Young. n.d. "EY Law Deals." Ernst & Young official German website. *https://ey-law.de/de_de/deals*

PepsiCo. 2021. *PepsiCo Annual Report 2021: Winning with pep+ PepsiCo Positive.* *https://www.pepsico.com/docs/default-source/annual-reports/2021-annual-report.pdf?sfvrsn=e04eec5e_0*

ProPublica. n.d.a. "COVID-19 Vaccine Distribution and Administration Tracking." Tracking Federal Purchases to Fight the Coronavirus, Coronavirus Contracts. *https://projects.propublica.org/coronavirus-contracts/contracts/75D30120C08239*

——. n.d.b. "VAMS." Tracking Federal Purchases to Fight the Coronavirus, Coronavirus Contracts. *https://projects.propublica.org/coronavirus-contracts/contracts/75D30121C10087*

Judging from Afar

NOTES

We use Moody's as an example of the three leading credit rating agencies. Locations of the lead rating analysts are accurate as of February 2021. All data was collected from the ratings page of each country on Moody's website (free and available upon subscription). The map would be similar, though not identical, if we used S&P or Fitch data instead. Sovereign credit ratings are indicators of creditworthiness (or else of likelihood of default) of national governments. Their importance lies in the fact that they usually provide a ceiling for ratings of all other entities in a country (e.g., subnational governments, banks, private and public firms). Empirical literature has shown that sovereign ratings exercise a significant impact on international capital flows (Ioannou 2017), banking stability (Gibson et al. 2017), and interest rates (Reisen and von Maltzan 1999; De Santis 2012).

For further information and discussion on credit rating agencies, see De Santis (2012), Fuchs and Gehring (2017), Gibson et al. (2017), Ioannou (2016, 2017), Ioannou et al. (2021), Reisen and von Maltzan (1999), Sinclair (2008), U.S. Securities and Exchange Commission (2018), and Sylla (2002).

REFERENCES

De Santis, Roberto. 2012. "The Euro Area Sovereign Debt Crisis: Safe Haven, Credit Rating Agencies and the Spread of the Fever from Greece, Ireland and Portugal." European Central Bank Working Paper Series, no. 1419. *https://www.ecb.europa.eu//pub/pdf/scpwps/ecbwp1419.pdf*

Fuchs, Andreas, and Kai Gehring. 2017. "The Home Bias in Sovereign Ratings." *Journal of the European Economic Association* 15 (6): 1386–1423. *https://doi.org/10.1093/jeea/jvx009*

Gibson, Heather D., Stephen G. Hall, and George S. Tavlas. 2017. "Self-Fulfilling Dynamics: The Interactions of Sovereign Spreads, Sovereign Ratings and Bank Ratings during the Euro Financial Crisis." *Journal of International Money and Finance* 73 (May): 371–85. *https://doi.org/10.1016/j.jimonfin.2017.03.006*

Ioannou, Stefanos. 2016. "The Political Economy of Credit Rating Agencies. The Case of Sovereign Ratings." PhD dissertation, University of Leeds.

——. 2017. "Credit Rating Downgrades and Sudden Stops of Capital Flows in the Eurozone." *Journal of International Commerce, Economics and Policy* 8 (3): 1750016. *https://doi.org/10.1142/S1793993317500168*

Ioannou, Stefanos, Dariusz Wójcik, and Vladimír Pažitka. 2021. "Financial Centre Bias in Sub-Sovereign Credit Ratings." *Journal of International Financial Markets, Institutions and Money* 70 (January): 101261. *https://doi.org/10.1016/j.intfin.2020.101261*

Reisen, Helmut, and Julia von Maltzan. 1999. "Boom and Bust and Sovereign Ratings." *International Finance* 2 (2): 273–93. *https://doi.org/10.1111/1468-2362.00028*

Sinclair, Timothy J. 2008. *The New Masters of Capital: American Bond Rating Agencies and the Politics of Creditworthiness.* Ithaca, NY: Cornell University Press.

Sylla, Richard. 2002. "An Historical Primer on the Business of Credit Rating." In *Ratings, Rating Agencies and the Global Financial System,* edited by Richard M. Levich, Giovanni Majnoni, and Carmen M. Reinhart, 19–40. New York: Springer. *https://doi.org/10.1007/978-1-4615-0999-8_2*

U.S. Securities and Exchange Commission (SEC). 2018. "Annual Report on Nationally Recognized Statistical Rating Organizations." Washington, DC.

Change at the Top

NOTES

The spreads focus on the leaders of the top 275 financial and business services companies in the world, comprising the 100 largest banks and 25 largest companies from insurance, asset management, real estate, accounting, law, consulting, and fintech sectors each. Banking has a bigger representation as the sector most central to finance. The largest companies in each subsector were identified based on the following sources (all as of the end of March 2021):

Banking—*https://en.wikipedia.org/wiki/List_of_largest_banks*
Insurance—*https://en.wikipedia.org/wiki/List_of_largest_insurance_companies*
Asset management—*https://www.advratings.com/top-asset-management-firms*
Real estate—*https://www.forbes.com/sites/samanthasharf/2020/05/13/the-worlds-largest-public-real-estate-companies-2020/?sh=9dedc1762f46*
Accounting—*http://www.crowe.ie/wp-content/uploads/2017/02/IAB-2017_World-Survey.pdf*
Corporate law—*https://en.wikipedia.org/wiki/List_of_largest_law_firms_by_revenue*
Consulting—*https://www.consulting.com/top-consulting-firms*
Fintech—*https://assets.kpmg/content/dam/kpmg/ch/pdf/fintech100-report-2019-en.pdf*

For each company, information regarding the location of the operational headquarters and CEO (or equivalent) name, gender, and year of appointment was hand-collected from their official website.

Source of information on each leader (in the order of appearance, from left to right) are as follows (all accessed at the end of June 2021):

Debra Cafaro

"CEO of Ventas since 1999" and "When Cafaro joined Ventas in 1999, the company was in dire straits. It is now a Fortune 1000 corporation. She credits her family and love of sports for her strong work ethic." —based on *https://en.wikipedia.org/wiki/Debra_Cafaro*

Jennifer M. Johnson

President of Franklin Templeton with effect from 2020—based on *https://www.franklintempleton.com/press-releases/news-room/2021/franklin-resources-inc.-appoints-jennifer-m.-johnson-as-president-and-ceo-gregory-e.-johnson-named-executive-chairman-and-continues-as-chairman-of-the-board*

"With over thirty years of experience, Johnson has won awards for leadership and performance and also for enhancing customer service practices in asset and fund management."—based on *https://www.franklintempleton.com/investor/profile-details?content-Path=common/04760_jennifer_m_johnson*

Barbara L. Becker

Chair & Managing Partner of Gibson, Dunn, & Crutcher since 2021—based on *https://www.gibsondunn.com/gibson-dunn-elects-new-york-ma-lawyer-barbara-becker-as-chair-and-managing-partner/*

"Made managing partner of a law firm at the age of 31"—based on *https://www.crainsnewyork.com/awards/barbara-l-becker*

"Becker is an advocate for executive involvement in the recruitment process."—based on *https://www.gibsondunn.com/lawyer/becker-barbara-l/*

Jami McKeon

Chair of Morgan Lewis since 2014—based on *https://www.morganlewis.com/news/2014/10/pr_mckeonbeginstermaschair_1oct2014*

"McKeon has rapidly expanded client reach into new regions, particularly East Asia."—based on *https://www.morganlewis.com/bios/jmckeon*

"She is an advocate of diversity in law."—based on *https://www.morganlewis.com/news/2015/12/jami-mckeon-ceo-evolution-video*

Jane Fraser

CEO of Citigroup since 2021, and "The first female CEO in the firm's history, Fraser is a published author on globalization in finance." —based on *https://en.wikipedia.org/wiki/Jane_Fraser_(executive)*

"She speaks frequently about maintaining a career while being a mother."—based on *https://www.reuters.com/article/us-citigroup-ceo-quotes-factbox-idUSKBN2613BH, https://www.citigroup.com/citi/about/leaders/jane-fraser-bio.html*

Martine Ferland

Heading up Mercer since 2019—based on *https://www.consultancy.asia/news/1886/mercer-appoints-martine-ferland-as-firms-next-president-and-ceo.*

"An advocate for improved opportunities for the LGBTQ+ community" —based on *https://www.lgbtgreat.com/role-model/martine-ferland*

"Ferland is passionate about inclusion, sustainability, and technology to improve productivity."—based on *https://www.mercer.com/about-mercer/martine-ferland.html*

Thasunda Brown

Has led TIAA since 2021—based on *https://www.prnewswire.com/news-releases/tiaa-appoints-thasunda-brown-duckett-president-and-ceo-301235787.html*

"The second Black woman to lead a Fortune 500 company"—based on *https://www.cnbc.com/2021/02/26/thasunda-brown-duckett-to-be-second-black-woman-fortune-500-ceo-in-2021.html*

"Brown also heads a foundation named after her parents that empowers individuals who help their communities."—based on *https://www.tiaa.org/public/about-tiaa/leadership-team/thasunda-brown-duckett*

Anne Richards

Has led Fidelity International since 2018—based on *https://www.fidelity.lu/search/tag/fil/global/authors/anne-richards*

"Richards is a chartered engineer"—based on *https://www.linkedin.com/in/annerichards/?originalSubdomain=uk*

"Dame Commander of the Order of the British Empire for services to women, education, and science"—based on *https://www.fidelity.lu/search/tag/fil/global/authors/anne-richards*

Jean Hynes

Head of Wellington Management since 2021—based on *https://www.linkedin.com/in/jean-hynes-310730148/*

"With a background in biotechnology and the pharmaceutical industry" —based on *https://www.linkedin.com/in/jean-hynes-310730148/*

"Hynes is known for fostering a culture of focusing on the long term and putting the client first."—based on *https://www.thinkadvisor.com/2020/09/01/jean-hynes-named-next-wellington-ceo/*

Julie Sweet

CEO of Accenture since 2019—based on *https://www.linkedin.com/in/julie-sweet/*

"The first female CEO of the firm"—based on *https://en.wikipedia.org/wiki/Julie_Sweet*

"Accenture is working toward equal representation of men and women on their staff by 2025."—based on *https://www.forbes.com/profile/julie-sweet/?sh=90cead1f3139*

Amanda Blanc

Heading up Aviva since 2020—based on *https://www.linkedin.com/in/amanda-blanc-4ba14a3a/*

"Hailing from a background in Wales" and "She is also an accomplished musician."—based on *https://en.wikipedia.org/wiki/Amanda_Blanc*

"Blanc has been the first woman to hold many positions, including chair of the Insurance Fraud Bureau."—based on *https://www.aviva.com/about-us/leader-profiles/amanda-blanc/*

Liza Robbins

Has led Kreston Global since 2018, and "Educated in Hong Kong" —based on *https://www.linkedin.com/in/lizarobbins/*

"Under her leadership, the firm has expanded from 70 countries to over 110." —based on *https://www.consultancy.uk/news/17220/liza-robbins-succeeds-jon-lisby-as-global-ceo-of-kreston*

Alison Rose

Head of NatWest Group since 2019—based on *https://www.linkedin.com/in/alison-rose-ab340b1b3/*

"An advocate for diversity" and "Rose was commissioned by the UK to report on the barriers women face to starting their own businesses."—based on *https://www.natwestgroup.com/who-we-are/board-and-governance/board-and-committees/profiles/alison-rose.html*

"She has also won many fintech awards."—based on *https://en.wikipedia.org/wiki/Alison_Rose_(banker)*

Georgia Dawson

Senior Partner of Freshfields Bruckhaus Deringer since 2020 —based on *https://www.globallegalpost.com/news/freshfields-becomes-first-magic-circle-uk-firm-to-appoint-a-woman-leader-14570590*

"the intent to change attitudes toward diversity within major law firms" —based on *https://www.freshfields.com/en-gb/contacts/find-a-lawyer/d/dawson-georgia/*

"Dawson has set diversity targets for Freshfields"—based on *https://www.fnlondon.com/articles/freshfields-boss-georgia-dawson-sets-race-and-gender-diversity-targets-for-magic-circle-firm-20210308*

Méka Brunel

Has led Gecina since 2017—based on *https://www.linkedin.com/in/mekabrunel/*

"With a background in civil engineering"—based on *https://press.gecina.fr/experts/meka-brunel.html*

"She also chairs the French Green Building Council."—based on *https://www.hammerson.com/about/board-governance/board-members/meka-brunel/*

Sirma Boshnakova

Head of Allianz since 2019, and "Boshnakova has held top positions in the pharmaceutical and insurance industries"—based on *https://www.linkedin.com/in/sirma-gotovats/*

"as well as in consulting"—based on *https://www.allianz-partners.com/en_US/who-we-are/board-of-management.html*

"She is passionate about supporting future generations."—based on *https://www.allianz.com/en/press/news/company/appointments/190328_allianz-partners-appoints-sirma-boshnakova-as-ceo.html*

Kjerstin Braathen

Leading DNB since 2019, and "She formerly worked at an aluminum company, chartering gas tankers."—based on *https://www.linkedin.com/in/kjerstin-braathen-9a1b888/*

"Braathen has over twenty years of experience at DNB, with clients in shipping and offshore logistics."—based on *https://www.nasdaq.com/partner/kjerstin-braathen*

Carina Åkerström

CEO of Handelsbanken since 2019, "With a background in law," and "Åkerström broke a 150-year-old rule by becoming the first female CEO of the bank."—based on *https://fi.wikipedia.org/wiki/Carina_%C3%85kerstr%C3%B6m*

"She joined the bank in 1986."—based on *https://www.marketscreener.com/business-leaders/Carina-kerstrom-12024/biography/*

People's Power?

NOTES

This spread focuses on social resistance and popular movements that explicitly or implicitly react to the excesses of global financial power. We selected four groups of social movements that in our view depict the clash between the power of the people and the power of finance in the most distinctive ways.

The first group is the debt-relief campaign, which united activists, academics, and civil-society organizations around a common demand: to achieve a massive debt reduction for poor countries with no conditionalities by the year 2000. In 1998, during the G7 summit in Birmingham, over 70,000 people formed a ten-kilometer human chain around the meeting point and demanded to "break the chains of debt." The same year the first international Jubilee 2000 conference was held in Rome and the Jubilee Afrika campaign was launched in Accra, Ghana, signaling the start of the movement in the Global South. In 1999, at another summit meeting of the G7 in Cologne, more than forty thousand activists protested. The same year, the movement expanded to South Africa (Jubilee South Africa), Asia (Jubilee Asia-Pacific), and Latin America (Declaration of Tegucigalpa) (Baillot, 2021; Collins, 1999).

The second group highlights the sociopolitical developments in Southeast Asia during the 1997–98 financial crisis. In 1997, the collapse of a Thai bank precipitated a domino-style financial crisis that spread all over Southeast Asia. Strong, open-market, and resilient economies, like those of Thailand, Korea, Indonesia, Laos, Malaysia, and the Philippines, were severely hit by bankruptcies and the austerity measures the IMF imposed on the region through stabilization programs (Crotty and Lee, 2006). In South Korea, grassroots movements and trade unions protested for the renegotiation of the IMF agreements and the establishment of social safety nets. In Thailand, unemployment increased by 1.6 million people after six months of IMF-designed austerity. In rural communities, farmers' organizations were asking for debt relief, whereas the urban population of the unemployed, the poor, and the working-class demonstrated in the streets (PBS, n.d.; Mydans, 1997; Sharma, 2003).

The third group centers around social movements in Latin America. During the 1980s and 1990s, the region suffered from unsustainable debt build-up and foreign-debt crises. This resulted in the intervention of financial institutions like the IMF, the World Bank, and the Inter-American Development Bank, which pressured countries to enact austerity measures, privatization, financial liberalization, and labor-market reforms, usually in the form of wage cuts and attacks on unionization. In 1992, mass mobilization in Uruguay led to a national referendum that rejected the privatization of the public ANTEL phone company with over 72 percent of the popular vote (Harding, 1992). Later, in 1999, Bolivians and Costa Ricans challenged the plans of their governments to privatize the water supply system and the public electricity and telecommunications companies, respectively (Almeida, 2007; Alphandary, 2000). A few years later, Argentina collapsed under the pressures of currency devaluations, capital flight, and economic recession. Political instability ensued as more than two-thirds of urban residents lost their jobs, and the IMF pushed for fiscal prudency and the liberalization of financial markets. In December 2001, workers and unemployed people were banging kitchen pots and pans in the streets of Buenos Aires and throughout the provinces in protest over government austerity measures (Almeida,

2007; Vilas, 2006). The same year, Guatemalans organized massive protests against tax increases suggested by the IMF. In 2004, Colombians demonstrated against austerity measures imposed by President Uribe, who was implementing the structural reforms dictated by the IMF; while in Brazil the landless workers' movement called MST (Movimento dos Trabalhadores Rurais Sem Terra) struggled for agrarian reforms that would enable a more equitable and democratic access to land and the means of food production (Latin America Data Base staff, 2004; Navarro, 2010). More recently, the IMF forced thousands in Argentina, Ecuador, and Costa Rica to rise up against austerity, anti-labor reforms, and tax hikes, signaling a new wave of social unrest in the region.

The fourth group describes events after the global financial crisis of 2007–9. Severely hit by the credit crunch in the international financial system, the global economy entered a prolonged period of recessionary pressure, political instability, and social unrest. In 2009, after a year of intense demonstrations by the people of Iceland, a referendum was held asking whether to spend almost 90 percent of the country's GDP to save the collapsed banks. An overwhelming majority of Icelanders (93 percent) rejected the deal (Wade and Sigurgeirsdottir, 2011). In early 2011, the governor of Wisconsin sparked a massive wave of protests when he attempted to pass a law eliminating collective bargaining for public-sector workers. Tens of thousands of workers, activists, and sympathizers, occupying the state capitol, gave birth to the Occupy movement that would sweep the country that year (Acar et al., 2011). A few months later, more than eight hundred protestors occupied Zuccotti Park, raising a banner that read, "We are the 99%. You are the 1%" (Earle, 2012; Loucaides, 2021; Lubin, 2012). In the meantime, the eurozone was experiencing its first sovereign debt crisis, with Greece, Ireland, Portugal, Spain, and Italy entering the spiral of economic deflation, austerity, and political instability. First in Spain and then in Greece, Portugal, Italy, Germany, and Belgium, millions of *indignados* (the outraged) occupied public spaces and challenged the power of banks and the Troika. The latter not only imposed harsh austerity measures but also interfered with the democratic processes in many countries, even promoting bankers as heads of governments (Gerbaudo, 2017; Mew, 2013).

On October 15, 2011, the United for #GlobalChange initiative called for demonstrations and protests all over the world, expressing international solidarity with crisis-ridden countries and demanding true democracy and a socially accountable and oriented financial system. On that day, 345 demonstrations took place all around the world. The data for the map with the locations of the protests of the United for #GlobalChange initiative was retrieved from the *Guardian* (2011). The comment by Micah White for the Occupy Wall Street movement was found in an interview with the Canadian newspaper *Globe and Mail* (Griffiths, 2016).

The English translations of the slogans found in the spread are as follows:

No Se Vende—Not for Sale
Que Se Vayan Todos—All Must Go
Democracia Real Ya—For a Real Democracy Now
Não Nos Mande Emigrar—Don't Tell Us to Emigrate
Unidad, Producción y Trabajo Argentino—Argentine Unity, Production and Work

REFERENCES

Acar, Taylan, Robert Chiles, Garrett Grainger, Aliza Luft, Rahul Mahajan, João Peschanski, Chelsea Schelly, Jason Turowetz, and Ian F. Wall. 2011. "Inside the Wisconsin Occupation." *Contexts* 10 (3): 50–55. https://doi.org/10.1177/1536504211418455

Almeida, Paul D. 2007. "Defensive Mobilization: Popular Movements against Economic Adjustment Policies in Latin America." *Latin American Perspectives* 34 (3): 123–39. https://doi.org/10.1177/0094582X07300942

Alphandary, Kim. 2000. "Report from Costa Rica on Mass Protests against Privatization of State-Owned Utilities." World Socialist Web Site, April 15. https://www.wsws.org/en/articles/2000/04/cr-a15.html

Baillot, Hélène. 2021. "A Well-Adjusted Debt: How the International Anti-Debt Movement Failed to Delink Debt Relief and Structural Adjustment." *International Review of Social History* 66 (S29): 215–38. https://doi.org/10.1017/S0020859021000146

Collins, Carole. 1999. "'Break the Chains of Debt!' International Jubilee 2000 Campaign Demands Deeper Debt Relief." *Review of African Political Economy* 26 (81): 419–22. http://www.jstor.org/stable/4006470

Crotty, James, and Kang-Kook Lee. 2006. "The Effects of Neoliberal 'Reforms' on the Postcrisis Korean Economy." *Review of Radical Political Economics* 38 (3): 381–87. https://doi.org/10.1177/0486613406290903

Earle, Ethan. 2012. "A Brief History of Occupy Wall Street." Rosa Luxemburg Stiftung, New York. http://crmintler.com/WWS/wp-content/uploads/2020/01/History-of-Occupy-Wall-Street-Earle.pdf

Gerbaudo, Paolo. 2017. "The Indignant Citizen: Anti-Austerity Movements in Southern Europe and the Anti-Oligarchic Reclaiming of Citizenship." *Social Movement Studies* 16 (1): 36–50. https://doi.org/10.1080/14742837.2016.1194749

Griffiths, Rudyard. 2016. "Micah White: 'Occupy Wall Street Was a Constructive Failure.'" *Globe and Mail*, March 18. https://www.theglobeandmail.com/opinion/munk-debates/micah-white-occupy-wall-street-was-a-constructive-failure/article29294222/

Guardian. 2011. "Occupy Protests around the World: Full List Visualised." https://www.theguardian.com/news/datablog/2011/oct/17/occupy-protests-world-list-map

Harding, Erika. 1992. "Uruguay: Upcoming Plebiscite on 'Privatization Law' Could Trigger Political Crisis." Albuquerque, NM. https://digitalrepository.unm.edu/notisur/10672

Latin America Data Base (LADB) staff. 2004. "Marches against President Uribe." October 22, Albuquerque, NM. https://digitalrepository.unm.edu/notisur/13311

Loucaides, Darren. 2021. "Did Occupy Wall Street Mean Anything at All?" *Financial Times*, September 17. https://www.ft.com/content/761f5219-f35e-43e6-88a2-4634f25fd1a9

Lubin, Judy. 2012. "The 'Occupy' Movement: Emerging Protest Forms and Contested Urban Spaces." *Berkeley Planning Journal* 25 (1): 184–97. https://doi.org/10.5070/BP325111760

Mew, Sue. 2013. "Contentious Politics: Financial Crisis, Political-Economic Conflict, and Collective Struggles—A Commentary." *Social Justice* 39 (1 [127]): 99–114. https://www.jstor.org/stable/41940970

Mydans, Seth. 1997. "Thousands of Thais Protest Bangkok's Inaction in Crisis." *New York Times*, October 22.

Navarro, Zander. 2010. "The Brazilian Landless Movement (MST): Critical Times." *REDES (Santa Cruz do Sul)* 15 (1): 196–223. https://www.redalyc.org/pdf/5520/552056847010.pdf

PBS. n.d. "Timeline of the Panic." *Frontline*. https://www.pbs.org/wgbh/pages/frontline/shows/crash/etc/cron.html

Sharma, Shalendra D. 2003. *The Asian Financial Crisis: Crisis, Reform and Recovery*. Manchester: Manchester University Press.

Vilas, Carlos M. 2006. "Neoliberal Meltdown and Social Protest: Argentina 2001–2002." *Critical Sociology* 32 (1): 163–86. https://doi.org/10.1163/156916306776150331

Wade, Robert H., and Silla Sigurgeirsdottir. 2011. "Iceland's Meltdown: The Rise and Fall of International Banking in the North Atlantic." *Revista de Economia Política* 31 (5): 684–97. https://doi.org/10.1590/S0101-31572011000500001

Chapter 8: Society & Environment

NOTE

The quote is from: Mooney, Annabelle. 2018. *The Language of Money.* London: Taylor and Francis, p. 59.

Finance and Inequality

NOTES

For housing prices in this spread, raw data on 2.6 million title deeds from the City of Cape Town in 2017 was collected for a PhD research project funded by the Ministère de l'Enseignement Supérieur et de la Recherche. Title deeds, which contain information on the date of the transaction and the selling price, have been geolocated and categorized (residential, commercial properties, etc.) using cadastral shapefiles provided by Cape Town's Valuation Department. The final sample contains 893,964 geolocated transactions for residential properties from 1984 to 2016. Prices have been adjusted for inflation at the 2016 rand value.

Spatial units used for the calculation and mapping of median house prices are based on those demarcated by Statistics South Africa for the 2011 National Census (Statistics South Africa, 2011). Some units have been manually modified to better account for un-urbanized areas. For each spatial unit, the zoning of the Group Areas Act was recreated using maps from Houssay-Holzschuch (1999), Graham (2007), Saff (1998), and Western (1981).

The demarcation of post-apartheid areas was created using historical topographic maps of Cape Town made available by Adrian Frith (2015) on his website. For this map, areas for Indians were grouped together with Coloured areas. This choice was made because of the very small number of areas reserved for Indians in Cape Town and, more importantly, because of close relationships between these two groups in the history of the Cape Colony, as exemplified by the case of the Cape Malays. More details on the data and methodology can be found in Migozzi (2020a).

For more information on how real estate professionals participate in the production of unequal housing landscapes and racial segregation, see Aalbers (2011), Korver-Glenn (2021), and Taylor (2019). For more discussion on the relationships between segregation, lending policies, and housing markets in Cape Town and South Africa during and after apartheid, see Kotze and Van Huyssteen (1991), Lemanski (2011), Mabin and Parnell (1983), Marais and Cloete (2017), and Migozzi (2020b).

REFERENCES

Aalbers, Manuel B. 2011. *Place, Exclusion, and Mortgage Markets.* Sussex, UK: Wiley-Blackwell.

Frith, Adrian. 2015. "Historical Topographic Maps of Cape Town." *https://adrian.frith.dev/historical-maps-of-ct/*

Graham, Nancy. 2007. "Race and the Post-Fordist Spatial Order in Cape Town." Master's thesis, University of Cape Town, Cape Town, South Africa. *http://hdl.handle.net/11427/7470*

Houssay-Holzschuch, Myriam. 1999. *Le Cap, Ville Sud-Africaine: Ville Blanche, Vies Noires.* Paris: L'Harmattan.

Korver-Glenn, Elizabeth. 2021. *Race Brokers: Housing Markets and Segregation in 21st Century Urban America.* New York: Oxford University Press.

Kotze, N. J., and Van Huyssteen. 1991. "Redlining in the Housing Market of Cape Town." *South African Geographer/Suid-Afrikaanse Geograaf* 18 (1–2): 97–122.

Lemanski, Charlotte. 2011. "Moving up the Ladder or Stuck on the Bottom Rung? Homeownership as a Solution to Poverty in Urban South Africa." *International Journal of Urban and Regional Research* 35 (1): 57–77. *https://doi.org/10.1111/j.1468-2427.2010.00945.x*

Mabin, Alan, and Sue Parnell. 1983. "Recommodification and Working-Class Home Ownership." *South African Geographical Journal* 65 (2): 148–66. *https://doi.org/10.1080/03736245.1983.10559681*

Marais, Lochner, and Jan Cloete. 2017. "Housing Policy and Private Sector Housing Finance: Policy Intent and Market Directions in South Africa." *Habitat International* 61 (March): 22–30. *https://doi.org/10.1016/j.habitatint.2017.01.004*

Migozzi, Julien. 2020a. "A City to Sell: Digitalization and Financialization of the Housing Market in Cape Town: Stratification & Segregation in the Emerging Global City." PhD thesis, Université Grenoble Alpes. *https://halshs.archives-ouvertes.fr/tel-03130133*

——. 2020b. "Selecting Spaces, Classifying People: The Financialization of Housing in the South African City." *Housing Policy Debate* 30 (4): 640–60. *https://doi.org/10.1080/10511482.2019.1684335*

Saff, Grant R. 1998. *Changing Cape Town: Urban Dynamics, Policy and Planning During the Political Transition in South Africa.* New York: University Press of America.

Statistics South Africa. 2011. "2011 Census." *http://www.statssa.gov.za/?page_id=3839*

Taylor, Keeanga-Yamahtta. 2019. *Race for Profit: How Banks and the Real Estate Industry Undermined Black Homeownership.* Chapel Hill: University of North Carolina Press.

Western, John. 1981. *Outcast Cape Town.* London: Allen & Unwin.

Microfinance

NOTES

Data on the location of MFI headquarters comes from the World Bank (2020b). Data on the location of self-help groups comes from the National Rural Livelihood Mission (2020). The number of self-help groups per 1,000 women was calculated using population data from the Indian government (Population Census, 2011).

In the main text, the quote "liberate people's dreams and help the poorest of the poor to achieve dignity" is based on BNP Paribas (2017). The statement "His idea was simple: lend small amounts of interest-free money to women there to improve their lives—roughly the equivalent of US$27 each" is based on Munir (2014).

Stories around the map have the following sources:

Palamaner, Andhra Pradesh—Paul and John (2010)
Yavatmal, Maharashtra—Global Round Media (2020)
Kerala—World Bank (2020a)
Harhua, Uttar Pradesh—International Finance Corporation (n.d.)
Kolkata, West Bengal—*Hindu* (2013)
Bhubaneshwar, Odisha—ANI News (2021)

For more discussion on microfinance in India, see Nichols (2022) and Sarkar and Chattopadhyay (2021).

REFERENCES

ANI New. 2021. "Mission Shakti Self Help Groups in Forefront of Urban Development in Odisha." *https://www.aninews.in/news/national/general-news/mission-shakti-self-help-groups-in-forefront-of-urban-development-in-odisha20210913101032/*

BNP Paribas. 2017. "History of Microfinance: Small Loans, Big Revolution." *https://group.bnpparibas/en/news/history-microfinance-small-loans-big-revolution*

Global Round Media. 2020. "The Role of Lenders and Loans in Maharashtra's Farmer Suicides." *https://www.globalgroundmedia.com/2020/02/06/the-role-of-lenders-and-loans-in-maharashtras-farmer-suicides/*

Hindu. 2013. "Cheat Funds, Again." Editorial, April 26. Updated December 4, 2021. *https://www.thehindu.com/opinion/editorial/cheat-funds-again/article4654467.ece*

International Finance Corporation. n.d. "For Women in India, Small Loans Have a Big Impact." *https://pressroom.ifc.org/all/pages/PressDetail.aspx?ID=15678*

Munir, Kamal A. 2014. "How Microfinance Disappointed the Developing World." *Conversation,* February 17. *https://theconversation.com/how-microfinance-disappointed-the-developing-world-23206*

National Rural Livelihood Mission. 2020. SHG Report. *https://nrlm.gov.in/shgReport.do?methodName=showIntensiveStateWiseReport*

Nichols, Carly E. 2022. "The Politics of Mobility and Empowerment: The Case of Self-help Groups in India." *Transactions of the Institute of British Geographers* 47 (2): 470–83. *https://doi.org/10.1111/tran.12509*

Paul, George, and Sara John. 2010. "Comparative Analysis of MFI and SHG-Banking Models." Paper submitted for manager traineeship segment, Institute of Rural Management, Anand.

Population Census. 2011. Indian Census for 2011. *https://www.census2011.co.in/*

Sarkar, Suparna, and Subhra Chattopadhyay. 2021. "Significance of the Microcredit Delivery Models for Livelihood Upgradation: A Comparison Between SHGs–Bank Linkage Model and Micro Finance Institutions Model with Case Studies from Rural West Bengal, India." *SEDME (Small Enterprises Development, Management & Extension Journal): A Worldwide Window on MSME Studies* 48 (2): 192–202. *https://doi.org/10.1177/09708464211068085*

World Bank. 2020a. "In India, Women's Self-Help Groups Combat the COVID-19 (Coronavirus) Pandemic." April 11. *https://www.worldbank.org/en/news/feature/2020/04/11/women-self-help-groups-combat-covid19-coronavirus-pandemic-india*

——. 2020b. "MIX Market." World Bank Data Catalog. *https://datacatalog.worldbank.org/search/dataset/0038647*

Learning Money

NOTE

For the rates of financial literacy around the world, we relied on Klapper et al. (2016). The data on the Human Development Index (HDI) comes from the United Nations Development Programme (n.d.). The HDI is a composite index that incorporates information about the human development of a country with respect to three dimensions: (1) long and healthy life, (2) knowledge, and (3) decent standard of living. The dimension of a long and healthy life is measured by the indicator of life expectancy at birth, whereas knowledge is quantified by the mean and expected years of schooling. Finally, the dimension of a decent standard of living is measured through the gross national income per capita in purchasing power parity (PPP) dollars. Data on population per country was taken from the World Bank (2019). For academic studies that investigate the introduction of financial education programs in Africa and Asia, see Fatoki and Oni (2014), Grohmann (2018), Lyons et al. (2020), Messy and Monticone (2012), Organisation for Economic Co-operation and Development (2019), Refera et al. (2016), and Yoshino and Morgan (2016).

REFERENCES

Fatoki, Olawale, and Olabanji Oni. 2014. "Financial Literacy Studies in South Africa: Current Literature and Research Opportunities." *Mediterranean Journal of Social Sciences* 5 (20): 409. *https://doi.org/10.5901/mjss.2014.v5n20p409*

Grohmann, Antonia. 2018. "Financial Literacy and Financial Behavior: Evidence from the Emerging Asian Middle Class." *Pacific-Basin Finance Journal* 48 (April): 129–43. *https://doi.org/10.1016/j.pacfin.2018.01.007*

Klapper, Leora, Annamaria Lusardi, and Peter van Oudheusden. 2016. "Financial Literacy Around the World: Insights from the Standard & Poor's Ratings Services Global Financial Literacy Survey." *https://responsiblefinanceforum.org/wp-content/uploads/2015/12/2015-Finlit_paper_17_F3_SINGLES.pdf*

Lyons, Angela C., Josephine Kass-Hanna, Fan Liu, Andrew J. Greenlee, and Lianyun Zeng. 2020. "Building Financial Resilience through Financial and Digital Literacy in South Asia and Sub-Saharan Africa." 1098. ADBI Working Paper Series. Tokyo, Japan. *https://www.adb.org/sites/default/files/publication/574821/adbi-wp1098.pdf*

Messy, Flore-Anne, and Chiara Monticone. 2012. "The Status of Financial Education in Africa." 25. OECD Working Papers on Finance, Insurance and Private Pensions. *https://www.oecd-ilibrary.org/docserver/5k94cqqx90wl-en.pdf*

Organisation for Economic Co-operation and Development (OECD). 2019. *OECD/INFE Report on Financial Education in APEC Economies: Policy and Practice in a Digital World.* Paris. *http://www.oecd.org/financial/education/2019-financial-education-in-apec-economies.pdf*

Refera, Matewos Kebede, Navkiranjit Kaur Dhaliwal, and Jasmindeep Kaur. 2016. "Financial Literacy for Developing Countries in Africa: A Review of Concept, Significance and Research Opportunities." *Journal of African Studies and Development* 8 (1): 1–12. *https://doi.org/10.5897/JASD2015.0331*

United Nations Development Programme. n.d. "Human Development Reports." *http://hdr.undp.org/en/content/download-data*

World Bank. 2022. "Population, Total." *https://data.worldbank.org/indicator/SP.POP.TOTL*. Data for this spread is from the 2019 version of this page.

Yoshino, Naoyuki, and Peter Morgan. 2016. "Overview of Financial Inclusion, Regulation, and Education." ADBI Working Paper, no. 591. *http://www.adb.org/publications/overview-financial-inclusion-regulation-and-education/%0A*

Weaponizing Finance

NOTES

Data on financial sanctions is available from the Global Sanctions Data Base (2021).

For more information on financial sanctions, see Arnold (2016), Drezner (2015), Felbermayr et al. (2020), Kirilakha et al. (2021), and Syropoulos et al. (2022).

REFERENCES

Arnold, Aaron. 2016. "The True Costs of Financial Sanctions." *Survival* 58 (3): 77–100. *https://doi.org/10.1080/00396338.2016.1186981*

Drezner, Daniel W. 2015. "Targeted Sanctions in a World of Global Finance." *International Interactions* 41 (4): 755–64. *https://doi.org/10.1080/03050629.2015.1041297*

Felbermayr, G., A. Kirilakha, C. Syropoulos, E. Yalcin, and V. Yotov. 2020. "The Global Sanctions Data Base." School of Economics Working Paper Series, 2020-02, LeBow College of Business, Drexel University.

Global Sanctions Data Base (GSDB). 2021. Data for this spread is from the 2019 version. *https://www.globalsanctionsdatabase.com/*

Kirilakha, Aleksandra, Gabriel Felbermayr, Constantinos Syropoulos, Erdal Yalcin, and Yoto Yotov. 2021. "The Global Sanctions Data Base: An Update that Includes the Years of the Trump Presidency." School of Economics Working Paper Series, 2021-10, LeBow College of Business, Drexel University.

Syropoulos, C., G. Felbermayr, A. Kirilakha, E. Yalcin, and Y. V. Yotov. 2022. "The Global Sanctions Data Base—Release 3: COVID-19, Russia, and Multilateral Sanctions." School of Economics Working Paper Series, 2022-11, LeBow College of Business, Drexel University. *https://ideas.repec.org/p/ris/drxlwp/2022_011.html*

Mining the Future

NOTES

Trade data for the main graph/map comes from the Observatory of Economic Complexity (OEC) (2022). The US-dollar trade values for each mineral traded by a country were totaled to calculate the percentage share of that country in the world trade of the six minerals. The color represents the mineral that has the largest value in imports or exports for a given country. For example, for China graphite has the largest share in exports and cobalt in imports.

Australia is the largest producer of lithium in the world and predominantly exports lithium concentrate in bulk to be further refined elsewhere. Australia was not included in the OEC data, as it only displays data for lithium carbonate and lithium oxide. Lithium concentrate was added into the calculation of global trade value by converting A$1.1 billion value of lithium exports (Industry Australia 2021) to US$ using the June 30, 2020, exchange rate.

Data on warehouses and exchanges is based on CityNet (n.d.) research, which identified the metals exchanges trading the EV minerals. Graphite and manganese were not yet being traded on metals exchanges as of April 2022. The other four minerals and metals were traded on the global exchanges. London trades copper, cobalt, and nickel physically and as futures. New York only trades cobalt as a future but offers physical and futures trading in copper and nickel (CME Group 2020). Lithium is physically settled on the Wuxi exchange in China (Reuters 2021) but is only available as futures in London and New York (CME Group 2021; LME 2021). Asia's appetite for lithium determines the mineral's futures pricing in London and New York. The pricing is based on spot prices of the lithium entering the harbors of China, Korea, and Japan. Rotterdam manages LME-traded cobalt warehousing, with the Netherlands taking a large share in its global export market. In addition, cobalt futures traded in London and New York are based on the "in-warehouse Rotterdam" price at Rotterdam harbor. LME-approved warehouses were identified based on LME (2022).

For reserves and production of minerals on the six smaller heatmaps, we use USGS (2022). Reserves are the identified geological deposits that can be extracted at a profit.

The statement "Glencore and Trafigura are key to the electric economy, trading EV minerals out of their headquarters in Switzerland" is based on Glencore (2021), Trafigura (2018), and Dobler and Kesselring (2019).

For more information, see the World Bank (2017) on the key role for minerals in the transition to a low-carbon future, the International Energy Agency (2021) highlighting that mineral production for EV batteries is more geographically concentrated than for fossil fuels, *Economist* (2022) on the geography of strategic minerals, Sovacool et al. (2020) on methods to develop sustainable minerals and metals for our low-carbon future, and Krauss (2021) and Narins (2017) on lithium in Bolivia.

REFERENCES

CityNet. n.d. Cities in Global Financial Networks: Financial and Business Services in the 21st Century [website]. *https://www.citynet21.org/*

CME Group. 2020. "Cobalt (Fastmarkets) Futures: A New Way to Manage Cobalt Price Risk." *https://www.cmegroup.com/markets/metals/battery-metals/cobalt-metal-fastmarkets.html*

——. 2021. "Lithium Futures: Take Charge of Price Risks Associated with Manufacturing Lithium-Ion Batteries." *https://www.cmegroup.com/trading/metals/other/lithium-futures.html*

Dobler, Gregor, and Rita Kesselring. 2019. "Swiss Extractivism: Switzerland's Role in Zambia's Copper Sector." *Journal of Modern African Studies* 57 (2): 223–45. *https://doi.org/10.1017/S0022278X19000089*

Economist. 2022. "The Transition to Clean Energy Will Mint New Commodity Superpowers. We Look at Who Wins and Loses." March 26. *https://www.economist.com/finance-and-economics/2022/03/26/the-transition-to-clean-energy-will-mint-new-commodity-superpowers*

Glencore. 2021. *Glencore Annual Report 2021.* *https://www.glencore.com/.rest/api/v1/documents/ce4fec31fc81d6049d076b15db35d45d/GLEN-2021-annual-report-.pdf*

Industry Australia. 2021. "Lithium. Resources and Energy Quarterly." June. *https://publications.industry.gov.au/publications/resourcesandenergyquarterlyjune2021/infographics/June21-Lithium-hr.png*

International Energy Agency (IEA). 2021. "The Role of Critical Minerals in Clean Energy Transitions." *https://iea.blob.core.windows.net/assets/ffd2a83b-8c30-4e9d-980a-52b6d9a86fdc/TheRoleofCriticalMineralsinCleanEnergyTransitions.pdf*

Krauss, Clifford. 2021. "Green-Energy Race Draws an American Underdog to Bolivia's Lithium." *New York Times,* December 16. *https://www.nytimes.com/2021/12/16/business/energy-environment/bolivia-lithium-electric-cars.html*

LME. 2021. "LME Lithium Hydroxide CIF (Fastmarkets MB)." *https://www.lme.com/en/Metals/EV/LME-Lithium-Hydroxide-CIF-Fastmarkets-MB#Trading+day+summary*

——. 2022. "Warehouse Rents April 1, 2022–March 31, 2023." *https://www.lme.com/Physical-services/Warehousing/Warehouse-charges*

Narins, Thomas P. 2017. "The Battery Business: Lithium Availability and the Growth of the Global Electric Car Industry." *Extractive Industries and Society* 4 (2): 321–28. *https://doi.org/10.1016/j.exis.2017.01.013*

Observatory of Economic Complexity. 2022. "Trade Data for 2020." March 25. *https://oec.world/en/profile/hs92*

Reuters. 2021. "China's First Exchange-Traded Lithium Contract to Launch on July 5." July 2. *https://www.reuters.com/article/us-china-lithium-contract-idUSKCN2E812U*

Sovacool, Benjamin K., Saleem H. Ali, Morgan Bazilian, Ben Radley, Benoit Nemery, Julia Okatz, and Dustin Mulvaney. 2020. "Sustainable Minerals and Metals for a Low-Carbon Future." *Science* 367 (6473): 30–33. *https://doi.org/10.1126/science.aaz6003*

Trafigura. 2018. *Meeting the EV Challenge: Responsible Sourcing in the Electric Vehicle Battery Supply Chain.* November 13. *https://www.trafigura.com/brochure/meeting-the-ev-challenge-responsible-sourcing-in-the-electric-vehicle-battery-supply-chain*

USGS. 2022. *Mineral Commodity Summaries 2022.* *https://doi.org/10.3133/mcs2022*

World Bank. 2017. "The Growing Role of Minerals and Metals for a Low Carbon Future." Washington, DC. *https://documents1.worldbank.org/curated/en/207371500386458722/pdf/117581-WP-P159838-PUBLIC-ClimateSmartMiningJuly.pdf*

A Drop in the Ocean?

NOTES

The map shows a satellite image taken on July 26, 2019. For clarity, it has been edited to remove clouds. Data on the nutrient input reduction status is from Helcom (n.d.). Captions on selected projects funded by the Nordic-Baltic Blue Bonds are based on Nordic Investment Bank (n.d.).

Sources for the blue-bonds table are as follows:

Republic of Seychelles 2018—World Bank (2018) and McFarland (2021)
Nordic Investment Bank 2019—Nordic Investment Bank (2019)
World Bank 2019—Credit Suisse (2019) and World Bank (2019)
Bank of China 2020—Crédit Agricole (n.d.a)
Nordic Investment Bank 2020—Nordic Investment Bank (2020)
Qingdao Water Group 2020—Cbonds (2021)
Seaspan Corporation (Hong Kong) 2021—Atlas Corp. (2021)
Industrial Bank of China 2021—Crédit Agricole (n.d.b)
Belize Blue Investment Company 2021—Maki (2021)
Asian Development Bank 2021—ADB (2021)
BDO Unibank Philippines 2022—BDO Unibank (2022)
Banco Internacional Ecuador 2022—Symbiotics Investments (2022)
Government of Barbados 2022—Credit Suisse (2022)

Data in the table is in USD. Calculations were made using historical FX currency rate conversions from local to USD on the bond issuance date.

In the main text, the statement "in 2010 generated an annual economic value of US$1.5 trillion" is based on World Bank (2023). "After their first bond was twice oversubscribed in 2019, the bank issued a second bond in 2020" is based on Nordic Investment Bank (2019, 2020).

For information on the Green Bond Principles, see International Capital Markets Association (2021). On the economic benefits of reducing eutrophication, see Roth et al. (2019) and Ahtiainen et al. (2014). On natural capital, see Nuveen (2022).

REFERENCES

ADB. 2021. "ADB Issues First Blue Bond for Ocean Investments." News release, September 10. https://www.adb.org/news/adb-issues-first-blue-bond-ocean-investments

Ahtiainen, Heini, Janne Artell, Mikołaj Czajkowski, Berit Hasler, Linus Hasselström, Anni Huhtala, Jürgen Meyerhoff, et al. 2014. "Benefits of Meeting Nutrient Reduction Targets for the Baltic Sea—a Contingent Valuation Study in the Nine Coastal States." *Journal of Environmental Economics and Policy* 3 (3): 278–305. https://doi.org/10.1080/21606544.2014.901923

Atlas Corp. 2021. "Seaspan Completes Significantly Upsized $750 Million Offering of Blue Transition Bonds." July 14. https://www.seaspancorp.com/wp-content/uploads/2021/07/2021-07-14-Seaspan-Completes-Significantly-Upsized-750-Million-Offering-of-Blue-Transition-Bonds.pdf

BDO Unibank. 2022. "BDO Issues First Blue Bond for US$100 Million." May. https://www.bdo.com.ph/news-and-articles/BDO-Unibank-Blue-Bond-USD-100-million-first-private-sector-issuance-southeast-asia-IFC-marine-pollution-prevention-clear-water-climate-goals-sustainability

Cbonds. 2021. "Domestic Bonds: Qingdao Water Group, 3.3%." https://cbonds.com/bonds/1040745/

Crédit Agricole. n.d.a. "Bank of China Issues Asia's Very First Blue Bonds." https://www.ca-cib.com/pressroom/news/bank-china-issues-asias-very-first-blue-bonds

———. n.d.b. "Inaugural Blue Bond and Covid-19 Resilience Bond Priced by the China Industrial Bank." https://www.ca-cib.com/pressroom/news/inaugural-blue-bond-and-covid-19-resilience-bond-priced-china-industrial-bank

Credit Suisse. 2019. "World Bank and Credit Suisse Partner to Focus Attention on Sustainable Use of Oceans and Coastal Areas—the 'Blue Economy.'" November 21. https://www.credit-suisse.com/about-us-news/en/articles/media-releases/world-bank-blue-economy-201911.html

———. 2022. "Credit Suisse Finances Debt Conversion for Marine Conservation in Barbados." Press release, September 21. https://www.credit-suisse.com/about-us-news/en/articles/media-releases/cs-finances-debt-conversion-for-marine-conservation-in-barbados-202209.html

Helcom. n.d. "Thematic Assessment of Eutrophication, 2011–2016." http://stateofthebalticsea.helcom.fi/pressures-and-their-status/eutrophication/

International Capital Markets Association. 2021. "Green Bond Principles Voluntary Process Guidelines for Issuing Green Bonds." https://www.icmagroup.org/assets/documents/Sustainable-finance/2021-updates/Green-Bond-Principles-June-2021-100621.pdf

Maki, Sydney. 2021. "Belize Cures $553 Million Default with a Plan to Save Its Ocean." Bloomberg, November 5. https://www.bloomberg.com/news/articles/2021-11-05/belize-cures-553-million-default-with-a-plan-to-save-its-ocean

McFarland, Brian Joseph. 2021. "Blue Bonds and Seascape Bonds." In *Conservation of Tropical Coral Reefs,* 621–48. Cham: Palgrave Macmillan. https://doi.org/10.1007/978-3-030-57012-5_15

Nordic Investment Bank. 2019. "NIB Issues First Nordic-Baltic Blue Bond." Press release, January 24. https://www.nib.int/releases/nib-issues-first-nordic-baltic-blue-bond

———. 2020. "NIB Launches Five-Year SEK 1.5 Billion Nordic-Baltic Blue Bond." October 7. https://www.nib.int/releases/nib-launches-five-year-sek-1-5-billion-nordic-baltic-blue-bond

———. n.d. "NIB Environmental Bonds." https://www.nib.int/investors/environmental-bonds#blue_bonds

Nuveen. 2022. "Alternatives: Investing in Natural Capital." https://www.nuveen.com/global/insights/alternatives/investing-in-natural-capital

Roth, Nathalie, Torsten Thiele, and Moritz von Unger. 2019. *Blue Bonds: Financing Resilience of Coastal Ecosystems. Key Points for Enhancing Finance Action.* Technical guideline, BNCFF. https://bluenaturalcapital.org/wp2018/wp-content/uploads/2019/05/Blue-Bonds_final.pdf

Symbiotics Investments. 2022. "Symbiotics Investments Brings World's First Ecuadorian Private Blue Bond to the Luxembourg Green Exchange." December 13. https://symbioticsgroup.com/symbiotics-investments-brings-worlds-first-ecuadorian-private-blue-bond-to-the-luxembourg-green-exchange/

World Bank. 2018. "Seychelles Launches World's First Sovereign Blue Bond." Press release, October 29. https://www.worldbank.org/en/news/press-release/2018/10/29/seychelles-launches-worlds-first-sovereign-blue-bond

———. 2019. "World Bank Launched Bonds to Highlight the Challenge of Plastic Waste in Oceans." Press release, April 3. https://www.worldbank.org/en/news/press-release/2019/04/03/world-bank-launches-bonds-to-highlight-the-challenge-of-plastic-waste-in-oceans

———. 2023. "Blue Economy." Updated April 25. https://www.worldbank.org/en/topic/oceans-fisheries-and-coastal-economies

The Alipay Ant Forest

NOTES

Data in the table on the right-hand side is based on the Policy Research Center for Environment and Economy (2019). Data for the map on the left-hand side is sourced from the same report from the Policy Research Center for Environment and Economy (2019) as well as Ant (Financial) Group Sustainability Reports 2016, 2019, and 2020 (Ant Financial 2017; Ant Group 2020, 2021), China Green Carbon Foundation (2020), the IUCN Ant Forest GEP accounting report (Chinese Academy of Sciences and International Union for Conservation of Nature, 2021), and several newspaper articles (Phoenix Public Welfare, 2017; Shengnan and Hong, 2019; T. Chen, 2018; Yinuo, 2020).

In the caption next to the digital tablet, "the equivalent of total emissions over this period by countries like Iceland or Namibia" is based on Worldometer (n.d.).

In the caption under the digital tablet, "since a real one absorbs 17,900 grams of carbon dioxide in its lifetime"—The Ant Forest energy calculation formula is a scientific algorithm provided by the Beijing Environmental Exchange certification, which is equal to the reduction of carbon dioxide emissions. The Nature Conservancy (n.d.) was involved in the design of the energy calculations for the app.

For caption above the map, "the scheme also creates employment opportunities and contributes to incomes, including those in remote rural areas"—According to Zhang et al. (2021), Ant Forest has created 730,000 rural jobs, adding to the gross economic product. Projects that can provide secondary agricultural produce are often selected. Sea buckthorn has been planted by Ant Forest since 2018, producing berries that are turned into juice, providing additional economic benefits to farmers.

In the main text, we used the following sources:

"600 million Alipay users have participated"—based on Pi (2019).

"which awarded Ant Forest the UN Champions of the Earth prize in 2019"—based on the press review by the United Nations (2019).

For more information on Ant Forest, see Chen et al. (2020), Yang et al. (2018), and Zhang et al. (2021).

REFERENCES

Ant Financial. 2017. *Ant Financial 2016 Sustainability Report: Moving Towards a Better Society for the Future*. *https://www.antgroup.com/en/news-media/media-library?type=Sustainability%20Report*

Ant Group. 2020. *Sustainability Report 2019: Towards a Better Society for the Future*. *https://www.antgroup.com/en/news-media/media-library?type=Sustainability%20Report*

——. 2021. 2020 *Sustainability Report: Digital Responsibility and Green Development Building a Better World Together*. *https://www.antgroup.com/en/news-media/media-library?type=Sustainability%20Report*

Chen, Bo, Yi Feng, Jinlu Sun, and Jingwen Yan. 2020. "Motivation Analysis of Online Green Users: Evidence from Chinese 'Ant Forest.'" *Frontiers in Psychology* 11 (June): 1–9. *https://doi.org/10.3389/fpsyg.2020.01335*

Chen, Tingyu. 2018. "Ant Forest Wins the 2018 China Corporate Social Responsibility Summit Green Award." *Sohu*, December 28. *https://www.sohu.com/a/285203255_267106*

China Green Carbon Foundation. 2020. *Annual Report*. *http://www.forestry.gov.cn/html/thjj/thjj_4929/20210412224012277833125/file/20210412224209990119619.pdf*

Chinese Academy of Sciences and International Union for Conservation of Nature. 2021. *Ant Forest 2016–2020 Gross Ecosystem Product (GEP) Accounting Report of Afforestation Projects*. 蚂蚁森林2016-2020年造林项目生态系统生产总值(GEP)核算报告.

Nature Conservancy. n.d. *Natural Climate Solutions: Unlocking the Potential of the Land Sector in China*. *https://www.nature.org/content/dam/tnc/nature/en/documents/TNC_Natural_Climate_Solutions_CHINA.pdf*

Phoenix Public Welfare. 2017. "'Ant Forest' Was Shortlisted for the 'Annual Charity Creativity' of the 2017 Charity Ceremony of the Activist Alliance." ifeng.com, November 15. *https://gongyi.ifeng.com/a/20171115/44762391_0.shtml*

Pi, Lei. 2019. "Internet Tree Planting Has Been Recognized by the State. Nearly 2 Million Netizens Have Received Certificates of Voluntary Tree Planting for the Whole People." *China Philanthropy Times*, January 7. *http://www.gongyishibao.com/html/gongyizixun/15830.html*

Policy Research Center for Environment and Economy. 2019. "Research Report on Low-Carbon Lifestyle of the Public under the Background of Internet Platform." *http://www.prcee.org/yjcg/yjbg/201909/W020190909692854952540.pdf*

Shengnan, Wang, and Huang Hong. 2019. "In 2019, the 'Ant Forest' Public Welfare Afforestation Project Passed the Review." *China Green Times*, January 18. *http://grassland.china.com.cn/2019-01/18/content_40647896.html*

United Nations. 2019. "Champion of the Earth 2019—Ant Forest." Video. UN Environment Programme. *https://www.unep.org/championsofearth/laureates/2019/ant-forest*

Worldometer. n.d. "CO2 Emissions by Country." *https://www.worldometers.info/co2-emissions/co2-emissions-by-country/*

Yang, Zhaojun, Xiangchun Kong, Jun Sun, and Yali Zhang. 2018. "Switching to Green Lifestyles: Behavior Change of Ant Forest Users." *International Journal of Environmental Research and Public Health* 15 (9): 1819. *https://doi.org/10.3390/ijerph15091819*

Yinuo, Liu. 2020. "In Addition to Planting Trees, the Carbon Trading Market behind the Ant Forest." OFweek, July 17. *https://mp.ofweek.com/ecep/a656714090027*

Zhang, Yufei, Jiayin Chen, Yi Han, Mengxi Qian, Xiaona Guo, Ruishan Chen, Di Xu, and Yi Chen. 2021. "The Contribution of Fintech to Sustainable Development in the Digital Age: Ant Forest and Land Restoration in China." *Land Use Policy* 103 (April): 105306. *https://doi.org/10.1016/j.landusepol.2021.105306*

Is Your Portfolio on Fire?

NOTES

All data on the carbon footprint and the temperature for individual companies and sectors is based on a proprietary methodology developed by Lombard Odier. For further details on the methodology, see Portfolio Alignment Team (2020).

Carbon footprint (y-axis of the chart) measures the exposure of the portfolio to climate change. The carbon footprint can be broken down into three scopes. Scope 1 accounts for all direct emissions from the activities of an organization or under their control. Scope 2 accounts for the indirect emissions from the consumption of purchased electricity, steam, or other sources of energy generated upstream from a company's direct operations. Scope 3 accounts for all other indirect emissions from activities of the organization occurring from sources that they do not own or control. Scope 3 emissions include several sources of indirect emissions both in the company's supply chain (upstream emissions) and downstream from the company's owned or controlled operations (e.g., the emissions from the in-use phase of a company's products or services, such as the driving of a truck manufactured by an automobile manufacturer).

Temperature alignment measures the expected evolution in emissions and does not reflect the overall scale of a company's current emissions, which is measured by carbon footprint. Temperature alignment, in other words, evaluates the trajectory of these emissions, whereas carbon footprint only measures the present volume of those emissions. The temperature alignment methodology allows us to estimate that, for instance, Volkswagen is aligned with a 2.0°C temperature outcome. This means that if the rest of the economy were to pursue a similar level of decarbonization ambition as Volkswagen, global temperatures would increase by 2.0°C by 2100.

Lombard Odier's analysis combines both carbon footprints and temperature alignment assessment. Considering only the carbon footprint would lead investors to concentrate investments in low-carbon industries and investments, but this approach neglects the need to identify solutions within higher-carbon industries, where a transition is most urgently needed and where the decarbonization impact is highest. In Lombard Odier's approach, we don't simply ignore carbon-intensive industries, which are often the most relevant to the climate because they are vital mainstays of our economy but most urgently need to decarbonize. These companies are in hard-to-abate industries such as agriculture, cement, steel, chemicals, energy, materials, construction, and transport. Lombard Odier gives the label "ice cubes" to companies in these carbon-intensive industries that understand the urgency of the transition and are decarbonizing towards net-zero alignment because they have the effect of disproportionately cooling down the economy's or a portfolio's overall temperature. Lombard Odier also seeks to identify carbon-intensive businesses that are not making progress toward net-zero alignment. The bank calls them "burning logs" as these are the companies that are "carbonizing," or generating huge emissions and failing to transition. These companies are not yet committed to the climate transition and may be exposed to significant risks connected to stranded assets or no longer being able to operate in a carbon-regulated world. Investing in such companies today will disproportionately raise the temperature of a portfolio unless effective active engagement can encourage a change in trajectory.

For a detailed methodological discussion and an empirical demonstration of temperature alignment, see Lombard Odier (2021).

This image (including the graph) is provided for informational purposes only and should not be interpreted as legal, fiscal, financial, economic, or any other advice and should not be utilized as an investment aid.

REFERENCES

Lombard Odier. 2021. "Designing Temperature Alignment Metrics to Invest in Net Zero: An Empirical Illustration of Best Practices." *https://am.lombardodier.com/sg/en/contents/news/white-papers/2021/july/designing-temperature-alignment.html*

Portfolio Alignment Team. 2020. *Measuring Portfolio Alignment: Assessing the Position of Companies and Portfolios on the Path to Net Zero.* *https://www.tcfdhub.org/wp-content/uploads/2020/10/PAT-Report-20201109-Final.pdf*

Lofty Goals

NOTE

The main source of data for this spread is the Public Development Banks Database (*https://www.nse.pku.edu.cn/dfidatabase/index.htm*), which was compiled by the Finance in Common initiative (*https://financeincommon.org/*) with the collaboration of the Institute of New Structural Economics of Beijing University and the French Development Agency. A research study, Xu et al. (2021), acts as the reference point of this project. The estimates for the annual financing needs for achieving the sustainable development goals by 2030 and net-zero emissions by 2050 were made by the Force for Good Foundation (2021) and the International Energy Agency (2021), respectively. For the indicators of world GDP, we used the World Economic Outlook Database from the IMF (n.d.), and for global credit and global financial assets, we relied on estimates from the Financial Stability Board (2020).

REFERENCES

Financial Stability Board. 2020. *Global Monitoring Report on Non-Bank Financial Intermediation.* *https://www.fsb.org/2020/12/global-monitoring-report-on-non-bank-financial-intermediation-2020/*

Force for Good Foundation. 2021. Capital as a Force for Good: Capitalism for a Sustainable Future. *https://www.forcegood.org/frontend/img/2021_report/pdf/final_report_2021_Capital_as_a_Force_for_Good_Report_v_F2.pdf*

International Energy Agency. 2021. *Net Zero by 2050: A Roadmap for the Global Energy Sector.* *https://iea.blob.core.windows.net/assets/20959e2e-7ab8-4f2a-b1c6-4e63387f03a1/NetZeroby2050-ARoadmapfortheGlobalEnergySector_CORR.pdf*

International Monetary Fund. n.d. World Economic Outlook database. *https://www.imf.org/en/Publications/SPROLLs/world-economic-outlook-databases#sort=%40imfdate%20descending*

Xu, J., R. Marodon, X. Ru, X. Ren, and X. Wu. 2021. "What Are Public Development Banks and Development Financing Institutions?—Qualification Criteria, Stylized Facts and Development Trends." *China Economic Quarterly International* 1 (4), 271–94. *https://doi.org/10.1016/j.ceqi.2021.10.001*

Where Is Money Going?

NOTES

Data on the distribution of satellites comes from the Union of Concerned Scientists (2005). Data on equity investments in the space economy is from Space Capital (2023).

More information on the Gaofen satellites is available from Jones (2022), on the Greenhouse Gases Observing Satellite from the GOSAT Project (n.d.), on the Cyclone Global Navigation Satellite System from NASA (2019). More information on spatial finance is available from the Spatial Finance Initiative (2021).

REFERENCES

GOSAT Project. n.d. "Instruments and Observational Methods." *https://www.gosat.nies.go.jp/en/about_%ef%bc%92_observe.html*

Jones, Andrew. 2022. "China Launches New Gaofen 12 Earth Observation Satellite." Space.com, July 1. *https://www.space.com/china-launches-gaofen-12-satellite*

NASA. 2019. "Cyclone Global Navigation Satellite System (CYGNSS)." Updated December 12. *https://www.nasa.gov/cygnss*

Space Capital. 2023. "Space Investment Quarterly Reports." Space Investment Quarterly. *https://www.spacecapital.com/quarterly*

Spatial Finance Initiative. 2021. *Report: State and Trends of Spatial Finance 2021.* *https://www.cgfi.ac.uk/wp-content/uploads/2021/07/SpatialFinance_Report.pdf*

Union of Concerned Scientists. 2005. "UCS Satellite Database." Reports & Multimedia. Updated January 1, 2023. *https://www.ucsusa.org/resources/satellite-database*

Cartographic Sources

To build the contextual layers underpinning our maps (roads, rivers, borders and so on), we used Natural Earth as our primary source, tweaking manually where necessary. For our most detailed maps, we used OpenStreetMap. These two sources were invaluable; we are grateful to those who maintain and contribute to them. In addition, we obtained terrain data from NASA's SRTM. Other map sources are listed throughout the Notes & References.

Image Credits

XVI BIBLIOTECA NAZIONALE MARCIANA **2–3** LIBRARY OF CONGRESS GEOGRAPHY AND MAP DIVISION **4** BEINECKE RARE BOOK AND MANUSCRIPT LIBRARY, YALE UNIVERSITY **5** © ASHMOLEAN MUSEUM, UNIVERSITY OF OXFORD **48–49, 178** OLIVER UBERTI

All photo illustrations on the following pages by Oliver Uberti. The original images used in the illustrations have been altered.

8 THE SCHØYEN COLLECTION, OSLO AND LONDON **9** BANISTER FLETCHER, *A HISTORY OF ARCHITECTURE ON THE COMPARATIVE METHOD,* 17TH ED. (NEW YORK: CHARLES SCRIBNER'S SONS,1946) **10** AMERICAN NUMISMATIC SOCIETY (CC BY-NC 4.0) • JEAN-MICHEL MOULLEC (CC BY 2.0) • © NATIONAL MUSEUM OF AUSTRALIA (CC BY-SA 4.0) • © THE TRUSTEES OF THE BRITISH MUSEUM (CC BY-NC-SA 4.0) **11** © THE TRUSTEES OF THE BRITISH MUSEUM (CC BY-NC-SA 4.0) • NUMISMÁTICA PLIEGO (CC BY-SA 3.0) **13** AMERICAN NUMISMATIC SOCIETY [ALSO ON P. 7] **14** *CATALAN ATLAS*/BIBLIOTHÉQUE NATIONALE DE FRANCE [ALSO ON P. 7] • DENIS TABLER/SHUTTERSTOCK.COM **15** WORLD IMAGING (CC BY-SA 3.0) • UNKNOWN (C.1023) • MASTER AFTER CHIANG HSUAN/BOSTON MUSEUM OF FINE ARTS • SYTILIN PAVEL/SHUTTERSTOCK.COM • YAROSLAFF/SHUTTERSTOCK.COM • CL2004LHY/SHUTTERSTOCK.COM **17** © THE TRUSTEES OF THE BRITISH MUSEUM (CC BY-NC-SA 4.0) • INTERFOTO/ALAMY STOCK PHOTO **18** ARCHIVE FARMS INC./ALAMY STOCK PHOTO [ALSO ON P. 6] **19** GORDON BAIRD/ART UK (CC BY-NC) **20** UNKNOWN (C.1800)/SCOTTISH NATIONAL GALLERY • PIETER JANSZ.SAENREDAM/RIJKSMUSEUM **22** FALKENSTEINFOTO/ALAMY STOCK PHOTO • JOHN JABEZ EDWIN MAYALL/INTERNATIONAL INSTITUTE OF SOCIAL HISTORY **24** BETTMANN VIA GETTY IMAGES • GOTTSCHO-SCHLEISNER COLLECTION, LIBRARY OF CONGRESS, PRINTS AND PHOTOGRAPHS DIVISION **27** APTYP_KOK/SHUTTERSTOCK.COM **34** MISTERSTOCK/SHUTTERSTOCK.COM **35** MORPHART CREATION/SHUTTERSTOCK.COM **36** PAULCLARKE/SHUTTERSTOCK.COM **39** OLIVER UBERTI [ALSO ON P. 29] **40–41** GROUND PICTURE/SHUTTERSTOCK.COM **42** CRAIG GALLOWAY/PROSPORTS/SHUTTERSTOCK.COM [ALSO ON P. 28] **45** JOSERPIZARRO/SHUTTERSTOCK.COM [ALSO ON P. 28] **52–53** GRESEI/SHUTTERSTOCK.COM **55** CHITTAKORN59/SHUTTERSTOCK.COM [ALSO ON P. 50] **57** MATAUW/SHUTTERSTOCK.COM **58** MPH PHOTOS/SHUTTERSTOCK.COM [ALSO ON P. 51] **60** KARRAMBA PRODUCTION/SHUTTERSTOCK.COM **62** ALBA_ALIOTH/SHUTTERSTOCK.COM **64–65** MODUSTOLLENS/SHUTTERSTOCK.COM **67** PHOTOCREO MICHAL BEDNAREK/SHUTTERSTOCK.COM [ALSO ON P. 50] **71** VIKTORISHY/SHUTTERSTOCK.COM **74–75** OLAVS/SHUTTERSTOCK.COM **77** GEORGIE GILLARD/ANL/SHUTTERSTOCK.COM **81** CERI BREEZE/SHUTTERSTOCK.COM [ALSO ON P. 73] **82** JOHN FABER JR., AFTER THOMAS MURRAY/© NATIONAL PORTRAIT GALLERY, LONDON (CC BY-NC-ND 3.0) **83** © THE TRUSTEES OF THE BRITISH MUSEUM (CC BY-NC-SA 4.0) • PIERRE SAVART/PEACE PALACE LIBRARY • *DEUTSCHE ACTA ERUDITORUM* (LEIPZIG: JOHANN FRIEDRICH GLEDITSCH AND SON, 1715) **88** I_AM_ZEWS/SHUTTERSTOCK.COM [ALSO ON P. 72] **90** RHJPHTOTOS/SHUTTERSTOCK.COM [ALSO ON P. 73] **92** OLEK LU/SHUTTERSTOCK.COM **93** IGOR SHIKOV/SHUTTERSTOCK.COM **97** PONTORMO/UFFIZI GALLERY • BRONZINO/NATIONAL GALLERY OF ART [ALSO ON P. 95] • THE MIRIAM AND IRA D. WALLACH DIVISION OF ART, PRINTS AND PHOTOGRAPHS: PRINT COLLECTION, THE NEW YORK PUBLIC LIBRARY **98** ARILD VÅGEN (CC BY-SA 4.0) • DXR (CC BY-SA 4.0) **102** NATTAPOLSTUDIO/SHUTTERSTOCK.COM [ALSO ON P. 95] **108** © SURONIN/DREAMSTIME.COM **111** PHOTO BY MUHAMMAD HASEEB SOHAIL • © YURII TYMCHUK/DREAMSTIME.COM • CALVIN TEO (CC BY-SA 3.0) [ALL ALSO ON P. 94] **112** BEN PRUCHNIE VIA GETTY IMAGES **114** RADOSLAW MACIEJEWSKI/SHUTTERSTOCK.COM **118** UNKNOWN (17TH CENTURY)/NORTON SIMON MUSEUM **120** TERESA ZABALA/THE NEW YORK TIMES/REDUX, © THE NEW YORK TIMES • GEORGE GRANTHAM BAIN COLLECTION, LIBRARY OF CONGRESS, PRINTS AND PHOTOGRAPHS DIVISION • WASHINGTON UNIVERSITY PHOTOGRAPHIC SERVICES COLLECTION, JULIAN EDISON DEPARTMENT OF SPECIAL COLLECTIONS, WASHINGTON UNIVERSITY LIBRARIES **121** © WORLD ECONOMIC FORUM, SWISS-IMAGE.CH/PHOTO REMY STEINEGGER (CC BY-NC-SA 2.0) **123** INKED PIXELS/SHUTTERSTOCK.COM **124** STEPHEN J. BOITANO/AP/SHUTTERSTOCK.COM • REUTERS/ALAMY STOCK PHOTO **126** GEOFF ROBINSON/SHUTTERSTOCK.COM **127** CHRIS RATCLIFFE/BLOOMBERG VIA GETTY IMAGES [ALSO ON P. 117] **128** GRANDEDUC/SHUTTERSTOCK.COM • ANDY DEAN PHOTOGRAPHY/SHUTTERSTOCK.COM **130** MATTPIX/SHUTTERSTOCK.COM • MEHANIQ/SHUTTERSTOCK.COM • PANAGIOTA ILIOPOULOU [ALL ALSO ON P. 117] **133** LOUISA GOULIAMAKI/AFP VIA GETTY IMAGES [ALSO ON P. 116] **139** FRANK_PETERS/SHUTTERSTOCK.COM **142** JEAN SCHWEITZER/SHUTTERSTOCK.COM **144** MICROSOFT PRODUCT SCREEN SHOT REPRINTED WITH PERMISSION FROM MICROSOFT CORPORATION **146** WOLFRAM WEIMER, *GESCHICHTE DES GELDES* (FRANKFURT: INSEL-VERLAG, 1997) **147** BANK OF ENGLAND **148** MANORIAL1/SHUTTERSTOCK.COM [ALSO ON P. 140] • CORNELL UNIVERSITY, PJ MODE COLLECTION OF PERSUASIVE CARTOGRAPHY **152** SV PRODUCTION/SHUTTERSTOCK.COM **155** ROMARIOLEN/SHUTTERSTOCK.COM **158–61** © DEUTSCHE BANK AG HISTORICHES INSTITUT, PHOTO LUTZ KLEINHANS **162** QUIETBITS/SHUTTERSTOCK.COM [ALSO ON P. 141] **167** KEVIN JACOBS/AFRICAN NEWS AGENCY **168** PRADEEPGAURS/SHUTTERSTOCK.COM [ALSO ON P. 164] **170** ABN AMRO ART & HERITAGE, AMSTERDAM **172** HUNINI (CC BY-SA 4.0) **174** AANBETTA/SHUTTERSTOCK.COM [ALSO ON P. 165] **176** ANIMAFLORA PICSSTOCK/SHUTTERSTOCK.COM **178** GE_4530/SHUTTERSTOCK.COM • EINBLICK/STOCK.ADOBE.COM **180** ROB WILSON/SHUTTERSTOCK.COM • OLEG GAWRILOFF/SHUTTERSTOCK.COM **181** DUSAN ZIDAR/SHUTTERSTOCK.COM • SPIDERMAN777/SHUTTERSTOCK.COM **183** CHUYKO SERGEY/SHUTTERSTOCK.COM **184** ASTRANIS SPACE TECHNOLOGIES (CC BY-SA 4.0) [ALSO ON P. 165]

Acknowledgments

MANY PEOPLE AND ORGANIZATIONS helped to make the *Atlas of Finance* possible. Dariusz Wójcik has drawn on funding from the Cities in Global Financial Networks: Financial and Business Services in the 21st Century (CityNet) project funded by the European Research Council under the European Union's Horizon 2020 research and innovation program (681337). The atlas was also funded by the School of Geography and the Environment, University of Oxford. Richard Holden offered critical help with managing the financial side of the project. Dariusz built on advice from Gordon L. Clark and has benefited from collaboration with Daniel Haberly, conversations with Danny Dorling, Henry Yeung, Phillip O'Neill, and Wei Wu, and exchanges within the community of the Global Network on Financial Geography (FinGeo) and with students who have taken his course on financial geographies. He worked on finalizing the atlas as a Rockefeller Foundation Bellagio Resident in April 2023, benefiting from conversations with Payal Arora, Chris Benner, Rose Boswell, Greg Fischer, Maria Floro, Caren Grown, Maria Kozloski, Shailendra Kumar, Alice Luperto, Sungi Mlengeya, Pilar Palacia, Manuel Pastor, Jasmeen Patheja, Emiliano Rodriguez-Neusch, Diah Saminarsih, Rajiv Shah, and Molara Wood. Viviana Di Leo offered great coaching on promotion strategy. Dariusz's wife, Anna Zalewska, has been immensely supportive throughout the thousands of hours he has dedicated to the atlas.

Panagiotis (Takis) Iliopoulos extends his appreciation to his colleagues and good friends Ashok Kumar, Giorgos Galanis, Giorgos Gouzoulis, and Harris Konstantinidis for their valuable advice. Takis is also heavily indebted to the unlimited patience and support given to him all these years by his beloved family: his wife, Danai; his parents, Elias and Pagona; and his sister, Teta.

Stefanos Ioannou would like to thank his mentor Gary Dymski. He also wants to thank his parents, Yanni Ioannou and Marica Frangakis, and his wife, Isabela Bertoni, as well as his son, León Ioannou, who was born during the writing of the atlas and allowed Stefanos to sleep well most nights.

Liam Keenan would like to acknowledge the creativity and collegiality of his co-authors, which made working on the atlas a labor of love. Liam also drew heavily on the unwavering support and compassion of his mother, Denise.

Julien Migozzi would like to thank everyone with whom he has collaborated along the atlas's long journey, including Ludwig Wier, Edoardo Ferlazzo, and Pierre Romera, with whom he had helpful discussions. He would also like to thank the staff from Il Sovrano for their delicious coffee and the R community for designing great packages and sharing useful tips to advance open science, without which this atlas would not exist. Finally, he would like to express his sincere gratitude to his friends and family, who provided support and lent their ears and eyes on numerous occasions.

Timothy Monteath would like to thank the CityNet team for welcoming him into financial geography and for all their support. He would also like to thank his partner, Danielle Cutts, for all her love and support as well as her suggestions, comments, and ideas, which have been invaluable in developing many of his contributions to the atlas.

Vladimír Pažitka would like to thank his research collaborators—including Isabelle Roland, Luke Milsom, Theodor Cojoianu, David Bassens, and Michiel van Meeteren—because their work together has been a great source of ideas and inspiration for the atlas. He would also like to thank his partner, Meg Barstow, for lending her artistic eye in reviewing many graphics and for reminding him just how lucky he is to have this opportunity. Finally, he would like to thank his parents, Vladimír and Rozália, for being his two most enthusiastic cheerleaders.

Morag Torrance drew on funding from the ClimateWorks Foundation, allowing her to develop stories on sustainable finance for the atlas. She would like to thank Gordon L. Clark for his encouragement and her husband, Collin McDonald, for supporting her return to the world of economic geography. She also thanks her children, who now assume maps and money are common topics of dinner table conversation.

Michael Urban would like to thank his colleagues Drs. Christopher Kaminker and Thomas Höhne-Sparborth as well as his academic mentor, Gordon L. Clark, for sharing their time and knowledge.

James Cheshire and Oliver Uberti wish to thank Dariusz for entrusting them with his vision. It has been a joy to design a book that bears the beauty of banknotes.

Our maps and visuals were inspired by many people beyond the team of co-authors, including

Amy Bogaard, University of Oxford
Ruishan Chen, Shanghai Jiao Tong University
Paul Collins, Ashmolean Museum, Oxford
Barrie Cook, British Museum, London
Elroy Dimson, Cambridge Judge Business School
Michael E. Drew, Griffith University, Australia
Chris Howgego, University of Oxford
Marek Jankowiak, University of Oxford
Paul Marsh, London Business School
Stephen Mullen, University of Glasgow
Mike Staunton, London Business School

We are grateful to Seth Ditchik from Yale University Press for believing in our project, Amanda Gerstenfeld and Josh Panos for their excellent assistance, Joyce Ippolito and Marnie Wiss for their eagle-eyed copyediting, Jenya Weinreb for guiding us through the production process, and Dustin Kilgore for his helpful suggestions to Oliver in the creation of the atlas's intricate cover design. We also owe a debt of gratitude to anonymous reviewers of our proposal and the first submission.

We have benefited massively from the work of nearly two hundred students. They amazed us with their skills, dedication, and creativity. Callum Buchanan and Karan Karasinska from the Micro-Internship Programme at Oxford University helped to arrange all these internships. We learnt about the programme from Dariusz's and Anna's dear friend Paulina Kewes.

OUR INTERNS

Fatimah Ahmadi
Hacer Akay
M. Ahsan Al Mahir
Vitor Alcalde
Alice Ardis
David Asamoah
Vittoria Baglieri
Bianca Barilla
Leo Bartels
Frederick Bate
Oana Bazavan
Joseph Beaden
Emil Beddari
Paula Bejarano Carbo
Enrico Benassi
Gabriele Brasaite
Catherine Brewer
Amy Brooks
Evangeline Burrowes
Edward Campbell
Matthew Campbell
Lucy Cawkwell
Ka Long Chan
Alexander Charters
Mary Chen
Chunfang Cheng
Ian Cheung
Jay Chitnavis
Madeline Connolly
Charles Croft
Tara Daemi
Alessandra David
Yasaman Davoudzadeh
Anas Dayeh
Ken Deng
Nina Djukanovic
Catherine Downie
Sarah Duffy
Baltazar Dydensborg
Jordan Edwards-Zinger
Jake Elliott
Ozan Erder
Harriet Eyles
Felix Fabricius
Manhon Fan
Chloe Fox-Robertson
Hanbo Gao
Zilin Gao
Hannah Gardner
Khanh Giang
Isabella Godley
Anthony Gosnell
Christopher Grassick
Brooklyn Han
Yang Han
Benjamin Harrison
Oliver Harvey-Rich
Thomas Hazell
Dominic Hill
Krisha Hirani
Daniel Hoos
Tianjie Huang
Louis Hudson
Yuedan Huo
Polina Ivanova
Leyi Jiang
Yuzhe Jin
Huw Jones
Daisy Joy
Alexa Kaminski
Daniel Kandie
Miles Keat
Edmund Kelly
Robert Kilgour
Halim Kim
Nile Kirke
Tarun Koteeswaran
Pierre Lanaspre
Woon Sing Lau
Nathan Lawson
Kaitlyn Lee
Antoine Levie
Benjamin Lewis
Haibei Li
Tianjin Li
Yu-Yang Lin
Harry Linehan-Hill
Rebecca Liu
Quentin Louis
Anisha Mace
Hamzah Mahmood
Karishma Malhotra
Megan Mantaro
Yingsu Mao
Ebba Mark
Sarah Marshall
Jasper McBride-Owusu
Nathanael McKibbin
Mika Erik Moeser
Samiha Mohsen
Georgi Nedyalkov
Filip Nemecek
Gabriel Ng
Thomas Noe
Natan Ornadel
Ishaan Parikh
Zachary Parsons
Jacobus Petersen
Anja Petrovic
Anna Polensky
Dylan Price
Natalia Puczek
Geoffrey Pugsley
Wei Qiang
Jiahe Qiu
Sunny Ramamurthy
Tanae Rao
Samuel Redding
William Reeves
Viggo Rey
Simone Rijavec
Phoebe Rodgers
Ifan Rogers
Dillon Roglic
Emily Rosindell
Heather Russell
Ipek Şahbazoğlu
Indrajeet Sahu
Simon Sällström
Mipham Samten
Piotr Sawicki
Avantika Sengupta
Arushi Sharan
Yujie Shen
Yiming Sheng
Junze Shi
Muyang Shi
Amita Singh
Nina Skrzypczak
Lunchen Song
Ruoxi Sun
Sawyer Suzuki
Emma Jiayue Tao
Nayah Thu
Christopher Uren
Beatrice Vernon
Hataipatara Vinaiphat
Natalie Vriend
Yuanjun Wan
Adrian Wang
Andrew Wang
Hanxi Wang
Yiqiao Wang
Yujie Wang
Lucy Weatherill
Moritz Weckbecker
Zhenhao Wen
Lumi Westerlund
Alexander Westwell
Bethan White
Timothy Williams
Hong Wong
Nicholas Wong
Harry Wright
Hung-Jen Wu
Yu Xiao
Qiuyi Xie
Chenhao Xue
Jiaqi Yu
Hanwen Zhang
Hengyi Zhang
Jingwei Zhang
Katie Zhang
Qingyang Zhang
Yang Zhang
Ziyang Zhang
Jiahe Zhu
Guy Zilberman

About the Authors

THIS ATLAS WAS CREATED BY an international team of researchers at the School of Geography and the Environment, University of Oxford, with Dariusz Wójcik as the lead author and project manager in collaboration with James Cheshire and Oliver Uberti, who designed the book and its maps and visualizations. The team built on an interdisciplinary background in geography (Liam Keenan and Julien Migozzi), economics (Stefanos Ioannou and Vladimír Pažitka), political economy (Panagiotis Iliopoulos), and sociology (Timothy Monteath), while Michael Urban and Morag Torrance also brought significant experience from the financial sector.

Dr. Dariusz Wójcik is a professor of financial geography at National University of Singapore and an Honorary Research Associate at the School of Geography and the Environment and St Peter's College, University of Oxford. He chairs the Global Network on Financial Geography and is the editor in chief of the journal *Finance and Space*. His awards include the Fellowship of the Academy of Social Sciences and the Fellowship of the Regional Studies Association.

Dr. Panagiotis (Takis) Iliopoulos is a postdoctoral researcher at the Faculty of Economics and Business at K. U. Leuven, Belgium. He completed his PhD at Birkbeck College, and his research interests include international economics, political economy, and financial geography.

Dr. Stefanos Ioannou is a senior lecturer in economics at Oxford Brookes University. He completed his PhD in economics at the University of Leeds in 2016 under the supervision of Gary Dymski and Malcolm Sawyer. His main research interests are macroeconomics, economic geography, and banking and finance.

Dr. Liam Keenan is an assistant professor in economic geography at the School of Geography, University of Nottingham. He completed a PhD in human geography at Newcastle University under the supervision of Andy Pike, Jane Pollard, Neill Marshall, and Paul Langley.

Dr. Julien Migozzi is an Urban Studies Foundation Postdoctoral Research Fellow at the School of Geography and the Environment, University of Oxford. He previously worked as a senior lecturer at the École Normale Supérieure, Paris. He was a student fellow at the École Normale Supérieure de Lyon and completed his PhD in geography at Grenoble Alpes University. His research interests lie at the intersection of financial geography, urban studies, and economic sociology.

Dr. Timothy Monteath is an assistant professor at the Centre for Interdisciplinary Methodologies, Warwick University. He received his PhD in Sociology at the London School of Economics and Political Science. His research interests include land ownership and registration, finance and real estate, and the use of big data and new digital methodologies in the social sciences.

Dr. Vladimír Pažitka is an assistant professor in banking and finance at Leeds University Business School. He completed his DPhil at the School of Geography and the Environment, University of Oxford. His research interests include fintech, investment banking networks, international trade in financial services, venture capital, and private equity.

Dr. Morag Torrance is a research associate at the School of Geography and the Environment, University of Oxford, and holds a DPhil in economic geography on the financialization of urban infrastructure. She has worked in finance in Amsterdam, London, New York, and Sydney. In her work she bridges the gap between academia and the private sector to pursue tangible solutions to benefit society.

Dr. Michael Urban is chief sustainability strategist at Lombard Odier Group, where he supports the group's managing partners in the design and implementation of their global sustainable investment strategy. Michael is also an honorary research fellow at the Smith School of Enterprise and the Environment and a member of Oriel College.

Dr. James Cheshire is a professor of geographic information and cartography at University College London. Oliver Uberti is a former senior design editor for *National Geographic*, who loves helping scientists translate their research into memorable visuals. James and Oliver have been making atlases together for more than a decade.